ROUTLEDGE HANDBOOK OF
SPORT AND POLITICS

D0074309

Sport is frequently considered to be an aspect of popular culture that is, or should be, untainted by the political. However, there is a broad consensus among academics that sport is often at the heart of the political and the political is often central to sport. From the 1936 Olympic Games in Nazi Germany to the civil unrest that preceded the 2014 World Cup in Brazil, sport and politics have remained symbiotic bedfellows.

The *Routledge Handbook of Sport and Politics* goes further than any other book in surveying the complex, embedded relationships between sport and politics. With sections addressing ideologies, nation and statehood, corporate politics, political activism, social justice, and the politics of sports events, it introduces the conceptual foundations that underpin our understanding of the sport–politics nexus and examines emergent issues in this field of study.

Including in-depth case studies from North America, South America, Europe, the Middle East, Africa and Asia, this is an essential reference for anybody with an interest in the social scientific study of sport.

Alan Bairner is Professor of Sport and Social Theory at Loughborough University, UK. He is co-author of *Sport, Sectarianism and Society in a Divided Ireland* and author of *Sport, Nationalism and Globalization: European and North American Perspectives*. He also edited *Sport and the Irish: Histories, Identities, Issues* and co-edited *The Politics of the Olympics: A Survey*. He is the founding editor and editor-in-chief of the *Asia Pacific Journal of Sport and Social Science* and serves on the editorial boards of a number of journals including the *International Review for the Sociology of Sport*.

John Kelly is the programme director for the undergraduate Sport and Recreation Management degree at the University of Edinburgh, UK, where he is a founding member of the Edinburgh Critical Studies in Sport (ECSS) research group. His research interests are varied and his articles have looked at "sectarianism" and the Scottish media, the sociology of rugby union, symbolic self-representations of ballet dancers, sport and militarism, and schoolchildren's virtual idealised body image. His previous books are *Sport and Social Theory: An Introduction* (co-written with Gyozo Molnar) and *Bigotry, Football and Scotland* (co-edited with John Flint).

Jung Woo Lee is Lecturer in Sport and Leisure Policy at the University of Edinburgh, UK. He is an associate editor of the *Asia Pacific Journal of Sport and Social Science* and a founding member of the Edinburgh Critical Studies in Sport (ECSS) research group. His research interests include sport media and communication, semiotics, sport mega-event studies, and globalisation of sport. He has published articles in various books and peer-reviewed journals including *Sociology*, the *International Review for the Sociology of Sport*, the *Journal of Sport and Social Issues*, the *International Journal of Sport Communication, Communication and Sport*, and *Sport in Society*.

ROUTLEDGE HANDBOOK OF SPORT AND POLITICS

Edited by Alan Bairner, John Kelly and Jung Woo Lee

Routledge
Taylor & Francis Group

LONDON AND NEW YORK

First published 2017 by Routledge

2 Park Square, Milton Park, Abingdon, Oxfordshire OX14 4RN
52 Vanderbilt Avenue, New York, NY 10017

Routledge is an imprint of the Taylor & Francis Group, an informa business

First issued in paperback 2020

British Library Cataloguing-in-Publication Data
A catalogue record for this book is available from the British Library

Library of Congress Cataloging in Publication Data
Names: Bairner, Alan.
Title: Routledge handbook of sport and politics / edited by
Alan Bairner, John Kelly and Jung Woo Lee.
Description: Milton Park, Abingdon, Oxon ; New York, NY :
Routledge, 2016. | Series: Routledge international handbooks |
Includes bibliographical references and index.
Identifiers: LCCN 2016014442| ISBN 9781138792548 (hardback) |
ISBN 9781315761930 (ebook)
Subjects: LCSH: Sports—Political aspects. | Sports and state.
Classification: LCC GV706.35 .R684 2016 | DDC 306.4/83—dc23
LC record available at https://lccn.loc.gov/2016014442

ISBN: 978-1-138-79254-8 (hbk)
ISBN: 978-0-367-89684-3 (pbk)

Typeset in Bembo Std
by Swales & Willis Ltd, Exeter, Devon, UK

CONTENTS

Contents

ILLUSTRATIONS

Figures

Tables

CONTRIBUTORS

Mary Louise Adams is a professor in the School of Kinesiology and Health Studies and the Department of Sociology at Queen's University. She is the author of *Artistic Impressions: Figure Skating, Masculinity and the Limits of Sport* (2011) and *The Trouble with Normal: Postwar Youth and the Making of Heterosexuality* (1997). She writes on issues related to the history of sexuality, queer and feminist social movements and on gender and sexuality in sport and physical activity. She has recently started work on two new projects: an oral history on the legacies of feminism in contemporary women's sport, and a study of the historical and cultural meanings of walking.

Lincoln Allison is currently Emeritus Reader at the University of Warwick. He is also an Ambassador at the National Forest Company and a tutor at Pembroke-Kings International Programme, University of Cambridge. Lincoln previously spent twenty five years at the University of Warwick. He is author or editor of eighteen books running into more than forty editions. He has also authored more than a thousand articles including regular features in *New Society*, *The Daily Telegraph*, *The Countryman*, *The Washington Times*, *Standpoint* and the Social Affairs Unit website. He is a regular contributor to national media programmes.

Mahfoud Amara is Assistant Professor in Sport Management and Policy at the College of Arts and Sciences, Qatar University. He was previously a lecturer in Sport Policy and Management in the School of Sport, Exercise and Health Sciences at Loughborough University and was the Deputy Director of the Centre for Olympic Studies and Research in the same School. Dr Amara's principal research area is comparative sports policy, and he has a specific interest in sport in Arab and Muslim contexts (society, history, culture, religion, economy, political and philosophical thoughts). He has published work on the politics of the Pan-Arab Games, sport in colonial and post-colonial Algeria, sport and media in the Arab world, sport and modernisation debate in the Gulf region, sport development and development through sport in the Arab World. His other research interests are sport, multiculturalism and intercultural dialogue. In 2012 he published *Sport, Politics, and Society in the Arab World*.

David Andrews is a professor in the Kinesiology department at the University of Maryland. His research focuses on the critical analysis of contemporary sport culture, with a particular focus on: the commercialisation and corporatisation of sport; sport and celebrity culture; the Olympic Games and other media sport spectacles; sport and globalisation; and sport and the built environment.

Will Atkinson, independent scholar, first became interested in the relationship between sustainability and sport in 2010 whilst focusing his Sports Science with Management degree on the Sociology of Sport at Loughborough University. In order to pursue this interest, he studied the Environment, Science and Society MSc in UCL's Human Geography department where his dissertation examined sustainability in the commercialised sport industry, using Wimbledon's Centre Court redevelopment as a case study. Since graduating from UCL, William has worked on a number of grassroots sustainability projects in London.

Alan Bairner was educated at the universities of Edinburgh and Hull, where he was awarded a PhD in political theory for his thesis on Antonio Gramsci's theory of the state. He is Professor of Sport and Social Theory at Loughborough University. He has written extensively on the relationship between sport and national identity. He is co-author of *Sport, Sectarianism and Society in a Divided Ireland* (1993) and author of *Sport, Nationalism and Globalization: European and North American Perspectives* (2001). He also edited *Sport and the Irish: Histories, Identities, Issues* (2005) and co-edited *Sport in Divided Societies* (1999), *The Bountiful Game? Football Identities and Finances* (2005) and *The Politics of the Olympics: A Survey* (2010). He is the founding editor and editor-in-chief of the *Asia Pacific Journal of Sport and Social Science* and serves on the editorial boards of the *International Review for the Sociology of Sport*, the *International Journal of Sport Policy and Politics*, the *Journal of Sport for Development and Soccer and Society* and the editorial advisory board of *Leisure Studies*.

Daphné Bolz, PhD, is Associate Professor (*maître de conférences*) at the University of Rouen, France. Her main research interests lie in the organisation of sport, in international influences and in sports architecture in interwar Europe (Germany, Italy, England). She is the author of *Les Arènes totalitaires. Fascisme, nazisme et propagande sportive*, 2008.

Claire Brewster is Senior Lecturer in Latin American history at Newcastle University in the School of History, Classics and Archaeology. She has published several books and articles on late twentieth-century Mexico including *Responding to Crisis in Contemporary Mexico* and *Representing the Nation: Sport and Spectacle in Post-Revolutionary Mexico* (2010). She is currently co-authoring a book on sport, politics and society in twentieth-century Mexico.

Keith Brewster is Senior Lecturer in Latin American history in the School of History, Classics, and Archaeology at Newcastle University. His research interests relate to the dynamics between sport, politics and society in twentieth century Mexico. He is the author of various articles on related topics, was editor of *Reflections on Mexico 68*, and co-author of *Representing the Nation: Sport and Spectacle in Post-Revolutionary Mexico*.

Michael Butterworth (PhD, Indiana University, USA) is Director and Associate Professor of the School of Communication Studies at Ohio University (USA). His research examines the relationships between rhetoric, democracy and sport, with a particular focus on nationalistic and militaristic discourses in the United States. He is the author of *Baseball and Rhetorics of Purity: The National Pastime and American Identity during the War on Terror* (2010), and co-author of *Communication and Sport: Surveying the Field* (2014). His research has appeared in journals such as *Communication and Critical/Cultural Studies, Communication and Sport, Critical Studies in Media Communication*, the *Journal of Sport and Social Issues* and the *Quarterly Journal of Speech*. He is also the founding Executive Director of the International Association for Communication and Sport (IACS).

Megan Chawansky is currently a senior lecturer at the University of Brighton. Her research focuses on socio-cultural power struggles around gender, and the way in which these struggles shape the subjectivities, bodies and lives of girls and women. She has worked and researched in the SDP sector since 2008.

Tzu-hsuan Chen is Associate Professor at the Graduate Institute of Physical Education, National Taiwan Sport University. His research interests currently focus on sport and the mass media, globalization, nationalism and cultural studies.

Olga Chepurnaya is currently a visiting professor at the University of Alberta, Edmonton, Canada. Her research focuses on critical theories of sport in relation to Soviet and Russian sports' policy and her recent publications include an analysis of the Moscow Olympics as a mega-event in the context of the Cold War and a case study focusing on the construction of a new soccer stadium in St Petersburg, Russia.

Christine Dallaire is an associate professor at the School of Human Kinetics at the University of Ottawa. She researches the role of sport in the discursive reproduction of minority and national identities in Canada, particularly among Francophone youth.

Paul Darby is a reader in the Sociology of Sport at the University of Ulster. He has written extensively on football in Africa, including the monograph *Africa, Football and FIFA: Politics, Colonialism and Resistance*, published in 2002.

Bevan Erueti is based in Te Kura Pūkenga Tangata/College of Humanities and Social Sciences at Te Kunenga ki Pūrehuroa/Massey University. His research incorporates two major foci linked by an overall theme of indigeneity with a particular convergence of Māori development in the areas of health, physical education and sport. The first focal point centres on promoting Māori knowledge in Health and Physical Education in mainstream education environments. The second focal area is based on his current research interests that examine how sport is understood in a Māori contemporary worldview, highlighting the characteristics of cultural identity for Māori elite athletes, and showing the impact cultural identity has on participation in sport at the elite level.

Eva Maria Gajek is a researcher in the Department of Journalism and History at the University of Giessen, Germany. Her research interests lie in European media and cultural history. She is the author of the book *Imagepolitik im olympischen Wettstreit* ("Image Politics and the Olympic Games" (2013)).

Paul Gilchrist, PhD, is Senior Lecturer in Human Geography at the School of Environment and Technology, University of Brighton. He has written widely on the politics of sport and leisure, and is co-editor of *The Politics of Sport: Community, Mobility, Identity* (2011). He is co-founder and joint convenor of the Political Studies Association's Sport and Politics Specialist Study Group.

Jonathan Grix is a Reader in Sport Policy and Politics in the School of Sport, Exercise and Rehabilitation Sciences, Director of the Sport Policy Centre and Head of the Sport Pedagogy and Sport Policy research and teaching group at the University of Birmingham. His latest books include *Sport under Communism: Behind the East German "Miracle"* (co-authored with Mike Dennis, 2012); *Understanding UK Sport Policy in Context* (co-edited with Lesley Phillpots, 2014) and *Sport Politics: An Introduction* (2016).

Spencer Harris is Assistant Professor at the University of Colorado, Colorado Springs' College of Business. He received his PhD in sport policy and sport management from Loughborough University, England. He researches the governance of sport and the sport policy process. His current research focuses on the governance of Olympic sport, specifically International Sport Federations and National Governing Bodies of Sport. Spencer has worked in various academic positions in the UK and the USA since 2008. Prior to academia, Spencer worked for sixteen years in community sports development in a variety of settings including sport development manager for Crawley Borough Council, Project Coordinator for Right to Play, and Head of Performance for Sport England.

Jean Harvey is a full professor at the School of Human Kinetics of the University of Ottawa. His research focuses on sport policy in Canada and on sport in the context of globalization. He recently co-authored *Sport and Social Movements: From the Local to the Global* published in 2014.

David Hassan is Head of the School of Sport and Head of Research Graduate School for Faculty of Life and Health Sciences at the University of Ulster in Ireland. He has published eleven books and 150 other research outputs, including eighty peer-reviewed articles in leading international journals and book chapters. He holds a Distinguished Research Fellowship from Ulster in recognition of his outstanding contribution to research, defined by its quality, breadth and impact. David has been Academic Editor of *Sport in Society* for over a decade. In 2008 he was invited to become an International Scholar with the International Football Institute, whilst he has delivered over twenty invited lectures, including at Oxford University, the University of London and Griffith University, Australia. In March 2014 he delivered a lecture to politicians and officials of the Northern Ireland Assembly on the role of sport in addressing issues of social marginalisation for young people in the country.

Susanna Hedenborg is Professor in Sport Science, Malmö University. Hedenborg has a background in Economic History and has studied gender relations in equestrian sports and horse racing both historically and currently. She has published several studies on contemporary children and youth sport. Hedenborg has written numerous textbooks on Swedish history and is a member of the ECSS scientific board. In 2015 she received the Swedish Sport Science reward for her achievements in Sport Science.

John Horne is Professor of Sport and Sociology at the University of Central Lancashire, UK. He is the author, co-author, editor and co-editor of numerous books, edited collections, journal articles and book chapters. His books include *Sport and Social Movements: From the Local to the Global* (2014), *Understanding Sport: A Socio-Cultural Analysis* (2013), *Understanding the Olympics* (2012), *Sports Mega-Events: Social Scientific Analyses of a Global Phenomenon* (2006) and *Sport in Consumer Culture* (2006).

Barrie Houlihan is Professor of Sport Policy at Loughborough University, UK, and Visiting Professor at the Norwegian School of Sport Sciences. He has authored or edited twenty books and authored over sixty journal articles. His most recent book is *Managing Elite Sport Systems: Research and Practice* (edited with Svein S. Andersen and Lars Tore Ronglan). He is the editor in chief of the *International Journal of Sport Policy and Politics*.

Kevin Hylton is Professor of Equality and Diversity in Sport, Leisure and Education, Carnegie Faculty, Leeds Beckett University, UK. Kevin is the first Black Professor to hold this title. Kevin was heavily involved in community sport development in the 1980s and early 1990s and works with marginalised groups and representative equality bodies in different settings. His early research focused on race equality in local government and has continued research into the nature and extent of "race" and racism in sport, leisure and education. Kevin has published extensively in peer-reviewed journals and high-profile book projects. Kevin's publications include *Sport Development: Policy, Process and Practice* (2013). Kevin also wrote *"Race" and Sport: Critical Race Theory* (2009) and is currently writing *Contesting "Race" and Sport: Shaming the Colour Line* for Routledge. Kevin is Patron of the Equality Challenge Unit Race Equality Charter Mark, Patron of Black British Academics, and Board Member for the *International Review for the Sociology of Sport* and the new *Journal of Global Sport Management*.

Grant Jarvie is Chair of Sport at the University of Edinburgh, where he is Head of the Academy of Sport. He is linked to the School of Education, the Academy of Government and the Centre for Cultural Relations. He is advisor to a number of governments (Scotland, the United Kingdom, Montenegro, Romania, Portugal, Monaco, Malaysia and Kenya) on key matters of policy and development. He acts as an international advisor to UNESCO. He was awarded the Glen Fiddich Scottish Literary Award for his book *Highland Games: The Making of the Myth* (1991) and more recently Routledge has published *Sport, Culture and Society* (2012) and re-issued *Class, Race and Sport in South Africa's Political Economy* (2014). Grant has spent his career combining research and teaching into sport, education, health and international development, while leading organisational change in higher education.

Nigel Jarvis completed his PhD in 2006 at the University of Brighton, which examined the meaning of sport in the lives of Canadian and British gay men. The research critically aids in understanding how the lived experiences of gay men taking part in sport relate to and inform relevant hegemonic and queer theoretical debates. Nigel undertook his MA in Leisure Management at the University of Sheffield (1996) and his BAA in Geography at Ryerson University in Toronto (1986). He has a keen interest in gender and sexuality issues in leisure and tourism. He is currently working on a series of research papers related to lesbian and gay men's perceptions of the cruise industry in general as well as the gay cruise sector specifically. He is also investigating how heterosexual staff working on gay cruise charters interact with customers.

Kevin Jefferys is Professor of Contemporary History at the University of Plymouth, UK. He has written widely on political and social history in post-1945 Britain, his publications including *Sport and Politics in Modern Britain: The Road to 2012* (2012), winner of the 2013 Lord Aberdare Literary Prize, and *The British Olympic Association: A History* (2014).

Dong Jinxia received her Bachelor and Master degrees from Beijing Sports University in the 1980s and PhD from the University of Strathclyde (UK) in 2001. She is the youngest scholar ever to receive the International Max & Reet Giwekk Award of NASSH. Her award-winning book

Women, Sport and Society in Modern China (2002) received international accolade. She was invited to become a visiting scholar at Yale, and selected as an advisor for ICSSPE and IWG Editorial Board and is a member of the extended Executive Board of ISSA. In the past decade and a half, she has been invited to universities and international conferences in Germany, Britain, Greece, Denmark, Canada, USA, Japan, Korea, India, Hong Kong and Taiwan to present in the area of sport/Olympics, women and society in China. She was an invited speaker at the Symposium of "Sport for children in the 21st century: opportunities and challenges" at the International Convention on Science, Education and Medicine in Sport 2012. She also organised a number of national and international conferences, including the ISSA 2014 World Congress. She has authored hundreds of articles both in Chinese and English on sport, Olympics, culture and gender.

John Kelly gained his masters at Brighton University and his doctorate at Loughborough University. He is the programme director for the undergraduate Sport and Recreation Management degree at the University of Edinburgh, where he is a founding member of the Edinburgh Critical Studies in Sport (ECSS) research group. His research interests are varied and his articles have looked at "sectarianism" and the Scottish media, the sociology of rugby union, symbolic self-representations of ballet dancers, sport and militarism and schoolchildren's virtual idealised body image. His previous books are *Sport and Social Theory: An Introduction* (co-written with Gyozo Molnar 2012) and *Bigotry, Football and Scotland* (co-edited with John Flint, 2013).

Hillary Kipnis is a qualified US attorney with a passion for human rights and with a variety of experiences in the field of international law and politics. Currently, she is a PhD candidate at the University of Brighton where she is engaged in a multidisciplinary research project that examines the ongoing occupation and its relationship to the role and meaning of sport in the lives of Palestinian women living in the Occupied Palestinian Territories.

David Clay Large is a senior fellow at the Institute of European Studies, University of California, Berkeley, and Professor of History, Fromm Institute, University of San Francisco. Previously he has taught at Smith College, Yale University, and Montana State University. His publications include *Nazi Games: The Olympics of 1936* (2007) and *Munich 1972: Tragedy, Terror, and Triumph at the Olympic Games* (2012).

Joshua J. H. Large is Assistant Professor of International Relations at Universidad EAFIT in Medellin, Colombia, where he teaches courses in Economic History, International Relations, International Political Economy and Economic Anthropology. His current research focuses on the international political economy of the Colombian peace process. He is currently writing a book on the history of the recreational *finca* (rural vacation house) in Colombia.

Jung Woo Lee is Lecturer in Sport and Leisure Policy at the University of Edinburgh, UK. He received a PhD in the sociology of sport from Loughborough University, UK. Dr Lee is an associate editor of *Asia Pacific Journal of Sport and Social Science*. He is also a founding member of the Edinburgh Critical Studies in Sport (ECSS) research group. His research interests include sport media and communication, semiotics, sport mega-event studies and globalisation of sport. He has published articles in various books and peer-reviewed journals including *Sociology, International Review for the Sociology of Sport, Journal of Sport and Social Issue, International Journal of Sport Communication, Communication and Sport*, and *Sport in Society*. Recently, Dr Lee edited the *Asia Pacific Journal of Sport and Social Science* special issue on "Examining Korean Nationalisms, Identities, and Politics through Sport."

Dominic Malcolm is Reader in the sociology of sport at Loughborough University, UK. He has written widely on the sociology of cricket encompassing themes such as race, nationalism, violence and gender. His most recent book, *Globalizing Cricket: Englishness, Empire and Identity* was published by Bloomsbury in 2013.

Udo Merkel holds degrees in the Social Sciences and Sport Sciences from the University of Cologne and the German Sport University. His MA in the Sociology of Sport is from the University of Leicester and his PhD from the University of Oldenburg. Before joining the University of Brighton in 1994 he contributed to the establishment of a new Research Centre for Comparative European Sport and Leisure Studies at the German Sport University in Cologne. He has spent extended periods of time in East Asia and South America working for several universities. After a short spell at Roehampton University in 2007 he re-joined the University of Brighton in 2008 lecturing at the School of Sport and Service Management. His research interests are in the sociology and politics of international sports events, comparative sport studies and football cultures.

William J. Morgan is a full professor in the Division of Occupational Science and has a courtesy appointment with the Annenberg School of Communication at the University of Southern California, Los Angeles. He has served as editor of the *Journal of the Philosophy of Sport* and has published extensively in refereed journals. He has authored two books *Why Sports Morally Matter* (2006) and *Leftist Theories of Sport: A Critique and Reconstruction* (1994), and edited several anthologies focusing on the philosophy of sport and sport ethics. He is a former president of the International Association of the Philosophy of Sport and was a recipient of its Distinguished Scholar Award in 1994. In the same year, he was elected active Fellow of the American Academy of Kinesiology. In 1988, he was awarded a Fulbright Senior Professor and Research Award to teach and conduct research at the Universitat of Marburg, in what was then West Germany.

Jacob Naish is both a PhD researcher at the University of Brighton's School of Sport and Service Management, and a practitioner from the world of Sport for Development and Peace. Over the past fourteen years, Jacob has worked on various SDP projects around the world as both an employee and a contractor. In doing so he's built up an in-depth knowledge of how SDP "works", based upon lived experience, and a critical perception of "common sense" understandings of it as a phenomenon. His research interests include Nikolas Rose's work on governmentality, Foucauldian conceptions of power, rationalities and biopolitics. He focuses empirically on Football for Development and Peace (FDP), Transnational Advocacy Networks (TANs), fundraising, "best practice", CSR, Monitoring and Evaluation, mobile applications, organisational management, social media, and data-management software.

Tomas Peterson is Professor in Sport Sciences (within the Social Sciences) at Malmö University, Sweden. His research interests include the professionalization of Swedish soccer, youth sport as education and upbringing, the relation between school sport and competitive sport, politics and sport.

Alexandra J. Rankin-Wright, PhD, is a research officer at Leeds Beckett University. She is an active member of the University's Research Centre for Diversity, Equity and Inclusion (DEI) and the Research and Enterprise Centre for Sport Coaching and Physical Education (SCOPE). Her research focuses on racial and gender equality, diversity and coaching development pathways in sport organisations in the United Kingdom. In particular, her research examines the experiences of Black and Minority Ethnic (BME) coaches using a Critical Race Theory framework.

Gavin Reid is the Director of the MSc Sport Management and International Development degree at the University of Edinburgh, where he lectures in sports development and sports policy. Gavin's primary research interests concern the policy and practice of sports development, with a particular focus on sport policy in the city. Within this general area, Gavin has the following main areas of interest: the politics of sport facility development/closure; the role of sport social enterprises in developing personal and social change; local government sport policy in an age of austerity; and the politics of sport event legacies.

Gabriel Silvestre is a visiting lecturer in tourism at the University of Westminster and a PhD candidate in Planning Studies at the Bartlett School of Planning, University College London. His research focuses on politics and the planning process, policy mobilities and the governance of the Rio de Janeiro 2016 Olympic Games. His publications include "An Olympic City in the Making: Rio de Janeiro Mega-Event Strategy 1993–2016" (IOC research report).

Alan Tomlinson is Professor of Leisure Studies at the University of Brighton, UK. He is a scholar and researcher on the social history and sociology of sport, leisure and popular culture. Professor Tomlinson has edited the *International Review for the Sociology of Sport* for four years, from 2000. He has been a pioneer of the critical social scientific study of sport, and is the author of numerous books on sport, leisure and consumption, including *Consumption, Identity and Style* (1990), *Sport and Leisure Cultures* (2005), *A Dictionary of Sports Studies* (2007) and *The World Atlas of Sport* (2011). His previous books include *Badfellas: FIFA Family at War* (with John Sugden, 2003), *The Game's Up* (1999), *FIFA and the Contest for World Football*, (with John Sugden, 1998), and *Consumption, Identity and Style* (1990). He has cultivated an investigative model of research into the power structures and ideological rhetoric of the powerbrokers of world sport, and written for many years on the politics of world football and the Olympic Games. His writings have drawn upon his interdisciplinary background, including social and cultural histories of working-class sport forms, studies of international sporting events and their power dynamics, and analyses of sport media.

Mick Totten is Senior Lecturer in Community Leisure and Recreation in the School of Sport at Leeds Beckett University. Originally a sociologist, he now mainly teaches Political Perspectives of Sport Development as well as Recreation and Community Development. Before teaching, Mick worked in community sport, community theatre, youth and community work and social work. For more than twenty years he has been a key club activist in a worldwide network of grassroots football clubs promoting Freedom through Football. His various interests are reflected in his recent writing on sport and grassroots club activism, inequality and community sports development, community action and empowerment, and fan power at FC Sankt Pauli.

Mariann Vaczi (University of Nevada, Reno) is an anthropologist and sociologist specializing in sport. Her geographical focus is the Basque Country and Spain, where she has done extensive ethnographic fieldwork. Her interests include the interfaces of soccer culture with identity, ethnicity, discourse, gender, ritual, politics and nationalism. Her publications have appeared in the *International Review for the Sociology of Sport*, *Sport in Society*, the *Journal of the Royal Anthropological Institute,* and the *South African Review of Sociology*. She is editor of the volume *Playing Fields: Power, Practice and Passion in Sport* (2014). Her monograph *Soccer, Culture and Identity in Spain: An Ethnography of Basque Fandom* was published in the Routledge Critical Studies in Sport series in 2015.

Devra Waldman is currently a Masters student at the University of British Columbia, Canada. Her thesis investigates how and why decisions are made by executives of the International Cricket Council to support international development work, and the potential implications of these decisions in recipient communities.

Stuart Whigham is a lecturer in Physical and Sport Education at the University of Worcester (UK), having previously been a lecturer in Physical and Sport Education in the School of Education, Theology and Leadership at St Mary's University College, Twickenham. He is also currently completing a doctoral thesis at Loughborough University on the political use of the 2014 Glasgow Commonwealth Games.

Thomas Zeiler is Professor of History and Director, Program in International Affairs at the University of Colorado, Boulder. Recent publications include *Ambassadors in Pinstripes: The Spalding World Baseball Tour* (2006), *Annihilation: A Global Military History of World War II* (2011), and *Jackie Robinson and Race in America* (2014). He is the former editor of *Diplomatic History* and President (2012) of the Society for Historians of American Foreign Relations (SHAFR).

ACKNOWLEDGEMENTS

As editors we would like to thank all of the contributors who have given up their time to provide excellent and thought-provoking chapters. Their patience and cooperation is very much appreciated. The volume reflects their interdisciplinarity and inter-cultural expertise and we are delighted to have included colleagues who are at different stages of their academic careers and from many parts of the world.

The Routledge Handbook series is well established and we are pleased to have been invited to contribute to this with the focus on Sport and Politics. We recognise that this task was challenging, not least due to the broad scope such a handbook could have. We realise too that this volume's range is unavoidably selective and limited, but we hope that readers will enjoy and engage with the chapters in positive and constructive ways.

We would like to thank Simon Whitmore, Joshua Wells and Cecily Davey for commissioning and developing the volume and for being instrumental in bringing the project to a successful completion. Thank you also to Mingxian Chen and Clare Murphy, who helped with the preparation of the final manuscript.

We are grateful to our students and colleagues who continue to challenge and enthuse us. Last, but by no means least, thanks to all those who care about freedom and equality and who continue to act in their name both inside and outside of sport.

Alan Bairner
John Kelly
Jung Woo Lee

EDITORS' INTRODUCTION

The sport–politics nexus

This handbook offers insights into the various ways in which two of the more prominent forms of human social intercourse – sport and politics – interact with each other. We take sport to consist of a number of competitive activities which operate according to well-defined rules and involve physical effort, albeit to varying degrees. Politics has been described by many as a series of activities through which it is decided, often by negotiation but frequently by force, who should get what, where and how. It is concerned with the resolution of conflict, the bestowing of rewards and the inflicting of punishments. It is often identified solely with reference to certain institutions, most notably the state. However, its reach is far greater than this, such that with a small "p", the word can be applied to any form of social organisation and, with a rather larger "P", to the everyday existence of people throughout the world. The contributors to the handbook collectively provide insights into the relationship between sport and politics as defined and understood in these different ways. In so doing, it is hoped they also make a fundamental contribution to a field of inquiry that has long been overlooked at least by those whose professional interest is in the study of politics.

Political studies (or political science, to use the term more favoured in North America) has been considerably slower than other cognate academic disciplines, including sociology, anthropology and history, to engage seriously with sport. Some attempts have been made to examine certain aspects of sport within specific branches of political studies, most notably policy analysis and international relations. Such work aligns itself to what has been described as "statist thinking" and is a major component of the edifice of contemporary political science (Magnusson 2010: 53). However, exponents of other elements of the discipline, including political sociology, the history of political thought, political philosophy, political theory and political ideology, have tended to either ignore sport completely or to mention it only as a passing aside. This collection of essays includes work that originates in those areas of political studies which have been more inclined to engage with sport. However, it also contains contributions that look beyond the state and attempt to discern the interaction between sport and politics in relation to ideologies, values and identities.

For many political scientists, sport is an important element in their lives – but often only of those lives as lived away from the lecture theatre, the seminar room and the computer screen.

Sport for them is something that goes on outside of the academic realm. As such it offers an escape from thinking constantly about *important* matters. But this in itself highlights a significant paradox because, if sport is important at all to them, for whatever reason, and we know that it is certainly of major significance to millions of people throughout the world, then it deserves to be regarded as a weighty issue rather than a relatively meaningless diversion. In any case, sport is closely linked to most, if not all, of those aspects of human society that political scientists clearly do regard as significant – policy-making, law and order, international relations, social class, gender, race, nationalism, ethnicity, and so on. Indeed, sport cannot be disentangled from these issues and consequently demands proper attention, if only because of the company that it keeps.

In fact, sport can offer an important avenue along which students of politics can travel in search of a deeper understanding of numerous aspects of human society. As Whannel (1983: 27) once put it, "sport offers a way of seeing the world". But arguably even this is to sell sport short. Matt Hern's (2013: 7) hope is that we:

> consider sports as seriously as we take other "high" art forms, to understand sports as sitting squarely within a spectrum of creative expression, and just as worthy of our serious attention, engagement, reflection, love, and respect.

As Hern suggests, sport is a hugely significant part of the contemporary world. Yet Whannel's point is also well made and incontestable and leads logically to the question, "Why has sport been so ignored by people whose profession it is to understand the political?" There is certainly no denying that "across the ideological, class, cultural, and sporting spectrum, there seems to be a consensus that sports are, at best, distractingly vapid" (Hern 2013: 9).

One reason for the academic neglect of sport, including that of students of politics, is to be found in the elitism of academia itself. In this regard, sport is by no means the only subject to have been treated in a cavalier fashion by the self-appointed guardians of what is deemed to be worthy of academic attention by a whole range of disciplines. In the world of musicology, pop music has often been dismissed as too frivolous for serious study. In literature, only the study of "good" writing has traditionally been encouraged. Elsewhere the question of what is or is not "good" art has exercised the minds of historians and critics alike. In such ways has a narrow definition of culture been constructed and reproduced even into an era in which popular culture has threatened to overwhelm its more esoteric opponents.

Second, the neglect of sport by political studies has much to do with the privileged position that has been assigned to sport and which the would-be custodians of sport's best interests have assigned to themselves. The myth of sport's autonomy has been so widely and successfully promoted as to effectively block attempts by all but the most tenacious to try to set it within a wider socio-political context. Arguably political science was always more likely to be seen by sports people as posing a threat to their world view than other disciplines for the simple reason that it must inevitably speak directly, rather than tangentially as might be the case with history and sociology, about the relationship between sport and politics which their myth of autonomy seeks to deny. As Lincoln Allison, one of the leading advocates of the political study of sport suggests:

> taking what has been said so far about the nature and development of sport and putting it alongside the assumptions in ordinary language about the concerns of politics – government, policy-making, social order and control – it would seem obvious that sport and politics impinge on one another.
>
> *(Allison 1986: 12)*

Despite this, or perhaps because of it, this "truth" is widely understood but not explicitly recognised; we are still constantly assailed with the claim by sports people, politicians and others that sport and politics do not or, at the very least, should not mix.

It is impossible for any handbook to include everything that could be considered to be relevant to its specific sphere of interest. Readers will note, and perhaps regret, for example that there are no chapters devoted specifically to the relationship between sport and politics in South Africa or the former Yugoslavia. However, the story of the former is arguably already well known to anyone with a serious, or even passing, interest in sport and politics. Above all, Nelson Mandela's willingness to be associated with the Springboks rugby team has become iconic in the eyes of those who would have us believe that sport has the potential to challenge and ultimately transcend political divisions. One might add, however, that ongoing debates about the use of quotas for the selection of national sport teams highlights the extent to which sport is just as likely, if not more so, to reflect and at times exacerbate division. The case of the former Yugoslavia is, of course, very different in so far as rather than sport being seen as a vehicle for healing old wounds and creating national unity, sport, and particularly football, played a significant role in reproducing those very national identities which directly contributed to the downfall of the unitary state, thereby ensuring that we now have formal international sporting rivalries amongst the Balkan peoples instead of internal ones. The issues raised by the cases of South Africa and the former Yugoslavia are discussed by the contributors to this handbook with reference to a range of other examples of the interaction between sport and the political.

Using sport to bolster political causes

It is quite obvious that sport occupies a prominent position in many, if not most, "developed" countries. This is something sponsors, for example, are well aware of. But sponsors, of course, are not the only ones to use sport to further their ideological causes. Various actors are afforded sporting platforms from which to promote political and ideological causes. This includes politicians using sport to gain political capital and charities using sport for financial and moral support. But it also includes non-official groups like supporters, consumers and athletes themselves who can also act in sporting environments in ways that push their cause/ideology or indeed challenge an official one that they are being incorporated by proxy into.

Politicians using sport to bolster their political ideology and/or profile

Perhaps one of the most recognisable forms of sport being used politically is when politicians become directly involved in sporting affairs. Vladimir Putin offers a clear contemporary example, promoting Russian statehood during the build-up to the Sochi 2014 Olympics when he personally received the Olympic torch in Red Square to mark its return from the contested territory on the North Pole via the Russian space station. Sport also offers opportunities for nations to support or challenge a particular nation's politics, with the Cold War era boycotts of the Moscow Olympics (1980) and Los Angeles Olympics (1984) being prime examples along with apartheid era sporting boycotts of South Africa before the racist policy ceased. More recently, during a period of Western antipathy towards Russia (regarding Ukraine, Georgia and concerns around the treatment of non-heterosexuals in Russia), a number of Western political leaders boycotted the Sochi Games. The potent political symbolism surrounding these Games made it unsurprising that one of the most high profile political figures to publicly embrace the Games, and by extension Russia, was China's President Xi Jinping.

Political leaders do not even need to be officially part of the sporting event to seek political leverage out of it. When the Scottish and British tennis player Andy Murray made tennis history winning Wimbledon in 2013, the year before the historic Scottish Referendum vote on independence/separation from the rest of the United Kingdom, the Scottish First Minister Alex Salmond and British Prime Minister David Cameron made explicit political capital out of the win. During the Wimbledon final, both leaders were present and highly visible in the venue's VIP box and once Murray secured the win, Salmond unfurled a Scottish saltire flag with David Cameron sitting a few seats away. These scenes were widely reported in the national media for days afterwards. Within hours of the win, Cameron used the victory to tweet that "Britain is proud".

The political power of sport is such that politicians sometimes act in advance of sporting competitions to offset and reduce potential political damage. For instance, in the lead up to the previously noted Referendum vote in Scotland, the union-supporting politician Jack McConnell recognised the political impact that the Glasgow 2014 Commonwealth Games could have on promoting Scottish identity and its political extreme of independence/separation from the rest of Britain. He called for a political truce during the Glasgow Games (see Devlin 2014). British Prime Minister David Cameron held no such fear. On the day of the Sochi Games opening ceremony, Cameron – who, in opposition to previously noted Russian policies, had avoided attending the Sochi event – was at the site of the London 2012 Games invoking an imagined "Team GB" spirit while pleading for Scotland to stay in the UK (see Wintour 2014). An additional politically motivated pre-emptive strike occurred with the release of the Pussy Riot activists (and Greenpeace activists) in Russia weeks before the start of the Sochi Games. This act was certainly viewed as politically motivated, aimed at reducing potentially embarrassing human rights protests. Indeed, on her release, one of the Pussy Riot women described it as a "disgusting and cynical act" (see Vasilyeva and Isayev 2014). Perhaps one of the more amusing examples occurred in the lead up to the London 2012 Olympics, with an Argentinian television advert showing an Argentine athlete training in the contested Islas Malvinas/Falkland Islands with the accompanying message, "To compete on English soil we train on Argentine soil" (see BBC News Online, May 2012).

Of course, sport is not only used to bolster political views or further political positions, it is also used to promote wider ideological causes, which are often presented as, or implicitly assumed to be, "non-political"; ranging from the United Nations' world food programme to anti-racism sport days, minute silences for those deemed worthy, to militarism being supported and appreciated through sport. Despite nearly all of these issues and causes being the direct result of political (in)action and despite existing in very real political contexts, they are accorded apolitical status thus enabling sport to enthusiastically and "legitimately" be used to promote and endorse what governing bodies, corporate media and politicians deem to be worthy causes.

Protest and non-conformity in sport

Yet there are examples where the actions of individual athletes have yielded politically powerful symbolism; the success of Jesse Owens in the 1936 Berlin Games challenged the racist ideology underpinning Nazism, while Muhammad Ali's stance in relation to the Vietnam War draft had racial, class and religious undertones. Ali famously commented that he refused to put on a uniform and go 10,000 miles from home and drop bombs and bullets on Brown people in Vietnam while so-called Negro people in Louisville are treated like dogs and denied simple human rights.

(Ali cited in Zirin 2004)

Athletes, therefore, have registered opposition to political acts both outside and inside of sport. When it is inside sport, it tends to be in opposition to the political stance, even when such acts are officially sanctioned, rather than to politicking in sport per se. In Britain, a number of (largely Black) Premiership footballers including Rio Ferdinand and Jason Roberts refused to join fellow players in wearing an officially sanctioned "anti-racism" t-shirt during their match warm-up. In the same competition, Irish footballer James McLean refused to wear the Earl Haig red poppy on his playing kit, deeming it a political symbol that he did not support. Displaying similar non-conformity, in the United States, college basketball player Toni Smith gained national attention[1] when she chose not to join her teammates in facing the United States flag for the national anthem before a match, choosing instead to bow her head away from the flag in protest of a range of American government policies (see Zirin 2004).

Other examples involve sports fans themselves and reveal the power of sport for organic supporter-based protest to occur. One of us remembers attending his first major sporting final at the 1988 Scottish Cup Final, where British Prime Minister Margaret Thatcher presented the cup; many of the 72,000 supporters of both clubs (Celtic and Dundee United) held up red cards and momentarily substituted sporting rivalry for political solidarity in chanting "Thatcher, Thatcher get to fuck." More recently, in 2013, Basel FC received a 30,000 euro fine from UEFA for its supporters unfurling a banner that was critical of prominent UEFA sponsor Gazprom, and which interrupted the live transmission of the high profile Champions League game. The 2011 Arab Spring witnessed popular grassroots uprisings, with football supporters being especially prominent in coordinating and participating in the Egyptian protests in particular (see Zacharias 2014).

If sponsors, politicians, athletes and fans all recognise sport's potential for spreading ideological messages, and if sections of the sporting world (athletes and fans) occasionally counter officially sanctioned politicking, it is hardly surprising that others beyond the sporting environs, often with counter-establishment views, also recognise sport's political utility. Sport, therefore, also provides high-profile stages for politically motivated direct action and protest, both peaceful and violent. There are those examples where terrorism occurred around the sporting event, such as the Munich 1972 Olympics and the Boston 2013 Marathon. Recognising the global mediated reach of sport, some protests occur before the event has begun in attempting to illegitimise the actual contest or nation competing, as the 2009 bus attack on the Sri Lankan cricket team in Pakistan illustrated.

Global sports mega-events

These events remind us that there are few higher-profile public stages globally than those occupied by sports events. Thus, global sports mega-events clearly exist as part of the political economy. The delivery of global mega sporting events has meaningful political implications, both domestically and diplomatically. More often than not, the decision to host a large-scale international sporting competition is the outcome of careful political considerations at national and provincial levels. Regarding internal political affairs, hosting a major international sport competition provides state officials with an important political opportunity to increase their approval and popularity rating. Frequently associated with the government's populist policy, news of winning an Olympics or World Cup bid is often perceived as a "feel good factor" with a nationalistic undertone, which potentially fosters a favourable attitude towards the incumbent president and his or her administration (or the prime minister and his or her cabinet) (Lee in press). In addition, a discourse on claimed positive legacies of hosting a mega sporting project such as the construction of new social infrastructure and the provision of new sport and leisure facilities can offer national and local governments a useful political resource for securing and justifying their current position, which may also positively influence their next election campaign. Yet, it should also be noted that not all citizens benefit from these presumed legacies, and sometimes negative consequences, such as huge economic deficit, can outweigh the alleged positives (Preuss 2015). In this case, sports mega-event populism may have a detrimental effect on the ruling party.

With regard to international relations, a global sports mega-event is often planned as part of a host nation's soft power strategy (Grix and Houlihan 2013). Soft power refers to the merit or attractiveness of a state frequently associated with its cultural resources (Nye 1990). By utilising this cultural power, a state can influence other states' behavior, or at least can make their voice heard in a diplomatic setting, without employing hard power tactics involving the military and the economy (for example). Hosting a global sports mega-event is often understood as an occasion not only for enriching the host's cultural capital, but also for displaying its rich cultural tradition to the world (Grix and Houlihan 2013). In addition, a number of humanitarian sport development programmes initiated in association with a global sports event can also increase the merit and attractiveness of the host. Yet, while it is believed that the delivery of global sports mega-events somehow contributes to enhancing the soft power of nations, it is somewhat unclear how to measure the soft power generated through being a host of the Olympic Games and the FIFA World Cup. At the same time, it seems that securing hard power resources represents the precondition for cultivating the effective soft power of the state. This means that, strictly speaking, sport mega-events taking place in emerging economies such as Brazil, South Africa and China are not so much related to boosting their soft power even if they claim it to be so. Instead, the events are more likely to function as their coming out party for joining an established political and economic order.

Surveillance and folk devils

Sport can, therefore, act as a device for securing soft and hard power, for both dominant and "emerging" states, and this power can sometimes be difficult to pin down, define and measure – one of the reasons that evidencing the material benefits of sports events is so problematic. Yet, in particular situations the political power of sport is tangible and quite unequivocal. This power is often exposed when non-official or oppositional ideological causes to the established order's political preferences are promoted in sport. It is in such circumstances that the truth of the dys-conscious political power of sport is often revealed, sometimes precipitating government and governing body action and this action often involves the increasing of surveillance.

Sport offers ripe environments for governments to increase and seek to legitimise state surveillance. This is clearly evident when terrorism and risk are perceived to have increased. Sporting events become prime examples where "surveillance capital" can be gained under the banner of protecting our security and safety. In the lead up to the Sochi Winter Olympics, Russia allegedly "upgraded" its internet and phone interception systems, leading to British and Dutch politicians raising fears of snooping in the European Parliament (see Walker 2013). In

London, it has been revealed that the surveillance cameras specially installed for the London 2012 Olympics are still functioning, "operating one of the biggest spy camera systems in the world in breach of national rules on surveillance" (Ungoed-Thomas 2016). In even more sinister developments, it has been alleged that Russian authorities collected the DNA of Muslim women in the lead up to the Sochi Games (De Carbonnel 2013). Sport continues to be politically valuable to those seeking to police and surveille citizens. As we are preparing the final manuscript for this volume, on the back of introducing a new anti-"offence" law for Scottish football, intended to criminalise Irish political expressions – Irish expressions by football fans in Scotland being framed by the authorities as politically impermissible – the Scottish football authorities have revealed plans to introduce facial recognition technology to "police" football supporters.[2] The transformation of safety and security into hyper-surveillance, censorship and the eroding of freedom of speech and movement are all potentially evident even in democratic societies and sport is often central to these processes.

History is littered with apparently well-intentioned political action in the name of protecting its citizens, and sport is one of the key arenas in which this occurs. For example, recent years have witnessed a rise in sport being used for peace and development. Yet caution is required when considering some of these wider political aims and objectives. At one end of the cautionary spectrum it can be assumed that there are various interest groups seeking to make capital out of their involvement. Who these people are and what type of capital they seek should be key concerns for critical thinkers. At the other end of the cautionary spectrum, apparently virtuous and non-political actions have become established features of the political manoeuvring of competing nation-states and interest groups yet involve highly political, non-disclosed, ethically questionable, personally intrusive and controversial actions. For instance, the CIA is reported to have embedded itself in a Christian charity in North Korea (see Cole 2015) and, in Pakistan in 2011, the United States was found to have set up a clandestine DNA collection operation in the guise of a medical vaccination programme in searching for Osama Bin Laden (see Winter 2014). The United States' government has also recently been exposed as using taxpayers' money to pay millions of dollars to numerous professional sports teams to advertise and endorse support for American militarism, when such endorsement was previously assumed (and often implicitly presented) as organic and grassroots public veneration. These and other examples remind us that we must be vigilant, curious and critical when apparently apolitical means are used and supported by governments and other political actors. Sport is one such means that is used by powerful actors and nation-states, even when it appears to be for virtuous reasons. These kinds of initiatives often occur in politically sensitive and contested arenas and it would be naïve if not foolish to assume that their sporting façade guarantees their practices and practitioners are universally virtuous or non-political. It remains the case, of course, that sport can and does offer genuine and authentic expressions of individuals, peoples and groups and it would be equally naïve and foolish to deny sport's utility and value in such cases. But as always, the questions remain: Who should get what? Where and how? How do we resolve conflict (even if it has been identified)? What rewards and punishments are fair? It may be the case that readers will be able to answer some of these questions after reading this volume, but we suspect and hope that it will raise further questions about the sport and politics nexus.

The chapters that follow will, we believe, inform, challenge and inspire readers to consider more carefully the relationships between sport and politics in a wide range of contextual circumstances. While there are unavoidable overlaps throughout, the volume is divided into six parts. Part I lays the theoretical groundwork for the study of sport and politics. Part II tackles some underpinning political ideologies, before Part III considers the positions of nations and states with regard to sport. The corporate politics and global community of sport, political activism and social justice are discussed in Parts IV and V, with the final Part VI focusing on sporting events.

Alan Bairner
John Kelly
Jung Woo Lee

Notes

1 Smith's actions gained national attention only after she was confronted on court by a military veteran who sought to challenge her actions.
2 At the time of writing, the Scottish government rejected funding the reported £4 million costs of the project but did not reject the concept.

References

Allison, L. (1986) Sport and politics. In L. Allison (ed.) *The Politics of Sport*. Manchester: Manchester University Press, pp. 1–26.

BBC News Online (2012) UK criticises "tasteless" Falklands Olympic ad. 4 May 2012. Accessed 6 May 2012. www.bbc.co.uk/news/world-latin-america-17946838.

Cole, M. (2015) The Pentagon's missionary spies. *The Intercept Online*. 26 October 2015. Accessed 27 October 2015. https://theintercept.com/2015/10/26/pentagon-missionary-spies-christian-ngo-front-for-north-korea-espionage/.

De Carbonnel, A. (2013) Putin targets Dagestan insurgents as Olympics loom. *Reuters Online*, 31 October 2013. Accessed 23 November 2015. http://uk.reuters.com/article/uk-olympics-sochi-dagestan-insight-idUKBRE99U04Q20131031.

Devlin, K. (2014) McConnell in call for halt to referendum campaigning during Games. *Herald Scotland Online*. 8 January 2014. Accessed 23 January 2016. www.heraldscotland.com/news/13139505. McConnell_in_call_for_halt_to_referendum_campaigning_during_Games/.

Grix, J. and Houlihan, B. (2013) Sports mega-events as part of a nation's soft power strategy: The cases of Germany (2006) and the UK (2012). *The British Journal of Politics & International Relations*, 16(4): 572–596.

Hern, M. (2013) *One Game at a Time: Why Sports Matter*. Oakland, CA: AK Press.

Lee, J. W. (in press) Do the scale and scope of the event matter? The Asian Games and the relations between North and South Korea. *Sport in Society*.

Magnusson, W. (2010) Seeing like a city: How to urbanize political science. In J. S. Davies and D. L. Imbroscio (eds) *Critical Urban Studies: New Directions*. Albany, NY: State University of New York Press, pp. 41–53.

Nye, J. S. (1990) Soft power. *Foreign Policy*, 80 (autumn): 153–171.

Preuss, H. (2015) A framework for identifying the legacies of a mega sport event. *Leisure Studies*, 34(6): 643–664.

Ungoed-Thomas, J. (2016) MET police still using Olympic spy cameras. *The Sunday Times online*. 14 February 2016. Accessed 21 February 2016. http://www.thesundaytimes.co.uk/sto/news/uk_news/article1667972.ece.

Vasilyeva, M. and Isayev, N. (2014) Amnestied Pussy Riot pair criticise Putin after release. *Reuters UK Online*. 24 December 2013. Accessed 4 January 2014. http://uk.reuters.com/article/uk-russia-pussyriot-release-idUKBRE9BM02B20131224.

Walker, S. (2013) MEPs raise concerns over Sochi Winter Olympics surveillance plans. *Guardian Online*, 13 November 2013. Accessed 13 November 2013. https://www.theguardian.com/world/2013/nov/13/meps-concerns-sochi-winter-olympics-surveillance.

Whannel, G. (1983) *Blowing the Whistle: The Politics of Sport*. London: Pluto Press.

Winter, M. (2014) CIA to stop using vaccinations as spy cover. *USA Today Online*. 20 May 2014. Accessed 13 February 2016. www.usatoday.com/story/news/world/2014/05/20/cia-vaccination-spying-pakistan/9339527/.

Wintour, P. (2014) Cameron urges Scots to stay part of "most brilliant country in history". *The Guardian Online*. 7 February 2014. Accessed 12 December 2014. www.theguardian.com/politics/2014/feb/07/cameron-scots-stay-brilliant-country-brand-britain.

Zacharias, A. (2014) Only a game? Not in Egypt. *The National Online*. 25 June 2014. Accessed 3 January 2016. www.thenational.ae/world/only-a-game-not-in-egypt#page2.

Zirin, D. (2004) Revolt of the black athlete: The hidden history of Muhammad Ali. *International Socialist Review (Online Edition)*. 33. Accessed 3 January 2016. www.isreview.org/issues/33/muhammadali.shtml.

Zirin, D. (2004) An interview with Toni Smith. *Counterpunch Online*. 12 March 2004. Accessed 13 December 2013. www.counterpunch.org/2004/03/12/an-interview-with-toni-smith/.

PART I

Sport and the study of politics

As noted in the *Handbook* introduction, political scientists have been slower than sociologists and historians to show an academic interest in sport. The probable reasons for this have already been rehearsed. However, as the opening section of the *Handbook* reveals, some branches of political studies have engaged with sport to a greater extent than others. This is made abundantly clear in the chapters by Grix and Harris on governance and governmentality, by Houlihan on policy-making and by Merkel on sport and international relations.

Governmentality represents the art of government, whereby governments manage to exert power over subjects by using techniques to ensure that individuals govern themselves, but in line with the government's objectives. Jonathan Grix and Spencer Harris note that issues linked to "governance" have become more prominent in sport over recent years not least because of the significant external funding (government and corporate) of sport, and the failure of institutions to effectively or appropriately govern sport. Their chapter takes a closer look at the governance of sport, with a specific focus on the governance of the London 2012 Olympic community sport legacy, drawing upon governance literature, specifically Foucault's notion of governmentality. The resultant narrative draws attention to the shift from centralist decision-making and big government to devolved governance and the passing of power to the local community level. These developments underscore an intentional government strategy that promotes the ideal of shifting power from central government to networked agents, whilst using a range of tactics to retain control and to ensure that actions are aligned with government expectations. Grix and Harris offer a valuable lens through which to analyse the governance context in which the policy process evolves rather than a specific approach to policy analysis. It is the latter that forms the central focus of the chapter that follows.

Barrie Houlihan locates sport policy-making within the broader sport policy analysis literature and proceeds to examine the distinctive features of the sport policy sub-sector. The chapter reviews the major factors that shape sport policy and briefly examines the four major macro-level theories: governance; neo-pluralism; neo-Marxism and market liberalism. The significance of macro-level theory as a foundation for the development of meso-level policy analysis frameworks is identified, thereby establishing the context for a review of three meso-level frameworks. Much sport policy-making takes place within individual nation-states. However, it is also an important feature of the international community.

In the next chapter, therefore, Udo Merkel considers ways in which the study of international relations has addressed the role of sport as a foreign policy and diplomatic tool. He offers a succinct account of the history of sport's use for diplomatic purposes, engages in a critical evaluation of selected International Relations (IR) theories that are able to embrace the world of sport, traces and outlines major trends in the post-World War II era, and assesses the changing role and efficacy of sports diplomacy, using contemporary examples. In addition to providing a stage for political and ideological rivalries, tensions and conflicts, international sports events have frequently been used as foreign policy and diplomatic tools. These high-profile events are able to facilitate cooperation, increase understanding, bridge profound differences, break down stereotypes, and confine conflicts to the playing field rather than the battlefield. Merkel develops this theme by looking specifically at the conciliatory gestures between North and South Korea in the context of the Asian and Olympic Games, whilst recognising that sport on its own cannot perform miracles.

These chapters amply demonstrate that sport has been of interest to groups of political scientists whose primary interest is in the role of institutions, particularly the state. We take the view, however, that the reach of the political extends well beyond the institutions of government and into the daily lives of billions of people, affecting the ways in which they think about the world and what sort of world they wish to live in. For this reason, the final chapter in this opening section addresses an area of political studies that has traditionally been more neglectful of the interaction between sport and politics.

Alan Bairner argues that there has always been room for debate about the aspirations of specific political ideologies and, even more commonly, about the strategies required to fulfil these aspirations. In almost every instance, but perhaps most markedly in the case of communism, gaps exist between the ideological ideal and the reality. Bairner's chapter examines the general relationship between political ideologies and sport. After a brief introduction to the concept of ideology, the chapter proceeds to consider the ways in which different ideologies have engaged and continue to engage with sport. With specific reference to sport, the actual influence and/or relevance of political ideologies varies enormously. Nationalism is arguably a constant presence. It is clear too that other ideologies have sought to directly affect the ways in which sport is organised and played. One thinks of fascism/national socialism and communism in this respect. In the case of most ideologies, however, the degree of direct influence is harder to detect. Feminism and environmentalism regularly attempt to influence sporting practices, albeit with limited success. As for conservatism, liberalism and socialism, it is perhaps easier to argue that their core values are often reflected in or antithetical to sport than that they have directly affected the world of sport over extended periods of time. By offering an overview of this kind, the chapter lays the foundations for contributions in the next section of the *Handbook*, which examine at greater length, and with reference to specific examples, the relationship between ideologies and sport.

1

GOVERNANCE AND GOVERNMENTALITY OF SPORT

Jonathan Grix and Spencer Harris

Introduction

A number of issues have ensured the rise in prominence of the term "governance" in relation to sport in recent years. First, a series of scandals have taken place associated with the governance of sporting structures commonly referred to as management corruption (e.g. FIFA). Second, a series of problems associated with competition in sport, commonly referred to as competition corruption (e.g. doping in sport), has occurred. Third, governments globally appear to be increasingly intervening in sport policy for non-sporting – and mostly political – ends. Finally, scholars have grappled with the term in order to explain a change in the manner in which public policy is delivered in a number of advanced democracies. "Governance", as a concept, has started to be used in sports studies to understand sport more often since the early 2000s. This is despite the fact that sports studies is relatively slow at taking on concepts from "main" academic disciplines, as the trajectory of the core terms from sociology, "social capital", and from international relations, "soft power", show. The rise to prominence of "governance" followed the development in most advanced capitalist states, and many "emerging" states, of a mixture of New Public Management – that is, a "devolved" central power and a desire to deliver public policy more efficiently. New Public Management appears to be an almost universally accepted governance type that is ideologically driven and purports to allow policy practitioners autonomy from a centralised state, while "steering" from behind the scenes.

Sport governance takes place at many levels, perhaps most clearly at the domestic and the international level of governance. The former concerns itself with how sport policy is delivered, how sport is funded and which type of organisations make up the so-called "sportscape", including National Sport Organisations (NSOs). International governance of sport concerns itself with those organisations that are responsible for transnational sport, for example, the World Anti-Doping Agency, the International Association of Athletics Federations (IAAF), FIFA (Federation Internationale de Football Association) and the IOC (International Olympic Committee). Such global organisations set the context within which NSOs operate; decisions made at a supra-national level often impact on and directly affect NGBs and their policies. The governance of sport is, therefore, not just a matter for individual nations. Key actors in world politics, for example, the United Nations (UN), and increasingly the European Union (EU) and the Council of Europe, have a direct impact on national sport. An example of agenda-setting policy at supra-national level is the European Commission's 2007 White Paper on sport, which suggests that member states ought to encourage a greater role for equal opportunities in sport. This is likely, in time, to force traditionally gendered sports such as golf to change their archaic policies and practices. The focus in this chapter is, however, on the domestic or national level of governance and we do so by arguing that the so-called "governance narrative", outlining a shift from big, central government to devolved "governance" of policy does not hold for the sport policy community. Further, we propose that fusing insights from the literature on "governance" – together with those from "governmentality" – can be fruitfully used to shed light on understanding the sport policy community. This offers a new analytical framework to assess the governance context in which the policy process evolves rather than a specific approach to policy analysis. The chapter unfolds as follows: after an overview of the "governance" debate, we introduce a "new governmentality" approach, we then set out the community sport policy context before analysing community sport from a new governmentality perspective.

Governance and the "governance narrative"

Issues around "governance" have become increasingly important in the last 30 years, as sport has become more politicised and as governments have invested more in sport. With heavy financial investment comes strict accountability and the need to modernise often archaic practices. In the world of sport this has led to a number of key tensions, for sport in many countries has been – and still is to a large extent – run by amateur volunteers. The delivery of sport policy in the majority of advanced capitalist states or advanced liberal democracies runs from government departments via NSOs (in the US the Olympic Organisation distributes monies to NSOs). It is clear to see how increasing levels of government funding and interest can give rise to difficulties in sport policy delivery: as modern, technocratic modes of governance meet archaic, amateur sport structures there is bound to be friction. Two strands of literature are of interest in understanding the manner in which sport is governed at the domestic level: the so-called "governance narrative" literature and Foucault's ideas about power encapsulated in the concept of "governmentality". Why this is of interest to sport politics is also clear: the domestic governance of sport covers key issues such as the funding for NSOs (who gets what, when and how), the mechanisms developed to monitor them (the checks and balances) and the effects such systems have on long-term sport development.

Only recently has sports studies looked to the mature debates in political science and public administration concerning the state's changing role in the delivery of public policy. Yet, the so-called "governance narrative", slowly becoming the new orthodoxy in political science (Marsh 2008a), is more often than not presented as *the* key approach to understanding recent developments in public policy in leading text books on the subject (see Coxall *et al.* 2003; Dorey 2005; Hill 2009). The "governance narrative" is a broad-brush approach that can usefully assist in "framing" particular studies of the sport policy area, ranging from those dealing with issues of meta-governance down to studies involving street-level bureaucrats, or both. The focus of the original work on "governance" was the "Westminster style" of government (for example, Australia, Canada and New Zealand), but general principles hold for the majority of advanced capitalist states investing heavily into sport. In particular, how governments fund elite sport, the mechanisms in place to make sports organisations accountable for the funds they receive, and the criteria and ideology upon which such a system rests.

In a nutshell, the "governance narrative" suggests a major shift in politics and public policy from "big" government to governance through networks, a wide array of "partnerships" and devolved bodies, thereby bringing policy closer to the street level and thus society.

"Partnership" working in particular, especially in sport policy delivery, has been championed strongly. This shift has led to the erosion of central governmental power and, with it, the state's ability to determine and deliver policy (Bevir and Rhodes 2006, 2008; Skelcher 2000). The diffusion of power moves from an hierarchical, top-down delivery of policy, to one that is sideways, with governance through a series of networks in which a wide variety of interests are represented.

The application of this approach to public policy in the UK has been critiqued for not capturing how the sport policy sector is governed. In particular Goodwin and Grix (2011) and Grix and Phillpots (2011) have shown that sport policy (and a number of other sectors) is a "deviant" case and as such does not fit this ideal type. This leads to a number of very interesting questions that shed light on the most salient aspects of the discussion around domestic governance. For example, why does sport policy (and others) not fit the notion of devolved, dispersed power among a variety of actors with increased autonomy from the central executive? After all, there is clearly a trend to "agencification" in the sport policy area, including arm's length agencies, the rapid growth of "partnerships", networks, charities, advisory bodies, boards, commissions, councils and other non-governmental bodies. The process described by the "governance narrative" does not result in a "hollowing out" of the state, but, perhaps paradoxically, rather in an increased capacity for central state control in most mature democracies (see Taylor 2000). The underlying, hierarchical power relations and resource dependence between networks, partnerships and government remain intact. The paradox arises between surface observation (the growth of devolved bodies) and the underlying power relations of networks and partnerships involved in policy-making and delivery. And this surface observation is usually enough evidence to confirm a shift from big, interventionist "government" to more autonomous governance by networks and partnerships (Bevir and Rhodes 2008; Marsh 2008b), a central tenet of the "governance narrative". Therefore, the "governance narrative" ideal type does not account for the continuance of "asymmetrical network governance" (Goodwin and Grix 2011) between government and resource-dependent actors, which exist in both elite and grassroots policy delivery in the UK (see Newman 2005, for a critique of elements of the "governance narrative"). This is an important point and one that has wider significance beyond the UK case. As discussed below, such an understanding of "governance" – whereby "devolved" bodies of public policy delivery do not lead to more open, democratic processes, but can be read as a state strategy for control – touches on many of the areas central to Foucault's notion of "governmentality".

On the surface the "governance narrative" would appear to accurately characterise the sport policy sector in the UK. There is no doubt that there is a multitude of organisations, committees and charities involved in sport delivery, resulting in one of the most "divided, confused and conflictive policy communities in British politics" (Roche 1993: 78) for this very reason. There is a bewildering array of actors – many with overlapping and unspecified roles – involved in the delivery of sport policy, including non-departmental public bodies (for example, the funding agencies for grassroots and elite sport, Sport England and UK Sport), a Sports Minister, an Olympics Minister, a UK Sports Institute, the British Olympic Association, 46 NSOs, 49 county sport partnerships and local authorities all working in one way or another together with the government department, DCMS (Department of Culture, Media and Sport) to deliver sport-related services. This is further complicated by the fact that there are private actors, charities, not-for-profit organisations, government-near bodies and so on making up the sportscape. However, inherent in this system – depending on how wealthy the NSOs are – are asymmetrical power relationships, mostly driven by dependency on central government resources. This ties in neatly with discussions around "governmentality".

Foucault put forward this term – which he coined "the art of government" (Foucault *et al.* 1991) – as a way of capturing how governments manage to exert power over subjects by using techniques to ensure that individuals govern themselves, but in line with the government's aims and objectives. That is, there is no overt use of force but, "increasingly, government seeks not to govern per se, but to promote individual and institutional conduct that is consistent with government objectives" (Raco and Imrie 2000: 2191). The manner in which this is carried out by governments is to offer autonomy, but with strings attached. And this is where sport policy comes in. The UK, Australia, Canada and New Zealand, to name but a few states, have introduced "modernisation" programmes to public policy delivery "designed (ostensibly) to empower and autonomize NSOs" (Green and Houlihan 2006: 49). This has been accompanied, however, by a growing regime of centrally set targets, directives and sanctions (Grix 2009). Sam's (2009) work on New Zealand sport states that through "modernisation":

> traditional, volunteer "kitchen table" administration is meant to be replaced with more formalized operations and an adherence to established management practices such as strategic planning, and the use of key performance indicators in monitoring and evaluations.
>
> *(p. 505)*

New governmentality

Our conceptualisation of new governmentality combines key elements from the governance narrative and governmentality. Specifically, we are interested in the macro context presented by the governance narrative. Policy agents today operate in an increasingly open, democratic and autonomous policy community. We also highlight the possibility that the ideals of a democratic and "newly" empowered policy community represent little more than the state's most recent strategy to retain control. In this respect, the process of governmentality reveals the art of government, the way in which governing authorities manage the conduct of individuals and groups: "to govern, in this sense, is to control the possible field of actions of others" (Foucault 2002: 341 in Bulley and Sokhi-Bulley 2014). Thus, new governmentality can be described as an intentional government strategy which promotes the ideals of shifted power from central government to networked agents, whilst using a range of tactics to retain control and to ensure that conduct is aligned with government objectives (Rose 1999).

Examples of new governmentality in England include such things as the Localism Act, the ostensible aspiration to move decision-making power and resources from central government to local communities. At the same time, governments maintain control by requiring that communities fulfil financial conditions and engage with ongoing performance management requirements. Alternatively, the key tenets of the "Big Society" reflect the essence of the governance narrative. The Big Society can best be described as a major programme of modernisation, a model representing a slimmer, more efficient government focused on engaging society, promoting social responsibility, actively encouraging community control and self-management (Bulley and Sokhi-Bulley 2014), and re-energising people power as the key solution to a broken society (Cameron 2009). These highly vaunted virtues reflect the key attributes of the governance narrative, not least the step away from the traditional, hierarchical Westminster mode of governance and the step toward a new democratic order. However, further examination reveals "the government as a series of tactics for managing conduct, as a mentality, [. . .] to spread responsibility as one of disseminating and diffusing the exercise of power as government"

(Bulley and Sokhi-Bulley 2014: 465). In other words, governments continue to govern; they just do so through the use of new and re-invented forms of control.

Before turning to an example of how a "new governmentality" approach could enlighten us on sport policy in the UK, it is important to stress how our conceptualisation differs from the original, post-modernist perspective. This is best explained in reference to our starting point, in fact, *the* starting point of all research, whether one likes it or not: that is, the ontological and epistemological position in which our new conceptualisation is grounded. We have argued at length elsewhere that researchers ought to be explicit about their "worldviews" (a "lay" way of summing up a researcher's meta-theoretical position) as this obviously informs the questions they ask, the methods they draw upon to answer those questions and the theoretical frameworks they use to shed light on social phenomena. The roots of our conceptualisation of "new governmentality" are to be found "on the border" between the research paradigms of "interpretivism" and "critical realism" and thus allow for an understanding of this new type of governance that seeks to take into account both actors' beliefs and ideas, but also leave room for structures and institutions in any explanation; such a perspective we term "hard interpretivism".

New governmentality in community sport in England

While sport policy in the UK is not a new phenomenon, the way in which it is presented, governed and delivered has changed considerably over the past 15 years. Relatively broad statements concerning indoor sports facilities, playing fields, school sport, inequality in sport and talent development have been replaced with precisely defined objectives, time-bound targets, and a relatively sophisticated (and, in some cases, costly) means of measurement. This is not to argue that all policy is presented this way or that this new form of public presentation is a prerequisite for all policy. Clearly, policy comes in many forms. That said, the key sport policy priorities of the central government since 2008, school sport, community sport and elite sport, have undoubtedly been subject to greater precision. This is due to three factors: (1) the increasing interest in sport at the highest political levels (Houlihan and Green 2012); (2) the considerable growth in the public monies (exchequer and lottery funding) allocated to sport; and (3) the broader influence of government attempts to modernise public services and its commitment to New Managerialism, involving the application of commercial sector ideas and practices to the public sphere (Green 2009; Grix 2009).

Community sport policy in England is led by Sport England under the direction of the Department of Culture, Media and Sport.[1] There are a number of policy directives that guide the work of Sport England, encompassing such matters as: supporting volunteers, encouraging talent, promoting public value (not private gain), involving the community in decision-making, and equally distributing funding across England (DCMS 2015). Central to these directives is the core policy for the period 2012–2017: a year-on-year increase in the proportion of people who play sport once a week for at least 30 minutes and, in particular, an increase in the percentage of 14 to 25-year-olds playing sport once a week, and a reduction in the proportion of 14 to 25-year-olds dropping out of sport. Implementation is led by National Governing Bodies of Sport (NGBs) with support from county sport partnerships and a range of national agencies including Street Games, Dame Kelly Holmes Legacy Trust, Sports Coach UK, Youth Sport Trust, English Federation of Disability Sport, Sporting Equals and the Women's Sports Foundation (see Figure 1.1). The specific action plans, programmes, and targets for increased participation reside within the Whole Sport Plan of each NGB. These plans are assessed by Sport England and funding allocations are awarded to each NGB based on goals and targets as well as the growth potential of each sport. For the period 2008–2017, a total of £950 million was invested in NGB whole sport plans and the support services of county sports partnerships (CSP) (Sport England 2015). The NGB-CSP partnership represents the institutional delivery arm of community sport policy insomuch as it is responsible for translating the NGB whole sport plan into local-level action (activities, programmes, promotional campaigns, etc.). In this way, the CSP is considered the strategic lead agency for sport for the sub-region and thus best placed to support the NGB in the implementation of its whole sport plan. Measuring progress against the policy objective is achieved through the Active People Survey. This survey collects a range of information about frequency and type of sports participation and allows analysis of changes in sports participation across the England population from 2005/6 to the present day.

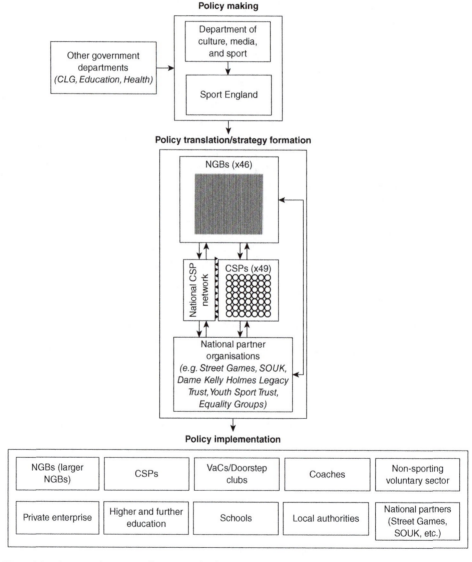

Figure 1.1 Community sport policy in England

The community sport policy process is an interesting case study when examining governance in England. On the one hand, the community sport landscape – that is, the range of agencies and partnerships that make up the delivery system for community sport – appear to present an apposite example of the governance narrative, in particular the creation of ostensible democratic network structures and the apparent shift of power from central government to local communities. However, these structural arrangements reveal significant power imbalances across the various agencies (Grix 2010). At the same time, against the broader governmental policy context of Localism, Big Society and power devolved to networks, NGBs and CSPs must respond to the various strategies of government that have been designed to influence, manage or control policy delivery (Harris 2013). In particular, we draw attention to three examples of strategies that reflect new governmentality: the structure of the community sport system, the whole sport plan process and the performance management system. These examples are drawn from empirical work focusing on the beliefs and ideas of actors within the networks themselves, specifically senior managers of NGBs, CEOs and board members of CSPs, and senior managers of local authorities.

The structure of the community sport system

The rhetoric relating to the community sport delivery system suggests a simplified, focused and democratic partnership combining sport and local community interests. On the surface the networked partnerships[2] "signify equalities of power, shared values and the establishment of common agendas and goals" (Newman 2005: 81) together with the provision of skills, expertise and financial resource – coordinated at the street level – to drive growth in community sports participation. In reality, the community sport policy community reflects the Weberian notion of bureaucratic rationality, a top-down policy led by a narrow coalition made up primarily of government departments and NDPBs (e.g. Sport England) down to NGBs.

> We have a very heavy top-down system . . . that is all well and good, but if you don't know what is going on at the local level, who has agreed to do what, what is working and what is not, you're not likely to be very successful.
>
> *(Principal Sports and Recreation Manager,*
> *Metropolitan Borough Council)*

> The experience of the last four years has shown that most NGB strategies were top-down, were focused on the national level, and most did not know what they wanted to do at the local level. You could go and sit down and have a meeting with them and they would not be able to articulate their priorities for [the area] or how they wanted us to help them.
>
> *(Operations Manager, CSP)*

Indeed, research into the community sport policy process underscores a top-down policy sub-system characterised by its hierarchy and consequent divisions (Harris 2013). The hierarchy or patterns of authority across the policy subsystem reflect the resource dependency of the agencies that make up the system. Thus, the authority of "the principal" cascades down the community sport structure whereby the various "principals" (the principal varies according to level) attempt to control and manage the behaviour of various "agents". To clarify, at the national level, the capacity and authority of the national-level agent (Sport England) is heavily dependent on the resources it receives from the principal (DCMS). Similarly, the ability of NGBs (agents) to secure funding for growing and sustaining sports participation is dependent on the resources it receives from the principal (Sport England). This pattern of authority and dependence cascades down the community sport structure and influences the nature of the relationships between NGBs, CSPs, local authorities and community sports clubs. Thus, from a rational perspective, it is in the agents' interest to cooperate and support the principal or governing authority, and reflect their ideals and norms, rather than bargain or enter into conflict regarding the nature of community sport policy. This is not to imply that agents unquestionably comply with principal requirements and refrain from subverting policy demands, but the hierarchical structure and the systems established to support principal control do reinforce the more centralised, traditional Westminster model of governance, as opposed to a shift of power to the local level.

The notion of democratic governance belies the nature of the enforced partnership between NGBs and CSPs and creates significant structural problems that hinder cooperation and collaboration across the community sport landscape. The partnership is described as enforced, as agencies, in particular CSPs, must comply with the minimum standards set out in Sport England's core specification in order to receive funding. While the networked partnership between NGBs and CSPs may work well in isolated cases, there are fundamental flaws in the structure, not least in the extent to which partners cooperate and engage with one another, and the degree to which there is consensus on the leadership role of NGBs and CSPs. The problem of engagement primarily relates to the broader conception of the CSP and its role in the strategic leadership of sport across the sub-region. When CSPs were created in the early 2000s, one of their core functions was to provide leadership and coordination for sport across their area. CSPs were conceived as broader partnerships, umbrella organisations that would represent local authorities, county sport associations and others involved in sport. The CSP would be the voice for sport for the area, the lead agency responsible for enhancing communication and coordinating efforts to grow sports participation and enhance talent. Whilst this broader conception of the partnership remains a feature of CSPs, to fulfill their role effectively two conditions must be met. First, the CSP must develop and pursue a strategic role. Second, it must be viewed and sanctioned as the strategic lead for sport by the agencies. Unfortunately, community sport appears to have a structure where, in some counties, the CSP assumes the former without the latter having taken place. For example: "first and foremost we are a strategic agency" (Director, CSP); "we have got to be seen in our area as taking the lead, we manage programmes and utilise local authorities and community networks to deliver" (NGB Lead Officer, CSP). In contrast, NGBs and local authorities reveal a range of perspectives, which underscore their independence and resistance to leadership from an outside source. Indeed, rather than representing a collective approach in which the CSP and local authorities work hand-in-hand, the local authority perspectives illustrate a more complex and, at times, divisive relationship where they feel that the CSP is attempting to take a lead role or dictate strategic and operational matters, where the local authority themselves felt better placed to do so:

> The CSP talks about being the strategic lead, strategic lead this, strategic lead that . . . but actually, strategic leadership comes at the local level . . . there is an argument that there is no need for CSPs. If NGBs worked more effectively with local authorities there would be more resources available to coordinate programmes in order to sustain and grow participation.
>
> *(Sports Development Manager)*

Adding to this, other local authority representatives stressed the local community development role of municipalities and their traditional role in facilitating sport development as a potential cause of tension and general lack of enthusiasm for the partnership:

I don't think we actually need the CSP . . . we could do the work ourselves if we had the funding. I would argue that we are better placed because we have the local links to make these things sustainable, we have the local knowledge and understanding to make sure it is needs-based and being delivered where it should be delivered, and to make sure that it is clearly coordinated with other services and programmes.

(Community Development Manager, City Council)

The credibility of the partnership is further weakened by some NGBs, who claim that the CSP's role in community sport is overstated: "If I'm honest, I don't spend a lot of hours with them through the year, it's not a priority, my priorities are schools and clubs, and places to play" (Regional Development Manager, Lawn Tennis Association); "while I'm mindful of the core funding that CSPs receive, it is difficult to drill down to clearly see what value and support the CSP can offer" (Regional Development Manager, Amateur Swimming Association). This reinforces the view from local authorities concerning the lack of consensus regarding the place of the CSP as the strategic lead for sport for the sub-region and underscores the pervasive nature of power and the way in which this intersects with seemingly rational and positive attempts to create strategic leadership for sport at the sub-regional level:

[A] lot of it is about the CSP wanting to be seen as the gatekeeper of sport in the area, but they're not necessarily seen as this. I mean, we would rather do the work ourselves than rely on a gatekeeper.

(County Director, England & Wales Cricket Board)

Thus, while the CSP may represent a partnership in name, the original, government-driven, broad conception of the partnership to provide a strategic lead and a voice for sport for the sub-region encompassing local authorities, county sport associations and others has not yet transpired. Rather than aiding policy implementation, the deep structures of power underpinning the partnership will more likely make the exercise of achieving policy goals more challenging than it otherwise might be (Bloyce *et al.* 2008).

The whole sport plan process

Despite the limited role of NGBs and CSPs in the formulation of national policy, NGBs play a significant role at the next level down, where they translate policy for their sport through their whole sport plan. This sets out the "community sport policy" for each NGB, detailing the targets and how the targets will be achieved. These plans are then assessed by Sport England and funding allocations agreed based on the details of the plan and the growth potential of each sport. Clearly, in the context of open and democratic governance, there is an opportunity for each NGB to engage key stakeholders in the formulation of its plan. However, the majority of NGBs reportedly pursued an insular approach, led by the upper echelons of the organisation. This is despite Sport England facilitating a series of roadshows with the aim of improving stakeholder engagement in the NGB whole sport planning process, an exercise which was largely viewed as being superficial, designed to create the illusion of engagement and consultation while allowing NGBs to continue their insular approach to planning. On reflection, this approach reinforces three key problems. First, it compromises the basic premise of network governance, that is, interacting with stakeholders on important decisions, and fails to secure commitment and consensus from implementing agents (such as local authorities, clubs, universities, schools, etc.). Second, it limits the insight of the NGB to a partial view of the broad context affecting policy, therefore remaining ignorant of significant issues that will inhibit policy implementation (Marsh and Smith 2000). Third, it illuminates the power imbalance across different levels of the community sport system, particularly between national-level NGBs, county sport partnerships, county sport associations, local authorities and local voluntary sports clubs. As one sport representative explained, making reference to the collapse of the British Athletics Federation and the creation of UK Athletics, "even in the bad old days there was more democratic decision making, more sense of ownership of the sport than there is today" (Chairman, County Athletics Association). Others reiterated the sentiment: "one of the big problems is that NGBs devise their own plans and programmes and become very attached to them without involving local partners" (Director, CSP); "the problem with many NGBs is that they don't even try . . . I mean why not come and talk to us? We know what is best for the local area, we represent it" (Head of Culture and Sport, County Council). Such comments not only underline the power imbalance inherent within the system but also the alienation that such behaviour cultivates. This, in turn, creates and perpetuates a "them and us" culture, and at its extreme, creates an apathetic or hostile environment where street-level workers seek to modify or subvert policy because it is unclear or fails to relate to the local context within which they operate (Barrett and Fudge 1981; Lipsky 1980). In sum, whilst the autocratic or insular approach of NGBs may offer a relatively quick and efficient means of translating policy, it does little to secure the participatory consensus of grassroots implementers and is likely to be far more effective in pushing partners apart rather than galvanising collective effort and collaborative capacity. Furthermore, it clearly fails to reflect the simplified and clearly coordinated system of delivery promoted by Sport England.

The core specification, the core funding agreement and the performance management system

In 2008, as a result of the revised strategy and structure for community sport, Sport England created a series of tools to strengthen the governance and accountability of the community sport system. These tools included the core specification, the core funding agreement, the performance management system and the payment by results scheme. These tools are pertinent examples of the techniques of modern managerialism (Newman 2005). However, they also epitomise the tactics of a govern/*mentality* (Barron 2005: 984) – the processes of governance – concerned with shaping, guiding and directing the conduct of agencies and individuals (Gordon 1991). While the resource dependency of most community sport agencies means that they conform with such requirements, they do so whilst reporting that such techniques adversely affect the bigger picture, namely cultivating the NGB–CSP relationship and focusing on participation growth. The core specification, core funding and performance management system were seen to be useful in some regards, particularly in relation to focusing attention, setting out expectations, minimum requirements and contractual obligations. However, such principles, specifically the creation of specifications and contracts, could be argued to contradict the very notion of network governance. Moreover, from an agent's perspective the overt emphasis on and demands of such processes was seen to unbalance the task-people management orientation of the NGB–CSP relationship toward a wholly task orientation, which in turn was generally viewed to be a major step back to the task-heavy days of an outdated public sector, stifling the softer skills and attention needed to broker and enhance partnerships and partnership interactions:

> Sport England has all those documents like the core specification that we as a CSP
> have to use, but they are just pieces of paper. What is more interesting for us is the

people behind the plan. The papers sit on the shelf, it's about getting beyond that to actually make it happen. We need to focus more on the relationship and how we can work together to achieve our goals.

(*NGB Lead Officer, CSP*)

I guess the final thing to say is about the target mentality that we all work in now. On the one hand it's fine, we need direction, we need it to help prioritise . . . The core specification is a little like that, okay, this is what I need to do, what I need to offer to be seen in a good light. But partnership working needs to be more genuine, it needs to go beyond this, it requires a more open conversation about vision, priorities and roles and responsibilities.

(*Chair/Trustee, CSP*)

Alongside this, the quarterly performance management system was seen to reinforce a short-term view where the priority was to turn in a "good report". A good report reflects good or outstanding performance in a range of specific tasks. The problem here is that many of the tasks included in the performance review do not naturally align with or contribute to growth in sports participation. For example, a CSP could submit quarterly performance reports over a four-year period that were judged to reflect outstanding organisational performance, yet at the same time the CSP could witness significant decreases in sports participation in the county. Thus, the process drives behaviours, such as focusing attention and allocating resources to achieving short-term goals, such as achieving "excellent" performance reports, rather than the more challenging, longer-term goal of driving growth in mass participation. Simultaneously, the process emphasises recognition and rewards for outstanding performance and high achievement as determined by the information provided in the performance report. This approach, which may be referred to as the "deadly disease of management", encourages agencies to do whatever is necessary to present themselves in the best possible light and reinforces an approach whereby "perception rules substance or reality":

We have to be honest about what is working and what is not. We tend to want to say what others want to hear. I think we are still caught up in trying to please everybody. I think we should just stop and focus on working with those CSPs where it's working well.

(*Regional Development Manager,*
England Basketball)

We like to present this idea that everything is rosy, everything is wonderful. We have to be more prepared to discuss the problems and the things that are not working as much as we do those things that are working well.

(*County Director, England and Wales Cricket Board*)

Thus, the performance management process underpins two significant problems. First, it drives a focus on perception over reality, where the desire to present oneself in the best possible light prevails over honesty, which in turn influences the norms and culture of the policy sub-system. Gaming the system for the purpose of submitting an excellent report becomes standard practice. Second, and more important, the façade of "excellence" inhibits the sharing of problems, mistakes and the more general policy learning that could emerge if a more genuine, democratic, and open epistemic community were to exist.

Summary

In this brief chapter we have attempted to highlight the value of a new approach to policy, "new governmentality", in analysing the governance context in which (sport) policy is made. We did so by drawing attention to the dominant position that the concept of "governance" has taken in debates on government set policy delivery. Further, we introduced a new "hard interpretivist" version of "governmentality", which draws on the concept of governance, but focuses very much on the government's attempt to shape and guide agents' behaviour according to government wishes through – ostensibly – devolving and dispersing power downwards closer to where policy is implemented. Such an approach is essential, we believe, especially given the unquestioned nature of the system of governance in the majority of advanced capitalist states: New Managerialism. Finally, we went on to show – using an empirical example of UK community sport policy – how this is not just a lofty academic debate: such a system of governance has a real-life impact on how policy is delivered and implemented; it also impacts greatly on the behaviour of the agents within the organisations and partnerships involved in delivering community sport policy.

Notes

1 Each of the home country Sports Councils (Wales, Scotland, Northern Ireland and England) has lead responsibility for community sports policy in their respective country.
2 We refer to these networks as networked partnerships as they bring together a range of existing sport-based partnerships (e.g. NGBs, county sports associations, clubs, etc.) and community-based partnerships (e.g. county sports partnerships, local authorities, Clinical Commissioning Groups, etc.) into a broader network focused primarily on community sport.

References

Barron, A. (2005) Foucault and law. In J. Penner, S. Schiff, and R. Nobles (eds) *Introduction to Jurisprudence and Legal Theory: Commentary and Materials*. Oxford: Oxford University Press, pp. 955–1034.

Barrett, S. and Fudge, C. (1981) *Policy and Action*. London: Methuen.

Bevir, M. and Rhodes, R.A.W. (2006) *Governance Stories*. London: Routledge.

Bevir, M. and Rhodes, R.A.W. (2008) The differentiated polity as narrative. *British Journal of Politics and International Relations*, 10(4): 729–734.

Bloyce, D., Smith, A,. Mead, R, and Morris, J. (2008) Playing the game (Plan): A figurational analysis of organizational change in sports development in England. *European Sport Management Quarterly*, 8(4): 359–378.

Bulley, D. and Sokhi-Bulley, B. (2014) Big society as big government: Cameron's governmentality agenda. *The British Journal of Politics and International Relations*, 16: 452–470.

Cameron, D. (2009) The Big Society: Hugo Young lecture. *The Guardian*. 10th November 2009. Accessed 12 November 2015. www.theguardian.com/politics/video/2009/nov/10/david-cameron-hugo-young-lecture.

Coxall, B., Robins, L. and Leach, R.L. (2003) *Contemporary British Politics* (4th ed.). London: Palgrave MacMillan.

Department of Culture, Media and Sport (2015) *Report of Triennial Review of UK Sport and Sport England*. London: DCMS.

Dorey, P. (2005) *Policy Making in Britain: An Introduction*. London: Sage.

Foucault, M. (2002) The subject and power. In J. Faubion (ed.) *Power: Essential Works of Foucault 1954–1984 (volume 3)*. Hammondsworth: Penguin.

Foucault, M., Burchell, G., Gordon, C., and Miller, P. (1991) *The Foucault Effect: Studies in Governmentality*. London: Harvester/Wheatsheaf.

Goodwin, M. and Grix, J. (2011) Bringing structures back in: The governance narrative, the decentred approach and asymmetrical network governance in the education and sport policy communities. *Public Administration*, 89(2): 537–556.

Gordon, C. (1991) Government rationality: An introduction. In G. Burchell, C. Gordon, and P. Miller (eds.) *The Foucault Effect: Studies in Governmentality*. London: Harvester/Wheatsheaf.

Green, M. (2009) Podium or participation? Analysing policy priorities under changing modes of sport governance in the United Kingdom. *International Journal of Sport Policy*, 1(2): 121–144.

Green, M. and Houlihan, B. (2006) *Elite Sport Development Policy Learning and Political Priorities*. London: Routledge.

Grix, J. (2009) The impact of UK sport policy on the governance of athletics. *International Journal of Sport Policy*, 1(1): 31–49.

Grix, J. (2010) The Governance debate and the study of sport policy. *International Journal of Sport Policy*, 2(2): 159–171.

Grix, J. and Phillpots, L. (2011) Revisiting the governance narrative: Asymmetrical network governance and the deviant case of the sport policy sector. *Public Policy and Administration*, 26(1): 3–19.

Harris, S. (2013) An analysis of the significance of the relationship between NGBs and CSPs in the delivery of community sport policy. Thesis (PhD). Loughborough University.

Hill, M. (2009) *The Public Policy Process* (5th ed.). Edinburgh: Longman.

Houlihan B. and Green, M. (2012) *Routledge Handbook of Sport Development*. London: Routledge.

Lipsky, M. (1980) *Street Level Bureaucracy: Dilemmas of the Individual in Public Services*. New York: Russell Sage Foundation.

Marsh, D. (2008a) Understanding British government: Analysing competing models. *The British Journal of Politics & International Relations*, 10(2): 251–268.

Marsh, D. (2008b) What is at stake? A response to Bevir and Rhodes. *The British Journal of Politics & International Relations*, 10(4): 735–739.

Marsh, D. and Smith, M. (2000) Understanding policy networks: Towards a dialectical approach. *Political studies*, 48: 4–21.

Newman, J. (2005) *Remaking Governance: Peoples, Politics and the Public Sphere*. Bristol: Policy Press.

Raco, M. and Imrie, R. (2000) Governmentality and rights and responsibilities in urban policy. *Environment and Planning*, 32: 2187–2204.

Roche, M. (1993) "Sport and community: Rhetoric and reality in the development of British sport policy". In J. Binfield and J. Stevenson (eds) *Sport, Culture and Politics*. Sheffield: Sheffield Academic Press.

Skelcher, C. (2000) Changing images of the state: Overloaded, hollowed-out, congested, *Public Policy and Administration*, 15(3): 3–19.

Sport England. (2015) About us. London: Sport England. Accessed 19 September 2015. http://archive. sportengland.org/about_us/what_we_do.aspx.

Sam, M.P. (2009) The public management of sport: Wicked problems, challenges and dilemmas. *Public Management Review*, 11(4): 499–514.

Rose, N. (1999) *Powers of Freedom: Reframing Political Thought*. Cambridge: Cambridge University Press.

Taylor, A. (2000) Hollowing out or filling in? Taskforces and the management of cross-cutting issues in British government. *British Journal of Politics and International Relations*, 2(1): 46–71.

15

2

SPORT POLICY-MAKING

Barrie Houlihan

The following four public policies have had an undeniably significant impact on sport either globally or within a particular country: Title IX of the 1972 Education Amendments legislation in the United States; the ruling by the European Court of Justice in the Jean-Marc Bosman case in 1995; the operation of apartheid in South Africa from 1948 to 1994 and the decision by the People's Republic of China to re-join the Olympic Movement in 1979. What the four policies have in common is that the primary motive for their implementation was not sport. Title IX was a part of an educational reform of access to United States' higher education institutions which "single-handedly revolutionised how American postsecondary institutions treat women and set the stage for women to outpace men as the recipients of bachelor's degrees" (Rose 2015: 158). However, the reform is also widely recognised as having radically impacted US college (and subsequently high school) sport and greatly expanded the opportunities for women to participate in competitive sport and contribute significantly to US success at Olympic Games (Lopiano 2000; Staurowsky 2003).

Footballer Jean Marc Bosman, due to a dispute over his transfer between clubs, took his case to the European Court of Justice (ECJ) on the grounds that the decision, by Standard Liège, to block his transfer to the French team Dunkerque, was a restraint of trade. The Court found in his favour, a decision which radically changed the power relations between players and their clubs and led subsequently to UEFA being forced abandon its rules on the number of foreign players that a club could field. From the point of view of the ECJ, it was simply enforcing the articles of the Treaty of Rome, the founding treaty of the European Union, in relation to the free movement of labour. Professional sport was required to operate within the same legal framework as other European businesses (Antonioni and Cubbin 2000; Binder and Findley 2012). The racial segregation policy of apartheid in South Africa, which affected every aspect of life in the country, not only hampered the development of non-white sporting talent, but imbued major sports such as rugby union and cricket with intense political symbolism (Lapchick 1977; Nauright 1997). Finally, the decision by the People's Republic of China to re-join the Olympic Movement was part of a much broader strategy aimed at achieving the diplomatic isolation of the Republic of China/Taiwan (Chan 1985; Lijun 2002).

It is evident that the dominant conceptualisation and metaphorical representations used in much of the analysis of public policy are of questionable value when studying sport policy. The dominant metaphors used in discussions of policy processes share a common, though exaggerated, language of policy territory, boundaries, policy-*making* and self-sufficiency. The image presented by the analyst is one of a series of relatively self-contained policy sub-sectors jostling for resources (including financial, political and organisational), but with significant though varying capacity to determine policy means and ends. Such an image is partly the result of the understandable preoccupation of governments and academics with the policy issues that command regular public and party political attention and consume substantial tax revenue such as defence, education, health and welfare. However, while the preference for exploring major sub-sectors/issues is understandable, it has the consequence of establishing a distorted template for the analysis of policy-making in less sharply defined areas such as sport and often obscures not only the extent to which sport policy is affected by external factors such as broader social and political values and history, but also the extent to which sport policy is affected by the "spillover" of decisions made in response to unrelated issues in more significant sub-sectors. Title IX, the Jean Marc Bosman case and China's decision to re-engage with the Olympic Movement were decisions driven by educational, trade and foreign policy actors respectively and were debated in non-sport forums, but nonetheless radically refashioned sport policy in the United States, the member states of the European Union and China. The example of apartheid reflects the extent to which a dominant ideology can affect policy outputs across the whole spectrum of public sector activity. Other examples of the significance of ideology would include the restrictions on women's participation in sport in Muslim countries (Amara 2008), the limits on young people's participation in elite competitive sport in Norway (Skille and Houlihan 2014) and the US federal government's extremely limited involvement in sports issues (Bowers *et al.* 2011).

Few policy sub-sectors, and certainly not sport in most countries, correspond to a mosaic metaphor in which clearly defined sub-sectors abut contiguous sub-sectors and are able to maintain their hard-edged boundaries. A more plausible alternative is to see sport as nested within more politically salient sub-sectors such as education, youth, tourism and economic development. A metaphor which refers to some sub-sectors nested within others is more persuasive and draws attention to the constraints on sport policy-making. However, a third metaphor is sport policy as residue – as the largely unplanned cluster of activities, initiatives and programmes created by default, inadvertence and spillover from other sub-sectors. In examining the sport policy process, it is useful to conceptualise policy sub-sectors as being located along a spectrum at one end of which are those whose issues present a clear profile to the public and policy-makers, which are populated by specialised and influential interest groups, where policy debate is located within recognised forums, and which possess an institutionalised policy history in terms of ends and means. At the other end of the spectrum are those sub-sectors, such as sport, which frequently struggle for recognition; whose issues are less distinct (from those associated with education, community welfare, economic regeneration and diplomacy for example) not only from the point of view of those actors considered integral to the sub-sector, but also from the perspective of external actors and interests; which are less likely to contain influential specialist interest groups or public agencies; which lack a stable forum for policy debate; and where policy stability and change is more likely to be shaped by the incidental and inadvertent decisions of contiguous policy sub-sectors. Policy sub-sectors at this end of the spectrum often travel in the slipstream of other policy sub-sectors. As was pointed out by the OECD in the mid-1980s "Public policy has become a crowded field, with complex, overlapping and even competing programmes addressing increasingly closely specified or targeted categories of client" (1987: 26). One important implication of the increasingly densely packed policy space is that "as the population of policies grows relative to the size of the policy space, individual policies necessarily become more interdependent.

The consequences produced by one policy are increasingly likely to interfere with the working of other policies" (Majone 1989: 159).

Majone's observation is clearly relevant to the study of sport policy in many countries where the dominant conceptualisation of sport is as an instrument to achieve non-sport objectives such as economic/urban regeneration, health improvement, community integration, positive nation branding and diplomatic advantage. The distinctive characteristics of sport policy means that established policy-making theories, concepts and analytical frameworks need to be utilised with care and with a recognition of a need for adaption and innovation. One example of valuable conceptual innovation was provided by Dery (1999), who drew a distinction between policy-*making* and policy-*taking*. Policy-making "implicitly presumes control over key variables that shape policy in a given area", whereas policy-taking

> denotes the pursuit of a given set of policy objectives, which is primarily or entirely shaped by the pursuit of other objectives . . . the resulting policy . . . [is] . . . the by-product of policies that are made and implemented to pursue objectives other than those of the policy in question.
>
> *(Dery 1999: 165–66)*

Thus rather than treating policies such as the hosting of major sports events, the inclusion of physical education in the school curriculum and the investment in developing a successful squad of Olympic athletes, as being primarily the product of the interplay between policy actors within the sport policy sub-sector it is more plausible to acknowledge that they are more likely to have been devised in the relatively remote sub-sectors concerned with economic development, health and international relations.

If Dery's concept of policy-taking resonates with the concept of spillover and is an apt description and explanation of the impact of Title IX, the Bosman ruling and China's re-engagement with the Olympic Movement, then the inter-related concepts of a hierarchy of beliefs (Sabatier 1998), mobilisation of bias (Schattschneider 1960) and the emphasis on historical institutionalism (Streeck and Thelen 2005) are valuable in explaining the extent to which sport policy options are constrained by ideology and history, as was the case with the apartheid regime. For Sabatier, shared beliefs (personal ideologies) are more significant in the policy process than rational self-interest. Shared beliefs bind advocacy coalitions together as effective policy actors and shape not only the way in which issues in sport are identified and defined as *public policy* issues, but also way policy responses are selected. Beliefs may be conceptualised as forming a hierarchy comprising, at the most profound level, "deep core" beliefs (ideology) that affect all policy sub-sectors including sport (the role of women in society, inter-personal trust, and individual rights and community responsibilities for example). "Policy core beliefs" include the balance in sport service provision between public agencies, civil society organisations and the market and the type of sport that should be valued (for example, traditional or Olympic, men's or women's) while "secondary aspects" refers to implementation strategies for public policy (for example, through commercial or public delivery agents and through the use of incentives or sanctions) (Sabatier 1998). In relation to "deep core" beliefs, the work of neo-pluralists such as Schattschneider and Lindblom is valuable as they refer to biases inherent in the socio-political system that constrain the policy process. According to Schattschneider (1960: 69):

> All forms of political organisation have a bias in favour of the exploitation of some kinds of conflict and the suppression of others because *organisation is the mobilisation of bias*. Some issues are organised into politics and others are organised out.

Mobilisation of bias might be a useful concept in explaining the slow acceptance of gender equity in elite sport, the lack of action on doping in many countries and the lack of apparent concern with the over-training and abuse of young elite athletes. Lindblom (1977) offered a similar analysis, except that he specifically identified business interests as the beneficiaries of organisational bias and argued that in relation to public policy, politicians and public officials instinctively seek to protect the long-term interests of business, whether in relation to major services such as healthcare and transport or in relation to sport.

The significance of historical institutionalism for the analysis of sport policy goes beyond the simple argument that "history matters", as it encourages the analyst to investigate why and under what circumstances history matters. As Howlett and Ramesh (2003: 27) argue, institutions as organisations or as sets of values and beliefs constitute "unique patterns of historical development and [impose] constraints . . . on future choices". The politicisation of sports clubs in Germany and Norway by the Nazis left a legacy of distrust of governmental involvement in sport, while for many ex-British colonies their current sport policy is clearly a product of the colonial experience. History is the accumulation of experiences and also the accumulation of "policy decisions [in which] . . . a process of accretion can occur in a policy area that restricts options for future policy-makers" – a process of path dependency (Kay 2005: 558). In a narrow application of the concept of path dependency, one would argue that early decisions in a policy area result in current policy being locked on to a particular policy trajectory. For example, the decision by a government to seek medal success in the summer Olympic Games can easily become a commitment to a path which involves spending ever larger sums of public money to retain or advance the national medal position. A broader application of the concept of path dependency would suggest that rather than the next policy choice being inevitable, it is more accurate to suggest that early decisions significantly constrain subsequent policy options and make policy reversal or termination progressively more difficult.

Factors influencing domestic sport policy

Figure 2.1 provides a summary of some of the factors that can influence the character and pattern of development of domestic sport policy. *Interests* refers to those organisations (and sometimes individuals) who have a concern with policy developments in sport because, for example, it is a source of profit (league, team owners, broadcasters), an opportunity for diplomatic advantage (government), a source of employment (IFs, NGB, club employees) or a passion (club volunteers, players). The capacity of these interests to exercise leverage over policy will vary considerably dependent upon resource control and the acceptability to other interests of their priorities. A closely related factor is the distribution of resources between non-state interests and the state with such resources including finance, expertise, organisational capacity, facilities and networks of contacts. While it is often the case that the state has substantial financial resource, it is often civil society sports clubs that have the resources of expertise, administrative capacity, organisational network and a voluntary labour force. *Cultural and historical institutions* were discussed above and can be summarised as the "weight of history" and the "power of tradition". *Constitutional and governmental arrangements* also constitute institutions which can have a substantial impact on domestic policy. For example, federal states often find it more difficult to develop national policies to support elite athletes and the central government ministry (education, youth and community or tourism for example) within which sport is located can significantly influence the development of policy. *Ideas and ideology* will also be important, for example in relation to the acceptable level of involvement of the state and the extent to which traditional sporting culture should be protected. Domestic developments can also affect sport

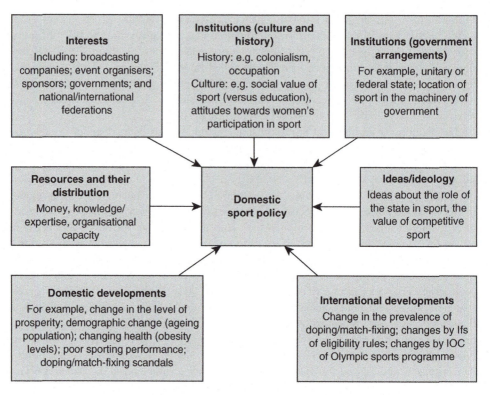

Figure 2.1 Selected factors influencing domestic sport policy

policy, for example as a result of a change in government, an economic recession, an increasing concern with children's health or a scandal. Developments exogenous to the political system may also be of domestic significance. The elite sport policy of many countries is affected by the decisions of external organisations, whether those are governmental, semi-governmental (the European Union or the World Anti-Doping Agency) or non-governmental bodies such as the major satellite broadcasters, the IOC or the major federations.

Explaining sport policy

The importance of macro-level theory

Most policy analysis utilises frameworks and theories designed to operate at the meso-level or sub-sectoral level, where the focus is on explaining particular policies, for example in relation to school sport, doping or crowd safety. However, it is important to bear in mind that valuable insights can be generated through the use of macro-level theories such as neo-pluralism, public choice and governance. Table 2.1 provides a summary overview of some of the major macro-level theories and illustrates how different theories direct the analyst's attention towards different aspects of the policy process, for example to investigate the role of the state in protecting commercial interest (neo-Marxism and neo-pluralism), the problems of managing complex networks (governance) or questioning the motives of public officials in influencing policy (market liberalism). The second important reason for acknowledging the importance of macro-level theories is that although meso-level analytical frameworks are often treated as though they were distinct from macro theories, they all have their roots in assumptions at the macro level – assumptions about the distribution of power at the societal level, the motives of public official, the significance of the pursuit and protection of sectional interests, the significance of ideas (whether as myths, evidence or ideology) and the relationship between the state and civil society. It is crucial to bear in mind that meso-level analytical frameworks are not value free and are derived from, often, highly contentious and partial theorisations at the societal level (see Dryzek and Dunleavy (2009) and Hay *et al.* (2006) for more detailed discussions of contemporary macro-level theories. See Giulianotti (2004), Morgan (1994) and Carrington and McDonald (2009) for discussions of their application to the study of sport).

Theories of policy stability and change

There are many theories designed to be applied at the middle-range or meso-level of policy analysis (see Sabatier 2007; Knill and Tosun 2012; Cairney 2012 for reviews) and, as with theories at the macro-level, they give emphasis to different factors identified in Figure 2.1. In very general terms, middle-range theories can be divided between those that give greater weight to structure (institutions) as opposed to (individual) agency and between those that emphasise the importance of ideas and evidence as opposed to the pursuit of self-interest. The three theories that will be reviewed: advocacy coalition framework, punctuated equilibrium and multiple streams, offer different combinations of these attributes.

Advocacy coalition framework

The advocacy coalition framework (ACF) (Sabatier 1998; Sabatier and Weible 2007) gives emphasis to the importance of ideas and learning as sources of change and is not only one of the more comprehensive frameworks but is also one of the most widely applied, including in the area of sport policy (see for example Green and Houlihan 2004). As mentioned above, shared beliefs are the ingredient that binds coalition partners and the ACF assumes that within each policy sub-sector two or more coalitions will normally emerge to compete for policy leadership. Bearing in mind the caveats about the problematic nature of the sub-sector concept in relation to sport in many countries, it would be possible to identify at least two competing coalitions: for example, community and elite sport, Olympic and non-Olympic sport, commercial and subsidised sport. How coalitions are defined and the extent to which they are in competition is a central question for empirical research.

Policy change or stability is affected by three factors, the first of which is competition between coalitions. At a common-sense level the identification of distinct coalitions in the sport policy area appears straightforward. However, this identification begs a number of questions: (1) How is a coalition distinguished from a looser network of policy actors? (2) in many countries coalitions overlap and are forming and reforming depending on the issue; and (3) How are coalitions organised and led? Where coalitions are present the ACF suggests that mediation between coalitions is often undertaken by policy brokers (thus giving a significant emphasis to agency), whose concern is primarily with sub-sector stability. The second factor is changes exogenous to the sub-sector, which would include both domestic and international developments that impact on sport, such as terrorist threats, economic crises and match-fixing scandals. Such exogenous developments are seen within the ACF as a catalyst for policy learning – that is, the search for effective responses to the developments adopted in other countries or policy areas which

Table 2.1 Selected major macro-level theories and sport policy

Dimension	Neo-Marxism	Governance	Neo-pluralism	Market liberalism
Unit of analysis	Social classes	Policy networks and subsystems	Interest groups	Markets and individuals
Role of the state	Under Marxism the state is an instrument of the ruling capitalist class. Under neo-Marxism the position and role of the state is less clear with some arguing that the state's role is to manage capitalism which might involve short-term actions which go against the interests of capital accumulation, for example provide welfare services through taxation to enhance legitimation.	Due to increasing complexity of social issues, governments seek to act in partnership with civil society organisations. Rhodes (1994) sees this as a loss of power (the hollowing out of the state), whereas Rose (1999) argues that we are witnessing an extension of state power, i.e. a "rolling out" of state power.	The state is an active participant in making policy, partly mediating between rival groups, but also protecting and promoting its own interests (especially in relation to problem definition and preferred solutions). The state has a bias towards business interests.	Argued that markets maximise social welfare and that individuals are rational utility maximisers. The role of the state is to enable markets to operate effectively (with as little regulation as possible). Market liberals, especially rational-choice theorists, have a deep suspicion of state action and argue that politicians and state officials will act rationally and consequently seek to maximise their budgets (through taxation) to secure organisational growth and therefore larger personal rewards. The role of the state should be limited to activities such as protecting property rights, defence, providing basic infrastructure and services (in cases of market failure) and regulating monopolies.
Dynamic for policy-making	Class conflict and/or the inherent instability of capitalism (e.g. the 2008 global banking crisis).	Accumulation of evidence and/ or external events (e.g. financial crisis).	Interaction between groups with unequal influence.	Market competition and the pursuit, by individuals, of personal interest.

Associated meso-level frameworks and approaches	None clearly, but elements of network theory in which business-dominated or business-oriented networks would manage policy subsystems; and institutionalism in which dominant power relations become institutionalised in the state.	Policy communities; institutionalism.	Advocacy coalition framework; punctuated-equilibrium theory; institutionalism.	Multiple streams.
Primary focus for the study of sport policy	Sport as a form of social control (i.e. diverting attention from the ills of capitalism) or sport as a source of profit (e.g. through broadcasting and commodification).	Sport policy networks/ community and their membership, values and decision processes.	Existence and influence of advocacy coalitions for interests such as elite, women, youth and community sport.	The regulatory role of the state. The relationship between the state, the market and the not-for-profit sector.
Orientation/key questions	How is the tension between sport as a "new industry" and as an element of welfare provision managed?	What are the dominant values in the community? How is the membership of the community decided? How insulated is the community from other policy subsectors?	To what extent do advocacy coalitions exist in sport? If they do, what is their relative strength and what is their relationship to government?	Is the state competing with the commercial sector by providing sports facilities? Is the expansion of state involvement in sport evidence in support of the public choice critique of public officials (seeking personal benefits, such as increased salaries, rather than social welfare)?

Source: Houlihan and Lindsey (2013).

might be transferred to the domestic sport policy context. Extensive policy transfer is evident in relation to talent identification and development, anti-doping policy, treatment of league monopolies and the promotion of community participation. The third factor is institutional parameters such as constitutional arrangements, tradition and history which, as discussed above, can constrain action in line with path dependency theory (Sydow *et al.* 2005). The emphasis on policy learning suggests a strong element of rationality in the sport policy process – that the accumulation of evidence (on childhood obesity rates, the economic impact of hosting major sports events and trends in gender equity in sport) will prompt a policy response. In the sport policy area this is an aspect of the ACF that needs rigorous empirical analysis for, as Coalter (2007) has demonstrated, sport policy debates are shrouded in elaborate mythologising which is, at times, impervious to evidence.

Operationalising the ACF as an analytical tool poses the problem of calibrating change – a problem which faces many analytical frameworks. Complementing the ACF with Hall's (1993) typology of "orders of change" provides a useful partial solution to this problem. First-order changes are alterations to the intensity or scale of an existing policy instrument, for example a decision to increase the funding of an existing initiative or programme. Second-order changes are those that introduce new policy instruments designed to achieve existing policy objectives: examples of which would include the decision to import foreign coaches to contribute to elite athlete development, or the decision to send talented athletes abroad to specialist training centres. Third-order changes are those that involve a change in policy goals of which the decision by China to re-engage with the Olympic Movement and the subsequent decision to seek substantial medal success would both be examples. In summary, the ACF provides a valuable framework for the analysis of sport policy, but one that still requires considerable conceptual refinement given the distinctive features of the sport policy area.

Punctuated equilibrium

The starting point for Baumgartner and Jones' (2009) theory of punctuated equilibrium (PE) (see also Baumgartner *et al.* 2009) is the observation that policy often exhibits long periods of stability, accompanied by only incremental change, which are interrupted, on occasion, by episodes of intense radical change. Central to the PE theory is the assumption that structures are conservative forces which provide institutional constraints on radical policy change. The scope for policy change originating from lobbying within the policy sub-sector is limited, as is the influence of evidence. This theory resonates strongly with the concepts of the mobilisation of bias and path dependency and the macro-level theorising of neo-Marxists and neo-pluralists. Baumgartner and Jones (1993: 7) explain periods of policy stability as partly due to the existence of "policy monopolies", which have two important characteristics: first, an institutional structure that enables control over access to the political agenda and which provides an institutional structure for policy deliberation; and second, a shared ideology which binds members (see also Bachrach and Baratz 1962). This definition of policy monopolies has much in common with Marsh and Rhodes' (1992) conceptualisation of a policy community which is characterised by: a stable membership comprising governmental and non-governmental actors who share a common view of issues and the appropriate response; regular contact; and the capacity to exclude incompatible actors. Membership of a policy community depends on the willingness of a policy actor to accept the dominant values of the community. In England it may be plausibly argued that a policy monopoly/community is dominated by commercial and Olympic elite sport actors and lobbies on behalf of youth sport and community sport; recreational as opposed to competitive sport is denied access to the decision process (Houlihan and Lindsey 2013).

While it is attractive to see long periods of policy equilibrium as the consequence of the exercise of power by particular actors/interests operating through policy monopolies/communities, it is also a consequence of the limited capacity of government to deal with the large number of issues it faces, especially the more complex ones. Policy equilibrium can, in part at least, be a consequence of the reluctance by governments to tackle complex issues in sport (such as homophobia and racism) where the prospect of a positive outcome is either remote or long term. Policy monopolies break down for two main reasons, the first of which is the accumulation of external pressure, for example resulting from the adoption by the media of a stance which challenges the current policy equilibrium. One example of the momentum that can be generated by media attention is the growing pressure on international sport federations to adopt higher standards of corporate governance. The second source of pressure is a consequence of excluded/critical interests pursuing a strategy of venue-shopping. Venue-shopping refers to the practice by lobbying groups (for example for gender equity in sport or the banning of professional boxing), who have received negative feedback from the primary venue such as the responsible ministry, to seek alternative venues such as the courts, media or a related policy sub-sector, in which to promote their cause.

Multiple streams

Kingdon's (2003) multiple streams (MS) theory (see also Zahariadis 2003) gives greater emphasis to agency over structure and downplays the rationality of the policy process in favour of an emphasis on chance and opportunism in agenda setting. Policy-making depends on the interconnection of three distinct streams or factors. The first, the problem stream, refers to the competition between advocates to bring their problem (such as the high cost of attending football matches or the loss of community sports fields) to the attention of government. The second stream contains solutions (policies) to problems. Kingdon challenges the common-sense assumption that the acknowledgement by government of a problem (i.e. that it has crossed the threshold from being a private concern to being a public issue) prompts the search for a solution and argues that the process can take place in the reverse order. In other words, he suggests that there are advocates of particular solutions (for example, using sport to address diplomatic, health or educational problems) who are looking for problems to which their solution can be attached (see DiMaggio and Powell 1983). Policy entrepreneurs play a key role in linking these two streams. The third stream relates to politics, particularly the attitude of the public and political parties towards a problem. If the national political mood is antipathetic to state involvement in sport, or concerned that school physical education will displace academic subjects, then the political agenda is likely to reflect those attitudes. The value of the MS theory is partly its parsimony and partly in its adaptability to suit a wide range of political systems. With its emphasis on contingency and the separation between problems and solutions, it provides a useful corrective to those theories which emphasise rationality (the power of evidence). However, the emphasis on chance and entrepreneurial skill needs to be tempered by an acknowledgement that these streams operate within an institutional framework that reflects the mobilisation of bias.

Conclusion

All policy sub-sectors have distinctive characteristics, but most also share many common features. While the sport policy sub-sector certainly does, in many countries, share some common characteristics of other sub-sectors (for example, a minister, specialist ministry or agency and a distinct budget – whether from taxation or lottery) the sub-sector exhibits many highly distinctive characteristics which not only make it a fascinating focus for study, but which also require that many of the established analytical frameworks need to be applied with care and often need to be adapted. However, the range of macro- and meso-level theories is both rich and adaptable and provides considerable opportunity for insightful analyses of sport policy decision-making. It is a common lament of the academic that "more research in needed", but in the case of sport policy the paucity of theory-informed research into the policy process and especially agenda setting, decision-making and policy implementation is both striking and regrettable. The regret is due not simply to the greater understanding of the social, economic and diplomatic significance of sport that could be provided, but also due to the insights that could be generated, which might benefit researchers working in other marginal policy sub-sectors.

References

Amara, M. (2008) "An introduction to the study of sport in the Muslim world". In B. Houlihan (ed.) *Sport and Society: A Student Introduction*. London: Sage, pp. 532–552.

Antonioni, P. and Cubbin, J. (2000) The Bosman ruling and the emergence of a single market in football talent. *European Journal of Law and Economics*, 9(2): 157–173.

Bachrach, P. and Baratz, M. S. (1962) Two faces of power. *American Political Science Review*, 56(4): 947–152.

Baumgartner, F. and Jones, B. (1993) *Agendas and Instability in American Politics*. Chicago: Chicago University Press.

Baumgartner, F. and Jones, B. (2009) *Agendas and Instability in American Politics* (2nd ed.). Chicago: Chicago University Press.

Baumgartner, F., Breunig, C., Green-Pedersen, C., Jones, B., Mortensen, P., Nuytemans, M. and Wagrave, S. (2009) Punctuated equilibrium in comparative perspective. *American Journal of Political Science*, 53(3): 603–620.

Binder, J. J. and Findley, M. (2012) The effects of the Bosman ruling on national and club teams in Europe. *Journal of Sports Economics*, 13(2): 107–129.

Bowers, M. T., Chalip, L. and Green, G. C. (2011) "United States of America". In M. Nicholson, R. Hoye and B. Houlihan (eds) *Participation in Sport: International Policy Perspectives*. London: Routledge, pp. 254–267.

Cairney, P. (2012) *Understanding Public Policy: Theories and Issues*. Basingstoke: Palgrave Macmillan.

Carrington, B. and McDonald, I. (2009) *Marxism, Cultural Studies and Sport*. London: Routledge.

Chan, G. (1985) The "two-Chinas" problem and the Olympic formula. *Pacific Affairs*, 58(3): 473–490.

Coalter, F. (2007) *A Wider Social Role for Sport: Who's Keeping the Score?* London: Routledge.

Dery, D. (1999) Policy by the way: when policy is incidental to making other policies. *Journal of Public Policy*, 18(2): 163–176.

DiMaggio, P. and Powell, W. (1983) The iron cage revisited: institutional isomorphism and collective rationality in organisational fields. *American Sociological Review*, 48(2): 147–160.

Dryzek, J. S. and Dunleavy, P. (2009) *Theories of the Democratic State*. Houndmills: Palgrave Macmillan.

Giulianotti, R. (ed.) (2004) *Sport and Modern Social Theorists*. Basingstoke: Palgrave Macmillan.

Green, M. and Houlihan, B. (2004) Advocacy coalitions and elite sport policy change in Canada and the United Kingdom. *International Review for the Sociology of Sport*, 39(4): 387–403.

Hall, P. E. (1993) Policy paradigms, social learning and the state. *Comparative Politics*, 25(3): 272–296.

Hay, C., Lister, M. and Marsh, D. (eds.) (2006) *The State: Theories and Issues*. Houndmills: Palgrave Macmillan.

Houlihan, B. and Lindsey, I. (2013) *Sport Policy in Britain*. London: Routledge.

Howlett, M. and Ramesh, M. (2003) (2nd ed.) *Studying Public Policy: Policy Cycles and Subsystems*. Toronto: Oxford University Press.

Kay, A. (2005) A critique of the use of path dependency in policy studies. *Public Administration*, 83(3): 553–571.

Kingdon, J. (2003) *Agendas, Alternatives and Public Policies*. New York: Longman.

Knill, C. and Tosun, J. (2012) *Public Policy: A New Introduction*, Basingstoke: Palgrave Macmillan.

Lapchick, R. E. (1977) Apartheid Sport: South Africa's use of sport in its foreign policy. *Journal of Sport & Social Issues*, March: 52–79.

Lindblom, C. (1977) *Politics and Markets*. New York: Basic Books.

Lijun, S. (2002) *China and Taiwan: Cross Strait Relations under Chen Shui-bian*. Singapore: Institute of Southeast Asian Studies.

Lopiano, D. A. (2000) Modern history of women in sports. *Clinics in Sports Medicine*, 19(2): 163–173.

Majone, G. (1989) *Evidence, Argument and Persuasion in the Policy Process*. New Haven: Yale University Press.

Marsh, D. and Rhodes, R. A. W. (1992) "Policy communities and issue networks: beyond typology". In D. Marsh and R. A. W Rhodes (eds) *Policy Networks in British Government*, Oxford: Oxford University Press.

Morgan, W. J. (1994) *Leftist Theories of Sport: A Critique and Reconstruction*. Chicago: University of Illinois Press.

Nauright, J. (1997) *Sport, Cultures and Identities in South Africa*. Leicester: Leicester University Press.

Organisation for Economic Co-operation and Development (OECD) (1987) *Administration as Service: The Public as Client*. Paris: OECD.

Rose, D. (2015) Regulating opportunity: Title IX and the birth of gender-conscious higher education policy. *The Journal of Policy History*, 27(1): 157–183.

Sabatier, P. (1998) The advocacy coalition framework: revisions and relevance for Europe. *Journal of European Public Policy*, 5(1): 98–130.

Sabatier, P. (ed.) (2007) (2nd ed.) *Theories of the Policy Process*. Boulder: Westview Press.

Sabatier, P. and Weible, C. M. (2007) "The advocacy coalition framework: innovations and clarification". In P. Sabatier (ed.) (2007) (2nd ed.) *Theories of the Policy Process*. Boulder, CO: Westview Press, pp. 117–167.

Schattschneider, E. E. (1960) *The Semisovereign People*. New York: Holy, Rinehart & Winston.

Skille, E. and Houlihan, B. (2014) "The contemporary context of elite youth sport: the role of national sport organisations in the UK and Norway". In D. V. Hanstad, M. M. Parent and B. Houlihan (eds) *The Youth Olympic Games*. London: Routledge, pp. 34–50.

Staurowsky, E. J. (2003) Title IX and college sport: the long painful path to compliance and reform. *Marquette Sports Law Review*, 14(1): 95–121.

Streeck, W. and Thelen, K. (eds) (2005) *Beyond Continuity: Institutional Change in Advanced Political Economies*. Oxford: Oxford University Press.

Sydow, J., Schreyögg, G. and Koch, J. (2005) Organisational Paths: Path Dependency and Beyond. 21st EGOC Colloquium, June 30–July 2, Berlin, Germany.

Zahariadis, N. (2003) *Ambiguity and Choice in Public Policy*. Washington, DC: Georgetown University Press.

3

SPORT AS A FOREIGN POLICY AND DIPLOMATIC TOOL

Udo Merkel

The so-called 'Christmas Truce' during the First World War (1914–18) made sport famous for pacifying the opposing sides (Brown and Seaton 1994; Jürgs 2003; Weintraub 2002) – albeit temporarily. Although this episode is often cited as evidence of sport's peace-making ability, the following three anecdotes are, at least, equally impressive and show different facets of the relationship between sport and international politics: The well-known ping-pong diplomacy made an important contribution to an improvement in Sino-American relations in the early 1970s (Carter and Sugden 2012; Hill 1996: 123; Kanin 1978). In 1998, a group of five American wrestlers and the same number of officials visited Iran to participate in the international Takhti Cup tournament. It was the first US delegation to visit Iran since before the Iranian Revolution. Symbolically, one of the most significant moments was the hoisting of the American flag in Tehran. Since 1979, the only images of the Stars and Stripes banner in Iran were those of flags being burned in anti-US demonstrations of animosity and resentment (Goldberg 2000). In spring 2004, the Indian cricket team toured Pakistan for the first time in 15 years. The tour followed a general agreement between the South Asian neighbours on a timetable for peace talks over the disputed province of Kashmir. It was initiated by an 'informal' visit of former Pakistani President Pervez Musharraf to watch a cricket match in India that the previous Indian Prime Minister, Manmohan Singh, and his Foreign Minister, Natwar Singh, also attended. It was the Indian government's willingness to let the cricketers tour Pakistan that convinced Pakistanis that Delhi's conciliatoriness was sincere and genuine (Bhaskaran 2006).

Ping-pong, wrestling and cricket diplomacy show that international sport encounters can be an effective foreign policy tool, and, in particular, a safe and gentle way of improving international relations. This view is widely, and uncritically, supported by high-profile and prominent politicians, sport administrators, the media and even musicians and singers, such as U2's front man Bono (Drezner 2006). Sport's ability to bring about global unity and peace, for example, has also been praised by former United Nations Secretary-General, Kofi Annan, who has repeatedly emphasised the potential of mega sports events, such as the Olympic Games and the Soccer World Cup, to unite citizens of different nations, 'rebuild fractured relationships . . . break down barriers and challenge stereotypes . . . and overcome the most deep-rooted conflicts' (Anan 2010: 30).

Although there is some truth in this statement, this chapter argues that only the systematic and lasting use of sport, both at grassroots and top levels, can make it a powerful diplomatic

28

tool. It also suggests that the use of sport as a foreign policy and diplomatic tool can be successful only if it is embedded in and supported by a wider strategy that pursues the same political goals. Otherwise, it is likely to fail, as Carter and Sudgen (2012) have convincingly shown in their analysis of baseball diplomacy between the United States and Cuba in the 1970s. On its own, or even at odds with the overall direction of a government's foreign policy, sports-led diplomacy is helpless and ineffective. This was, and continues to be, most evident on the politically divided Korean peninsula, where a variety of sport exchanges, in the late twentieth and early twenty-first century, between the Republic of Korea (ROK), in the South, and the Democratic People's Republic of Korea (DPRK), in the North, were a prominent and integral part of both countries' foreign policy agendas and had a significant impact on the political climate in Korea. This case study offers a unique opportunity to examine critically the changing role and political efficacy of contemporary sport diplomacy as the global sport order takes shape in the twenty-first century.

Sport diplomacy, in the context of this chapter, is defined as the whole range of international contacts between athletes, teams, spectators, fans, coaches, administrators and politicians in the context of sports competitions, events, exchanges, cooperations and collaborations that are motivated by broader foreign policy concerns and have implications for the general relations between and the overall political climate in the countries involved. For governments, the involvement of non-governmental and non-state actors is convenient and relatively risk-free. If their efforts are unsuccessful, politicians will not suffer from embarrassment and the political fall-out will be minimal. Beach suggests that any analysis of foreign policy, including diplomatic activities, needs to address three main areas: first, what those actors involved in foreign policy prioritise and want; second, the decision-making processes; and third, the output or what those actors eventually do (2012: 12–13). This chapter focuses on the results and outcomes and links these to wider governmental foreign policy goals, but will have to ignore the second field as 'most foreign policy decisions take place behind closed doors' (Beach 2012: 3).

Prior to the 2018 Winter Olympics in South Korea's Pyeongchang, which is located close to the border with North Korea, it is timely to focus on sport diplomacy on the divided Korean peninsula. Even relatively recent publications on sport and international relations (Levermore and Budd 2004) hardly mention this interesting and contemporary example. Although there has been an increased academic interest in the study of socio-economic, cultural and political aspects of sport in South Korea (Ahn 2000; Horne and Manzenreiter 2002; Manzenreiter and Horne 2004; McBeth 1988; Ok 2007), boosted by the successful staging of the 1988 Summer Olympics and the 2002 FIFA World Cup, hosted together with Japan, the role of sport as a foreign policy tool has been largely ignored, with the notable exceptions of Bridges (2012) and Jonsson (2006), who touch on this issue.

Conceptual considerations

Political tensions, rivalries and international conflicts have long accompanied and impacted the development of modern sport (Riordan and Krüger 1999), whether it is capitalism versus communism (Riordan 1999), separatism versus integration (Hargreaves 2000; Sugden and Bairner 1995) or nationalism versus internationalism (Merkel 2003). Since the beginning of the twentieth century, political agendas and ideological conflicts (Hoberman 1984; Riordan and Arnaud 1998) have disrupted a large number of international sports events. States and governments frequently used international competitions as high-profile public forums to validate their political systems and ideological preferences, and to pursue specific foreign policy goals. In its broadest sense, foreign policy is defined as, the particular actions taken by a state or other collective actor as directed toward other collective actors within the international system. Foreign policy actions can be undertaken using a variety of different instruments, ranging from adopting declarations, making speeches, negotiating treaties, giving other states economic aid, engaging in diplomatic activity such as summits, and the use of military force.

(Beach 2012: 3)

Any analysis of sport as a diplomatic tool needs to be embedded within the broader fields of foreign policy and international relations. Within the academic study of international relations, the three major theoretical approaches are Realism, Pluralism and the more radical Marxist perspective (Mingst 1999: 60–108). At first sight, there appears to be no place for sport in any of these paradigms, as they are primarily concerned with trade, security, international terrorism, the armed forces, foreign policy and economic relations. The Realist approach can make little contribution to a better understanding of the role of international sport in global politics, as it almost exclusively focuses on the state, as the primary unit of analysis, and its military capabilities, in the wider context of an international system that is characterized by uncertainty and insecurity:

> What makes realist theory unattractive for the exploration of the diplomatic value of sport is the scant attention it gives to the role of non-governmental organisations such as governing bodies of sport that are central to the utilisation of sport for diplomatic purposes.
>
> *(Houlihan 1994: 40–1)*

This paradigm would be very limiting, as it is unable to capture the complexity and subtleties of the Korean people that exists in two nation-states with very different socio-economic and political systems, standards of living and levels of contact with the outside world (Cumings 2004, 2005).

Like Realism, the capacity of the Marxist paradigm as an overall theoretical framework is limited. This approach acknowledges the impact of non-state actors and the importance of non-security issues, but it almost exclusively focuses on economic structures, developments and inequalities. Although there is no doubt that many aspects of international sport are highly commercialised and driven by the greediness of international governing bodies, the commercial interests of multi-national sponsors and corporations, the Marxist approach offers only limited scope for assessing the efficacy of sport as a diplomatic resource as the latter has limited economic value in the Korean context.

Pluralism appears to provide a much more helpful theoretical framework for the study of sport diplomacy. It has several advantages over the other paradigms. First, it acknowledges the central role of the state within international relations but also recognises the input of non-state actors, for example non-governmental organisations and civil society initiatives that have no formal political status and diplomatic powers. Second, Pluralism acknowledges that the policy agenda of foreign offices is multi-layered and tends to include exchanges and negotiations addressing social, cultural, economic and environmental issues. Third, the increasingly 'porous nature of territorial boundaries' and 'the multiplicity of international connections . . . and interactions based on trade, tourism, media communications, and migration' (Houlihan 1994: 42) are usually taken into consideration. Furthermore, Pluralism does not treat the state as an autonomous actor, but as an organisation that tries to accommodate various, sometimes conflicting, interests. One major concern of most modern states is to avoid large-scale military conflicts, since security and self-preservation are deemed absolutely essential. It is, therefore, in the self-interest of each state to cooperate with others. Such cooperation, through diplomatic dialogue with others, requires continuous interactions in a variety of realms. The general public tends to be excluded from most of these activities. However, foreign policy initiatives that occur in the world of international sport tend to be highly visible and allow ordinary citizens, to some extent, to participate and experience both the symbolic and real elements of foreign policy.

International politics and foreign policies on the divided Korean peninsula

During the Cold War (1947–1991), international sports events provided both North and South Korea, both founded in 1948, with an impressive public stage for their ideological battles. Both countries claimed to be the true representative of the Korean people, their distinctive culture and 5,000-year history. They either did not participate, in protest at the other's presence, or, when they engaged with each other, the competition was fierce (Ha and Mangan 2002). That changed considerably after the 1988 Summer Olympics in Seoul, which North Korea boycotted. This event is widely considered a 'major factor in South Korea's emergence on to the world stage' (Cho and Bairner 2012: 285). South Korea's capital put on a spectacle that celebrated the country's technological progress, modernisation, democratisation and wealth that the North was unable to match. While South Korea nowadays boasts Asia's fourth largest economy, on a par with many developed nations, the North is one of the poorest countries in the world. In addition to 'a large economic disparity, a democracy gap, [and] a vastly different culture' (Feffer 2003: 57), the North has rather limited contact with outsiders. What ties both countries closely together is the purity of their ethnic roots, a deep sense of shared injustice and external threats.

'The start of the Seoul Games . . . truly marked the end of inter-Korean competition for legitimacy' (Cha 2009: 59), which used to be one of South Korea's major foreign policy goals. Currently, security and trade are at the top of the country's international political agenda. Despite the DPRK's secretive and often apparently irrational behaviour on the international stage, North Korea's political aspirations and foreign policy objectives are crystal clear. First, the political regime is most concerned about a peace treaty, as it would guarantee the territorial sovereignty of the state and, finally, end the infamous chapter of the Korean War (1950–1953), which cost the lives of three million Korean civilians and 700,000 soldiers. Such an agreement would also reduce the risk of military action from outside forces that could lead to regime change. Second, and going hand in hand with the first objective, North Korea's rulers want respect through recognition of its legitimacy – however absurd that might appear to the international community (Tisdall 2010). More recently, the North's foreign policy agenda appears to be overshadowed by the government's desire for the socialist system to survive, improving its reputation, as a politically stable country, and attracting desperately needed foreign investment.

The only foreign policy goal both countries share is their desire to reunite the divided Korean people (Ministry of Unification 2005). In July 2014, South Korea's president, Park Gyeun-hye, set up a new committee, comprising more than 70 members from government, private sector organisations and universities and chaired by herself, which was tasked with preparing for Korean reunification. In September of the same year, at a meeting of the United Nations General Assembly in New York, North Korea's Minister for Foreign Affairs proposed a confederation between the two countries to prevent war and secure peace. However, there are currently several insurmountable political barriers that make the reunification of the divided

Korean people an unrealistic political vision (Chamberlin 2005). Furthermore, several polls over the last few years have repeatedly shown that young South Koreans are considerably less enthusiastic about reunification than their parents and grandparents.

Inter-Korean sports events, exchanges and cooperation

In the aftermath of the 1988 Seoul Olympics, political relations between the two Korean states gradually improved. Reunification initiatives proposed in 1998 by former South Korean President Kim Dae-jung succeeded for about ten years in moving the divided Korean peninsula in a new direction. His innovative and pragmatic foreign policy towards the North, known as the 'Sunshine Policy', favoured rapprochement and engagement, included economic assistance and encouraged cultural exchanges and political cooperation in order to normalise relations and, ultimately, achieve reunification. The 'Sunshine Policy' focused on peace, reconciliation and prosperity for the whole Korean nation through multi-faceted people-to-people contacts. This was clearly reflected in, and strengthened by, various forms of cooperation in the world of sport. Most notable and of great public interest were sport exchanges and the so-called 'unification sports events'. They became important diplomatic tools to engage with the other, foster a sense of pan-Korean unity and keep the reunification issue in the public discourse.

The first ever 'Unification Football Matches' were held in October 1990 and took place in both countries' capitals, Seoul and Pyongyang. The friendly tournament had become possible through talks between the sports ministers of the two Koreas during the Asian Games in Beijing earlier that year. Ten years later, Pyongyang and Seoul hosted the first 'Unification Basketball Tournament', with two matches played in both capitals. Two years later, in 2002, the 'Inter Korean Unification Soccer Match' took place in the sold-out World Cup Stadium in Seoul. The display of national flags was strictly prohibited, and North and South Korean football players carried the unification flag, a white banner with the shape of the Korean peninsula embroidered in a deep blue. In November 2005, a group of 150 South Korean marathon runners flew directly to the North Korean capital to participate in the 'Pyongyang-Nampho Marathon for Reunification'.

Both Koreas have been deadly serious about the use of sport as a diplomatic tool in order to improve relations and promote unity between the two countries. Therefore, a number of unusual and innovative measures were taken to avoid any uncertainties or ambiguities. In February 2006, for example, when the national women's ice hockey sides of both countries met for a friendly match in Seoul, one of the South's best players, Hwang Bo-young, did not play. She had to watch the game from the stands as she had fled from North Korea in 1997 aged 19. In the spirit of peace and friendship, even the rules had been modified and checking on the ice was not allowed (Yoon 2006). Only one month later, another North Korean ice hockey team was invited to play a friendly match in the South. On this occasion, it did not lead to a competition between North and South, as two mixed teams were formed, each comprising players from both countries. Even the teams' names, URI (meaning 'we') and HANA (meaning 'one'), reflected the reconciliatory spirit of this event.

This incomplete but exemplary list of 'unification sports events' and the various forms of sporting cooperation and exchanges between the North and the South, prior to the 2008 Summer Olympics in Beijing, clearly demonstrates that both countries were keen to promote, grow and intensify dialogue, celebrate commonalities and unity, and demonstrate to their respective populations their commitment to reunification. That was certainly also the rationale for the state-controlled North Korean media occasionally reporting on the outstanding performance of the South Korean soccer team during the 2002 World Cup finals. The media discourse in North Korea (Merkel 2012b), which is exclusively orchestrated and strictly controlled by the state-run Korean Central News Agency (KCNA), suggested that South Korea's surprising success in 2002 should be seen as a continuation of the North's impressive achievement at the 1966 World Cup in England (Polley 1998). The same strategy, that is, exploiting the symbolic potency of high-profile sports events, can also be found in the context of international competitions.

Contact and dialogue at global sports spectacles

Both Koreas have regularly used the global media attention that mega sports events tend to attract to remind the world and their respective people of their commitment to reunification. On various occasions, both countries formed a unified team for the official opening and closing ceremonies (Bridges 2012: 94–107; Choi 2002: 107–115; Jonsson 2006: 97–150). When the two Korean teams marched together at the 2000 Sydney, 2004 Athens and 2006 Turin Olympic opening ceremonies, at the 2002 Busan Asian Games, the 2003 Aomori Winter Games and the 2003 Daegu Summer Universiade, they displayed the above-mentioned white flag with the shape of the Korean peninsula embroidered in a deep blue and used the name 'Korea'. The presidents of both nations' Olympic committees usually followed the two flag bearers (one from each country) in front of the athletes and coaches. Bridges suggests that, 'for both Koreas a desire to pass a political message to the United States may have contributed to this continued cooperation through joint entries to sporting mega-events' (2012: 101). As long as Washington does not take 'North Korea's security fears as seriously as those of the United States and understands that division in the region ultimately undermines democracy, human rights, and economic progress' (Feffer 2003: 164), the political tensions on the divided Korean peninsula will remain high.

Furthermore, by participating regularly in international sporting events the North Korean rulers hope to gain from the political legitimacy conferred automatically on any country invited to participate. In 1999, North Korea's women's soccer team qualified unexpectedly for the Third FIFA Women's World Cup in the United States. However, the even bigger surprise was that the North Koreans accepted the invitation to travel to North America, although the two countries do not have formal diplomatic relations. The North Korean regime appears to believe that sports diplomacy will boost their attempts to establish formal government-to-government or international non-governmental relations while maintaining strict control over the limited and selective people-to-people contacts. At the same time, it is important for the North to create and globally convey an image of political stability favourable for foreign trade and investment in order to achieve system survival.

Almost as significant as the first Pyongyang summit between the two leaders of North and South Korea in 2000, Kim Jong-il and Roh Moo-hyun, respectively, were the 2002 Asian Games, hosted by the city of Busan in South Korea. North Korea sent 312 athletes, 111 sport officials and around 250 cheerleaders to Busan.

> Such a large delegation had never been dispatched before or been allowed to stay for such a long period. [. . .] watching the games provided repeated one on one contacts between North and South Koreans making them an important opportunity to dissolve the Cold War popular culture.
>
> *(Jonsson 2006: 86)*

Although North Korea's flag and anthem are officially banned in the South, the DPRK was allowed to raise its flag outside the buildings of the local media centre and organising committee in Busan. Since the division of the Korean peninsula in 1945, this was the first time that the official banner of the DPRK was exhibited on South Korean territory. Even North Korea's anthem was played on several occasions and North Korean visitors were given permission to use official DPRK insignia. As before, the public display of both countries' desire to reunite was most visible, and emotionally reinforced, at the opening ceremony. Athletes from the North and South used the unification flag, wore identical outfits and walked together hand in hand into the stadium.

After previously marching together at the opening ceremonies of several international competitions, in November 2005, sport administrators from North and South Korea agreed, in principle, to form a unified team for the 2008 Beijing Olympics. The deal was struck on the sidelines of the 2005 East Asian Games in Macau and fully supported by the IOC. Taking the symbolic reconciliation of the divided Korean people one step further seemed to be the logical extension to years of inter-Korean rapprochement and an important milestone towards fulfillment of the ultimate foreign policy goal of reunification. The South Korean National Olympic Committee was skeptical and predicted four major challenges: first, the principles determining the actual selection of athletes; second, harmonising training methods; third, agreeing lines of communication and responsibilities; and finally, finances. After two years of intense negotiation, the two Koreas did not compete as one team at the Beijing Olympics as they could not agree on the principles guiding the selection of athletes. Nevertheless, many political commentators saw the declaration of intention itself as a major breakthrough and a new milestone for inter-Korean efforts to travel one step further in their cooperation (Kim 2006). North Korea's willingness to engage constructively with the South and gradually to abandon its isolationist politics, was, however, undermined by two significant events that caused a severe deterioration of their political relationship.

First, the outcome of the general elections in South Korea in February 2008 had a huge impact on inter-Korean relations. South Korea's new president, Lee Myung-bak, took a much tougher stance than his liberal predecessors Roh Moo-hyun (2003–2008) and Kim Dae-jung (1998–2003) who had won the Nobel Peace Price for his 'Sunshine Policy' in 2000. Lee abandoned their successful strategy and replaced it with his 'Vision 3000', which tied economic aid and political cooperation to the de-nuclearisation of the North. Second, the killing of a South Korean tourist by a North Korean soldier in July 2008 in the south-east of North Korea played an important role. The 53-year-old woman was shot after wandering into a fenced-off military area near the Mount Geumgang resort, a popular tourist destination and symbol of cross-border reconciliation, which was accessible to South Koreans. Both events meant that the two countries did not even march together at the opening ceremony of the 2008 Beijing Olympics.

Two years later, China hosted the 2010 Asiad in Guangzhou. This event was marked by the absence of any reconciliatory gestures, signs of goodwill and cooperation between the two Koreas. The South Korean basketball team turned their backs when North Korea's anthem was played, whilst DPRK fans ignored South Korea's anthem and remained seated. Although only a railing in the stadium separated the spectators from both Korean countries, there was no interaction between them. At the same time, in November 2010, North Korea fired dozens of artillery shells onto the island of Yeonpyeong, approximately 120 km west of Seoul. The surprising attack set more than 60 houses ablaze, killed two South Korean soldiers and two civilians, and sent the local population fleeing in terror. The artillery strike was the first of its kind since the end of the Korean War in 1953 and provoked angry reactions from the international community.

What these examples show clearly is that, during the decade before the 2008 Beijing Olympics, sport as a diplomatic tool did not only 'promote détente between the two Koreas'

(Levermore and Budd 2004: 3) but was also used to keep the issue of reunification in the public discourse. Despite the two Koreas marching together at various opening ceremonies of high-profile international events and the popular 'unification sports events', these kind of exchanges were not a cure-all for political tensions, animosities and conflicts that have existed for over half a century. They constitute only small steps that can have positive effects beyond the playing field and onto the chessboard of international relations.

North Korea's mass games as a foreign policy tool

North Korea does not only rely on symbolic gestures, people-to-people contacts and joint activities with the South as diplomatic tools. The country's unusual but spectacular mass games also contribute to its foreign policy. Although the North has regularly hosted mass games over the last decades, since the beginning of this millennium, these more or less annual events have grown grander, more sophisticated and prominent (Burgeson 2005). Most notable is the Arirang Festival, which premiered in 2002, and the 'Prosper our Motherland' show of 2008, which celebrated the sixtieth anniversary of the foundation of the DPRK.

They usually take place in Pyongyang's gigantic May Day stadium, which can host up to 150,000 spectators. The shows comprise and combine three distinct elements: first, in the centre of the stadium, complex and highly choreographed group routines performed by tens of thousands of young gymnasts (with large artificial flowers, flags, hoops, balls, ropes and clubs), acrobats (with poles, ladders, springboards, trampolines and huge metal-framed wheels) and dancers in colourful costumes. Second, the backdrop, a giant human mosaic forming elaborate and detailed panoramas of historical and contemporary events, achievements, landscapes, architecture, portraits of individuals, such as the country's previous leaders, Kim Il-sung (1912–1994) and Kim Jong-il (1941–2011), slogans and cartoons. More than 20,000 schoolchildren hold up coloured cards that are part of a book with almost 200 pages. They turn them so quickly and in such complete unison that these images appear to be animated. The music constitutes the third element and links the performance in the centre of the May Day stadium with the backdrop. The combination of these three elements offers an impressive spectacle and a highly politicised package with a complex and multi-layered political agenda (Merkel 2008 and 2010), which goes far beyond propaganda 'crude, didactic propaganda . . . we associate with totalitarianism' (Hill 2003: 152).

This spectacle is full of political meanings and messages. Most prominent are the themes of Korean division, unity, nationalism and reunification. They feature more frequently than any other issue. The celebration of Korean unity is not restricted to the North Korean population, but includes South Koreans and promotes 'an extreme form of ethnocentric Korean national-ism . . . that expresses pride and self-esteem based on the greatness of the Korean nation' (Lee and Bairner 2009: 394).

One of the sets depicted a dramatic theatrical representation of the division of the Korean people. Several hundred young performers magically assembled into the perfect shape of the whole Korean peninsula. Subsequently, the southern and northern halves of the peninsula inex-orably drifted asunder; aching arms were outstretched in futility as unseen forces pulled the two halves apart. At the same time, the backdrop created a colourful panorama of Korean children repeatedly uttering, 'How much longer do we have to be divided due to foreign forces?'

More recently, the reunification theme has become more prominent than ever before. This is largely due to the above-mentioned leadership and fundamental policy changes in South Korea. The Arirang Festival even describes the unification of the divided Korean penin-sula as the ultimate achievement that will secure a prosperous future for the whole nation.

The 'Prosper our Motherland' show, went beyond the emotional celebration of Korean nationalism and unity and referred explicitly to specific meetings and treaties that were intended to drive the reunification of the two countries forward but have not yet been fully implemented (Merkel 2012a).

One of the fundamental preconditions for successfully communicating these foreign policy messages is, of course, the presence of witnesses, preferably large numbers of foreign and local spectators as well as the international media. This is particularly important for another key foreign policy objective; namely, to generate an alternative global discourse about North Korea that distracts from the country's autocratic political system, the prevalent militarism and economic hardship. In 2002, only a small number of foreigners were allowed to attend the Arirang Festival (Watts 2002); three years later, more foreigners than ever before experienced this extravaganza first-hand (Watts 2005). Even Americans were issued with short-term visas, allowing them to visit Pyongyang. 'The festival brought official delegations from China, Russia and Cuba as well as high ranking visitors from Mexico and a host of other nations' (Cho and Faiol 2005: 37). Along with a growing number of curious Western spectators, in 2005 ordinary South Korean citizens were, for the first time, allowed to fly directly from Seoul (Incheon) to Pyongyang and watch the Arirang spectacle. That degree of openness was clearly intended to show the strength and stability of North Korea. This message would not be heard loudly and clearly unless there were select groups of foreigners there to witness it. In 2012, the hundredth birthday celebrations of Kim Il-sung and the Arirang Festival attracted several thousand tourists from all over the world, particularly from Europe (Paris 2013).

Conclusion

For most of the post-Second World War period, the hosting of and participation in international sports events have been dominated by three major patterns: first, during the Cold War, when both capitalist and communist countries, for example the United States (Sage 1998), West Germany, the former Soviet Union (Riordan 1978 and 1980) and East Germany (Merkel 1999), used the often outstanding success of their top-level athletes to demonstrate the ideological superiority of their political systems, consolidate and/or gain international recognition, and promote relations with and win support among developing countries; second, as a cheap but high-profile means of publicly expressing disapproval of another country's actions, for example through boycotts or attempts to marginalise states in the world of international sport; and, third, as a vehicle for building, reinforcing and promoting a distinctive national identity and gaining international recognition.

However, sports events can also facilitate international cooperation, increase understanding and bridge profound differences. This potential has been systematically exploited on the divided Korean peninsula, where the use of sport as a diplomatic tool by both governments, as well as non-governmental organisations, has helped to build contacts and improve relations. For almost a decade prior to the 2008 Beijing Olympics, sport was an integral and highly visible element of their overarching foreign policy agenda and provided a multi-layered network for engagement and dialogue between the two Korean states. National and international sports events were used systematically to send diplomatic signals and pursue specific foreign policy goals. These efforts show that sport is able to make considerable contributions to international relations – not as spectacular one-off gestures, but as planned, thought-through, structured and meaningful activities at both grassroots and higher levels. Inter-Korean sport encounters were an efficient way of keeping the highly emotional issue of reunification, currently an unrealistic political dream, in the public discourse. Considering the declining support for reunification among young people in South Korea, the world of sport also offers an opportunity to test, reinforce and gather domestic support for a specific foreign policy goal.

The lack of symbolic and practical cooperation at, and in the years after, the 2008 Beijing Olympics was an accurate reflection of the general deterioration of inter-Korean relations caused by the introduction of a new, much more confrontational, foreign policy agenda. This development clearly shows that the efficacy of sport as a diplomatic tool largely depends on the overarching foreign policy framework and rationale.

Enhancing North Korea's international profile and improving the country's reputation are two of the many tasks of the contemporary domestic mass games. These impressive spectacles provide the North Korean rulers with a rare opportunity to present the usually secluded country to the rest of the world and to showcase the strength and stability of its socialist system. For the North Korean government, this is an inexpensive symbolic gesture demonstrating more openness and improving its questionable reputation.

References

Ahn, M.S. (2000) Studying the managerial prospect of Seoul Olympics Sports Promotion Foundation. *Journal of KAHPERD*, 39(1): 727–737.

Anan, K. (2010) The World Cup is Africa's chance to show how it has changed. *The Guardian*. 26 April 2010, p. 30.

Beach, D. (2012) *Analyzing Foreign Policy*. Basingstoke: Palgrave Macmillan.

Bhaskaran, G. (2006) Indo-Pakistan cricket diplomacy. *Seoul Times*. 10 March 2006.

Bridges, B. (2012) *The Two Koreas and the Politics of Global Sport*. Leiden/Boston: Global Oriental.

Brown, M. and Seaton, S. (1994) *The Christmas Truce: Western Front, December 1914*. London: Papermac Books.

Burgeson, J.S. (2005) Triumph of the Dear Leader? Pyongyang mass games take spectacle to another level. *Korea Times*. 25 October 2005.

Carter, T.F. and Sugden, J. (2012) The USA and sporting diplomacy: comparing and contrasting the cases of table tennis with China and baseball with Cuba in 1970. *International Relations*, 26(1): 101–121.

Cha, V. (2009) *Beyond the Final Score: The Politics of Sport in Asia*. New York: Columbia University Press.

Chamberlin, P.F. (2005) 'Peaceful Korean unification: is it feasible; is there a U.S. role?' In Korean Overseas Information Service (ed.) *Two Years of Roh Moo-hyun Administration: Achievements and Challenges*. Seoul: Government Publications, pp. 50–57.

Cho, J.H. and Bairner, A. (2012) The socio-cultural legacy of the 1988 Seoul Olympic Games. *Leisure Studies*, 31(3): 271–289.

Cho, J. and Faiol, A. (2005) North Korea sends a 'message to the world': secretive state welcomes visitors for month-long celebration of patriotism. *Washington Post Foreign Service*, 27 October 2005, p. 12.

Choi, D. (2002) Building bridges: the significance of Inter-Korean sports and cultural exchange. *East Asian Review*, 14(4): 107–115.

Cumings, B. (2004) *North Korea: Another Country*. New York and London: The New Press.

Cumings, B. (2005) *Korea's Place in the Sun: A Modern History*. New York: W.W. Norton and Company.

Drezner, D.W. (2006) The soccer wars: 'Bono says the World Cup is a peacemaker. Not quite'. *Washington Post*. 4th June 2006.

Feffer, J. (2003) *North Korea/South Korea: U.S. Policy at a Time of Crisis*. New York: Seven Stories Press.

Goldberg, J. (2000) Sporting diplomacy: boosting the size of the diplomatic corps. *Washington Quarterly*, 23(4): 63–70.

Ha, N.G. and Mangan, J.A. (2002) Ideology, politics and power: Korean sport-transformation, 1945–1992. *The International Journal for the History of Sport*, 19(2–3): 213–242.

Hargreaves, J. (2000) *Freedom for Catalonia?: Catalan Nationalism, Spanish Identity and the Barcelona Olympic Games*. Cambridge: Cambridge University Press.

Hill, C.R. (1996) *Olympic Politics*. Manchester: Manchester University Press.

Hill, C.R. (2003) *The Changing Politics of Foreign Policy*. Basingstoke: Palgrave Macmillan.

Hoberman, J.M. (1984) *Sport and Political Ideology*. Austin: University of Texas Press.

Horne, J. and Manzenreiter, W. (2002) (eds.) *Japan, Korea and the 2002 World Cup*. London: Routledge.

Houlihan, B. (1994) *Sport and International Politics*. New York: Harvester Wheatsheaf.

Jonsson, G. (2006) *Towards Korean Reconciliation: Socio-cultural Exchanges and Cooperation*. Aldershot: Ashgate.

Jürgs, M. (2003) *Der kleine Frieden im Grossen Krieg. Westfront 1914: Als Deutsche, Franzosen und Briten gemeinsam Weihnachten feierten*. München: Bertelsmann.

Kanin, D.B. (1978) 'Ideology and diplomacy: the dimension of Chinese political sport'. In B. Lowe, D.B. Kanin and A. Strenk (eds.) *Sport and International Relations*. Champaign, IL: Stipes Publishing Company, pp. 263–278.

Kim, H.C. (2006) ANOC gives Korea Olympic boost. *Korea Times*. 6 April 2006.

Lee, J.W. and A. Bairner (2009) The difficult dialogue: Communism, nationalism and political propaganda in North Korean sport. *Journal of Sport and Social Issues*, 33(4): 390–410.

Levermore, R. and Budd, A. (2004) (eds.) *Sport and International Relations: An Emerging Relationship*. London: Routledge.

Manzenreiter, W. and Horne, J. (2004) (eds.) *Football Goes East. Business, Culture and the People's Game in China, Japan and Korea*. London: Routledge.

McBeth, J. (1988) Sporting Seoul awaits the five-ring circus. *Far Eastern Economic Review*, April: 42–44.

Merkel, U. (1999) 'Sport in divided nations: the case of the old, new and "re-united" Germany'. In J. Sugden and A. Bairner (eds.) *Sport in Divided Societies*. Aachen: Meyer and Meyer, pp. 139–166.

Merkel, U. (2003) The politics of physical culture and German nationalism: *Turnen* versus English sports and French Olympism. *German Politics and Society*, 21(2): 69–96.

Merkel, U. (2008) The politics of sport diplomacy and reunification in divided Korea: one nation, two countries and three flags. *The International Review for the Sociology of Sport*, 43(3): 289–312.

Merkel, U. (2010) Bigger than Beijing 2008: politics, propaganda and physical culture in Pyongyang. *The International Journal of the History of Sport*, 27(14–15): 2467–2492.

Merkel, U. (2012a) Sport and physical culture in North Korea: resisting, recognising and relishing globalisation. *Sociology of Sport Journal – Special Issue*, 29(4): 506–525.

Merkel, U. (2012b) North Korean media accounts of the Olympic and Asian Games. *The International Journal of the History of Sport*, 29(16): 2326–2337.

Mingst, K. (1999) *Essentials of International Relations*. New York: W.W. Norton & Company.

Ministry of Unification (2005) Peace and prosperity. *White Paper on Korean unification 2005*. Seoul: Ministry of Unification Republic of Korea.

Ok, G. (2007) *Transformation of Modern Korean Sport: Imperialism, Nationalism, Globalization*. Seoul: Hollym International Corporation.

Paris, N. (2013) North Korea welcomes increase in tourism. *The Telegraph*. 20 February 2013.

Polley, M. (1998) The diplomatic background to the 1966 football World Cup. *The Sports Historian*, 18(2): 1–18.

Riordan, J. (1978) (ed.) *Sport under Communism*. London: C. Hurst and Co.

Riordan, J. (1980) *Soviet Sport*. Oxford: Basil Blackwell Publisher.

Riordan, J. (1999) 'The impact of communism on sport'. In J. Riordan and A. Krüger (eds) *The International Politics of Sport in the 20th Century*. London: E & FN Spon, pp. 48–66.

Riordan, J. and Arnaud, P. (1998) *Sport and International Politics: The Impact of Fascism and Communism on Sport*. London: E & FN Spon.

Riordan, J. and Krüger, A. (1999) (eds.) *The International Politics of Sport in the 20th Century*. London: E & FN Spon.

Sage, G.H. (1998) *Power and Ideology in American Sport*. Champaign, IL: Human Kinetics.

Sugden, J. and Bairner, A. (1995) *Sport, Sectarianism and Society in Divided Ireland*. Leicester: Leicester University Press.

Tisdall, S. (2010) The keys to Pyongyang. *The Guardian*. 23 November 2010, p. 24.

Watts, J. (2002) Despair, hunger and defiance at the heart of the greatest show on earth: surreal North Korean party opens isolated state to the world. *The Guardian*. 17 May 2002.

Watts, J. (2005) Welcome to the strangest show on earth: reclusive regime opens its doors with a spectacular to make Hollywood envious. *The Guardian*. 1 October 2005.

Weintraub, S. (2002) *Silent Night: The Remarkable Christmas Truce of 1914*. New York: Simon and Schuster.

Yoon, F. (2006) Hwang skates on thin ice between 2 Koreas. *The Korea Herald*. 14 April 2006.

4

SPORT AND POLITICAL IDEOLOGY

Alan Bairner

Introduction

As Hoberman (1984: 1) observed, 'The idea that sport is somehow an intrinsically political phenomenon has never been explained. In fact, sport is less known for its political character than for its legendary effects.' There is certainly no denying that 'across the ideological, class, cultural, and sporting spectrum, there seems to be a consensus that sports are, at best, distractingly vapid' (Hern, 2013: 9). Yet if we are to understand fully the intrinsic political character of sport, there is arguably no better place to begin than with the ideological spectrum to which Hern refers. This chapter outlines the trajectory of the concept of political ideology before offering an overview of the relationship between political ideologies and sport.

Political ideologies

According to Finlayson (2012: 751), 'The political theory of ideologies is an established sub-field of political theory, distinguished by a commitment to studying political ideas as they are found "in the wild".' It can be argued that 'ideologies are ubiquitous, intrinsic and necessary components of political life' (Finlayson 2012: 752). Thus, 'The political theory of ideologies is concerned with the ubiquity, propriety and creativity of political thinking' (Finlayson 2012: 757). The concept of ideology itself, however, has a chequered history. The word was first used in public in 1796 by Antoine Destutt de Tracy, who regarded *ideologie* as a new 'science of ideas' (Heywood 2003). His goal was to establish scientific truths on the basis of rational thought. However, although the European Enlightenment laid the foundations for the use of the word 'ideology' in social scientific analysis, it was the development of the concept by Karl Marx and his followers that influenced subsequent theorisation to a greater extent.

For Marx, ideology involved delusion and lay at the heart of what was to become known as false consciousness, specifically the false consciousness of the working classes in capitalist societies (Marx and Engels 1970). It is therefore central to the maintenance of power in class societies. Marx also assumed that ideology's role is temporary and will disappear in the course of the transition to a communist world. To that extent, therefore, although influential, the Marxist use of the term differs markedly from its function in contemporary political science.

Karl Mannheim (1936) developed the concept still further, agreeing with Marx that ideological thinking is the product of social conditions, but removing the concept's negative implications. Even with this revision, however, ideologies were still presented as thought systems which tend to defend the interests of dominant elites. Moreover, they offer partial, distorted and self-interested versions of social reality.

This understanding of ideology was given added credence with the rise of totalitarian regimes in the years between the First and Second World Wars. For some indeed, the twentieth century can legitimately be described as 'the age of ideologies' even though most, if not all, of the significant ideologies, had their roots in the nineteenth century or even earlier. Since the 1960s, however, as Heywood (2003: 11) notes, 'the term ideology has gained a wider currency through being refashioned according to the needs of conventional social and political analysis.' Thus, ideologies become action-oriented systems of thought. They are 'neither good nor bad, true nor false, open nor closed, liberating nor oppressive – they can be all these things' (Heywood 2003: 11). So what precisely does the term political ideology mean in the twenty-first century?

According to Heywood (2003: 5), 'To examine "ideology" is to consider a particular type of political thought, distinct from, say, political science or political philosophy.' On the other hand, 'To study political ideology is to analyse the nature, role and significance of this category of thought, and to reflect on questions such as which set of political ideas and arguments should be classified as ideologies' (Heywood 2003: 5). Here, one can argue along with Marx, and to a lesser extent with Mannheim, that political ideologies are partial and distorted ways of seeing the world which are propagated by certain people to ensure that others, often an overwhelming majority of the population, accept a view of the world which allows the former to maintain their positions of power. Are some ideologies truer than others? Yes – but only if they serve one's own interests and/or accord with how one envisages what the world is now and what it could be.

Ideologies, according to Müller (2009: 213), 'were really a result of the loss of a belief in progress towards the end of the nineteenth century; they were an expression of "crisis thinking", made up of dispersed and often incoherent fragments from "decayed thought systems".' Although they are often located on a spectrum running from right to left, it might be more accurate to identify them at different points of a circle, thereby helping us to maintain an appropriate distance between those ideologies (communism and fascism) which in practice, if not necessarily in theory, were more likely to promote the idea of a strong, interventionist state. 'The age of ideologies' is often equated with 'the age of extremes.' Yet, as Müller (2009: 213) observes,

> seeing the twentieth century as an age of ideological extremes or as an 'age of hatred' is to fail to understand that ordinary men and women – and not just intellectuals and political leaders – saw many of these 'ideologies' and the institutions that were justified with their help as real answers to their problems.

There are those who would have us believe that ideologies are increasingly irrelevant to the contemporary political landscape. For them, ideologies emerged in the late eighteenth century and reached a crescendo during the twentieth century when most global political issues were linked in some way or another to competition between certain ideologies. It is certainly arguable that the function that has historically been served by ideologies is less needed in a world in which individualism appears to have become the dominant world view at least in most of the developed world. After all, to all intents and purposes ideologies offered people the means whereby they could think collectively or, if one was to be really harsh, not think at all but simply take the ideological manual down from the shelf and apply it to each and every circumstance that was faced.

As early as 1960, Daniel Bell announced the end of the concept of ideology.

> The historicity of the term has lost its context, and only the pejorative
> and invidious penumbra, but no conceptual clarity, remains.
> Ideology has become an irretrievably fallen word.
>
> *(Bell 1960: 447)*

According to Bell (1960) ideology, which once was a road to action, has come to be an end. It should be noted that most of Bell's opprobrium was directed towards socialism and, above all, Marxism. His successor, Frances Fukuyama, on the other hand, questioned the relevance of *all* systems of thought other than those which advocated liberal democracy coupled with a commitment to capitalist economics. In 1992, Fukuyama (2006: 39) argued that 'On both the communist Left and the authoritarian Right, there has been a bankruptcy of serious ideas capable of sustaining the internal political cohesion of strong governments, whether based on "monolithic" parties, military juntas, personalistic dictatorships.' Fukuyama (2006: 51) had arrived at the conclusion that

> The success of democracy in a wide variety of places and among many different peoples would suggest that the principles of liberty and equality on which they are based are not accidents or the results of ethnocentric prejudice, but are in fact discoveries about the nature of man as man, whose truth does not diminish but grows more evident as one's point of view becomes more cosmopolitan.

It should be noted that Fukuyama (2010) himself has subsequently abandoned some of the neo-conservative implications of his analysis which, to all intents and purposes, represented an alternative ideological mode of thought as opposed to a sustainable argument that ideologies had become things of the past. In any case, to argue that the age of ideological conflict is now complete and what remains is ideological convergence is surely premature at a time when people all over the world are still happy to admit to being supporters of particular ideological perspectives, many of them at odds with other ways of thinking. As in the past, however, this does not mean that they agree with their fellow adherents on every issue. There has always been room for debate about the aspirations of specific ideologies and, even more commonly, about the strategies required to fulfil these aspirations. It is also worth bearing in mind that, in almost every instance, but perhaps most markedly in the case of communism, gaps exist between the ideological ideal and the practical reality.

According to Hoberman (1984: 12), 'Sportive expressionism appeals to all ideological temperaments. In other words, it is a universal aesthetic before it is differentiated into divergent ideological messages.' However, the actual influence on and/or relevance to sport of political ideologies varies enormously. It is not the purpose of this chapter to pre-empt what follows in chapters dealing with specific ideologies. Rather, the aim is to provide a discursive overview of the ways in which ideologies and sport may interact. In the case of some ideologies, the degree of influence is relatively difficult to detect although the extent to which the core values of these ideologies are reflected in sport is of great significance. It is clear, however, that some ideologies have sought to directly affect the ways in which sport is organised and played. In the first category, there is a place for conservatism, liberalism and socialism. Here sport is discussed as a repository of ideological thinking, reflecting as it does some key ideological elements. In the second category, we can locate communism, fascism/national socialism and nationalism. The focus here is on sport as a direct product of ideological thinking. The third category recognises that feminism and environmentalism also seek to exert influence but in rather different ways such that we can talk about sport as a site for aspirational ideological thinking.

Sport as a repository of ideological thinking

It would be fair to say that in countries such as the United Kingdom, there has been relatively little deviation on the part of mainstream political parties in relation to sport. That is not to suggest, however, that the core values which underpin these mainstream parties have little or no relevance for sport. Indeed, it can be argued that conservative ideas have been highly influential in Britain, and elsewhere, in the development of sport and in many of its current practices, to such an extent that at times it looks as if conservatism and sport are natural bedfellows.

Conservatism

Conservatism's belief in the importance of authority and order has been reflected over the years in the imposition of restrictions and even bans on specific leisure pursuits including rough-and-tumble football games and various activities involving cruelty to animals. Conservatism's emphasis on hierarchy, competition and tradition also sits well with sport as generally understood. Edmund Burke, the founding father of modern British conservatism, is almost certainly best remembered for his critique of the French Revolution. According to Burke, the revolutionaries were acting on the basis of what he described as 'abstract principles' – namely liberty, fraternity, equality. In his view, this was a disastrous approach to promoting change. Of course, as a conservative, he was no great admirer of change in any circumstance. He accepted, however, that it is sometimes necessary. The important thing for Burke was that necessary change should always be effected cautiously. It should never be a leap in the dark, which, for him, was precisely what change based on abstract principles involved. According to Burke, we should never overlook the value of tradition and of the tried and tested. As Hampshire-Monk (1992: 264–5) explains,

> Burke's major purpose is to evoke, in a way that would have been familiar to most eighteenth-century readers, the way in which an established church, a particular kind of social order and a particular arrangement of property rights contributed to the stability of public opinion necessary for settled and civilized life.

This attitude of mind remains a fundamental element of conservative thinking and, it can be argued, it is also an ever present, albeit regularly contested, feature of sport. Tradition is highly important in the world of sport, not only because many of the people most directly involved in overseeing and managing sport are themselves Burkean conservatives (perhaps with a small 'c') but also because, in certain circumstances, tradition sells.

Other elements of conservative thinking, such as respect for authority, the idea of an organic society and the inevitability of social hierarchy also have relevance for sport, but these themes can arguably be best addressed, even if indirectly, in a later discussion of socialism. For the time being, it is worth commenting on the fact that conservatives in the United Kingdom were by no means in the forefront of advocating a free-market economy, even though the Conservative Party has now embraced it with considerable enthusiasm. This transition is captured in the manner in which professional cricket has developed from the traditional, almost backward-looking activity that it once was to the commoditised product that it has increasingly become. The question for traditional conservatives is whether the advent of Twenty-Twenty or Big Bash cricket represents a necessary change for marketing reasons or a revolution based on abstract principles which might lead who knows where. As a socio-economic system, capitalism owes far more to liberal economic theory, the irony being that modern liberals from the end of the nineteenth century onwards have been much less willing to allow free rein to market forces. What then for liberals should be the role of the state in other human endeavours, amongst them sport and leisure?

Liberalism

Apart from upholding the virtues of the market economy, liberalism has had less direct impact on sport than has conservatism. Arguably the liberal contribution to political debate about sport has been more philosophical than ideological. My starting point here is another key figure in the history of political debate in Britain: John Stuart Mill.

Mill's *On Liberty*, published in 1859, appears on an initial, cursory reading to be a classic and incontestable defence of individual freedom. Mill (1974: 69) argues that 'Over himself, over his own body and mind, the individual is sovereign.' This would seem to offer each of us a considerable amount of leeway in all aspects of our lives, including the use of leisure time. However, Mill has already qualified this defence of individual freedom, having asserted that 'the only purpose for which power can be rightfully exercised over any member of a civilised community, against his will, is to prevent harm to others' (Mill 1974: 68). If the body politic is entitled to restrict out activities when harm to others is a factor, then everything hinges on how harm to others is to be defined. This is particularly relevant to many sporting practices, none more so obviously as (professional) boxing.

The British Medical Association espouses a long-standing policy aimed at the banning of boxing 'because of the serious health risks involved' (British Medical Association (BMA), 2008: 2). More recently, this has been extended to apply also to Mixed Martial Arts. The number of deaths during or immediately after contests is relatively small, but nevertheless significant. The incidence of non-fatal injuries is considerably greater. The BMA claims that 80 per cent of professional boxers have serious brain scarring and many retired boxers suffer from neurodegenerative disorders. As a consequence, boxing 'cannot be justified on health and safety grounds as an appropriate or legitimate sport' (BMA 2008: 7).

Any ensuing debate necessarily highlights the conflicted character of Mill's defence of liberty. The overwhelming majority of professional boxers are consenting adults, even if there is concern that, in many parts of the world, they are driven to this potentially dangerous activity through economic necessity. They intend to do harm to another, but in so doing they accept that harm will almost certainly be done to them. Over their own bodies, are they not sovereign? On the other hand, if we extend the concept of harm and also the definition of 'the other,' the argument becomes rather different. At this point, we are no longer concerned with physical harm and/or the well-being of the two combatants. Rather our concern is with the moral harm that is done to society as a whole if we accept that two people inflicting harm on each other can be regarded as both a sport and a form of entertainment.

This is not the place, of course, to pronounce on the arguments for and against professional boxing. The purpose of the preceding discussion is simply to demonstrate the extent to which, in practice, ideologies – in this instance liberalism – can turn from being unquestioned political manuals to amalgams of sometimes mutually contradictory ideas. In the case of the next ideology to be considered, the contradictions are embedded in questions about what it wishes to achieve and how it intends to do so.

Socialism

As Berki (1975) observed, we all think we know what socialism is. According to Berki (1975: 23), 'Socialism is almost exactly coeval with classical liberalism: it is its reverse side, giving expression to the spiritual traumas and social and economic dislocations which were the effects of bourgeois-liberal victories.' For Berki, socialism is made up of four basic tendencies – rationalism, moralism, libertarianism and egalitarianism – of which the fourth is arguably the most important. All socialists would proclaim an interest in the idea of equality. But what can that possibly mean in the context of sport, which almost always pits one individual against another, one team against a rival team, the end result being the emergence of winners and losers? Much depends here on what is meant by equality, the crucial distinction being between equality of reward and equality of opportunity. Whilst few socialists, let alone their critics, would argue today that winners and losers in sport should be rewarded equally or perhaps not rewarded at all, most would accept the argument that there should be equality of opportunity in relation to playing and watching sport. But even this argument is open to further qualification. Although the 'Sport for All' mantra is regularly recited in the corridors of political power and within the policy statements of sports governing bodies, this normally means that everyone, especially when they are young, should have a chance to play sport. It does not suggest that all people should have access to all sports. This is particularly significant in a country such as Britain, where social class continues to cast a long shadow over people's leisure experiences.

Nowhere was this more apparent in the past than in the distinction made between amateurs and professionals. Well into the second half of the twentieth century in Britain, the word 'amateur' was still a complimentary description of someone who played sport, in large part, for its own sake and according to certain standards of proper behaviour, irrespective of the accuracy of these underlying assumptions. Professionals, on the other hand, played sport to earn a living or to supplement an otherwise meagre income and could not be trusted to behave as honourably. But things have changed. Who, as D. J. Taylor (2006) asks, would care to be described as an 'amateur' today?

> If there is one state to which the average twenty-first-century worker aspires it is the glossy, cast-iron prestige of the 'professional', with its imputations of expertise, competence and status.
>
> *(Taylor 2006: 32)*

But is this to suggest that elite sport must inevitably reflect the values inscribed in capitalist economics at their most stark?

It is tempting to look to the Nordic countries and, in particular, to Sweden to search for an approach that is more compatible with socialist values. Although Skille (2011: 335) is right to describe the so-called Scandinavian model as 'debatable, and debated,' he is equally correct to point out that 'historically there has been a fairly harmonic relationship between the voluntary and public sides of sport in all Scandinavian countries based on a mutual dependency' (Skille 2011: 331) and to remind us that 'compared to most other countries, participation rates in sport are considered high in Scandinavia' (Skille 2011: 332). One can add that sport in Sweden and in the other Nordic countries has been less bedevilled than in some countries by the cult of celebrity which is so prevalent in British and North American sport.

However, as the cultural gap between the Nordic region and the rest of the developed world grows ever narrower, it becomes much harder to maintain the distinctiveness of a system or systems which have relied so heavily on values which many might think are increasingly outmoded. Individualism constantly threatens social solidarity and cooperation. Furthermore, even though the Nordic countries are still worthy of emulation in the world of sport, any idea of simply importing the systems that are in place there is hopelessly idealistic (Bairner 2010).

Sport as a product of ideological thinking

Nationalism

At the most basic level of analysis, it is easy to see the extent to which sport, arguably more than any other form of social activity in the modern world, facilitates flag waving and the playing of national anthems, both formally at moments such as medal ceremonies and informally through the activities of fans. Indeed there are many political nationalists who fear that by acting as such a visible medium for overt displays of national sentiment, sport can actually blunt the edge of serious political debate. No matter how one views the grotesque caricatures of national modes of behaviour and dress that so often provide the colourful backdrop to major sporting events, one certainly cannot escape the fact that nationalism, in some form or another, and sport are closely linked. It is important to appreciate, however, that the precise nature of their relationship varies dramatically from one political setting to another and that, as a consequence, it is vital that we are alert to a range of different conceptual issues (Cronin and Mayall 1998; Smith and Porter 2004; Bairner 2008).

For example, like the United Nations, sport's global governing bodies, such as the International Olympic Committee or the *Fédération Internationale de Football Association* (FIFA), consist almost exclusively of representatives not of nations but rather of sovereign nation-states. It is also worth noting that pioneering figures in the organisation of international sport, such as Baron Pierre de Coubertin who established the modern Olympics in 1896, commonly revealed a commitment to both internationalism and the interests of their own nation-states. Thus, whilst de Coubertin could write enthusiastically about a sporting event that would bring together young (male) athletes from across the globe, he was also specifically concerned with the physical well-being of young French men in the wake of a demoralising defeat in the Franco-German War.

Whilst in most cases, these nation-states that constitute international sporting bodies are coterminous with nations, the fact remains that numerous nations throughout the world, as well as other forms of collective belonging, are stateless and are consequently denied representation in international sporting competition just as they are in the corridors of global political power. When considering the relationship between sports and nationalism, therefore, it is important to think in terms both of nation-states and of nations and to be sensitive to the variety and con-testation within accepted nations and nation-states regarding what their shared nationhood and statehood constitutes. This also provides the means whereby sport's connection with nationality and also with national identity can be separately explored. It is also useful to bear in mind that sport often acts as a window through which we are able to examine a whole range of social developments and to test a variety of theoretical concepts and perspectives. With specific refer-ence to the relationship between sports and nationalism, observing the world of sport offers insights into the relevance and reliability of such concepts as ethnic and civic nationalism and the validity of explanatory approaches to the rise of nations and nationalism such as primordialism and modernism. Sport can also provide important insights into varieties of imperialism, the cultural politics of anti-imperialist struggle and postcolonial legacies.

Communism

Marx had nothing to say about sport *per se*, although Marx and Engels do make reference to the potential contribution of exercise and games to worker satisfaction (Grant 2014). Lenin, too, was an advocate of physical activity, which Grant (2014) appears to conflate with sport when she argues that he thereby validated the Soviet sports system. For example, Lenin advocated the establishment of a High School for Sport and Physical Culture, believing that mass participation in physical culture could help in the creation of the new 'communist man' (Bunck 1994). However, as Grant (2014: 729) herself admits, in the years immediately following the Russian revolution, 'Competitive sport was looked upon unfavourably and did not receive official sanction until the late 1920s and 1930s.' Thus, physical activity in the post-revolution Soviet Union was largely military training or exercise for the sake of improving the health of the population. Only gradually did team sports become acceptable as vehicles of social solidarity in specific workplaces and occupational groups. The most dramatic shift in thinking arrived with the Cold War, when sport was recognised as a highly effective source of what has come to be known as 'soft power.' Competition between the Soviet Union and the United States in the quest for Olympic medals became one of the most compelling narratives of the Cold War, together with the space race. In pursuing sporting success, however, the Soviet Union was arguably retreating still further from the original aims of the revolution, above all an egalitarian society which did not seek to divide people into winners or losers.

Another revolutionary leader who recognised the importance of physical activity was Mao Zedong (1917) who, in one of his earliest publications, sounds more like a nineteenth-century English public school headmaster than a future communist leader, arguing that 'when the body is strong, then one can advance speedily in knowledge and morality, and reap far-reaching advantages.' It is now the Peoples Republic of China's (PRC's) turn to face a challenge similar to that previously encountered by the Communist Party of the Soviet Union, having already recognised the 'soft power' appeal of sport by hosting the Olympic Games in Beijing in 2008 when the country topped the medal table, and having won the highest number of golds and coming second to the USA in the table for the 2012 Games held in London.

There is, of course, an additional problem linked to the inherent character of sport. Writing with specific reference to Cuba, Carter (2014: 1) argues that 'sport is often a conservative set of institutional practices used to reinforce existing power relations.' It has certainly tended to be associated far more with conservative values, such as tradition, than with radical politics. The question arises, therefore, given the trajectory described above, 'are communist ideals and sporting success compatible?'

The answer, at least in theory, is that these are not compatible objectives. As Hoberman (1984) notes, the idea of the athletic nation does not appear in Marxist writing or the rhetoric of communist societies. On the other hand, 'It is an image which still retains its primitive character and appears frequently in fascist writings and almost never in the rhetoric or the political literature of Marxist societies' (Hoberman 1984: 72). Moreover, perhaps no single event has so clearly encapsulated the close ties between sport and ideology as the Berlin Olympic Games of 1936. As Mandell (1971: xii) asserts, 'all the athletes who competed at Garmisch-Partenkirchen and at Berlin were made to feel that they were the corporeal manifestations of intellectual and political forces let loose to compete in other spheres later in that troubled decade.' But why were fascists, and more specifically Nazis, with their common desire to subjugate the individual to the greater glory of the state, the race, the land, and its people, so interested in a sphere of human activity in which individual excellence is so often the central ingredient, even in team games?

Fascism

First, fascism is an essentially action-oriented ideology. Indeed, it has been credited with having invented an entirely new activist style of politics (O'Sullivan 1976). Second, it places great emphasis on body culture. In this respect, the fascists asserted their sympathy with classical antiquity in which the human form, particularly the male form, was an object of admiration and, in some cases, adoration. Hoberman (1984: 83) comments, 'no other modern political culture has produced a doctrine of physicality for its own sake.' Third, the fascists were preoccupied with symbolism and, as we shall see, the symbolic power of sporting spectacle was soon identified. Finally, the fascists recognised earlier than most the propagandist potential of sport. According to Krüger (1999: 67), 'sport for the sake of national fitness and the demonstration of it was nothing new at the time of the fascist governments in Europe, but the extensive use of it for indoctrination to establish a totalitarian system was new.' The national socialists in Germany employed sport for political purposes far more than their fascist comrades elsewhere in Europe. According to Krüger (1999: 67), 'historically, the use of sport by the Nazis seems to have been the most extensive and efficient of the fascist regimes (in spite of the fact that the so-called thousand year empire lasted only twelve).' But Hitler himself was no athlete. Conversely, Mussolini did much to present himself as an active sportsman and even a cursory examination of the Francoist years in Spain reveals evidence of the extent to which sport and, above all, football, became implicated in ideological struggle (Burns 2009). Nevertheless, it is the Nazi era that provides us with most insights into the authoritarian right's close relationship with sport.

As early as 1925, Hitler (1971) had demanded that young men should receive one hour of physical training in the morning and one hour in the afternoon daily, covering every type of sport and gymnastics. He was neither the first nor the last strict disciplinarian to recognise sport's role in personal development as such diverse experiences as those of nineteenth-century English public schools and twentieth-century Hindu fundamentalism testify. But, as Hoberman (1984: 83) notes, 'Hitler's endorsement of the body is a specifically fascist one.'

In part, the Nazi interest in sport, like that of the communists, was related to the need for military preparedness. Indeed, throughout Europe, modern sport's development had been closely linked to military training. However, because of the Nazi belief in the superiority of the Aryan race it was vitally important, ideologically as well as strategically, to encourage physical fitness. To quote Krüger (1999: 76) again, 'the Nazis as a male-dominated cult of youth and strength, who believed in genetic and racial endowment, on the survival of the fittest, used the sports movement for their purpose on national unity.'

Although the Third Reich itself extended into the 1940s, all of the main roles that Nazism had assigned to sport were brought together in the 1936 Olympics. For example, as Mandell (1971: x) argues, 'Hitler's success as a whole is inconceivable without the application of the contrived festivity that enveloped Nazism from beginning to end.' This was expressed through a variety of vehicles which brought the militants together, helped to unify their style, and sought to win the attention and subsequently the support of sympathisers. Thus, sport and other popular events became subsumed within the broader ideological enterprise. In the intervening years, the festive qualities of the Olympics and other major international competitions, particularly as revealed in a series of increasingly outrageous opening ceremonies, have been emphasised by every host nation. In many respects, however, the Nazis set the early pace as they did in anticipating yet another modern phenomenon – the symbiotic relationship between sport and the media. Leni Riefenstahl was commissioned to film the event in the hope that 'her cinematic record of the Nazi Olympics would bring the splendor of this unique festival to the whole German race and to the whole world' (Mandell 1971: 251).

Sport as a site for aspirational ideological thinking

Feminism

There are arguably two possible ways of viewing the current status of women's sport and of women in sport. The first is to argue that considerable advances have taken place, that the media now take women's sport more seriously than in the past, and that the future is relatively bright. The alternative view is that despite superficial appearances to the contrary, sport remains one of the last powerful bastions of patriarchy. One could add to the latter that gender power relations are simply rawer in the world of sport than in areas such as politics where, in reality, advances in most countries have been few in number and relatively inconsequential. What saves the day for most professions is a kind of polite sexism. In sport, on the other hand, sexism is altogether less polite.

Take for example the failings of the National Football League to respond quickly and decisively to domestic violence meted out by some of its highly prominent players such as Ray Rice and Adrian Peters. The evidence suggests that the NFL has long ignored this subject. As Harry Edwards, Emeritus Professor of Sociology at the University of California at Berkeley and adviser to the San Francisco 49ers put it, 'The NFL is essentially a money-making machine based on the creation of illusion and entertainment, and anything other than the marketing, growth and expansion of the game has been a low priority' (quoted in Luscombe 2014: 33). Needless to say, this wilful neglect is by no means confined to the NFL, American football or the US in general. As Krien (2014) reveals, similar problems exist in Australian Rules football as they do in the overwhelming majority of male team sports. This is not to suggest that all men who play team sports or, indeed, sport more generally, are potential wife beaters or rapists. Nor is it to argue that such men do not exist in other walks of life. There remains something insidious, however, about a culture where some men appear to believe that the power they exude on the field of play can legitimately be transferred to their personal relationships away from sport.

By seeking to identify alternative examples of sporting heroism, Jennifer Hargreaves (2000: 3) quite properly looked beyond 'the violence, corruption, commercialization and exploitation that plague men's sports.' In so doing, however, perhaps unwittingly, she may also have denied a voice to women as national sporting beings. The contribution of women to the relationship between sport and national identity formation has undeniably been largely ignored. This is particularly apparent in discussions on so-called national sports, including Gaelic games in Ireland, baseball in the United States, cricket in England, taekwondo in Korea, and wushu in China. Just as men are customarily regarded as the real warriors who fight for their nations, so too are they identified in most of the relevant literature as proxy national warriors in the world of sport. Having identified this particular example of gender blindness, we can go on to outline the extent to which this problem is part of a wider theoretical and discursive disregard for the role of women in the construction and reproduction of national identities.

Much has been made in the British media of the achievements of the country's female Olympians at London 2012, with gold medals being won in such disparate sports as rowing, boxing, dressage, cycling and taekwondo. Commentators remarked on the fact that women were being celebrated for doing something more with their bodies than model the latest clothes. It was also noted that one of the rowing gold medallists, Heather Stanning, was a captain in the British Army and was being cheered on from afar by her battalion then serving in Afghanistan. War and sport brought together in perfect harmony, it seemed. But to what extent can we expect female athletes to assume the traditionally male role of proxy warriors who represent the nation and whose deeds are treated by many as matters of life and death?

This may, of course, be the wrong question. Rather than have as a central aim a world of sport in which women emulate men with all that this implies for good and ill, perhaps feminists should look instead towards an alternative approach to sport in which the true heroines are of the kind identified by Jennifer Hargreaves (2000: 232) who wrote that 'Different women across the world are struggling for identity, and sport has become an increasingly significant way for women to assign meaning to their lives.' This does not mean that women should treat sport as men have done. As Hargreaves (2000: 233) concludes, 'Global sport feminism is *defined* by difference and requires a language and strategy that takes *account* of difference.'

Environmentalism

The emergence and subsequent development of environmentalism challenges the assumptions of those who hail the end of ideology by arguing that people are increasingly individualistic and have no truck with schools of thought that demand solidarity. After all, nothing could be more contrary to naked self-interest than the desire to protect the planet for future generations instead of simply ignoring such phenomena as climate change because it suits our present lifestyle to do so. The questions that environmentalists ask us to consider are as follows – Are we the masters of nature? Are we the stewards of nature? Are we equal partners with the rest of the natural world? But what is the relevance of these questions to sport?

According to Lenskjy (1998: 341),

> With the exception of golf and downhill skiing, which have regularly come under criticism for the obvious damage that they inflict on the natural environment, most sporting activities and venues escaped the attention of environmental activists and researchers until the 1980s.

Today, however, greater attention is paid to the question of what happens when sport and nature meet. As Mincyte *et al.* (2009: 103) point out, it is important to recognise that '*nature* . . . is intricately woven into human activities, and that human activities, including movement of sporting bodies through space and time, can and do deeply affect the environment.'

It is perhaps asking too much of sport that it become an equal partner with the natural world, but one can at least hope that the people who run global sport can recognise that helping to look after the natural world is preferable to arrogantly assuming that we can do what we like with it – by building more golf courses, by holding mega events, by having Formula 1 motor racing teams travel the world at huge expense, causing considerable environmental damage along the way.

On the positive side, the IOC has certainly begun to make the right noises about the environment, with potential host cities promising sustainability and 'green Games' being lauded. The cynic might add that most of this amounts to window dressing rather than a genuine desire to act as stewards of nature. There may certainly be a tendency to give with one hand and take away with the other. That said, it is possible that the Winter Olympics have been more successful in this regard than their summer counterparts for several reasons. First, they tend to take place in countries, such as Norway, which have relatively good environmental records. Second, they are smaller. Third, the relationship between the competitors and nature is generally more intimate than that which exists in sports that take place in outdoor stadia and indoor arenas. Good explanations all. But then there was Sochi, with its undeniable environmental damage. What hope for the environment when the Games are used by power hungry politicians with little or no concern for the environment? There is a long way to go before sport is able to meet the aspirations of environmentalism.

Conclusion

Other chapters in this collection will examine the relationship between specific ideologies and sport in detail. As revealed above, the influence on and/or relevance to sport of political ideologies vary enormously. In the case of some ideologies, the degree of influence is relatively difficult to detect, although the extent to which the core values of these ideologies are reflected in sport is of great significance. It is clear, however, that some ideologies have sought to directly affect the ways in which sport is organised and played. Feminism and environmentalism also seek to exert influence but in rather different ways and to date with only limited success. Each of them still has many battles to fight.

References

Bairner, A. (2008) 'Sports and nationalism.' In G. H. Herb and D. H. Kaplan (eds) *Nations and Nationalism: A Global Historical Overview: Volume 3 1945–1989*. Santa Barbara, CA: ABC-CLIO, pp. 991–1004.

Bairner, A. (2010) What's Scandinavian about Scandinavian sport? *Sport in Society*, 13 (4): 734–43.

Bell, D. (1960) *The End of Ideology: On the Exhaustion of Political Ideas in the Fifties*. Cambridge, MA: Harvard University Press.

Berki, R. N. (1975) *Socialism*. London: Dent.

British Medical Association (BMA) (2008) *Boxing: An Update from the Board of Science*. London: BMA Science and Education Department.

Bunck, J. M. (1994) *Fidel Castro and the Quest for a Revolutionary Culture in Cuba*. University Park: The Pennsylvania State University Press.

Burns, J. (2009) *Barça: A People's Passion*. London: Bloomsbury.

Carter, T. F. (2014) Game changer: The role of sport in revolution. *International Journal of the History of Sport*, 31 (7): 735–46.

Cronin, M. and Mayall, D. (eds.) (1998) *Sporting Nationalisms: Identity, Ethnicity, Immigration and Assimiliation*. London: Frank Cass.

Finlayson, A. (2012) Rhetoric and the political theory of ideologies. *Political Studies*, 60 (4): 751–67.

Fukuyama, F. (2006) *The End of History and the Last Man*. New York: Free Press.

Fukuyama, F. (2010) The 'End of History': 20 Years Later. *New Perspectives Quarterly*, 27 (1): 7–10.

Grant, S. (2014) Bolsheviks, revolution and physical culture. *International Journal of the History of Sport*, 31 (7): 724–34.

Hampshire-Monk, I. (1992) *A History of Modern Political Thought: Major Political Thinkers from Hobbes to Marx*. Oxford: Blackwell.

Hargreaves, J. (2000) *Heroines of Sport: The Politics of Difference and Identity*. London: Routledge.

Hern, M. (2013) *One Game at a Time: Why Sports Matter*. Oakland, CA: AK Press.

Heywood, A. (2003) *Political Ideologies. An Introduction* (3rd ed.). London: Palgrave Macmillan.

Hitler, A. (1971) *Mein Kampf*. Mumbai: Jaico Publishing House.

Hoberman, J. (1984) *Sport and Political Ideology*. Austin, TX: University of Texas Press.

Krien, A. (2014) *Night Games: Sex, Power and a Journey into the Dark Heart of Sport*. London: Yellow Jersey Press.

Krüger, A. (1999) 'Strength through joy: the culture of consent under fascism, Nazism and Francoism'. In J. Riordan and A. Krüger (eds) *The International Politics of Sport in the Twentieth Century*. London: Spon, pp. 67–89.

Lenskjy, H. J. (1998) Sport and corporate environmentalism: The case of the Sydney 2000 Olympics. *International Review for the Sociology of Sport*, 33 (4): 341–54.

Luscombe, R. (2014) Scandal and rows encircle US football as it makes its annual trip to Wembley. *The Observer*, 28 September 2014, p. 33.

Mandell, R. D. (1971) *The Nazi Olympics*. New York: Macmillan.

Mannheim, K. (1936) *Ideology and Utopia*. London: Routledge and Kegan Paul.

Mao, Z. (1917) A study in physical education. Hsin ching-nein, April. Accessed 13 December 2010. www.marxists.org/reference/archive/mao/selected-works/volume-6/mswv6_01.htm.

Marx, K. and Engels, F. (1970) *The German Ideology. Part One*. London: Lawrence and Wishart.

Mill, J. S. (1974) *On Liberty*. Harmondsworth: Pelican Classics.

Mill, J. S. (1983) *Fascism*. London: Dent.

Mincyte, D., Casper, M. J. and Cole, C. L. (2009). Sports, environmentalism, land use, and urban development. *Journal of Sport and Social Issues*, 33 (2): 103–10.

Müller, J. W. (2009) The triumph of what (if anything)? Rethinking political ideologies and political institutions in twentieth century Europe. *Journal of Political Ideologies*, 14 (2): 211–26.

O'Sullivan, N. (1976) *Conservatism*. London: Dent.

Skille, E. Å. (2011) Sport for all in Scandinavia: sport policy and participation in Norway, Sweden and Denmark, *International Journal of Sport Policy and Politics*, 3 (3): 327–39.

Smith, A. and Porter, D. (eds.) (2004) *Sport and National Identity in the Post-War World*. London: Routledge.

Taylor, D. J. (2006) *On the Corinthian Spirit: The Decline of Amateurism in Sport*. London: Yellow Jersey Press.

PART II

Sport, politics and ideologies

The chapters in this section examine the interrelationship between sport and several political ideologies – fascism, communism, conservatism, liberalism, socialism (specifically Swedish social democracy), and feminism. Nationalism and environmentalism are discussed in later sections.

Writing on fascism, Daphné Bolz describes the feelings of frustration and appetite for revenge in post-World War I Europe, which prevented the establishment of balanced relationships in and between the nations. On the sport scene, this led to the exclusion of the war losers from the Antwerp (1920) and Paris (1924) Olympics. With the subsequent rise of fascism in Italy and Germany, the identity of the individual became secondary to the destiny of the people and the state. In both countries, sport gradually became an instrument to support these "fascist" regimes and their search for international recognition and supremacy. The chapter looks at the ways in which this process unfolded.

Jung Woo Lee and Alan Bairner discuss the relationship between sport and communism (or state socialism), not by revisiting the relatively familiar terrain of the experience of this relationship in the Soviet Union and its closest allies but by considering how this relationship has developed in North Korea and Cuba. They argue that whilst, as in other state socialist societies, sport has been used in these countries as a propaganda tool, it has also been closely associated with attempts to develop a new kind of citizen – the socialist man or woman. A major difficulty, however, lies in the fact that the pursuit of elite achievement, which is undeniably consistent with the former objective, might inevitably be at odds with the latter. To that extent, the fate of sport in communist societies has proved to be a microcosm of the fate of communism itself, at least in the form of state socialism.

One of the pioneers of the political study of sport, Lincoln Allison offers a range of insights into the relationship between conservatism and sport, He discusses a range of conservative ideas and reveals the degree to which concepts such as authority and tradition are important elements in the organisation and appreciation of sport. It could even be argued that, for better or ill, more than any other ideology, conservatism enjoys a special, and largely supportive, relationship with many of those who administer, sell and play sport.

William Morgan's chapter focuses on sport and liberalism and makes the case that a properly fashioned liberal theory of sport, one which takes seriously calls for liberalism to become radical, is better equipped and positioned than its present main leftist alternatives (Marxism, hegemony theory, and cultural studies/critical theory) to shed critical light on sport and to effect genuine change in its practice. Morgan argues that attempts to cordon off social practices such as sport to protect them from market intrusions exacerbate rather than ameliorate the corrosive effects of such intrusions. On the other hand, a liberal theory of sport, that takes its cue from the conventional social meanings that attach to and inform its practice, suggests a potential means by which the market can be thwarted from appropriating sport for its own economic purposes.

In the next chapter, Susanna Hedenborg and Tomas Peterson consider the relationship between socialism (or, to be more precise, Nordic social democracy) and sport. They note that this relationship is closely linked to what is often called the Nordic Sport Model, according to which sport has historically been comparatively well supported by the state. For all sports clubs fostering top athletes is an essential pursuit. However, in youth sport activities, a characteristic contradiction can be found, as these have to balance democratic values, particularly equality in participation, and elitism in the form of competitiveness. To develop democracy means to make sport available to everyone, regardless of age, sex, social and ethnic affiliation, of physical and mental condition, and place of residence. State support for youth sport in the Scandinavian countries is both a huge economic investment and an important ideological commitment. In turn, children are supposed to learn both democratic ways of thinking and acting, based on respect, cooperation and equality while simultaneously acquiring the principles of competing and winning. The ways in which this contradiction has been handled tells us a great deal about the sport politics of social democracy in the Nordic countries.

Over the past half century, the landscape of women's sport has changed beyond recognition. While the sporting world remains dominated by men and boys, the participation of girls and women has increased tremendously. Female athletes now regularly have experiences that would have been well beyond the possibility for many of their grandmothers. Mary Louise Adams argues in her chapter that the transformation of women's sport – especially the expansion of opportunities to play and the increased visibility of the athletic female body – would not have been possible without the rise of second wave feminism during the second half of the twentieth century. Her chapter begins with a discussion of feminism as a multiplicity of movements and ideas that have had different histories in different political and social contexts. There follows an overview of some of the ways that feminist thinking and feminist practice have shaped contemporary sport. Illustrative examples, from a variety of national contexts, demonstrate the range of issues and strategies addressed by feminists who are concerned about sport on the playing field and in the media. A feminist intersectional analysis is used to assess contemporary women's sport and campaigns around equality of opportunity and the gendered ideological dimensions of sport discourses.

5

SPORT AND FASCISM

Daphné Bolz

In the humanities and social sciences, few concepts are as difficult to define as "fascism", the term having been used for various political, social or cultural systems in both the past and present. As George L. Mosse has written, there is no workable definition of fascism that can suit all historical experiences and analyses (Mosse 1999). In modern times, the expression was first used in Italy after World War I, when a group of political activists created a "fascist" movement and eventually founded the Fascist National Party (PNF) in 1921. Their leader, Benito Mussolini, seized power in 1922. From the 1930s, the significance of the concept was extended and more widely used to characterise a specific political form that included German National Socialism, whose leader Adolf Hitler ruled Germany from 1933 to the end of World War II in 1945 (Kershaw 1985). The holistic vision of society, the objective to breed a New Man and the idea of a Third-Way state are considered as the core components of fascist ideology (Eatwell 2013). However, the concept itself has a turbulent history as an interpretation tool (Musiedlak 2010). It is closely related to other concepts such as "totalitarianism", which was much used in the first post-war interpretations of the interwar dictatorships (Arendt 1951). From the 1970s, the coming of a generation of historians who developed new ways of writing history allowed daily life under fascism to be considered in a different way. This was a significant turn in historiography, because researchers questioned the role of the masses. The reference to terror now seemed insufficient to explain the success of fascism. Scholars rather focused on the way the regimes sought the populations' consent (De Grazia 1981). Given the strong importance of emotion in sport and sport's extraordinary development in the interwar years, it is not surprising that the new "social" approach to fascism examined the specific role of sport. This chapter aims at giving an overview of the place of sport in fascist regimes and relies on historical examples taken mainly from Italy and Germany.

Changing minds and bodies: education in the fascist revolution

After the slaughter of the "war that ended all wars", the people of Europe hoped for a better future. Aspirations were great, but the concrete developments disappointed many. The Treaty of Versailles made Germany responsible for the war, obliged this country to pay for it and limited the size of the German army. The German population would not accept this and others, like the British leaders, also disapproved of it. Even if peace was back, internal socio-political orders and international relations between nations were immediately put to the test. This fragile situation was ideal for the development of reactionary movements, especially in Germany, which refused to accept the humiliating defeat imposed on it by its hereditary enemy, France, and in Italy, which had hoped that its participation in the war on the side of the winners would give it international recognition.

As far as post-war sport was concerned, it had definitely grown beyond continental anglophile circles and increasingly reached the masses during the interwar period. Its simplicity made it a perfect tool to assert identity and political opinions. In spite of claims of political independence, sport and fascism quickly found each other, for they both stood for a "modern" way of life. Fascist leaders and their followers despised the pre-war political elites, whom they considered to be passive and cowardly, because they had been unable to give satisfaction to their people both before the war and in handling the armistice after it. Fascists wanted to introduce a radical break in the history of the nations. Italian fascists in particular were obsessed with the modernisation of their country. The determination of all fascist activists to introduce a Revolution was boundless and they developed an ambitious programme that was not limited to politics but embraced all areas of social life. It implied a "new attitude of mind" that had a direct influence on what people did in both the public and private spheres. This was nothing less than an "anthropological revolution" to be achieved through a vast education programme. In this process, physical training was an important component of the regimes' policies because it implied "action", which was a key concept of fascism.

In Fascist Italy, the first attempt to promote physical education to children was carried out shortly after the fascists came to power. In 1923, as part of the large education reform by Giovanni Gentile, the responsibility for physical education was given to a new body called *Ente Nazionale di Educazione Fisica* (ENEF). However, ENEF was unable to meet this challenge, as it lacked the organisational skills required to work on a national level. In 1927 all its missions were transferred to the youth organisation *Opera Nazionale Ballila* (ONB), which had been founded the year before. This new organisation had a much better grasp of the Italian situation and was highly successful. It relied on a specific pedagogy developed by Eugenio Ferrauto, and on the political leader and gifted organiser Renato Ricci. As far as sport was concerned, the Fascist leaders had little interest in it at first. Sport had no great tradition in the country and the Fascists, who were first and foremost interested in educating the New Italian, rather considered sport as a foreign activity that was uncontrollable, sometimes violent, and foreign to national habits. However, the subordination of sport to politics was to come shortly. In 1925, Lando Ferretti was elected head of the national sports body, the Italian National Olympic Committee (CONI). Ferretti considered sport as an education tool to be used for the fascist Revolution. In December 1926, CONI became dependent upon the Fascist National Party. The domination of sport by politics occurred through forced centralisation (most federations moved to Rome) and several significant reforms, like the *Carta di Viareggio* (1926), which reorganised football to satisfy the political objectives of the regime (Simon 2005).

While all these measures were being taken in Italy, Germany was still a democratic country. The Weimar Republic experienced one of the most developed sports systems in the world. Participation boomed, clubs (*Vereine*) multiplied and many new and modern facilities were built, showing the way for other countries. Since the beginning of the twentieth century, German sports enthusiasts like Carl Diem had been working to obtain public funding for sport. The proposed daily hour of physical education in schools and their request for a law stipulating a *per capita* minimum sports space were widely debated during the 1920s. The town councils were a driving force in the construction of sports venues. This was not imposed by legislation, but by motivation rooted in the conviction that physical activity was necessary for the well-being of the German people. However, the ambitions could not be completely fulfilled as they fell victim to economic instability and the crisis of 1929. So when the Nazis came to power, contrary to the Italian Fascists, they found a highly developed sports network and a population which was sensitive to the idea of a harmonious development of mind and body. This attitude dated back to the philanthropist movement and had been successfully used in the *Turnen* movement – combined with a nationalist sensitivity not to displease the Nazis. The development of commercial sport and sport as entertainment was also inevitable in Germany, an evolution which was regretted by many sports teachers and theorists. However, the drawing of large crowds was also typical of the *Turnen* festivals. The Nazi inherited multiple experiences and influences from these. They adopted elements which fitted in with their ideology and could be used for political purposes. All the sports organisations were united in the *Deutscher Reichsbund für Leibesübungen* (DRL) headed by Hans von Tschammer und Osten.

Whatever their sporting heritages, fascist movements basically considered sport as an education tool to reach a further aim. The programmes they developed aimed at strengthening populations physically and mentally. What is more, this educative mission was not to be perceived as oppressive. Of course, the new leaders saw it as the duty of each individual to exercise and to be fit in order to be able to represent and serve his/her country. Pressure was more or less strong, for example in imposing a compulsory sports test on students in Germany, which had to be passed if they were to pursue their education. But the ultimate aim of these measures was to get people to "experience" the benefits of health and of community life, and to win them over to the fascist cause. In this sense, the youth organisations were typical of the fascist regimes because they gave children the opportunity to leave the family circle in order to enjoy physical activity and experience new friendships. Of course, not all children liked sport and even fewer were interested in the political framework and discourses. In the same way as the youth, workers' organisations were used to access the people's feelings, both in making them active (through sport and tourism) (Da Rold 1994) and in diverting them (with cinema for example) (Krüger 2007). Seeking consent was essential, for the regimes' strength relied on the participation of the masses (Freeden 2003).

This is why propaganda – understood as a kind of mass education (or *Volksaufklärung*, as Goebbels' Ministry was called) – was so central to fascist regimes. The achievements of the Revolution had to be made visible. This was particularly true for sport, where successes were immediately broadcast, the best example being the preparation, organisation and dissemination of the Berlin Olympic Games through the "Ministry of Propaganda and *Volksaufklärung*". As Tony Collins (2013: 86) writes, "sport underwent a second industrial revolution, underpinned by technological developments in the media" during the interwar period. The fascist regimes fully participated and took advantage of this evolution. Lando Ferretti for example, was not only President of CONI, but also the head of propaganda (Bacci 2002). He conceived his illustrated magazine *Lo sport fascista* as a means of furthering the acceptance of fascism through sport. The radio, which allowed for a mass audience all around the world, was not absent either, although it seems its massive use for sports events was rather limited during this period. Finally, the newsreels – which were shown in all Western countries at that time – participated in the visual transmission of a propaganda message in which sport and fascism merged together.

Fascism in action: the New Man in sport

The emphasis on the media reveals that the education issue was more than just a "socialist" measure for the well-being of the people. Physical training and sport were, rather, techniques to direct individuals and impress observers. In fact, fascist movements shared a theological vision of history insofar as they conceived the history of mankind as a succession of phases, the final aim of which was the holist organisation of society according to fascist principles (Gentile 2013). The conception of history and the use of the past were central to fascist ideologies, as in the end all the efforts served to establish these new "ideal" societies.

Unlimited ambitions

The New Man was meant to be the direct result of fascist education. He was the prototype of the "new race" who exemplified the achievements of fascism. As a product of fascist education, his characteristics were physical strength and commitment to the fascist cause. To fulfil his duty as a fascist, he "lived dangerously". Obedience and respect of hierarchy were understood. The figure of the New Man had roots in the traditional idea of the citizen-soldier and more recent roots in the experience of comradeship in the trenches during World War I, which had first been glorified by the futurist movement. Ideally, all men (and women) were to belong to the "new race" once they had undergone fascist education. Here again, the various organisations of the regimes played a leading role in controlling the entire population, including older children out of school, students, and of course workers and their families. In Italy, the ONB was most active in out-of-school activities and was responsible for the education of physical education teachers. As for the *Hitler Jugend*, it offered all kind of activities, especially those useful during war (like broadcasting techniques). Enrolment of children became compulsory in 1936. The ambition to raise convinced fascists was not kept secret. Indeed, the fascist leaders were proud of modelling a new generation.

As the fascist regimes confirmed their leadership in Europe in the 1930s, they also shared a tendency to radicalisation. Education increasingly gave way to complete indoctrination. This had consequences for sport. As early as 1928, the Italian Charter for Sport started reorienting the function of sport in society: physical education was still fine, but competitive sport was not to be forgotten. The Charter therefore introduced competitions for children aged 14 and above. When the Italian team ranked second in the 1932 Olympic medal table, the fascists realised the propaganda power of sport. The image of the New Man and the role of sport also changed during this contest. As a result, the organisations were reformed. In Italy, ONB and several other organisations were merged into the *Gioventù Italiana del Littorio* (GIL) in 1937. In Germany, the national sports body became dependent upon the Party in 1938 and changed its name to *Nationalsozialistischer Reichsbund für Leibesübungen* (NSRL). Top athletes were increasingly considered as representatives of the regimes. Their strength was the regime's strength. Accordingly, high-level sport was promoted and supported as part of the propaganda plans of the fascist regimes. The Italian soccer team, which was to win the 1934 World Cup organised in Fascist Italy itself, went to a training camp before competition, free from any other professional obligation. In Nazi Germany, the Olympic athletes – except for those who were Jewish – could also train for the 1936 Games in exceptional privileged conditions.

Nation, race and international domination

The evolution towards a greater emphasis of domination in sport was not surprising with regard to the fascist theological visions of history. The core of fascist ideologies was an ideal organisation of society which was immutable and absolute. But the contribution of sport to the establishment of this harmonious community life had severe implications. The systems put in place were rigid. Neither the ideological background nor the practical organisation imposed on the population in general and on the athletes in particular, were to be questioned. Criticism was out of the question and people were expected to be submissive.

Control over sport – as over most other social activities – increased with the stability of the regimes. This control was organised through a centralised system. At first, it was state guided. But as the regimes became established and the ambitions of the leaders increased, sport became subject to Party control. There was no alternative to the imposed system. Respect of hierarchy was particularly evident in the rituals and new traditions that these fascist regimes put in place. Symbols became increasingly important and were to be shown on sports clothes and during the many rituals and celebrations of the sports meetings. Representatives of the Party were always present in order to underline the official presence and political support (and influence) in sport. In short, sport under fascist regimes was completely integrated into the sacralisation of politics (Gentile 1996). For Emilio Gentile, Italian fascism had created a new religion which had its roots in modernity. The regimes were based on the assumption that they held the key to a perfect organisation of society. But if harmonious unity was the most important principle in fascist regimes, not everybody was to be included.

Most of the time, fascist regimes claimed to want peace and to welcome all comers, as the Nazis did in the run up to the Olympic Games. However, they also placed a high value in war, which was ultimately considered a necessary action to disseminate the benefits of fascism. Sport could justify peace and war, comradeship and combat. Fascists of all sorts saw their political activism as right and moral because it conformed to the idea that they were acting for the benefits of their people, if not of humanity. Indeed, the Nazis were convinced that the Aryans were a superior race, and it was this conviction that rationalised their policies and murders to justify the Revolution. Fascist leaders also relied on history (notably on past glories) and a vision of the future. Sport was just one activity amongst others that were used to further the global fulfilment of humanity. These were considered as natural laws and were therefore indisputable – as were the fascist laws. The Italian Fascists wanted to "civilise" Ethiopia, while the Nazis believed the Aryans were selected and had the duty to impose their supremacy on the world. The support given to sport, physical education and body care (like medicine) were directly dependent upon these visions of a "world order". This also explains why members from the fascist states tried to be elected within international sports bodies, quite often with success. The exclusiveness and irrationality of fascist ideology found fertile ground in sport. Both expected (physical) commitment, were ritualised and, in the end, represented an ultimate fight. Both were also ambiguous on many issues such as race and peace. The relationship between sport and fascism was one of mutual exploitation. As war approached, the militarisation of sport increased dramatically. The disciplines which were most supported by the fascist regimes were those of military relevance such as alpinism, skiing, mechanical sports and swimming.

The aesthetics of fascism in sport: architecture and representations

The newly created institutions to educate the physical education teachers are an excellent example of the fusion of sport and fascist policies. Fascist education principles applied to all areas in the countries, but more elite leaders were needed if the system was to continue. Therefore, a few selected individuals were educated in special schools. In these places, the curricula went far beyond the mere topics of physical education and sport, also including a large element of political education and fascist doctrine. In Italy, the appropriate institution was the Fascism Academy for Physical Education, which opened its doors in 1928 (Ponzio 2009). In Germany, the future elite Nazi leaders were educated from childhood in *Nationalpolitische*

Erziehungsanstalten (NAPOLA). But there was also the Higher School for Physical Education, which was founded anew in a Nazi version in 1936, its "democratic" ancestor having been created in Berlin in 1920. Both were located in the National Stadium in Berlin, which later became the Olympic Stadium.

As part of the transformation of the country, new facilities were built in fascist countries (Bolz 2008). This was particularly visible and significant in Italy, where the regime remained for a longer period. As far as physical activity is concerned, the most important were the *Case del Ballila*, i.e. the venues of the youth organisation ONB. These were designed to meet the purpose of the physical and moral education of children and youth. Depending on the local situation, they were made up of simple meeting facilities or were endowed with a library and proper venues for physical education, including a swimming pool and a stadium. However, some ONB facilities did not respect sports norms because the ONB leaders considered proper sports competition as an obstacle to its education goals. Nevertheless, sport was boosted in Italy and the number of normed sports facilities rose significantly parallel to the development of the ONB. From 1928, a law allowed financial support to towns that were willing to have a stadium built, based on the model of the *Stadio del Littorio*. A Commission for Sports Facilities (*Commissione Impianti Sportivi* – CIS) was founded in 1933, and having venues to train champions became a priority. A number of Italian architects specialised in sports architecture and obtained significant fame at home and abroad. This was not unjustified, as architects were given a lot of freedom and were able to develop a singular and modern architecture, for example at the stadia of Bologna, Florence and Turin. All venues displayed a modernist style, which was an expression of both the fascist modernity aspiration and the international artistic tendency (Gentile 2007). The expertise of Italian architects was one of the reasons why the country was chosen to organise the 1934 football World Cup. The stadia contributed to the success of the competition, the highlight of which was certainly the final won by the Italian team in the presence of Mussolini. With the radicalisation of the regime, architecture was considered a political tool too. The regime's ambition in organising international sports events to promote its image went hand in hand with the development of a monumental and neoclassical style, as exemplified in the new urban area called *Esposizione Universale di Roma* (EUR), which was designed as a centre for the Expo in 1942 and the planned Olympics of 1944 (Bolz 2015). In Germany, the rather numerous venues that the Nazis had inherited were considered as places for the Aryan community to exercise and recover its dignity, which had been stained during the previous decades. The style was often modern too, which was not in line with Nazi taste but which was tolerated because political education had to be carried out there, along with the physical training of the people. The Olympic stadium, however, and the park which surrounded it were completely built anew. The monumentality of the complex obscures the fact that the venue was indeed technologically advanced and modern, whereas Hitler had favoured a massive, medieval-like construction in a more typical Nazi style.

In both countries, a new aesthetics of the body was also developed, which supported the idea of the New Man. Sculpture was a powerful means to represent the New Man in a sporting pose. Indeed, the Forum Mussolini (now Italico), which hosted the Academy, is richly decorated with statutes – most of them blank white – and mosaics of active athletes. The reference to antiquity is plain and traces a direct link from the glorious Roman past to the glorious fascist Empire (founded in 1936). In Germany, sculptures especially by Arno Brecker, photographs, and films such as *Olympia* by Leni Riefenstahl (McFee and Tomlinson 1999) presented scenes of the vigorous Aryan, strong in body and mind. Under fascist rule, women's sport was encouraged up to a point, although not as much as men's. It was fine for women to practise sport in order for them to strengthen their bodies, but their first role was to act as mothers and wives.

Nevertheless, German female athletes were admired internationally, at least in other fascist countries. And Italy's Ondina Valla, who won a gold medal in Berlin, was obviously celebrated by the Italian press (Gori 2001; Morgan 2004). Technical progress in the media allowed for the fast transmission of photographs and collages, which were very popular, especially in sports periodicals. The fascist aesthetics of sport was also developed in films, in particular those of the Italian LUCE Institute, which contributed to the dissemination of a new artistic taste – in particular in architecture – and general knowledge on sport in the country. Mass displays were important events, as these were occasions to showcase the regimes' achievements. The Berlin Olympics, with thousands of people and athletes marching in the decorated streets and places of Berlin, set a milestone. In Italy, one of the most famous displays was the parade of Italian athletes on 28 October 1934 in Rome on the occasion of the twelfth anniversary of the March on Rome. In a speech to athletes at the parade, Mussolini made this famous declaration in which he clearly uses sport as a political tool by elevating its status and linking it with concepts such as nation and honor:

> You must be tenacious, chivalrous, daring, [you must] remember that when you fight outside the country, at that very moment the honour and the sporting prestige of the nation are entrusted to your muscles and above all to your spirit.
>
> *(Mussolini 1934, cited in Gori 1999: 22)*

Sport and fascism: an ideal alliance?

An opportunist sports movement

To some athletes, sports leaders and institutions which had not been banned by the regimes, fascist regimes offered welcome support to their cause. Health and physical training specialists had often called for better hygiene education and practices among the population. Since the nineteenth century, the effects of industrialisation and poverty had seriously limited the population's potential. In the aftermath of World War I, this situation was still critical although various groups had been created in order to support healthy physical activities (Hau 2003). Sport was one of these. In countries like Germany, where the state played a central part in organising or supporting the peoples' social activities, it is not surprising that sports leaders begged public bodies for support. The Nazis were at first rather reluctant to promote sport, and when Hitler came to power the Weimar leaders were anxious about its future. But once the top hierarchy of Nazism had understood how powerful sport could be for propaganda purposes, they fully supported the sports movement. The organisers of the Berlin 1936 Olympics were delighted to receive all they had ever dreamt of from the Nazi government. Sports institutions and top leaders were responsible for this fusion of sport and fascism, because in claiming the political independence of sport – with reference to the Olympic Charter for example – they gave the Nazis a free hand. This also applied to the famous 1935 and 1938 football matches between the German and English teams (Beck 1999; Bolz 2014). In the pure amateur tradition, the British Foreign Office felt little concerned with sports matters. This was an error, for all social activities were political in Nazi Germany. The Olympic celebration was actually a highlight of Hitler's political success. The impressive Olympic park, the propaganda in Germany and abroad and the breathtaking celebration were all part of a seduction offensive on the part of a Nazi regime which spared no expense to show its best profile and to impress international audiences. The official non-exclusion of Jews from the German team was a major concession by a system which only worked in the interest of "Aryan" people. But Nazi ideology remained untouched by Olympic regulations. Fascist ideology is even stronger when not apparent, at least for those who do not want to see. Many of these people could be found in the IOC, either because they shared an admiration for the achievements of the new regimes, or because they were blinded by their own Olympic ideology, or, finally, because they felt powerless in the face of the growing strength of the "New Germany", as was the case with IOC President Baillet-Latour (Carpentier 2004). The full success of the Nazi regime in manipulating the IOC was evident when Garmisch-Partenkirchen was allocated the 1940 Winter Games on the eve of World War II.

There are many other examples of the successful cooperation between sport and fascism – especially as fascist activism was often a condition for being awarded responsibilities in sport! The 1934 Football World Cup in Fascist Italy was probably the first major international sports event where fascist interests were so explicit. Here too, Mussolini first had to be convinced of the event's value for the international image of his country before the propaganda and publicity machine could start. The victory of the Italian team was the best service the players could do for the regime. Even if the event and propaganda were relatively moderate in comparison to today's practices, the competition was still a significant milestone in sports history.

The readiness of the regimes to support sport was grasped by all kinds of sports leaders. In Germany, Carl Diem's career may have been uneven, but it was continuous from long before 1933 to long after the war. Pleading for the political independence of sport, his sports activism during the regime made him a supporter, if not a frontrunner, of fascist ideology. Fascist regimes naturally engaged the athletes by praising the New Man's physical strength. The Danish gymnast Niels Bukh, for example, was fascinated by Nazi Germany and "He was ideologically uninterested in states with democratically founded forms of government [. . .] he was conspicuously negative about Soviet Communism. All in all, these considerations corresponded with the reactions of the various states towards his gymnastics" (Bonde 2009a: 1432). As such, in supporting sport, the fascist regimes responded to the calls and needs expressed by a large part of the sports community. The ideological position and the racial approach to the sports "cause" was not always pointed out. But the relationship of fascism to sport also had ideological limits.

The limits of success

The limits of the alliance between sport and fascism were those of fascist ideology itself. The self-proclaimed superiority of fascist regimes was hardly compatible with the "values" of sport, which originated in the culture of the British upper class. With racial purity being at the core of their doctrine, the Nazis were never really prepared to tolerate stand out of the mix of "human races" during the practice, training and competitions in sport. Their ideological position was so extreme that they encouraged marriage between athletes to produce babies with the best possible pedigree. This was in accordance with their "racial hygiene" theory (Krüger 1999). The leaders themselves had ambiguous attitudes towards sport. Mussolini genuinely practised horse riding and fencing, but his love of sport was exaggerated by propaganda. As for Hitler and Franco, they were no sportsmen. Hitler was above all such practical issues anyway, because no one would question the purity of his genes.

Looking at it superficially, the overlapping of fascist and sports principles was of course possible – as best exemplified by the 1936 Olympics. However, fascist leaders committed themselves to sport only once they had realised the propaganda power of major sports events. It is important to stress that the fascist regimes relied on a certain amount of flexibility in their ideologies and doctrines and that they were continuously adapting to concrete situations, hence for example the changing nature of the Italian state organisations. There were also many incoherencies within fascist doctrines and regimes. As a homosexual, Bukh certainly should not have been a respectable figure for the Nazis. However, he was invited to tour Germany and "For the Nazis, Bukh's gymnasts were the incarnation of a perfection of the Aryan race" (Bonde 2009b). Under the Franco regime in Spain, sport was in theory a much-valued activity to promote the regime. Concretely, it lacked competent sports leaders and funding because Franco was not willing to invest a lot of money into the sports system in the way Mussolini and Hitler had done. The result was a complete failure (Gonzalez Aja 1998).

What is more, fascist regimes could only take advantage of sport as long as the populations were willing to participate. Most people certainly welcomed changes like stronger state support in terms of the economy, working conditions, health care and leisure opportunities. But not all were willing to be "active", to train and to fight for a fascist cause to which they did not necessarily adhere. It is clear that the Italian population became increasingly uncertain as to whether its government was going in the right direction when the country underwent a period of sanctions (due to the conquest of Ethiopia in 1936) and when Mussolini signed the Pact of Steel in May 1939. In the face of the heightening of international tensions, sport played above all a role as entertainment. Hard training for military combat was not the preoccupation of most Italians. The man in the street certainly enjoyed the success of the Italian football players at the 1934 and 1938 World Cups and at the 1936 Berlin Olympics, as well as Gino Bartali's win of the 1938 Tour de France. These were of more interest than reports on the Spanish Civil War (1936–1939), the *Anschluss* (1938) and the Munich Crisis (1938).

Ultimately, the discrepancy between the fascist regimes and the sports movement was best brought to light by the international boycott movements. The international community was not willing to accept the fascist manipulation of sport. The reason why the Nazis developed such massive propaganda was in part to battle against the immense criticism that was coming from all over the world and seriously jeopardising the holding of the grand celebration of the "New Germany" through sport (Krüger and Murray 2003). Cancelling the Games would have been a terrible blow to their prestige.

Conclusions

The fascist movements were obsessed with changing the habits of the population and with training athletes who would be loyal to the fascist cause. Education was the key to the implementation of the Revolution. The New Man was the result of fascist education, which laid as much emphasis on physical as on intellectual development. However the alliance between sport and fascism was not immediate. It came gradually. In Germany, Italy and Spain the political leaders first had to be convinced of the power of sport to boost their international prestige. A new relationship between the fascist regimes and physical training then started, as best illustrated by the 1934 football World Cup in Italy and the 1936 Berlin Olympics. Emphasising mass participation and preparing top-level athletes had a twofold aim. First, it gave the people a sense of belonging to the community and convinced them of the validity of the fascist ideology. Second, impressive displays and successful sports results were presented to foreign observers as achievements of the fascist regimes and helped them to strengthen their diplomatic profiles.

It is undeniable that fascism promoted sport and used it for its own political and ideological purposes. Sport was of interest to fascist movements because it gave their ideologies a forum where they could visibly concretise their social and possibly racial plans. But in return the sports movement benefited from it to some extent and some sports leaders saw the new regimes as opportunities for sport.

Sport fitted well into the new environments which fascist leaders wanted to create, but which basically consisted of an eclectic use of old and modern elements fused in irrational discourses. Indeed, fascist regimes were constantly adapting to the changing realities of their situations. As a socio-historical construct, sport has historically been home to a variety of conflicting ideologies. In the end, however, fascism never managed to get a complete hold of the people and a complete "fascistization" of the sports movement did not take place.

References

Arendt, H. (1951) *The Origins of Totalitarianism*. New York: Harcourt Brace & Co.

Bacci, A. (2002) *Lo Sport Nella Propaganda Fascista*. Turin: Bradipolibri.

Beck, P. (1999) *Scoring for Britain: International Football and International Politics, 1900–1939*. London: Cass.

Bolz, D. (2008) *Les Arènes Totalitaires: Fascisme, Nazisme et Propagande Sportive*. Paris: CNRS Éditions.

Bolz, D. (2014) Reversing the influence: Anglo-German relations and British fitness policies in the 1930s. *Sport in History*, 34(4) : 569–594.

Bolz, D. (2015) "The legacy of the unsuccessful Olympic ambition of fascist Rome". In R. Holt, and D. Ruta (eds) *Routledge Handbook of Sport and Legacy: Meeting the Challenge of Major Sports Events*. London: Routledge, pp. 339–351.

Bonde, H. (2009a) Nationalism in the age of extremes: Taking Danish gymnastics to the world. *The International Journal of the History of Sport*, 26(10): 1414–1435.

Bonde, H. (2009b) The struggle for Danish youth: Fascism, sport, democracy. *The International Journal of the History of Sport*, 26(10): 1436–1457.

Carpentier, F. (2004) *Le Comité International Olympique en Crises: La Présidence de Henri de Baillet-Latour, 1925–1940*. Paris: L'Harmattan.

Collins, T. (2013) *Sport in Capitalist Society: A Short History*. London and New York: Routledge.

De Grazia, V. (1981) *The Culture of Consent: Mass Organization of Leisure in Fascist Italy*. Cambridge: Cambridge University Press.

Da Rold, E. (1994) *Turismo e Sport Nella Provincia di Belluno Durante il Fascismo. Economia, Ideologia, Società e Consenso*. Belluno: Istituto Bellunese di Ricerche Sociali e Culturali.

Eatwell, R. (2013) "Fascism". In M. Freeden, L. Tower Sargent, and M. Stears (eds) *The Oxford Handbook of Political Ideologies*. Oxford: Oxford University Press, pp. 474–492.

Freeden M. (2003) *Ideology: A Very Short Introduction*. Oxford: Oxford University Press.

Gentile, E. (1996) *The Sacralisation of Politics in Fascist Italy*. Cambridge: Harvard University Press.

Gentile, E. (2007) *Fascismo di Pietra*. Rome-Bari: Laterza.

Gentile, E. (2013) "Total ideologies". In M. Freeden, L. Tower Sargent, and M. Stears (eds) *The Oxford Handbook of Political Ideologies*. Oxford: Oxford University Press, pp. 56–72.

Gonzalez Aja, T. (1998) "Spanish sports policy in republican and fascist Spain". In P. Arnaud and J. Riordan (eds) *Sport and International Politics: The Impact of Fascism and Communism on Sport*. London: Spon, pp. 97–113.

Gori, G. (1999) *Italian Fascism and the Female Body: Sport, Submissive Women and Strong Mothers*. London: Routledge.

Gori, G. (2001). A glittering icon of fascist femininity: Trebisonda "Ondina" Valla. *The International Journal of the History of Sport*, 18(1): 173–195.

Hau, M. (2003) *The Cult of Health and Beauty in Germany: A Social History, 1890–1930*. Chicago: Chicago University Press.

Kershaw, I. (1985) *The Nazi Dictatorship: Problems and Perspectives of Interpretation*. London: Edward Arnold.

Krüger, A. (1999) Breeding, rearing and preparing the Aryan body: Creating the complete superman the Nazi Way. *The International Journal of the History of Sport*, 16(2): 42–68.

Krüger A. (2007) "Strength through joy: The culture of consent under fascism, Nazism, and Francoism". In J. Riordan, A. Krüger (eds) *The International Politics of Sport in the Twentieth Century*. London: Spon, pp. 67–89.

Krüger, A. and Murray, W. (ed.). (2003) *The Nazi Olympics: Sport, Politics and Appeasement in the 30s*. Urbana-Chicago: University of Illinois Press.

McFee, G. and Tomlinson, A. (1999) Riefenstahl's Olympia: Ideology and aesthetics in the shaping of the Aryan athletic body. *The International Journal of the History of Sport*, 16(2): 86–106.

Morgan, S. (2004) Inventing the Latin body: The reception of the Olympic athletes Valla and Beccali in the Italian press. *Annual of CESH*: 17–27.

Mosse, G. L. (1999) *The Fascist Revolution: Toward a General Theory of Fascism*. New York: Howard Fertig.

Musiedlak, D. (2010) Fascisme, religion politique et religion de la politique. Généalogie d'un concept et de ses limites. *Vingtième Siècle. Revue d'histoire*, 4(108): 71–84.

Ponzio, A. (2009) *La Palestra del Littorio. L'Accademia della Farnesina; un Esperimento di Pedagogia Totalitaria nell'Italia Fascista*. Milan: Franco Angeli.

Simon, M. (2005) *Football and Fascism: The National Game under Mussolini*. Oxford and New York: Berg.

6

SPORT AND COMMUNISM

The examples of North Korea and Cuba

Jung Woo Lee and Alan Bairner

Introduction

Although this chapter is headed 'Sport and Communism', it might be more accurate to note from the outset that we are interested here in state socialism as opposed to democratic socialism or democratic social democracy as practised in countries such as Sweden over an extended period of time or, more importantly, communism as envisaged in the writings of Karl Marx. Our reasoning is that no country to date has witnessed the completion of all of the aims that Marx anticipated for a communist society, the withering away of the state being arguably the most significant, but by no means the only, lacuna. This was true of the former Soviet Union and its satellite states, including the German Democratic Republic (GDR), and it remains true today of the People's Republic of China (PRC). Rather than revisit those countries where the relationship between sport and the dominant ideology has been examined at length and in depth elsewhere (Riordan 1980, 1991; Riordan and Jones 1999; Dong 2003; Grix and Dennis 2012), we have chosen to focus in this chapter on two countries, North Korea and Cuba, which, at the time of writing, possess most of the characteristics of state socialism and which exhibit some similarities although they are also very different in numerous respects. Before we turn to these case studies, however, it is worth reminding ourselves of the, sometimes, difficult relationship that communists in general have had with sport and how this has been addressed.

Marx had nothing to say about sport *per se*, although Engels and he did make reference to the potential contribution of exercise and games to worker satisfaction (Grant 2014). Lenin, the main architect of the 1917 Russian Revolution, was also an advocate of physical activity, which Grant (2014) appears to conflate with sport when she argues that he thereby validated the Soviet sports system. Lenin did indeed advocate the establishment of a High School for Sport and Physical Culture, believing that mass participation in physical culture could help in the creation of the new 'communist man' (Bunck 1994). However, as Grant (2014: 729) herself admits, in the years immediately following the revolution, 'Competitive sport was looked upon unfavourably and did not receive official sanction until the late 1920s and 1930s.' Thus, physical activity in the post-revolution Soviet Union was largely restricted to military training or exercise for the sake of improving the health of the population. Only gradually did team sports become acceptable as vehicles of social solidarity within specific workplaces and occupational groups. The most dramatic shift in thinking, however, arrived with the Cold War when sport came to be recognised as a highly effective source of what has come to be known as 'soft power' (Nye 2005). Competition between the Soviet Union and the United States in the quest for Olympic medals became, along with the space race, one of the most compelling narratives of the Cold War. In pursuing sporting success, however, the Soviet Union was arguably retreating still further from the original aims of the revolution, above all an egalitarian society which did not accept that people should be divided into winners or losers.

Another revolutionary leader who recognised the importance of physical activity was Mao Zedong who, in one of his earliest publications, sounds more like a nineteenth-century English public school headmaster than a future communist leader, arguing that 'when the body is strong, then one can advance speedily in knowledge and morality, and reap far-reaching advantages' (Mao 1917). However, it is now the PRC's turn to face a similar challenge to that previously encountered by the Communist Party of the Soviet Union, having already recognised the 'soft power' appeal of sport by hosting the Olympic Games in Beijing in 2008 when the country topped the medal table with the highest number of gold medals and by subsequently coming second to the USA in the medal table at the 2012 Games held in London. As with the earlier example of the Soviet Union, it is difficult to reconcile this pursuit of sporting success with a communist commitment to equality. Furthermore, there is an additional problem linked to the inherent character of sport itself.

Writing with specific reference to Cuba, Carter (2014: 1), argues that 'sport is often a conservative set of institutional practices used to reinforce existing power relations'. It has certainly tended to be associated far more with conservative values, such as tradition and hierarchy, than with radical politics. Thus, the question arises: given the trajectories described above, are communist ideals and sporting success compatible? In this chapter, we seek to address, if not necessarily definitively answer, that question, through an examination and comparison of two of the smaller countries in the world to have embraced communism or state socialism.

As Gordy and Lee (2009: 229) have observed, 'Since the beginning of the 1990s, Cuba and North Korea have devoted most of their resources to economic and political survival, hoping to integrate into the capitalist world system and normalise relations with the United States'. Arguably both regimes now emphasise nationalism more than communism or socialism, although 'nationalism was always an essential ingredient of their revolutionary ideologies' (Gordy and Lee 2009: 229–230). Nevertheless, their demonisation by the United States has continued to be narrated with specific reference to what is regarded as their totalitarian style of communism. They are similar, therefore, insofar as they have been identified by the US as 'rogue states'. But there are other similarities, not least the fact that 'Both Cuba and North Korea insist that their socialism is a form unique to that nation's historical and cultural needs, rather than a Marxism-Leninism imported from abroad' (Gordy and Lee 2009: 231). In relation to sport in both countries, nationalism casts a long shadow (see Lee and Bairner 2009). There are also differences, of course, which is hardly surprising when one takes into account the character of their respective historical conditions and revolutionary missions. In examining the role of sport in North Korea and Cuba, therefore, we endeavour to discover if similarities and differences are also apparent within the context of an activity, sport, that other state socialist regimes have found so problematic.

North Korea

North Korea is the last remaining hard-line totalitarian communist state. Although it initially adopted Marxist–Leninist ideology as a ruling political doctrine, the North Korean communist leaders gradually revised its governing principle several times, and they have finally developed its unique political system, namely the *Juche* (self-reliant) ideology, which displays a strong nationalist undertone and, at the same time, underpins the permanent leadership of Kim Il-sung and his offspring (Mceachern 2010). In fact, according to the North Korean political statement, the entire people of communist Korea are regarded as symbolic sires of the Kim ruling family, and, on this basis, the communist state has developed the notion of 'Kim Il-sung nationalism' as one of the core components of the ruling ideology through which the cult of Kim's family emerged (Kim 2014; Lee 2009). In order to understand this peculiar nature of North Korean communism more precisely, it is worth looking at a brief history of the Korean communist movement.

Historical development of the Korean communist movement

Communism was first introduced to Korea in the early twentieth century when the nation was ruled by Japanese imperialists, and the Korean communist movement at that time largely emerged as part of anti-colonial independent struggle (Scalapino and Lee 1960). As Marxist–Leninist ideology criticises imperialism for being the highest stage of capitalism, international communist groups materially and spiritually assisted the national liberation movement occurring in the colonies because liberation from imperial domination is an essential precondition for the establishment of a communist state (Lenin 1920/1966). This support from the communist international was an example of the rare external assistance on which Korean resistance groups relied and the left-wing independence fighters, in particular, were deeply influenced by Lenin's anti-colonial thesis (Scalapino and Lee 1960). In spite of this international communist alliance, however, the Korean communists were concerned more with national liberation itself than with building a communist state on the Korean peninsula (Suh 1967). This meant that, from the outset, nationalism constituted the major element of the Korean communist movement.

When Korea was liberated from Japan in 1945, the nation was divided into two parts by UN mandate. With direct military and political support from Moscow, communism flourished in the Soviet-led North Korea. Kim Il-sung, who had led one of the most militant independent armies during the colonial period, seized political power soon after partition and the Soviet Union authorised Kim to be the legitimate leader of the Korean Communist Party. In 1948, the Democratic People's Republic of Korea was founded under Kim's leadership and, in the same year, the Soviet army completely left the Korean peninsula as a sign of its recognition of North Korea as a sovereign communist state (Armstrong 2003). However, US troops continued to be stationed in US-backed South Korea, and the United States heavily influenced the South's political affairs. Kim Il-sung's communist regime perceived this situation as a symptom of American imperialism in the South, and finally declared a war with South Korea in 1950 so as to liberate its southern neighbours and compatriots from the American imperialists. The resultant Korean War ended without a peace treaty, which has resulted in an almost permanent partition of the Korean peninsula. Because the US government subsequently displayed a hostile attitude towards Kim's socialist regime and because US forces remain in South Korea to the present day, the political and military struggle against American imperialism still represents one of the major tenets of North Korean communist ideology (Feffer 2003).

In the 1960s, Kim Il-sung developed *Juche* ideology and claimed this philosophy of self-reliance as an official political doctrine of North Korea. *Juche* ideology has four major principles, namely indigenous ideology, autonomous politics, self-sustaining economy, and self-defence (Helgesen 1991). Hence, building a self-determined and self-reliant communist nation–state is the ultimate aim of this political dogma which is, in reality, a highly nationalistic variant of communism (Armstrong 2003). North Korea's situation necessitated this new governing ideology for two major reasons. First, when the tension between North Korea's closest communist allies, the Soviet Union and the People's Republic of China, began to develop in the 1960s, Kim's regime was no longer able to depend on these two communist giants simultaneously (Feffer 2003). Consequently, North Korea decided to adopt its own, more or less neutral, third way which was underpinned by the principle of self-reliance. Second, the 1960s was a period during which Kim-Il-sung attempted to accomplish the political project to establish an almost absolute totalitarian regime (Cumings 2005). By introducing this Korean-style communist ideology, he sought to create the circumstances in which he and his followers could legitimately purge potential political rivals, particularly those who still ardently supported Marxist–Leninist principles and those who were closely associated with Maoism, all of whom were stigmatised as anti-revolutionaries opposed to the *Juche* ideology (Mceachern 2011). The North Korean red terror was completed in the mid-1960s. Subsequently, members of the Korean communist party unanimously adopted this *Juche* ideology as a fundamental principle of the North Korean socialist society (Helgesen 1991).

The implementation of policy based on the *Juche* ideology also involves the idolisation of the 'Great Leader' and his family (Mceachern 2011). In the 1970s, the North Korean Communist Party further updated this self-reliant principle and also began to call it 'Kim Il-sung-ism' thereby offering a fundamental framework for the development of 'Kim Il-sung nationalism' (Kim 2013). This implies that only Kim Il-sung and his sons who have inherited power from him are able to interpret and apply this principle to North Korean communism without error, which ultimately justifies and legitimates the Kim dynasty's eternal despotic rule. In addition, by constructing and disseminating a nationalistic discourse based on the ruling ideology, the Kim regime effectively integrates and mobilises the people under the banner of 'Kim Il-sung-ism' and 'Kim-Il-sung nationalism' (Kim 2006). This personified form of nationalism, or the cult of Kim's family, is particularly workable in the post-Cold War era when North Korea experiences almost complete economic isolation from the world and faces direct political and military challenges from its old foes, mainly the US and South Korea.

Sport and politics in North Korea

Sport and politics are inseparable concepts in North Korea. According to a North Korean dictionary, sport is 'a means to develop strong will power and revolutionary comradeship amongst its people so that sport can contribute the construction of the communist state' (Political dictionary cited in Sung 2008: 6). Hence, the fundamental aim of sport and physical activities in North Korea is to foster patriotic socialist individuals. At the same time, high-performance sport operates as an important vehicle for propaganda (Lee and Bairner 2009; Merkel 2012). In particular, the occasional international successes of North Korean elite athletes provide useful material that the communist regime can exploit so as to propagate the excellent leadership of the 'Great Leader' and to show the greatness of North Korean nation to its people (Hong 2012; Lee 2009). In this section, we look at the connection between sport and politics during the series of Kim regimes in communist Korea.

The Kim Il-sung regime and sport

During the formative stage of the North Korean communist state, Kim Il-sung actively used sport and physical activities as political tools. Like Mao Zedong in China, Kim Il-sung believed that physical education could help foster physically and mentally strong communist individuals who could be mobilised in the nation-building project following the destructive Korean War (Hong 2015). Yet, in order to promote an active sporting culture, the communist regime needed to overcome two cultural barriers. First, given that sport had been regarded as a set of leisure activities for the bourgeoisie during the Japanese colonial period, it was a relatively new activity for the majority of people (Lee and Kim 1995). Second, due to the remnants of Confucianism, which had operated as a dominant ideology for more than 500 years, sport was perceived as an even more unfamiliar practice for women (Lee and Kim 1995). In effect, therefore, North Korean sport policy in this formative period mainly focused on the dissemination of socialist physical culture in which every individual took part in sport without discrimination and restriction (Sung 2008).

Reflecting this, at the Party's central committee meeting in 1953, Kim Il-sung initiated a nationwide sport promotion campaign including the provision of various sport facilities (Sung 2008). In order to oversee the sport development programme more systemically, the North Korean government launched the Sport Development Supervisory Committee in 1954. From February 1954 to August 1955, this committee implemented a planned sport promotion programme, major goals of which included the organisation of local sport governing bodies, the provision of sport equipment and facilities, and the measurement of the physical strength of the people (Lee and Kim 2004). This policy also recommended regular provincial sporting competitions and introduced a mass gymnastics culture. However, it should be noted that the policy fundamentally aimed to equip stubborn socialist individuals with strong willpower and revolutionary comradeship rather than improving the welfare of the people (Sung 2008).

From the 1960s, North Korea also began to focus on developing high-performance sport. Kim Il-sung stressed that it was important to display the superiority of the socialist state by fostering highly skilled athletes, and called for the adoption of a more scientific method for training its athletes (Lee and Kim 1995). This was not unrelated to the fact that Kim-Il-sung also introduced the self-reliant *Juche* principle in this period. With the new political doctrine, the North Korean regime required an ideological apparatus which helped to legitimate this indigenised nationalistic communism. Few activities could perform this political function better than international sport. The most distinctive example was the North Korean football team's surprising achievements in the 1966 Football World Cup. In this competition, the North Korean footballers beat the top-notch Italian team and advanced to the quarterfinals. This was a pivotal moment in terms of proclaiming the existence of communist Korea to an international audience and displaying the nation's greatness under Kim's excellent leadership of his people (Lee 2016). In addition, North Korea attempted to participate in the 1964 Olympic Games in Tokyo for the first time in its history (Bridges 2007) and, although the country had to wait eight more years before its athletes would enter an Olympic stadium, the communication and negotiation with the IOC during the 1960s aimed at joining the Olympic Movement clearly indicated the North's awareness of the political value of being a participant in the Games.

The Kim Jong-il regime and sport

Kim Il-sung died in 1994. After a three-year period of silence, Kim Jong-il officially succeeded his father and became a 'Dear Leader' of the state. Throughout his regime, North Korean communism displayed a radically nationalistic and aggressively militaristic character (Kang 2012). This was closely linked to communist Korea's post-Cold War survival strategy in the context of internal economic hardship and external political pressure to reform. Using highly emotive nationalistic policies underpinned by fostering strong military power, Kim Jong-il attempted to break through such economic and political difficulties (Kwon 2003).

North Korean sport directly reflected the communist state's radical nationalism and hostile militarism. Among other events, the redevelopment of taekwondo aptly encapsulates the political situation. Until the early 1990s, the communist government disregarded the nation's cultural and historical traditions from the period before the foundation of the communist state because those were seen as legacies of feudalism and imperialism. Understandably, taekwondo, a martial art which arguably originated in the mediaeval Korean kingdom, received only scarce attention until the 1980s (Lee and Bairner 2009). Yet, with the introduction of radical nationalism, which stresses that the Korean people are the greatest ethnic group in the world, the Kim Jong-il regime began to take its historical artefacts seriously even though the value and meaning of these relics were somewhat distorted in order to propagate the superior quality of the 'Kim-il-sung nation'. Thus, the communist state actively cultivated the taekwondo tradition, highlighting that this is one of the greatest martial arts, which had been developed by one of the smartest peoples in the world (Lee and Bairner 2009). In the 1990s, the Kim Jong-il regime funded a number of research projects which investigated the historical legacy of taekwondo, and the ruling Party also published 15 volumes of a taekwondo encyclopaedia in 1998. In addition, in 1992, the National Taekwondo Hall, which comprises a museum and training facilities, was opened. The series of taekwondo developments that occurred throughout the 1990s in North Korea sufficiently evidences the ideological connection between the implementation of nationalist policy and the cultivation of the martial art. In short, it is a North Korean variant of invented tradition.

Mass gymnastics, which involves a number of complicated synchronised movements, represents an important component of socialist physical culture (Roubal 2003). The North Korean mass gymnastics performance, *Arirang*, functioned to display the idea of 'military first' or North Korean militarism to the world (Lee and Bairner 2009; Merkel 2013). Communist Korea has enacted a series of mass gymnastic displays since its foundation and has activity utilised these as a means of propaganda (Lee and Kim 1995, 2004). The *Arirang* is North Korea's most spectacular mass gymnastics performance and it first took place in 2002 (Merkel 2013). On the field, a large number of participants perform military drills and demonstrations, and in the grandstand, cards and posters exhibit political slogans that boast of North Korea's military power, including its nuclear programme. In celebration of the ten-year anniversary of this mass gymnastics performance, one of the Party's organs claimed that 'it is the great pride of our nation and our people to have an ability to perform a forceful and beautiful display of the *Arirang*, which symbolises the power of militant North Korea' (Rodong Shinmun 2012). In effect, this spectacle is a political instrument for disseminating the 'military-first' ideology.

The Kim Jung-un regime and sport

Kim Jung-un is the third supreme leader of North Korea, officially coming to power in April 2012. Unlike his father and grandfather, he was educated in Switzerland and is therefore familiar with Western popular culture. In particular, Kim Jong-un is known as a passionate follower of the NBA, which is somewhat paradoxical given North Korea's ardent anti-American sentiment. He even invited a former NBA player, Dennis Rodman, and his amateur basketball team to North Korea in 2014 to take part in an unofficial friendly match between US and North Korean players (Shearlaw 2014). It appears that Kim-Jung-un is the most sport-loving North

Korean leader to date. In 2012, he declared that making North Korea a sporting powerhouse is one of his regime's key political objectives and highlighted the necessity of stimulating 'sport fever' in the state (Uriminzokkiri 2014). Unlike his predecessors, Kim-Jung-un has always pointed out in his new-year messages his firm willingness to develop an active sporting culture, including fostering elite athletes. For instance, on New Year's Day 2015, Kim-Jung-un proclaimed that 'sport fever must grip the entire nation, and our athletes must raise our national flag high on the international stage so that we can propel our efforts to construct a sport power-house further' (Joongang Ildo 2015).

In relation to North Korea's new policy, one of the notable political reforms that Kim Jong-un has introduced has been to assign more power to the State Sport Development Supervisory Committee (the SSDSC). In 2012, Kim appointed his uncle and the second most powerful figure in North Korean politics, Jang Song-thaek, to chair the SSDSC. Yet, the supreme leader then brutally purged his uncle in December 2013 and installed the North Korean military second-in-command Choe Ryong-hae in the position of SSDSC chair in the following year. The appointment of such high-ranking officials is evidence that the development of sport has become a major North Korean political project. In fact, the SSDSC is not simply a sport governing body but also the state's propaganda machine for formulating ways by which to exploit sport as an ideological tool. In this regard, an editorial published in Rodong Shinmum, the official organ of the Communist Party, is worthy of note:

> Our effort to make North Korea a sporting powerhouse constitutes one of the sig-
> nificant political struggles in the construction of a strong socialist state . . . Sport is by
> no means someone's hobby or leisure time activity but is a matter of expressing one's
> patriotism. And, more importantly, taking part in sport is an important means of mea-
> suring loyalty toward the Party.
>
> *(2015: 1)*

Therefore, it is evident that sport under Kim Jong-un's leadership has come to be an important element of the North Korean political project to establish a socialist state on the Korean peninsula. Put simply, sport is not simply a physical activity but a political act or perhaps politics itself, in the Korean communist movement's unfolding development.

Cuba

Although we have referred to Cuban communism as an example of state socialism, one can also argue that 'true' socialism exists in Cuba in two linked but distinct forms. On one hand, there are the principles of Marxism–Leninism espoused by political leaders and, according to Cuba's critics, many of them Cuban exiles in the US, imposed on the population from above. On the other hand, there is what Gordy (2015: 9) refers to as a 'living and lived ideology' which also assumes two related but distinct forms. For Gordy (2015: 9) living ideology, in the case of Cuban socialism 'refers to an ideology that lives because people use it and think about its meaning, even when its relationship to conspicuous facts seems tenuous'. In addition, it refers to the actual experience of an ideology as opposed to its existence as an abstract canon of beliefs. According to Gordy (2015: 13), 'To live an ideology is both to negotiate a world where choices are not entirely determined by that ideology, and also to re-conceptualise that ideology as one encounters particular sets of conditions.' This would appear to indicate that the Cuban people have enjoyed more opportunities to reflect on their socialist selves than has tended to be the case in state socialist societies. Amongst the factors that have contributed to this situation are (1) the fact that, unlike the transition which took place in many former communist societies, the Cuban revolution was the result of struggle for national liberation and attachment to the nation has remained strongly held even in difficult economic times, with the United States still cast in the role of 'the historical predator' (Morris 2014: 11) and (2) the fact that although 'Cubans have suffered severe hardship since 1990 . . . in terms of social outcomes, other ex-Comecon countries had it worse' (Morris 2014: 5–6). For example, Cuba has one of the highest life-expectancy rates of the ex-Soviet bloc and amongst the highest in Latin America.

Nevertheless, according to Salazar (2014: 15), 'the Cuban socialist transition has accumulated a series of endogenous weaknesses that may endanger its continuity in the more or less immediate future'. Indeed, he goes on to suggest that 'If the current political/state leadership does not comprehensively address the objective and subjective causes of the increased deterioration of moral and civic values in Cuban society, it will be very difficult to eradicate them' (Salazar 2014: 22). On the other hand, in an analysis of recent developments in Cuba, Harnecker (2013: 120) argues that 'In the current process of redefining the kind of socialism that is desirable for Cuba, there is an alternative to "state socialism" and "market socialism"'. This will involve the opening up of public discourse and an emphasis on the role of direct, participatory democracy. Given that the achievements of Cuba in health and education are well known, one might anticipate that sport is another field where negotiation and the re-conceptualisation of communism will have to take place in the years ahead. Before looking to the future, however, it is necessary to understand the development of sport in Cuba since the revolution (1953–1959).

We have already noted the influence exerted by certain leaders in promoting physical culture in communist or state socialist societies. In addition to the roles played by successive members of the Kim dynasty, we also have the examples of Lenin and Mao Zedong. In the case of Cuba, the influence of Fidel Castro and Ernesto 'Che' Guevara is also considerable and arguably relates more directly to competitive sport than to the kind of activities favoured by Lenin and Mao. Indeed, when Castro refers to physical education, it would appear that he almost always has sport in mind (Bairner 2014).

Before the revolution

Sport had flourished in Cuba long before the revolution. Baseball came to Cuba in the 1830s, before US intervention in the island's political affairs and was 'just as much Cuban as it was American' (Huish 2011: 423). By the 1920s, it was already the national sport, 'situated at the heart of Cuba's 19th century nationalist movement against Spanish imperialism and later its American variant' (Huish 2011: 424). From 1947 onwards, numerous Cuban players joined teams in the US (Pettavino and Brenner 1999). Thus, by the time of the revolution, sport was a highly visible component in the construction of Cuban identity. It was against this backdrop that 'the revolutionary government lost no time in putting sports to use as a political tool, both internally and externally' (Pettavino and Brenner 1999: 524).

Like Mao, Castro spoke on occasions as if he was a private school educator in the muscular Christian tradition which, during the late 1850s in England, became an integral part of the public (i.e. private) education system (Watson *et al.* 2005). Furthermore, Parrish (2014) argues that 'Guevara's sport and leisure experiences, more than simply "forming a bitter sense of humour", significantly contributed towards his development and revolutionary accomplishments'. Not surprisingly, therefore, as Carter (2014) demonstrates, 'sport became a principal mechanism for inculcating the revolutionary ethos and imagined Cuban revolutionary'.

Castro recalls that, as a boy, he 'had had no conflict at Dolores College' (Castro and Betto 2006: 108). However, he decided for himself that he wanted to be transferred to Belén College, a Jesuit school with excellent facilities which was 'attended by the cream of the aristocracy and the Cuban bourgeoisie' (Castro and Betto 2006: 108). According to Castro, 'the Jesuits' spirit of self-sacrifice and austerity, the kind of life they led, their work and effort made a school of that caliber possible' (Castro and Betto 2006: 109). It was, he remembers, 'a wonderful school' with 'several basketball courts, baseball fields, track and field facilities, volleyball courts, and even a swimming pool' (Castro and Betto 2006: 109). Castro had just turned 16 at the time and quickly began to take an active part in school sport, claiming later that he was quite good at basketball, soccer, baseball and track and field – indeed 'nearly everything' (Castro and Betto 2006: 109). Given earlier comments, this emphasis on competitive achievement is itself worth noting.

Like Mao, however, Castro also believed that 'physical exercise and participation in sports can teach us a lot: rigor, endurance, determination, and self-discipline' (Castro and Betto 2006: 118). Interestingly, he makes this observation within the context of a more general appreciation of the Spanish Jesuits and their approach to education – regardless of their political views. Castro claimed that his temperament, which was 'partly inborn, was also forged by the Jesuits' (Castro and Ramonet 2008: 67). The Jesuits, for their part, were equally generous in return, describing Castro in the school yearbook on the occasion of his graduation from Belén as 'an outstanding athlete always courageously and proudly defending the school's colors' (cited in Castro and Betto 2006: 240). Castro himself believed that the Jesuits made kind remarks about him largely because he was good at sports (Coltman 2003).

Despite suffering from asthma, Castro's fellow revolutionary, Ernesto 'Che' Guevera exhibited a similar enthusiasm for a variety of sports – swimming, soccer, rugby, golf and also chess (Parrish 2014). After Guevera was killed in Bolivia in 1967, Castro gave a speech in which he described his fallen comrade as 'the man of ideas and the man of action' (Castro 1968: 22). Indeed, Guevara (1961: 48) himself had written that the guerrilla fighter needs 'a series of physical, mental, and moral qualities', not unlike those that Castro believed he had acquired in the course of a Jesuit education.

In Castro's case, what comes to light are essentially what might generally be regarded as relatively conservative views about the value of sport. Although this is not quite so apparent in Guevara's thinking, some of the sports about which Che was most enthusiastic might seem unusual for a future revolutionary leader. These included golf and rugby. With reference to the former, Parrish (2014: 4) argues that

> the socialisation the golf club provided Guevara was not restricted to a cultural indoctrination of Córdoba's high society. On the contrary, the most meaningful relationships he developed in the golf club were with individuals of modest means whose purpose was specifically related to labor.

The fact remains, however, that his access to these sports had been eased because of his relatively privileged background. Thus, it was almost certainly only his interest in football that allowed him to engage in a sporting context with working-class South Americans on a more equal footing. On his travels around Peru and Colombia, Guevara and his friend Alberto Granado organised football matches, and the sport itself 'provided an opportunity to build rapport and gain the trust of those who looked upon the "peculiar travelling doctors from Argentina" with scepticism' (Parrish 2014: 5).

After the revolution

In light of all of the foregoing, it is little surprise that, in the years immediately following the Cuban revolution, Castro and his comrades were keen to build sports and recreational facilities with what at that time was the relatively novel and undeniably progressive aim of providing access to all. In the words of Pettavino and Brenner (1999: 523), 'Cuba's national sports program, initiated in 1961, was aimed at two mutually reinforcing goals'. Sporting triumphs on the international stage would attest to the success of the revolution. But, in addition, the sports programme would contribute to internal development. As Carter (2014: 7) notes, 'the 1976 Cuban constitution, modelled on the earlier short-lived 1933 revolutionary constitution, clearly enshrined sport into this reshaped Cuban society'. According to Carter (2014: 8), Castro and his colleagues 'saw sport as a vital vehicle for the inculcation of revolutionary and socialist values'. In addition, the symbolism and practice of sport allowed them 'to demonstrate their "natural" Cubanness as means of legitimating their usurpation of the existing order while also indicating the new order of things' (p. 5).

However, in an otherwise comprehensive and contemporary account of Cuban socialism, Gordy (2015) makes only one reference to baseball and none at all to sport in general, perhaps because of an acceptance of the widely held and largely compelling belief that sport, by its very nature, is inimical to radical politics. Yet, other researchers have demonstrated the almost symbiotic relationship between sport and socialism in Cuba. According to Huish (2011: 421), 'One of the most distinctive features of the Cuban sports model is that it is entirely state-driven', the state's controlling arm being the Instituto Nacional de Deportes, Educación Fisica y Recreación (the Institute of Sports, Physical Education and Recreation). In this respect at least, it differs little from the model adopted in the former Soviet Union, the GDR and elsewhere. Nevertheless, as Pye (1986: 119) has argued, 'The Cuban regime rejects the neo-Marxist argument that sport promotes elitism and anti-collectivist ideas'. This is not to deny that Cuban sportsmen and sportswomen have had remarkable success in the post-revolution era, particularly in baseball, boxing, and track and field. However, according to Huish (2011: 426), 'Balancing the nationalisation of professional sport in Cuba as a mechanism of anti-imperialism with the goal of achieving elite success for nationalistic goals challenges the dominant trends of equating high achievements in sport with zealous individualism'. Playing for the nation represents a rather different set of emotions than playing for the state, the system or the ideology. In addition, Cuban sport has paradoxically been more outward facing, and hence more internationalist, than the sport systems of other state socialist countries.

Writing in 2011, Huish (2011: 427) argued that 'The outreach of Cuban sport personnel closely mirrors medical internationalisation programmes that currently place 38,000 Cuban healthcare workers in 76 countries around the world'. At the same time, the Escuela Internacional de Education Fisica y Deporte (the International School for Physical Education and Sport) offers free physical education scholarships to students from around the world. Such interventions alone allow Huish (2011: 431) to assert that the Cuban sport model is a unique example of an approach that 'conceives of sport as part of broader transformative projects aiming to enable economically hobbled countries to overcome underdevelopment through solidarity and co-operation'.

Facing the future

Sport will have an important part to play in the next stage of Cuba's development, as it has done at various earlier stages in the island's history. According to Nauright and Wiggins (2014: 693),

Given the overt focus on the functionalism of sport being taught around the world in sport management programmes, it is crucial that we stand against the tide of the neoliberal juggernaut and bring alternative ways of thinking in and through sport and physical activity to bear on our field.

The Cuban case demonstrates that there are ways in which sport can be harnessed to alternative ways of thinking not only about sport itself but also about the organisation of human societies both domestically and globally. What the future holds for Cuban society in general and Cuban sport in particular is impossible to predict. No matter what takes place, however, the Cuban approach will shine like in a beacon in the history of communism's otherwise vexed relationship with sport.

Conclusion

North Korean sport has always been linked to the political project to build and maintain a strong and sovereign socialist state, from the moment the communist state was found in 1948 to the present. During the formative stage, Kim Il-sung used sport as a means of fostering physically and mentally stubborn communist individuals. With the emergence of the nationalistic *Juche* ideology, he also exploited international sport to display the existence of the Korean communist state to the world. His successor Kim Jung-il had to lead the communist state in unfavourable external political circumstances and consequently the second supreme leader introduced militant nationalism to fight against American hegemony. Sport played an important role in disseminating and reinforcing nationalism and militarism in the Korean communist state. The current supreme leader, Kim Jung-un, is believed to be a keen sports person, and he appears to be a master of the political manipulation of sport with help from the State Sport Development Supervisory Committee. His aspiration to make the communist Korea a sporting powerhouse is bound up with defending North Korea's sovereignty and its own communist ideal. Put simply, in North Korea, sport is a significant political instrument for realising the Kim dynasty's vision of a self-reliant, nationalistic and militaristic communist state. While this variant of communism is rather different from what Karl Marx envisioned, such a hard-line approach may be an inevitable choice for North Korea if it is survive in circumstances in which global capitalism and Western hegemony are forcefully pushing communism to the fringes of world politics. If this trend continues, North Korean sport will flourish but it will do so in very different ways than it flourishes in the capitalist world.

Cuba's achievements in the world of sport should not be underestimated. Elite performance has been accompanied by the promotion of sport for all and a commitment to international cooperation. The immediate future of Cuban socialism, however, is arguably even more uncertain that that of the North Korean variety due to undeniable differences between the two regimes. In both countries, however, the linkage of communism and nationalism has been of major significance, as has the cult of personality surrounding the revolutionary leadership. As in other state socialist societies, sport has been used in North Korea and Cuba as a propaganda tool but it has also been closely associated with attempts to develop a new kind of citizen – the socialist man or woman. A major difficulty, however, lies in the fact that the pursuit of elite achievement, which is undeniably consistent with the former objective, may inevitably be at odds with the latter. To that extent, the fate of sport in communist societies has proved to be a microcosm of the fate of communism itself, at least in the form of state socialism.

References

Armstrong, C. K. (2003) *The North Korean Revolution: 1945–1950*. Ithaca: Cornell University Press.

Bairner, A. (2014) Conservative physical education for radical politics: The example of Fidel Castro. *Movimento. Revista da Escola de Educação Física da UFRGS*, 20, Special Issue: 57–66.

Bridges, B. (2007) Reluctant mediator: Hong Kong, the two Koreas and the Tokyo Olympics. *The International Journal of the History of Sport*, 24(3): 375–391.

Bunck, J. M. (1994) *Fidel Castro and the Quest for a Revolutionary Culture in Cuba*. University Park, PA: The Pennsylvania State University Press.

Carter, T. F. (2014). Game changer: The role of sport in revolution. *International Journal of the History of Sport*, 31(7): 735–746.

Castro, F. (1968). In Tribute to Che. In Che Guevara *Reminiscences of the Cuban Revolutionary War*. London: Allen and Unwin, pp. 15–27.

Castro, F. and Betto, F. (2006) *Fidel Castro and Religion: Fidel Castro in Conversation with Frei Betto on Marxism and Liberation Theology*. Melbourne: Ocean Press.

Castro, F. and Ramonet, I. (2008) *Fidel Castro: My Life*. London: Penguin Books.

Coltman, L. (2003) *The Real Fidel Castro*. New Haven: Yale University Press.

Cumings, B. (2005) *Korea's Place in the Sun: A Modern History* (updated ed.). New York: W. W. Norton & Company.

Dong, J. X. (2003). *Women, Sport and Society in Modern China: Holding Up More Than Half the Sky*. London: Frank Cass.

Gordy, K. (2015). *Living Ideology in Cuba: Socialism in Principle and Practice*. Ann Arbor: University of Michigan Press.

Gordy, K. and Lee, J. S. E. (2009) Rogue specters: Cuba and North Korea at the limits of US hegemony. *Alternatives*, 34: 229–248.

Grant, S. (2014) Bolsheviks, revolution and physical culture. *International Journal of the History of Sport*, 31(7): 724–734.

Grix, J. and Dennis, M. (2012). *Sport under Communism: Behind the East German 'Miracle'*. London: Palgrave Macmillan.

Guevara, C. (1961). *Guerrilla Warfare*. New York: Monthly Review Press.

Feffer, J. (2003). *North Korea South Korea: U.S. Policy at a Time of Crisis*. New York: Seven Stories Press.

Harnecker, C. P. (2013). Cuba's new socialism: Different visions shaping current changes. *Latin American Perspectives*, 40(3): 197–125.

Helgesen, G. (1991). Political revolution in a cultural continuum: Preliminary observations on The North Korean Juche ideology with its intrinsic cult of personality. *Asian Perspective*, 13(1): 187–213.

Hong, E. (2012) Women's football in the two Koreas. *Journal of Sport & Social Issues*, 36(2): 115–134.

Hong, S. B. (2015) *Bukhan Sungun Cheyuk ui Kiwon Yeonkoo: 1945–1970* (the origin of militaristic North Korean sport: 1945–1970). Seoul: Sunin.

Huish, R. (2011) Punching above its weight: Cuba's use of sport for South–South co-operation. *Third World Quarterly*, 32(3): 417–433.

Joongang Ildo (2015) Kim Jung-un 2015 shunnyunsa junmoon (2015 Kim-Jung-un New Year message). 1 January. Accessed 24 February 2016. http://news.joins.com/article/16834384.

Kang, J. W. (2012) North Korea's militant nationalism and people's everyday lives: Past and present. *Journal of Historical Sociology*, 25(1): 1–30.

Kim, G. S. (2006) North Korea's nationalism in the making: Its emphasis on inter-Korean cooperation. *The Journal of Unification Studies*, 45(1): 149–177.

Kim, C. H. (2013) An analysis on the governing ideology of North Korea: 'Kim Il Sung-Kim Jong Ilism'. *Journal of Korean Politics*, 22(3): 187–211.

Kim, G. C. (2014) *The Political Strategies of 'Kim Il-Sung Nationalism': A Critical Analysis*. Seoul: Book Lab.

Kwon, S. Y. (2003) State building in North Korea: from a 'self-reliant' to a 'military-first' state. *Asian Affairs*, 34(3): 286–296.

Mao, Z. (1917) A study in physical education. Hsin ching-nein, April. Accessed 13 December 2010. www.marxists.org/reference/archive/mao/selected-works/volume-6/mswv6_01.htm.

Lee, H. R. and Kim, D. S. (1995) *Bukhan Cheuk Jaryo-jip* (the collection of North Korean documents on sport). Seoul: Saram gwa Saram.

Lee, H. R. and Kim, D. S. (2004) *Bukhan ui Cheuk* (Sport in North Korea). Seoul: KSI.

Lee, J. S. (2016) *A History of Football in North and South Korea C. 1910–2002: Development and Diffusion*. Oxford: Peter Lang.

Lee, J. W. (2009) Red Feminism and propaganda in communist media: Portrayals of female boxers in the North Korean media. *International Review for the Sociology of Sport*, 44(2–3): 193–211.

Lee, J. W. and Bairner, A. (2009) The difficult dialogue: Communism, nationalism and political propaganda in North Korean sport. *Journal of Sport and Social Issues*, 33(4): 390–410.

Lenin, V. I. (1920/1966) *Essential Works of Lenin: 'What is to be Done' and Other Writings*. New York: Bantam Books.

Mceachern, P. (2010) *Inside the Red Box: North Korea's Post-Totalitarian Politics*. New York: Columbia University Press.

Merkel, U. (2012) Sport and physical culture in North Korea: Resisting, recognizing and relishing globalization. *Sociology of Sport Journal*, 29(4): 506–525.

Merkel, U. (2013) 'The grand mass gymnastics and artistic performance Arirang' (2002–2012): North Korea's socialist–realist response to global sports spectacles. *The International Journal of the History of Sport*, 30(11): 1247–1258.

Morris, E. (2014) Unexpected Cuba. *New Left Review*, 88: 5–45.

Nauright, J. and Wiggins, D. K. (2014) Sport and revolutionaries: Reclaiming the historical role of sport in social and political activism. *International Journal of the History of Sport*, 31(7): 693–695.

Nye, J. (2005) *Soft Power: The Means to Success in World Politics*. New York: Perseus Books.

Parrish, C. (2014) Building character and socialising a revolutionary: Sport and leisure in the life of Ernesto 'Che' Guevara. *International journal for the History of Sport*, 31(7): 747–759.

Pettavino, P. and Brenner, P. (1999) More than just a game. *Peace Review: A Journal of Social Justice*, 11(4): 523–530.

Pye, G. (1986) The ideology of Cuban sport. *Journal of Sport History*, 13(2): 119–127.

Riordan, J. (1980) *Sport in Soviet Society*. Cambridge: Cambridge University Press.

Riordan, J. (1991) *Sport, Politics and Communism*. Manchester: Manchester University Press.

Riordan, J. and Jones, R. E. (eds) (1999) *Sport and Physical Education in China*. New York: Taylor and Francis.

Rodong Shinmun. (2012) Sunkun Chosun ui dank-yul-ryuk gwa kook-ryuk ul him-it-gae gwa-shi (Forcefully showing off the militant Korea's power and unity). 23 September. Accessed 24 February 2016. www.uriminzokkiri.com/index.php?ptype=gisa2&no=59179.

Rodong Shinmum. (2015) Cheyuk-kangkuk-kunsul ui kyul-sung-sun ul hyang-ha-yeo deowook himcha-gae naedalrija (Let's run faster towards the finish line of constructing a sport powerhouse). 2 May, p.1.

Roubal, P. (2003) Politics of gymnastics: Mass gymnastic displays under communism in Central and Eastern Europe. *Body and society*, 9(2): 1–26.

Salazar, L. S. (2014) Updating Cuban socialism: A utopian critique. *Latin American Perspectives*, 41(4): 13–27.

Scalapino, R. A, and Lee, C. (1960). The origins of the Korea communist movement. *The Journal of Asian Studies*, 20(1): 9–31.

Shearlaw, M. (2014) Dennis Rodman to go back to North Korea: again. *The Guardian*. 30 September 2014. Assessed on 24 February 2016. www.theguardian.com/world/2014/sep/30/short-history-dennis-rodman-north-korea.

Suh, D. (1967). *The Korean Communist Movement, 1918–1948*. Princeton: Princeton University Press.

Sung, M. J. (2008) *Bukhan ui Cheyuk Siltae (the reality of North Korean sport)*. Seoul: The Ministry of Unification.

Uriminzokkiri (2014) Juche ui cheyuk kangkuk kunsul ul wehayeo (Building a self-reliant sport powerhouse). 29 January. Assessed on 24 February. www.uriminzokkiri.com/index.php?ptype=gisa1&no=81453.

Watson, N. J., Weir, S. and Friend, S. (2005) The development of Muscular Christianity in Victorian Britain and beyond. *Journal of Religion and Society*, 7. Accessed 16 August 2014. http://moses.creighton.edu/jrs/2005/2005-2.pdf.

7

SPORT AND CONSERVATISM

Lincoln Allison

The suffix "ism" has two distinct implications, though they may be combined. The first is doctrinal: "Marxists" are defined by beliefs, propositions derived from the thought of Karl Marx, even though the meaning and relative importance of those propositions is likely to be interpreted diversely and contested. The second implication suggests tendencies of attitude and behaviour rather than belief as such: "racism" means a tendency to react in a discriminatory way towards people perceived as being racially different rather than any conscious beliefs about race. Thus many "racists" could truthfully deny that they believed overtly racist propositions about racial difference or inferiority, but it is not beliefs that make them racist. "Conservatism" in most of its ordinary usages is logically much more like "racism" than it is like "Marxism". It is much easier to describe typically conservative responses and to outline the context in which conservatism has developed than it is to list any defining beliefs of conservatism. (For a fuller account of the nature of conservatism see Allison 2009.)

The origins of conservatism lie in eighteenth-century Europe during a period in which religious disputes ceased to be the prime determinant of the political agenda and the secular doctrines of the "Enlightenment" shaped the intellectual agenda. These doctrines were typically about "natural" rights (later "human" rights) – generally those rights which a person is said to possess simply on account of their existence – and about political equality and universal suffrage. Conservatism can be identified as a variety of combinations of scepticism about and opposition to the claims of the Enlightenment, including a view that they may be ultimately correct, but could only be implemented slowly and carefully. In particular, conservatism in Britain was defined by opposition to the French Revolution of 1789 and to a large-scale extension of the franchise. In retrospect, Edmund Burke's *Reflections on the Revolution in France* is considered to be one of the defining texts of conservatism, though Burke's objections were not so much to the revolution as a change of regime (he had not objected to the American "revolution" and the subsequent establishment of a republic), but to the abstract and supposedly universal principles claimed by the French revolutionaries as the basis of their new republic (Burke 1907). The "Tory" Party, which had evolved from a parliamentary faction supporting the previous, Stuart, regime to one whose uniting principle was opposition to the ruling, "Whig", oligarchy, further evolved into the Conservative Party by the early 1830s. The name "Conservative" was first heard in the debate about reform of the suffrage in 1831 and when the "Great Reform Act" of 1832 was passed the name became generally applied to opponents of the Act by both themselves and their opponents. Sir Robert Peel's speech at Tamworth in 1834 – the "Tamworth Manifesto" – is generally seen as the event which finally and inexorably transformed the Tory Party into the Conservative Party (Hume 1985).

Of course, if one opposes a set of beliefs or propositions it might be from several different points of view; an "ism" so defined might turn out to contain not just very different doctrines, but also opposites. For example, universal suffrage and declarations of natural rights might be opposed because they are in flagration of what is believed to be a natural order headed by a divinely appointed monarch: such was the conservatism of the French anti-revolutionary writer, Joseph De Maistre. But you might also oppose these claims because you thought they were the kind of irrational nonsense which could only be justified by religion rather than by reason. God might have decreed the equality of persons, but if he didn't neither our capacity for logic nor that for observation suggests that people are equal. This is closer to the kind of conservatism which could claim descent from the philosopher David Hume or from the modernist, consequentialist Jeremy Bentham, who described natural rights as "nonsense on stilts" and argued that the existence of any right could only be justified by its consequences for human happiness as assessed in a particular context; he specifically denied, for instance, a right not to be tortured (see Twining and Twining 1973). Thus, when it comes to a fundamental aspect of human belief, the truth of revealed religion, conservatism can be derived from both faith and its opposite.

It follows that any attempt to characterise conservatism must start with a list of the numerous and considerable difficulties facing such an exercise. Much conservatism "durst not speak its name", to borrow Oscar Wilde's elegant phrase; that is, for historical reasons it cannot be self-ascribed. In much of continental Europe after 1918 "conservatives" were authoritarian clerical-monarchists, harking back to pre-war regimes, but closely allied in practice with fascism and similar tendencies and thus disgraced after 1945. As a result, when a "Conservative" group was formed in the European Parliament in 1989 its only members were from the United Kingdom and Denmark. Both of these countries had remained monarchies and neither had experienced a home-grown authoritarian regime. Most republics are in some sense or other post-revolutionary and their constitutions define them as egalitarian and progressive, moulded by Enlightenment values. Thus to be overtly conservative would be to define oneself as being in opposition to the existing state, which would be a paradoxical and problematical way of being a conservative. Political scientists, on the other hand, tend to classify quite large numbers of political parties as "conservative": it can become something of a residual category, those that are left over when socialists, liberals, radicals, etc. have been listed. "Christian Democrat" parties are the most likely to be classified as conservatives against their will, so to speak, though Christian Democrats, at least in principle, base their politics on beliefs quite different from those of conservatives.

Conversely, in the United States, the paradigm and exemplar of a modern republic, about 40 per cent of people now identify themselves as "conservatives" and this term is also generally used to describe a large faction of the Republican Party. Given that the prolegomenon to the Constitution of the United States embraces the main propositions of the Enlightenment, such as natural rights and equality as "self-evident" (even if it was interpreted in practice for two centuries to mean only the equality of white males) this is an odd ascription for a loyal American. Most American conservatives would describe themselves as both "fiscal" and "social" conservatives, though it is possible to be one without the other: Gerry Brown as Governor of California has described himself as a fiscal conservative and social liberal since the 1970s and many have followed him in this self-ascription. "Fiscal" conservatism means prioritising the containment of public expenditure and it can be considered a legitimate aspect of conservatism, albeit one which non-conservatives often have to adopt. But for several reasons "social" conservatism may be a misnomer. Conservatives, it might be argued, above all accept the realities and imperfections of society; they believe that there will always be inequalities – and they believe that there will always be crime, infidelity and a variety of sexual preferences and activities. "Social" conservatism in its American form fails to accept reality and seeks to legislate about things that should not be subjects of legislation. Thus it is often a form of Republican idealism, aspiring to a much-improved form of society imbued with Republican virtues, rather than a true variant of conservatism. As a result we find in contemporary global politics both conservatives who cannot call themselves by that name and idealists who insist that their idealism is conservative.

At least in a trivial sense one can be "conservative" in respect of any established regime. Journalists covering the Soviet Union in its later stages frequently identified as "conservatives" those who opposed the reforming spirit of *glasnost* and *perestroika* introduced after 1985 by the regime of Mikhail Gorbachev. A similar language has been used about the theocratic and revolutionary regime in power in Iran since 1979. This raises the question of whether one can be "conservative" in respect of a regime which is, in another way, fundamentally opposed to conservatism. The answer must be "yes", though only in a trivial and limited sense, just as an individual can be "conservative" in respect of fashion or finance. This might also be extended into a more significant sense when modes and rates of change are discussed. For example, it might be considered properly conservative to argue that a regime such as the Soviet Union was never going to work – that is, work well – in the long term. But it did last seventy years, traditionally the normal length of a human life, and a majority of the population had known no other regime. Under these circumstances a conservative might legitimately argue in favour of a slow and rather evolutionary form of change rather than the "big bang" collapse, which actually occurred. The "big bang" was favoured by many economists, who cited abstract and fundamentalist arguments about how economies should be run and how economic change should occur. This author has heard many people in the former Soviet Union express envy of China's relatively ordered and linear progress towards capitalism.

Just as there may be conservatives, in a sense, within radical regimes, it is also true that non-conservatives often express and embrace conservative sentiments. Indeed, many of the ideas which have come to define conservatism as opposition to the radicalism and progressivism fostered by the Enlightenment have been developed by thinkers who could not themselves be described as conservatives. Edmund Burke is the most important example of this. In his *Reflections* he sought to show how Englishmen had "real rights", slowly acquired under a constitution grounded in the development of their society. Merely declaring that all men had abundant and equal rights, as the French revolutionaries had, was a dangerous fantasy and no substitute for the real rights which were allocated by social hierarchies and historically acquired obligations. When the revolution degenerated into the Reign of Terror, Burke's arguments became impossible to ignore. Yet Burke had favoured the American Revolution on much the same intellectual basis as he detested the French and his views on India and Ireland were liberal and reformist. His anti-revolutionary arguments are as liberal as they are conservative and it is worth remembering that until well into the twentieth century he featured more prominently in books and essays on liberalism than on conservatism.

George Orwell is parallel in many respects to Burke. In the twenty-first century, his works can be found recommended prominently on self-ascribed conservative websites. These include some of his essays, but especially his novels *Nineteen Eighty-Four* and *Animal Farm*; both are assumed to be powerful propaganda against any kind of totalitarianism, especially communism. Yet Orwell always described himself as a "democratic socialist", albeit one who disapproved of communism after his experiences in the Spanish Civil War of 1936–39. As with Burke, Orwell offers us well-expressed conservative ideas without, himself, being a conservative. These include an acceptance of at least some English constitutional traditions and a rejection of everything which fell under the heading of "smelly little orthodoxies", a phrase he coined while praising Charles Dickens (Orwell 1937/1994). It is not just that non-conservatives express conservative sentiments, it is that the most prominent and definitive of conservative ideas have been expressed by non-conservatives. Perhaps we should bear in mind John Stuart Mill's (1866) description of the Conservative Party as "the stupid party", though Mill would have been the first to concede that his description was not intended to imply that the party was always wrong.

An aspect of that stupidity was always an instinctive rejection of new ideas and therefore a reliance on "tradition". The English word tradition, like the word tractor, is derived from the Latin verb *trahere*, which means to drag or to derive. It is, of course, pretty stupid to believe that the way things are done now and/or have been done in the past is either the only or the best way in which they might be done. But it is much less stupid to be sceptical about proposals to replace arrangements which work to at least some people's satisfaction (including, perhaps, one's own) by alternatives derived from reason or theory. In some cases the objection might be that the proposed arrangements were untried; in others cases it might be that such arrangements had been shown to work, but only in different conditions. Burke's arguments against the French revolutionary ideologues were of the former type and can be seen as stressing the virtues of reliance on tradition against the dangers of reliance on theory: we do not have to know why something works to know that it works. Being a traditionalist in this way makes one also a relativist. Liberals, democrats and socialists naturally tend to be fundamentalists in that they believe that liberalism and so forth represent political forms that should be implemented always and everywhere. Conservatism leaves much more room to allow that aristocracy, dictatorship or imperialism may be better forms of government – in particular, that they may evolve more beneficially – in particular circumstances.

But it should be noted that conservative traditionalism is political rather than cultural: it prioritises tradition in legal and constitutional matters, including status systems and property rights. It is not typically conservative to be preoccupied with folk traditions and cultural practices, still less to want to revive semi-defunct linguistic and musical forms. Those are more the preoccupations of populists and nationalists. The important sentiment attributed to Sir Thomas Beecham, that a man (person) should try everything at least once, apart from morris dancing and incest was (if said by him)[1] an opposition to folk-nationalist fashions in music and a preference for a grand, classical, international tradition. But it might also be taken in the twenty-first century to be an opposition to government sponsoring of folk traditions (as practised variously by the Soviet Union under Stalin's influence and by the European Union) on the grounds that only constitutional traditions are worthy of public attention. Naturally, these distinctions between senses of tradition and conservatism have applications in sport: a simple sporting conservative might want to keep things exactly as they are, but there is also a more complex argument that much of the appeal and commercial value of sport is dependent on its maintenance of continuity with its traditions.

A further complication to the understanding of conservatism is that, whereas, as we have seen, some people of conservative disposition can be described as naive or simple conservatives in that they just want to keep everything as it is, virtually every intellectually or politically active conservative in modern conditions must also be a "conservative reformer". That is, they must accept that some changes must be made in order that some other, valued, things remain. Although the phrase "conservative reformism" is of mid-nineteenth-century continental origin, the founding father of conservative reformism in the Anglophone world was undoubtedly Benjamin Disraeli, who perceived that to preserve what he, as a Jewish semi-outsider, valued about English life it was necessary to make important changes primarily to improve the condition of the lower classes by extending the franchise and improving working conditions (Blake 1966). As a result, his Conservative Party became more of an agent for change than its Liberal rival in certain respects. Most sportsmen will be familiar with the essential logic of conservative reformism even if they have little interest in politics in its everyday sense. This is because in much sport what is valued is what Pierre De Coubertin called "the spirit of sport" (1901/2000), the honesty, comradeship and gentlemanly conduct without which he believed sport would be pointless. But what he called the "tendency of sport" – the desire to do things better than other people and to win – compromises sporting practice, which tends to become "sharp" practice: sports and games become more aggressive, more defensive, more deceitful and more influenced by extraneous factors such as coaching and doping. Typically, rules must be changed to penalise such practices and to restore the underlying spirit.

Finally, anything construed as conservative belief must be compromised with the needs of two institutions which are usually important to conservatives, the nation and the party. The continued existence of nations and national identities are part of the reality which conservatives seek to embrace and preserve. But they may contradict other aspects of conservatism. For example, a belief in free trade and the free movement of labour may come into conflict with aspirations to preserve national identity and to enhance national strength. A Conservative Party leadership is also bound to regard the winning of elections as a necessary condition of any kind of success. Thus there is a natural conflict between "purists", who want the party to stick to its principles and "pragmatists", who emphasise that principles are of no value in practice if you are never going to have an opportunity to implement them. Thus, whatever members might believe privately the acceptance of a National Health Service has been part of Conservative policy in Britain for generations. Of course, this natural conflict is at the heart of most political parties and it was minimal in the British Conservative Party in the period when they were in competition with a Labour Party nominally committed to socialism. The dilemma has been more of a problem for the "conservatives" in the Republican Party in the United States.

All of these considerations reinforce the view that conservatism is best identified as a tendency rather than as a body of doctrine and that attempts to outline a conservative creed are doomed to failure. It cannot be said (though it has been claimed) that conservatives believe in an "organic society", nor that they (particularly) believe in "free" markets: these sorts of claims are vague and unhelpful rather than clearly false. But there are doctrinal consequences of the historical nature of conservatism, even if these tend to be also vague and negative. Karl Mannheim was right to suggest that conservatives reject "natural law thinking" (1925/1986). They do not believe in arrangements which can be applied universally or can only be justified by reference to abstract reason or universal rights. They cannot believe there will be societies in the foreseeable future which are markedly different from those we already know or clearly better than the best we have already had. They must have more faith in well-established procedures than in anything newly invented or untried. Philosophically, as I have argued elsewhere, they must be "conceptual sceptics", giving the ideas of equality or human rights (in particular) little value in determining policy. They cannot, at least in an important sense, be humanists if by that term is meant a kind of post-religious religiosity which emphasises mankind's unlimited potential or intrinsic worth. The sceptical conservative is always going to doubt that a declaration of human rights or a project for socialism is really going to be of benefit, given the realities of local circumstances (Allison 1984).

Conservatism and the amateur hegemony

Modern sport and organised games were largely the creation of English public schoolboys in the period 1815–63. In general the creation was the re-invention and amalgamation of ancient practices, which had been rowdy and lacking in formal discipline as modernised, codified and respectable games. They were constrained not only by written rules, but by an unwritten *grundnorm* of "gentlemanly conduct". The ancient folk games which were replaced had been mostly in decline, often a terminal or near-terminal decline. In an urbanising and industrialising society, there was a shortage of space, but also of time for such pastimes. The traditional forty-four "high days and holy days" were reduced to the mere four "bank" holidays eventually recognised by legislation in 1868. Above all, traditional games were an embarrassment to the middle classes, who from the 1830s held power in many aspects of English life and who tended to see many folk traditions, including games, as enemies of progress and respectability. Nowhere was this as fully evident as in Derby, where the traditional football rivalry between the parishes of All Saints and St Peter's has given its name to close local rivalries throughout much of the world. The game had grown in scale with the city and by the 1840s was considered a serious threat to public order. The prophets of order and respectability were eventually able to rid themselves of the turbulence (Delves 1981).

The significance of the elite "public" schools is that they did possess the resources to develop games. These included large spaces, such as the "Close" at Rugby, long, "free" afternoons and a relatively broad geographical knowledge by the boys of different games. Above all, they had official tolerance for their activities: it was at first, as in the case of Dr Thomas Arnold, headmaster of Rugby from 1828 to 1842, no more than tolerance. For a later generation of headmasters, the cult of games became a kind of ethical enthusiasm (Mangan 1981).

When a sub-committee of boys met at Rugby in 1845 to produce a printed rule book for a code of football they were an important part of a complex process of development, argument and schism which led to the foundation of the Football Association in 1863. The FA became the model and exemplar for sporting organisation: a national association loosely ruling an ill-defined structure of clubs, competitions and local associations. To fail to adopt this model was to fall behind. The period 1863–95 was one in which an enormous range of sporting practices, ranging from the role of the goalkeeper in Association Football to the list of events recognised in track and field athletics, were in effect set in stone, including most of the competitions and institutions which have lasted into the twenty-first century. But as well as being the golden age of codification, this can also be described as the period in which the amateur hegemony was established as in almost every case procedures were put in place which instituted the primacy or superiority of amateurism in sport (Allison and McLean 2012).

Amateurism is a complex concept with a range of meanings. Even in the apparently simple sense in which it is commonly used, meaning, roughly, "unpaid", it is highly ambiguous. W. G. Grace, for example, as the greatest star of Victorian cricket, made far more money from his game than most of his contemporaries, who were professional footballers, made from theirs and made gains in a wide variety of ways, all of which were prohibited by the much stricter code of amateurism that prevailed in Rugby Union. The term "hegemony" in reference to an amateur hegemony is used in the sense given currency by Antonio Gramsci (1971), meaning a kind of moral and intellectual authority which is internalised by its objects (as opposed to a coercive form of power which succeeds over overt opposition). The "amateur hegemony" allowed a variety of responses to professional sportsmen. In rugby, rowing and athletics, for instance, they were marginalised by schism. In the already established sports of horse racing, boxing and cricket, professionals were distinguished from amateurs but not barred from competition with them. The most rapidly growing sport, Association Football, followed this pattern, but severely limited the earnings of footballers according to a "maximum wage" regulation. I have argued that the amateur hegemony showed a partial tolerance towards the idea of professional sportsmen; what it could not tolerate was a fully *commercial* model of sport in which (for example) clubs would relocate to the most profitable venues (Allison 2001). The abiding and underlying principle was that sport was the province of gentlemen, not tradesmen, even if those who were gentlemen on Saturdays were actually tradesmen on Mondays.

The precepts and procedures of amateurism originated in London and the surrounding "Home" counties in England. They fitted most naturally into the social structures which existed there and generated greater tensions even when transmitted to other regions of England, let alone to the United States or the Soviet Union. Yet they did achieve a kind of global suzerainity and if there was a single individual who transmitted them to the world, it was Baron Pierre De Coubertin through the modern Olympic Movement. Thus the largest sporting organisation in the United States, the National Colleges Athletic Administration, has resolutely clung to its claim to embody amateur values and after 1945 the Soviet Union abandoned its previous contempt for "bourgeois" amateurism in order to flex its muscles in the Olympic Games. Soviet and other communist athletes also competed in prestigious English amateur events such as the All-England Lawn Tennis Championships at Wimbledon (amateur until 1968) and the Henley Royal Regatta. As a visual image of the amateur hegemony this author treasures a vivid memory of Henley in the 1960s: an East German eight had won the "Grand" and they stood, in identical suits, rigidly to attention saluting the Union Jack as the band played "God Save the Queen".

The most significant single date marking the retreat of the amateur hegemony was 1961 when the maximum wage in English Association Football was abolished. The immediate stimulus for this reform was the emergence of a global labour market in footballers, with English and other British players moving abroad. (Given the nature of the amateur hegemony they were initially reviled by the British press for their "greed".) But the more powerful underlying force for change was the development of television: as the technology improved, stage by stage, to make the watching of a game on the screen comparable to being a live spectator – and even superior in some ways – a market was created for watching many sports that was on a different scale from anything which had existed previously. Bob Lord, chairman of the Football League Management Committee, saw the potential for some clubs to use television to move into a different financial dimension.[2] Lord was also chairman of Burnley Football Club, a small club which had thrived in the conditions of the amateur hegemony. He saw television as football's greatest enemy and correctly predicted a world in which Manchester United would develop a global fan base if the commercial power of television were not restricted (Lord 1963).

We cannot talk of a "collapse" of the amateur hegemony; events moved slowly and it was a retreat, never a surrender. But events did move in the same direction on all fronts: the major tennis tournaments became "open" in 1968, track and field athletes began to receive money prizes and appearance fees overtly in the 1970s and the presidential regime of Juan Samaranch at the IOC from 1980 introduced a more devolved and relaxed approach to the idea of the Olympics being an event for amateurs. Finally, in August 1995 the International Rugby Board voted to allow professionalism in Rugby Union, a sport which had effectively defined itself as amateur. But although in one respect most of sport had changed its nature, there had been no revolution: in most cases the institutions and competitions remained those which had been established between 1861 and 1895 and governing bodies remained determined to aspire to "love of the game" and "gentlemanly conduct".

Thus a kind of conservatism is an important aspect of contemporary sport. It involves an appreciation of the value of what was created by the amateur hegemony and a mission to preserve and perpetuate that achievement where possible. Such conservatism is not specific to conservatives: many socialists and liberals – in fact, almost anybody except a free-market libertarian ideologue – are likely to bemoan and regret aspects of the commercialisation of sport. Some widely held values are incorporated into the amateur conception of sport. And there is also a kind of basic conservatism which attaches to systems which persist. This is unlikely to be perceived in terms of my broad periodisation of 1863–95 and 1895–1961. Most sports fans would see this in terms of the history of their favoured sport; for example, in Lawn Tennis that would be 1869–1968, in Rugby Union 1871–1995 or in track and field athletics 1882 to approximately 1976. Most fans of football clubs apart from the very wealthiest are likely to look back on the period 1863–1961 as one in which there was much greater security and stability and less fear of winding-up orders, administrations and extinctions.

However, for most non-conservatives there are bound to be ideological reservations about the creations of the amateur hegemony. For egalitarians and socialists, however they might embrace some of the principles involved, the amateur hegemony itself is bound to be seen as essentially elitist. Most liberals are going to have reservations about something which systematically cuts off commercial possibilities and earning opportunities. The fullest embrace of the amateur hegemony was always going to be – and must remain – from conservatives who lack these reservations. There was a system which ring-fenced most sport from both the state and the market, which allowed people to get on with their sporting lives and to enjoy the physical and spiritual satisfactions of the sporting life. Conservatives find it easier to accept what De Montesquieu called "mixed government" (De Montesquieu and De Secondat 1752/1913). He argued that the best form of government was not one which embodied a coherent set of principles derived, for example from the idea of the divine right of kings or from popular sovereignty, but one which combined contradictory principles, as the British Constitution combined monarchy with liberty and elements of popular representation. David Hume (1778/1983) and Voltaire (1952) both made similar remarks about the advantages of the British Constitution in the eighteenth century. Commitment to the elusive and even contradictory values of the "British Constitution" has been an important element in the continuity of British conservatism and it has an important analogue in the protection of sporting institutions from any unmixed government or smelly little orthodoxies, whether they come from commercialism, egalitarianism or even amateurism.

The ideology of performance

The market forces generated by television were, arguably, inexorable in the long term in their effect on the governance of sport. But the structures of British sport came under an earlier pressure from failures on the field of play and the public and press reactions to them. Of course, the two things were connected because television (literally) brought home such failures to a much wider public. During the period 1948 to 1954, just as sport was re-establishing itself after the war, English and British teams met with a series of historic humiliations. These included a comprehensive loss to the Australian cricket team in the "Ashes" series of 1948, a defeat by the United States at the football World Cup in 1950 and thrashings (3–6 and 1–7) by the Hungarian football team in 1953 and 1954. At the 1952 Summer Olympic Games in Helsinki, Britain's only gold medal was in an equestrian event. The press, which pre-war had been supportive of sporting authorities and generally apologist about failure, became more critical. The sole university physical education department in the country (at Birmingham) initiated a debate about comparative standards in sport and alternative methods of organisation. This was followed by a government report, *Sport in Society*, in 1960 chaired by the *doyen* of government reports, Sir John (later Lord) Wolfenden. What I have called the "Why are we so crap?" debate was underway and it was to lead ultimately to the existence of ministers for sport, councils for sport and programmes for funding athletes which re-established Britain as a major sporting power, at least in Olympic terms, third in the medals table in 2012.

Much of this process has taken place under Conservative governments, especially during the period when John Major was prime minister between 1990 and 1997. This included the introduction of a National Lottery in 1994, with part of the profit devoted to investment in sport. Originally, this was limited to investment in the physical infrastructure of sport, but after the publication of *Raising the Game* (Department of National Heritage 1995) the following year, lottery funding was also available to develop elite performance. It is fair to call this the Sovietisation of British sport, since before the success of Soviet sport it would not have occurred to a Conservative government to create such a programme, but in fairness it must be pointed out that a substantial minority of countries followed similar patterns. The initial reaction of a Conservative government to the Wolfenden recommendations (CCPR 1960) had been completely different and, arguably, more conservative. Harold MacMillan's cabinet discussed the recommendations in December 1962; Quintin Hogg, Lord Hailsham, whose ministerial responsibilities already included being Lord Privy Seal, Minister for Science and a special responsibility for north-east England, volunteered to be Minister for Sport, but made it clear that he had no intention of doing anything (Bloyce and Smith 2010). This minimalist spirit of leaving well alone was not replaced until the Labour victory of October 1964 and the appointment of the former football referee Dennis Howell as a much more pro-active minister for sport.

Hailsham's approach can be said to have been authentically conservative: there was a system of clubs and associations; it was, in itself, a stable system; it provided sport for those who wanted it and could afford it at no cost to the public purse. But the trouble with identifying an authentic conservative sports policy is that Conservative politicians in office are always going to act more as politicians than as conservatives. They are not unusual in this respect: for many years the world has been full of socialist idealists bemoaning the pragmatism and compromise of socialist politicians once in office. Even so, the British Conservative Party has a reputation in comparative politics as having a high level of capacity to compromise its principles in order to gain or retain office, particularly when compared with the Republican Party in the United States, many of whose activists also describe themselves as conservatives. The attitude of the two parties to state involvement in health care would be the prime example of this comparison.

Sport is intensely subject to what Hoberman (1984) calls "the performance principle", which we can recast here as *the performance imperative*. Success and failure are clear-cut, defined by victory and defeat. Ever since Harold Wilson made a connection between England's defeat by West Germany in the 1970 World Cup and the subsequent defeat of the Labour Party at the general election (a connection one imagines would have been inconceivable to his predecessor Harold MacMillan only a few years previously) politicians have been aware of a "feelgood factor" arising out of sporting success (Keating 2010). Although irrational and immeasurable, the theory is that national sporting success tends to act as a kind of rosy glass through which other aspects of national life are seen and that this reflects on the perception of a government's achievement (whether the success is a consequence of government policies or not or seen as such). To some degree the successful holding of major events such as Olympic Games and FIFA World Cups, though obviously less well defined, has been appended to this idea of the feelgood factor.

If one considers the differences between the two major parties that have held office in Britain over the last fifty years in respect of sports policies, one sees an apparent opposition of approach modified by a strong tendency to convergence. As early as 1966, a year after the formation of the first Council for Sport, the Labour government was defining its policy in terms of "Sport for All". This slogan has never been repudiated and was also taken up by the European Union (as it now is). Of course, being against "Sport for All" is a bit like being against children or happiness, so the extent to which it was a slogan with substance, taken to mean the maximisation of freely and equally available facilities, has varied enormously. The Labour government of 1974–79 was in a sense the high period of substance and excited opposition from Conservatives who tended to believe that the sports councils were obsessed with getting Muslim women into swimming pools and insufficiently concerned with serious sporting competition, especially in schools. The eventual Conservative response came under a Prime Minister, John Major, who was the most genuinely committed sportsman – at least in the modern sense in which "sport" is taken to include organised games – of any British Prime Minister. The combination of the lottery funding and the Department of National Heritage's (1995) *Raising the Game* has been considered effective and been praised by many non-Conservatives.

"New" Labour governments after 1997 embraced these policies. Conservatives formally embrace "Sport for All". For several elections, the two parties' manifesto sections on sport have embraced both aspects and have given the same reasons for fostering sport: it benefits health, decreases crime and fosters patriotism and community spirit. There is no mention of the truly amateur, Kantian, idea that one might sail a boat or hit a ball as an *end-in-itself*; governments have extreme difficulty with that sort of concept. Mass participation and elite success are always portrayed as symbiotic despite the obvious geographical evidence that China has elite success without mass participation and that Argentina, in Olympic terms at least, has mass participation without elite success. Or the historical evidence that Rugby Union in England, for example, has prospered at elite level since professionalisation in 1996, but has declined massively in terms of the number of adult males playing the game. The differences between the two parties tend to be nuanced, unstated or differences of emphasis rather than clear substance.

Conclusion: the elusiveness of conservatism

Suppose one asks the questions, "What should a conservative believe about sport?" and "What should a conservative want to do about sport?" In the absence of any kind of electoral or political constraints there are several different positions from which to approach these questions. The "classical" liberals who found their political home in the Conservative Party from the 1920s onwards would naturally suggest a *laissez-faire* policy: sporting facilities should be bought and sold on the open market and professional sport is a form of "entertainment" also best left to market forces. Though occasional Conservative MPs have expressed these sentiments, they have never been a mainstream view and are certainly not the only alternative. A more typical view would be a defence of the amateur hegemony, seen as a kind of ancient constitution embodying well-rooted values. This would share with the *laissez-faire* response a desire to limit the role of the state, but the ring-fencing in this case would be also from market forces. Or the starting point might be the simple scepticism which perceives that principled change is more likely to make things worse that better: "If it ain't broke, don't fix it!" though with the inevitability of long debate and reflection on what constitutes "broke". And there are increased difficulties if it's already been broke and suffered an attempt to fix.

If these approaches are not already diverse enough you then add in the needs of a Conservative *Party* with professional politicians who need to be elected it becomes very difficult to define what is distinctive about Conservative policy. Perhaps, as usual, the differences between conservatism and other beliefs are best expressed in terms of absences and negatives. They consist primarily of having less concern about equality and "human" or "natural" rights thought to be predicated on existence and therefore more priority to those rights occurring because of existing obligations, including especially the rights of private property and private clubs.

Notes

1 As with Albert Camus' thoughts on football and morality it seems impossible to track down Beecham's statement about incest and morris dancing to a definitive version or particular origin. It is reasonably certain that he said it, probably in different versions at different times.
2 Apart from the statement in his memoir the author also heard Bob Lord talking on this and related topics. It would be fair to say that the oral version was more emphatic than the printed.

References

Allison, A. (1984) *Right Principles: A Conservative Philosophy of Politics*. Oxford: Basil Blackwell.

Allison, A. (2001) *Amateurism in Sport: An Analysis and a Defence*. London: Frank Cass.

Allison, L. (2009) "Conservatism". In I. McLean and A. McMillan (eds.) *The Concise Oxford Dictionary of Politics* (3rd ed.). Oxford: Oxford University Press.

Allison, A. and McLean, R. (2012) There's a deathless myth on the close tonight: Re-assessing rugby's place in the history of sport. *The International Journal of the History of Sport*, 29(13): 1866–1884.

Blake, R. (1966) *Disraeli*. London: Faber and Faber.

Bloyce, D. and Smith, A. (2010) *Sport Policy and Development: An Introduction*. London: Routledge.

Burke, E. (1907) *The Works*. Oxford: Oxford University Press.

Central Council for Physical Recreation. (1960) *Sport in the Community: The Report of the Wolfenden Committee on Sport*.

De Coubertin, P. (1901/2000) *Olympism*. Lausanne: International Olympic Committee.

Delves, A. (1981) "Popular recreation and social conflict in Derby, 1800–1850". In E. Yeo and S. Yeo (eds.) *Popular Culture and Class Conflict, 1590–1914*. Harvester: Humanities Press.

De Montesquieu, and De Secondat, C. (1752/1913) *The Spirit of the Laws*. George Bell and Sons.

Department of National Heritage (1995) *Sport: Raising the Game*. Cmdn. 3999, HMSO.

Gramsci, A. (1971) *Prison Notebooks: Selections from the Prison Notebooks*. London: Lawrence and Wishart.

Hoberman, J. (1984) *Sport and Political Ideology*. Texas: University of Texas Press.

Hume, D. (1778/1983) *The History of England, Volume VI*. Liberty Fund Classics.

Hume, D. (1985) *Essays: Moral, Political and Literary*. Liberty Fund Classics.

Keating, F. (2010) The World Cup defeat that cost an election. *The Guardian*. 21 April 2010. Accessed 10 March 2015. www.theguardian.com/football/blog/2010/apr/21/world-cup-1970-harold-wilson.

Lord, B. (1963) *My Fight for Football*. London: Stanley Paul.

Mangan, J. A. (1981) *Athleticism in the Victorian and Edwardian Public School*. London: Frank Cass.

Mannheim, K. (1925/1986) *Conservatism: A Contribution to the Sociology of Knowledge*. London: Routledge.

Mill, J. S. (1866) *Hansard*. Vol. 183, C01.

Orwell, G. (1938) *Homage to Catalonia*. London: Secker and Warburg.

Orwell, G. (1945) *Animal Farm*. London: Harcourt Brace and Co.

Orwell, G. (1949) *Nineteen Eighty-Four*. London: Secker and Warburg.

Orwell, G. (1937/1994) "Charles Dickens". In G. Orwell (ed.) *The Penguin Essays of George Orwell*. London: Penguin, pp. 35–77.

Twining, W. L. and Twining, P. E. (1973) Bentham on torture. *Northern Ireland Legal Quarterly*, 24(3): 305–356.

Voltaire. (1952) *Lettres sur les Anglais*. Cambridge: Cambridge University Press.

8

THE SOCIAL CRITICISM OF SPORT

A "radical" liberal approach

William J. Morgan

In his book, *Liberalism and Social Action* (1991), John Dewey argued that because of significant changes in the economic, social, and political makeup of twentieth-century liberal democratic societies like the United States "liberalism must now become radical." That his call for liberalism to become radical was not a mere rhetorical flourish is apparent when he exclaims a few sentences later, "If radicalism be defined as the perception of the need for radical change, then today any liberalism which is not also radicalism is irrelevant and doomed" (1991: 66). What Dewey specifically had in mind in urging liberalism to go radical will inform an important part of my central argument to come that not only is a liberal theory of sport a genuinely radical theory of sport, but, more strongly, that it is our best hope for ridding elite sport of the present ills that beset it. For now, however, I mention Dewey's exhortation only to point out how jolting and bizarre it must seem to contemporary ears, especially to the current crop of leftist critics of elite sport who claim Marx, or Gramsci, or Raymond Williams, or Stuart Hall, or Foucault, or some combination of them, as their muses, and regard Dewey, if, improbably, they think of him at all, as a useless, uncritical apologist of the status quo. To be sure, the idea that Dewey is anything but a radical social critic or the liberal outlook he espoused anything but a radical doctrine is not a new one, for the leftists of Dewey's time had much the same dim view of the man and the theory as the current generation does. But the entrenched opposition to liberalism and its supposed radical pretensions is especially acute nowadays, not least among leftist theorists of sport.

That is why it was not surprising that one of Dewey's most enthusiastic, if not most well-known, contemporary liberal admirers, the philosopher and social critic Richard Rorty, was summarily dismissed recently by a contemporary leftist theorist of sport as a "conservative left-ist" (Carrington 2007: 61). I have no doubt that Rorty's own twentieth-century liberal heroes, which number William James, Herbert Croly, John Kenneth Galbreath, Arthur Schlesinger, and Sidney Hook, would have been similarly dispatched had this same leftist theorist or any of his peers troubled to peruse their work – presuming, again improbably, they thought their published writings warranted perusing in the first place. That is why I was also not surprised that my own admittedly flawed, overly formalistic, and abstract attempt to make the case for a critical liberal account of sport (1994) was further written off as "essentially idealistic and social democratic" by these same leftists theorists of sport, in other words, as not sufficiently radical because of its reliance on the "liberal tradition" (Carrington and McDonald 2009: 6).[1]

I remain persuaded, nevertheless, that Dewey's plea for liberalism to become radical, and that a liberal approach to sport that takes his call to radicalism to heart is better equipped and positioned than its present main radical alternatives (Marxism, hegemony theory, cultural studies, Foucauldian-based critiques) to effect genuine change in sport. My aim in the present chapter is to argue for just such a radical liberal alternative to the social criticism of sport.[2] My argument will proceed in two stages. In the first, I show that a radically re-tooled liberal theory of sport can defeat the three main objections leftist critics in general and leftist critics of sport in particular press against such a theory (that it is hopelessly implicated in the very neoliberal agenda that plagues modern capitalist societies and athletic practices, that it is reformist rather than radical, and that its efforts to wall off individuals and social practices to protect them from market intrusions exacerbates rather than ameliorates the corrosive effects of such intrusions). In the second, I sketch out a liberal theory of sport that attempts to protect sport from the long arms of the market by erecting boundaries between them that take their cue principally from the deep conventional meanings that inform cultural practices like sport.[3]

Leftist objections to liberal theories of sport

As noted, leftist theorists of sport criticize liberal theories of sport, and, like their leftist counterparts who target different human fare, liberal theories of anything, on three principled grounds. The first of these grounds argues not only that the very idea of a radical liberal theory of sport is absurd on its face value, a contradiction in terms, but that it is itself a major impediment to transforming sport into a force for the good rather than a tool of repression. After all, the neoliberal economic, social, and political theory and agenda that leftists single out as the major culprit for all that is wrong with present society and social practices like sport is called such for a good reason – because liberal ideas of freedom and social welfare reside at the very center of its toxic ideology. That noxious theory and agenda burst on the political scene in a big way in the late 1970s when Deng Xiaoping in China initiated a capitalist makeover of a communist-based economy, when Margaret Thatcher became Prime Minister of Britain in 1979 on a campaign of weakening trade union power, and when Ronald Reagan won the presidency of the US on the promise of revitalizing the economy by deregulating industries. Their ascension to political power was a testament to the growing influence of a neoliberal world view that confidently touted human welfare is best served by freeing individual entrepreneurs to ply their craft as they alone best see fit, backstopped by strong legal protection of private property and a minimalist state that confines its attention and efforts to military defense and creating favorable economic climates for free markets to flourish. Such unleashing of economic forces required weakening not just labor unions but all forms of association (social solidarity) that obstruct capital accumulation, rolling back the welfare state and consumer protections, lowering taxes especially on the "job-creating" entrepreneurial class, a monetary policy fixated on fighting inflation no matter its affects on employment, and, perhaps most importantly given our focus on sport, commodifying anything and everything to include public services and utilities, cultural endeavors, and even war itself (as evidenced in the US invasion of Iraq by the unprecedented reliance on private contractors).

The liberal piece of this neoliberal agenda, leftist critics assert, is as unmistakable as it is vital to its rise and eventual triumph. For the idea that it is individual ambition and enterprise that is the key to a free and prosperous society and that an interventionist state is its archenemy is something that nineteenth-century English and American liberals drummed into the heads of our grandparents every chance they got. These early liberals successfully ingrained in their consciousness that the natural rights of individuals are the bedrock upon which their economic opportunities and political fortunes rest, and that it is the main duty of the state to safeguard these rights come hell or high water. This is the source of the now commonplace idea that we are most free when we are allowed to pursue our own egoistic desires and wishes, to chase our own dreams, unimpeded by others. Hence the divinization of the so called free (unregulated) market as the most hallowed place in which to exercise and realize our individual freedoms and the defamation of the state as the place in which our freedoms are most imperiled, which is why these first wave liberals were given to characterize the state as something we are not so much free *in* as free *from*. According to these early liberals then, the ethic of personal freedom, initiative, and responsibility is the recipe for individual success and social welfare as well as the best deterrent against political tyranny. It is also their recipe for success for the conduct, organization, and financing of cultural practices like sport, which also need to be protected from an over-reaching state.

The left's charge that liberal theorists of this era were guilty of promulgating a conception of individual freedom and rights congenial to the ascent of neoliberal economic and political regimes is true as far as it goes. And John Stuart Mill's claim that

> Men are not, when brought together, converted into a different kind of substance, as hydrogen and oxygen differ from water . . . [but rather] in society have no properties but those which are derived from . . . the laws of individual men
>
> *(Dewey 1991: 47)*

is a particularly egregious example of the lengths to which they defended their unreconstructed account of the sanctity of individual agency. However, the liberal championing of the autonomy of human agents, it should not be left unsaid, was mainly directed at the then-reigning political class of wealthy landowners, and aimed not just to liberate capital from the harsh constraints such landowners placed on moveable wealth, but as well on the no less harsh constraints they imposed on workers that prevented them from moving about and choosing their own line of work. By including workers' rights as part of their liberal agenda, these thinkers gave birth to the important notion of the career open to talent, which in making things like nepotism moral wrongs did much to advance the labor movement. This same liberal notion of a career open to talent played a large role in the development of a professional conception of sport that first gained a foothold in North America in the early twentieth century, and that was the historical successor to the conception of amateur sport championed in England. On this predominantly American version, therefore, sport was cast primarily as a vocation (a career open to talent), rather than a leisurely pastime, which is why its proponents, unlike its amateur rivals, considered sport a serious endeavor that demanded they become the most accomplished competitors they could be, that is, well-trained, well-coached (by the best coaches money could buy), strategically savvy, extremely efficient, and highly specialized performers. Former amateur constraints on such serious regard and pursuit of athletic excellence, which included, of course, their exclusion of working-class athletes, thus became moral wrongs to be corrected rather than moral rights to be safeguarded. And at least in this first, incipient wave of professional sport, this emphasis on the individual liberty of athletes was combined with a healthy skepticism of an unchecked profit motive, since they were of the view, as Rader notes, that there were "higher purposes than merely making or spending money" (2004: 131).

It should also not go unsaid in this regard that these leaders of the "new" liberalism were themselves not economic men, that is, interested in their own material gain, but were mainly political agitators interested in promoting the greatest good of the greatest number. One of their prominent members, Jeremy Bentham, known today mostly for Foucault's famous account of him as the inventor of the panopticon, was a tireless muckraker in law and politics, and his justly famous dictum "every individual is to count as one and only as one" became the rallying cry of emergent democracies of the time and remains to this day a fundamental plank of democratic thought.

All that said, however, the left is surely right in claiming that none of their more progressive ideas would have seen the light of day were it not for the comfort and aid their notions of individual agency and responsibility gave to the new ascendant class of capitalists, to include, of course, capitalist owners of professional sport franchises. The greatest failure of these early liberals then was not seeing that the private control of the economy their ideas of individual freedom emboldened would produce the same liberty destroying effects on the entire population that the private control of the state by wealthy landowners, whose tyrannical effects they were well acquainted with, did.

There are good reasons, nonetheless, for not taking this leftist indictment of liberals' blind spot on economic tyranny, on their complicity in promoting the neoliberal agenda, too far by turning it into a wholesale indictment of liberalism per se. For one, this criticism of early liberal leaders overvaluing economic freedom was forcefully made by their liberal heirs, in particular by Dewey (1991: 44), and by contemporary liberals like Walzer (1983), who trenchantly criticized their failure to understand that "what [political] power takes by force, money merely purchases, and the purchase has the appearance of a voluntary agreement between individuals" (p. 325). For another, Dewey's prescience on how economic liberty can easily turn into nothing more than a freedom to exploit the economically disadvantaged is what prompted the second wave of American liberalism, in particular the twentieth century liberal progressive movement, to use the state not to advance capitalist interests but to protect the rest of the population from being exploited by them. The achievements of liberal progressives in this regard include, among others, factory laws limiting the workday to eight hours, labor laws for the protection of children and women, workmen's compensation, employers' liability laws, and the welfare state, and in sport the elimination of onerous restrictions like the "reserve clause" in professional baseball that bound players to their current teams in perpetuity, effectively turning them into indentured servants – no shabby accomplishments if I must say so myself. There is the further matter that the tension between individual freedoms and collective, social initiatives and actions evident between the earlier and later proponents of liberalism is also apparent, though in reverse historical order, between leftist proponents of individual freedoms that fueled the 1968 Berkeley free speech movement and more traditional leftist proponents of unions and political movements that leaned heavily on social solidarity to push their major initiatives (Harvey 2005: 41). If the latter tension between leftist camps is no reason to ditch the entire left, the similar tension between liberal camps is surely no reason to reject liberalism wholesale. The final good reason why the left should not think that its legitimate criticism of some liberals for not seeing the dangers of economic tyranny constitutes grounds for dismissing liberalism root and branch is that Dewey's call for liberalism to become radical is intended in the first instance to correct that very mistake; that is, rather than keeping the state small to safeguard individual freedoms, to keep it sufficiently strong to prevent the United States and other advanced capitalist societies from becoming established oligarchies.

The second major brief leftist sport theorists and their peers bring against liberal sport theorists and their peers is their unwillingness and/or inability to seek the radical changes in the status quo needed to turn around the alienation and exploitation that presently plague sport and larger society. Liberals, they assert, are content instead to tinker with the status quo, to make adjustments here and there to make things more equitable and just, but their reformist efforts and half-measures fall well short of the revolutionary changes needed to do the job.

The left's indictment of liberalism in this respect for failing to go to the "root" of the problem, the intrinsic bankruptcy of bourgeois social practices and institutions themselves, grows out of its previous criticism of the role liberal ideals played in the ascent of the neoliberal agenda. Neither liberal individualism nor its civic successor that produced the Progressive Movement in the US is spared a leftist tongue-lashing in this regard. Connelly's criticisms of both strains of liberalism are representative of the left's view on this matter. He singles out the former variant for failing to see "the cruelty in its own constructs," which was brought to light only when Foucault came on the scene. Connelly's takedown of civic-minded liberals like Dewey and Rawls focused on what he called their shallow appeal to the ideals of the public political culture of the US, which, once again, concealed the dangers and denials that also reside within them (1991: 81). And Connelly's criticisms are echoed in leftist sport theorist Bairner's considered view that although legislative efforts to eradicate discrimination in and outside of sport (one of the favorite devices of liberals to achieve social justice), have accomplished a great deal, the "logic of capitalism is such . . . that no legislation exists or is likely to come into existence [to] maximize[e] the sporting opportunities of the poor" because the plight of the "economically deprived requires [a] full-scale economic transformation" (2007: 46, 47). Connelly's disdain for liberal remedies is further echoed in leftist sport critic Andrew's bolder claim that "The emancipatory potential of language is rarely, if ever, realized within the vernacular" (2007: 38), the most important and prominent concepts of which, of course, are drawn from the normative vocabulary of liberalism. The problem with this liberal vernacular that shapes and colors our discourse about sport and everything else these days, opines Andrews, is that it "routinely neutralize[s]" whatever gets said to conform to the dominant order's own normalized "view of the world and the idealized subjectivities that inhabit it" (2007: 38).

Once again, however, I am not persuaded that the left's charge of liberalism isn't radical enough to undo the shackles that presently bind and corrupt contemporary sport and society is on the mark. That is because its indictment of liberalism's supposed weak reformism commits the same mistake it often accuses its own critics of making over and over again no matter the issue, namely, not taking history seriously enough. For what counts as genuinely radical change is a historical matter through and through, and in the current historical setting, I want to argue, the social measures Deweyean liberals propose to resolve our current social ills, suitably updated as I suggest in the next section, would, if successfully enacted, have the requisite radical effect. In claiming otherwise, I think the left is guilty, as noted, of applying context-free criteria of radicalism unsuited for our times, and, therefore, unsuited to warrant its summary dismissal of liberalism.

That history must always be reckoned with to gauge whether or not some proposed change qualifies as radical or reformist (the continuation of the status quo by other means) is what Dewey was driving at in the second instance in goading liberalism to become radical. For to call an economic or political remedy radical means that the change it is supposed to bring about is both extensive enough to warrant the label and, as Harvey nicely puts it, "soberly anchored in the realities of its time and place" (2005: 188). To Dewey's way of thinking then, radical emancipatory change is "always relative to forces that at a given time and place are . . . oppressive. . . . [to forces] once taken as a normal part of life but now experienced as bondage" (1991: 54). So attaching the adjective radical to some proposed emancipatory program is always a contextual judgment, which is why, he goes on to say, at one time emancipation signified liberation from chattel slavery; at another, "release of a class from serfdom"; later in the seventeenth and early eighteenth centuries, "liberation from despotic dynastic rule"; and a century later, freeing industrialists from constraining "inherited legal customs" (1991: 54). And in Dewey's own time, radical change meant emancipation from unfettered economic forces and a corresponding equally unfettered conception of individual ambition that leaned heavily on state-based legislative measures to curb market abuses. This is, of course, what accounted for his shift from liberalism's early focus on individual autonomy, which in its own time was also deemed radically subversive, to his championing of civic fraternity to rein in a runaway market.

That Dewey's civic turn and the Progressive Movement it gave rise to in the US in the middle decades of the twentieth century deserves a radical designation is, I think, incontestable, so long, as Dewey forcefully, and I think rightly, argued, the historical context in which it occurred is duly noted. Consider for a moment in this regard one of the leading figures of the Progressive Movement, US President Franklin Roosevelt's, very public and emphatic denunciation of excessive market freedoms as the cause of the country's serious economic and social problems in the 1930s. He made that charge the centerpiece of his 1935 annual address to the Congress in which he urged Americans to "foreswear the conception of the acquisition of wealth which, through, excessive profits, creates undue private power" (quoted in Harvey 2005: 183), and followed it up with "New Deal," state-based initiatives designed to break up private power. I can't imagine a living prime minister, president, or major political figure of similar position in North American or Europe uttering such an unqualified sentence, not, that is, without suffering widespread recrimination from most quarters of his or her constituents save the most alienated and disaffected among them.[4] The reason why is the same reason why we contemporaries have no trouble grasping the radical portent of his remark, since we find ourselves once again in the grip of economic forces and the private power that comes with the concentration of wealth in a few hands, which threaten to privatize sport and most everything else that we care about. There was, of course, nothing natural about this return to the bad old days of the Gilded Age, because it was precisely the triumph of neoliberalism over progressive liberalism that led to this explosion of inequality in both income and wealth and all the bad things that come with it. So it was no accident that the United States and most European countries were at their (economic) egalitarian best in the period from the 1950s to the 1970s, and at their (economic) inegalitarian worst in the Thatcher–Reagan era from the 1980s to the present. Indeed, Piketty says of present-day United States that its level of inequality of income from labor is "probably higher than any other society at any time in the past, anywhere in the world, including societies in which skill disparities were extremely large" (2014: 265). The key point here is that this alarming rise in inequality cannot be chalked up to the laws of capitalism per se, but to political policies that enabled it, and to which Deweyean liberal remedies represent a radical point of departure. The fact that they once worked, that they have a familiar ring to them but none of the romantic charm and novelty of what often passes for radical politics nowadays, is no reason, as I see it, to abjure their radical character.

What is to be said about the leftist sport's own programs of change when judged against this neoliberal background is not as easy to say. To be sure, there is no doubt that the Marxist side of this left's call for an end to private capital and its hold over cultural practices like sport envisages a far more extensive transformation of the status quo than Dewey's liberalism, and to my own modified version discussed in the next section. But I have my doubts about how "soberly anchored it is" in the present realities we face. I am not alone in this respect, since the Cultural Studies left is also unconvinced that we presently live in a revolutionary period, one in which a "radical" transformation of the sort Marx envisaged is in the offing. For instance, Andrews contends that "comprehensive social reformation" is presently unfeasible (2007: 42), and Carrington seconds his assessment, embracing Williams's and Hall's skeptical view that a "self-conscious and revolutionary working-class subject" is nowhere to be found today (2009: 19). Part of the blame here must be laid at Marx's feet, since he had little to say about what a society that completely abolishes private capital would look like and how its economy and politics would work. The abysmal failure of state-based efforts to create such a society are an especially egregious example of what can go wrong when there is no clear way forward to create something entirely new. What it did show is that neither the rich nor self-appointed political bureaucrats can be trusted to keep their grubby hands off of the surplus value generated by the societies they preside over. That leaves me all the more unsure just what specific measures the Marxist left would actually be willing presently to advocate and implement in or outside of sport, and whether they have any ideas about how to cure the present economic malaise that are better than progressive liberal measures such as proposals for a living wage, universal healthcare, equal educational opportunities, an increase in earned income credit payments, campaign finance reform, consumer protections, a robust progressive tax system (which would include Piketty's call for a global tax on capital gains), and, as we shall see, building a firewall between sport and the market to curb unwarranted market intrusions into athletic practice.

The Cultural Studies side of this left and their call for strategic wars of position that pick up on resistance to the dominant moment of sport certainly looks more soberly conversant with and anchored in present realities. My doubts here, however, have to do with the strategic wars of position they wish to wage, specifically, about how these strategic wars and the forms of resistance that they are intended to harness are to be packaged into some tangible program of action. To be sure, it is always important to keep one's critical eye on those occasions in sport in which its dominant moment is challenged, but unless there is some plan of action or policy in which these forms of resistance can be put to effective political use, I am not optimistic that they will lead to any real change. And no less contemptuous regard for liberal remedies of any sort further dampens my optimism that such strategic wars of position will get us anywhere any of us dissatisfied with the status quo want to be.

The third, and for my purposes final, quarrel the left has with liberalism involves its heavy reliance on what Walzer aptly calls the "liberal art of separation" (1983). Separating different social practices and institutions is the liberal response to what its proponents regard as the main scourge of a truly free and well-ordered society, the emergence of private power vested in the hands of the few who are able to control and dominate society as a whole. What form private power takes depends on the historical circumstances. At one point in our history it was wielded by a clerical elite, at another by a political oligarchy, and presently by a moneyed plutocracy. The reason liberals resorted to walling off spheres of life in response to such eruptions of private power has always been the same: to prevent the reigning private power in question from having its way, as is its wont, with everything else human beings do and really care about in these different spheres. This is why they erected barriers between the Church and the state to keep the former from lording its authority over the latter and vice versa; in other words, to allow religiously inclined people to profess their faith without interference from the state and citizens to conduct their political affairs without interference from the Church. They did the same for university academics by insulating them from both religious zealots and political demagogues so that they could pursue their intellectual inquiries wherever they might take them no matter how unconventional or heretical. And this is also what I propose, in the last section of my chapter, we do to shield contemporary sport from the corruption of a runaway market hell bent on imposing its laissez-faire norms on anything and everything it can get its arms around.

To say that the left finds this liberal effort to divvy up society and individuals in this fashion loathsome is something of an understatement. After all, they are firmly wed to an organic view of society, one in which its various parts are able to function at all only as an integrated whole. So the idea that carving up the social world is the "radical" solution to the problems of today's advanced capitalist societies is not something that leftists can take seriously, which is why they dismiss it as an impractical, illusory exercise. That they go further and excoriate it as a fundamentally ideological exercise is also unsurprising, since to their mind pretending there are differences where none exist is not only a grievous mistake but one that conveniently blinds us to the indissoluble connections that do exist, that explain why nowadays neither clerics, nor politicians, nor academics, nor athletic types can practice their respective crafts free from market meddling, from the imperatives of the ubiquitous and ominous "bottom line" that hangs over everything they do.

The left thus speaks with one voice on this matter of liberal partitioning. In the case of the Marxist left, trying to safeguard the integrity of social practices like sport in this distinctly liberal fashion is unthinkable because Marx never waivered in his conviction that society "is always ruled as a whole, now by a single class, ultimately by all of its members working together" (Walzer 1984: 315). Liberal separation is also unthinkable for the Cultural Studies left, since its adherents, too, steadfastly maintain that what goes on in one sphere of life is inescapably connected to what goes on in every other sphere, that "institutions like the family" are one and all "tied to the mode of production itself" (Carrington 2007: 52). The idea that social practices are radically continuous with one another, that it is not possible to say with any confidence where one leaves off and the other begins, comes straight from the pen of Williams and Hall, the two aforementioned main theoretical heroes of Cultural Studies sport theorists. Williams was emphatic in this regard, arguing that social practices cannot be split into "independent sphere[s]" (1977: 145). In his view, social practices are "real practices, elements of a whole, [indissoluble] material social process, not a realm or a world or a superstructure" (1977, 94). Hall was equally emphatic in rejecting such mapping of the social world because it violated what he dubbed his theory of "radical interactionism: in effect, the interaction of all practices in and with one another . . . The distinction between practices is overcome by seeing them as variants of praxis – of a general human activity and energy" (1981: 23). This same wariness of liberal social division lies behind Gruneau's criticism of any effort by either liberal or "left-wing" theorists (he had Brohm directly in mind) to separate "culture" from material life, which has always been the dominant tendency in idealist cultural analysis (1983: 37).

There is thus no mistaking the left's antipathy for the way liberals take their scalpel to the social world in the attempt to stem and nullify the pernicious effects of private power. Nor is there any mistaking that their commitment to the "indissolubility of the social process" means that the only remedy to our present economic malaise that they could countenance as a genuinely radical remedy is not one that merely cordons off the market from sport and larger culture, but one that abolishes the market altogether. As they see it, putting an end to market intrusions that sully sport and everything else they come into contact with is synonymous with putting an end to the market itself, and with it to the direct and indirect causal links that emanate from it.[5]

Dewey and his contemporary fellow liberals like Walzer remained wary of such left-based totalizing calls for wholesale revolutionary change. In fact, to their minds it is these totalizing revolutionary leftists who are guilty of having their heads in the abstract clouds of theory, of pushing illusory agendas of change. They were so persuaded not only because, as previously claimed, no such revolutionary change was currently in the offing, but because contemporary society is the end product of what Walzer called "a long term process of social differentiation," one in which different forms of life were able to achieve relative autonomy from one another. He was referencing here, among other things, the gradual secularization of society, the pace of which accelerated and its effects greatly accentuated in the last decades of the twentieth century, in which social practices like sport came out from under the shadow of religion and, as a consequence, developed a normative conception of themselves as separate spheres of action with their own particular aims, ideals, and values. The secularization of sport, like the secularization of other cultural fare, "does not mean that an originally religious phenomenon becomes worldly but rather that an athletic game, originally laden with religious significance, concentrated itself upon its own . . . elements" (Kamphausen as cited in Guttmann 1978, 23). What concerned Dewey and Walzer was that this gradual process of social differentiation was now under threat of being co-opted by the long and covetous arms of the market, and they were persuaded that the way to eliminate this threat was to put the market in its proper place, that is, to confine its egoistic rational calculus exclusively to the economic realm.

To Walzer's way of thinking then, slotting social practices according to their internal social logic and the social meanings of the goods they traffic in is "a morally and politically necessary adaptation to the complexities of modern life," rather than an ideologically evasive effort to disguise if not deny the complex realities of modern life (1984: 319). As such, it offers, he thinks and I concur, the best critical hope to stopping the market in its tracks, to prevent it from tyrannically trespassing the boundaries of social practices like sport and from installing its own normative brand of rational egoism in place of social norms of athletic excellence and the like.[6] Further, Walzer thought that applying the liberal art of separation in this socially targeted way, focusing on the social institutions themselves rather than the particular individuals that populate them, would steer liberalism in a democratic socialist direction. But the socialism he envisioned, he hastened to point out, is "a democratic socialism of a liberal sort," because "it doesn't require the abolition of the market . . . but rather the confinement of the market to its proper space" (1984: 323). This accent on social separation strikes just the right chord because earlier liberals armed with their theory of individualism and natural rights too often viewed boundary setting as primarily a matter of protecting individuals from every sort of external interference. That is, they viewed protecting religious freedom as having more to do with ensuring the right of individuals to worship God as they see fit than safeguarding the institution of religion itself from unwanted and unwarranted outside intrusions. Similarly, they viewed protecting academic freedom as mainly ensuring the right of individuals to say or write whatever they please rather than shoring up the institutional parapets of the university to ward off the anti-intellectual forces arrayed against it. The problem with understanding and deploying the liberal art of separation in this narrow way is that it gives us a false picture of both individuals and institutions. It gives us a false picture of individuals because there are no such asocial individuals to be found, that is, individuals who are able somehow to stand completely outside all social institutions and choose only the ones they desire to be involved with. And it gives us a false picture of social institutions by insinuating they are wholly the product of willful agreements among individuals. Of course, it was precisely to correct for this ill-conceived individualist focus, and the sham description of social institutions it encourages, as previously noted, that Dewey had in mind in pushing liberalism to become radical. And that same socially accentuated call to become radical when applied to liberal separation itself gives us yet a third sense in which Dewey's exhortation to go radical should be understood.

If I have understood Dewey's and his fellow liberals' resistance to totalizing revolutionary agendas correctly, then it is not owed to any blindness on his or their parts that social practices like sport are not bound by external systemic imperatives but only by their internal logics of action and goods. Rather, their stout resistance concerns what even Williams conceded in a sober moment, namely, that describ[ing] productive forces as all and any activities in the social process as a whole . . . [invites an] opposite kind of error . . . in which the generalizing and connecting impulse is so strong that we have lost sight of real specificities and distinctions of practice, which are then neglected or reduced to simulations of more general forms.

(1977: 145)

The problem with eliding such "differences, specificities, and distinctions of practice" is not only that it deprives the left of a crucial critical resource to fight off the systemic imperatives emanating from private power wherever and whenever it emerges, but, as I have intimated, paints the left into a corner from which it can alight only by a leap of revolutionary faith – that it is indeed a leap of faith is borne out by the left's own previously cited self-professed doubts about the likelihood of such a total transformation of the status quo.

So it is a serious mistake to reject liberal separation on the grounds that it seeks, *per impossible*, to isolate completely sport and other such practices from one another or from the systematic imperatives of the prevailing private power of the market. On the contrary, the aim of such separation in bringing back these differences, specificities, and distinctions of practice back into the picture is to change the instrumental character of their relationship to one another and especially to the market (as simply other means of profit-taking) by changing the terms of their interaction. That is, by restricting the reach of the market to the economic realm, to the buying and selling of economic goods proper (commodities), the state, as the overseer and arbiter of all other social spheres, is freed up to flex its regulatory muscle to steer commerce to serve democratic rather than plutocratic ends; the Church is freed up to use its public bully pit, as the Pope has recently done, to condemn the excesses of wealth that contravene its vision of the good life, and the radical dissidents harbored by the university are freed up to unleash their critical slings wherever and whenever they detect the market encroaching upon the borders of the Church, or state or, indeed, the university itself. In all of these instances, the point and purpose of liberal separation is to open up a social space in which these differences, specificities, and distinctions of practice are allowed to play the distinctive roles they are designed to play in the different social practices in which they figure, to exercise the particular social logics that drive them and attend to the particular goods that define them, and thereby to respond to current economic systemic imperatives on their own specific terms rather than on the market's exclusive terms. That means that whenever the market seeks to commodify yet another social practice and its trademark goods, it must first rather than after the fact answer to what is the aim of that social practice and the social meanings of its particular goods. And when the answer is to cure the sick, or to ensure the equal dignity of all citizens, or to pursue athletic excellence, the market must be denied a free pass. That may mean in some cases blocking it altogether, in others sidelining it to accommodate the internal goods of these social endeavors, and in yet others to heavily monitor and regulate it once again to protect the internal goods of these at bottom non-economic activities.[7]

A radical liberal theory of sport: concluding postscript

In the little space I have left, I want to sketch what a radical liberal theory of sport would look like and how it would put liberal separation to work to achieve its critical, emancipatory aims. As one can already gather from my affirmation of Dewey's call for liberalism to become radical, the lines on my map of sport are social ones through and through. That means they must be drawn mindful both of the logic of action that informs its internal workings as a form of life and the social meanings we attach to the ideals and goods that guide and enliven its conduct. The overarching aim of my socialization of the liberal art of separation is to achieve something approximating what Marx once described as the signature feature of a truly human society (which for Marx, of course, was a post-capitalist society and for me, following Dewey, a successfully socialized liberal society), namely, a society in which

> love can only be exchanged for love, trust for trust, etc. If you wish to enjoy art you must be an artistically cultivated person; . . . If you wish to influence other people, you must be a person who really has a stimulating . . . effect upon others.
>
> *(Walzer 1983: 18)*

In my earlier book *Leftist Theories of Sport* (1994), I followed Suits in arguing that the social logic of sport can be read off of its distinctive constitutive rules. These all-important rules, Suits explained, require we forsake the easiest, most expedient ways to achieve the goal of athletic games in favor of less efficient, less expedient ways of doing so (it is, for example, useful but prohibited to trip one's opponent in a footrace). The crucial feature of these rules is, therefore, the limitations they place on the means allowed to pursue game goals, which mandate that the *permissible* ways of achieving such goals must always be narrower in scope than the *possible* ways of achieving them. The point of such means-limiting rules, of course, is to create the challenges that make athletic games the captivating affairs they are for the impressive number of people eager to take them up. And I dubbed the logic that lies behind the contrivance of such athletic challenges, the "gratuitous logic" of sport to distinguish it from the quite different instrumental logic that lies behind most of the other human activities people pursue in which they seek to accomplish their goals as efficiently as possible. This gratuitous logic of sport, I earlier claimed and still claim, does not somehow paradoxically enmesh sport in the prevailing social logic of everything else that goes on in society, as some on the left have argued, but, contrarily, is what explains its special allure in a society like ours in which, as just noted, instrumental reason is the rational coin in which most of our other social practices are minted. It is this distinctive social logic of sport that for me explains why, as Whannel nicely puts it, sport "can never be totally subsumed by [attempts to] commod[ify it]" (2009: 84).

However, leaning too heavily on the social logic of sport alone to set the borders of my social map of sport is, as I now realize, too formalistic and abstract to do the normative work that I asked it to do. That is, it is too thin socially and historically speaking to adequately protect sport from being swallowed whole by the market. In order to thicken these social borders, therefore, the incorporation of the social meanings of athletic ideals and goods is needed to ensure the boundaries of this social map are not too porous. That means accounting for the ways in which our identification with athletic practice communities (which includes players and spectators alike as well as those who follow sport in various media and talk and write about it) gives us a sense of who we are, of what beliefs we think are worth holding, and of what reasons we regard as central to understanding what sport is all about and in justifying what conceptions of sport we come to hold. Membership in such groups explains why, to cite a different example, members of a union would never cross a picket line, and if they inexplicably did would no longer be able to respect themselves because they would no longer be able to gain the respect that only the people they most identify with and care about could give them. Similarly, membership in and identification with athletic practice communities explains why, as Carrington notes, the English Premier Football League's attempt to schedule regular-season games played outside of England failed because of the English fans' unwavering attachment to their local football teams (2009: 23). In this case, Carrington avers, the fans' strong identification and emotional attachment to their home teams simply would not yield to the mighty economic logic of the Premier League's effort to globalize football, which is just a hifalutin way of saying they couldn't live with themselves if they stood idly by as the captains of the sport industry tried to milk yet more revenue from football by seeking a yet larger market. This is a perfect illustration of how the market is prevented from having its way not by the gratuitous logic of football itself, or at least not wholly by this strange game logic, but by the social meanings the fans attributed to football and its central goods. And when these social meanings are put to work to wall off baseball and its athletic kin from an avaricious market, the resistance they offer to the powers that be becomes a tangible policy directive.

The same sort of communal attachment to sport is apparent in an example I featured in *Why Sports Morally Matter* (2006), in which the fans strong allegiance to baseball and the social meanings of the game they attributed to it accounted for why they steadfastly refused to regard the impending Major League Baseball strike in 2002 as simply another garden variety labor strike. The fans' obstinate refusal to view the threat of a baseball strike as business as usual led David Grann, a *New York Times* correspondent, to upbraid the baseball public as hopelessly naïve if not delusional. As he acidly put it, as

> the latest strike loomed, it has become harder and harder to deny the true nature of baseball – that it is, at its core, a business. . . Still, rather than view the strike as the ordinary jostling of competing self-interests, it has been [publicly] spoken of as a moral catastrophe and a violation of some sacred trust.
>
> *(Morgan 2006: 56)*

But what Grann takes to be the baseball public's infuriating lack of critical judgment, its inability to see the economic drama unfolding before its very eyes, is better understood and interpreted, I argued, as a perfectly understandable and appropriately critical moral expression of its outrage over how baseball was being treated as if it were just another business. If there is a problem here, it does not lie, as I see it, with the fans' supposed colossal naiveté, but with the illegitimate inference Grann draws from the fact that because professional baseball is plagued by the same labor disputes that plague other business enterprises, it is, therefore, "at its core," a business. The blind spot is thus Grann's not the fans'; for while they were all too aware that a baseball strike is an economic matter not an athletic one, in refusing to speak of it solely in such terms they were voicing their contrary view that baseball deserves better, that it ought to stand for something beyond competing economic self-interests, something akin to what we expect of other perfectionist social practices like art, in which athletic excellence and virtues such as courage, perseverance, and dedication are what matter above all else. Far then from being the naïve know-nothings that Grann makes them out to be, I interpret the baseball public's pointed moral take on the impending strike, that it ranks as a "moral catastrophe," as the just right response to what they rightly sized up to be Major League Baseball's misplaced priorities, to its putting its narrow economic interests ahead of those that the fans had invested in the game.

The takeaway from examples like these is that the social meanings we attribute to athletic aims, ideals, and values by way of our socialization into and identification with them forms an important and indispensable part of what, at bottom, they normatively stand for, and, therefore, should figure centrally in our efforts to protect them from market incursions. By enlisting them in the "radical" liberal partitioning of sport and other cultural practices from the market they cease to be merely episodic interruptions in the market's unremitting co-optation of non-market endeavors, but part of a larger strategy and policy of reining in runaway markets.

What is surely the most comprehensive and fully worked out liberal theory of sport that also takes its point of departure from the social meanings of practices like sport is LaVaque-Manty's *The Playing Fields of Eton: Equality and Excellence in Modern Meritocracy* (2012). His masterfully argued but, alas, largely overlooked book aims to show that the cultural and political salience of sport has to do with the light it sheds on "how actual human beings" at specific times and places "try to understand what it means to be . . . equal [and] excellent" (p. 5). These two central notions of the normative vocabulary of contemporary liberalism are best understood, he argues, not as "abstract conceptions" but as "value systems embedded in historical social practices" like sport. And what is distinctive about sport in this regard is that it problematizes the widely held view that equality and excellence are two different things entirely and often at loggerheads with one another; after all, "Excellence is comparative and hierarchical; [and] equality is, well, egalitarian" (p. 4). But, in fact, what is apparent in competitive sports if one troubles to give them a critical look is "that something can only count as excellent against some basis of equal comparison" (p. 2). This is no minor insight, the author argues, because it serves as a corrective to traditional Marxist left views that "cultural" politics – concern with issues of equality in cultural fare like sport, is a distraction from genuinely important political concerns with equality regarding the fair distribution of "real goods," things like income and health care (p. 3). Taking note of the fact that equality and excellence in sport are joined at the hip also serves as a corrective to the political right's view that legislation like Title IX that gave women the legal right to press for equal opportunity in sport is bogus because it has nothing to do with equality as such but rather with a supposed oppressed group's envy and discontent at the athletic benefits men have garnered through hard work. The damage of running together envy with equality, it claims, is that it glosses over the "fact" that women are just not as interested in sports as men, and, worse, dumbs down excellence by failing to appreciate salient natural as opposed to social differences – the "fact" that biological males are more capable athletes than biological females (for the right this sexual binary is as well an unassailable natural "fact"). As noted, however, athletic excellence is meaningless if it is based on an unequal comparison, which is why the attempt to level the playing field in sport for women did not, in fact, dumb down athletic excellence but changed its meaning. So segregating already existing (masculine) sports where sexual differences disfavor women not only gives them a fair opportunity to obtain athletic benefits but changes the perfectionist character of these sports – to wit, women's tennis is a game of finesse with long rallies, whereas men's tennis is a matter of scorching serves with short rallies. Calling the former a ridiculous parody of the latter is simply mistaken, not to mention ridiculous. Further, creating equal opportunities for women to engage in sport by designing new sports that privilege the female body, as Jane English has urged (2007), also and more radically changes our notion of the meaning of athletic excellence. The same, of course, holds for so called disability sports. The most far reaching critical achievement of liberal theories like LaVaque-Manty's that take seriously the changing social meanings we attach to equality and excellence in different spheres of life such as sport is that it affords us, in the author's own words, "an entirely different vision . . . [of] the meaning of practices in civil society" that counters the capitalist ideology that market forces have so thoroughly penetrated civil society "that most things people d[o] in it" amount to "an implicit stamp of approval for capitalism" (p. 119).

But why, it might be objected in closing, should we entrust these attributions of social meanings to sport to do a significant part of the normative work necessary to carve out a social space in which sport can flourish without undue interference from market imperatives? After all, how can we be confident that such social meanings will be able to hold their own against the powerful conservative social forces arrayed against them, to keep dominant parties intent on maintaining the status quo from passing off sport as just another market-friendly form of entertainment, and thus breaching any wall we construct to keep them separate. This question, no doubt, deserves a paper in its own right. All I can offer for now, however, are two brief, but, I hope, reasonably persuasive replies.

My first reply is that my confidence in this social, communitarian dimension of sport, and confidence rather than unattainable certainty is the operative word here, does not come from any illusion on my part that dominant social parties had and have no hand in fashioning our social conceptions of sport. For the different conventional meanings we attach to sport are never just bottom-up matters. But the fact that such meanings are decidedly mixed ones, comprising both top-down and bottom-up views of athletic enterprise, should not dampen the critical potential of what they say about sport. For as Marx himself pointed out long ago, every ruling class "is compelled, merely in order to carry through on its [ruling] aim, to represent its interest as the common interest of all the members of society," and, therefore, "to give its ideas the form of universality" (1976: 60). I take Marx's point here to be that because the ruling class can't expect to get its way simply by asserting that its particular view of the social world is, in fact, the way the social world is, not, that is, without significant pushback from the ruled, it must claim to speak for all of society. However, in trying to pass itself off as speaking for all of society, it will, *per necessity*, end up saying things, making claims, and setting standards, that it won't and can't possibly live up to because they contramand its own particular interests. And what holds for society in general holds for sport in particular. That means that because the ruling class will feel equally compelled to disguise its economic designs on sport by speaking about it in this same universalist way, by claiming, among other things, that sport is not just another business but something *sui generis*, it gives social critics of sport all the ammunition they need to take it to task for its failure to match its lofty words with the requisite lofty standards and actions required to make good on its claims. This gives critics a crucial foothold within the dominant culture to unleash their critical attacks using its very words against them.

My second reply as to why we can be reasonably confident in the conventional views peddled by the athletic community despite the dominant parties in their midst is a corollary of the first. For it follows from the fact that because the dominant party fraction of this athletic "we" is compelled to talk about sport, however disingenuously, in ways that often chime with the way the dominated talk about it – in extra-economic terms, then we can be reasonably confident that the bottom-up fraction of that community will get to have its voice heard loud and clear. That is because the dominant parties will not only have to claim things they can't deliver on, but will have to take seriously the ideas of those whom they wish to dominate if they are to have any credibility at all with the latter. As Walzer nicely puts it, the ruling class will "have to make the case for the ideas they are defending among men and women who already have ideas of their own" (1983: 41). It can't, therefore, avoid internalizing the contradictions and tensions of the alternative views it is compelled to take on board. This was clearly the case in the two examples I cited earlier, in which the athletic community stoutly resisted efforts by the powers that be to commodify their respective sports. Alongside, then, the critical foothold within the dominant culture social critics gain by virtue of the ruling class's own disingenuous universalist posture, we can add the critical foothold within the dominated culture social critics gain by virtue of the dominated culture's own resolute ideas about the point and purpose of athletic endeavor. This should give us confidence enough, I should think, to rely on the athletic community's pronouncements on what sport is all about and what social meanings should define its central goods to help us get the lines right in our social mapping of sport.

Notes

1 I am grateful, however, that Carrington and McDonald saw fit to mention my work at all, since it was mostly ignored by the rest of their peers, and that despite their judgment that it was "politically problematic" because of its liberal slant nevertheless declared it "an essential read for any critical theorist of sport" (2009: 6).

2 Although the tone of my chapter in this regard is critical throughout, my effort to find a place for a liberal theory of sport in what presently passes for a leftist theory of sport should make clear both my admiration for the theoretical work currently done under this banner and my sympathy in general with leftist accounts of sport and society. It is in this sense that I view my present attempt to get liberalism recognized as a genuine left-oriented theory as doing for it what Carrington tried to do to by trying to persuade self-identified Marxist theorists of sport and their Cultural Studies counterparts to "engage in less dogmatic rejections of each other's work as either being not properly 'critical' or as in some sense . . . anachronistic" (2009: 16).

3 By arguing for a thoroughly contextualized liberal theory of sport, one mindful of historical and social conceptions of sport, I attempt to correct my earlier attempt to provide sport normative protection purely in terms of its formal features, in particular, its distinctive constitutive rules and logic of action.

4 As I write this chapter, the so far surprising strength of Bernie Sanders' campaign for the US presidency is a notable exception. But I have serious doubts, alas, that his strong criticism of the capitalist class makes him electable. I hope I'm wrong about this.

5 Of course, that once again raises the leftist conundrum already noted of how to reconcile its radical aim with its self-professed pessimism that such a revolutionary change is not presently, nor in the foreseeable future, in the offing.

6 It bears mentioning that Walzer's socialist version of liberal separation is virtually indistinguishable in this respect from Habermas's own version of socialism. As Habermas avers,

> What constitutes the idea of socialism, for me, is . . . overcoming the onesidedness of the capitalist process of rationalization . . . Onesidedness . . . in the sense of the rise to dominance of cognitive-instrumental aspects . . . *With the overcoming of that system, these aspects would be shifted to their proper place . . . one [could then] live with an economic system which operates exactly like a partial system which is separated out of the political context.*
>
> *(1986: 91, my emphasis)*

That Walzer and Habermas not only see contemporary society in the same complex and socially differentiated way, but offer the same remedy to put it right should, I presume, given Habermas's impeccable leftist credentials among most members of this circle, make it easier for self-identified leftist sport theorists of both the Marxist and Cultural Studies varieties to stomach the idea that Walzerian liberalism is indeed a radical social theory.

7 Whether to block, sideline, or regulate the commodification of these practices and goods is a case-by-case matter. But that blocking their commercialization is not the only option is because the market is not always a bad thing and sometimes even a good thing. For example, allowing athletes to earn a living from the sports they play is a good thing in the sense in which it allows them to pursue their passion full time, to make it their vocation rather than, depending on their private wealth, a part-time avocation. The same can't be said, of course, when financial considerations crowd out the goods internal to sport and, as a consequence, no longer figure in how it is treated or organized.

References

Andrews, D. (2007) Response to Bairner's "back to basics": Class, social theory, and sport. *Sociology of Sport Journal*, 24: 37–45.

Bairner, A. (2007) Back to basics: Class, social theory, and sport. *Sociology of Sport Journal*, 24: 20–36.

Bairner, A. (2007) Rebuttal. *Sociology of Sport Journal*, 24: 46–48.

Carrington, B. (2007) Merely identity: Cultural identity and the politics of sport. *Sociology of Sport Journal*, 24: 49–96.

Carrington, B. (2009) Sport without final guarantees. In B. Carrington and I. MacDonald (eds.) *Marxism, Cultural Studies and Sport*. New York: Routledge, pp. 15–27.

Carrington, B, and McDonald, I. (2009) Marxism, cultural studies and sport: Mapping the field. In B. Carrington and I. MacDonald (eds.) *Marxism, Cultural Studies and Sport*. New York: Routledge, pp. 1–12.

Connelly, W. E. (1991) *Identitity/Difference: Democratic Negotiations of Political Paradox*. Ithaca, NY: Cornell University Press.

Dewey, J. (1991) *Liberalism and Social Action*. New York: Prometheus Books.

English, J. (2007) Sex equality in sport. In W. J. Morgan (ed.) *Ethics in Sport*. Champaign, IL: Human Kinetics. pp. 303–308.

Gruneau, R. (1983) *Class, Sport and Social Development*. Amherst: University of Massachusetts Press.

Guttmann, A. (1978) *From Ritual to Record: The Nature of Modern Sports*. New York: Columbia University Press.

Habermas, J. (1986) The political experience and the renewal of marxist theory. In P. Dews (ed.) *Habermas: Autonomy and Solidarity*. London: Verso, pp. 73–92.

Hall, S. (1981) Cultural studies: Two paradigms. In T. Bennett, G. Martin, C. Mercer and J. Woollacott (eds.) *Culture, Ideology and Social Process*. London: Open University Press, pp. 19–37.

Harvey, D. (2005) *A Brief History of Neoliberalism*. New York: Oxford University Press.

LaVaque-Manty, Mika. (2012) *The Playing Fields of Eton: Equality and Excellence in Modern Meritocracy*. Ann Arbor, MI: University of Michigan Press.

Marx, K. (1976) *Karl Marx, Frederick Engels: Collected Works, Volume 5*. New York: International Press.

Morgan, W. J. (1994) *Leftist Theories of Sport: A Critique and Reconstruction*. Urbana and Chicago: University of Illinois Press.

Morgan, W. J. (2006) *Why Sports Morally Matter*. New York: Routledge.

Piketty, T. (2014) *Capital in the Twenty-First Century*. Cambridge, MA: Harvard University Press.

Rader, B. (2004) *American Sports: From the Age of Folk Games to the Age of Televised Sports*. Upper Saddle River, NJ: Prentice Hall.

Walzer, M. (1983) *Spheres of Justice*. New York: Basic Books.

Walzer, M. (1984) Liberalism and the art of separation. *Political Theory*, 12 (3): 315–330.

Whannel, G. (2009) Between culture and economy: Understanding the politics of media sport. In B. Carrington and I. MacDonald (eds.) *Marxism, Cultural Studies and Sport*. New York: Routledge, pp. 68–84.

Williams, R. (1977) *Marxism and Literature*. New York: Oxford University Press.

9

SPORT AND THE SWEDISH WELFARE STATE

Susanna Hedenborg and Tomas Peterson

Introduction

In Sweden the majority of all children and young people participate in organised sports. Approximately 20,000 sport clubs in the country are affiliated with the Swedish Sport Confederation (SSC). Voluntarism characterises the work done by the approximately 650,000 unpaid coaches and leaders within the SSC. The Swedish government supports the SSC financially with an annual 1.7 billion SKR so as to enable the SSC to organise sporting activities, especially for children and young people. The SSC has a strong position in Swedish society, and is largely autonomous from the state (Norberg 2002; SOU 2008: 59). The Swedish Olympic Committee organises Swedish participation in the Olympic Games. Support for Swedish elite sports is, however, relatively small. With the exception of an allocation of the Olympic Games in Stockholm (1912), a talent development program (1998–2004) and an elite support program (2009) the Swedish government has not given extra support to elite sport. Instead decisions about investments in elite sport have been taken within the SSC.

The purpose of this chapter is to describe and analyse the development of the Swedish sport model in relation to the development of Swedish Social Democracy and the welfare state in order to explain the strong position of the SSC. The sport model will be problematised, as several conflicting ideas have and continue to influence the model, including the notion of "Sport for all", elite sport, voluntarism, amateurism, professionalisation and commercialisation. In addition, societal expectations regarding the competencies that children and young people should learn and develop while participating in organised sports will be elucidated and problematised. Finally, the sport model will be discussed in relation to patterns of gender relations.

The forming of the social democratic party and the welfare state

During the nineteenthth century, agriculture was modernised, proto-industrialisation and industrialisation processes took off, and new groups were claiming power. In 1866 a two-chamber parliament was instated in Sweden and in 1889 the first modern party was founded. This was the Social Democratic Party (SAP), which was formed mainly by the trade union movement. In the early 1900s, it gained a significant influence on Swedish politics. In 1909 a decision on universal suffrage for men was instated. A liberal cabinet initially presented the proposal, yet a right-wing government laid the final proposal. Still, women were excluded from political power and citizenship. The general election in 1921 was the first election conducted in Sweden when suffrage was not linked to gender or social class.

In 1922 Hjalmar Branting formed the first elected social democratic government. The period 1921–1932 was, however, politically turbulent and eight prime ministers and six governments were in power. Each ministry was dependent on being able to mobilise support in the parliament for different issues. Not until 1932 was the political situation stabilised, when Per Albin Hansson, the SAP leader formed a new government based on political coalitions. At that time the SAP made an agreement with the Farmers League (now the Centre Party). The content of the agreement made it possible for the SAP to carry through policies against unemployment in a Keynesian spirit – a policy reminiscent of the American president Roosevelt's "New Deal". In order to support this, the Farmers League received protection of Swedish agricultural products, through tariffs and subsidies. An important measure was the introduction of the construction of a welfare state model called the "People's Home" (Folkhemmet) by SAP leader Hansson.

Post-war Sweden was, for a long time, led by the SAP, either in league with the former Farmers League or with the support of the Swedish Communist Party. A characteristic of the post-war Swedish welfare state was that previously tested social policies became general. Danish sociologist Gösta Esping-Andersen (1990) distinguishes between three types of welfare states that differ in terms of taxes, social security systems and social policies: corporatist-statist, liberal, and social democratic welfare states. According to Esping-Andersen, Sweden was governed by a social democratic welfare state, which is characterised by a public, tax-funded social security system. Insurances within the social security system are income related and taxes and benefits are individual. Social policy is redistributive and equalising. Income inequality is moderate, especially after taxes and contributions. Women have a high level of labour force participation in the social democratic welfare state regime. A social democratic welfare state regime characterises the other Nordic countries as well as Sweden.

An early example of policies in the Swedish social democratic welfare state model was the child allowance instated in 1947, which included all families regardless of their social situation. Furthermore, a general and compulsory health insurance was installed in 1955. The first retirement pension was introduced in 1913, but questions related to the pension system were extensively debated in the post-war period. In a public report from 1955, a compulsory supplementary pension was suggested (the ATP). After a referendum (1957) voting was carried out in government and an abstention by one of the liberals made it possible for the SAP to win and to instate the ATP in 1960. Another key social policy issue was housing policy. In the 1930s and 1950s several efforts and investments were made to solve the housing situation. In the early 1960s the so-called "One million homes" program was implemented. In ten years the program was finished and several new residential areas had been built.

During the latter half of the 1960s the political landscape changed. Radicalisation and the student revolution affected Sweden, as it did many other countries. So did economic stagnation, competition from the newly industrialised countries and the oil crises. The SAP lost the elections in 1976 for the first time since 1932. For just over a 40-year period (1932–1976), Sweden had been ruled by the SAP. During the period 1976 to 2015 governments varied and right-wing parties were in power from 1976 to 1982, 1991 to 1994 and from 2006 to 2014. Important political issues during this period were economic growth, environmental challenges, the introduction of a private social insurance system and the privatisation of the public sector at large.

The Swedish sport model

In Sweden, the sports movement has been seen as a popular movement similar to the suffrage or temperance movements, and the basic preconditions for it are very similar to those underpinning the social democratic welfare state. However, the history of modern Swedish sport has not been devoid of internal disagreements. Until the late nineteenth century, physical culture was dominated by Ling gymnastics, and the SSC was not established until 1903. At this time, advocates of Ling gymnastics and proponents of modern sports argued about the ideals of physical culture. While the former emphasised gymnastics, correct movements, and cooperation, the latter stressed modern sporting activities and competition. Mainly upper-class men participated in sporting activities during this period (Blom and Lindroth 1995; Lundquist 2004).

The ruling parties' perception of the sports movement has changed over time. In the early twentieth century, the Swedish Social Democrats regarded the emerging modern sport movement as a competitor when it came to recruiting members of the working class, and condemned various competitive aspects within sports. This attitude shifted dramatically in the late 1920s and 1930s when the ideological construction "People's home" was introduced (Andersson 2002; Bairner 2001; Goksoyr 1998; Lindroth 1987; Norberg 2004; Pålbrant 1977).

After World War II, state support to organisations was directed towards youth organisations, particularly sports clubs, whose activities take place on an everyday volunteer basis, offering leisure activities for children and youth in the Scandinavian countries. The government regarded financial support to sport associations as one of the best ways of imparting democratic values to young people, as well as providing a meaningful pastime. Along with physical education and corporate health care, the sports movement (including inter-company athletics) has been considered beneficial to youth socialisation as per the formula "a healthy mind in a healthy body", but also more generally by forging ties between people from different levels of society and strengthening national identity (Lindrot 1987).

In 1969 a public report introducing the idea "sports for all" was presented. The meaning of the concept was that sport activities were to be offered to all citizens and should be organised to make this possible. This idea was in line with the welfare state's structure in the post-war era.

The relationship between the state and sport has since its beginning relied on an "implicit contract": the state supports the autonomy of the sport movement, trusting that the sporting organisations will use this financial support to promote certain societal values. From a social economic point of view, material support of sports and other popular movements provides an inexpensive complement to other types of supervision and care regarding children and young people. When it comes to state support of youth activities in the post-war period, sports has been one of the major beneficiaries. Support to study circles, recreation groups, counsellors/instructors, municipal activity support and support to education of youth leaders have all shaped today's sports movement. In addition to the establishment of certain university curricula such as Physical Education Teachers' Education (PETE) and, more recently, programmes in Sport Sciences and Sport Management, this material support has created a strong infrastructure for organised sport. A possible consequence of this is the disappearance of spontaneous sports. Simultaneously, new forms of sports and physical activity have emerged outside sports organised by the SSC (Bäckström 2007).

Amateurism, professionalisation and commercialisation

As in many other countries, the emergence of the Swedish sport movement was strongly influenced by English amateurism. Amateurs and gentlemen were the ideal sports*men*. At that time,

Sweden was a relatively poor country with a small upper class. Thus, it is not immediately obvious why the British ideals became a model for the Swedish sport movement. However, the development can be explained in terms of a fusion between the ideology formulated by the English upper class and the ideals created as an action ethos for the sport movement in Scandinavia.

Professionalisation of sport, that is, sport as paid labour, was forbidden in all Scandinavian countries as late as the 1960s. Athletes who were found guilty of accepting payment for competing were suspended from organised competitions, sometimes for life. Professionalisation was regarded as inimical to sport up until the very end of the twentieth century, and this attitude still persists to an extent (Peterson 2000). In practice, however, there were several exceptions to the amateur rules.

Strong amateur ideals, coupled with a sport movement built on voluntarism, could potentially explain why the professionalisation of sport occurred relatively late in the Scandinavian countries. Nevertheless, the development is complex. In order to explain the process, the concept of professionalisation must be discussed. In the history of sport, the term "professional" has mainly referred to those who have practiced sport as an occupation, as paid employees, such as professional jockeys or football players. In addition, having a specific license is connected to the professional sport role. Outside of the sporting context, professionalisation has also been connected to other features. Aside from monetary payment and licensing, education is an important characteristic of professions such as medical doctor, nurse, and lawyer. In addition, people within a profession often form interest groups. The concept also includes a strongly specialised organisation where rationality, efficiency and predictability govern both the organisation and the actual activities (Brante 1992; Collins 1979; Juliani 1973; Parkin 1979; Sarfatti-Larsen 1979).

The contemporary Swedish sport movement is mostly not professionalised, as education, interest groups, and the above-mentioned characteristics of a professional organisation are lacking. However, parts of it are undergoing a process of professionalisation. The professionalisation process requires substantial financial resources, which is where commercialism enters the stage. In contrast to most other countries, capitalist market forces have had little influence over Swedish sports. So far, the professionalisation of sport organisations has largely taken place with governmental support. However, some sports, especially men's football, have undergone a gradual transition from a popular movement towards a capitalisation of leisure activities (Peterson 2007). The internal activities of some of the associations (like soccer and ice hockey) have changed, and the elite clubs resemble medium sized companies. In such associations activities became gradually professionalised, hierarchical and specialised in order to meet new needs. Feelings of community, idealism, and solidarity are difficult to emphasise in a market-governed organisation where productivity and liquidity must come first. A medium-sized company cannot be maintained with voluntarism and amateurism. There is a need for rationality, effectiveness and predictability in both organisation and sports activity. Therefore, the professionalisation of sports leadership is closely connected to the commercialisation of sports. Managing sports training on the elite level – whether the aim is to achieve the best possible results from the active members to handle a multimillion money-flow, negotiate contracts consisting of hundreds of pages, or create a suitable media image showcasing the activities of the organisation – demands a different set of competences than those necessary in the former non-profit people's movement (Billing *et al.* 2004).

The degree of commercialisation varies between the Scandinavian countries. Previous research has indicated that the sport movement in Denmark shows the highest degree of professionalisation. The Norwegian sports movement is the least professionalised, and Sweden lands somewhere in between (Hedenborg 2013a). Even child and youth sport has become increasingly commercialised in the last few decades (Norberg and Redelius 2012). The gradual transition from activities based on amateurism and popular movement ideals to market forces and paid labour means that sporting activities practised and organised by volunteers in the form of a popular movement are threatened, and have become capitalised in some sports. Within the higher leagues of men's football, players receive full or partial wages, and paid coaches, office personnel, accountants, and club directors are in charge of the associations' activities. In addition, players are bought and sold on the market. This activity has been facilitated by professional representatives: agents, intermediaries, and legal experts. The development of the sport movement has been criticised and discussed. It is, however, coupled with a dramatic change of the social democratic welfare state towards a more neoliberal state since the 1980s.

Fostering in sports

Popular movements have been regarded as the cornerstones of Scandinavian democracy, as participation in voluntary associations has been seen as an important means to fostering democratic citizens (Peterson 2008). State support for children and youth sport in the Scandinavian countries is a tremendous economic investment as well as a substantial ideological commitment. Through this engagement, children are ideally taught democratic ways of thinking and acting based on respect, cooperation and equality. In addition, a crucial aim has long been to welcome anyone who seeks out the sports association, and allow each individual to develop in accordance with his or her own capabilities (Peterson and Norberg 2008). All this, in line with the ideological construction of "People's home", means that everybody should be welcomed and find their place.

Nonetheless, sports clubs have held conflicting ideals and values in relation to the fostering of children and young people. Shaping new top athletes has always been an essential aim. Aside from enhancing participants' athletic and sporting abilities, this is also accomplished by teaching them to handle competition: winning and losing, following the rules and focusing in order to reach one's goals. Competing and winning are basic principles, and selection, ranking and elitism are developed through competition fostering (Peterson 2008). There is thus a paradox in child and youth sport activities, which are somehow supposed to balance democratic values, especially equality in participation, with elitism in the form of competitiveness (Peterson 2007).

How sports organisations actually handle fostering of children and youth in practice has been studied for some sports. In 1948, the Swedish Football Association was the first to establish a specific youth committee in order to increase the number of boys playing football. Some young men already played football within the associations, and the aim of the initiative was to improve the organisation of the youth footballers. In addition to its sports-related objectives, the committee was expected to work to prevent youth criminality and alcohol abuse (Peterson 1993).

Other federations developed similar committees, and the number of young members increased in several sports. The issue of youth was discussed as early as the 1940s within the equestrian federation. In contrast to football, however, the equestrian federation had no designated committee in charge of this group, and young people were not seen as more important than any other horse-riding group. The year 1948 witnessed the formation of a new equestrian association, specifically aimed at promoting horse riding as a leisure time activity. The work of this association made a difference to young people who wanted to ride, as the organisation granted subsidies for the construction of indoor riding schools, and provided discount tickets to young people. Horse riding and participation in a horse-riding school were then seen as an important form of socialisation. The equestrian association, like many other sports associations, received governmental subsidies for its youth activities, and a large amount of its work was devoted to education (Hedenborg 2009a).

Studies of equestrian sports in Sweden have demonstrated the complexity of the ideals held by sports associations in regards to their activities. It has been demonstrated that education aimed at developing competitiveness is important for understanding the development of youth football. Unlike the Swedish Football Association's courses that soon after their introduction developed a competitive focus, courses arranged by the equestrian association focused on citizenship education and democracy. Another concept must be used in order to characterise the educational strivings of the equestrian association: education for caretaking. The caretaking characteristics emphasised in the equestrian organisation could possibly be connected to the process of feminisation. However, this characterisation is problematic; equestrians can attest to the strenuous and dirty work performed in the stable, the risks associated with interaction with large prey animals, and the many difficulties involved in riding them (Hedenborg 2009a, 2009b). Previous research has indicated that stable work may be seen as a way of training young women to be leaders (Forsberg 2012a, 2012b).

Patterns of gender relations within the Swedish sport model

The *Eurobarometer for Sport and Physical Activity* from 2009 shows that people in Sweden and the Nordic countries are relatively physically active compared to people in other countries in Europe. In Sweden, 22 per cent of the respondents claim that they practise sports (organised, spontaneous or commercialised sports) five times a week or more. In addition, 86 per cent of young people between ages 13 and 20 in Sweden are current or former members of a sports club. In addition, it is relatively common to be engaged in voluntary sport associations. These high numbers can partly be explained by the fact that in Sweden both women and men participate in sport and are members of the SSC. Forty-two per cent (1,179,000) of SSC members aged 6 to 80 are women, and 58 per cent (1,620,000) are men. Participation rates for women are somewhat higher in the younger age groups. Forty-four per cent of the members between 6 and 25 years of age are female.

The relatively high sport participation rates for women in Sweden can likely be connected to the fact that Sweden is one of the most gender-equal countries in the world. In the *Global Gender Gap Report 2012*, Sweden is ranked as number four (2012, Table 3a, 8). Women's high participation numbers in the labour market has been connected to the social democratic welfare state (Sommestad 1995).

Even though both men and women have been physically active in many different ways for a long time, the modern sport movement began as an organisation for men. In that way, its resemblance to the popular movements can be questioned. However, the sport movement has changed over time. In 1953, 15 per cent of the members were women. The greatest increase occurred in the 1970s and 1980s (Olofsson 1989, 2003).

Although an increasing number of women become members of SSC-affiliated sports clubs, there are gender differences in regards to the sports men and women practise and the positions they are engaged in. Men's economic and material conditions are also generally more favourable than women's, and the media treats male and female athletes differently. Men's sports generally receive more coverage, and male sports practitioners are often presented as more serious (Tolvhed 2008, 2012; Hedenborg 2013b; Hellborg and Hedenborg 2014).

Today, women are in majority in 8 of the 71 sport federations connected to the SSC. The greatest majority of women can be found in equestrian sports, gymnastics, and figure skating (Olofsson 2003). There are also differences when it comes to positions of authority within the organisations; women only amount to 23 per cent of the leaders, coaches, officials and referees.

In the early twentieth century, so-called "women's gymnastics" was seen as one of the most appropriate physical activities for women. The same was true of swimming and diving. Up until World War II, discussions of sports activities highlighted the differences, rather than the resemblances, between women and men. As in other countries, medical research was often used to argue that women should not be engaged in certain sports. A national women's football league was not established until the 1970s. Today, the Swedish football associations have a high number of members among both boys and girls.

Many sports are more or less associated with masculinity or femininity. In Sweden, ice hockey is likely one of the sports that are perceived as the most masculine, whereas horse riding is connected to femininity. Some sports have changed gender coding over time. In the early twentieth century, synchronised swimming was seen as masculine, whereas today it is perceived as feminine. A century ago, riding and caring for horses was connected to men and masculinity, while today equestrianism is one of the most popular sports among women and girls (Hedenborg 2009b, 2011).

Conclusion

The purpose of this chapter is to describe and analyse the development of the Swedish sport model in relation to the development of Swedish social democracy and the welfare state in order to explain the strong position of the SSC. Since World War II, the Swedish state has supported the sport movement economically. The sport movement has been given an autonomous position in relation to this support, as its activities have been believed to benefit society as a whole. The support to elite sport is in comparison to many other countries relatively small. Instead the idea "sports for all" has been strong and it has been up to the federations within the SSC to decide to what degree they have been willing to support elite sports. It seems likely that the strong connection between the Swedish welfare state can be explained by the ability of the SSC to harbour ideological constructions shared with the state – universality and being a "People's home".

In this chapter the notion of the Swedish sport model as a unified concept has been problematised. It has been demonstrated that the sport model comprises several contradicting ideas about the purpose of sport and the ways in which it is supposed to educate children and young people. In addition, it has been stressed above that patterns of gender relations in sport must be uncovered if a sport model is to be understood. Over time, the relatively gender-equal Scandinavian societies have made it possible for both men and women to participate in sports activities, although men's and women's conditions still differ in terms of economic resources, power relations and media coverage.

References

Andersson, T. (2002) *Kung Fotboll*. Stehag. Stockholm: Symposion.

Bairner, A. (2001) *Sport, Nationalism, and Globalization*. Albany, NY: State University of New York Press.

Billing, P., Franzén, M. and Peterson, T. (2004) "Paradoxes of football professionalization in Sweden: A club approach". *Soccer & Society*, 5(1): 82–99.

Blom, K. A. and Lindroth, J. (1995). *Idrottens Historia: Från Antika Arenor till Modern Massrörelse.* Farsta: SISU idrottsböcker.

Brante, T. (1992) *Expert Society: The Origins and Development of Professions in Sweden.* Stockholm: Council for Studies of Higher Education.

Bäckström, Å. (2007) *Spår: om Brädsportkultur, Informella Lärprocesser och Identitet.* Stockholm: HLS förlag.

Collins, R. (1979) *The Credential Society: An Historical Sociology of Education and Stratification.* New York: Academic Press.

Esping-Andersen, G. (1990) *The Three Worlds of Welfare Capitalism.* Princeton, NJ: Princeton University Press.

Forsberg, L. (2012a) "Gender and entrepreneurship in the horse-related industry". In Forsberg, L. (ed), Manegen är Krattad: Om Flickors och Kvinnors Företagsamhet i Hästrelaterde Verksamheter (diss). Luleå: Luleå University of Technology.

Forsberg, L. (2012b) "The horse stable as a leadership school for girls". In Forsberg, L. (ed.), Manegen är Krattad: Om Flickors och Kvinnors Företagsamhet i Hästrelaterde Verksamheter (diss). Luleå: Luleå University of Technology.

The Global Gender Gap Report (2012). World Economic Forum, https://www.weforum.org/reports/global-gender-gap-report-2012/.

Goksoyr, M. (1998) "The popular sounding board: Nationalism, 'the people', and sports in Norway in the inter-war years". In H. Meinander and J. A. Mangan (eds), *The Nordic World: Sport in Society.* London: Frank Cass, pp. 100–114.

Hausmann, R., Tyson, L.D. and Zahidi, S. (2010) *The Global Gender Gap Report 2010.* Geneva: World Economic Forum.

Hedenborg, S. (2009a) "Till vad fostrar ridsporten? En studie av ridsportens utbildningar med utgångs-spunkt i begreppen tävlingsfostran, föreningsfostran och omvårdnadsfostran", *Educare* 2009: 1.

Hedenborg, S. (2009b) "Unknown soldiers and very pretty ladies: Challenges to the Social order of sports in post-war Sweden". *Sport in History,* 29 (4): 601–622.

Hedenborg, S. (2011) "The horse in Sweden: Workmate and leisure pursuit". In Antonson, Hans and Ulf Jansson (eds.) *Agriculture and Forestry in Sweden since 1900: Geographical and Historical Studies.* Stockholm: The Royal Swedish Academy of Agriculture and Forestry.

Hedenborg, S. (2013a) "På jakt efter den goda idrotten: lärdomar från Norden och Australien". In C. Dartsch and P. Johan (eds), *Spela Vidare: Centrum för Idrottsforskning.* Stockholm: Centrum för idrotts-forskning, pp. 43–58.

Hedenborg, S. (2013b) "The Olympic Games in London 2012 from a Swedish media perspective". *The International Journal of the History of Sport,* 30 (7): 789–804.

Hellborg, A. and Hedenborg. S. (2014) "The rocker and the heroine: Gendered media representations of equestrian sports at the 2012 Olympics". *Sport in Society,* 2: 1–14.

Juliani, S. (1973) "Social change and the athlete". In J. Gerstl (ed.), *Professions for the People: The Politics of Skill.* Cambridge, MA: Schenkman Publishing CO.

Lindroth, J. (1987) *Idrott Mellan Krigen: Organisationer: Ledare och Idéer i Den Svenska Idrottsrörelsen 1919–1939.* Stockholm: HLS.

Lundquist, W. P. (2004) *Kroppens Medborgarfostran: Kropp, Klass och Genus i Skolans Fysiska Fostran 1919–1962.* Stockholm: Stockholms Universitet.

Norberg, J. R. (2002) "Riksidrottsförbundets hegemoni". In J. Lindroth and J. R. Norberg (ed.), *Ett Idrottssekel: RiksidrottsförBundet 1903-2003.* Södertälje: Fingraf. pp. 59–93.

Norberg, J. R. (2004) *Idrottens väg till Folkhemmet.* Mölndal: SISU idrottsböcker.

Norberg, J. R. and Redelius, K. (2012) "Idrotten och kommersen: marknaden som hot eller möjlighet?" In F. Wijkström (ed), *Civilsamhället i Samhällskontraktet: En Antologi om vad Som Står på spel.* Stockholm: European Civil Society Press.

Olofsson, E. (1989) *Har kvinnorna en sportlig chans?* Umeå: Pedagogiska Institutionen.

Olofson, E. (2003) "RF och kvinnorna". In J. Lindroth and J. R. Norberg (eds.), *Ett Idrottssekel. Riksidrottsförbundet 1903–2003.* Stockholm: Inbunden, pp. 379–395.

Parkin, P. (1979) *Marxism and Class Theory: A Bourgeois Critique.* London: Tavistock.

Peterson, T. (1993). *Den svengelska modellen: svensk fotboll i omvandling under efterkrigstiden.* Lund: Arkiv.

Peterson, T. (2000) Split visions: The introduction of the Svenglish model in Swedish football. *Soccer & Society,* 1(2): 1–18.

Peterson, T. (2007) "Landskrona BoIS as an environment for nurturing and education". *Soccer & Society,* 8(1): 125–139.

Peterson, T. (2008) "The professionalisation of sport in the Scandinavian countries". Accessed 2 March 2016. http://idrottsforum.org/articles/peterson/peterson080220.pdf.

Peterson, T. (2014) "The double articulation of relative age effect". *Idrottsforum*. 15 December 2015. Accessed 2 March 2016. http://idrottsforum.org/peterson141216/.

Peterson, T. and Norberg, J. R. (2008) *Föreningsfostran och Tävlingsfostran: En Utvärdering av Statens Stöd till Idrotten: Betänkande av Idrottsstödsutredningen*. Stockholm: SOU.

Pålbrant, R. (1977) *Arbetarrörelsen och Idrotten 1919–1939*. Uppsala: Studia historica Upsaliensia.

Sarfatti-Larsen, M. (1979) *The Rise of Professionalism*. Berkeley, CA: University of California Press.

Sommestad, L. (1995) *Privat eller offentlig välfärd?: ett genusperspektiv på välfärdsstaternas historiska formering*. Stockholm: Svenska historiska fören.

SSO. (2008) Swedish Government Inquiry Public report: Association Fostering or Competition Fostering. An Evaluation of Public Support to the Sport Sector, p. 59.

Toftegaard Støckel, J., Strandbu, A., Solenes, O., Jørgensen, P. and Fransson, K. (2010) "Sport for children and youth in the Scandinavian countries". *Sport in Society*, 13 (4): 625–642.

Tolvhed, H. (2008) *Nationen På Spel: Kropp, kön och Svenskhet i Populärpressens Representationer av Olympiska Spel 1948–1972*. Umeå: Bokförlaget h:ström.

Tolvhed, H. (2012) "The sports woman as a cultural challenge: Swedish popular press coverage of the Olympic Games during the 1950s and 1960s". *The International Journal of the History of Sport*, 29 (2): 302–317.

10

FEMINIST POLITICS AND SPORT

Mary Louise Adams

Over the past half-century the landscape of women's sport has changed beyond recognition. Since the 1970s the numbers of women participating in a broad range of sports has increased exponentially. In some parts of the world female athletes routinely have experiences that would have been unthinkable for many of their grandmothers, and sport has become an unremarkable activity for girls, as it has been for boys for generations. The transformation of women's sport is among the most visible legacies of second wave feminism, the global social movement that came to prominence in the 1960s to address the social, economic and political inequalities between women and men. Many feminists have seen sport as an institution with the potential to challenge sexism and hierarchical notions of gender and to promote equality between women and men. Too frequently, however, sport fails to meet this potential.

Despite dramatic increases in women's participation, sport remains an institution dominated by men and rife with discriminatory practices. In general men have more opportunities to participate in sport. Even at the London Olympics, which were lauded as the most gender equal Games in history, men competed in 30 more events than women did, and many events required men and women to compete under gender-specific rules (Donnelly and Donnelly 2013). Men have more opportunities to play sport professionally and, when they do, they make more money than women do – sometimes a lot more. In golf, in 2014, the prize money available for the men's Professional Golf Association (PGA) Championship was £1.1 million, while for the women's PGA Championship it was £212,000. In World Cup football the prize money for the men's tournament was £22 million and for the women's it was £630,000 (BBC 2014). Men also have more opportunities in sport administration and coaching. A 2014 European Union study on gender and sport noted that 20 of 52 European sport federations had no women on their governing boards (European Commission 2014: 14). The study noted that, for example, in Germany only 10 per cent of 500 national team coaches were women; in Sweden the figure was 11 per cent across 34 national sports; in Slovenia women made up 15 per cent of national team coaches at the junior level and higher (European Commission 2014: 19).

International research also shows that women's sports receive significantly less media coverage than men's sports. The 2010 Gender and Media Progress Study in South Africa found that 'sport is the most covered topic in South African media. . . . Yet only 10% of this coverage is of women's sport or women athletes' (Philip 2013). A 2013 study of six daily newspapers in the UK found that only 2.9 per cent of sport articles referred to women (Packer *et al.* 2014). In the United States a longitudinal study found that coverage of women's sports on television sports news programmes has declined over the past 20 years. On the television programmes that were included in the study, women's sports now account for just 1.3 to 1.6 per cent of the total content (Cooky *et al.* 2013: 209). While social media offers new opportunities for women to promote their sports, it can also reproduce the inequities of more traditional media, adding to these the misogyny and cruelty so often evident in online comments (Hardin 2009).

Despite huge gains made by advocates for women's sport, sport remains an institution that too often privileges men over women and provides men with more and better resources. Moreover, the expansion of women's sport has benefitted some groups of women more than others, particularly able-bodied women in middle-class communities in wealthier nations. Persistent inequalities have kept sport on the feminist agenda for the past half-century. But feminists are not just concerned about who gets to play or which athletes get which resources, they are also concerned about the way sport operates symbolically in cultures in which it is a highly valued realm of achievement. Popular narratives about sport keep in circulation understandings of sex and gender that position men and women in a hierarchical relationship. Such discussions help to prop up ideologies of male supremacy and, therefore, to maintain inequality between women and men in the broader culture. Until such narratives change, sport will remain a feminist issue.

One of the major political forces of the twentieth century, feminism has influenced all levels of society. And yet today many women who believe in gender equality feel little connection to feminism itself. The reluctance of people who believe in equality to call themselves feminists is, in part, due to mischaracterization and the vilification of feminists and the feminist project. It is also a consequence of the mistaken view that feminism's time has passed, such politics are no longer necessary, gender equality has been achieved and we are now in a post-feminist era. This chapter argues that feminist politics remain not just relevant but necessary to the development of a socially just sport. The chapter offers an overview of the relationship of feminist politics to sport over the past century. It looks at why feminists have found sport to be such an important political target and at the way sport has been conceptualized through different feminist frameworks.

What is feminism and what does it have to do with sport?

Feminism is an international social justice movement that aims to bring about equality between women and men. American feminist critic bell hooks writes, simply, that feminism 'is a movement to end sexism, sexist exploitation, and oppression' (hooks 2000: viii). hooks makes the point that the feminist project is much bigger than simply working for equality between the sexes, because women are not just oppressed due to their sex. Thus feminism is a movement that must address oppression on many levels. hooks writes that the aim of feminism is 'not to benefit solely any specific group of women, any particular race or class of women. It does not privilege women over men. It has the power to transform in a meaningful way all our lives' (hooks 1984: 26). For hooks, the goal of feminism is a world without oppression and domination.

As in any major international political movement, there are many versions of feminism and these have had different histories, goals and strategies; some of these build on one another, while others conflict. Some English-language writers use the metaphor of 'waves' to distinguish between feminist movements in different time periods, referring to first, second and third wave feminisms. The metaphor can make it seem that there was no feminism before the 'first wave' or that the feminist projects identified in each wave were unique or distinct from women's organizing in other political projects. Like any classificatory system this metaphor has exclusionary effects and tends to reinforce the dominance of certain groups – in this case, white middle-class women in the West (Springer 2002). That said, distinct feminist projects have emerged in different eras.

The term 'first wave feminism' refers to the women's rights movements that existed in many parts of the world from the mid-nineteenth into the early twentieth centuries. In some national contexts these movements drew on the organizing and rhetorical strategies developed by black women in abolitionist movements. They also had links to socialist, trade union, temperance, and political and religious reform movements. Among the primary goals of first wave feminism was women's suffrage, that is, the vote for women; hence these movements are often referred to as suffragist movements. Yet early feminists were also concerned with property rights, access to education and economic freedoms, including access to the employment opportunities brought about by industrial capitalism. By the 1920s and 1930s, some feminists were working toward legalizing birth control, reforming men's sexual behaviours and giving women options for controlling their fertility. Feminist interest in women's self-determination and physical autonomy also led to calls for women to be able to participate in a range of leisure time activities like sport.

Second wave feminism is what most people think of as the contemporary women's movement. It emerged in the 1960s and came to prominence alongside other social and activist movements, like anti-racism and civil rights movements, the peace and student movements, socialist and labour movements and, in some contexts, nationalist, anti-imperialist and independence movements (Jayawardena 1986). Second wave feminism is an umbrella term that refers to a diverse collection of organisations, strategies and ideas that arose in response to pervasive and persistent inequalities related to sex, gender and sexuality. In Western countries, the major schools of thought and practice in second wave feminism have included liberal feminism (sometimes referred to as mainstream feminism), socialist feminism and radical feminism. These forms of feminism tended to be dominated by and to give priority to the concerns of white, middle-class women. Separate forms of feminism emerged among black and third world women, in part as critiques of the exclusionary practices and universalizing theories developed by white women.

It is important to note that the different tendencies are not as easy to separate in practice as they are in a textbook. Similarly, the labels for the different feminisms are also more likely to be found in textbooks than in the everyday conversations of feminists. In the present day – an era of reduced explicit public discussion of feminism – the labels sound quaint or outdated, and yet the principles and approaches that they identify continue to shape feminist practices.

Liberal forms of feminism are concerned with issues related to rights and equality of opportunity. Do women and men have equal access to resources? Do women and men have similar opportunities to participate in their society and benefit from that participation? A liberal feminist organization might campaign for equal pay or equal opportunities in the workplace. Liberal feminist proposals for resolving gender inequalities tend to rely on education, laws and policies as ways of ensuring that women have the same opportunities as men. This strand of feminism has been the primary driver of efforts to increase the numbers of women and girls who participate in sport.

In some jurisdictions feminists have launched court cases or taken their concerns to human rights tribunals to force sports governing bodies to accommodate female athletes and address discrimination based on sex or gender. In Canada, for instance, a series of cases, launched by young female athletes, have won for girls the right to try out for and to play on boys' teams in schools and minor sports leagues (Canadian Association for the Advancement of Women and Sport and Physical Activity 2012). Feminists have also pushed government agencies and sports organizations to change practices that have disadvantaged female athletes. They have pushed for the implementation of policies to ensure that resources go to women's teams or that women get opportunities to develop skills as coaches or sport administrators. For example, between 2012 and 2016, the Union of European Football Associations (UEFA) will provide extra funding to its 54 member organizations to develop the women's game, particularly at the grassroots level (Union of European Football Associations 2013). Although they are not always explicitly acknowledged, liberal approaches to feminism have tended to ground the work of national and international organizations that promote women's sport, such as the Australian Women Sport and Recreation Association, Women in Sport in the United Kingdom, the Japanese Association for Women and Sport and the International Working Group on Women and Sport, among others.

Socialist feminism is a broader project than liberal feminism; it is concerned not just with inequality between men and women, or male domination of society, but with class exploitation. Socialist feminists draw attention to the way that gender inequality is related to the economic oppression that is a consequence of capitalism. They believe that one cannot understand the oppression of women without also understanding women's relationship to capitalist forms of production and the political and social systems that these engender. Socialist feminists also recognize that, in addition to gender oppression, capitalism contributes to racism, heterosexism, imperialism, and colonialism – and that all of these constrain women's lives. The goal for socialist feminists, therefore, is not simply to gain more equality for women in the existing society but to transform social structures to achieve more equality for all people. In 1976, the feminist writer Barbara Ehrenreich suggested that the label 'socialist feminism' was an inadequate reflection of the movement it represented, which she pegged as 'socialist internationalist anti-racist, anti-heterosexist feminism' (Ehrenreich 1976).

In terms of sport, a socialist feminist perspective has influenced strong critiques of the ways that the recent rise of women's sport has been tightly linked to consumer capitalism and to corporate efforts to develop new markets for women's athletic apparel (Helstein 2003). Feminists have noted how companies like Nike have appropriated feminist language to commodify women's athleticism and female athletes and to render women's sport a new source of profit (Heywood and Dworkin 2003). Socialist feminist analysis has contributed to questions about, for instance: the relationship between women's domestic labour and their ability to participate in leisure (Bray 1988); working conditions for women employed in factories that supply athletic shoes or clothing for markets in the West (Enloe 1995); and the imposition of Western sporting practices on indigenous women and their communities (Hargreaves 2000).

Like socialist feminism, the type of feminism that is known as radical feminism has also aimed at broad social transformation. But where socialist feminists focus on the effects of a patriarchal capitalism, radical feminists focus specifically on the effects of patriarchy. In anthropology a patriarchal household is one in which a male father figure holds authority. In feminist theory and politics the term has a broader meaning. Historian Gerda Lerner defines patriarchy as

> the manifestation and institutionalization of male dominance over women and children in the family and the extension of male dominance over women in the society in general. It implies that men hold power in all the important institutions of society and that women are deprived of access to such power. It does *not* imply that women are either totally powerless or totally deprived of rights, influence and resources.
>
> *(Lerner 1986: 239)*

Nor, we might add, does it imply that all men are equally powerful. The objectives of radical feminism are to overcome men's domination of women, to end women's oppression, and to remove gender as a key organizational feature of society.

While radical feminists are less visible than they were in the 1970s and 1980s, radical feminist ideas have been influential in reshaping popular understandings of gender and in contributing to the monumental, if incomplete, shifts in gender relations that have taken place over the past decades. Radical feminism has drawn public attention to men's violence against women, to women's right to define their sexuality and control their bodies, to the way that language represents men as more central to the culture, for example the use of the generic 'man' to refer to humans of both sexes or the distinct marking of women's activities as not the norm, as in 'football' vs 'women's football'. Radical feminist analyses address both the material circumstances of women's lives, like access to birth control, and the cultural meanings of sex and gender in specific contexts. They have helped to make visible the tenaciousness of ideas and practices through which male supremacy has been constituted.

While this strand of feminism has certainly contributed to arguments around increasing sporting opportunities for women, it has made a greater impact on the sports world by drawing attention to how normative ideologies about gender and sexuality are central to everyday sport cultures. It has led to discussions about how such ideologies are oppressive not just to women but also to many men. We can see the legacy of radical feminist ideas in sport policies that address the sexual abuse of athletes and in recent projects to eliminate homophobia from sporting cultures. Similarly, we can see the influence of radical feminism in commentaries that ask why twenty-first century sport continues to be so gendered. Why do so few boys and men feel comfortable with aesthetic sports like figure skating or diving (Adams 2011)? Why do so many female athletes and coaches try so hard to emphasize their femininity off the field (Festle 1996: 265)? Why, do so many men's team sport cultures seem to promote such macho versions of masculinity (Pringle and Markula 2005)? Radical feminist perspectives have also contributed to important work by male scholars that has brought to light the troubling consequences of some men's and boys' contact team sport environments – bullying of weaker players, sexualized hazing rituals, violence off the field, and too-frequent injuries on it (Messner 1995).

In the 1990s, some feminists began to talk and write about what they called the third wave of feminism, a movement for younger women that is often presented as a critique of the feminisms that preceded it. Third wave feminism is said to take for granted racial, sexual and class diversity among women. It eschews what some women have seen as the too strict ideologies of earlier movements, instead promoting individuality and, for some proponents, a bit of irreverence and sassiness. Some writers have argued that the third wave is feminism for a generation that has grown up benefitting from previous feminist efforts: 'For our generation feminism is like fluoride. We scarcely notice that we have it – it's simply in the water' (Baumgardner and Richards 2000: 17). Third wave feminists put a heavy emphasis on analysis and production of media, on sexual empowerment, and on styles of personal expression. American sports scholars Leslie Heywood and Sherri Dworkin have taken a third wave perspective to suggest that sport could be seen as a kind of 'stealth feminism', a form of expression that can, under certain circumstances, produce strong independent young women and help to change representations of women in popular culture (Heywood and Dworkin 2003). Heywood and Dworkin's work shows how complicated 'progress' has been in the realm of women's sports. In many industrialized countries, female athletes are increasingly visible in popular culture, and yet representations of them are as likely as other images of women to be sexualized or to reinforce narrow conceptions of femininity that marginalize racialized women, women with disabilities and women whose bodies do not meet contemporary body ideals. Nevertheless, the authors argue that in the right context sport itself – the physical experience of it – has the possibility to lead to personal and social changes that might foster change in the world outside the gym (Heywood and Dworkin 2003: 54). Hence its usefulness as a feminist tool.

In the West, feminism been dominated by white middle-class women and discussions of their interests. In response, racialized women and 'third world' women developed their own distinct feminisms, in part to represent specific experiences but also to critique the exclusions and limitations of much feminist practice and theory. From black feminist critique emerged the key concept of intersectionality – the recognition that gender cannot be understood independently of other relations of power like race or class (Collins 1993). An intersectional analysis of, for instance, women's (or men's) experiences in a particular sport, would require attention not just to gender but to how gender is produced through other social relations, like race and class. Such an analysis draws out the salience of race and class to the gendering of athletes of colour or athletes from economically marginal backgrounds; it also shows how race and class privilege constitute the gendered experiences of white middle-class athletes. In figure skating, the sport that I study, relations of race and class are most evident in the overwhelming whiteness of what is a very expensive sport and in the particularly limited notions of gender that are constantly reproduced in performances (Adams 2011). For female skaters the style that is most often rewarded is a kind of clichéd elegance drawn from Western styles of dance or Hollywood glamour. In popular culture this is a style most frequently expressed by white bodies, a fact that privileges white skaters, who embody the ideal. Racial stereotypes that position black women as naturally more athletic and as less naturally graceful than white women put black skaters at a disadvantage in a sport where narrow aesthetic norms determine success. To adopt an intersectional approach in research or advocacy work is to acknowledge that gender is not a universal category and that any given social context produces layered formations of inequality and privilege. Thus as we consider the transformation of the world of women's sport, an intersectional approach means that we cannot assume this change has been experienced equally by women of different racial or class backgrounds or women who live with and without disabilities.

Why have feminists been interested in sport?

The simple reason feminists came to be interested in sport is because it is a site of gender inequality; men have more opportunities to participate in and excel at it. In cultures that put high value on athletic achievement, women are, therefore, at a disadvantage. Feminists have also been interested in sport because sport works ideologically to keep in circulation ideas about the so-called 'natural' differences between women and men and about the norms of femininity and masculinity that set the bounds of appropriate attitudes, behaviours and appearance. As a site of inequality, sport is not unique; there are many sectors of society that support the binary gender system and that restrict the participation of women and girls. What makes sport unique is its physicality. In social contexts in which women have been declared to be weak or fragile, and have been deemed incapable of participating fully in public life, physical activity and sport have held out the possibility for women to challenge prevailing opinion and transform gender ideologies.

In the late 1800s and the early 1900s, women's involvement in sport and their development of athletic skills was considered by some first wave feminists to be a key element in their liberation. In 1896, American women's rights campaigner Susan B. Anthony told a New York newspaper:

Let me tell you what I think of bicycling. I think it has done more to emancipate women than anything else in the world. It gives women a feeling of freedom and self-reliance. I stand and rejoice every time I see a woman ride by on a wheel . . . the picture of free, untrammeled womanhood.

(Bly 1896: 10)

In an era of chaperones, corsets and long skirts, cycling helped to shift notions of acceptable feminine behaviour – for middle-class white women. It helped to reform conventions of fashion that impeded women's mobility, and it gave some women access to both urban and rural landscapes that had previously been off limits (Strange and Brown 2002). The ability to ride a bicycle provided a freedom of movement and a sense of independence and competence that would have been for many women both unprecedented and exhilarating.

The notion that athletic ability and physical confidence can contribute to women's emancipation has been drawing feminist interest in sport for more than a century. In 1979, as the massive expansion of women's sport was underway, historian Stephanie Twin wrote, 'Sport is part of a larger movement for female physical autonomy, a movement in which efforts to gain control over pregnancy, birth, family size, and individual safety figure prominently. As this movement proceeds, athletics may well form its backbone' (Twin 1979: xxxix). In the face of long-standing expert and popular discourses about female frailty and incompetence, some feminists have promoted sport and other forms of physical activity, including self-defense, as a way of changing how women understand their bodies and their place in the world. The confidence and pleasure that may result from feeling physically powerful have been seen as useful resources for women as they confront issues around sexuality, body image and sexual violence.

The belief that sport might help empower and perhaps, more importantly, politicize women – by making obvious the contradictions between their own physical strength and ideologies about female frailty – has been key to feminist interest in sport. But feminists have also engaged with sport because of the contribution it makes to popular understandings of the differences between female and male bodies, women and men, femininity and masculinity. In some versions of feminism, the main political goal is to reduce the power of sex and gender to diminish the role sex and gender play in the organization of daily life. Hence the concern about sport – a highly valued and pervasive cultural institution in which sex and gender differences are, especially at the highest levels, not just present but fundamental to its structure and social meaning.

Sex and gender differences are made prominent in sport in a number of ways, the most obvious being the routine segregation of the sexes. One of the defining characteristics of Western liberal democracies is supposed to be a principled commitment to equality between the sexes. This commitment is often thought to be evident in equal provision of education to boys and girls, in integration of women into the military, in incorporation of women into the workforce. The general trend in such societies over the past century has been towards sex and gender integration in the public sphere. Yet in sport the default position, at all but the lowest levels, is sex segregation. Most sports have separate events for men and women; thus, female and male athletes rarely compete against each other. Historically, women and men have also been kept separate by assumptions about the gender appropriateness of certain sports. While attitudes are definitely changing (more for women than for men), there are still sports that are considered to be more suitable for one sex than the other, like synchronized swimming and rhythmic gymnastics for women, and Canadian or U.S. football for men. Therefore it is still the case that women and men are constrained in their ability to develop skills that represent the full range of human physical possibility.

Of course other institutions, besides sport, contribute to constructions of gender. Commerce, religion, and education also contribute to understandings of masculinity and femininity that emphasize the differences rather than the similarities between men and women. This binary view of gender is both a product and a requirement of the normative heterosexuality that pervades Western cultures. When heterosexuality is a primary organizing principle of social relations, masculinity and femininity must not grow too similar. Refracted through popular discourses of biology, men and women are constructed as 'opposite sexes', as the 'two halves of a whole'. The segregation of men and women in sport lends support to gender polarization in the culture at large.

The physicality of sport can make it seem like differences between men and women are natural, that they are not socially constructed but the product of differently shaped male and female bodies. It is rarely acknowledged that sporting practices themselves contribute to the production of differently shaped bodies with different capacities. For instance, throughout much of the twentieth century, women were steered towards and men away from aesthetic sports, and thus it came to appear as if the qualities demanded by those sports – expressiveness, grace, flexibility – were feminine qualities by virtue of the fact that male athletes in typical male sports were unlikely to be called upon to display them (which is not to say they never did). Similarly, until quite recently, some women have been prohibited from playing sports that highlight so-called masculine qualities. In Brazil, a law was in effect between 1941 and 1975 that prohibited women from participating in sports that were seen to be 'incompatible with their natural [feminine and reproductive] condition'. In 1965, the Brazilian National Sports Council developed explicit regulations that prohibited women's participation in 'fights' of any nature, soccer, indoor soccer, beach soccer, polo, weightlifting and baseball (Votre and Mourão 2001: 199). While such a law seems a striking demonstration of gender ideology, the perspective behind it is reflected in the more general international history of prohibitions on women's participation in elite level sport. For instance, women were long considered incapable of running significant distances – despite considerable evidence to the contrary – and were excluded from the Olympic marathon until 1984. Indeed in only a small number of events did women and men enter Olympic competition at the same time; full equality in terms of the sports and the number of events available to women and men has yet to be reached. Women ski-jumpers, for instance, will not have their Olympic debut until 2018.

One of the most troubling consequences of the segregation of the sexes in sport is the practice of testing female athletes to verify their sex, a practice to which male athletes are not subject. While major sport organizations like the IOC have stopped general testing of female competitors, they continue to charge themselves with the task of determining who is or is not a woman. In 2009, South African runner Caster Semenya was prohibited from competing and subject to intensive medical testing and humiliating treatment by the press after other competitors accused her of not being a 'real' woman. More recently, Indian sprinter Duttee Chand has been told that she may not compete unless she undergoes medical treatment to lower her natural testosterone levels, which International Association of Athletic Federation (IAAF) officials have decided are too high. A report put out by the Canadian Centre for Ethics in Sport argues that 'the overall evidence from genetics and science support dismantling the structures of suspicion towards athletes with variations of sex development' (Canadian Centre for Ethics in Sport 2012: 8).

Efforts to police the boundaries between female and male bodies are also visible in the difficulties experienced by transgender and transexual athletes, who are not always accommodated by sport organizations. As more trans people 'come out' at younger ages, their inclusion in sport may force a re-thinking of the current default organization of sport along lines of sex.

Do all sports at all levels need to separate male and female bodies? If sex segregation is intended to promote fairness in sport, how must our notions of fairness change when we think about the accessibility of sport to people who do not conform to normative categories of sex or gender?

At all but the lowest levels, contemporary sport is inconceivable without the notions of sex and gender through which it is organized. The heavy emphasis on sex and gender differences in sport puts it at odds with a feminist politic that seeks to diminish the power of these categories to constrain daily life. Physical differences between men and women have often been used to justify differences in other realms of life; in a hierarchically structured society, differences tend to be the ground of inequality. The proposition that men, on average, are stronger than women, on average, has often served to symbolize and justify men's political and economic domination of women – despite the fact that there are many women who are stronger than many men or that physical strength, as a human quality, has little importance in the political and economic structures that are dominant in the current moment. The results of sex-segregated sporting contests – men's and women's events and men's and women's sports – advertise and perpetuate the gender binaries that continue to be so apparent in North American societies and that feminists, along with queer and transgender people, have been working hard to eliminate.

Conclusion

The purpose of this chapter has been to show conceptual and practical links between feminism and sport. The argument here is that feminism provided the groundwork that has made possible the recent transformations of women's sport. Broad-based international movements for the liberation of women made possible the advocacy and organizing that ushered in monumental shifts in the meanings of sport and who could play and benefit from it. There is not the space here to discuss the many recent issues in sport that have drawn feminist interest, like: sexual abuse; hazing; the limited accessibility of sporting opportunities for people with disabilities or people who are poor or who live in marginalized communities; eating disorders; homophobia and heteronormativity; the sexualization of female athletes by the media; the exclusion from competition of athletes who wear hijab, among many others. The fact that these issues are now on the sporting agenda is itself a product of a half-century of diverse feminist advocacy and thought.

It is clear that feminism has made a huge impact on sport. What is less clear is the extent to which sport has helped to achieve feminist goals in the broader society. Has sport helped to diminish the racism and class oppression that shape so many women's lives or to reduce the dominance of whiteness as the signifier of normative behaviour? Has sport helped to expand women's ability to challenge the inequities in the world around them? Has sport made gender a less important category in daily life? It is good but it is not enough that sport can help individual women to feel stronger. Over the past decade there has been a proliferation of sport-related projects designed to empower girls. As sport sociologist Lyndsay Hayhurst writes, we need to ask whether such programmes simply prepare girls to function better in an unjust world or do they actually help change the structural inequalities that shape girls' lives (Hayhurst 2013)?

There is nothing inherently good or bad about sports themselves. As an institution, sport can reinforce the existing social organization or it can challenge it. Historically, it has done both, with different effects for people of different genders, physical abilities, ages, nationalities, and racial, ethnic or class backgrounds. Sport is neither liberating nor oppressive; it is the context in which sport is experienced that produces its political effects. A feminist political perspective is one means of assessing the social effects of sport and of thinking about how to change it so that it contributes to the construction of a more just world.

References

Adams, M. L. (2011) *Artistic Impressions: Figure Skating, Masculinity and the Limits of Sport.* Toronto: University of Toronto Press.

BBC News. (2014) Prize money in sport – BBC study. 14 October. Accessed 15 January 2015. www.bbc.com/news/uk-29665693.

Baumgardner, J. and Richards, A. (2000) *Manifesta: Young Women, Feminism, and the Future.* New York: Farrar, Straus & Giroux.

Bly, N. (1896) Champion of Her Sex. *New York Sunday World.* 2 February 1896, p. 10.

Bray, C. (1988) Sport and social change: Socialist feminist theory. *Journal of Physical Education, Recreation and Dance,* 59(6): 50–53.

Canadian Association for the Advancement of Women and Sport and Physical Activity. (2012) *Sex Discrimination in Sport: An Update.* Ottawa: Canadian Association for the Advancement of Women and Sport and Physical Activity.

Canadian Centre for Ethics in Sport. (2012) *Sport in Transition: Making Sport in Canada More Responsible for Gender Inclusivity.* Ottawa: Canadian Centre for Ethics in Sport.

Collins, P. H. (1993) Toward a new vision: Race, class, and gender as categories of analysis and connection. *Race, Sex, and Class,* 1(1): 25–46.

Cooky, C., Messner, M. A., and Hextrum, R. H. (2013) Women play sport, but not on TV: A longitudinal study of the televised news media. *Communication and Sport,* 1(3): 203–230.

Donnelly, P. and Donnelly, M. K. (2013) *The London 2012 Olympics: A Gender Equality Study.* Centre for Sport Policy Studies Research Report. Toronto: Centre for Sport Policy Studies, Faculty of Kinesiology and Physical Education, University of Toronto.

Ehrenreich, B. (1976) What is socialist feminism? *Marxists.* Accessed 24 January 2015. www.marxists.org/subject/women/authors/ehrenreich-barbara/socialist-feminism.htm.

Enloe, C. (1995) The globe-trotting sneaker. *Ms* March/April, pp. 11–15.

European Commission (2014) *Gender Equality in Sport: Proposal for Strategic Actions, 2014–2020.* Brussels: European Commission.

Festle, M. J. (1996) *Playing Nice: Politics and Apologies in Women's Sports.* New York: Columbia University Press.

Hardin, M. (2009) Does new media bring new attitudes toward women's sports. *Tucker Center.* 24 September 2009. Accessed 15 January 2015. https://tuckercenter.wordpress.com/2009/09/24/does-%E2%80%98new-media%E2%80%99-bring-new-attitudes-oward-women%E2%80%99s-sports/.

Hargreaves, J. (2000) *Heroines of Sport: The Politics of Difference and Identity.* London: Routledge.

Hayhurst, L. (2013) Girls as the 'new' agents of social change? Exploring the 'girl effect' through sport, gender and development programs in Uganda. *Sociological Research Online.* 18(2): 8. Accessed 29 January 2015. www.socresonline.org.uk/18/2/8.html.

Helstein, M. (2003) That's who I want to be: The politics and production of desire within Nike advertising to women. *Journal of Sport and Social Issues,* 27(3): 276–292.

Heywood, L. and Dworkin, S. L. (2003) *Built to Win: The Female Athlete as Cultural Icon.* Minneapolis, MN: University of Minnesota Press.

hooks, b. (1984) *Feminist Theory: From the Margin to the Center.* Boston, MA: South End Press.

hooks, b. (2000) *Feminism is for Everybody: Passionate Politics.* Boston, MA: South End Press.

Lerner, G. (1986) *The Creation of Patriarchy.* New York: Oxford University Press.

Jayawardena, K. (1986) *Feminism and Nationalism in the Third World.* London: Zed Books.

Messner, M. A. (1995) *Power at Play: Sports and the Problem of Masculinity.* Boston, MA: Beacon Press.

Packer, C., Geh, D. J., Goulden, O. W., Jordan, A. M., Withers, G. K., Wagstaff, A. J., Bellwood, R. A., Binmore, C. L. and Webster, C. L. (2014) No lasting legacy: No change in reporting of women's sports in the British print media with the London 2012 Olympics and Paralympics. *Journal of Public Health.* Accessed 25 January 2015. http://jpubhealth.oxfordjournals.org/citmgr?gca=jphm%3Bfdu018v1.

Philip, S. (2013) Women's sport in the spotlight with gsport, *Media Club South Africa.* 15 November 2013. Accessed 24 January 2013. www.mediaclubsouthafrica.com/sport/3554-women-s-sport-in-the-spotlight-with-gsport#ixzz3Pksju4n4.

Pringle, R. and Markula, P. (2005) No pain is sane after all: A Foucauldian analysis of masculinities and men's experiences in rugby. *Sociology of Sport Journal*, 22(4): 472–497.

Springer, K. (2002) Third wave black feminism? *Signs*, 27(4): 1059–1082.

Strange, L. S. and Brown, R. S. (2002) The bicycle, women's rights and Elizabeth Cady Stanton. *Women's Studies*, 31: 609–626.

Twin, S. L. (1979) *Out of the Bleachers: Writings on Women and Sport*. Old Westbury, NY: The Feminist Press.

Union of European Football Associations (2013) *UEFA Women's Football Development Program: A Review of National Association Projects*. Accessed 10 January 2015. http://www.uefa.com/women/womens-football-development/programme/news/newsid=2032691.html.

Votre, S. and Mourão, L. (2001) Ignoring taboos: Maria Lenk, Latin American inspirationalist. *The International Journal of the History of Sport*, 18(1): 196–218.

PART III

Sport, nation and statehood

The existence of a close relationship between sport, nations and nationalism is widely accepted. This relationship manifests itself in many different ways including the enduring popularity of international competitions, events and contests, in the myriad ways in which politicians and politically motivated groups have sought to harness sport to national causes, and in the idea of national sports. In any discussion of the relationship between sport and nationalism, it is important to define carefully those concepts (nation, nation-state, nationality, national identity) that are most frequently used. Thus, when we refer to the prestige that nations and their politicians can derive from sport, it is necessary to think in terms not only of internationally recognised states but also of submerged nations (Scotland, Wales, Québec, the Basque nation, Catalonia, and so on) for which sport has commonly been one of the most effective vehicles for cultural resistance. For nationalists in such contexts, sport provides athletes and fans with opportunities to celebrate a national identity that is different from and, in some cases, opposed to, their ascribed nationality. These two forms of engagement need not be mutually exclusive. Depending on which sport is involved, it is possible, for example, to support both British teams and Scottish ones or to represent Wales and also the United Kingdom.

The desire, particularly on the part of fans, to express their national identity in the realm of sport is clearly linked to nationalism in the broadest sense or, at the very least, to patriotism. For George Orwell, international sport was war minus the shooting, a constant source of enmity. Yet a British Member of Parliament, Jim Sillars, once famously dismissed the support of his fellow Scots for national sporting representatives as mere 'ninety-minute patriotism'. It is undeniable that expressions of solidarity for players and teams that represent one's nation are closely linked to cultural nationalism. Whether or not they are also bound up with political aspiration is a different matter.

There are some grounds for believing that the link between nationalism and sports is becoming weaker and that the very existence of international competition is threatened by the twin forces of globalisation and consumer capitalism. For the time being, however, the relationship between sport, nation-states and nations remains strong as manifested in a wide variety of ways, a number of which are addressed in the chapters that constitute this section.

Michael Butterworth discusses the United States of America, often regarded as the civic nation state *par excellence*, the melting point in which, in theory at least, nationality takes precedence over national identity as exemplified in affinity felt by immigrants towards 'home'

127

countries. Performances such as the playing of the national anthem before sports events are intended to underline the idea of inclusivity. Amongst other things, Butterworth examines the promotion of patriotism, nationalism, and militarism through sport and the interpretation of global sport as a means to diplomacy and/or imperialism, including the United States' history in international events such as the Olympic Games.

The United Kingdom (UK), discussed here by Kevin Jefferys, is a very different type of nation state. Jefferys traces the interaction between sport and politics in post-1945 Britain, concluding with the 2012 London Olympics. Being multinational, not least in the context of sport, the UK provides space for the celebration both of British nationality and national identity and also of Scottish, Welsh and Irish (and, indeed, English) national identities. The Scottish case is examined here by Grant Jarvie, who discusses the 2014 Commonwealth Games, held in Glasgow, alongside the referendum on Scottish independence which took place later that year. Another challenge to the UK's current constitutional arrangements has come from Northern Ireland and nationalism in both parts of Ireland is the focus of David Hassan's chapter which offers the view that sport is contributing to what can become a more normalised society, part of the UK albeit with a devolved assembly. A comparable example to the UK is Spain where nationalists in stateless nations such as the Basque country and Catalonia, use sport, amongst other vehicles, to celebrate their distinctiveness and make the case for independent statehood. These issues are addressed here by Mariann Vaczi. As Vaczi reveals, while Basques and Catalans have been central to the development of football in Spain, they remain at odds with the idea of a centralised Spanish state. Compared with the UK and Spain, the challenge from Québec to Canada's indivisible nation-state constitutional status has receded in recent years. However, it is noteworthy that Christine Dallaire and Jean Harvey remind us here of the important role that is so often played by language in the politics of nation-states. The intersection of sport and language politics and identities is examined here through case studies of two different sporting events in Canada.

The part opens with chapters written by Mahfoud Amara and Paul Darby on nation-states in the Arab world and on Ghana respectively. Amara examines the post-independence period when sport became an arena for the consolidation of national unity as understood by one-party military regimes and royal families and goes on to consider the legacy of those years. Darby describes how football was used by colonial powers, not only in Ghana but throughout Africa, to secure their hegemony over the continent. In turn, however, football clubs became important vehicles for anti-colonial politics that led to the establishment of independent nation states, Ghana included, and the game remains an important mechanism through which politicians seek to secure support.

11

SPORT AND POLITICS IN THE ARAB WORLD

Mahfoud Amara

This chapter examines the interaction between sport and politics in the Arab World. In post-independence, in the 1950s and 1960s, sport was an arena for the consolidation of national unity, at least the way it was defined by the one-party, military-led regimes and royal families. Sport has been a terrain of ethno-nationalists rivalries within and between Arab countries despite the institutional (top-down) discourse on Arab unity and all Arab-nation (*Arab Ummah*). Sport is also a tool for international relations and diplomacy. Countries in the Arabian Peninsula, particularly the United Arab Emirates (UAE), Qatar and Bahrain, are adopting sport today as part of their strategy to build alliances with the world of finance and repositioning the region in the global sporting arena. Finally, sport in general, and football in particular, is at the centre of the political turmoil and multifaceted transitions occurring today in Arab countries.

Introduction: sport, a legacy of colonial history and globalisation

During the colonial period sport was used in some parts of the Arab World as means of resisting, in symbolic terms at least, French and British colonial presence, and defending the Arab cause in the international arena. The boycott of the 1956 Melbourne Olympic Games by Lebanon, Egypt, and Iraq, in protest against the tripartite invasion of Egypt by British, French, and Israeli troops, was the first instance (and may be the only example) of a joint Arab sport-based diplomatic action against foreign military intervention in the region. Sport clubs such as *Al-Ahly* in Egypt (established in 1907), *Espérance* in Tunisia (1919), Mouloudia in Algeria (1927), *Al-Kramah* in Syria (1928), *Al-Hilal* in Sudan (1930), and *Al-Widad* in Morocco (1937) – to name but a few – were also schools for the formation of Arab nationalist movements to resist colonial hegemony (Amara 2012).

In post-independence, despite the existence of some pockets of resistance (in the name of anti-apartheid, *Third-Worldism* and non-aligned movement), one can argue that the appropriation of the Western dominant model of sport was seen as a necessity. The adoption of sport was accomplished through the integration of Arab countries, to different degrees, into the homogeneous and pre-established sporting and administrative structure, rules and regulations of the international sports federations (particularly FIFA and the IOC). Integrating with international sports organisations, such as FIFA and the IOC, was important internally to strengthen nationalist sentiment and externally for the purpose of international relations and international prestige

(Fatès 1994). This is true today in relation to Palestine, which since its recognition by the IOC (in 1995) and FIFA (1998) could be argued has taken a first (symbolic) step toward the recognition of Palestine as an independent political entity.

A useful concept, which captures identities at national and individual levels and in the context of global sport and local dynamics, is that of 'transnationalism'. According to Giulianotti and Robertson (2007: 197) 'transnationalism is an ensemble of processes that connect individuals and social groups across specific geo-political borders'. To reflect on the transnational political dynamics of sport in the Arab World, we will first discuss the interaction between business and politics in sport. We then move to examine the politics of football (or soccer). Football has been at the centre of political agitation before and during the so-called 'Arab Spring'. The last section is devoted to the question of body (gender) and politics in sport. The female body in sport has been a significant factor in the debate on identity politics in Arab countries as well as among Arab diaspora in the West.

Business (and politics) of sport

European sport clubs are expanding their identity, including in the Arab World, so as to maintain local ties with local markets while developing brand awareness globally. They are opening football academies (such as Manchester United Academy in Abu Dhabi, Real Madrid and FC Barcelona in Morocco). They take part in pre- and post-season international football tournaments (such as the Mohammed bin Rashid International Football Championship, also known as the Dubai Cup). They set up their training camps, usually financed by local sponsors such as Emirates, Etihad or Qatar Airways, in Doha or Dubai (mainly during the winter break), which offer better weather conditions and competitive prices for hospitality and medical services. The other strategy is to move some of their domestic competitions to the region or to open official shops, for instance L'Olympique Marseille in Algiers and PSG in Doha, or Real Madrid coffee shop in Dubai.

To sense the impact of globalization of sport on Arab societies, one should travel to Morocco during Spain's El Classico. The derby divides the country and Moroccan families between Merengue and Barça fans. A similar phenomenon takes place in Lebanon every four years, during the FIFA World Cup. Neighbourhoods and balconies in Lebanese towns become divided, not necessarily on the basis of traditional political/religious sectarianism, but according to loyalty to a European or a Latin American national team. To comprehend this phenomenon, one should examine Lebanese migration to Europe and to Latin America during the civil war (Al-Arabia.net 19 June 2014). With 10,452 square kilometres, and a population of less than 10 million, embracing 18 different religious communities, this offers a unique context to the study of the interplay between sport and politics (Reiche 2011; Nassif and Amara 2015).

In the Gulf region, named also the Arabian Peninsula, there is a pattern of integrating sport and putting it onto the economic agenda of political and business elites to negotiate the region's transition toward a post-oil era. This strategy is tailored around urban regeneration, the exploration of new venues for investment in banking, tourism, retail and hospitality, as well as networking with multinationals including in sport (e.g. car racing, sport products, and sport TV broadcasting). One case in point is the Qatari state-owned sport TV network beIN Sports (formerly Al-Jazeera Sport), which is now dominating sport TV broadcasting in the Middle East and North Africa and is currently present in Europe (beIN Sports France), the USA (beIN Sports US in English and Spanish), Asia (beIN Sports Indonesia), and, more recently, Australia since beIN Sports took over the pay-TV sports provider Setanta Sports Australia (Amara, 2013a). Sport is also becoming an integrated part of monarchy-states' agenda in the

Arabian Peninsula for soft power and public diplomacy. Surrounded by political instability and having to face the so-called Iranian growing influence in the region, business and political leaders in the Gulf Cooperation Council (GCC) are keen to tie their economic and political destinies with that of the world's economy (in trade, banking, and finance). On the one hand, the entry of Gulf countries into the global sport industry is welcomed, particularly by international sport organisations such as FIFA and the IOC, which perceive this as a new opportunity to expand the global reach of sport (including the global consumption of sports products). On the other hand, it is viewed with scepticism by some media and investors in sport industry, which see in the growing influence of oil-rich countries a threat to 'traditional' balance of power between 'centre' and 'periphery' in the world's sport system (Dorsey 2014). The continuous debate about/questioning of legitimacy over the hosting of the FIFA 2022 World Cup and the ethno-religious tensions surrounding the Formula 1 Gulf Grand Prix are being used as examples to delegitimise the international sport strategy of countries such as Qatar and Bahrain. Opposition to/or celebration of the visibility of these nations in sport offers an interesting venue for research on international power relations in sport between the so-called traditional 'centre' and emerging 'centre(s)' (Garcia and Amara 2013; Reiche 2014).

Football, culture and identity

We cannot discuss sport and politics in Arab societies without mentioning football, the most politicised sport in the region (Tuastad 2014a; Raab 2012). Football stadia have been used by Arab regimes to provide, in a Marxist sense, a distraction from societal realities and to promote some kind of 'normality'. Football offers the opportunity to celebrate national unity and national prestige around the national team. The victory is usually presented as a result of harmony in society and product of economic and development policies. This discourse is not unique to Arab countries; it is also applicable to democratic and authoritarian regimes alike. However, the use of football for political legitimacy can have a reverse impact. A case in point is the Gaddafi regime in Libya. To raise its international profile after years of isolation following the bombing of Pan Am flight 103 over Lockerbie in 1988, the Libyan regime, represented by the Libyan Arab Foreign Investment Company (Lafico), bought a 7.5 per cent stake in Juventus for an estimated fee of £14 million (Marzocchi 2002). Subsequently, the 2002 Italian Super Cup final was played in the Libyan capital, Tripoli. In addition to the business dimension, Libya's direct investment in one of the most prestigious clubs in Italy was also promoted by the Libyan regime as a symbolic victory against the former coloniser. This was not enough though to prevent the heat of Arab protest from reaching Libya. I will come back to the role of sport/football in the recent popular uprising in Arab countries in the next section.

Football has been a site for contestations and identity claims. It is one of the few spaces where the Arab population, and particularly the youth can mock the ruling class and the privileged minority; to express also their frustration over the harsh social, economic, and political conditions. It is also a source of fractions, fuelled by political, ethnic, and religious tensions within the national community and between Arab nations. This tension reached an unprecedented level with the 'battle' between Algeria and Egypt over qualification to the 2010 FIFA World Cup. It turned into a clash between the two nations over legitimacy; in other words the legitimacy to be the only representative of the Arab World in South Africa. Social media was turned into a platform by Algerian and Egyptian fans to insult each other's culture, language, and history. Even internet hackers from the two countries entered the battle to attack Egyptian and Algerian governments and media websites. The tension over football turned into a quasi-diplomatic incident between the two states (Amara 2011). In a way, this signalled the decline of the over-manipulated propaganda around Arab nationalism and Arab unity (traditionally constructed around the Arab–Israeli conflict) and the subsequent events which took place in the region, starting from the end of 2010.

Violence and hooliganism are becoming common phenomena in major football stadia, obliging governments and sports governing bodies to introduce more legislation and disciplinary procedures to maintain their control (and authority) over the national sport system. A recent example is the death of 75 football supporters in Egypt following a football match between rival clubs Al-Ahly and Al-Masry. Twenty-one fans received the death sentence for their involvement in one of the world's deadliest incidents of football violence. Rivalry between football clubs in Egypt has been recently fuelled by the political divide following the fall of Mubarak regime and, later, the military coup against the Muslim Brotherhood-led government. In Jordan, the rivalry between Al-Faysali, being seen to represent Jordanians, and Al-Wihdat Palestinian refugees, is also a product of the contemporary political discourse in Jordan about national identity and citizenship, particularly in relation to the ongoing question of Palestinian refugees (who, demographically, represent an important segment of Jordanian society) and their right of return (Tuastad 2014b).

With reference to Arab culture and identity politics, it is worth examining sport culture among the Arab diaspora and its contribution to the construction of meanings around sport, culture (including religion), and ethnicity. The question of sport and diaspora destabilises the debate on identity both in the country of origin and in the country of birth (Amara 2006, 2013b). An illustrative example is Zidane's famous headbutting of Metarazzi in the final of the 2006 FIFA World Cup – a global media event par excellence, experienced by millions of spectators. The incident was extensively debated in the media as being somehow the by-product of (or symptomatic of) the 'clash of civilizations' between Islam and the West. On the one hand, Zidane, with his Algerian immigrant origin, representing 'the Muslim World' (emotional, irrational, and aggressive), and on the other hand, Metarazzi, from Italy, representing 'the West' (victim, rational, and triumphant) (Jiwani 2008; Dauncey and Morray 2008; Rowe 2010).

Sport and 'the Arab Spring'

One-party state regimes, which ruled their countries for more than 30 years (41 years for Gaddafi), collapsed in a matter of months as consequence of popular demonstrations in the case of Tunisia and Egypt, and military conflict in the case of Libya. Events since 2011 have changed politics in the region and will have a profound and lasting impact. Revolutionary and counter-revolutionary movements, as well as other internal and external forces with different ideological (religious and ethno-nationalists) agendas, are at war over, or engage in proxy-war to reshape territories and zones of influence in the region. This could provoke further fragmentation and the emergence of even smaller entities founded exclusively on ethno-religious identities (Sunni, Shi'a, Aloui, Yazidi, etc.).

Sport is not immune to this upheaval. For some, the time had come to judge those (sport officials, coaches, referees, and even players) who benefited from the former regimes' favours, and to evaluate the level of intervention from former political-business lobbies, in the corruption of the national sport system. The political transition, with the exception of Tunisia, is not happening in a smooth manner. The Port Said event in Egypt is an illustrative example of current fragile political and security conditions. Many Egyptian football clubs (including Zamalek and Al-Ahly) who played an active role in toppling Mubarak's regime are now divided over the new military-led government which pushed (temporarily at least) the Islamic Brotherhood movement outside the political arena. The raising of Libya's new flag in the 2012

Olympic Games was celebrated as a symbolic moment for the re-integration of the country (post-Gaddafi) into the international community, although the path toward the (re-)building of the nation-state is yet to be seen. For the Syrian authority led by Bashar Assad, despite the civil war, participating in the 2012 Olympic Games and the FIFA 2014 World Cup qualification tournament was presented as a form of resistance against the enemies of the Baath party, declared by the regime to be 'the sole legitimate representative of the Syrian people'. The Assad regime's power to maintain its authority over the national sport system and Syrian territory will depend on the outcome of the civil war. As a consequence of the military conflict, 'more than 200 [football] players have left the country, with the most popular destination being Iraq. Among the 25 players representing the national side in the last tournament, only three of them reside in Syria' (*The Guardian* 7 September 2014). There have also been some attempts by the Syrian National Coalition (a coalition of opposition movements in exile), to form a competing national sport system, including the Free Syrian National Football Team (Associated Press 20 June 2014).

For other Arab countries which were not directly affected by the popular uprising, such as Morocco, organising the World Cup of club winners in 2013 (and 2014) is promoted as a sign of a country's political and economic stability under the leadership of the monarchy-state, in opposition to military and the one-party state rules which are in crisis today. Algeria's qualification for the second consecutive time to the 2014 FIFA World Cup (after 2010 in South Africa), as the only Arab country in the tournament, and qualifying to the second round for the first time, is presented by the political establishment as a key moment in the reconciliation between Algerians (in Algeria and abroad) after a decade of political violence which caused the death of thousands (200,000 according to some estimates). For the Bahraini authorities, maintaining the Formula 1 Grand Prix despite the mounting popular protest and discontent (particularly among the Shi'a community) is a form of resistance against 'so called forces of instability', in reference to Iran's political influence in the region.

For the majority of Arab people, particularly the youth, who are still dissatisfied with politics, but not seduced by the call of 'global jihadism', watching the FIFA World Cup, or consuming sport in general, is one way to seek some 'normality' in uncertain times.

Sport and body politics

The question of body politics in the Arab context has been dominated by the debate on (Arab/Muslim) women's bodies. There is a competition (continuous struggle) between secular and other movements in the Arab world in defining and even controlling/shaping women's bodies. The participation of women in sport is promoted by secular-nationalist movements as a sign of 'progress' and 'modernity'. For conservative movements in the Arab world, resisting female participation in international sport competition and women revealing parts of their body (examples are Boulemerka from Algeria during the 1992 Barcelona Olympic Games or Ghribi from Tunisia in the 2012 London Games) is another form of resistance against the 'Westernisation' of Arab societies. As an alternative to those two conflicting ideologies there are individuals among female athletes who are re-claiming ownership over their bodies and their right (including theologically) to the re-interpretation of the veil (hijab) in sport. Some veiled athletes are publicly voicing their aspiration to achieve their ambition to be top athletes while accommodating religious belief (Farooq and Sehlikoglu 2004).

There are also women who want to be present in male-dominated sports such as football. There is increasing interest among girls in practising football and in being part of the football experience as players, referees, coaches, and journalists. This is even true in so-called conservative countries such as Saudi Arabia (*Time Magazine* 10 August 2012). Female foot-ballers have to battle against social stereotypes, the lack of human and financial resources, and the quasi-absence of media coverage. Moreover, up until recently, female footballers in the Arab world were also restrained by FIFA's decision to ban the hijab shortly before the 2010 Youth Olympics in Singapore. The ban was finally lifted in 2014 after a series of negotia-tions and the influence of Arab football personalities such as the example of Prince Ali bin Al-Hussein, the FIFA Vice President from Asia (also a candidate for the FIFA presidential election in 2015).

The IOC is also taking a more inclusive policy toward the participation of veiled women athletes. As a result, the 2012 Olympic Games witnessed for the first time the participation of female athletes from Saudi Arabia and Qatar. To capitalize on this event, the Qatari, as part of their strategy to brand the country's readiness and inclusive strategy to host major sport competitions, organised an exhibition in the heart of London devoted to female sport in the Arab World. The exhibition, produced by the award-winning French photographer Brigitte Lacombe and her sister, independent documentary film-maker Marian Lacombe, included portraits and short films of veiled and non-veiled Arab athletes (*The Guardian* 27 July 2012). However, the question of the veil surfaced again during the 2014 Asian Games, when the Qatari women's basketball team decided to withdraw from competition after some players were refused permission to cover their hair. In response, the International Basketball Federation (FIBA) declared that 'while certain groups have interpreted the provisions of the official bas-ketball rules as a ban against the participation of players of certain faiths in basketball compe-titions, the uniform regulations are of a purely sporting nature' (BBC 24 September 2014). Subsequently, FIBA is introducing a testing phase for the next two years that will consist of:

> relaxing the current rules regarding headgear in order to enable national federations to request, as of now, exceptions to be applied at the national level within their territory without incurring any sanctions for violation of FIBA's Official Basketball Rules. National Federations wishing to apply for such an exception to the uniform regulations shall submit a detailed request to FIBA. Once approved, they shall submit follow-up reports twice a year to monitor the use of such exceptions.
>
> *(FIBA 16 September 2014)*

Conclusion

Sport is an integral part of the modern history of the Arab world. Sport, the product of colonial history, was integrated – to different degrees – into the struggle for independence and resistance against foreign occupation. This is also true today with regards to the recognition of Palestine. To this end, the qualification of Palestine to the 2015 Asian Cup of Nations in Australia is his-toric for a divided nation under occupation (*The Independent* 28 April 2015).

During post-independence, sport was a significant tool for the national state's formation and diplomacy. The participation of national teams or local clubs in regional or international com-petitions is considered as a showcase for the country to promote its development project and sense of unity. The victory of Iraq in the 2007 Asian Cup of Nations was an important moment for Iraqi people to celebrate their sense of togetherness as Sunni, Sh'ia, and Kurds, Muslims and Christians. This partly explains why states in the Arab World and elsewhere cannot ignore sport. Sport is an important matter, politically, ideologically, and of course economically. In addition to sponsorship and direct investment in top European football clubs (Manchester City, PSG), the other growing sector that symbolises the emergence of Qatar (and to a lesser extent

UAE and Bahrain) as new (contested) 'centres' in the global sporting arena, is sport TV broadcasting. The Qatari state-owned TV sport network, Aljazeera sport (now beIN Sport), has embarked on an aggressive strategy for the acquisition of TV rights of major football leagues and competitions. It is now broadcasting from almost all the worlds' continents. Arab nations, an example of which is Qatar, also want to have a share of the sport media space as well as equal opportunities to host international sport events. Of course more visibility comes with more international scrutiny and criticism, as with the case of labour rights of construction workers involved in the building of sports infrastructures, and the allegation of corruption surrounding Qatar's bid for the 2022 FIFA World Cup. The international spotlight can also be utilised internally for civic protest against Arab regimes' policies. As discussed in this chapter, sport is a space for social mobilisation, political contestation, and identity claims. For Arab youth (particularly male), sport, and football in particular, is a site for the expression of masculinity (or to reclaim manhood, which is being delayed because of unemployment and housing shortages) that manifests itself in football chanting, which is becoming a political tool of resistance against the state's control over political and moral legitimacies.

Last and least, the study of sport can offer useful insights into different political dynamics occurring in Arab societies. It can be used as a lens through which to undertake a historical analysis of nation-state formation. Sport is a useful context for the analysis of nationalism and ethnic identity in Arab countries; their expression (construction and deconstruction) in times of crisis, political transitions, and sporting victories. Sport can provide a valuable insight into the political analysis of power dynamics within Arab states, including rivalries over leadership in political, economic, and sporting domains, and between Arab states and other nations or international organisations: the GCC countries and Iran, former colonised and colonising nations, such as between Algeria and France; and engagement/disengagement of Arab countries with the Olympic movement. These are only examples of possible venues for further studies about the fascinating topic of sport and politics in the Arab World.

References

Amara, M. (2006) Soccer, post-colonial and post-conflict discourses in Algeria: Algérie-France, 6 Octobre 2001, 'ce n'était pas un simple match de foot', *International Review of Modern Sociology*, 32(2): 217–239.

Amara, M. (2011) Football: the new battlefield of business in Algeria, *The Journal of North African Studies*, 16(3): 343–360.

Amara, M. (2012) *Sport, Politics and Society in the Arab World*. London: Palgrave Macmillan.

Amara, M. (2013a) The political economy of sport broadcasting in the Arab world. In J. Scherer and D.D. Rowe (eds) *Sport, Public Broadcasting, and Cultural Citizenship*. London: Routledge, pp. 209–220.

Amara, M. (2013b) Sport, Islam, and Muslims in Europe: in between or on the margin? *Religions*, 4(4): 644–656.

Al-Arabiya.net (2014) World Cup fever beats politics in Lebanon. 19 June 2014. Accessed 1 October 2014. http://english.alarabiya.net/en/views/news/middle-east/2014/06/19/World-Cup-fever-beats-politics-in-Lebanon-.html.

Associated Press (2014) Ex-Syrian players form opposition team in exile. *Daily Mail* Online. 20 June 2014. Accessed 1 October 2014. www.dailymail.co.uk/wires/ap/article-2664046/Ex-Syrian-players-form-opposition-team-exile.html.

BBC.com (2014) Asian games: Qatar women's team pull out over hijab ban. 24 September 2014. Accessed 24 September 2014. www.bbc.co.uk/sport/0/basketball/29342986.

Dauncey, H. and Morrey, D. (2008) Quiet contradictions of celebrity Zinedine Zidane, image, sound, silence and fury, *International Journal of Cultural Studies*, 11(3): 301–320.

Dorsey, J.M. (2014) The 2022 World Cup: a potential monkey wrench for change, *The International Journal of the History of Sport*, 31(14): 1739–1754.

Farooq, S.S and Sehlikoglu, S. (2014) Strange, incompetent and out-of-place, *Feminist Media Studies*. Accessed 1 September 2014. www.tandfonline.com.

Fatès, Y. (1994) Sport et Tiers-Monde. Paris: Presses universitaires de France FIBA.com: PR N°56 – Key appointments headline first meeting of newly-elected Central Board, FIBA press release 16 September 2014. Accessed 5 October 2014. www.fiba.com/news/pr-n56—key-appointments-headline-first-meeting-of-newly-elected-central-board.

FIBA (2014) International Basketball Federation statement on rules of game. 16 September 2014.

Garcia, B. and Amara, M. (2013) Media perceptions of Arab investment in European football clubs: the case of Málaga and Paris Saint-Germain, *Sport & EU Review*, 5(1): 5–20.

Giulianotti, R. and Robertson, R. (2007) Recovering the social: globalization, football and transnationalism, *Global Networks*, 7(2): 166–186.

Jiwani, Y. (2008) Sports as a civilizing mission: Zinedine Zidane and the infamous head-butt, *TOPIA*, 19(Spring): 11–31.

Marzocchi, M. (2002). Gaddafi joins board of Juventus. *Scotsman Newspaper Online*. 29 October 2002. Accessed 24 February 2011. http://sport.scotsman.com/football/Gaddafi-joins-board-of-Juventus.2373398.jp.

Nassif, N. and Amara, M. (2015) Sport, policy and politics in Lebanon, *International Journal of Sport Policy and Politics* [online]. Accessed 27 January 2015. www.tandfonline.com/doi/full/10.1080/19406940.2014.914553#.

Raab, A. (2012) Soccer in the Middle East: an introduction, *Soccer & Society*, 13(5–6): 619–638.

Reiche, D. (2011) War minus the shooting? The politics of sport in Lebanon as a unique case in comparative politics, *Third World Quarterly*, 32(2): 261–277.

Reiche, D. (2014) Investing in sporting success as a domestic and foreign policy tool: the case of Qatar, *International Journal of Sport Policy and Politics* [online]. Accessed 20 December 2014. www.tandfonline.com/doi/full/10.1080/19406940.2014.966135#.

Rowe, D. (2010) Stages of the global: media, sport, racialization and the last temptation of Zinedine Zidane, *International Review for the Sociology of Sport*, 45(3): 355–371.

The Guardian (2012) Hey'Ya: Arab women in sport exhibition – in pictures. 27 July 2012. Accessed 30 July 2012. www.theguardian.com/lifeandstyle/gallery/2012/jul/27/hey-ya-arab-women-sport-exhibition-in-pictures.

The Guardian (2014) Once full of promise, Syrian football has been destroyed by civil war. 7 September 2014. Accessed 15 October 2014. www.theguardian.com/football/blog/2014/sep/07/syrian-football-civil-war.

The Independent (2015) Asian Cup 2015: Palestinians flying the flag for a nation of two halves. 28 April 2015. Accessed 28 April 2015. www.independent.co.uk/sport/football/international/asian-cup-2015-palestinians-flying-the-flag-for-a-nation-of-two-halves-9978829.html.

Time Magazine (2012) The secret life of a Saudi women's soccer team (short documentary). 10 August 2012. Accessed 20 August 2012. www.youtube.com/watch?v=5ZN-Fpw3j9I.

Tuastad, D. (2014a) From football riot to revolution: the political role of football in the Arab world, *Soccer & Society*, 15(3): 376–388.

Tuastad, D. (2014b) 'A threat to national unity': football in Jordan – ethnic divisive or a political tool for the regime? *The International Journal of the History of Sport*, 31(14): 1774–1788.

12

FOOTBALL AND IDENTITY POLITICS IN GHANA

Paul Darby

Introduction

It has become somewhat of a truism to say that football in Africa is political. During the early twentieth century, the game featured prominently in the wider political, cultural and economic agendas of various colonial powers as they sought to entrench their hegemonic position on the continent. Subsequently, the Africanisation of the game was accompanied by its use as a powerful medium for anti-colonial politics and dissent. In the post-colonial era, African clubs and national teams became bulwarks for the wider political ambitions of a succession of African leaders as they sought to root fledgling nation-states in the international arena and accrue the political capital that came from association with successful football teams. Since then the game has continued to function as a space where local, regional, national and international politics are quite literally *played* out (Onwumechili and Akindes 2014; Alegi 2010; Armstrong and Giulianotti 2004). In the current decade the extent to which football connects to and inter-twines with the political has been clearly visible and visceral. Nowhere has this been more apparent than in Egypt, where the game has become mired in post-revolution politics and deployed by oppositional factions to express their political views and conflicting identities. This has had damaging repercussions for football, with the Egyptian league being suspended on several occasions since 2011. Much more problematically, this has also led to significant loss of life inside Egyptian football stadia as was the case in Port Said in 2012 when 74 football fans died following rioting during a game between local club Al-Masry and their Cairo-based counterparts, Al-Ahly whose 'ultras' had been prominent in the protests which led to the overthrow of the former President, Hosni Mubarak (Dorsey 2015).

This chapter seeks to examine the multifarious ways in which football connects to and is shaped by broader political forces. Space does not permit a wide-ranging analysis that explores a range of examples. Thus, this chapter focuses on football's relationship with ethnic, regional, national and international politics in colonial and post-colonial Ghana. Ghana constitutes one of the clearest cases of the overt politicisation of the game on the African continent and while the nature of its politicisation and the drivers for this were specific to the Ghanaian context, broadly similar processes have been at play in the game's development elsewhere on the African continent (Fair 1997; Ndee 1996; Boer 2006; Hawkey 2009; Alegi 2010). This chapter begins by examining football's emerging political pedigree in colonial Gold Coast in the opening decades of the twentieth century and exploring the ways in which it became entwined in local ethno-regional chauvinisms in the 1940s and 1950s. Thereafter, the focus switches to the relationship between football and anti-colonial sentiment in the lead up to independence. The chapter moves towards its conclusion with a discussion on the mixed value of the game as a tool to overcome internal political division, build a unified sense of Ghanaianness and encourage buy-in to the broader notion of Pan-Africanism.

Football and ethno-regional politics in colonial Gold Coast

Football was transported to the Gold Coast in the late 1870s and was initially played around Cape Coast, the administrative capital at the time (Vasili 1998). The first club in the colony, Cape Coast Excelsior, emerged in 1903 from the playing fields of the Government Boys School and during the remainder of the decade other clubs, with names that revealed a British influence such as Everton Energetics, Sports Swallows and Bolton Wanderers, were founded (Goldblatt 2006). While British schoolmasters were important in the popularisation of the game in this period, Africans returning to the Gold Coast following educational sojourns in Britain were key in its promotion (Jenkins 1990). While they viewed football as an enjoyable pastime, in the context of their exclusion from the higher reaches of the colonial administration they also saw it as possessing counter-hegemonic potential. However, others, most notably many of the business and intellectual elite and influential Euro-African elders, felt that it was morally corrupting and interfered with the business of capital accumulation in what was a rapidly expanding trading metropolis (Quarcoopone 1993). While these attitudes highlighted that football was imbued with political meaning from its inception, they did little to stunt the growth and popularity of the game and organised clubs continued to emerge. The two most prominent, at least in the capital, were the Accra Invincibles, founded in 1910 and based in the Jamestown area and Accra Hearts of Oak, established a year later in neighbouring Ussher Town. A strong rivalry quickly developed between them and this was the first indication of the extent to which football in the Gold Coast could generate oppositional identities (Fridy and Brobbey 2009). It is likely that the relationship between these two clubs in this period reflected broader urban tensions between chiefs and residents from Jamestown and Ussher Town as they struggled to position themselves favourably, socially and politically, with the introduction of indirect rule in the Gold Coast colony (Parker 1995). Indeed, the emergence and rapid popularisation of the pugilistic sport of *asafo atwele* ('group fighting') among the urban poor around the time that these two clubs formed was partially rooted in the fact that it facilitated the expression of competing community and political identities between residents of both parts of the city (Akyeampong 2002).

Until the late 1920s, football activities remained centred along the coastal belt, particularly in Accra and Cape Coast. However, the establishment of clubs such as Sekondi Eleven Wise and Cape Coast Venomous Vipers in the early 1930s gave the game a much more geographically diverse complexion. The game's appeal had also begun to spread north and by the early 1930s, it was well entrenched in the Asante region. This was largely a consequence of the establishment of the Rainbow Football Club in Kumasi in 1924, who were subsequently renamed Ashanti United in 1926 before finally assuming the famous moniker Kumasi Asante Kotoko in 1935 (Kwateng 1985). The renaming of this club was not a mere cosmetic measure but rather reflected a broader political context in the region characterised by a revival of Ashanti pride and identity. Between 1896 and 1924, the British had held the Ashanti King Prempreh I and a number of other important chiefs in exile and had replaced them with other local rulers who helped to facilitate colonial interests. This process was initiated with British success in

Anglo-Ashanti wars in 1896 and 1901 and cemented with the formal annexation of Ashanti in 1902. In 1926, the year of Kotoko's first name change to one that more adequately captured regional pride (Ashanti United), Prempreh I was reinstalled as King, albeit of Kumasi rather than Ashanti. In 1935, Prempreh II was returned to the Golden Stool of Ashanti by the British, a move that was symbolically important for the Ashanti people (Allman 1993). The renaming of Ashanti United, Kumasi Asante Kotoko in the same year can clearly be located within this broader revival of Asante nationalism. Indeed, the club quickly came to be viewed as representative of the Asante 'nation', a fact evidenced by the naming of Asantehene Prempeh II as life patron in 1935 and the adoption of the porcupine (Kotoko), the symbol of the Asante army, as the team's nickname (Bediako 1995).

The close association of Kotoko with the Asante region and people prompted deep rivalries with some of its southern counterparts, particularly Accra Hearts of Oak, and highlighted the role of football in contributing to broader senses of regional distinctiveness and competition. These fissures were reflected in, and indeed reinforced through, the fragmented governance of the game in this period. By the early 1940s, there were a number of administrative units which oversaw the game in particular parts of the country. Richard Akwei, an Oxford-educated, Accra-based schoolmaster who became president of the Accra Football Association in 1943, grew increasingly concerned at a lack of unity and the transfer of wider regional tensions into the administration of the game. As a consequence, he began canvassing for the idea of a single governing body. Despite his best efforts, a serious split in his Accra Association led to the emergence of two bodies: the Gold Coast Football Union, based in Accra and led by Akwei and the Gold Coast and Ashanti Football Union, situated in Kumasi and controlled by John Darkwa, the first chairman of Asante Kotoko (Bediako 2010). The relationship between these associations was often characterised by the sort of posturing and attempts to assert primacy that were evident in the broader ethno-regional politicking between the Asante and those from other ethnic groups from the capital. This was particularly evident during the planning for the Gold Coast football tour of Britain in 1951.

This football tour to Britain was one of five during a ten-year period from 1949 by the colonies of Nigeria, the Gold Coast, Trinidad, Uganda and the Commonwealth region of the Caribbean. These tours were conceived by British diplomats as an opportunity to balance emerging nationalism in Africa and the Caribbean with a desire to ensure that any transition to self-rule would be managed in a manner that protected British economic interests (Vasili 2000). Of course, the tour also provided an opportunity for representatives of the Gold Coast to demonstrate their readiness for self-government. It might reasonably have been anticipated that Kwame Nkrumah's victory and the success of his Convention People's Party (CPP) in the Gold Coast's first general election in 1951 and his desire to see the 'nation' unite around his election platform of 'freedom' would help to focus the minds of indigenous football administrators and allow them to overcome regional self-interest. When the idea of a tour was first mooted, it did appear to have the potential to ameliorate regional fissures and at a meeting in Kumasi in 1949, the Accra- and Kumasi-based associations came together to form the United Gold Coast Amateur Football Association (UGCAFA) with Darkwa appointed chairman and Akwei the vice-chair. However, any hopes that this would bring about harmony in the governance of the game were short-lived and preparations quickly became mired in ethno-regional arguments with the UGCAFA and the Kumasi Football Clubs Union, a body linked to the Ashanti FA, engaging in bitter recrimination and counter-recrimination over the composition of the touring party.

The decision of UGCAFA in 1954 to discontinue the Guggisberg Shield, the primary colonial competition, seemed to indicate that the football authorities were at least capable of uniting around the shedding of British influence in the local game. However, football was unable to insulate itself from wider fragmentary currents. Despite the CPP's election success in 1951 and 1954, and what had become an inexorable march towards independence, Gold Coast politics became riven with sectional self-interest, militancy and political violence (Allman 1990). As had been the case in previous years, regional fissures filtered into football. This was particularly apparent in events surrounding an attempt to organise a national league in 1956. In a heady atmosphere of anti-colonial sentiment and anticipation of self-rule, it might have been expected that there would be unanimous support for the establishment of a league that would be completely controlled and run by Ghanaians. However, Richard Akwei's involvement in this initiative tempered enthusiasm for the league, especially amongst Asante-based clubs, because it led to a perception that the league would be organised and structured in a way that favoured teams from Accra and the south. This view resonated with broader Asante discontent at what was considered a wider accretion of power in the capital (Rathbone 2000). In light of this sort of resentment and in the context of fierce local political division, it was little surprise that Kotoko as well as four other Kumasi-based teams, Cornerstone, Great Ashanti, Kumasi Dynamos and Evergreens, decided to boycott the competition. When the UGCAFA suspended these clubs, they responded by persuading others to withdraw from the league, leaving the inaugural competition with only two teams, Accra Hearts of Oak and Sekondi Eleven Wise (Bediako 1995).

Football and the politics of anti-colonial dissent

In light of the previous discussion, it may appear somewhat incongruous that Nkrumah identified in football the raw material with which to help forge a unified national consciousness and build support for Pan-Africanism. The fractured organisation of football and the tendency for in-fighting between regional football bodies was anathema to his broader aspirations to rid Ghanaian political and social life of ethnic and regional divisions. Nonetheless, the broader politicisation of football across the continent resonated with Nkrumah and helped to convince him of the logic of using it to build popular support for his nationalist and Pan-African aspirations. Not only did he recognise that football had significant popular appeal in the Gold Coast, particularly amongst young, urban working-class men but Nkrumah also understood the fact that elsewhere on the continent the game had been gradually wrested from European control, had become Africanised and had come to represent an important vehicle for local self-expression and popular resistance against colonial rule. This process accelerated significantly in the post-war period and football became a focus for the articulation of anti-colonial sentiment and aspirations for independence (Ndee 1996; Fair 1997; Darby 2002; Boer 2006; Alegi 2010).

Given the popularity of football in colonial Gold Coast and Nkrumah's place at the vanguard of political opposition to British rule, the game slowly became entwined with populist mobilisation and the agitation for independence, and he sought to politicise football and sport more generally in an explicit fashion. This was clear from his response to a visit to Accra by the noted British Olympian, Lord Burghley, in the late 1940s, which he interpreted as a subtle attempt on the part of the colonial administration to use sports to engender bonds of Empire and divert the city's populace from their efforts to end colonial rule. His response, published in an editorial of an Accra-based newspaper, revealed that even at this time, he viewed sport as having considerable potential in contributing to Ghanaian nationhood:

> We like sports, but we want self-government first so that we can be masters not servants in our own country. When we get self-government, you will be amazed at what

we can put into the field at the next Olympic Games; and you will also be amazed at the stadiums that will glorify sporting activities in the new Ghana.

(James 1977: 118)

These sentiments suggest that Nkrumah would have viewed the emergence of pseudo 'national' football teams in the Gold Coast and opportunities to participate in international competition as symbolically important in the broader context of his 'self-government now' campaign. Thus, the organisation of football matches between representative teams from Accra and Nigeria in the late 1940s, the sanctioning of an inter-colonial competition between the Gold Coast and Nigeria for the Jalco Cup in 1951 and the inception of an annual match against Sierra Leone in 1953 provided opportunities to give vent to a fledgling sense of national identity. As independence neared, Nkrumah sought to position himself more closely to a cultural form that he recognised could capture and mobilise the youth movement in the Gold Coast's urban centres, build populist approval for the political agenda of his Convention People's Party and help solidify an embryonic nationalism. When it became clear that independence was imminent, Nkrumah assumed much more direct responsibility for the management of football and this allowed him to project his vision for the game as a vehicle for generating the sort of emotional and cultural bonds that he believed were necessary both for the creation of a harmonious Ghanaian state and building Pan-African unity.

Football, nation-building and Pan-Africanism

On Ghana's inauguration as an independent nation in March 1957, Nkrumah opined of a 'new African in the world . . . ready to fight his own battles and show that the black man is capable of managing his own affairs' (Mazrui and Tidy 1984: 40). Central to this 'new African' was the concept of Pan-Africanism, which for Nkrumah should function as the bedrock of liberation across the continent and the subsequent promotion of African interests on the world stage (Nkrumah 1963). If Ghana was to take the lead in this movement, he was acutely aware of the need to build unity at home. While football had become embroiled in regional political chauvinisms, on achieving independence the government quickly identified the game as invaluable in building a sense of *Ghanaianness* that they felt would transcend all divisions.

The placing of the game centre stage in the country's independence celebrations in the first half of 1957 was a clear sign of Nkrumah's intention to use it for nationalistic purposes. Aided by the Ministry of Education and Information, which also had responsibility for sport, he quickly set about forging a sound base for the game at both the international and domestic level. The Ghanaian Amateur Football Association (GAFA) was established in 1957 to replace the UGCAFA and, at a meeting in Accra in September, Richard Akwei was replaced by Ohene Djan as chairman. Djan would go on to become an instrumental figure in implementing Nkrumah's ambitious plans for football and his first step was to establish a new eight-team national league (Bediako 1995). In a move that revealed a shrewd understanding of the need to portray the GAFA as an organisation that had the 'national' interest to the forefront of its policymaking, the league was comprised of two teams from each of the four major municipalities of Accra, Kumasi, Sekondi and Cape Coast.

Beyond the local game, the GAFA played its part in registering Ghana's presence in the international community of sovereign nation-states by affiliating to the continental and world governing bodies for football, the Confédération Africaine de Football (CAF) and the Fédération Internationale de Football Association (FIFA) in 1957 and 1958 respectively. These affiliations not only cleared Ghana's path to participate on the international stage but also provided the platform for Nkrumah to use the newly formed national team to mobilise the youth of the country around a common identity and sense of pride. Nkrumah's government and the GAFA also aspired to have their national team function as a representative of the whole continent. In a move replete with Pan-African symbolism, the team adopted the moniker, the 'Black Stars', deliberately evoking the name of the shipping line established by Marcus Garvey, the Jamaican-born Pan-Africanist, that not only facilitated travel and trade between the Americas and Africa but also became a symbol of black pride (Hawkey 2009).

Whilst the naming of the national team in this way was hugely symbolic, it was the organisation of the 'Kwame Nkrumah' Gold Cup in 1960 that perhaps did most to exemplify the Ghanaian head of state's intention to use football to promote his Pan-African agenda. On the eve of the tournament featuring Ghana, Nigeria, Sierra Leone and Portuguese Guinea, Tommy Thompson, a correspondent for the Accra-based daily, the *Evening News*, gave voice to the underlying principle of the competition; 'With the coming of tomorrow our prospects of uniting Africa through soccer . . . gradually and steadily grow better' (*Evening News* 30 January 1960). The Chairman of the GAFA Supporters Union, Prince Yao Boateng echoed these sentiments by calling for local fans to put aside parochial loyalties and support 'all the visiting teams as brothers' (*Evening News* 29 January 1960). Following Ghana's 6–2 victory over Sierra Leone in the final of the tournament at Accra's Independence Stadium on 7 February 1960, Nkrumah again underscored his commitment to use football as part of his Pan-African aspirations: 'I selected and donated this cup not for its intrinsic value, but rather because it is symbolic of the sound foundation upon which we can build the unity of West Africa' (*Evening News* 8 February 1960).

While football was singled out for specific state support, given its wide popular appeal, Nkrumah was also convinced that sport more generally possessed great value in building bonds of fraternal brotherhood across West Africa. For example, two weeks after the final of the Gold Cup, Nkrumah sent a message of support to a meeting of the cricket associations of Ghana, Gambia and Sierra Leone which had been convened to discuss the possibility of establishing regular international cricket matches in the region. The tenor and substance of his comments made it clear that he saw other sports forms playing a role in his Pan-African project: 'I cannot imagine a better means of preparing the way for unity than by Africans from all parts of the continent joining hands in an atmosphere of brotherhood in the arena of sports' (*Evening News* 20 February 1960). Shortly afterwards, at the opening ceremony of the Kumasi Sports Stadium, Nkrumah provided his clearest policy statement on sport, making explicit his aspirations for sport:

> When, therefore, progress towards the attainment of African unity is made at the political and economic level, one can hope that interchange of sports and cultural activities will have made its influence felt in the creation of a healthy atmosphere for African unity and independence.
>
> *(Obeng 1979: 29–30)*

The national football team remained a focal point for the government's strategy of using sports to generate an 'atmosphere for African unity' and Nkrumah increasingly cast it in an ambassadorial role. For example, he personally sanctioned the participation of the Black Stars in exhibition games as part of both Kenya's and Zambia's independence celebrations and during General Joseph Désiré Mobutu's inauguration as President of the Congo in 1965. The GAFA also welcomed a number of prominent club and national teams from Europe and South America to Ghana to play friendly matches against local club teams, regional select sides and the Black Stars.

The Black Stars also played friendly fixtures in the Soviet Union, Germany, Austria, England, Italy and Spain between 1960 and 1962. For Nkrumah, these matches against European teams were more than mere football contests and he felt that Ghana's creditable performances were useful not only for instilling national confidence at home but also as a means of challenging prejudices about Africans in Europe (Versi 1986).

While these ventures were important, the biennial African Cup of Nations, inaugurated in 1957 by CAF, was to become a focal point for the state's support of football. Ghana acquired hosting rights for the 1963 tournament and conscious of the opportunities that this offered to showcase itself on the African and international stage, Nkrumah took a close interest in the Black Stars preparation and personally stressed to the players the importance of a favourable outcome for the host nation. Spurred on by their head of state's personal investment and interest in the tournament, Ghana secured their first continental crown, a victory that did much to engender a strong sense of patriotism amongst the Ghanaian populace and further wedded football to Ghanaian nationhood. As Versi observed in the aftermath of the tournament, 'their [the Ghanaian national team] picture, with the late Dr Kwame Nkrumah, first president of Ghana sitting in the middle, adorned almost every Ghanaian home' (ibid.: 75).

While Ghana's successes in inter-continental competition were most welcome, the government had loftier ambitions for the Black Stars and it increasingly recognised FIFA's World Cup competition as the platform towards which the national team should be aspiring. Indeed, in launching a three year 'soccer development plan' in 1960, Kojo Botsio, then chairman of the GAFA and Minister of Foreign Affairs declared 'we are determined to be world soccer champions one day' (*Evening News* 4 April 1960). In order to fulfil their aspirations, Ghana and other African national teams required access to the World Cup tournament. Up until this point though, FIFA was imbued with a deeply embedded Eurocentrism, evidenced not least in the allocation of places for the 16 team finals which were dominated by European nations (Darby 2000). Despite the rapid growth in FIFA's African constituency during the early 1960s, the continent did not have an automatic qualification berth at the competition. Instead, after winning the African qualifying tournament, the continent's best team was required to participate in a play-off game against the best Asian team in order to make it through to the finals. Under such circumstances, opportunities for African nations to play on the game's premier international stage and accrue the visibility and prestige that this would furnish were extremely limited.

In keeping with his cherished Pan-African principles, Nkrumah advocated a continent-wide response, which involved boycotting the qualifying rounds for the 1966 tournament. This idea quickly gained approval from CAF and at its executive committee meeting in Cairo in July 1964 a boycott was announced (CAF 21 August 1964). The Pan-African nature of the boycott vindicated Nkrumah's view that acting in unison, African nations were stronger politically. Indeed, their unity contributed significantly to FIFA's decision to grant the continent its own qualifying berth for the 1970 World Cup. Although qualifying from what was likely to be an intensely competitive African pool remained a stern challenge, Nkrumah's aspirations of seeing the Black Stars one day take their place on the game's most prestigious international stage had at least become more achievable. Were Ghana to qualify for the 1970 tournament, the capacity of Nkrumah to maximise the symbolic capital that would come with this was of course dependent on whether or not he would remain as Ghanaian head of state. To ensure this, he clearly had to seek ways to shore up his popularity on the one hand and tackle political fragmentation on the other. Nkrumah was clearly able to wring significant political value from football. However, as cracks in his personal and political persona widened during the 1960s, he was unable to control the extent to which opponents at home were able to draw on the game to support their own agendas.

Football, internal dissent and the politics of fragmentation

In the six years preceding independence, Nkrumah had successfully negotiated a path from self-government within a colonial framework to an independent Ghanaian state, one that was welcomed by the majority of the populace. Nonetheless, despite the euphoria that greeted freedom, the politics of fragmentation that had become particularly marked between 1954 and 1956 lingered just below the surface of the Ghanaian polity. The defeat of the NLM in the 1956 election may well have put an end to organised, coordinated opposition to Nkrumah but resentment remained amongst the Asante aristocracy and across the region more broadly (Birmingham 1998). In this context, Nkrumah and Ohene Djan would have been conscious of the fact that football had the potential to widen or at least reflect ethno-regional schisms and they sought to use the game within Ghana to supersede division. As noted earlier, measures were put in place to ensure that the domestic league would encourage a shared sense of Ghanaianness rather than parochial ethnic or regional loyalties. However, Nkrumah's most significant effort in this regard was his establishment of the Real Republikans Sporting Club in March 1961.

Real Republikans, based in Accra, covered a breadth of sports, including cricket, athletics, boxing, hockey, volleyball, and of course football, and its aims were in keeping with his broader policy of using sport to build internal unity and promote Pan-Africanism and 'the new spirit of the African man' (Quansah 1990: 36). Unsurprisingly, Nkrumah closely associated himself with the football wing. Indeed, as well as being dubbed the 'mother' club of Ghana, from the 1962/63 season onwards, Real Republikans became known as 'Osagyefo's Own Club' with the letters OOC emblazoned on their playing kit and tracksuits (Bediako 1995). In a move intended to encourage Ghanaian's from across the country to identify with Real Republikans, the club's recruitment strategy involved the government selecting two players from each side in the national league. The team were entered into the national championship initially only on a non-points scoring basis and many of the players who competed for them subsequently formed the nucleus of the Black Stars squads that lifted African Cup of Nations' crowns in 1963 and 1965.

The inception of Republikans then was rooted in a concern to help develop a cohesive, successful Black Stars squad and, hence, contribute to the national interest and a unitary vision that *all* Ghanaians might buy into. Ultimately though, the extent to which the populace would consume this vision was always going to be determined by the popularity of Nkrumah and the success or otherwise of his programme for government. Despite considerable early progress, opponents grew vocal at the emergence of a 'cult of personality' that began to evolve around Nkrumah. Others complained about corruption and cronyism at the highest political levels. The establishment of the Republic in 1960 which gave Nkrumah the power to rule by decree and his relentless pursuit of critics and opponents through the Preventive Detention Act introduced in 1958, raised concerns about the general slippage towards an authoritarian approach. A sharp dip in the world price for cocoa in 1961 brought economic difficulty and the imposition of high levels of taxation by the government engendered much resentment. Those who organised widespread strikes against the resultant decline in living standards were swiftly imprisoned, further revealing growing authoritarian inclinations (Meredith 2005). While Nkrumah argued that all of this was necessary in the interests of the Republic (Nkrumah 1963), there was no shortage of public, political dissent, particularly in Asante, the traditional heartland of anti-Nkrumahism.

Despite his intentions for Real Republikans to function as a symbol of unity, its strategy for recruiting players increasingly featured in the broader groundswell of criticism that precipitated the end of Nkrumah's presidency in 1966. While it is difficult to determine with certainty whether the bitter disputes that followed the Republikans played a direct role in Nkrumah's downfall, it is clear that his use of football had unanticipated, contradictory political implications that proved counter-productive to his vision for Ghana and his capacity to hold on to power. Within one year of the establishment of Republikans, those clubs that lost their key players as part of the government controlled selection process began to speak out, arguing that the whole concept was illustrative of Nkrumah's broader centrist, autocratic tendencies (Darby 2013). It was no surprise that Asante Kotoko were amongst the most vociferous critics of the Republikans' approach to player recruitment and, indeed, the CPP's control of football more generally. As noted earlier, Kotoko had long functioned as the club of the Asante 'nation' and had come to be considered as representative of the interests of the Asante people in independent Ghana. This growing politicisation of Kotoko was augmented by the fact that Dr J. B. Danquah, who helped establish and lead the NLM and who remained a vocal critic of the government, was closely aligned with the club in the period immediately prior to and following independence (Fridy and Brobbey 2009).

In this context, the relationship between the state-controlled GAFA and Kotoko was often prickly but with the establishment of the Republikans, Kotoko's relationship with the GAFA rapidly deteriorated. A recruitment strategy that effectively forced the Kumasi giants to transfer its two best players each season to its closest rival was viewed not only as a threat to their football pedigree but also as a challenge to the place of the Asante people in the emerging nation-state. Thus, just prior to the commencement of the 1962 season, Kotoko threatened to boycott the national league in protest. The GAFA responded by suspending Kotoko from playing home fixtures for the first half of the season, a move that further reinforced a perception that the game had become an adjunct to Nkrumah's authoritarianism. Tensions persisted for the remainder of Nkrumah's reign, largely because Kotoko officials perceived the GAFA and Djan's Central Organisation of Sports to be acting in the interests of Republikans and seeking to blunt the sporting threat posed by their Kumasi rivals and, hence, the extent to which the team could serve as a rallying point for the Asante people (Darby 2013).

The fractious relationship between the country's two biggest clubs clearly undermined Nkrumah's desire to see domestic football contribute to his unitary vision. As noted earlier, he was more successful in employing the national team for this end and in promoting his Pan-African agenda. He viewed the African Cup of Nations as a particularly invaluable vehicle for developing cross-continent sporting exchanges that would contribute to the Pan-African project and he soon looked to the potential that the club game offered in this regard. In 1963, Nkrumah was proactive in discussions around the possibility of establishing a continent-wide competition between Africa's most prominent club teams. This aim was realised at CAF's sixth annual congress in Accra in November 1963 and at a reception for the CAF delegates at Flagstaff House, the official presidential residence, Nkrumah presented General Abdel Mustapha, president of CAF, with a 205-guinea trophy for the first edition of the African Cup of Champions Clubs, the final of which was to be staged in Accra in 1964 (*Ghanaian Times* 25 November 1963). In outlining the rationale for involving himself in this venture, Nkrumah again spelt out in explicit terms his views around the relationship between football and the broader Pan-African agenda:

> It is encouraging to note that with progress towards the attainment of African unity at the political and economic levels, the interchange of sports and cultural activities is making its influence felt in the creation of a healthy atmosphere for African unity and total independence. It is for this reason that I, as a citizen of Africa, have donated the

Osagyefo trophy for the annual African clubs' championship to help consolidate the foundation of a continental movement to bring all Africa together in the field of sports.

(Versi 1986)

For the remainder of his presidency, Nkrumah's commitment to his cherished Pan-African philosophies and his belief in the power of sport to contribute to their fruition continued to manifest itself in Ghana's sporting life. It was no coincidence that the second match in a two-game series against Congo Brazzaville in Accra in October 1965 was timed to coincide with a summit of the Organisation of African Unity (OAU) in the city, thus allowing most African heads of state to attend the game (*Ghanaian Times* 24 October 1965). Locally, Nkrumah's CPP continued to invest significantly in both 'constructive mass participation' and high performance across a range of sports. The latter approach brought Ghana further success in the international arena, as evidenced in the Black Stars retention of its African Cup of Nations crown in 1965. The response to this victory appeared to indicate that Nkrumah's political ambitions for football were still being realised. For example, shortly after the tournament, Kwaw Ampah, National Secretary of the Trades Union Congress (TUC) used the *Ghanaian Times* to argue that the Black Stars had helped challenge lingering prejudice against Africans around the world and in so doing had gone some way to 'expunge the contempt that history had poured on the African' (*Ghanaian Times* 30 November 1965).

Despite investment in grassroots sport, the continued success of the Black Stars and the rousing nationalist rhetoric that accompanied their feats, by the close of 1965 Nkrumah's popularity was at its lowest ebb. A number of major economic misjudgements and wasteful-ness, a 60 per cent drop in the global price in cocoa, dwindling support for African unity across the continent and a rapid decline into outright authoritarian rule, precipitated by the establishment of a one-party system in 1964, combined to generate unprecedented levels of public dissatisfaction and political opposition (Meredith 2005; Agbodeka 1992). This disaf-fection had seeped into football in ways that reflected long-standing divisions in the country. It is distinctly possible that this contributed to the president's diminishing reputation at the level of civic society in Ghana. Ultimately however, it was other forces that heralded his unseemly demise. On 24 February 1966, just a matter of months following the Black Stars successful defence of its African title, and with Nkrumah out of the country on a state visit to North Vietnam and China, power was seized by the Ghanaian military and police, led by Lieutenant General Joseph A. Ankrah. Thus, Nkrumah's reign was brought to an abrupt end and with it, his employment of football in processes of nation-building and the promotion of Pan-Africanism.

Conclusion

This chapter is informed by Bea Vidacs's assertion that 'studying sports can yield important insights about non-sporting aspects of African societies' (Vidacs 2006: 337). While the analy-ses here have centred on Ghana, the broad thrust of the chapter, that football is intimately connected to local, regional and national politics, is as applicable to South Africa, Angola, Nigeria and many other states in sub-Saharan Africa as it is to Ghana. The significance of football clearly extended beyond the purely sporting and its growth and development reveals much about politics in colonial Gold Coast and post-colonial Ghana. By the late colonial period, the game had become an important social, cultural and political resource that the colonial administration, local politicians, nationalists, chiefs, the Asante royalty and the urban populace had drawn on for various and at times conflicting political ends. As this chapter

reveals, Kwame Nkrumah was the key protagonist in imbuing the game with deeply politicised meaning.

This is not to say that the politicisation of football in support of the fledgling Ghanaian state
was without risk or was an uncontested process. As was the case elsewhere in the world, sport in
Ghana was capable of arousing powerful, contradictory emotions that not only had the capacity
to connect individuals to large-scale entities such as the nation but also allowed them to give
vent to much more localised expressions of identity. Thus, during the 1960s football became
implicated in the broader tensions between an authoritarian, unitary vision for Ghana and an
assertive federalist political discourse. Nkrumah may well have been misguided and perhaps
arrogant to presume that he could completely control and channel the powerful emotions that
football is capable of unleashing. His deployment of the game in the process of nation-building
and shoring up his own political position ultimately proved to be counter-productive because it
came to be viewed by opponents as a further illustration of his autocratic, centrist inclinations,
and it was this perception that ultimately led to his downfall.

The capacity of football to generate unpredictable emotional attachments and counter-
hegemonic currents was writ large through Nkrumah's experiences with the game. Despite
this those political and military opponents who eventually succeeded him continued to seek
to avail of the political capital that this most pervasive and popular cultural form offered. On
assuming power following the coup d'etat, General Ankrah's military government recognised that it could not be seen to be supporting acolytes of or institutions heavily backed by
Nkrumah. Thus, some of Nkrumah's highest profile football-related initiatives were quickly
reversed by the new regime. However, a year after he came to power, General Ankrah closely
associated himself with Asante Kotoko's success in reaching the final of the African Cup of
Champions Clubs in 1967 in order to shore up popular support for the military government (Bediako 2010). His successor, Lieutenant General Akwasi Amankwa Afrifa, did likewise
and was pictured on a number of occasions being introduced to Black Stars players prior to
international fixtures (Kwateng 1985). Dr Kofi Busia, the long-standing anti-Nkrumahist and
Ghanaian Prime Minister between 1969 and 1972 followed suit, hosting the Black Stars and
a GAFA delegation at Osu Castle, the official seat of government, in January 1970 and welcoming the Kotoko squad to the same venue following their victory in the African Cup of
Champions Clubs a year later (Bediako 2010).

Since then, virtually every Ghanaian head of state, democratically elected or otherwise and
regardless of their political hue, has recognised the political utility of football. This was exemplified as recently as February 2012 when in his State of the Nation Address to the Ghanaian
parliament, former president, John Atta Mills, reserved part of his speech to laud the Black
Stars for their performances at the African Cup of Nations in Gabon and Equatorial Guinea,
suggesting that this was linked to the broader governmental programme of 'building a better
Ghana' (Ghana Soccer Net 26 March 2012). The fact that the relationship between football
and Ghana's polity remains close at the national, regional and local level is clearly a legacy of
the Nkrumah era and those holding or aspiring to hold high political office continue to view
it as part of a broader armoury to win hearts and minds and curry political favour.

References

Agbodeka, F. (1992) *An Economic History of Ghana*. Accra: Ghana Universities Press.
Akyeampong, E. (2002) Bukom and the social history of boxing in Accra: warfare and citizenship in pre-
colonial Ga society. *The International Journal of African Historical Studies*, 35(1): 39–60.
Alegi, P. (2010) *African Soccerscapes: How a Continent Changed the World's Game*. London: C. Hurst and
Co Publishers Ltd.

Allman, J. M. (1990) The youngmen and the porcupine: class, nationalism and Asante's struggle for self-determination, 1954–57. *Journal of African History*, 31(2): 263–279.

Allman, J. M. (1993) *The Quills of the Porcupine: Asante Nationalism in an Emergent Ghana*. Madison, WI: University of Wisconsin Press.

Armstrong, G. and Giulianotti, R. (2004) *Football in Africa Conflict, Conciliation and Community*. London: Palgrave Macmillan.

Bediako, K. (1995) *The National Soccer League of Ghana: The Full Story, 1956–1995*. Accra: Self published.

Bediako, K. (2010) *Black Stars: The Long Road to Greatness*. Tema: Self published.

Birmingham, D. (1998) *Kwame Nkrumah: The Father of African Nationalism*. Athens, OH: Ohio University Press.

Boer, W. (2006) Football, mobilisation and protest: Nmandi Azikiwe and the goodwill tours of World War II. *Lagos Historical Review*, 6: 39–61.

CAF. (1964) *Circular Letter to FIFA From the CAF Executive Committee*, 21 August 1964.

Darby, P. (2000) Colonial doctrine and indigenous resistance: mapping the political persona of FIFA's African constituency. *Culture, Sport, Society*, 3(1): 61–87.

Darby, P. (2002) *Africa, Football and FIFA: Politics, Colonialism and Resistance*. London and Portland, OR: Frank Cass.

Darby, P. (2013) 'Let us rally around the flag': football, nation-building and pan-Africanism in Kwame Nkrumah's Ghana. *Journal of African History*, 54(2): 221–246.

Dorsey, J. M. (2015) *The Turbulent World of Middle East Soccer*. London: C Hurst & Co Publishers Ltd.

Evening News (1960) 29 January.

Evening News (1960) 30 January.

Evening News (1960) 8 February.

Evening News (1960) 20 February.

Evening News (1960) 4 April.

Fair, L. (1997) Kickin' it: leisure, politics and football in colonial Zanzibar, 1900s–1950s. *Africa*, 67(2): 224–251.

Fridy, K. S. and Brobbey, V. (2009) Win the match and vote for me: the politicisation of Ghana's Accra Hearts of Oak and Kumasi Asante Kotoko Football Clubs. *Journal of Modern African Studies*, 47(1): 19–39.

Ghanaian Times (1963) 25 November.

Ghanaian Times (1965) 24 October.

Ghanaian Times (1965) 30 November.

Ghana Soccer Net. (2012) 'Ghana President Atta Mills congratulates the Black Stars'. Accessed 26 March 2012 www.ghanasoccernet.com/ghana-president-atta-mills-congratulates-black-stars/.

Goldblatt, D. (2006) *The Ball is Round: A Global History of Football*. London: Penguin Books.

Hawkey, I. (2009) *Feet of the Chameleon: The Story of African Football*. London: Portico.

James, C. L. R. (1977) *Nkrumah and the Ghana Revolution*. London: Lawrence Hill and Co.

Jenkins, R. (1990) Salvation for the fittest? A West African sportsman in Britain in the age of the new imperialism. *International Journal of the History of Sport*, 7(1): 23–60.

Kwateng, W. (1985) *Asante Kotoko Football Club: Golden Jubilee, 1935–1985*. Kumasi: Self published.

Mazrui, A. and Tidy, M. (1984) *Nationalism and New States in Africa*. Nairobi: Heinneman.

Meredith, M. (2005) *The State of Africa: A History of Fifty Years of Independence*. London: Simon and Schuster.

Ndee, H. (1996) Sport, culture and society from an African perspective: a study in historical revisionism. *International Journal of the History of Sport*, 13(2): 192–201.

Nkrumah, K. (1963) *Africa Must Unite*. London: Panaf Books.

Obeng, S. (1979) *Selected Speeches of Kwame Nkrumah, Vol. 1*. Accra: Afram Publishers.

Onwumechili, C. and Akindes, G. (2014) *Identity and Nation in African Football Fans, Community and Clubs*. London: Palgrave Macmillan.

Parker, J. (1995) Ga state and society in early colonial Accra, 1860s–1920s. Unpublished PhD thesis, University of London.

Quansah, E. (1990) The fall of a soccer empire. *West Africa: Special Edition* (March): 36–38.

Quarcoopone, S. S. (1993) A history of urban development of Accra, 1877–1957. *Research Review*, 9(1–2): 20–32.

Rathbone, R. (2000) Kwame Nkrumah and the Chiefs: the fate of 'natural rulers' under nationalist governments. *Transactions of the Royal Historical Society*, 10: 45–63.

Vasili, P. (1998) *The First Black Footballer, Arthur Wharton 1865–1930: An Absence of Memory*. London and Portland, OR: Routledge.

Vasili, P. (2000) *Colouring Over the White Line: The History of Black Footballers in Britain*. Edinburgh: Mainstream Publishing.

Versi, A. (1986) *Football in Africa*. London: Collins.

Vidacs, B. (2006) Through the prism of sports: why should Africanists study sport? *Afrika Spectrum*, 41(3): 331–349.

13

SPORT AND POLITICS IN THE UNITED STATES

Michael Butterworth

In the months preceding the 2014 Winter Olympic Games in Sochi, Russia, voices from opposite ends of the political spectrum in the United States called for a boycott. Some conservative leaders, such as South Carolina Senator Lindsey Graham, were angered that Russian officials allowed National Security Administration (NSA) whistle-blower Edward Snowden safe harbor within the country. A boycott, he contended, "would just send the Russians the most unequivocal signal" that protecting Snowden was "a slap in the face to the United States" (Harris 2013). Meanwhile, some liberals, especially advocates for lesbian, gay, bisexual, and transgender (LGBT) rights, objected to homophobic violence and Russian laws that appeared to sanction discrimination (Smith-Spark 2013). Ultimately, the prevailing wisdom suggested that a boycott would only hurt the wrong people, as Katrina vanden Heuvel put it, "the athletes who have spent lifetimes training for this event" (vanden Heuvel 2013). Moreover, competing in the Games was understood as an opportunity to make a counter-statement. In the words of President Barack Obama:

> One of the things I'm really looking forward to is maybe some gay and lesbian athletes bringing home the gold or silver or bronze, which would, I think, go a long way in rejecting the kind of attitudes that we're seeing there.
>
> *(Smith-Spark 2013)*

Although a boycott did not materialize, the suggestion of one nevertheless mandates a consideration of the ways sport and politics intersect. The very context of an international sporting event is entangled in various geopolitical conflicts, in this case made more salient by the national security questions raised by Snowden's actions. Additionally, the issue of how a nation cares for its citizens of diverse backgrounds provides a political norm against which Russia's homophobia may be evaluated. Each of these concerns reminds us that the presumed separation between sport and politics is an illusion. Indeed, sport is political and politics, too often, is sport.

The mythology that hails a division between sport and politics is nearly as universal as the games and governments themselves. However, in light of the notorious individualism of American society and its citizens' embrace of "American exceptionalism," it is felt in particularly acute ways in the United States. In particular, Americans have long embraced the idea that sport provides an "escape" from political and social troubles, even as they celebrate their nation's athletic accomplishments as evidence of superior character. Participation in the early iterations of the modern Olympics, for example, gave rise to triumphant narratives about the "New World" and the American "melting pot." As S.W. Pope (1997) details, after the 1900 Games in Paris:

> President Theodore Roosevelt exploited the occasion to pay homage to the virtues of the frontier, westward expansion, and America's policy of manifest destiny. In a world alive with social Darwinism, displays of material and natural abundance became an outward sign of inner strength and a high level of culture.
>
> *(p. 42)*

Although few today would embrace the language of social Darwinism, contemporary American observers still routinely see the Olympic Games as a showcase for the virtues of the United States.

The Olympic Games provide an appropriate context for introducing a chapter about sport and politics in the United States. Of course, even a cursory review of American sporting culture reveals that they are far from alone. Baseball, the so-called "national pastime," has bolstered American foreign policy aims since its inception (Butterworth 2010a; Elias 2010); American football has long been a vehicle for "American distinction, power, and nationalism" (Gems 2000: 20); basketball has promoted players such as Michael Jordan as symbols of the nation's ability to welcome people of all backgrounds to the spoils of capitalist competition (Andrews 1998); other international events, such as golf's Ryder Cup or tennis's Davis Cup and Federation Cup, provide a platform for patriotic declarations (or laments). Even when the United States is not dominant in a sport, such as the globally celebrated soccer, American mythology provides an exceptionalist rationale to explain the apparent inferiority:

> In short, all major American professional sports that defined the dominant sports culture in the United States in the course of the twentieth century exhibited a much more unimpeded capitalist style and ethic than their European counterparts, particularly in the world of soccer.
>
> *(Markovits and Hellerman 2001: 45)*

In more blunt terms, former U.S. Senator Jack Kemp once declared, "[American] football is democratic, capitalism, whereas soccer is a European socialist [sport]" (Foer 2004: 241).

Discourses of nationalism provide a meaningful context for understanding the relationship between sport and politics in the United States, yet other contexts also warrant our attention. In this chapter, I outline four dimensions of this relationship: (1) the development of sport as political language, and the efforts of American politicians to exploit sport; (2) the use of sport as a means for fostering community identifications, including efforts to center economic development in and around sporting contexts; (3) the promotion of patriotism, nationalism, and militarism through sport, including the use of sport to valorize American exceptionalism and legitimate war; (4) the use of sport within the United States as an expression of political identity and activism.

The language of sport and politics

In the summer of 2012, the Washington DC insider publication, *The Hill*, offered an analysis of the presidential election between incumbent Barack Obama and challenger Mitt Romney grounded in the language of sport. Although the column, premised on hypothetical political scenarios that may or may not have been realistic, included military metaphors to describe the campaign – "uncertainties of the battlefield," for example – it was heavy on references to events that could be a "game changer." In case the metaphor was not clear enough, the column even quoted one Republican strategist who directly invoked boxing: "A large gaffe in a debate by either team could make a difference," said Ron Bonjean; "The debates are going to be widely-watched prize fights" (Bolton 2012). Such references are common in U.S. politics, especially during high-profile campaigns. The specific phrase, "game change," was used often enough to provide a suitable title for John Heilemann's and Mark Halperin's book about the 2008 election, *Game Change: Obama and the Clintons, McCain and Palin, and the Race of a Lifetime* (2010).

The use of sport metaphor in U.S. politics was hardly new to the 2008 presidential election. Indeed, political cartoons depicted presidential candidates as boxers in the ring as early as 1836, and the portrayal of campaigns as horse races was the dominant frame for political journalism throughout the twentieth century. In a longitudinal study of *New York Times* coverage of presidential elections from 1952 to 2000, for example, horse-race coverage occupied more print space (40 percent) than any other topic (Benoit *et al.* 2005). Scholars worry that the competitive focus of the horse race conditions voters to be passive observers rather than active democratic citizens. As Kathleen Hall Jamieson (1992) writes, "so enmeshed is the vocabulary of horse race and war in our thoughts about politics that we are not conscious that the 'race' is a metaphor and 'spectatorship' an inappropriate role for the electorate" (p. 165). Even as some scholars have identified a potential decline in the horse race emphasis (Jarvis and Han 2011), it nevertheless remains a dominant focus of political discourse in the United States.

Perhaps the ubiquity of the horse race metaphor owes something to the currency of sport more broadly. As I will discuss in the next section, sport is an institution with a potential to constitute community and bridge differences, so it is of little surprise that an often divisive arena such as politics might benefit from a site of such identification. To this end, politicians in the United States frequently seek to appeal to audiences by demonstrating their affinity for sport. As Watterson (2006) describes it, with respect to the presidency, "Sporting interests help to define the presidents, and they use sports to connect with the electorate" (p. 3). Theodore Roosevelt embodied the rugged individualist; John F. Kennedy tossed the football on the beach; and Ronald Reagan hailed his days as a radio broadcaster for minor league baseball.

Specific rituals have connected politics, especially the presidency, with sport. For example, Jimmy Carter began the tradition of inviting championship teams to the White House, a ritual Hester (2005) terms the "presidential sports encomia." The *encomium* is a classical rhetorical genre in which speakers offer praise as a means to affirm the shared values of a community. Values such as dedication, perseverance, and teamwork are all assigned to championship teams, with whom the president becomes symbolically linked. Much the same can be said of another familiar ritual, the ceremonial first pitch in baseball. William Howard Taft was the first president to "throw out" a pitch at a Washington Senators game in 1910. More than a century later, every president but Carter has thrown out at least one pitch. As historian Harold Seymour (1989) contends, the first pitch is a ritual that "gives the appearance of conferring upon [baseball] the presidential stamp of approval" (p. 63).

Arguably, no U.S. president has better performed these rituals and capitalized on the public's passion for sport than George W. Bush. Prior to his election as the governor of Texas in 1994, Bush achieved his greatest professional success as the Managing General Partner of Major League Baseball's (MLB) Texas Rangers. Many have noted that his experience with the Rangers helped his political career. As Trujillo (2000) suggests, "it is obvious that [his ownership] helped him to become a viable (and successful) candidate for governor of Texas and a viable nominee for president of the United States" (p. 315). Bush's recognition of baseball's symbolism was on full display in the immediate aftermath of the 9/11 terrorist attacks in 2001. At Game Three of the World Series, played in New York's famed Yankee Stadium, the president performed the ceremonial first pitch ritual at a time of intense anxiety and uncertainty. Even the president's critics largely conceded that his appearance – and perfect aim – demonstrated strength and resolve at a time when the nation needed it most.

As Markovits and Rensmann (2010) observe, "The central role that sports play in the lives of most American male politicians is significant" (p. 10), therefore reminding us that the intersection of politics and sport occurs largely in masculine terms. In addition to this gendered bias, politicians' references to sport are not without other risks. In their efforts to foster identification with the public, candidates may actually damage their credibility if they appear not to understand the sporting context. When Senator John Kerry, a Democrat from Massachusetts, challenged George W. Bush for the presidency in 2004, for example, he was asked to name his favorite player from his home town baseball team, the Boston Red Sox. He responded with "Manny Ortez," a hybrid of two of Boston's best players, Manny Ramirez and David Ortiz. Although he later made efforts to demonstrate his real knowledge of baseball, "The damage had been done" (Fleer 2007: 55), and Kerry never earned the kind of sporting credibility granted to Bush. Eight years later, Republican nominee Mitt Romney faced a similar dilemma. Much like his Democratic counterpart, Kerry, Romney had a reputation for being an elitist who was out of touch with average American citizens. One attempt from Romney to connect with voters was an appearance at auto racing's premier event – NASCAR's Daytona 500. Asked by a reporter if he followed stock car racing, he replied, "Not as closely as some of the most ardent fans. But I have some great friends that are NASCAR team owners" (Rucker 2012). By identifying with wealthy owners instead of (also wealthy) drivers or, more effectively, fans, Romney confirmed for many their suspicions that he was out of touch.

Sport and community

Among the virtues of sport is its capacity to develop a sense of community. As O'Rourke (2003) writes:

> In this country, professional sports represent something more than political or economic games between wealthy and powerful team owners. Professional and amateur sports are part of our collective culture and represent one of the symbolic threads that can either bring communities together or tear them asunder.
>
> *(p. 64)*

O'Rourke's conclusion stems from his study of fans of the National Football League's (NFL) Cleveland Browns, who were dismayed to learn in 1995 that the franchise would be moved to Baltimore. For decades, the Browns had served as a metaphor for a city that celebrated its identity as a multicultural, industrial center. The potential loss of the team, therefore, represented a threat to the community's identity. In an unusual circumstance, community outrage led NFL officials to grant Cleveland an expansion franchise. Although the new Cleveland Browns, who began play in 1999, have had little success, their presence nevertheless unifies segments of the community who otherwise might have little connection to one another.

The example of the Cleveland community reminds us that sport's symbolic significance can have material consequences. The unity felt among otherwise disconnected individuals is important, yet it is also fragile. Uszynski (2014) demonstrates that this collective identity is rooted in a series of sporting disappointments that has come to symbolize the decline of the city's status more broadly. As he writes:

> Cleveland fans are marked by professional sport team losses that have mythological proportions within the greater sports community, with defeats by each of the three main teams – the NFL Browns, the MLB Indians, and the NBA Cavaliers – at moments when each were on the brink of championships.
>
> *(p. 3)*

These historic defeats provide a context for a particularly acute crisis for the Cleveland community: the 2010 departure of National Basketball Association (NBA) superstar LeBron James. A savior-turned-traitor, James's decision to sign with another franchise exposed the social fissures among Clevelanders. More specifically, it raised questions in general about the role of sport in any major city and in particular about race – James is African American, and Cleveland's claim to multiculturalism is based on the diversity represented by generations of (mostly White) immigrants from Europe – as well as the economic impact of a highly successful athlete or team. Indeed, this narrative came full circle in 2014, as James returned to Cleveland, prompting a series of articles speculating on the millions of dollars he would generate for the city (Gregory 2014).

The experience of another city in the United States spotlights the political complexities revealed by sport. After New Orleans and much of the Gulf of Mexico Coast was devastated by Hurricane Katrina in 2005, many found hope in the NFL's New Orleans Saints as a symbol of community revival. When the Saints qualified for their first Super Bowl appearance in January 2010, Louisiana native and political consultant James Carville remarked that "the team has become a symbol for not only what can be but what is. New Orleans is moving. She's recovering" (Carville 2010). Thus, in the wake of a natural disaster understood by many as a commentary on the failures of President George W. Bush's leadership, Carville offered sport as a metaphor for the recovery of the city.

The Saints-as-hope narrative actually found its origins in the very first game played in New Orleans after the tragedy. The most visible site for the anguish of those displaced by the storm was the Superdome, the massive indoor facility that is home to the Saints, which has hosted several Super Bowls. Along with New Orleans' famed French Quarter tourist district, the Superdome was among the first locations in the city to be refurbished, and the Saints played on *Monday Night Football* just over a year after the horrors of Katrina. Grano and Zagacki (2011) interpret the reopening of the Superdome as a kind of spiritual revival, one that energized portions of the community but, more importantly, did so by failing to attend to the paradox of playing football before a mostly White audience in the very location where the majority of those seeking refuge from the hurricane were African American. Restoring one of New Orleans' most iconic structures might have been an opportunity to push beyond the Saints-as-metaphor and toward more material changes that addressed the city's economic inequities. Instead, the re-opening of the Superdome constituted a "paradox of purity," a purification ritual that concealed:

> assumptions about the transcendent, "pure" position of White over Not White, limiting critical self-reflexivity about white status and maintaining the invisibility of categorically "lower class" (nonwhite) terms and positions.
>
> *(Grano and Zagacki 2011: 219)*

In subsequent years, national sports media have pointed to the revival of the Superdome and tourism in New Orleans as signs of recovery, all too often without acknowledging the substantial devastation that remains. In a rare exception, Wright Thompson (2015) reflects on the tenth anniversary of Katrina and acknowledges the work yet to be done in a wide-ranging, long-form piece, "Beyond the Breach." There are no simple narratives he insists, for "The hurricane lives in a complicated place. Everyone's experience is both communal and personal, obvious and hidden." As is evidenced by both his essay and the critiques leveled by Grano and Zagacki, however, the role of sport in post-Katrina New Orleans demonstrates that its capacity to unify a community may reinforce socio-political divisions just as much as it fosters identifications.

The focus on a downtown arena like the Superdome points also to the politics of stadium development and construction. In a city like Detroit, for example, politicians and entrepreneurs began as early as the late 1960s thinking of stadium development projects as catalysts for urban renewal. A riverfront dome project that would have housed both the MLB Tigers and NFL Lions failed (Betzold and Casey 1992), but downtown facilities eventually opened for both franchises, in 2000 and 2002, respectively. In 2014, the National Hockey League's (NHL) Red Wings finalized a deal to build a new arena to debut in 2017 (Shea 2014). All of these projects take place in the context of a city experiencing a well-documented economic and political decline, and much of the support for stadium development rests on the idea that it can jump-start a revival. In spite of such claims, a substantial body of research concludes that any economic benefit to the larger community is minimal (Bennett 2012; DeMause and Cagan 2008; Trumpbour 2006). In the words of Friedman *et al.* (2004):

> Beneath the rhetorical veneer of improving the welfare of low-income urban residents through income derived from increased tax revenue . . . the true beneficiaries of this use of increasingly scarce government resources have been the upper and middle classes.
>
> *(p. 131)*

Although the stadium boom of the 1990s and early 2000s has somewhat abated, the development of $1 billion-plus projects in markets such as New York and Atlanta brings into sharp relief the politics of class struggle facilitated by the economics of sport.

Patriotism, nationalism, militarism

The preceding section limits our understanding of community to local contexts; however, given Anderson's (1991) oft-cited definition of a nation as an "imagined community," we should also attend to sport as a political expression of national values. Indeed, sport is often most obviously political in the context of national and international sporting events, if only because athletes are seen as competing for their countries. Perhaps this is why Allison (2000) declares, "National identity is the most marketable product in sport" (p. 346), since spectators eagerly follow medal counts and seek national bragging rights. In the United States, sporting success is commonly attributed to a broader mythology about the nation's historic role. Rooted in an evangelical calling that proclaims the United States to be the embodiment of Jesus's "shining city on a hill," American exceptionalism "is the distinct belief that the United States is unique, if not superior, when compared to other nations" (Weiss and Edwards 2011: 1). As I observed at the outset of this chapter, as the United States emerged as a global leader at the turn of the twentieth century, sport was among the most visible mechanisms for the demonstration of the nation's virtues.

For example, a strong showing at the 1912 Stockholm Olympic Games "bolstered nationalist appraisals that the United States was surpassing its old-world rivals. Jim Thorpe's brilliant performance at Stockholm, in particular, appeared to legitimize America's melting-pot ideology" (Pope 1997: 50). In subsequent Olympics, athletes such as Jesse Owens, Mark Spitz, and Mary Lou Retton became heroic figures whose gold medal performances affirmed exceptionalist mythology.

Perhaps the definitive nationalistic moment for the United States came during the 1980 Winter Olympics, in which the men's hockey team stunned the Soviet Union on the way to an unexpected gold medal. The significance of the victory was magnified by the political context of the time: a struggling U.S. economy, American hostages held captive in Iran, and the Soviet Union's invasion of Afghanistan as the latest chapter in the Cold War. Against this backdrop, U.S. coach Herb Brooks assembled a team of amateurs and adopted tactics specifically designed to challenge the Soviet style of play. The result was more than a sporting triumph; rather, it was at the time, and continues to be, understood as a metaphor for American resilience in the ideological struggle against communism. Years later, the memory of the 1980 team continued to resonate for Americans still coping with the tragedy of 9/11, first with the team's appearance at the Opening Ceremonies for the 2002 Winter Olympics in Salt Lake City and second with the release of *Miracle*, a 2004 film that cultivated a feel-good nationalism by appropriating the legacy of the "miracle on ice" (Butterworth 2010b).

The shock of 9/11 and the subsequent "war on terror" led to an explosion of rituals and ceremonies at sporting events designed to rally spectators/Americans around the flag (see Kelly's chapter in this collection for some wider discussions of this). The "cult of the 'Star Spangled Banner'" was especially prominent at events such as Super Bowl XXXVI and the 2002 Winter Olympics (Silk and Falcous 2005: 453), but also ubiquitous in daily rituals at baseball games (Butterworth 2005). Even as 9/11 has somewhat receded from memory and the "war on terror" has been redefined, sporting events in the United States continue to feature patriotic imagery as a standard part of the experience. On the tenth anniversary of 9/11, for example, each of the major sports leagues and organisations devoted considerable time and resources toward the remembrance of the lives lost in the terrorist attacks. As has too often been the case in the past 10 to 15 years, however, these ceremonies provided only temporary unity at the expense of an honest account of political divisions that continue to threaten democratic societies (Butterworth 2014). Nevertheless, it is clear that ritualistic expressions of American patriotism continue to galvanize fans and provide positive public relations for sports leagues and media.

The military plays an especially prominent role in these patriotic productions. A range of scholars have identified the ways that sport, media, and the military have developed a mutually beneficial relationship, especially in the past decade (Butterworth and Moskal 2009; Jenkins 2013; King 2008; Stempel 2006). The concerns expressed in these studies coalesce around the problems that arise when the spectacle of sport desensitizes audiences to the harsh realities of war. Noting that such concerns first arose during the short-lived Persian Gulf War of 1991, when Super Bowl XXV was awash in patriotic symbolism and media reports of the war frequently characterized it as they might a video game, Stahl (2010) argues:

> The sports metaphor casts war as a clean, two-sided affair conducted under egalitarian rules-based strictures that eventually determine a winner based on merit. In the case of the Persian Gulf War, the sports metaphor deflected attention from certain aspects, such as the fact that the war resembled less a fair competition than a high-tech, illegal, one-sided slaughter. Arguably, the number of such mismatches has increasingly called forth the sports metaphor in the interest of maintaining a veneer of the "just war."
>
> *(p. 53)*

Meanwhile, as sport reduces war to a game, leagues and media celebrate military personnel through myriad tributes designed to "support the troops." These events include on-field enlistment ceremonies, surprise reunions between military members and their spouses (usually a male soldier and his young wife), military recruitment efforts, aircraft flyovers, and military charity promotions. There are too many such events to summarize in this space, but one example condenses many of these features. Fans of American football are well acquainted with the memory of Pat Tillman, a member of the Arizona Cardinals who gave up his NFL contract so he could serve in the Army Rangers after 9/11. When Tillman was killed in Afghanistan in 2004, his death became a symbol of heroic sacrifice immediately exploited by sports media and political figures alike. Even as details emerged about his death – revealing that he had been killed by "friendly fire" and that he actively questioned the purpose of the war he was fighting – the mythologizing of Tillman continued unabated. An especially vivid illustration of this is on display in a Pro Football Hall of Fame exhibit called "Pro Football and the American Spirit," in which Tillman's sacrifice is absorbed into a larger narrative about football and the virtues of war. Through pictures, anecdotes shared by other players, and even (incomplete) interview comments from Tillman himself, the exhibit defaults "to the common mythic image that has been discredited" (Butterworth 2012: 253).

Sport and the activist athlete

The common assumption that sport and politics do not mix is perhaps felt most obviously when it comes to athletes voicing political opinions. As sportswriter Dave Zirin (2011) notes, fans want athletes to entertain, to "shut up and play." Meanwhile, others insist that "no population in society is less qualified" to comment on politics than professional athletes (Pearlman 2006). Kaufman and Wolff (2010: 165) counter by asking, "How are athletes different from business people, doctors, and office workers"? To the extent that they are citizens with a democratic right to free expression, it is true that athletes are no different. Given their visibility, however, politically minded athletes have a unique platform, and it is clear that substantive social change can be facilitated within the sporting context.

How can one understand the Civil Rights Movement in the United States, for example, without accounting for Jackie Robinson? Robinson "broke the colour barrier" in Major League Baseball when he played for the Brooklyn Dodgers in 1947, becoming the first African American player of the modern era and thus opening the door to hundreds and later thousands of athletes in subsequent years; 1947 is seven to eight years before other events more often associated with the start of the Civil Rights Movement: the 1954 *Brown v. Board of Education* Supreme Court case, the murder of Emmet Till in 1955, and the refusal of Rosa Parks, also in 1955, to give up her bus seat to a White patron. Indeed, the symbolism of African American players such as Robinson playing alongside Whites in the "national pastime" inspired movement activists. As Martin Luther King, Jr. once told pitcher Don Newcombe, one of the prominent African American players to follow in the steps of Robinson, "You'll never know what you and Jackie and Roy [Campanella] did to make it possible to do my job" (Dreier 2001: 48). Years later, President Barack Obama declared to baseball legend Willie Mays, "Let me tell you, you helped us get there. If it hadn't been for folks like you and Jackie, I'm not sure that I would get elected to the White House" (President Barack Obama 2013).

Robinson has long been heralded as a figure of positive social and political change. It has been more complicated for other athletes. Muhammad Ali, for example, went from Olympic hero (as Cassius Clay) to feared spokesman for the Nation of Islam. His refusal to submit to the draft in 1967 earned him scorn and cost him three years of his career during his prime.

Decades later, Ali is lionized not only as "the greatest" boxer but also as a champion for peace and human rights, as the "prototype against which the modern athlete is often publicly shamed" (Grano 2009: 192). Similarly, Olympians John Carlos and Tommie Smith were stripped of their medals and forced to leave the 1968 Mexico City Games after their controversial gesture on the medal stand, in which they bowed their heads and raised their black-gloved fists in the air as a statement against the impoverishment of African American citizens. Although Carlos and Smith were marginalized upon their return to the United States, the iconic photograph of their protest has become,

> the defining image of Mexico City, an image that has had residual effects on the sports world as well as a more generalized historical and cultural resonance that fuses the racialized anger of 1968 with the broader imagery of black masculinity in American society.
>
> *(Bass 2002: 25)*

In recent years, as nostalgic reconsiderations have cast more favorable light upon figures such as Ali, Carlos, and Smith, various authors have lamented the decline of the "activist athlete," especially those among the African American community (Powell 2007; Rhoden 2006). These laments call out contemporary athletes, such as Michael Jordan and Tiger Woods, for neglecting the sacrifices made by previous generations and refusing to engage in political issues. One athlete frequently mentioned in such arguments is Curt Flood, the baseball player who challenged MLB's "reserve clause," a rule that allowed franchise owners complete control over player contracts and prohibited free agency. Flood's case eventually made its way to the United States Supreme Court. Although he lost the case, and was largely estranged from baseball as a consequence, his actions set in motion a series of events that led to free agency in U.S. professional sports. It is now common to hear older athletes or members of the sports media suggest that contemporary players owe their considerable salaries to the activism of Curt Flood. Yet, as Khan (2012) contends, today's players are a logical byproduct of capitalism and liberal progressivism. In his words:

> Instead of demanding more from the framework of our political culture, we take our shots at Michael and Tiger for their refusal to be Jackie and Curt, when perhaps who they are is exactly who liberalism hoped they would be.
>
> *(p. 25)*

More than failing to connect the dots between players of today and those of the past, criticisms of athletes as insufficiently political neglects the range of activism in which players *are* engaged: football players such as Brendon Ayanbadejo, Scott Fujita, and Chris Kluwe have been outspoken advocates on behalf of gays and lesbians; basketball player Steve Nash has been vocal in his opposition to war; Venus Williams lobbied for equal pay for women at the Grand Slam championships in tennis; and players in a range of sports have used their platforms to express their views on specific issues, from NHL player Tim Thomas's refusal to visit the White House because of his criticisms of the Obama administration, to the entire roster of the Miami Heat showing solidarity with the memory of slain teen Trayvon Martin, to players across sports speaking out against domestic violence. These moments of advocacy are all the more impressive because they often express resistance to the very organizations that might otherwise support these athletes. Williams's challenge to the major tennis tournaments makes plain the inequity in the previous system, just as NFL players critiquing domestic violence spotlights the league's unwillingness to confront the issue. Individual acts of protest are not the only answer, of course, but, in these moments, it is undeniable that politics and activism occupy a central space in the U.S. sporting landscape.

Conclusion

Given the range of political symbols in U.S. sport, this chapter could be considerably more detailed. The examples provided here are designed both to highlight broad themes and provoke additional thinking about the relationship between politics and sport. Even as many continue to insist that politics and sport are distinct institutions, or that sport is especially designed to provide an "escape" from the political, it should be clear that the two co-exist and are often mutually dependent. To conclude, let me return to the context with which I began – the Olympic Games. When Germany prepared to host the Summer Games in 1936, various critics in the United States called for a boycott. Instead of confronting the political realities of the Nazi regime, the head of the United States Olympic Committee, Avery Brundage, defended American participation on the grounds that the Olympics could not, "with good grace or propriety, interfere in the internal, political, religious or racial affairs of any country or group" (Zirin 2008: 77). Brundage made this statement, apparently, without any sense that the claim to avoiding politics was, in and of itself, a political statement.

Decades later, the Olympics remain among the most prominent reminders of the ways that the languages of sport and politics intersect, the investments in community associated with host cities and the stories of individual athletes, the persistent nationalism that characterizes so much spectatorship and media coverage of the events, and the occasion for activism that the international stage provides. In the wake of controversy in Brazil over the expenses associated with hosting the 2014 World Cup, for example, we might expect to see renewed protest as Rio de Janeiro prepares to host the 2016 Summer Olympic Games. In the United States, such unrest may take a more subtle form, but it nevertheless may affect the playing field – as it obviously did in the case of Boston's failed bid to host the 2024 Summer Games. Opponents organized a group, "No Boston Olympics," that, as Boston's National Public Radio affiliate reported, was small but "had an out-sized effect on the public debate over the Olympics – driven largely by the group's ability to tap into social media and its consistent presence at public meetings about the bid" (Enwemeka 2015). Thus, as evidenced by this instance of public protest, as well as the various examples cited throughout this chapter, the question with respect to the United States should not be *if* it will see sport as political, but *how*.

References

Allison, L. (2000) Sport and nationalism. In J. Coakley and E. Dunning (eds.) *Handbook of Sports Studies*. London: Sage, pp. 344–355.

Anderson, B. (1991) *Imagined Communities: Reflections on the Origin and Spread of Nationalism*. London: Verso.

Andrews, D. (1998) Excavating Michael Jordan: notes on a critical pedagogy of sporting representation. In G. Rail (ed.) *Sport and Postmodern Times*. Albany, NY: State University of New York Press, pp. 185–219.

Bass, A. (2002) *Not the Triumph but the Struggle: The 1968 Olympics and the Making of the Black Athlete*. Minneapolis, MN: University of Minnesota Press.

Bennett, J.T. (2012) *They Play, You Pay: Why Taxpayers Build Ballparks, Stadiums and Arenas for Billionaire Owners and Millionaire Players*. New York: Springer.

Benoit, W.L., Stein, K.A., and Hansen, G.J. (2005) *New York Times* coverage of presidential campaigns. *Journalism & Mass Communication Quarterly*, 82: 356–376.

Betzold, M. and Casey, E. (1992) *Queen of Diamonds: The Tiger Stadium Story*. West Bloomfield, MI: Northmont Publishing.

Bolton, A. (2012) Ten game changers that could decide the race between Obama and Romney. *The Hill* June 3, 2012. http://thehill.com/homenews/campaign/230583-ten-game-changers-that-could-decide-the-presidency.

Butterworth, M.L. (2005) Ritual in the "church of baseball": Suppressing the discourse of democracy. *Communication and Critical/Cultural Studies* 2: 107–129.

Butterworth, M.L. (2010a) *Baseball and Rhetorics of Purity: The National Pastime and American Identity During the War on Terror.* Tuscaloosa, AL: University of Alabama Press.

Butterworth, M.L. (2010b) Do you believe in nationalism? American patriotism in Miracle. In H. Hundley and A.C. Billings (eds.) *Examining Identity in Sports Media.* Thousand Oaks, CA: Sage, pp. 133–152.

Butterworth, M.L. (2012) Militarism and memorializing at the Pro Football Hall of Fame. *Communication and Critical/Cultural Studies,* 9: 241–258.

Butterworth, M.L. (2014) Public memorializing in the stadium: Mediated sport, the 10th anniversary of 9/11, and the illusion of democracy. *Communication & Sport,* 2: 203–224.

Butterworth, M.L. and Moskal, S.D. (2009) American football, flags, and "fun": The Bell Helicopter Armed Forces Bowl and the rhetorical production of militarism. *Communication, Culture & Critique,* 2(4): 411–433.

Carville, J. (2010) Saints' parade has room for fans. *ESPN.com,* February 4, 2010. http://sports.espn. go.com/espn/commentary/news/story?id=4887061.

DeMause, N. and Cagan, J. (2008) *Field of Schemes: How the Great Stadium Swindle Turns Public Money into Private Profit.* Lincoln: Bison Books.

Dreier, P. (2001) Jackie Robinson's legacy: Baseball, race, and politics. In R. Elias (ed.) *Baseball and the American Dream: Race, Class, Gender and the National Pastime.* Armonk: ME Sharpe, pp. 43–63.

Elias, R. (2010) *The Empire Strikes Out: How Baseball Sold U.S. Foreign Policy and Promoted the American Way Abroad.* New York: New Press.

Enwemeka, Z. (2015) 7 reasons why Boston's Olympic bid failed. *WBUR,* July 27, 2015. Accessed January 3, 2016. www.wbur.org/2015/07/27/why-boston-olympics-bid-failed.

Fleer, J. (2007) The church of baseball and the U.S. presidency. *Nine: A Journal of Baseball History and Culture,* 16: 51–61.

Foer, F. (2004) *How Soccer Explains the World: An Unlikely Theory of Globalization.* New York: HarperCollins.

Friedman, M.T., Andrews, D.L., and Silk, M.L. (2004) Sport and the façade of redevelopment in the postindustrial city. *Sociology of Sport Journal,* 21: 119–139.

Gems, G.R. (2000) *For Pride, Profit, and Patriarchy: Football and the Incorporation of American Cultural Values.* Lanham, MD: Scarecrow Press.

Grano, D.A. (2009) Muhammad Ali versus the "modern athlete": On voice in mediated sports culture. *Critical Studies in Media Communication,* 26: 191–211.

Grano, D.A. and Zagacki, K.S. (2011) Cleansing the Superdome: The paradox of purity and post-Katrina guilt. *Quarterly Journal of Speech,* 97: 201–223.

Gregory, S. (2014) Economist: Lebron James worth almost $500 million to Cleveland. *Time,* July 14, 2014. Accessed October 28, 2014. http://time.com/2981583/lebron-james-cleveland-cavs-money/.

Harris, M. (2013) Sen: Lindsey Graham's call for boycott of Sochi Olympics is out to lunch. *Washington Times,* July 17, 2013. Accessed October 28, 2014. www.washingtontimes.com/news/2013/jul/17/sen-lindsey-graham-boycott-sochi-olympics-russia/?page=all.

Heilemann, J. and Halperin, M. (2010) *Game Change: Obama and the Clintons, McCain and Palin, and the Race of a Lifetime.* New York: HarperCollins.

Hester, M. (2005) America's #1 fan: A rhetorical analysis of presidential sports encomia and the symbolic power of sports in the articulation of civil religion in the United States. Unpublished doctoral dissertation. Georgia State University.

Jamieson, K.H. (1992) *Dirty Politics: Deception, Distraction, and Democracy.* New York: Oxford University Press.

Jarvis, S.E. and Han, S.H. (2011) The mobilized voter: Portrayals of electoral participation in print news coverage of campaign 2008. *American Behavioral Scientist,* 55: 419–436.

Jenkins, T. (2013) The militarization of American professional sports: How the sports-war intertext influences athletic ritual and sports media. *Journal of Sport and Social Issues,* 37: 245–260.

Kaufman, P. and Wolff, E.A. (2010) Playing and protesting: Sport as a vehicle for social change. *Journal of Sport and Social Issues,* 34: 154–175.

Khan, A.I. (2012) *Curt Flood in the Media: Baseball, Race, and the Demise of the Activist-Athlete.* Jackson, MS: University Press of Mississippi.

King, S. (2008) Offensive lines: Sport-state synergy in an era of perpetual war. *Cultural Studies – Critical Methodologies*, 8: 527–539.

Markovits, A.S. and Hellerman, S.L. (2001) *Offside: Soccer & American Exceptionalism*. Princeton, NJ: Princeton University Press.

Markovits, A.S. and Rensmann, L. (2010) *Gaming the World: How Sports Are Reshaping Global Politics and Culture*. Princeton, NJ: Princeton University Press.

O'Rourke, D.J. (2003) The talk of the town: A rhetorical analysis of the Browns' departure from and return to Cleveland. In R.S. Brown and D.J. O'Rourke (eds.) *Case Studies in Sport Communication*. Westport, CT: Praeger, pp. 63–79.

Pearlman, J. (2006) Pro athletes, politics a bad mix. *ESPN.com*, November 7, 2006. http://sports.espn. go.com/espn/page2/story?page=pearlman/061107.

Pope, S.W. (1997) *Patriotic Games: Sporting Traditions in the American Imagination, 1876–1926*. New York: Oxford.

Powell, S. (2007) *Souled Out? How Blacks are Winning and Losing in Sports*. Champaign, IL: Human Kinetics.

President Barack Obama and Willie Mays on Air Force One (2013) *YouTube*. www.youtube.com/watch?v=v_l6VSWxyL0.

Rhoden, W.C. (2006) *Forty Million Dollar Slaves: The Rise, Fall, and Redemption of the Black Athlete*. New York: Crown.

Rucker, P. (2012) Mitt Romney at Daytona 500: "I have some great friends that are NASCAR team owners." *Washington Post*, February 26, 2012. Accessed February 26, 2012. www.washingtonpost.com/blogs/post-politics/post/mitt-romney-trades-campaign-trail-for-daytona-500/2012/02/26/gIQAMsHpcR_blog.html.

Seymour, H. (1989) *Baseball: The Golden Age*. New York: Oxford University Press.

Shea, B. (2014) On cost, financing of Wings arena: Here are answers. *Crain's Detroit Business*, September 22, 2014. Accessed September 22, 2014. www.crainsdetroit.com/article/20140921/NEWS/309219990/on-cost-financing-of-wings-arena-here-are-answers#.

Silk, M. and Falcous, M. (2005) One day in September/a week in February: Mobilizing American (sporting) nationalisms. *Sociology of Sport Journal*, 22: 447–471.

Smith-Spark, L. (2013) Why Russia's Sochi Olympics are now a battleground for gay rights. *CNN.com*, August 10, 2013. Accessed October 28, 2014. www.cnn.com/2013/08/10/world/europe/russia-gay-rights-controversy/.

Stahl, R. (2010) *Militainment, inc.: War, Media, and Popular Culture*. New York: Routledge.

Stempel, C. (2006) Televised sports, masculinist moral capital, and support for the U.S. invasion of Iraq. *Journal of Sport and Social Issues*, 30: 79–106.

Thompson, W. (2015) Beyond the breach: A summer in search of saints, sinners, and lost souls in the New Orleans that Katrina left behind. *ESPN The Magazine*, August 24, 2015. Accessed September 22, 2015. http://espn.go.com/espn/feature/story/_/id/13479768/wright-thompson-life-loss-renewal-new-orleans-10-years-hurricane-katrina.

Trujillo, N. (2000) Baseball, business, politics, and privilege: An interview with George W. Bush. *Management Communication Quarterly*, 14: 307–216.

Trumpbour, R.C. (2006) *The New Cathedrals: Politics and Media in the History of Stadium Construction*. Syracuse, NY: Syracuse University Press.

Uszynski, E.T. (2014) Implicit religion and the highly-identified sports fan: An ethnography of Cleveland sports fandom. Unpublished doctoral dissertation. Bowling Green State University.

Vanden Heuvel, K. (2013) Sochi boycott would hurt the wrong people. *Washington Post*, August 27, 2013. Accessed October 28, 2014. www.washingtonpost.com/opinions/katrina-vanden-heuvel-sochi-boycott-would-hurt-the-wrong-people/2013/08/27/41d55b1c-0ea1-11e3-8cdd-bcdc09410972_story.html.

Watterson, J.S. (2006) *The Games Presidents Play: Sports and the Presidency*. Baltimore, MD: The Johns Hopkins University Press.

Weiss, D. and Edwards, J.A. (2011) Introduction: American exceptionalism's champions and challengers. In J.A. Edwards and D. Weiss (eds.) *The Rhetoric of American Exceptionalism: Critical Essays*. Jefferson NC: McFarland, pp. 1–10.

Zirin, D. (2008) *A People's History of Sports in the United States: 250 Years of Politics, Protest, People, and Play*. New York: The New Press.

Zirin, D. (2011) Shut up and play? Patriotism, jock culture and the limits of free speech. *The Nation*, May 4, 2011. Accessed May 4, 2011. www.thenation.com/blog/160408/shut-and-play-patriotism-jock-culture-and-limits-free-speech.

14

SPORT AND LANGUAGE POLITICS IN CANADA

Christine Dallaire and Jean Harvey

As illustrated through several previous chapters in this collection, countless accounts of the use of sport as a tool for the promotion of national as well as minority identities abound in sport studies literature (among many others see Bairner 2001). From Nazi Germany propaganda to post-apartheid South African nation building, from expressions of political minorities community life to minorities resistance, to the reproduction of dominant nations, sport can play a contrasted and significant role in the promotion/repression/resistance of diverse forms of national and ethnic communities. Arguably, among the less frequent accounts of such expressions or strategic collective initiatives, are the ones illustrating how sport can be bound up with language politics and collective expressions/strategies of community belonging. The aim of this chapter is precisely to examine the intersection of sport with language politics and identities, using examples of two different sporting events in Canada. In contrast with an earlier contribution on identity politics in Quebec (see Harvey 1999), the focus here is not on how sport contributes to political divisions in Canada, but rather on how sporting games are contributors to contrasted Francophone identities in Canada.

Canada has two official languages, French and English, meant to be equal in status, rights and privileges within federal institutions, as well as intended to benefit from full recognition within the larger Canadian society (Canada 1985). In reality, however, despite different protective measures adopted as part of Canadian nation-building strategies, the standing of French language has been and remains vulnerable since the creation of the federal state in 1867. In the Anglo-dominant context of North America, the proportion of Canadians with French as their mother tongue has steadily declined since 1951 and the ratio of those who speak French at home or who converse in French more frequently than in English has also been decreasing since 1981 (Lachapelle and Lepage 2011; Statistics Canada 2012). The last census showed that 7.7 million Canadians claimed French as their first official language spoken, representing 23.2 per cent of the total population. Most of them (86.9 per cent) live in Quebec where they constitute a majority in the lone province with French as the only official language, emphasising Quebec's position as a distinct society. Over three quarters of the remaining million or so Francophones reside in Ontario and New Brunswick (Statistics Canada 2012), the latter being the only officially bilingual province in the country, whereas English is the sole official language in Ontario and the rest of the provinces.

In the context of ongoing concerns for the sustainability of the French language in Canada, the Jeux de la francophonie canadienne (JFC) and the Finale des Jeux du Québec (FJQ) are two large youth sporting events exclusively held in French in order to safeguard the vitality of this official language. Yet, their influence in giving meaning to the *francophonie* differs in light of their specific political context and their differing role in nation building. The Jeux de la francophonie canadienne (JFC) is a pan-Canadian youth festival that celebrates French language, culture and identity as a focal feature of a Canadian nationalism that highlights its linguistic duality despite the minority status of Francophones. Conversely, French language and its cultural dimensions are taken for granted rather than fêted at the Finale des Jeux du Québec (FJQ). This large-scale multisport competition convenes youths from across Quebec, yet it does not necessarily foster a greater sense of belonging to this Francophone society. This chapter discusses the politics of language at both games to illustrate the complexity of promoting French language and Francophone belonging not only in a bilingual Canada but also in the only officially Francophone province. We start by providing a brief historical context to situate French language policies with regards to nationalism in Canada and in Quebec. Drawing on document analysis, interviews with civil servants, organisers and youths, as well as youth survey results and participant observation from the 2008 JFC and the 2010 FJQ, the specific circumstances in encouraging French language use and in fostering a Francophone collective identity among youths at the JFC are then discussed followed by an outline of language idiosyncrasies at the FJQ.

Language policies and nationalisms in Canada and Quebec

The status of the French language became an issue after the 1760 British conquest of Nouvelle-France introduced English in this former French colony. It has remained disputed throughout the homogenising nation-building efforts of the subsequent North American British provinces (Martel and Pâquet 2010). Canada can be said to be born out of a political compromise between these original four provinces, but the 1867 Confederation was also purported to have been a pact between two founding nations defined on the basis of language and religion: French Canadians (Catholic) and English Canadians (Protestant) (Martel and Pâquet 2010; Rocher 2009). Indeed, language concerns date back to negotiations to create this new country and were articulated in the Constitution Act of 1867 to ensure the use of both French and English in judicial and parliamentary systems at the federal level, in addition to the obligation to adopt laws in both languages. This legal framework meant to provide equal access to legislative bodies, laws and tribunals to both Francophones and Anglophones was however lacking and did not adequately safeguard the use of French language (Foucher 2011). In the 1950s and early 1960s, confronted with nascent calls for Quebec independence because the Canadian federation was not successful at protecting French language rights, the federal government created the Royal Commission on Bilingualism and Biculturalism in 1963 (known as the B&B Commission). This Commission advocated for the idea of two founding nations but transformed it into the concept of an "equal partnership" between two linguistic communities, focusing on the imperative to actually achieve this equality through legal means while recognising the historical contribution of other "ethnic groups" to the Canadian nation and encouraging their integration in either of the two linguistic communities (Canada 1967). In a bid to foster Canadian unity and curtail Quebec nationalism, the federal government endorsed the B&B Commission's recommendation and adopted the Official Languages Act in 1969, thereby giving a new meaning to Canadian nationalism characterised by bilingualism and the official status of French and English (Martel and Pâquet 2010).

It is in this context that traditional French Canadian nationalism centred on the Catholic Church collapsed during the 1950s through the 1970s in the face of a rising Quebec nationalism prioritising language as the fundamental vector of identity and investing the provincial government as the ultimate self-determination political tool to defend and enhance French language. This period of modernisation of the Quebec provincial government led to the fragmentation of old French Canada as a founding nation, into the new Quebec nation with other French Canadian communities spread across the rest of the country becoming Francophone minorities (Thériault 2003). Following the advent of official bilingualism in federal institutions, Quebec opted for a different political and linguistic nation-building approach, firmly establishing French as a common good across its territory rather than an individual right (Martel and Pâquet 2010). French was first legislated in the Quebec parliament as the exclusive official language of the province in 1974, followed in 1977 by the adoption of the Charte de la langue française (known as the loi 101) during the first government of the separatist Parti québécois (i.e. between 1976 and 1985),[1] reinforcing the status of French as the public language, complemented in 1978 with an extensive cultural development policy to enrich the common and collective project of creating a modern society, thus strengthening civic bonds within the *Québécois* nation.

In Ottawa, the 1982 Constitution Act was accompanied by the adoption of the Canadian Charter of Rights and Freedoms entrenching French language individual rights within the new Canadian foundational document. This new language regime rejected the theory of the two founding nations and thus offered no constitutional amendments to the division of powers between the provinces and the federal government. No special status was given to Quebec as a founding nation or as a distinct society. Instead, the Charter was founded on the burgeoning principles of equality between the two linguistic communities and multicultural diversity, as proclaimed through the 1969 Official Languages Act and the 1971 multiculturalism policy (Martel and Pâquet 2010; Rocher 2009). In 1988, the federal government reinforced the new symbolic order by adding provisions to the Official Languages Act and adopting the Canadian Multiculturalism Act. Finally, it again strengthened the Official Languages Act in 2005 with regards to the federal government's obligation to support and enhance the development of minority Francophone communities outside Quebec, as well as the Anglophone minority in Quebec.

In light of the minimal margin that separated the proponents of sovereignty from those voting to keep Quebec within Canada in the second Quebec referendum of 1995, the federal government pursued a judicial and then a legislative strategy to constrain secession. These measures promptly elicited a reaction from Quebec to reassert the fundamental rights and entitlements of the Québécois nation and the Quebec provincial state. The 2000 loi 99 stipulated that a majority of Francophones compose the Québécois nation, reinforced the Charte de la langue française (loi 101) and reaffirmed French as the unique official language of the province. The existence of the French Canadian nation, later replaced by the Québécois nation, has been historically widespread in Quebec, where it is believed that this national community deserves official recognition as a distinct society and merits a special constitutional status as a founding nation or total independence. As a compromise between Quebec independence proponents and the constitutional status quo, the Canadian Parliament passed a motion in 2006 acknowledging that the "Québécois form a nation within a united Canada" (House of Commons Debate 2007). This symbolic gesture served the federal government's national unity objectives, even though it did complicate the form of Canadian nationalism dominant among Anglophones, by conceding to the interpretation privileging the multinational character of the country long defended by the Québécois (McRoberts 2001; Pelletier 2009).[2]

In short, French language policies have been used as a nation-building tool in contradictory ways in Canada and in Quebec. Initially designed to curb Quebec nationalism, today's federal official languages regime is embedded in Canadian nationalism in spite of the inadequacy of its implementation and its shortcomings to protect and reinforce the French language at the federal level (Foucher 2011). In Quebec, linguistic policies frame the central vector of the Québécois identity and have been successful at instituting French as the shared public language although the linguistic regime remains tenuous (Plourde 2003) and the promotion and enhancement of the French language remains an ongoing project (Langlois 2003). How do these complex linguistic features of nation building translate to amateur sport? The former and current Commissioner of Official Languages summarised the issues raised in various reports since the 1980s, confirming that required linguistic reforms have not been fully implemented in Canadian amateur sport in spite of undeniable progress (see Adam 2007; Fraser 2013). In fact, linguistic issues remain an afterthought and stay unresolved, notwithstanding efforts to ensure the bilingualism of sport institutions or the materialisation of both official languages in major games hosted in Canada. Conversely, Francophone games do provide a space to compete in French and to highlight the French language and culture. Yet, the politics of language still emerge in such events staged exclusively in French by Francophones. The following analysis illustrates how language concerns are played out on the one hand at the Jeux de la francophonie canadienne (JFC), an event rooted in Canadian nationalism emphasising linguistic duality, and on the other hand at the Finale des Jeux du Québec (FJQ), games framed by the loi 101.

Language policies and the Jeux de la francophonie canadienne[3]

First held in 1999, the Jeux de la francophonie canadienne (JFC) attract up to 1,000 youths from across Canada on a triennial basis for sporting and artistic competitions as well as leadership training. The games are the biggest and most visible endeavour of the Fédération de la jeunesse canadienne-française (FJCF), the umbrella youth organisation that brings together provincial and territorial minority Francophone youth groups. The FJCF initiated the pan-Canadian games following its enquiry on the "crisis" of assimilation uncovered by the 1986 census and the ensuing call to action to ensure the sustainability of Francophone minorities. Betting on the appeal of leisure practices, the JFC were designed as an enjoyable experience to encourage the use of the French language and foster Francophone belonging among youths, as well as a source of stimulation for the host Francophone community (Dallaire 2014). But the event is not restricted to minority Francophone youths. Since their inception, Quebec youths have been invited as well. Drawing on the idea of French Canada as a founding nation, this inclusion of a Quebec delegation was a genuine intent of the founders of the JFC to promote a pan-Canadian francophonie composed of diverse communities. The games would then showcase their different accents and cultural specificities but still highlight the coast-to-coast dimension of the francophonie canadienne. Youth leaders and organisers still insist on this pan-Canadian vision and would not imagine the JFC without Quebec. In this sense, their project certainly endorses federal nation-building efforts. Nevertheless, including Quebec was a purposeful decision to reflect the FJCF's vision of today's francophonie canadienne; it was not merely a strategy to meet federal funding criteria aimed at fostering Canadian nationalism through the Official Languages Act, nor were the games designed to be entrenched within the Canadian sport system and funded under the Canadian sport policy.

Indeed, the JFC would not exist without subsidies obtained through federal responsibility for the development of linguistic minorities and the promotion of the Canadian linguistic duality. While the local organising committee obtains revenues from other sources, such as the host city and province, the federal government provides the majority of the financial resources sustaining the overall JFC undertaking. This covers not only the actual staging of the event and the travel costs to bring delegations, which in a large country like Canada represents a sizeable portion of the total budget, but also the upstream planning by the FJCF and the groundwork by Francophone youth associations in selecting and training delegations. Since grant decisions are framed by official language policies, the FJCF tailors funding applications to emphasise specific features of the games that match federal criteria. The JFC in turn benefit from unanimous collaboration with civil servants assigned to official languages programs as they work with the FJCF to ensure their success in meeting ministerial objectives, as well as achieving managerial and financial success. In fact, had it not been for federal intervention, the first JFC would have been cancelled because of a lack of funding and organisational readiness. They were "saved" on the one hand by the Minister of Canadian Heritage, responsible for Official Languages, who strongly backed the project and on the other hand by public servants committed to the project. The JFC emerged at an opportune time when youths were targeted as a priority area of intervention and represented one of the rare initiatives allowing the federal government to address challenges regarding minority Francophone youth isolation through an enjoyable experience. Moreover, official language bureaucrats endorse the formula of expanding the JFC's program to include arts and leadership activities. Even though the majority of participants and most of the competitions are sport related, they appreciate how the JFC remain a youth gathering focused on sociability as opposed to adversity among competitors. They recognise the impact of the games on enhancing French language use and increasing Francophone belonging through bonding with youths from diverse regions of the country that share a common language and culture. That the event also attracts youths who learned French at school rather than at home also contributes to the federal focus on linguistic duality. The inclusion of Quebec youths is similarly underlined as a valued feature of the JFC. The addition of Quebec youths contributes to Canadian nationalism imperatives in the sense that the games serve to integrate Quebec youth in a pan-Canadian francophonie, yet federal monies are distributed through programs specifically aimed at sustaining minority Francophone communities.

While the amounts are quite limited compared to federal grants, the Quebec government also contributes financial resources to the JFC through its intergovernmental policies aimed at maintaining ties with Francophone communities outside the province. One form of funding is meant to bring Quebec expertise to Francophone communities; in the case of the JFC, it is used to share sports know-how. A second Quebec financial contribution covers the selection process and travel expenditures of the Quebec delegation, managed through *Sports Québec*, the non-profit organisation responsible for the Jeux du Québec program and the FJQ. Similarly to federal funding, the financial resources provided by Quebec are tied to the Francophone character of the JFC, not their sport content.

Despite a consensus amongst organisers, funders and participants that the JFC are essentially an event to reinforce French language use and Francophone identity among youths, the minority status of the francophonie in Canada gives rise to different challenges that complicate efforts at providing an all-embracing Francophone environment at the games. The first issue concerns participant recruitment. The Quebec delegation is composed entirely of youths who fluently converse in French. Francophone youth associations in Ontario and New Brunswick benefit from a comprehensive and large network of Francophone schools from which they recruit participants. Francophones are however much less numerous in all other Francophone communities, thus youth associations have expanded their activities in some provinces to attract adolescents from French immersion schools. These schools provide educational programs meant to progressively teach French to non-French-speaking students and were created across Canada as a means to increase bilingualism following the adoption of the Official Languages Act. Despite different participant selection practices from one delegation to another, organisers and youth leaders agree on a basic tenet: participants must be able to speak French as well as demonstrate the desire to take part in an event held exclusively in French. The point then is not to ensure a Francophone environment by selecting participants on the basis of mother tongue, ethno-cultural antecedents or quality of the spoken language. Instead, the aim is to invite youths who have the required linguistic competencies to understand and communicate in French throughout the games and who manifestly want to live a Francophone experience. Such recruitment criteria also recognise the fact that in some parts of the country, even youths who have French as a first language[4] and speak French at home[5] may be more fluent in English or at least communicate spontaneously in English rather than in French. Indeed, many Francophone youths declare in interviews that they have to "work on" or "practice" speaking French. Thus, discerning among youths who have some form of family tie to French as opposed to those who learn it exclusively in school may be difficult and in any case irrelevant if the point is to ensure a French-speaking environment. These recruitment practices further give smaller youth associations the potential to enrol a full delegation despite the smaller Francophone population of their province/territory. While recruiting French immersion students fulfils linguistic duality objectives framing the funding of the games, broadening recruitment beyond Francophone schools was initiated by Francophone youth associations to meet their own goals and their inclusive understanding of the francophonie rather than a practice adopted as a means to obtain federal resources. Despite a minority of participants communicating at times in English and a handful of youths not fluent enough in French to easily exchange and meet youths from other delegations – thus unable to live the full Francophone experience as opposed to a mere youth competition – the JFC are without a doubt successful in their participant recruitment to establish an overall ambiance that encourages the use of the French language.

While no one questions that the ability to converse in French is the crucial requirement in selecting participants, the same cannot be said about recruiting sport officials. This second challenge again is a result of the minority status of French, which means a lack of sport expertise in the host Francophone community or access to bilingual referees in the host province and is exacerbated by limited funds when the JFC are held outside Quebec, Ontario and New Brunswick. Indeed, the only way to ensure that all sport competitions are officiated in French is to recruit referees beyond the host province, which increases the costs of staging the JFC. This challenge is also complicated by the impetus to ensure a certain sporting legitimacy to attract competitive athletes. Organisers and youths prefer that the sport competitions be officiated in French. But when faced with limited human and financial resources, there is no consensus on the precedence of French fluency over sport credentials. FJCF youth leaders underline the importance of French as the language of the games, which should also be manifested throughout official communication during sport competitions, not just in the socio-cultural dimension of the program or in conversations among and within delegations. Among organisers involved in staging the JFC, some believe that the event should act as a platform to increase sport expertise in Francophone communities. Until the FJCF can rely on a sufficient number of French-speaking referees accredited to officiate national-level competitions, they emphasise that the Francophoneness of the games should be privileged by providing French-speaking referees with certification for lower levels of competition. Others argue instead that it is best to ensure a high level of officiating in order to meet athletes' and coaches' expectations. They contend that proving that a competition held in French can offer sporting excellence would contribute to increasing the sense of Francophone pride and belonging among athletes. Local organising committees try to manage these competing interests the best they can.

It is relevant to note that this issue of aiming for discipline-specific "legitimacy" at the possible cost of undermining the Francophoneness of the JFC does not emerge with regards to the credibility of officials and other organisers responsible for the delivery of the artistic and leadership activities. Judges and other officials are expected to communicate in French in their interactions with the visual artists, dancers, singers, improv competitors or apprentice chefs de mission. Similarly, the socio-cultural program, including the opening and closing ceremonies as well as activities offered at the participants' village, is meant to showcase Francophone talent and cultural products. The only English "officially" heard (other than potentially non-French-speaking sport referees) might be from government officials or representatives of major corporate sponsors during ceremonies. Such occasions may be rare, yet delegations react to the presence of English in protocol events – the crowd of participants will mutter and whisper, not being as attentive, which again underscores the focus everyone, including youths, puts on the JFC as an exclusive Francophone space. Notwithstanding occurrences where English may be spoken "officially" or informally, this limited emergence of English is insufficient to undermine the Francophoneness of the games. It is rather perceived by organisers, youth leaders, youth participants and civil servants as unavoidable in a country where English is inescapable. But they contend that it must remain minimal.

The success of the JFC depends not only on regulating the use of language both spoken and in print, but more importantly on their capacity to provide an ambiance that enhances and values the French language and culture rather than one that exposes its tenuous position in Canada (Dallaire 2003). This is where the expertise of the Francophone youth associations is critical in guiding the local organising committee and even more significantly in shaping the selection and preparation of their mission team, including coaches and other volunteers, as well as their work in raising awareness among participants to prepare them for the JFC. As a result of this know-how, the endeavour has proved popular among youths since 1999 and also achieves the purpose of reinforcing Francophone belonging. Surveys and interviews of the 2008 JFC participants confirm that participants undeniably enjoy the experience, emphasising the fun they had and the friends they made as they describe the event as a large Francophone youth gathering. In fact, over 40 per cent of youth survey responses accentuate the Francophone feature of the JFC in explaining what the games mean to them and what they most appreciate about their experience. Among the most frequent participant open-ended responses identifying what they gained from the JFC are Francophone belonging and pride. While they were also attracted by the sports, arts or leadership components of the program and clearly benefited from those competitions/activities, it is the Francophone ambiance and the focus on youth sociability that stands out and defines the event. The JFCs' overt celebration of Francophoneness and their impact on reinforcing Francophone belonging and identity is what distinguishes them from the FJQ with regards to language matters and nation building.

Language and nationalism at the Finale des Jeux du Québec[6]

The Finale des Jeux du Québec (FJQ) is the crowning event of the Jeux du Québec program. This amateur sport initiative emerged during the period of Francophone mobilisation to modernise the Quebec government and expand its role in various sectors. A department dedicated to youth, leisure and sports, modelled on the one then in place in France, was first instituted in 1968 and was compelled along with amateur sport organisations to create the Jeux du Québec program in 1969, inaugurating regional multisport competitions that led to a provincial-wide final held for the first time in 1971. Quebec's participation in the 1967 and 1969 Canada Games was the main factor that contributed to rallying amateur sports groups in founding a comparable sport development undertaking throughout the province. Although the Jeux du Québec program has always been managed through an independent sports body, initially the provincial government was heavily involved, not just in funding but also in providing human resources for the planning and operationalisation of the program and the ultimate event, the FJQ. At a time of growth in provincial government action on the one hand and on the other hand of amateur sport organisations' efforts at consolidating their network, both the government and sport groups mutually sought each other's support and endorsement. Amateur sport organisations would eventually balk at what was considered provincial interference but as the main financial backer of the overall program, Quebec did influence the JFQ for nation-building purposes during the years a government of the Parti Québécois was in power.

As opposed to the JFC, who receive no monies from Sport Canada but are largely funded through federal official language programs in addition to smaller contributions from Quebec, the FJQ obtains Quebec and municipal funding predominantly targeting sport. Governed by Sports Québec, a private non-profit corporation representing provincial sport federations and regional sport and leisure groups, the Jeux du Québec program is embedded in the amateur sport system, whereas few JFC competitions have been sanctioned by the relevant sport federations. Yet, despite being conceived as a sport event that annually showcases more than 3,000 of the best teenage athletes of the province, the FJQ are nevertheless influenced by Québécois nationalism. For one thing, the presence of Canadian symbols at the FJQ is proscribed. Only Quebec symbols are to be displayed in print, on stage or at medal ceremonies. After the close 1995 Quebec referendum vote, the Canadian government created a sponsorship program to increase its visibility in Quebec. Federal funding was hence offered to a FJQ local organising committee, but Quebec blocked the grant and instead increased its own funding to compensate for the potential lost revenue. The Canadian government may not be an official supporter of the FJQ to ensure the absence of the maple leaf, but federal funding is sometimes provided through indirect means, for example through government programs supporting youth employment. Furthermore, without explicitly stating that Canadian government representatives are excluded, the Sports Québec protocol procedures indicate specifically which dignitaries are to be invited on stage and who can speak during opening and closing ceremonies. This document itemises technical, logistical and procedural instructions, including which flags are to be displayed as well as a list of possible government officials, which includes only municipal and Quebec representatives; the Canadian flag and federal representatives are omitted.

A second illustration of nation-building initiatives through the FJQ is the vocabulary promoted by the Parti Québécois minister responsible for sport in 1978 in documenting a series of decisions regarding the Jeux du Québec program. The province-wide games bringing together winners of regional competitions were now referred to as "finales nationales", denoting the national character of Quebec. This terminology still emerges spontaneously in discussions with or among FJQ organisers and it is occasionally included in documents prepared by delegations. It does not however appear in official documentation from Sports Québec, as the name of the ultimate event in the Jeux du Québec program omits both "nationale" and "provinciale" as qualifiers. An organiser explained that the intention was to avoid giving a "political" connotation to the sport endeavour. The term "national" did however make its way later when the former FJQ delegation representing the larger Quebec city region was divided in two, with one delegation assigned to the municipal region becoming "Capitale nationale" reflecting the new terminology used for tourism purposes and other municipal and provincial governmental affairs since the mid-2000s.

Following debates about the status of cultural activities, one of the minister's decisions put forth in 1978 was to define the Jeux du Québec as a sport program, nevertheless outlining that the Quebec government believes in the fundamental contribution of the cultural dimension of the program to both regional and "national" competitions and adding that sport cannot be divorced from Quebec popular culture. It has indeed been a principle since the 1970s that the cultural program of the games should highlight local and regional talents and it is still understood as a stage to showcase local artists and Quebec French language culture. For instance, the 2010 FJQ organisers had identified Eva Avila, a local singer who had won the 2006 Canadian Idol champion, as an artist that would add celebrity status to the opening ceremony. However, she was renowned for singing in English and thus when approached, organisers first made sure that she did have French language material. Similarly to the JFC, performances were to be exclusively in French. Although it is largely implicit that the FJQ will feature French language culture, matters do arise that force the organisers to explicitly manage the emergence of English, whether it be through popular culture features of the games or as a language of communication.

Similarly to the JFC, the French language environment of the FJQ is not only governed by an unspoken endorsement, it is managed through rules or statutes targeting language use in Québec. However, provisions regulating French language at the FJQ are more detailed and exhaustive. The Jeux du Québec were developed at a time of rising Quebec nationalist sentiment and they participate in the collective project, in the context of the loi 101, of establishing the French language as a common public good to be enhanced and valued. The comprehensive language policy of Sports Québec respects the prescriptions of the loi 101 and is replicated by the local organising committee of the FJQ. French is the exclusive official language, mandatory for all activities of the organisation. Among the various stipulations, some target the quality of the language and others regulate the use of English in communication with non-French-speaking athletes and volunteers as well as the translation of administrative documents. As opposed to the JFC aiming to promote the use of French among participants, yet allowing English to be officially spoken, even if minimally, at ceremonies and by sport officials, the FJQ are to formally operate in French exclusively, thus only French-speaking referees work at the games. Nonetheless, athletes may communicate informally in English, as it is understood that some Quebec athletes are non-Francophones and converse among each other in English. As prescribed in Quebec legislation, English may be used in private conversations, but the games themselves are to be run officially in French only. This of course complicates communication with non-Francophone parents and athletes. Most delegations function exclusively in French, but a few *chefs de mission* for delegations with larger proportions of English-speaking athletes undertook the translation of the registration/consent form that parents must sign for their teenager's participation at the FJQ and shared it among themselves. It is not an officially translated document provided through Sports Québec. Conversely, at the JFC, the registration documents are officially translated in order to facilitate communication with English-speaking parents. What matters at those games is that youths speak French during the event, whereas the opposite is true at the JFQ – English is not to be used officially by organisers, referees or at ceremonies but may be spoken informally among participants.

Despite the greater formalisation of language policies at the FJQ, the success of these games is not at all related to their contribution to reinforcing French language as the common good, nor is it linked to promoting a Québécois belonging. That French language and culture predominate at this event is instead widely perceived as a given in light of the majority status of Francophones in Quebec and the exclusive official status of French in the province. It is not viewed as a feature that necessitates further proclamation, as it is at the JFC. The FJQ clearly is a Québécois institution operating under loi 101 and, like the JFC, it brings together youths in a Francophone environment that strengthens the legitimacy of the French language. Unlike the JFC though, the FJQ is not a site where Québécois or Francophone identity are necessarily reinforced nor do organisers attribute such a role to the games. Quite the opposite, they conceive of the FJQ as strictly a "sport" phenomenon that ought not be "used" for nationalist purposes, as if sport was indeed apolitical, which of course this book demonstrates it is not, nor are the FJQ as illustrated above. That French language should predominate at the games is not thought of as a political issue, but that the games should promote a "national" identity is considered political interference. This inconsistency illustrates the current situation where the significance of the French language in Quebec is broadly endorsed, but meanings attributed to "national" belonging and its civic focus on French as a public good remain contested, as was poignantly shown through deliberations regarding how to accommodate for cultural and religious differences in Quebec (Bouchard and Taylor 2008) and more recent debates about the ensuing Parti Québécois proposed bill to identify central Quebec values regarding religious neutrality and gender equality.[7] The reticence of FJQ organisers to venture onto this disputed terrain is unsurprising, yet the games presumably do enhance bonds among athletes. However, rather than consolidating an attachment to Quebec or Francophoneness, the games spur a regional sense of attachment among participants and volunteers within delegations. Even if the *chefs de mission* do not extend the efforts deployed by delegations at the JFC, they report that the structure of the games, where athletes travel and share accommodations as part of a delegation and where their sport performance contributes to the overall results of the delegation, is an uncommon occurrence in youth sport experiences and one that they do emphasise. Athletes at the FJQ do report developing new relationships with peers from their delegation, and conversely rarely describe the games as a place where they meet other athletes from across Quebec. When they speak of making new friends and of enjoying the socialisation aspects of the event, they refer mainly to connections made within the delegation and none describe the games as an occasion that underlines Québécois belonging or Francophoneness which is in stark contrast to how JFC participants depict their experiences. The JFC also follow a similar model that reinforces identification to the Francophone community represented through the delegation. However, the delegations, the LOC and elements of the JFC program also put much effort into promoting the pan-Canadian francophonie. This emphasis on the coming together of youths who share something in common – living in Francophone Quebec – is absent from FJQ organisers' discourse. Correspondingly, athlete interviews and surveys reveal that youths focus on their sport performance and on the opportunity to be part of a large, mediatised multisport event. Youths were actually puzzled by interview questions about the possible impact of the games on their sense of self as Francophones or as citizens of Quebec, even if they recognised that they were held exclusively in French. While 37.2 per cent of youth survey respondents agreed that the FJQ contributed to establishing Francophoneness, 37.9 per cent disagreed, noting that Anglophones did take part in the games, English was heard (even if minimally) or that there is no link between language and sport. They took for granted that the games would be held in French and failed to connect this linguistic feature of the FJQ and promoting Francophoneness in Quebec. Despite the fact that 81 per cent of FJQ participants declared having French as a first language and 6.4 per cent stated having both French and English as mother tongues, 55.5 per cent identified as Québécois and another

9.9 per cent of survey respondents identified predominantly as Francophone, which, at a total of 65.4 per cent, is less than at the JFC where less youths shared French as a first language. JFC survey results show that 68.3 per cent of participants underscored their Francophoneness, despite 57.4 per cent respondents stating that French was a first language, 17.9 per cent claiming English as a first language and 21.3 per cent declaring both French and English as mother tongues. Clearly, while the FJQ do validate the prevalence of French language and culture as central in Quebec, they play a limited role in sustaining Francophoneness as a source of identity.

Conclusion

The JFC and the FJQ are, first and foremost, eloquent reminders of the metaphoric power of sport, which can be an instrument of emancipation as well as a vector of alienation. The metaphoric power of sport illustrated here is its ability to draw attention to the representations communities have of their identities or those they want to promote, in this instance on the one side Francophone minorities in Canada and on the other side the Québécois French majority. Thus our case studies illustrate how language, identities and nationalism intersect in sport, or rather how sport acts as a vehicle for the expression of contrasted forms of Francophoneness in Canada. The JFC are only one example of sporting festivals that are explicitly designed for the promotion of Francophoneness in Canada. The *Jeux de l'Acadie*, for example, is the oldest such sporting event. Even if they were modelled on the FJQ and were developed with expert assistance from Sports Québec, the Jeux de l'Acadie differentiated themselves as they were designed specifically to boost Acadian identity (Lamarre 2000). In contrast, the FJQ has been put in place right from its inception as a sport event and is entrenched and sanctioned within the Canadian sport system. In the FJQ, French as the official language is assumed as a reality in a province where the language regime is governed by the loi 101. In so doing, despite all attempts at avoiding being politicised by federalists and/or by sovereignists, the FJQ are nevertheless, albeit involuntarily, an instance of expression of Québécois nationalism through the dominance of French as the sole official language of the games.

Notes

1 The Parti Québécois has also been in power between 1994 and 2003, as well as between 2012 and 2014.
2 This concession to the multinational character of Canada may not be unanimous across the country, but it is the first parliamentary interpretation of Canada that allows a legitimate recognition of First Nations and their claim to nationhood. The earlier premise of the two founding nations (or of two linguistic communities as proposed in the B&B Commission) simply ignored Canada's Indigenous Peoples. Despite this 2006 formal recognition of the Québécois nation, thus of the existence of internal nations within Canada (Pelletier 2009), the country's political institutions are not organised on the basis of comprehensive multinationalism. Canada remains a nation-state, not a multinational state (McRoberts 2001).
3 The analysis of language issues at the JFC draws on: 2008 and historical JFC documents; interviews with 6 federal and provincial officials, 37 organisers (youth leaders, LOC, delegation personnel) in addition to 115 participants during the 2008 games; 612 participant surveys at the 2008 games; and participant observation of the 2008 JFC and some prior planning meetings.
4 Whether French is their sole first language or whether it is considered a first language alongside another first language. These youths usually have both French and English as first languages, but French could be combined with another language in recent immigrant communities.
5 Again, it is possible that more than one language is spoken at home, but French would be one of them.
6 The analysis of language issues at the FJQ draws on: 2010 and archival Jeux du Québec documents; interviews with two provincial officials, 15 organisers (Sports Québec LOC, *chefs de mission*) in addition to

82 athletes at the 2010 FJQ; 438 athlete surveys at the 2010 games; and participant observation of the 2010 FJQ and some prior planning meetings.

7 This bill was a key feature of the Parti Québécois platform in calling a spring election in 2014 that it lost to the Quebec Liberal party. See www.assnat.qc.ca/en/travaux-parlementaires/projets-loi/projet-loi-60-40-1.html for more information on the proposed charter (accessed 1 June 2016).

References

Adam, D. (2007) "Les langues officielles et la participation des athlètes Francophones dans le système sportif canadien." In J.P. Augustin and C. Dallaire (eds.) *Jeux, sports et francophonie: L'exemple du Canada.* Pessac, France: Maison des Sciences de l'Homme d'Aquitaine, pp. 27–50.

Bairner, A. (2001) *Sport, Nationalism and Globalization.* New York: SUNY Press.

Bouchard, G. and Taylor, C. (2008) Building the future: A time for reconciliation. *Final Report of the Consultation Commission on Accommodation Practices Related to Cultural Differences.* Quebec: Gouvernement du Québec.

Canada (1985) *Official Languages Act* R.S.C., 1985, c.31 (4th Suppl.). Ottawa: Minister of Justice.

Canada, Royal Commission on Bilingualism and Biculturalism (1967) *Report of the Royal Commission on Bilingualism and Biculturalism, Book I: The Official Languages.* Ottawa: Government of Canada.

Dallaire, C. (2003) Sport's impact on the Francophoneness of the Alberta Francophone Games. *Ethnologies*, 25(2): 33–58.

Dallaire, C. (2014) "La FJCF et ses Jeux de la francophonie canadienne: s'investir pour mousser l'engagement Francophone des jeunes". In A. Pilote (ed.) *Francophones et citoyens du monde: identités, éducation et engagement.* Québec: Presses de l'Université Laval, pp. 183–209.

Foucher, P. (2011) "The Official Languages Act of Canada: A historical and contemporary review". In J. Jedwab and R. Landrey (eds) *Life after Forty: Official Languages Policy in Canada.* Montreal and Kinston: McGill-Queen's University Press, pp. 89–101.

Fraser, G. (2013) "Official languages and the Canadian sport system: Steady progress, constant vigilance needed". In L. Thibault and J. Harvey (eds) *Sport Policy in Canada.* Ottawa: University of Ottawa Press, pp. 351–379.

Harvey, J. (1999) "Sport and Quebec nationalism: Ethnic or civic identity?" In J. Sugden and A. Bairner (eds) *Sport in Divided Societies.* Aachen, Germany: Meyer and Meyer, pp. 31–50.

House of Commons Debate (Friday 24 November 2007) 39th Parliament, 1st session, Official Report (Hansard), Volume 141, Number 086. www.parl.gc.ca/HousePublications/Publication.aspx?Language=E&Mode=1&Parl=39&Ses=1&DocId=2539452&File=0.

Lachapelle, R. and Lepage, J.F. (2011) *Languages in Canada: 2006 Census.* Catalogue no. CH3-2/8-2010. Ottawa: Statistics Canada and Heritage Canada.

Lamarre, J. (2000) "Les Jeux de l'Acadie et le Québec". In F. Harvey and G. Beaulieu (eds) *Les relations entre le Québec et l'Acadie: de la tradition à la modernité.* Québec: Les Presses de l'Université Laval, pp. 277–291.

Langlois, S. (2003) "L'avenir de la langue française". In M. Plourde, H. Duval and P. Georgeault (eds) *Le Français au Québec: 400 Ans d'Histoire et de Vie.* Montréal: Fides, pp. 430–439.

Martel, M. and Pâquet, M. (2010) *Langue et Politique au Canada et au Québec.* Montréal: Éditions du Boréal.

McRoberts, K. (2001) Canada and the multinational state. *Canadian Journal of Political Science*, 34(4): 683–713.

Pelletier, R. (2009) "La dynamique fédérale au Canada". In B. Fournier and M. Reuchamps (eds) *Le Fédéralisme en Belgique et au Canada: Comparaison Sociopolitique.* Bruxelles: Éditions De Boeck Université, pp. 73–88.

Plourde, M. (2003) "La langue, ancre et moteur d'un monde en mutation". In M. Plourde, H. Duval and P. Georgeault (eds) *Le Français au Québec: 400 Ans d'Histoire et de Vie.* Montréal: Fides, pp. 441–455.

Rocher, F. (2009) "L'avenir de la fédération, l'avenir du fédéralisme: deux enjeux distincts au Canada". In B. Fournier and M. Reuchamps (eds.) *Le Fédéralisme en Belgique et au Canada: Comparaison Sociopolitique.* Bruxelles: Éditions De Boeck Université, pp. 231–254.

Statistics Canada (2012) Census in Brief: French and the Francoponie in Canada. Catalogue no. 98-314-X2011003. Ottawa: Minister of Industry.

Thériault, J.Y. (2003) "La langue, symbole de l'identité québécoise". In M. Plourde, H. Duval and P. Georgeault (eds) *Le Français au Québec: 400 Ans d'Histoire et de Vie.* Montréal: Fides, pp. 254–259.

15

THEIR SKIN IN THE GAME

The Basques, the Catalans and the 'body politic' of the Spanish national football team[1]

Mariann Vaczi

In 2010, a highlight of Spanish nation building during the South African FIFA World Cup was an Adidas commercial promoting the Spanish national team jersey. The commercial was titled *Nace de dentro*, 'It is born within.' It featured two Basque players and an Asturian standing with naked upper bodies, handsome, muscular and sweaty. The players start stripping their own skin digitally, from under which emerges the national symbol of Spain, and the colours red and yellow: the Spanish national team jersey. Against the backdrop of slow-motion soccer field images and dramatic music, a voiceover speaks the words: 'This jersey is history. It is everything that we suffer for, that we fight for, that we feel and live for. That which unites us is born within.' Skin is particularly symbolic in Spain. The country is also called *piel de toro* 'bull's skin', since the shape of the skin cut off from the animal after the bullfight is similar to the shape of Spain. The digital strip of the skin connotes a Spanish expression often used in sports: *dejarse la piel*, 'leaving the skin', or doing one's best. Skin is the imaginary link between the two ludic spectacles that constitute a temporal axis of Spanish identity, the bullfight of the past, and football of the future.

Rarely is the embodiment of a nation rendered so literally. The national team player's body emerges as a primordial metaphor for a Spain, where all are Spanish 'under their skin', in essence, whether they are Basque, Asturian, Catalan, Andalusian, and so on, on the surface. In its splendours and miseries, the Spanish national team has been Spain's 'body politic': a metaphor where the team's sport performance is considered as a reflection of the country's social-political state. Historically, the under-performance of the national team, also known as *la Furia Española* and *la Roja* (the 'Spanish Fury' or the 'Red One'), was sometimes attributed to a lack of patriotism on the part of players from ethno-regional peripheries. Basques and Catalans have been instrumental in the development of Spanish football and the national team, while they remain at odds with the idea of a central Spain. After major international disappointments the suspicion would often emerge: do Basques and Catalans really have their skin in the game when playing for Spain?

Winning the 2008 and 2012 UEFA European Championships and the 2010 FIFA World Cup finally silenced the decades-long 'Quixotic failure narrative' (Quiroga 2013: 19–48), and spoke of a different country. Pro-Spain fans and commentators believed that the spectacular performance of the *Roja*, with Catalan football as its core identity, reflected a new 'unity in diversity'. The successes of the national team were celebrated as evidence that Spain had become a modern country that was politically and socially united at last, and had overcome its regional divisions. Or had it? As of 2015, Spain faces the greatest political challenge in the post-Franco era to the nation's constitutional unity. In June 2014, King Juan Carlos abdicated in anticipation of a 'hot fall' as Catalans prepared to vote on the question of independence on the 9 November, despite a constitutional ban. Basques and Catalans have been claiming regional rights and liberties with varying degrees of intensity since the late nineteenth century. The 2011 permanent ceasefire of ETA (*Euskadi Ta Askatasuna* 'Basque Land and Freedom') and the current economic crisis have led to significantly greater support among Basques and Catalans for political movements that pursue independence.

The Spanish constitution and its discontents

This chapter examines Spain's basic, and ultimately most urgent, political question through football: the constitutional unity of the country. Spain's centuries-long centre–periphery conflict is characterised by the contradictory impulses of unification, espoused by Spanish centralist nationalists who argue that Spain is one and indivisible, and diversification, espoused by peripheral nationalities driven by various degrees of secessionist or Republican nationalism. The wording of the Constitution itself reflects that tension. After the death of Franco, the 1978 draft set as its priority the democratisation of Spain rather than the resolution of regional problems. In an attempt to reconcile unity and diversity, the document sought to strike a compromise between the supporters of a unitary state, and the proponents of a federal state (Comas 2003). The compromise led to an ambiguous definition of centre–periphery relations in Article 2:

> The Constitution is based on the indissoluble unity of the Spanish Nation, the common and indivisible country of all Spaniards; it recognises and guarantees the right to autonomy of the nationalities and regions of which it is composed, and solidarity among them all.
>
> *(Comas 2003: 39)*

While the Constitution promises a balance of central unity and regional autonomy, it results in asymmetrical arrangements in practice. Basques secured an economic agreement with Madrid right after the Transition, and got to manage their own treasury. Catalans, however, are estimated to lose about 8 per cent (16,400 million euros) of their GDP to the Spanish treasury each year, which motivates Catalonia to secede from Spain, and motivates Spain to prevent that secession. Once in conflict, centralist interests prevail over regional autonomy. Similarly, Catalonia and the Basque Country can label themselves 'nationalities' but not 'nations', an attribute reserved only for Spain, which created a constitutional crisis when Catalans referred to themselves as a 'nation' in their 2006 Statute of Autonomy. There is a sense, therefore, in which the double standards resulting from the paradoxical impulses of the Constitution remind periphery nationalists of the Seventh Commandment of George Orwell's *Animal Farm*, which stipulates that 'all animals are equal, but some are more equal than others'.

Football is the most visible social arena of these political tensions, which this chapter analyses through two concepts that affect processes of unification and diversification: 'works of hybridisation' and 'works of purification' (Latour 1993; Bauman and Briggs 2003). Works of hybridisation allow for the proliferation of heterogeneous voices and life worlds, and recognise their interconnectedness. Works of purification, however, disregard alternative affective histories, and/or reduce them to a single essence by imposing a single authorial conscious-ness from a particular perspective of domination. Spanish football and politics are a terrain for both works. 'Our country counts with a king, a prime minister, and eleven gods. The eleven gods wear a red-fury jersey – Spanish, of course', Rosa Montero wrote in *El País* in 1983. The 2010 FIFA World Cup success was discursively constructed as 'a much delayed, "normal" enjoyment of Spanishness' (Delgado 2010: 266): Spain became a modern state that has finally 'defeated its ghosts' (Delgado 2010: 270). By defeating ghosts and becoming mod-ern, do centralists celebrate the 'de-provincialising', (Chakrabarty 2000) of the Spanish national team – the negation of regional loyalties and affective histories? 'Normal', 'modern' and 'de-provincialised' become works of purification whose aim is to establish the national team as a meta-discursive regime representing one culture, one language, one territory, one people – Spanish. This chapter explores the Spanish national team as a conflicted ideological terrain between Spanish, Basque and Catalan nationalism. It traces antagonistic impulses of unity versus diversity, purification versus hybridisation as a process called 'schismogenesis' (Bateson 1958): a dialectic process of differentiation between centre and periphery which might be contained under repressive regimes but, once those restraints are removed, increasing sym-metry of power between the parties threatens with a breakaway situation. Analysing sport and politics through the logic of schismogenesis informs how the current constitutional crisis about the unity of Spain emerged, and how football has contributed to the current Catalan independence process.

The class, gender and ideology of early Spanish sport (1870–1936)

The late emergence, slow institutionalisation and spread of sport in Spain may be attributed to various factors. The Spanish state had political and economic difficulties, and did not pri-oritise the educational system, sport's main context elsewhere. Progressive political factions distrusted sports for their militarist connotations in Europe, while traditionalists opposed them in an effort to protect traditional cultural performances like bullfighting. The Catholic Church, which played a crucial role in education at the time, was not particularly convinced, either (Domínguez Almansa 2011: 61). Lacking state and institutional support, sport in Spain emerged and spread through two main channels: the industrial elite and its economic exchange with Britain, and the grassroots initiatives of *asociacionismo*, or the popular-associative world. The arrival of sport from Britain and elsewhere favoured maritime locations and the capital: Bilbao (Basque Country), Barcelona (Catalonia) and Madrid. These centres quickly grew into distinct football cultures: by the 1930s, two-thirds of the total number of players of the peninsula played in Catalonia, the Basque Country, Asturias and Madrid (Bahamonde Magro 2011: 100).

The first *gimnasios* were centres of urban bourgeois sociability: they had diverse cultural functions, and were associated with political, social and economic sensibilities, including nationalism and Republicanism. The first sports reflected bourgeois tastes and world views: tennis was adopted as the fashionable European sport, rowing reflected the maritime elite's economic attachment to the sea, cycling suited capitalists' penchant for the competitive exploi-tation of time and motor racing reflected their fascination with new technology. The bour-geois elite embraced sport for its values related to entrepreneurship: 'the effort of work, the capacity for calculated risk taking, the embrace of innovation, a sense of leadership, the spirit of the company, and the pride of being agents and protagonists of modernity' (Bahamonde Magro 2011: 98).

The Second Republic of Spain (1931–1936) affected a new relationship between sport and citizenship: the general democratisation of political life helped sport conquer the non-elite, non-urban sectors, the working classes, universities and women (Pujadas i Martí 2011). Though based on essentialist, biological determinism with regards to gender and 're-generationist' discourses with regards to 'race', sport associations fostered such wide-ranging political ideologies as communism, anarcho-syndicalism, Marxist socialism, Basque and Catalan nationalism, feminism and the fascism of the Spanish Falange. This was an epoch of associative public spheres characterised by the burgeoning of syndicalist unions, youth platforms, and cultural and popular organisations. Many sport organisations were openly linked to political ideologies: the Federación Cultural Deportiva Obrera to communism, the Comité Català pro Esport Popular to Republican-Catalan nationalism, the Salud y Cultura to socialism, and the Juventud Vasca to Basque nationalist youth platforms. A most important manifestation of sport based on working-class associative culture (*asociacionismo popular y obrero*) and left-wing ideologies was the organisation of the Olimpiada Popular in Barcelona in 1936 by an international alliance of anti-fascist popular movements in protest of Hitler's Games (Large 2007). With athletes already in town, the Olimpiada Popular was eventually cancelled due to the outbreak of the Spanish Civil War (1936–1939).

Sports became an important public arena of women's emancipation during the Second Republic (1931–1936). The 1931 Constitution's voting rights to women, the 1932 Divorce Law granting juridical equality to women in marriage, and increased female literacy enabled greater public participation for women in general. Some women's *gimnasios*, such as the emblematic Club Femení i d'Esports de Barcelona (1928) made no secret about their feminist agenda to provide a platform of 'civic, Republican sociability' (Pujadas i Martí 2011: 157) for the modern woman who was independent, responsible and Republican. Concomitantly to these popular, grassroots, developments elite women's sport gained international admiration. Overall, sport was a cultural arena of social progress and women's emancipation, while it remained predicated on essentialist discourses: women could participate in sports that fitted their 'fragile' biological constitution, else their role was reduced to the passive role of the 'beautiful spectator' (Pink 1997: 61).

The Basque and the Catalan nationalist movements crystallised around the end of the nineteenth century, and represented progressive Republican ideas vis-à-vis the Spanish monarchy. The emerging Basque and Catalan industrial bourgeoisie espoused a position against Madrid, making dialogue increasingly difficult. Catalonia mobilised around 'cultural Catalanism', affected by the flourishing, cosmopolitan cultural life and renaissance of fin-de-siècle Barcelona, as well as language as a community-marking factor (Conversi 1997: 42). Basque nationalism was nourished by a sense of ethno-linguistic difference and economic-administrative autonomy, historically reinforced by such state-granted privileges as local statutes and charters (Conversi 1997: 178). Early on in the twentieth century, Basque and Catalan nationalisms aligned with two major clubs of the Spanish *Liga*: Athletic Club and Barcelona FC. Athletic became 'the flagship football club of the Basque Country' (Walton 2011: 458), and Barcelona FC the most important Catalan symbol (Llopis-Goig 2008). Both clubs had shared leadership with the local, economic-nationalist elite, often members of Basque and Catalan nationalist parties and organisations.

The beginnings of the Spanish Fury: 'race', ethnicity and national virility in Spain

A mí el pelotón, Sabino, que los arrollo 'Sabino, give me the ball, and I'll wipe them out!' This phrase by the Basque José Mari Belausteguigoitia ('Belauste') gained transcendence in the history of Spanish soccer. The first Spanish national team played an especially physical game against

Sweden at the 1920 Olympic Games in Amberes, Belgium. Such was the physicality, passion and force of the squad that the following day the Italian press called it *Furia Rossa* or 'Red Rage', after the colour of the players' jersey. Soon they were called 'Spanish Fury'.

'It is quite ironic', Belauste's daughter Lorea Belausteguigoitia writes, 'that the "Spanish Fury" should come from this Basque nationalist, director of the football team of the Basque Nationalist Party youth' (Bacigalupe 2005: 29). The man who inspired the identity of the Spanish national team was an anti-Spain Basque nationalist. Belauste was a member of the youth section of the Basque Nationalist Party (PNV), where he was responsible for the organisation of a series of sport events. He was forced into exile to France and Mexico for his Basque nationalist activities. Furthermore, there was little that was strictly speaking 'Spanish' about the game that came to identify Spanish football. The team consisted of thirteen Basque, four Catalan, and four Galician players, headed by coach Paco Bru of undisguised Barcelona sympathies. The physical football that inspired the word 'fury' reflected the dominant style of the squad: *la manera inglesa*, 'the English style' of the Basques, inherited from early British players and coaches. It was a physical, forceful game that suited well the more robust and taller constitutions of the northern peoples of Spain. Belauste was himself a veritable force of nature: 6 feet 3 inches tall and 210 pounds of muscle. The Basque player's game provided the adjectives that came to describe the 'Spanish Fury' for several decades to come: his '"nobility", "courage", pressure, enthusiasm and vigour . . . energy and spirit' (Díaz Noci 2000: 5).

While the national team was mobilised in the service of a Spanish national identity, Basques and Catalans mobilised football for the construction of their own national characters. The Basque and Catalan nationalist press devoted particular efforts to promote football. The youth section of the Basque Nationalist Party (PNV) was a most active agent in the merger of football, politics, and 'racial' health. An article titled 'Art and Sport' in *Euzkadi* in 1915 welcomed football for its regenerative powers against 'the mortal enemy . . . the destruction of the Basque soul, of our pure and national idiosyncrasy' (Unzueta 1999: 160). The Catalan *La Rambla* openly linked Catalan identity and civic nationalism to football under the editorship of Josep Sunyol, Barcelona FC's emblematic president shot by Francoist forces, in an article titled 'Sport and Citizenship':

> To speak of sport is to speak of race, enthusiasm, and the optimistic struggle of youth.
> To speak of citizenship is to speak of the Catalan civilisation, liberalism, democracy, and spiritual endeavour.
>
> *(Burns 2012: 88)*

For some fifty years therefore, between the appearance of football on the peninsula and the establishment of the Franco dictatorship in 1939, we see works of both purification and hybridisation in Spanish football. While the beginnings of the Spanish Fury indicates impulses of centralist unification and Hispanicisation, the nationalist peripheries added diversity to the overall football arena by their own, local works of purification. The result was a hybrid narrative that Bakhtin (1981) would call *heteroglossia*: the co-existence of various tones and voices within a single arena. The Franco regime would put an end to that diversity.

'The dove of peace is a ball': ideology and identity under Franco

The Franco dictatorship endorsed football for two related purposes: first, to construct a unified national character, and second, because it helped 'opiate' regional-political discontent

(Shaw 1987). The challenge was to establish football as an agent of nationalism for the centre, but a non-agent for the peripheries. These objectives resulted in the purification of not only the national team, but the entire football scene as exclusively Spanish.

Virility, impetuousness and fury continued to determine a Spanish style that celebrated masculine Hispanic values. The Spanish Fury connoted Spain's imperial past of conquest and glory, as the name itself was first inspired by the 1576 Spanish pillage of Antwerp. At the 1950 FIFA World Cup group stage against England, after the winning goal by Telmo Zarra, a Basque forward who set several records in the Liga, Spanish football's top official Armando Muñoz Calero told Franco: 'Excellency: we have vanquished the perfidious Albion' (Burns 2012: 4), as if the victory finally served historical justice for Britain's 1588 defeat of the Spanish Armada. Again, the Spanish Fury was embodied by a tall and forceful Basque, Zarra. 'Zarra scored the goal of the most glorious Spanish victory', wrote *Marca* after the group stage victory:

> A splendid demonstration to the whole world that the traditional Hispanic virtues of passion, aggression, fury, virility and impetuosity have been completely recovered in the 'New Spain' born out of that bloody conflict – the Civil War.
>
> *(Burns 2012: 139)*

The swan song of the Spanish Fury was the 1964 victory against the Soviet Union. For Franco, winning was imperative for his anti-communist agenda. The winning goals were authored by a Basque: Txus Pereda, who scored the first goal, and delivered an assist for the second one. The final 2–1 victory was celebrated as the return of the Spanish Fury: of passion, aggression and courage. Then the Fury quietened down for the next forty-something years.

Franco set out to purify the entire football arena as Spanish. He ordered all sports clubs to Castilianise their names in 1942. Athletic Club, which had assumed the English name in homage to its British roots, was now called Atlético de Bilbao. Franco also controlled club leadership and made sure club presidents were close to his regime. A prime example of such a president was Santiago Bernabéu, a Civil War veteran who turned Real Madrid into Europe's most successful football club, and Spain's 'national team'. It was Bernabéu who famously said: 'The dove of peace is a ball', tacitly equating football with distraction from political discontent. A few years after the collapse of the regime, at the 1982 FIFA World Cup inaugural ceremony in Barcelona, the world witnessed the reproduction of that maxim: a boy walked up midfield holding a football, removed its cap, and out flew a white dove. 'The spectacle of the dove flying out of the football was incredibly impacting', an informant told me. It was also an evocation of the political utilisation of football only a few years before.

'Athletic, Only Spanish Blood': the contention over purity

The Basque Athletic Bilbao has a special patina in the Spanish league: besides Barcelona FC and Real Madrid, it is one of the three teams that has never descended to the second division – and, for a hundred years now, it has only played Basque players. I address the pleasures and pains of this special recruitment *filosofía*, its evolution and consequences for Basque fandom, identity and nationalism elsewhere (Vaczi 2015). Suffice it to say here that Athletic only signs players who were born or bred in the historical (i.e. Spanish and French) Basque Country, making it a major Basque symbol.

In January 2002, the following text appeared on the front page of the daily *La Razón* under the title 'Athletic, Only Spanish Blood':

Athletic, the only team of eleven Spanish players . . . [the club that has] always preferred the national purity, the national product. And it seems they have not been
mistaken if we judge it by the accumulated successes of its history. Athletic presumes
to achieve something no one else can . . . It will continue its politics of Spanish
players that have given it such good results, and it will make everyone envious of its
youth academy.

(*Gómez* 2007: 122)

Spanish nationalist journalist Luis María Anson would make a particular ritual of repeating
this argument during his tenure at *ABC* and later *La Razón*: 'Athletic, the only team of eleven
Spanish players.'

Praising Athletic as 'the only team of eleven Spaniards', which Basques find a provocation,
resonates with Franco's works of purification. Franco tolerated, respected and even liked Athletic
Club. During my interviews with elderly fans, I inquired about what first seemed a conundrum:
Franco criminalised all manifestations of Basque identity, while he never touched Athletic's
philosophy of recruiting from Basque land. The Bilbao club was not just acceptable, but even
welcome for Franco's Hispanicising agenda because, like it is today, it could always be conveniently called Spanish. Spain could always turn to Athletic for local heroes for the nourishment
of the Spanish Fury, which was not always the case with Real Madrid or Barcelona FC. These
two giant clubs had foreigners as some of their most paradigmatic historical personages: Puskás
and Di Stéfano for the former, Kubala and later Cruyff for the latter. These players changed the
course of football in Spain; what they could not do as Hungarian, Argentine or Dutch, however,
was to serve as an embodiment of Spanish Fury. This was an acute problem. As *Marca* wrote in
1962 after Spain was yet again eliminated from the World Cup:

the national team is now so full of foreigners and so conditioned by foreign tactics that
it no longer plays like a team of real Spaniards, with passion, with aggression, with
courage, with virility, and above all with fury.

(*Burns* 2012: 121)

During its golden age (1940s–1960s), Athletic Club produced world-class players, who in
Madrid were seen as 'real Spaniards' due to the club's localist recruitment policy.

The appropriation of a Basque-only recruitment philosophy as 'Spanish' reveals centralist impulses of purification. Limiting their player pool to the Basque Country, Basques were
recreating their own version of purity. In the 1950s, the club hymn already exalted Bilbao's
football as *limpia tradición*, a 'clean tradition'. 'We haven't lost our virginity yet', a fan told me
with reference to the club's purity. Basques produced an ideal of purity that Spanish centralists
desired for the Spanish Fury.

Calling Spain 'Spain': when things dare not speak their name

In November 2012, the Basque Markel Susaeta was called up for the Spanish national team.
At his first press conference he said: 'I am very happy and proud to be here, the dream of
my life . . . Here we are representing . . . *una cosa* "a thing" . . . that we have to respect' (*El
Mundo* November 2012). Susaeta provoked nation-wide indignation among centralists because
he seemed to avoid saying that he represented Spain.

Naming and de-naming, anthropologists tell us, have the capacity to fix, steal, trade, suspend and erase identities; naming practices are a performance that 'do' as well as 'say' things,

a privilege that perpetuates power (Bodenhorn and Bruck 2006). During the Franco regime, that privilege lay with the regime. With the democratic transition after the death of the dictator in 1975, a new challenge of naming and de-naming catalysed spectacular debates over how to insert phenomena into the new social-political matrix (Raento and Watson 2000; Mees 2012).

In the Basque Country, the new nationalist media faced the challenge of transition acutely. Some of the first Basque nationalist daily newspapers avoided using the word 'Spain', and chose to use 'Spanish State' instead. The idea behind that strategy was the contention that Spain was not a nation but a political category. The initial desire of these editors was to give news of the 'Spanish State' in a limited fashion, and possibly avoid it altogether. With the 1980 Moscow Olympic Games, however, pro-Basque papers had to recognise that people wanted to read more extensively about Spanish athletes. On the one hand, they had been socialised into state-level sports; on the other, there was always a few Basque athletes in the Spanish delegations. 'This was a situation that caught Basque nationalists off guard as if in self-contradiction', a journalist told me. 'There we were rejecting Spain even in its name, while many of our readers followed Spanish sports and national teams.' Basque nationalist news portals expanded their coverage, but continued to call Spain the 'Spanish State', even in the rankings of nations. Another revealing naming practice emerged: dropping any reference to Spain altogether. Instead of 'Spanish national team' or even the 'national team of the Spanish State', coaches' names were introduced: 'the national team of Kubala', 'the national team of Suárez'. This practice suggests that for Basque nationalists, following the Spanish team was unbearable under that name. They faced a dilemma: stop following the national team, or drop the name. Euphemisms like the 'national team of Kubala' were a coping mechanism to somehow reconcile contradictory mandates: the hybridising mandate to follow the Spanish team as well (for which many Basques, and even Basque nationalists continued to play), and the purifying mandate to taboo everything Spanish.

Naming has been a problem for the centre as well. After the Franco regime, when the idea of a united Spain became increasingly problematic as a result of re-invigorated regional nationalisms, the designation *selección española* 'Spanish team' became untenable. The Basque and Catalan peripheries continued to delegate a substantial number of players to the 'national' team, although they were increasingly antagonistic to the idea of 'Spain'. The term *selección nacional*, 'national team', had been used during the Franco regime. The *Furia* character became increasingly obsolete in the light of a new soccer style that thrived on technique and imagination rather than pure force: a shift from the Basque roots towards a Catalan style. When national team coach Luis Aragonés started to call his squad *la Roja*, a loud radical right-wing minority opposed the name, as for them red was the colour of communism, a major enemy under Francoism. Another minority suggested this was Aragonés' way of warming up to the newly elected socialist government of José Luis Zapatero. But overall, *la Roja* became a designation that was abstract enough not to conjure up major historical-ideological antagonisms, while it retained an allusion to life-giving vitality in its resemblance to wine or blood. De-naming the Spanish Fury was what Bodenhorn and Bruck would call 'a form of political annihilation' (Bodenhorn and Bruck 2006: 1): a break with earlier impulses of purifying Hispanicisation.

Feeling Spanish: purity and danger in the national team

In January 2013, the Catalan player Xavi received criticism implying that he might not be entirely devoted to the Spanish team because of his unconcealed Catalan sympathies. Coach Vicente del Bosque stepped up to defend him: 'Xavi's devotion to the Spanish team is unquestionable. The numbers are there. We cannot cite his Catalan condition, either. This would mean having a *dirty mind*' (Segura January 2013).

A history of purification reminds us of the anthropologist's argument: where there is purification there is also dirt or at least a perceived threat of it, for the concepts of cleanliness and pollution constitute a binary system that reflects a culture's basic idea of order and disorder (Douglas 1966). The *Roja* is such a reflection: unity in diversity is the Spanish 'fantasy of normalcy', of order, while the prioritisation of ethno-regional sentiments at the expense of Spanish-ness is by extension contamination and disorder. By shovelling dirt back on them, Del Bosque's is a riposte to those who consider Xavi's 'Catalan condition' as possibly contaminating.

That a player should not feel Spanish has been perceived as a source of danger. Anxiety over whether players 'feel the Spanish colours', whether they 'have their skin in the game' is palpable, and leads to a constant policing of allegiances. When Susaeta had troubles calling Spain Spain and said 'thing' instead, public reaction was intense: many saw it as proof that he did not 'feel Spanish', and therefore he should not play in the national team. Feelings, comments, flags and gestures become elements of potential contamination, a threat to order as conceived from a particular perspective. The Spanish national anthem has no lyrics, allowing no opportunity to debate which players, and with how much conviction, sing it. Instead, other destabilising demons such as socks emerge. In 2007, the pro-Spanish media was shocked to see that the Catalan player Xavi concealed the Spanish colours of his socks, and Puyol somehow fabricated a Catalan national flag (*senyera*) out of them (20 Minutos 4 June, 2007). Fear about the colour of players' socks was most marked when the 1980s Basque goalkeeper Luis Arconada would wear plain white socks instead of the official black ones featuring the Spanish colours. For some, it was out of superstition; others interpreted it as a sign of the Basque goalkeeper's *anti-españolismo*. Players' political activism is similarly scrutinised. When Barcelona FC and Spanish team defender Gerard Piqué were photographed in a massive rally in September 2014 in Barcelona for the right to vote about Catalan independence, the player received so much criticism he had to give explanations: 'I am not asking for [Catalan] independence, I am asking for the right to vote . . . I feel very committed, and will be always happy to play for the Spanish national team' (*La Vanguardia* 10 October, 2014). At the same time, at the 2014 Christmas friendly between the unofficial Basque and Catalan national sides, a game of ample pro-independence proclamations, the Spanish media was happy to spot that the Catalan Busquets did not hold on to the Catalan team banner saying 'one nation, one national team'. Was it a secret sign, a gesture against the Catalan *independentista* fervor? In the Spanish football scene, minor incidents may become major fetishistic fixations.

The Spanish national team remains a site of tension. On the one hand, there are few ways that the Basque and Catalan regions can feel comfortable with it. An impasse of identification emerges for fans and players and the following questions arise: 'Do I feel Spanish?' 'Does this really represent me?' 'Why can't we have our own regional-national teams?' When the game is over, Basques and Catalans are declared Spanish world champions, and are celebrated as the finest Spaniards amidst cries of *Viva España!* and the chant *Yo soy español, español, español,* 'I am Spanish!' For some players, it results in an irreconcilable contradiction. Among the few known cases of a football player's refusal to play in the Spanish national team – which the Spanish Football Federation has the right to sanction with cancelling the player's licence – is that of the Basque goalkeeper Iribar from the 1970s and 1980s. Iribar was the undisputed goalkeeper of the Spanish national team for several years. However, as he gradually got involved with Basque nationalism, ran for office and attended political rallies, there came a point when playing for the Spanish team became untenable. 'For me, there arrived a moment of contradiction', Iribar said in an interview in 1980. 'I could no longer ask for the release of Basque political prisoners, and then be ambassador of Spain with the Spanish national team' (Gómez, 2007: 66). A recent Catalan example is the former Barcelona defender Oleguer Presas, who explained to national team coach Luis Aragonés 'how he saw the world', and told him 'when there is no sufficient commitment or sentiment, it is better to call other persons'. While there have been other cases, it remains in everybody's best interest to treat these withdrawals from the national team with discretion.

Centralists and pro-national team fans also feel the vulnerability of their situation reflected by the contingency of the country's greatest national brand, the *Roja*, on players that are often openly anti-Spanish. On the eve of the 2010 FIFA World Cup final, one and a half million Catalans protested in favour of independence and against a constitutional court decision to curtail regional autonomy. That particular night before the historic game that won the championship for Spain, the question of what would become of the country without one of its economic motors, Catalonia, gained another frightful dimension: what would become of the Spanish national team without its Catalan players?

Schism under the skin

The main motif of the commercial that started this chapter, skin and the implied underlying national essence, also brings awareness that something may be brewing under the surface: an alarming sense of division and schism. Spanish football is a 'field' in Bourdieu's (1984) sense: a system of social positions and agents whose interaction is determined by power relations, and the specific character of the field. The specific character of sport fields is *agôn*, or competitive combat (Caillois 1961). Spanish, Basque and Catalan nationalists are agents of this field who, by way of their varying historical trajectory, have aligned in a competitive–antagonistic relationship over the symbolic and political capital of mobilising power through football.

In this political geography, we see a process whose logic was analysed by Bateson (1958) as 'schismogenesis': a 'process of differentiation in the norms of individual behaviour resulting from the cumulative interaction between individuals' (p. 175). Football and politics in Spain have been a historically accumulating, agonic dialectic. As each party reacts to the reaction of the other in the process of progressive differentiation, and unless there are restraining factors, the end result will be schism. Historically, the equilibrium of both the political system between centre versus periphery, as well as the sport system of Madrid versus Barcelona and Bilbao, was restrained by state domination and purifying discourses. The system did not disintegrate because there was a situation of 'complementary schismogenesis': a competitive relationship between categorical unequals, as was the centre and the periphery. Both politics and sports have been part of a system with clear tendencies for schism, but the parties remained in complementary antagonism held together by submission to a national hierarchy fixed by works of purification.

The current possibility of disintegration lies in a shift from complementary towards 'symmetrical schismogenesis': a shift towards a competitive relationship between categorical equals, which, in the absence of restraining factors, may lead to a breakaway situation. Indeed, we see an unprecedented constellation of circumstances. In a supra-national democratic Europe where Great Britain has recently allowed Scotland to vote on its independence in September 2014, Spain's ban on regional self-determination is increasingly untenable. As Catalan football continues to weigh heavily for the national team, and Spanish football receives more media scrutiny than ever, we see increasing symmetry: the symbolic capital of Catalan soccer turns the periphery into a categorical equal. Catalans make no secret of what they wish for the future: at the 2012 October *el Clásico*, the derby between Real Madrid and Barcelona FC that was broadcast by 680 journalists from thirty countries and viewed by 400 million television spectators, the Camp Nou terraces displayed the message 'Catalonia, Europe's Next State' on its large screens.

The result of the increasing symmetry of power relations is often open confrontation. On May 13, 2009, Valencia's Mestalla stadium filled every one of its seats for the King's Cup final between Barcelona FC and Athletic Bilbao. As the Spanish national anthem was played through the loudspeakers, 55,000 Basque and Catalan fans whistled so intensely that the anthem could not be heard. In 2012, Athletic and Barcelona once again qualified for the King's Cup final, this time held in Madrid. The game became a major security concern: the Madrid Court of Justice allowed the demonstration of pro-Spain Falangist (neo-fascist) organisations in Madrid on the same day. With about 100,000 Basque and Catalan fans in town, including their radical nationalist segments, and Falangists marching through the streets of Madrid, the King's Cup final became a paradigmatic spectacle that condensed the antagonistic impulses of centralist unification and regionalist diversification.

The king's two bodies

It was a 'peculiar conversation', as the media put it. On June 17, 2014, just as the Spanish national football team was resting before the crucially important game that it needed to win to continue in the FIFA World Cup finals in Brazil, the Spanish King Juan Carlos was preparing his abdication. As he said goodbye to the representatives of political powers and Prime Minister Mariano Rajoy amid gentlemanly handshakes and courtesies, the cameras caught Rajoy joking: 'Tomorrow the game is all fixed!' And the king, maintaining the joking tone: 'And how much did it cost us?' 'Gratis!' Then they proceeded to discuss goal-keeping feats and failures, penalties, referee decisions and players' conditions. The conversation at the last official act of King Juan Carlos revolved around the national team's upcoming FIFA World Cup game.

Doing fieldwork in Catalonia just then, I found it difficult to decide what drew more attention: the game that would decide the *Roja*'s future in the World Cup, or the abdication of the old, and the coronation of the new king. It was also difficult not to suspect a purpose behind such a 'coincidence' of events. On the one hand there was the World Cup and the *Roja*, whose successes had been actively constructed as 'uniting' Spain; on the other hand there was the abdication and coronation, which provoked anti-monarchy, pro-Republican demonstrations in Catalonia and the Basque Country. Was the *Roja*'s presumed World Cup success supposed to suture the political divisions caused by the coronation of the new king? Was the World Cup going to serve as a distraction from highly controversial political events?

In his acclaimed medieval political theology *The King's Two Bodies* (1957), Ernst Kantorowicz explores the maintenance of monarchical power through distinguishing between the 'body natural', and the 'body politic' of the king. While the natural body of the king may die and decay, he also has another, 'spiritual' body that transcends death, and continues to symbolise his office. Through its centralist connotations as described in this chapter, and through its discursive presence at the king's abdication, the national team was invoked and deployed as that other, spiritual body: the 'body politic' that served to remind people that, while the king abdicated, the symbolic power of his office continued through the *Roja*'s global reign. Ironically, it happened the other way round: the celebrations of the coronation served to suture the wound of the humiliating, record-fast elimination of the epoch-making champion team. As the 'end of Juan Carlos' reign' emerged in chilling parallel with 'the end of Spanish football's reign', the new king and his bright red sash of military power served to symbolise the continuity of both Spain and its football in the face of Catalans who, emboldened by the Scottish referendum, threaten their unity.

Note

1 Parts of an earlier version of this chapter appeared in "'The Spanish Fury": a political geography of soccer in Spain'. *International Review for the Sociology of Sport*, published online ahead of print February 2013, doi:10.1177/1012690213478940.

References

Bacigalupe, A. (2005) *Belauste: el caballero de la furia*. Bilbao: Muelle de Uribitarte.

Bahamonde Magro, Á. (2011) 'La escalada del deporte en España en los orígenes de la sociedad de masa, 1900-1936'. In X. Pujedes i Martí (ed.) *Atletas y ciudadanos: historia social del deporte en España 1870–2010*. Madrid: Alianza Editorial, pp. 89–125.

Bakhtin, M.M. (1981) *The Dialogic Imagination: Four Essays*. Austin, TX: University of Texas Press.

Bateson, G. (1958) *Naven*. Stanford, CA: Stanford University Press.

Bauman, R. and Briggs, C.L. (2003) *Voices of Modernity: Language Ideologies and the Politics of Inequality*. Cambridge: Cambridge University Press.

Bodenhorn, B. and Bruck, G.V. (eds) (2006) *The Anthropology of Names and Naming*. Cambridge: Cambridge University Press.

Bourdieu, P. (1984) *Distinction: A Social Critique of the Judgment of Taste*. Cambridge, MA: Harvard University Press.

Burns, J. (2012) *La Roja: How Soccer Conquered Spain, and How Spanish Soccer Conquered the World*. New York: Nation Books.

Caillois, R. (1961) *Man, Play, and Games*. New York: Free Press of Glencoe.

Chakrabarty, D. (2000) *Provincializing Europe: Postcolonial Thought and Historical Difference*. Princeton, NJ: Princeton University Press.

Comas, J.M. (2003) 'Spain: The 1978 constitution and centre–periphery tensions'. In J. Ruane, J. Todd and A. Mandeville (eds) *Europe's Old States in the New World Order: The Politics of Transition in Britain, France and Spain*. Dublin: University College Dublin Press, pp. 38–61.

Conversi, D. (1997) *The Basques, the Catalans, and Spain: Alternative Routes to Nationalist Mobilisation*. London: Hurst and Co.

Delgado, E.L. (2010) The sound and the red fury: the sticking points of Spanish nationalism. *Journal of Spanish Cultural Studies*, 11(3–4): 263–276.

Díaz Noci, J. (2000) 'Los nacionalistas van al fútbol: deporte, ideología y periodismo en los años 20 y 30'. *Revista de estudios de comunicación = Komunikazio ikasketen aldizkaria*. Accessed June 2, 2016. www.ehu.es/zer/hemeroteca/pdfs/zer09-13-diaz.pdf.

Domínguez Almansa, A. (2011) 'La práctica de la modernidad: orígenes y consolidación de la cultura deportiva en España'. In X. Pujedes i Martí (ed.) *Atletas y ciudadanos: historia social del deporte en España 1870–2010*. Madrid: Alianza Editorial, pp. 55–89.

Douglas, M. (1966) *Purity and Danger: An Analysis of the Concepts of Pollution and Taboo*. London: Ark.

Gómez, D. (2007) *La patria del gol: fútbol y política en el Estado español*. Almed: San Sebastián.

Kantorowicz, E.H. (1957) *The King's Two Bodies: A Study in Mediaeval Political Theology*. Princeton, NJ: Princeton University Press.

Large, D.C. (2007) *Nazi Games: The Olympics of 1936*. New York: W.W. Norton & Company.

Latour, B. (1993) *We Have Never Been Modern*. Cambridge, MA: Harvard University Press.

Llopis-Goig, R. (2008) National orientation, universal outlook: the symbolic capital of FC Barcelona in the global era. *European Journal for Sport and Society*, 5(1): 63–71.

Mees, L. (2012) 'A nation in search of a name: cultural realities, political projects, and terminological struggles in the Basque Country'. In P. Salaburu and X. Alberdi (eds) *The Challenges of a Bilingual Society in the Basque Country*. Reno, NV: University of Nevada Press, pp. 11–33.

Pink, S. (1997) *Women and Bullfighting: Gender, Sex and the Consumption of Tradition*. Oxford: Berg.

Pujadas i Martí, X. (2011) 'Del barrio al estadio: deporte, mujeres y clases populares en la Segunda República, 1931–1936'. In X. Pujedes I. Martí (ed.) *Atletas y ciudadanos: historia social del deporte en España 1870-2010*. Madrid: Alianza Editorial, pp. 125–169.

Quiroga, A. (2013) *Football and National Identities in Spain: The Strange Death of Don Quixote*. London: Palgrave Macmillan.

Raento, P. and Watson, C. (2000) Gernika, Guernica, *Guernica*? Contested meanings of a Basque place. *Political Geography*, 19: 707–736.

Segura, M. (2013) Del Bosque alucina con Messi. In *El Mundo Deportivo*, January 15, 2013. Accessed January 15, 2013. www.mundodeportivo.com/20130115/fc-barcelona/espana-seleccion-la-roja-del-bosque-messi-xavi-iniesta_54360890808.html.

Shaw, D. (1987) *Fútbol y franquismo*. Madrid: Alianza Editorial.

Unzueta, P. (1999) 'Fútbol y nacionalismo vasco'. In S. Segurola (ed.) *Fútbol y pasiones políticas*. Madrid: Editorial Debate, pp. 147–169.

Vaczi, M. (2015) *Soccer, Culture and Society in Spain: An Ethnography of Basque Fandom*. London, New York: Routledge.

Walton, J.K. (2011) Sport and the Basques: constructed and contested identities, 1876–1936. *Journal of Historical Sociology*, 24(4): 451–447.

20 Minutos. (2007) Por qué la bandera española no está en las medias de Puyol y Xavi? Accessed October 15, 2012. www.20minutos.es/noticia/243094/0/Espana/bandera/polemica/.

16

SPORT IN A DIVIDED NORTHERN IRELAND

Past and present

David Hassan

Introduction

It is a universal truism that when politicians fail to agree and division becomes manifest that the effects of such discord are witnessed across civic society and impact upon the everyday lives of its citizens. Nowhere is this truer than in Northern Ireland, a country synonymous with internal conflict, violence and mistrust between its two major ethnic groupings, Irish nationalists and Ulster unionists (McEvoy 2008). The country is one part of the United Kingdom of Great Britain and Northern Ireland but its positioning, adjacent to the Republic of Ireland, offers a clue as to the social, political and cultural issues at the heart of a long-standing dispute, underwritten in many cases by thinly veiled sectarianism (at other times this is tragically manifest), that led to a violent guerrilla-style conflict between Irish republican paramilitaries, loyalist factions (Unionist paramilitaries) and functionaries of the British state, specifically the locally based police force, the Royal Ulster Constabulary (RUC), which began in the late 1960s (Bew 2007).

This violence grew out of a frustration being experienced by ordinary Catholics in Northern Ireland at that time who felt that a Unionist-dominated government in Northern Ireland treated them in a discriminatory fashion and, inspired by a global civil rights movement that was taking hold then, took to the streets to vent their frustration. From there events spiralled out of control and, sensing an opportunity to revisit an unrelenting desire for the re-unification of Ireland (between Northern Ireland and the Republic of Ireland), which had been established following the signing of the Anglo-Irish Treaty in 1921, republican paramilitaries waged a war against their pan-Unionist opponents that only reached an agreed cessation with the signing of the Belfast Agreement in 1998 (Ó Dochartaigh 2004). This simultaneously brought an end to widespread violence in Northern Ireland, introduced a broad policy of demilitarisation and established a power-sharing executive in the country that allowed proportionate representation for different shades of political opinion there and which became acceptable to most (if not all) sides (Bew 2007).

That said, it would be incredibly naïve to expect a sophisticated network of subversive paramilitary activity simply to cease as if somehow bringing down the shutters on a defunct shop front. As recently as late 2015, the devolved executive sitting at Stormont was placed in jeopardy following the murders of two former IRA volunteers in the Markets and Short Strand areas of Belfast respectively, the second of which was widely believed to have been carried out by members of the Provisional Irish Republican Army (IRA), which had officially been stood down in 2005. As Sinn Féin had been the political wing of the IRA and had approved the organisation's commitment to non-violence, a precursor to engagement in the locally formed power-sharing executive, the future of the executive remained in the balance even within sight of the twentieth anniversary of the signing of the Good Friday Agreement.

At the heart of much of this dispute was the issue of national identity and even those for whom expressions of allegiance were a secondary consideration, perhaps because they did not experience the sense of loss that conflict can exercise upon a people, were almost obliged to adopt a partisan stance. Indeed, in this case, some (albeit a minority) had to effectively acquaint themselves with markers of ethnic identity in Northern Ireland so as to variously deploy these in the company of like-minded individuals or, perhaps more commonly, use this knowledge to orientate themselves around uncomfortable social situations when in the company of the 'other side'. Social class was not the only means by which people could sidestep many of the problems that beset Northern Ireland over the course of the last three decades (and more) of the twentieth century. In reality it was only certain parts of the country that experienced the full effects of the conflict, which meant that other regions (despite its modest size) of Northern Ireland escaped relatively unscathed. Those who lived in rural parts of North Antrim, South Down, North Derry and West Tyrone appeared to go about their lives in a manner largely untouched by events that they otherwise consumed through their televisions and radios. Of course there were some terrible atrocities in these districts as well, but they were comparatively few and far between and, as these parts were similarly bereft of the presence of security forces, it was possible to live out one's life there in a benign form of relative isolation (McVeigh 1994).

Thus, as this chapter will make clear, many of the unresolved issues that remain in Northern Ireland are not exclusively political in form but in fact have more to do with cultural identity and expression, such as the flying of certain flags and establishing an agreed narrative concerning the country's divided past to permit its telling in a public forum. In recognising this, it should not be overlooked that many of these cultural markers are of course underwritten by political symbolism and meaning. Activities such as the flying of flags and banners, the playing of certain songs, not to mention participation in certain sports remain ostensibly cultural acts but they retain defined political meanings as well, the exact degree of which is dependent upon a host of historical and contextual factors peculiar to the setting in which they are being performed. Alongside this a range of other agencies have attempted to play their part, many again operating outside established political structures, focusing instead on popular expressions of identity promoted through sport, cultural pastimes and other similar pursuits (Bairner 2002). In so doing they recognise the need to respect cultural differences, in relation to such matters as membership of social organisations and clubs. As in all societies, individuals and groups pursue entirely legitimate forms of cultural expression in Northern Ireland, even if these carry particular weight in such divided settings where they constitute both a form of political allegiance 'by proxy' and are an important aspect of community expression for many, including those who feel disenfranchised from wider society (Boyd 2001; Brewer and Higgins 1998).

As such, despite the signing of the aforementioned Belfast Good Friday Agreement in 1998 and a wide range of significant developments in the peace process since then, Northern Ireland remains a polarised society. Nearly half of all council wards in Northern Ireland (47 per cent) have a population that is over two-thirds Catholic or Protestant, and the vast majority of children and young people (92.6 per cent) attend schools that are segregated on the basis of religion. These deep divisions are also evident in the realm of sport and the close relationship between sport and national identity in Northern Ireland is, by now, well established. However, this picture is more complicated than some commentators suggest and while sport undoubtedly reflects social divisions, it also has the capacity to cross these boundaries and contribute to social cohesion.

Nevertheless it is perhaps not surprising that of all available forms of cultural expression, sport has often been the site where the underlying community divisions that historically have existed in Northern Ireland have found a hostile public expression, taking such forms as verbal sectarian abuse, the chanting of songs designed to demonise 'the other' and, occasionally, spectator violence between supporters of clubs aligned with competing ethnic traditions (Bairner and Darby 1999). In addition, some sports continue to be perceived as being associated with one part of Northern Ireland's community only, so that Gaelic games (such as hurling and Gaelic football) are still thought to be for Catholics and nationalists, while games originating in the main from Britain (such as hockey and rugby) are broadly understood as being solely for Protestants and unionists (Bairner 1999). That being said, there is some 'shifting of the sands' around the edges of this historical analysis in recent times, largely the result of social class issues, for example, the sporadic interest in rugby union shown by the growing Catholic middle classes as a legitimate expression of their comparative wellbeing and general *bonhomie*.

That is not to say that any attempt to straddle the issue of divided identities in Northern Ireland (to ride two horses, to use an appropriate sporting metaphor) is an entirely pain-free process. In September 2012, Rory McElroy, by then the World's Number 1 golfer, was asked whether he would wish to play for Team GB or Ireland when golf is played at the Summer Olympics in Rio 2016 for the first time. In response McElroy recognised that he owed the Golf Union of Ireland a great debt of gratitude for its support in his early career development but remarked 'I've always felt more British than Irish. Maybe it was the way I was brought up, I don't know, but I have always felt more of a connection with the UK than with Ireland' (RTE online, 12 September 2012). The crucial phrase here is 'the way I was brought up', as for McElroy, a Catholic from North Down, the decision should have been straightforward in the apparently dichotomised world of contested identities in Northern Ireland. He was Catholic, which means he sees himself as exclusively Irish and thus, wanting nothing to do with Team GB, would choose instead to declare for Ireland. But McElroy's prevarication on the issue (he would eventually declare for Ireland in 2014 to considerably less fanfare) suggests that there are other factors at play in shaping individual identities through sport, such as the locale in which people grow up, their exposure to members of the 'other side' and, again, their social class.

Instead we must return to the major team sports in Northern Ireland to gain a more accurate understanding of the current state of community relations, as evident through the prism of sport, in the country. Indeed, in the face of periodic violent outbursts at, and in the vicinity of, its matches and conscious that, all too often, sport does present the most obvious expression of ethnic division in any country, the major sporting bodies in Northern Ireland, namely the Irish Football Association (IFA), the Ulster Council of the Gaelic Athletic Association (GAA) and the Ulster Branch of the Irish Rugby Football Union (IRFU), began to assume a wider community development role following the historic political settlement of 1998 and, virtually in unison, launched a series of outreach activities aimed at encouraging those who might have traditionally pursued other sporting interests to become acquainted with theirs (Boyd 2001). It is of course admirable, even ambitious, work and, as will be made clear, it is possible to point to meaningful developments from this well-intentioned endeavour and to where positive outcomes have been realised. However is it not equally timely to suggest that significantly more should have been achieved by the major sporting bodies in Northern Ireland around advancing the cause of 'good relations' in the country almost two decades after the signing of the Belfast Agreement? Specifically, on the key markers of sporting division in the country – Catholic support for the Northern Ireland football team, Protestant engagement with Gaelic games and working-class involvement in rugby union – whilst there have been undoubtedly some useful, if largely ephemeral, initiatives undertaken, precisely how impactful these have been over the long term remains unproven.

Thus whilst key stakeholders, including the various sporting organisations, have invested considerable time and resources in this area over recent years and there are perhaps some indications that certain cross-community sporting schemes and initiatives have had positive outcomes, work still remains to be done. Put simply, without broad agreement about the aims and objectives, and in the absence of a set of benchmarks against which to evaluate these, it is difficult to measure the success of these initiatives with any confidence. For example, while the 2013 Northern Ireland Life and Times Survey module on 'Sport and Social Exclusion' produced some interesting results, these are open to a raft of competing interpretations. The fact that 38 per cent of Protestant respondents expressed a willingness to attend a GAA match at Casement Park, Belfast (compared to 78 per cent of Catholics), could either be viewed as a cause for concern or as evidence of the first steps to progress. However, set against the figures for a willingness to attend an Ulster Rugby match at the Kingspan Stadium, Ravenhill (67 per cent of Protestants and 70 per cent of Catholics), these results appear more perturbing. By contrast, the fact that relatively few Protestant respondents (16 per cent) disagreed with the statement that 'I would like to see more Protestants playing Gaelic Sports' suggests a softening of attitudes towards the GAA on the part of that community. The limitations of the social attitude surveys are also evident here, however, and the significance of this apparent shift might be called into question if actual membership and participation rates remain polarised along ethno-sectarian lines.

In fact, one of the main challenges for researchers is the lack of clarity around what constitutes 'success' or 'progress' in this area and the existence of different perspectives among stakeholders. Moreover, although the concept of cross-community sport is multi-faceted, many of the nuances between the different levels of involvement in sporting activity are glossed over. For example, the strategies designed to increase the proportion of children from a Protestant background playing Gaelic games are likely to be very different to those aimed at tackling anti-social behaviour in interface areas in Belfast or of increasing the number of Protestant spectators at GAA inter-county games. However these are often grouped together under the general umbrella of cross-community sport with little consideration of the differential implications for the individual and society.

Thus to adequately grasp the changing nature of the interplay between sport and politics amongst Northern Ireland's foremost participatory sports, there follows an overview of these throughout the remaining part of this chapter. This is designed to illustrate the genesis of their link to forms of political activity and, more optimistically, how this process has evolved and ultimately changed for the better (in some cases) as the country begins to move beyond its troubled past to a more settled and tolerant future. To begin with, the focus turns to the game of association football or soccer. Despite the apparent omnipotence of the indigenous Gaelic sports in Ireland as a whole, in Northern Ireland soccer still retains a strong hold on the sporting interests of that society, not least because members of the majority Unionist community rarely frequent Gaelic games or have any particular interest in them. It is with a close examination of soccer therefore that this focused overview begins.

Association football

The founding of association football in Ireland was, for the most part, a Unionist project, which in every way sought to locate its cultural epicentre in the Protestant-dominated northern part of the island (Garnham 2004). Yet this did little to quell interest in the game on the part of Irish nationalists who, albeit sceptically at first, gradually started to take a firm interest in the sport, even in the face of the growing strength of the indigenous GAA, which often spoke in grave tones about how fraternising with soccer folk somehow constituted a form of Irish cultural heresy (Hassan 2002). Over time, and especially in urban areas such as Belfast, Dublin, Cork and Derry, soccer became extremely popular for many nationalists, who played and attended matches alongside others, including the majority Unionist population, in Northern Ireland. In the latter case, however, difficulty arose for some as all forms of popular pursuits in the country, including sport, became appropriated by one side or the other, that is by either Irish nationalists or Ulster unionists. Within the space of less than a decade, from the mid-1980s until the early 1990s, playing soccer, supporting certain teams and the relationship between politics and sport in Northern Ireland changed irrevocably (Cronin 1999). Whereas young Catholic boys ran through the streets of Derry, Belfast, Armagh and Newry recounting imaginary commentary of their part in Northern Ireland's relative triumphs at the 1982 and 1986 FIFA World Cup finals, by now adolescents they began acquainting themselves instead with a series of relative unknowns, born and brought up in England, Scotland and Wales, who, as a result of a generous interpretation of eligibility criteria on the part of the Football Association of Ireland (FAI), had managed to find themselves playing for the Republic of Ireland and, under their new English manager, the 1966 World Cup winner, Jack Charlton, appeared to be sweeping all before them (Cronin 1999). Compared with the sombre, stale, sectarian soccerscape of Northern Ireland, the excitement surrounding the Republic of Ireland national team was much too attractive for nationalist fans north of the border to ignore (McGee and Bairner 2011). More significant, however, is the fact that in subsequent years, a growing number of players born in Northern Ireland have opted to represent the Republic of Ireland. Not all nationalists in Northern Ireland made this most unusual of international transfers. Some have retained what once appeared to be an unbreakable bond of allegiance to 'the north' as if informed by the very sense of loyalty that goes to the core of football fandom itself (Hassan *et al.* 2009). However, issues of identity were transformed with the signing of the Good Friday Agreement, which formalises the right of Northern Irish citizens to align themselves to the national identity of their choice. In a number of instances, this has encouraged young footballers to refuse to play for Northern Ireland representative teams, with perceived discrimination and exclusion of the part of IFA coaches and officials and the continued use of the British national anthem at Northern Ireland games being cited as significant factors (McGee and Bairner 2011). It is for this reason, and in light of many more apparent contradictions, that soccer, possibly more than most other cultural pastimes and certainly more than any other sport in Northern Ireland, sheds light into the dark crevasses of nationalist ambitions, both culturally and politically. As such, the late 1980s were a turning point in football allegiances for northern nationalists and almost three decades hence, battle lines established back then show little sign of abating (Bairner 2013).

Expressed differently, despite Northern Ireland being an altogether changed place from the ravages of the 1970s and 1980s, most Catholics and seemingly all nationalists, show little sign of supporting the country's international football team so long as the Republic of Ireland remains comparatively vibrant, progressive and altogether more inclusive – to their minds at least. Little consideration is given to the fact that the Republic of Ireland team, in some ways at least, only represents 26 of the 32 counties in Ireland and thus is as partitioned – in an Irish Republican sense – as the team taking to the field in the colours of Northern Ireland. To quote an interviewee the author encountered in the late 1990s when researching this subject, '26 is as bad as 6' in terms of how soccer reflected the aspirations of at least some Irish nationalists in 'the north'. Instead they point to the fact that Martin O'Neill, from south Derry, a Catholic and former manager of Celtic FC (a Scottish football club with Irish and Republican connections), and thus someone with impeccable credentials for the job, is the current manager of the Republic of Ireland team. The fact that he is a former captain of Northern Ireland, representing the country in two World Cup tournaments, is only interpreted as further proof – if this was indeed required – of a justification for their actions.

Whilst a discussion of how soccer reflects the divided identities of sports fans in Northern Ireland may appear perfectly logical, what of the activities of the GAA? It is tempting to conclude that the GAA remains the most obvious example of a homogenised, all-island sporting form on account of its underpinning ideology and guiding principles. However, such analysis is too simplistic and instead the Irish identity evident in Northern Ireland and displayed through the auspices of the GAA, is markedly different to that revealed by their contemporaries in the Republic of Ireland.

GAA: a united organisation

Simply put, the approach taken by the GAA is such that it regards its legitimate presence across the 32 counties of Ireland to be unfettered by the presence of a legal boundary demarcating 6 counties in the north-east of the island, as they remain part of the United Kingdom of Great Britain and Northern Ireland, from the 26 counties of the Republic of Ireland. By not officially recognising the legitimate presence of Northern Ireland, or at least not doing so for much of its long history as reference to its existence is by now widely accepted by GAA members and officials, the association sought to advance the myth that the way the organisation is experienced, and the views held by its members on a range of policy issues, remains common across both parts of the island. This is patently not the case and plenty of evidence exists to support this thesis, from differing attitudes on the part of representatives in Northern Ireland towards the removal of Rule 21, which until its repeal in 2001 had prevented members of the British police and army presence in Ireland from becoming members of the association, and also the playing of sports other than Gaelic games at GAA grounds (Rule 42). That the GAA would be different in Northern Ireland compared to the Republic of Ireland is not a surprise and would even be widely understood and appreciated by its membership. Yet a reluctance to fully embrace this reality has implications for the role the GAA performs in a divided Northern Ireland, in relations between its members on either side of the political divide on the island and upon its supposed role in assisting a latent push towards the reunification of Ireland.

The simple fact is that the majority of Protestants in Northern Ireland do not understand the GAA, consider it an almost exclusively Catholic organisation and one with an unhealthy degree of sympathy for the cause of Irish republicanism. The Ulster Council of the GAA, based in Armagh, Northern Ireland, has been engaged in very positive outreach work with its counterparts in other sporting bodies and with schoolchildren from the state sector (i.e. Protestant and Unionist). But this work only appears to be having a limited impact, as breaking down long-standing barriers, maintained by a cocktail of truth, misperceptions and myths, is an onerous undertaking, which will take considerably more time and effort to deliver upon.

Boxing

As has already been suggested in this chapter, plying one's trade as a professional sportsman in the 1980s in Northern Ireland was far from a straightforward undertaking. Sport could not escape the ethno-sectarian divide that so defined the country and any attempt to subvert the established dichotomy between nationalists and unionists appeared naive at best (Sugden 1996). If anything, one risked the wrath of one's own community by becoming overly acquiescent with 'the other side' so most athletes, teams and governing bodies of sport engaged in an endless round of self-justification, of listing unresolved grievances and generally keeping their distance for risk of alienating their own constituency. Yet individual athletes appeared to be able, at least in part, to remain outside this unseemly process and receive the support of a representative sample of both Catholics and Protestants in Northern Ireland. One such individual was the boxer Barry McGuigan, who, on a famous night at Loftus Road, the home of Queens Park Rangers Football Club, in 1985 claimed the World Featherweight championship to the unbridled joy of his legions of followers. What set McGuigan apart were his deliberate attempts to position himself as a representative of all the people of Northern Ireland, and indeed of Ireland as a whole for he was after all born and brought up in County Monaghan, on the southern side of the Irish border (Hassan 2005). Few athletes, including boxers, had attempted to make a virtue out of their cross-community support and McGuigan was by no means the most high-profile athlete to emerge from Ulster. The Pentathlete Dame Mary Peters had, of course, claimed Olympic Gold in Munich in 1972 whilst during the same era George Best was celebrated worldwide for his achievements on and indeed off the football field. Thus there was something significant about the man himself, but also the sport, that allowed McGuigan to occupy a role that was part sportsman, part peace campaigner, and whose often-quoted plea 'Leave the fighting to McGuigan' remained an honourable, if not particularly impactful, plea amid a Northern Ireland torn asunder by internal strife (Hassan 2005).

Nevertheless McGuigan's capacity to set himself apart from the sports–politics nexus in Northern Ireland, to command a genuine cross-community following and to reject symbols and anthems that could be interpreted as divisive was a brave and worthy crusade, all the more so when understood in the context of his sporting heroism. After I wrote an article on McGuigan, in an edition of the journal *Sport in History* (2005), the response of those who read it only confirmed the special standing enjoyed by McGuigan amongst sports fans worldwide. I received correspondence from boxing fans in many remote parts of the globe, including those who had heard about the piece but hadn't been able to read it. Then one day I returned to my office after teaching a class of undergraduates to be met by a voicemail message from McGuigan himself who had read the article and wanted to express his gratitude to me for penning it. Shortly after, a signed copy of the opening page of the article arrived in the mail from McGuigan and now adorns a wall in my office. Almost three decades after McGuigan was carried shoulder high through the then-divided streets of Belfast his legacy still lives on in the minds of many sports fans in Ireland, and indeed amongst the boxing fraternity worldwide.

It is almost poetic therefore that McGuigan would play such a telling role in the rise of the Belfast boxer Carl Frampton who, by 2014, had become the IBF World Super Bantamweight champion. Frampton's ascent to global boxing stardom reflects a lot of the experiences of McGuigan himself. Both men form one half of so-called 'mixed marriages', a remarkably dated term meaning they are married to women who come from the opposing religious persuasion to them. In addition, like McGuigan before him, Frampton is keen to promote cross-community support for his work and remains impressively adept at communicating this in his public interviews and through his broader civic engagement across Northern Ireland. He is, in many ways, a modern incarnation of his mentor McGuigan. What distinguishes Frampton of course is that he grew up in Tiger's Bay, a staunchly loyalist part of north Belfast, while his wife Christine, a criminology graduate, was raised in Poleglass, a republican estate on the western fringe of the city.

Sporting infrastructure

Whilst McGuigan (and now Frampton) managed to at least bring to the fore some debate about the potential unifying capacity of sport in a divided society, the reality is that much about this realm only exacerbates and consolidates separation, as opposed to helping ameliorate it (Bairner 2001). In this regard sports stadia, with all their associated resonance, their imbued meanings and exclusionary infrastructure, constitute very real examples of division in Northern Ireland. Earlier the dilemma facing many Irish nationalists in Northern Ireland around which international team to support on the island of Ireland – the Republic of Ireland or Northern Ireland – was outlined. A large part of the stated resistance of northern nationalists to engage with football in Northern Ireland, to play for the team but mostly to support it, is due to the Unionist iconography associated with Windsor Park, the ground where Northern Ireland plays its home games (Hassan 2002). Simply put, many nationalists interpret the atmosphere at Windsor Park to be unwelcoming for them and thus they choose to stay away.

Of course other events in the troubled history of Northern Ireland have also played a role in this process. In 1994, the murder of six civilians in the Heights Bar, Loughinisland, a village previously largely untouched by the Troubles, during the Republic of Ireland versus Italy World Cup group game in the U.S., struck at the very heart of the interplay of sport, politics and division in the country. As local men and women had congregated in the public bar to watch the game – all residents of the small County Down village – the Ulster Volunteer Force (UVF), a loyalist paramilitary grouping, entered shooting randomly at those gathered in front of the television screens viewing the match. As those present were assumed to be Catholics supporting the Republic of Ireland, an act viewed by some within the loyalist community as somehow indicative of a broader antipathy towards Northern Ireland, they were considered a 'soft target' by loyalist terror groups intent on sending out a much wider message about the future of Northern Ireland and, in particular, its status within the United Kingdom.

Unionists, of all shades, are being increasingly encouraged to consider engaging with the GAA in Northern Ireland, while the Ulster Council of the GAA for its part is pursuing an on-going courtship of Unionist politicians so as to convey a sense of openness to the Unionist people as a whole. Whereas such work is of course long and often arduous in nature, albeit certainly better than doing nothing, quite what has been achieved from well over a decade of endeavour in the broad field of 'sport and good relations' in Northern Ireland remains unproven. Maybe this is ultimately because the major governing bodies of sport in Northern Ireland, rugby union, GAA and association football, continue to play their games in relative isolation (Sugden and Harvie 1995).

When the British government announced in early 2004 that it believed a multi-sport stadium was financially viable most observers interpreted this as meaning that should the authorities governing GAA, football and rugby union in Ulster come to some accommodation regarding ground sharing, and this proposal gain the backing of the devolved Northern Ireland Assembly, that the UK Exchequer would not be found wanting in providing the finance necessary to build a new, and much needed, sports stadium. It was, to use an appropriate euphemism, something of an 'open goal' (Hassan 2006). The machinations of what happened next are far too complex to recount here but suffice to say the stadium was not built; the funding was reallocated to each of the aforementioned sports that, at the time of writing, are engaged in various stages of reconstruction of their existing, partionist and thus ultimately exclusive stadia. Therefore a form of sporting apartheid remains in Northern Ireland for all but a small upwardly mobile, culturally inquisitive elite who may well oscillate between Belfast's Ravenhill and Casement Park, between the sports of rugby and GAA, even if Windsor Park, with its dated, dark and increasingly historic sporting past, continues to be a step too far for most.

The 'new' Irish

The internal conflict in Northern Ireland occupied the attention of those near and far in such a way as to largely overlook the growing numbers of people born outside the British Isles who gradually began arriving there. Understandably this number could initially be categorised in the hundreds (or even fewer) but certainly after some degree of acceptable 'peace' took hold in Northern Ireland and the borders of the European Union expanded, many new arrivals made Ireland, north and south, their home. Immigrants are themselves a disparate collective, with some coming to Ireland to find work, to relocate for family reasons, or because they are refugees or asylum seekers. Regardless of the precise reason underlying their relocation to Ireland most immigrants are keen to secure employment, settle into a normal way of life and contribute to the communities in which they now reside. Yet all too often their story is markedly different from this idyll as some are subject of racism, discrimination of a variety of forms and experience subsequent isolation (Garner 2004). It is a regrettable, if all too predictable, response in a world seemingly incapable of accepting the outworking of global migration and resettlement.

Again sport can be a useful tool in helping to integrate new arrivals into a country, if handled appropriately. In Northern Ireland an enlightened approach adopted by the Irish Football Association meant that those people, initially males but more recently females as well, who were new to Belfast and had an interest in football could join a team, whose purpose was only partly the winning of soccer matches. Instead the club, entitled World United FC, constituted a useful information and advice centre for those seeking employment, a safe and welcoming place to live and the type of support network any person arriving from overseas could benefit from. The success of World United, which has been recognised by UEFA as a programme worthy of wider dissemination, is itself a statement about the evolving nature of sport and society in Northern Ireland (Hassan and McCue 2013).

The same could be said of the situation in the Republic of Ireland, which is mercifully free of the legacy of inter-ethnic violence that has so besmirched Northern Ireland, yet nonetheless remains a conservative and largely insular nation-state. Here however it seems the real challenge is around finding accommodation with a significant minority of talented young men, some of whom are refugees and asylum seekers, on the part of those who govern association football in the Republic of Ireland (FAI) and appear reticent to actively pursue citizenship on behalf of some of these young immigrants. Certain organisations, such as the grassroots body Sport against Racism Ireland, have sought to draw attention to this issue not least as they recognise the very important role sport can play in helping to alleviate the concerns and fears some 'new arrivals' have about settling into a new locale (Hassan and McCue 2013).

What consideration of this development ultimately achieves is to track the evolution of life and sport in Ireland, especially Northern Ireland, over the past 40 years. Whereas sport began as a convenient means of demarcating 'us' from 'them', it now also serves to highlight the changing nature of society in Northern Ireland and the many benefits such plurality can provide in a society that is otherwise sadly bound by myopia and latent political self-interest.

The future

All of which brings the situation in Northern Ireland up to the present day with some degree of optimism that a better future may yet unfold in the years ahead. There is some evidence of a cultural thawing in the country with sport again seemingly leading the way. Unionist politicians, who previously studiously avoided any reference to the work of the GAA, are now enthusiastically attending Gaelic football matches, speaking in praiseworthy tones about its community relations work and generally proving wholly receptive to its overtures. Likewise, Sinn Féin ministers in the Northern Ireland Executive, including the Deputy First Minister Martin McGuinness, are now publically attending matches at Windsor Park, including games featuring Northern Ireland. All the while there appears to be a very profitable working relationship being established between the three major sporting bodies in the country that now seem capable of negotiating a fine line between continuing to serve their own constituencies without unduly alienating others who otherwise approach their activities with caution.

At the same time a growing sense of 'Northern Irishness' appears to be making a resurgence, and this is communicated variously from certain sections of society there. Thus, having reached the apparent depths of despair during the late 1980s in Northern Ireland a critical examination of sport in the country might actually contains the seeds of an altogether more peaceful future. Historically, sportsmen and women have become embroiled, for better or worse, in the politics of identity in Northern Ireland but as the political situation there appears finally to have found some common ground it is little surprise that sport too is gradually moving to reflect this uneasy peace. In another decade or more it is a distinct possibility, perhaps remarkably so, that sport may contribute to an even more normalised society and that the divisions of the past may be confined, where arguably they should always have been, to the annals of history.

References

Bairner, A. (1999) Civic and ethnic nationalism in the Celtic vision of Irish sport. In G. Jarvie (ed.) *Sport in the Making of Celtic Cultures*. Leicester: Leicester University Press, pp. 12–25.

Bairner, A. (2001) *Sport, Nationalism, and Globalization: European and North American Perspectives*. Albany, NY: State University of New York Press.

Bairner, A. (2002) *Sport, Sectarianism and Society in a Divided Ireland* revisited. In J. Sugden and A. Tomlinson (eds) *Power Games. A Critical Sociology of Sport*. London: Routledge, pp. 181–195.

Bairner, A. (2013) Sport, the Northern Ireland peace process, and the politics of identity. *Journal of Aggression, Conflict and Peace*, 5(4): 220–229.

Bairner, A. and Darby, P. (1999) Divided sport in a divided society. In J. Sugden and A. Bairner (eds) *Sport in Divided Societies*. Aachen: Meyer and Meyer, pp. 51–72.

Bew, P. (2007) *The Making and Remaking of the Good Friday Agreement*. Dublin: Liffey Press.

Brewer, J.D. and Higgins, G.I. (1998) *Anti-Catholicism in Northern Ireland, 1600–1998: The Mote and the Beam*. London: Palgrave Macmillan.

Cronin, M. (1999) *Sport and Nationalism in Ireland: Gaelic Games, Soccer and Irish Identity Since 1884*. Dublin: Four Courts.

Garner, S. (2004) *Racism in the Irish Experience*. London: Pluto.

Garnham, N. (2004) *Association Football and Society in Pre-Partition Ireland*. Belfast: Ulster Historical Foundation.

Hassan, D. (2002) A people apart: Soccer identity and Irish nationalists in Northern Ireland. *Soccer and Society*, 3(4): 65–83.

Hassan, D. (2005) A champion inside the ring and a champion outside it: An examination of the socio-political impact of the career of Barry McGuigan. *Sport in History*, 25: 221–236.

Hassan, D. (2006) An opportunity for a new beginning: Soccer, Irish nationalists and the construction of a new multi-sports stadium for Northern Ireland. *Soccer and Society*, 7: 339–352.

Hassan, D. and McCue, K. (2013) The 'silent' Irish: Football, migrants and the pursuit of integration. *Soccer and Society*, 14: 1–13.

Hassan, D., McCullough, S. and Moreland, E. (2009) North or south? Darron Gibson and the issue of player eligibility within Irish soccer. *Soccer and Society*, 10(6): 740–753.

McEvoy, J. (2008) *The Politics of Northern Ireland*. Edinburgh: Edinburgh University Press.

McGee, D. and Bairner, A. (2011) Transcending the borders of Irish identity? Narratives of northern nationalist footballers in Northern Ireland. *International Review for the Sociology of Sport*, 46(4): 436–455.

McVeigh, R. (1994) *'It's Part of Life Here....': The Security Forces and Harassment in Northern Ireland*. Belfast: CAJ publishers.

Ó Dochartaigh, N. (2004) *From Civil Rights to Armalites: Derry and the Birth of the Irish Troubles*. Basingstoke: Palgrave Macmillan.

RTE. (2012) *RTE Online*, 12 September 2012. Accessed 8 December 2014.

Sugden, J. (1996) *Boxing and Society: An International Analysis*. Manchester: Manchester University Press.

Sugden, J. and Harvie, S. (1995) Sport and community relations in Northern Ireland. Coleraine: Centre for the Study of Conflict. http://cain.ulst.ac.uk/csc/reports/sport.htm.

17

SPORT AND POLITICS IN GREAT BRITAIN

Kevin Jefferys

Introduction

The London Olympics of 2012 were a spectacular global phenomenon. Extravagant pledges were made in advance by politicians and officials of a tangible Olympic "legacy", promising sustainable regeneration in east London and lasting improvements for British sport. Huge sums of public money, in excess of £9 billion, were committed for the construction of purpose-built venues and to help ensure the success of a few weeks of sporting endeavour. Although some criticised the scale of funding ahead of the Games, the medal-winning exploits of British Olympians and Paralympians – seen by television audiences around the world – helped to create a favourable public reaction. The whole picture was very different when London previously staged the Games. In 1948 Britain was still recovering from the ravages of the Second World War. The government of the day provided moral but little financial support, television coverage was in its infancy and the idea of building a dedicated Olympic park or making expansive legacy promises was a non-starter. The 1948 Games proved successful but are commonly remembered as "the austerity Olympics" (Hampton 2008).

The contrasts between the London Games of 1948 and 2012 are striking, not only in the scale and cost of the two events – one hastily put together at a time when much of world sport was based on amateur principles and the other meticulously planned in an era of commercialisation and professionalism – but also in the degree of involvement by political leaders. Before the age of the post-war welfare state, sport in Britain was largely a voluntary enterprise, overseen by independent bodies such as the British Olympic Association (BOA), the Central Council for Physical Recreation (CCPR) and individual national governing bodies, responsible for running hundreds of separate sports (Baker 1995). What happened on the athletics track, the tennis court or the football pitch was not considered the preserve of the state. Direct and sustained interest of the type shown by Labour's Tony Blair in the framing and winning of the 2012 Olympic bid was unimaginable in the era of his 1940s predecessor, Clement Attlee (Beck 2008).

The differences between 1948 and 2012 exemplify a broader trend towards increased interaction between sport and politics over the past sixty years. This is often most noticeable in relation to international sport. Far from engaging tentatively in sporting affairs, as was the case until and beyond the 1948 Games, present-day British politicians are often found showcasing the virtues of the nation staging major sporting events such as the Olympics and football's World Cup.

But a convergence between sport and politics can also be traced in other ways: in the evolution since the 1960s of central government machinery for oversight of sport and in incremental rises in state funding. Such funding was minimal at the end of the Second World War, whereas today hundreds of millions of pounds are directed annually to sport via delivery bodies such as UK Sport and through government departments, notably the Department for Culture, Media and Sport (DCMS) and the Department for Education (DfE), which has responsibility for sport in state schools (Jefferys 2012c).

The aim of this chapter is to examine how successive British governments have approached sport from 1945 to the present day and to assess what the prospects are for securing Britain's Olympic sporting legacy. "Sport" comes of course in multiple guises, embracing the competitive and strenuous to the recreational, and particular sports can only be selectively touched upon within the confines of a single chapter. In what follows, the emphasis is mostly on traditionally amateur sports: Olympic disciplines such as athletics which sought state financial assistance in the post-war period, whereas professional-dominated sports including football were expected to manage their own affairs and pay their own way. Although priority is accorded to national policy determined in London, some attention is also directed towards Wales and Scotland (with more on the implications of the 2014 Scottish referendum in Grant Jarvie's chapter that follows), though not Northern Ireland (discussed in Hassan's chapter in this volume).

The key overarching argument that emerges in the chapter is that although assisting Olympic athletes, improving local recreational facilities and increasing participation rates were accepted as legitimate objectives from the 1960s onwards, state policy towards sport frequently remained hamstrung by funding constraints, shallow levels of political support and an unstable policy-making environment. Against this backdrop, securing the sporting legacy of London 2012 remains in the balance.

Sport policy in historical context, 1945–97

Contemporary sport policy reflects past practice. In order to understand the nature and level of state involvement today, we first need to gauge how and why the sport–politics relationship became closer after the Second World War. It was not of course the case that sport and politics operated in entirely separate compartments before 1945. Britain had a tradition stretching back to the Victorian period of local authorities providing (on a permissive and so highly variable basis) parks and other recreational facilities such as swimming baths. And with the spread of international competition in the first half of the twentieth century, government ministers sometimes found themselves embroiled in unwelcome diplomatic disputes arising from sporting controversy; the "Bodyline" controversy in cricket and the 1936 "Nazi Olympics" were both examples of this. But the reality remained that, in an age when the role of the state was much less intrusive than today, it was commonplace to assume that sport and politics did not "mix". This assumption was only slowly eroded in the post-1945 period, and this section of the chapter briefly outlines the evolution of policy during the half-century after the war through four broad stages.

In the 1945–64 period, as before the war, there was no government "sport policy" as such. The Attlee administration's extension of welfare principles did not extend to the sporting arena. Ministerial backing for the 1948 Olympics was driven primarily by a desire to bolster post-war economic recovery, and for several years thereafter it was left to a small number of MPs to make the case that Britain's infrastructure of sporting facilities, for both elite performers and casual participants, was deeply inadequate compared with some other advanced industrialised nations.

Concern arose that Britain's unpaid amateur athletes, in particular, had little chance of competing successfully on the international stage against the likes of state-sponsored Soviet athletes at the Olympics. More broadly in society, reformers argued that sport was a valuable means of countering problems such as youth alienation at a time of rising affluence, and required much increased investment at community level (Binfield and Stevenson 1993).

But Conservative governments of the 1950s maintained a minimalist approach, believing sport should be left to run its own affairs. This stance largely prevailed despite the publication in 1960 of the influential Wolfenden Report, which called for a range of state initiatives to enhance "sport in the community" (Central Council of Physical Recreation 1960). This clarion call for improved facilities was sponsored by one of the major independent umbrella organisations, the CCPR, rather than being a direct government initiative, and as a result ministers were not obliged to take up its main recommendations. Although there was some movement on the Wolfenden proposals, by the time the Conservatives lost office in 1964 nothing had been done to act on the central recommendation: that of introducing a Sports Development Council to act as a focal point for the development of a new generation of athletic tracks, swimming pools and sport centres (Hailsham 1975, 1990).

In the years spanning the Wilson-Heath-Callaghan administrations of 1964–79, the second of the four broad stages, we can identify with hindsight government sport policy becoming more than a misnomer. This was partly because Labour's Harold Wilson was the first prime minister to sense the potential electoral resonance of sport. He knew that sport was never likely to be a front-line electoral issue, although it came close in 1970, when sporting links with apartheid South Africa threatened to overshadow the campaign. A proposed tour to England by the South Africans provoked sustained, highly publicised protests by the anti-apartheid movement, dividing political opinion and raising the prospect of an election, in the words of Wilson, being "fought and won on and around the cricket pitch at Lord's" (Wilson 1971). The crisis was only resolved at the eleventh hour when the English cricket authorities, with behind-the-scenes prompting from ministers, agreed to call off the tour (Hain 1971; Butler and Pinto-Duschinsky 1971). Despite the adverse headlines generated by this sporting controversy, Wilson sensed that for the most part it did no harm to his party's popularity to be associated with something more than the uncoordinated and low key approach of previous governments. Hence, for example, he sanctioned an unprecedented intervention in professional sport, providing Treasury funds to help ensure the organisational success of the 1966 FIFA World Cup on English soil (Wilson 1971; Howell 1993).

It was in relation to amateur sport that fresh departures were most apparent after 1964. Labour thinking in opposition had long echoed Wolfenden's view that state funding was required to increase the range and availability of sporting facilities. With this in mind, Wilson appointed Denis Howell as the first Minister for Sport in 1964, and within months the energetic and populist Howell established a Sports Council, initially as an advisory body with the Minister as Chairman (Howell 1993). Despite periodic bouts of retrenchment, continuing and intensifying in the 1970s, both Labour and Conservative administrations between 1964 and 1979 engendered a sense of momentum in sports development. The Sports Council was granted executive status in the early 1970s and pushed forward on various fronts: providing travel costs and expenses to British amateur teams competing overseas at events such as the Olympics; funding coaching schemes across a range of sports; assisting clubs in updating their facilities; and aiding local authorities with the capital costs of new projects. Between 1973 and 1977, facilities for indoor sport in Britain almost trebled and, on a decade-long timescale, there were notable advances particularly in relation to the construction of multi-purpose leisure centres, up from 12 in 1971 to 449 in 1981 (Coghlan and Webb 1990).

In the 1980s – the third of our four stages – the process of steadily developing ties between sport and politics was abruptly interrupted. Many of the tensions of this period reflected Prime Minister Thatcher's indifference towards sport, and the lasting effects of her attempt to persuade British athletes not to attend the 1980 Moscow Olympics in protest at the Soviet invasion of Afghanistan. While many nations fell in behind an American-led boycott of the Games, in Britain the majority view was that Olympians should not be singled out when trade links with the Soviets remained largely unaffected. After a bruising encounter, occupying a prominent place in public debate for several months, a British team went to the 1980 Moscow Games having inflicted a rare bloody-nose on Thatcher (Sarantakes 2011; Jefferys 2012a). For the remainder of her long premiership she fought shy of involvement with sport unless it was unavoidable. Elite-level sport could not rely, as was later the case, on sustained ministerial backing for bids to host the Olympics; failed attempts were made by both Birmingham and Manchester in the 1980s (Hill 1992).

On the domestic front, as Thatcherism gained in strength and looked to reduce state involvement in social and economic life where possible, sections of Conservative parliamentary opinion questioned the need for either a Sports Council or for a Minister for Sport, preferring a return to a 1950s-style, hands-off approach. And after years of progress for school sport under the terms of the 1944 Education Act, ministers anxious to reduce public spending embarked on a policy that was held up in future years as a symbol of Thatcher's disregard for sport: the sale of school playing fields. Some 5,000 fields across the country were lost during the 1980s to new building developments, and with teachers in dispute over pay and conditions school sport went into a period of pronounced decline. Many staff, including non-PE teachers, having hitherto volunteered their time to assist with after-school games, ceased to participate in extra-curricular activities as part of the dispute, with the result that for a time much competitive sport went into abeyance in the state sector (Holt and Mason 2000).

Finally, in the fourth stage of development since the end of the Second World War, Thatcher's successor John Major went some way towards repairing the damage of the 1980s during his seven-year premiership after 1990. Much of what took place stemmed initially from Major's personal love of sport and his sense (like that of Harold Wilson) that political opportunities were being missed by not at least attempting to tap into sport as a popular social and cultural phenomenon (Major 1999). As well as introducing a new department of state under a Minister of Cabinet rank to help improve the profile of sport, Major personally endorsed the landmark policy paper *Raising the Game*, which placed particular emphasis on the themes of reviving school sport and boosting elite performance (Department of National Heritage 1995). His most lasting achievement was to find significant new sources of revenue for sport, especially for capital projects, via the introduction of the National Lottery in 1994 (Henry 2001). Whereas the Treasury grant to the Sport Council remained at around the £50 million mark annually in the mid-1990s, Lottery funding for sport quadrupled in the first few years of operation to reach over £200 million in 1997.

Yet despite his best efforts, there was always a sense that Major promised more than he delivered. Although fee-paying, independent schools were unaffected by the difficulties of the previous decade (and continued to provide a high proportion of British Olympians in relation to the nation's total numbers of pupils), sport in the state sector remained in the doldrums. Only a quarter of pupils in secondary schools were doing two hours of Physical Education (PE) per week in the mid-1990s. And generous new funding systems for elite athletes came on stream too late to influence Britain's poor showing at the 1996 Atlanta Olympics, at which Team GB finished a lowly thirty-sixth in the medal table. The advances of the 1990s were arguably the product less of evolving maturity in the system of governance for sport than of the exceptional personal interest of the Prime Minister (Houlihan 1991). According to a top official quoted by Major's biographer, his Cabinet[1] colleagues "were variously indifferent to, amused or irritated by, his passion for sport" (Seldon 1997: 595).

Policy lessons: advances and limitations

By the time John Major left office in 1997, sport occupied a place in political discourse that was inconceivable at the time of the 1948 Olympics. Prompted by a mixture of ideological, electoral and practical impulses, state involvement in sport had been transformed, not uniformly over the whole post-war period, but with discernible leaps forward between 1964 and 1979 and from the mid-1990s onwards. Sports administrators and governing bodies still prized their independence, but they valued assistance (not control) from politicians prepared to sanction funding for sport from the grassroots up to international level. More people than ever before had access to local recreational amenities such as pools and sport centres, and structures were in place to enable elite athletes to compete seriously at future Olympics. On the other hand, optimistic 1970s talk of "sport for all" remained a long way from becoming a reality. Only about a quarter of adults took part in sport regularly, school sport was still at a low ebb, and several perennial problems remained unresolved. In considering the limitations of policy development across the 1945–97 period as a whole, four enduring difficulties especially stand out.

In the first place, funding constraints were a major source of ongoing concern. Starting from a tiny base, direct exchequer funding for sport did rise after 1964, but by the end of the 1970s had still not reached the levels proposed by the Wolfenden Report in 1960. In the mid-1990s, the entire budget of the Department of National Heritage (the departmental home of the Minister for Sport at that time) amounted to just 0.4 per cent of all central government spending, a proportion not dissimilar to what was spent on equivalent services a decade earlier (Jefferys 2012b).

Second, recurrent funding problems stemmed in part from the unstable administrative framework in which sport policy was set after 1945. Making the case for state investment was not helped by the junior status of the ministers appointed (never above mid-ranking Minister of State level and usually below that) and frequent concern over where, within Whitehall, the role of Sports Minister best fitted: the post variously resided after 1964 at the Education Department (on two separate occasions), the Ministry of Housing and Local Government, the Department of the Environment and the Department of National Heritage before becoming part of the DCMS in 1997 (McMaster and Bairner 2012). This picture of fragmentation at ministerial level was compounded by other departments retaining responsibility in specific areas: the education ministry, as noted, for school sport and the Foreign and Commonwealth Office for international-related sporting matters.

In a similar vein, achieving continuity of policy was difficult in the face of ongoing disputes over the role, status and functions of the delivery bodies charged with day-to-day oversight of sport. The Sports Council was granted executive status in the 1970s largely on the grounds that it would be less prone to ministerial interference, but by the 1980s the Council was under attack for lacking independence. Arguments continued to rage into the 1990s as to whether the Sports Council needed strengthening, adapting or abolishing. In 1993, Major's government shelved plans for restructuring, only to decide a couple of years later that it would separate out responsibility between new bodies such as UK Sport and separate home country bodies such as Sport England and its counterparts in Scotland and Wales (Pickup 1996).

Funding shortages and disputed administrative structures contributed to a third debilitating problem, that of determining where the balance should lie in prioritising the needs of recreational and international-standard sport (Houlihan and Lindsey 2013). In the 1964–79 period, when the emphasis was on building new facilities, community initiatives held sway as the top priority. "Sport for all" was at least a rhetorical aspiration, if not a rigorously defined or measured feature of policy. By the early 1990s the Sports Council was inclined to give a higher priority than in the past to developing Olympic sports, a trend that intensified when John Major diverted large-scale lottery funding towards the training needs of elite athletes (Pickup 1996).

Reflecting and underpinning the perennial difficulties of sport policy, finally, was the issue of shallow levels of political support – among MPs at Westminster, across Whitehall, and around the Cabinet table. Sport policy also exhibited a high degree of dependence on the personal interest (or lack of it) among successive prime ministers. The periods of most discernable progress came under sympathetic leaders such as Wilson and Major. At other times sport suffered from calculated hostility. Thatcher's only prolonged intervention came when there was little choice but to react to events, as in the case of football hooliganism in the 1980s (Coghlan and Webb 1990; Macfarlane and Herd 1996). For the most part, sport occupied a lowly place in the political pecking order; its profile was only occasionally raised by one-off events, and those dealing with sport as ministers found themselves heavily outgunned in the battle for resources by bigger spending Whitehall departments.

New Labour and sport

How far, we next consider, were the Blair–Brown governments of 1997–2010 – commonly referred to as "New Labour" administrations, referring to efforts to rebrand Labour by abandoning traditional notions of state socialism – willing and able to transcend the inherent weaknesses of pre-1997 British sport policy? With the economy in reasonable shape for the bulk of Tony Blair's ten-year premiership, and with the luxury of huge parliamentary majorities in 1997 and 2001, the prospects for sport were more promising than at any time in the previous generation. But progress was slow in coming. In the short term, spending on sport was constrained by the desire of Labour's powerful Chancellor, Gordon Brown, to work within the financial framework laid down by the previous administration.

But over time New Labour established a creditable record, and in the process overcame – partially at least - the characteristic shortcomings of previous policy as outlined above. In terms of political support, sport received a sympathetic hearing in Downing Street: Blair, like Major before him, felt there was political capital to be gained. Critics accustomed to bemoaning government indifference were, in the words of Houlihan and White, "taken aback" by the ambitious and prescriptive target setting contained in policy statements such as *A Sporting Future for All* (Houlihan and White 2002: 103). After 2001, the duo of Tessa Jowell as Culture Secretary and Richard Caborn as Sports Minister forged close links with key figures at the heart of government, such as Deputy Prime Minister John Prescott, helping to explain why sport policy temporarily established a profile in the corridors of power to which it was unaccustomed.

More generous levels of investment were one product of high-level backing for sport. Direct Treasury funding doubled between 2001 and 2005, with wide-ranging effects. The proportion of state secondary students undertaking two hours of PE per week rose to nine out of ten by 2007. In addition, the government created almost 450 School Sports Partnerships (SSPs), responsible for stimulating inter-school games in local areas, and were widely regarded as doing much to reverse the decline of school sport associated with the Thatcher–Major era.

Progress was also facilitated by a more stable administrative framework than was the case in the past. Caborn remained for longer at the DCMS than most of his predecessors as Minister for Sport. And he also worked hard to ensure that the roles and expectations of the main delivery agencies were settled and clarified: Sport England and its Welsh and Scottish equivalents concentrated on increasing participation, UK Sport on high performance sport, and the Youth Sport Trust monitored school sport. Above all, what distinguished New Labour policy was its attempt at a more integrated approach: a conscious strategy of trying to knit together school, community and elite-level sport and to regard recreation as part of a "joined up" approach aimed at delivering on wider welfare goals such as improved health, civic renewal and social cohesion. Blair described sport as a pro-education policy, a pro-health policy and an anti-crime policy (Bloyce and Smith 2010; Houlihan and Lindsey 2013).

Solid foundations were thus in place when in 2005 the Blair administration secured its single most high-profile success in sport policy: winning the right to host the 2012 Olympics (Lee 2006). Protracted arguments followed over whether the scale of public investment – increased from earlier figures to £9.3 billion in 2007 – represented value for money, and whether Britain could deliver on the range of ambitious legacy promises that were essential to winning the race to stage the Games (House of Commons, Committee of Public Accounts 2008). One of these, that Britain would maintain its high ranking in the Olympic medal table, looked to be readily achievable. Lottery funding on a scale that dwarfed what had gone before, together with UK Sport's "no compromise" targeting of funds at likely medal winners, helped to transform Britain's performance. At Beijing in 2008, Team GB (having improved on its dismal Atlanta showing in 2000 and 2004) surged to fourth in the medals table, behind only China, the USA and Russia. The British medal tally had only ever been bettered at the 1908 London Games, and ministers were able to hail triumphs across a range of well-financed Olympic sports including cycling, rowing, sailing, boxing, swimming and athletics.

On the other hand, it became apparent after Gordon Brown took over the reins of power from Blair in 2007 that it would be difficult to deliver on ambitious targets relating to increased participation: pledges of a million more people taking part regularly in sport and another million taking up physical activity on a more casual basis. The creation of "Sport Action Zones" in areas of inadequate inner-city provision, and the reinvigoration of "sport development" under local authority auspices were success stories for grassroots sport after 1997. But these advances were overshadowed by Sport England data showing that while the numbers playing sport three times a week rose by half a million during 2005–08, the increase had stalled by 2009. Even so, by the time New Labour lost office it could boast a creditable record on sport. There were measurable improvements in school and community sport and preparations were well underway for hosting London 2012: the Olympic park was taking shape and well-funded elite athletes looked on course to deliver British medal success at the Games (Jefferys 2012b).

Wales and Scotland

Although associated in complex ways with separate national identities, sport in Scotland and Wales also shared many characteristics with England in the early post-war years, for example a continuing reliance on voluntary leadership that valued independence from government. Legislation passed in London applicable to sport, as to many spheres, was automatically administered by Secretaries of State for Scotland and Wales. The 1960 Wolfenden Report claimed that all parts of Britain had broadly similar needs: for improved facilities, better coaching and higher levels of funding, though the Report side-stepped the question of whether the creation of a Sports Development Council required the establishment of matching bodies in different parts of the UK (CCPR 1960).

A key feature of Denis Howell's approach as Sports Minister after 1964 was his desire to enhance regional and local coordination, and with this in mind advisory Sports Councils were established in Scotland and Wales in 1965 alongside newly created English Regional Councils. These were designed to bring together representatives of local councils, voluntary sports organisations and assessors of government departments to survey needs and lay out plans for the building of new facilities. Despite funding constraints in the late 1960s, the Sports Council for Wales (SCW), based in Cardiff, in consequence oversaw in its first few years of operation a range of initiatives: recommending to the main GB Council nearly 100 grants to sports clubs to help with the capital cost of developing facilities, offering assistance to twenty governing bodies for administrative costs, and encouraging the appointment of full-time coaches for the likes of the Welsh Rugby Union to develop the game at the grass roots (Sports Council 1969).

By the time Wilson's Labour government lost power in 1970, the Scottish and Welsh advisory councils were established features of the policy framework for sport. Hence it came as no surprise that when the main GB Council received executive status via Royal Charter in 1972, Scotland and Wales were granted their own equivalents. This move reinforced their involvement with the development of sport at "national level". The opening of the National Sports Centre for Wales in Cardiff, for instance, provided a recognisable base for Welsh sport as well as a physical home for the SCW. Under the energetic guidance of Chairman Colonel (Sir) Harry Llewellyn, a gold medallist at the 1952 Olympics, the Welsh Sport Council successfully operated for many years as both a national and local funding agency, developing facilities and coaching programmes often with limited resources (Coghlan and Webb 1990). In spite of the distinctiveness associated with the pre-eminence of Rugby Union, however, Welsh sporting developments as pursued by governing bodies, municipal authorities and local education authorities continued as before to largely follow the English pattern, as set by legislation, White Papers and Whitehall directives. According to John Coghlan, a senior figure at the GB Sports Council in the 1970s and 1980s, there was much "overlapping and duplication" with the Scottish and Welsh bodies, which many London-based civil servants considered to be "resources wasted" (Coghlan and Webb 1990: 168).

The potential for fresh departures appeared to be significantly increased following Labour's legislation to create devolved assemblies in Scotland and Wales in 1998. This led to the transference of formal responsibility for sport from London to Edinburgh and Cardiff. In reality, however, according to one recent study, the outcome was a continuation of the long-term trend towards greater autonomy rather than a clear break with the past. At most, the record since 1998 suggests "a modest impact on sport policy" (Houlihan and Lindsey 2013: 101). A variety of factors contributed to the strong degree of continuity: pressures for convergence at the levels of both domestic and international sport (in relation to the latter, for example, the need to adhere to regulations set by global authorities such as the International Olympic Committee and the world doping agencies); the existence of common sporting provision and socio-economic features across the home nations; and broadly similar ideological approaches of the governing parties throughout Britain for at least a decade after the introduction of devolution.

In the case of Scotland, a sharp rise in funding for sport was detectable following the transfer of powers to the Scottish executive after 1997, though from a low base. While considerable rhetorical importance was attached by politicians to sport, its salience for Scottish ministers was variable and – as elsewhere in the UK – tended to assume a high priority only at times of crisis (associated with sectarian controversies in football in particular) or as a result of one-off episodes such as preparing for the Olympics or the 2014 Commonwealth Games, held in Glasgow. Labour's strength in Scotland, at least in the early post-devolution years, meant that following the concern of the national leadership in London, much effort was directed towards using sport as a tool to address wider social issues, notably those of poor health and rising obesity levels. The major policy pronouncements of these years by the Scottish Sports Council (later Sport Scotland), such as *Sport 21* and *Reaching Higher*, "exhibited a broad similarity to policy found in England and to a large extent also in Wales" (Houlihan and Lindsey 2013: 82). Although there were some organisational differences – notably Scottish local authorities having a statutory duty to provide recreational facilities – elite and community sport continued upon familiar lines; it was only in the sphere of school sport that Scotland diverged markedly from England after 1998 (Thomson 2010).

The coalition, London 2012 and beyond

This final section of the chapter briefly assesses the development of sport policy under David Cameron's Conservative-Liberal Democrat Coalition, although perspectives on the recent past will inevitably evolve and change as the 2010–15 government passes into history. The first six months of the Coalition were dominated by discussions about how to tackle Britain's massive public debt, which had spiralled to a post-war high following the onset of recession in 2008. A huge programme of spending cuts announced in October 2010, totalling over £80 billion over five years, placed considerable question marks over whether the advances secured for sport in the New Labour era were sustainable.

From the outset, the Coalition partners were determined not to jeopardise preparations for the London Games. Like his predecessors, Cameron believed that hosting the Olympics would secure a range of benefits over and above the impact on sport, embracing trade, regeneration and national well-being. As a result, New Labour's £9 billion budget survived the Spending Review and the Games took place to generally widespread acclaim. The long-term preparations and investment appeared vindicated when "Team GB" put in its best performance for a hundred years, winning a total of 65 medals, including 29 gold. Opinion polls indicated that four out of five Britons – across all ages, classes and regions – believed the Games were worth the money (Clark 2012) and funding providers such as UK Sport were confident that momentum could be maintained. With hundreds of millions of pounds continuing to be invested each year from exchequer and lottery sources, the prospects were reasonable for Britain continuing to shine at the 2016 Rio Olympics in sports such as athletics, cycling, rowing and sailing.

But other elements of the Blair–Brown sporting legacy fared less well after 2010: a reflection not only of the bleak economic backdrop, but also of the enduring fissures in the policy-making framework. The DCMS was initially powerless to prevent the announcement by the Coalition Education Secretary, Michael Gove, that Labour's £162-million a year strategy of supporting School Sports Partnerships was to be scrapped. After concerted opposition from well-known Olympic athletes, teachers, opposition MPs and sections of the press, the Cabinet decided that many of the 450 SSPs would be temporarily reprieved. Gove was forced to retreat, but he balked at the reinstatement of the full budget for the Partnership programme, and instead smaller sums were committed to the holding of annual "schools Olympics". A Department for Education spokesman said there was no longer a need for "centralised PE strategy" (Helm 2010).

Dark clouds also hung over the provision for community sport after 2010. Labour's target of getting an extra million adults each year doing general physical activity was quietly dropped soon after the Coalition came to power. Similarly endangered in the wake of the Spending Review was the aim of increasing by a million the numbers taking part in sport three times a week. By 2012 the Culture Secretary Jeremy Hunt preferred a measurement based on numbers participating once a week and directed at encouraging more young adults to get involved, rather than aiding the population as a whole (Jefferys 2012b). Although ministers claimed the government was delivering on Olympic legacy, critics pointed to some worrying trends. Sport England reported in 2013 that among governing bodies, 17 registered declining participation rates since 2007–08, with only four recording significant increases.

The Cameron regime thus delivered on long-promised plans to make a success of the Olympics, but viewed in the round, sport policy under the 2010–15 coalition became increasingly disjointed, losing much of the sense of integration and coherence that had grown steadily since the mid-1990s. Despite various failings and an obsession with arbitrary targets, there was at least a conscious effort in the latter stages of the Major administration and in the Blair–Brown years to adopt a comprehensive strategy, aimed at linking together school, community and elite-level sport and in so doing seeking to deploy sport in the interests of wider welfare and community goals – an aspiration that fell by the wayside as austerity took hold after 2010. While public investment remains steady in hard times and ensures that much good work continues, British sport policy looking forward would benefit from an injection – or a renewal – of urgency, direction and cohesion. The jury remains out on the sporting legacy of London 2012.

Note

1 In Britain, "the Cabinet" is the collective term used to describe the government's senior politicians who sit at the government's top table and shape government policy.

References

Baker, N. (1995) The amateur ideal in a society of equality: change and continuity in post-Second World War British sport 1945–48. *International Journal of the History of Sport*, 12(1): 99–126.

Beck, P.J. (2008) The British government and the Olympic movement: the 1948 London Olympics. *International Journal of the History of Sport*, 25(5): 615–47.

Binfield, J.C. and Stevenson, J. (1993) (eds) *Sport, Culture and Politics*. Sheffield: Sheffield Academic Press.

Bloyce, D. and Smith, A. (2010) *Sport Policy and Development: An Introduction*. Abingdon: Routledge.

Butler, D. and Pinto-Duschinsky, M. (1971) *The British General Election of 1970*. London and Basingstoke: Macmillan.

Central Council of Physical Recreation. (1960) Sport and the community. *The Report of the Wolfenden Committee on Sport*. London: CCPR.

Clark, T. (2012) 'Britain's end-of-year Olympic verdict: it was worth every penny', *The Guardian*, 26 December 2012, p. 2.

Coghlan, J. and Webb, I. (1990) *Sport and British Politics since 1960*. Brighton: Falmer.

Department for Culture, Media and Sport. (2000) *A Sporting Future for All*. London: DCMS.

Department of National Heritage. (1995) *Sport: Raising the Game*. London: DNH.

Hailsham, Lord. (1975) *The Door Wherein I Went*. London: Collins.

Hailsham, Lord. (1990) *A Sparrow's Flight*. London: Collins.

Hain, P. (1971) *Don't Play with Apartheid: The Background to the Stop the Seventy Tour Campaign*. London: Allen and Unwin.

Helm, T. (2010) 'Children launch national protest against sport cuts', *The Observer*, 5 December 2010, p. 19.

Hampton, J. (2008) *The Austerity Olympics: When the Games Came to London in 1948*. London: Aurum.

Henry, I. (2001) *The Politics of Leisure Policy*. Basingstoke: Palgrave.

Hill, C.R. (1992) *Olympic Politics*. Manchester: Manchester University Press.

Holt, R. and Mason, T. (2000) *Sport in Britain 1945–2000*. Oxford: Blackwell.

Houlihan, B. (1991) *The Government and Politics of Sport*. Abingdon: Routledge.

Houlihan, B. and Lindsey, I. (2013) *Sport Policy in Britain*. Abingdon: Routledge.

Houlihan, B. and White, A. (2002) *The Politics of Sports Development: Development of Sport or Development Through Sport*. Abingdon: Routledge.

House of Commons, Committee of Public Accounts. (2008) *The Budget for the London 2012 Olympic and Paralympic Games*. London: HMSO.

Howell, D. (1993) *Made in Birmingham*. London: Queen Anne Press.

Jefferys, K. (2012a) Britain and the boycott of the 1980 Moscow Olympics. *Sport in History*, 32(2): 279–301.

Jefferys, K. (2012b) *Sport and Politics in Modern Britain: The Road to 2012*. Basingstoke: Palgrave Macmillan.

Jefferys, K. (2012c) On Your Marks . . . Formulating sports policy and Britain's Olympic legacy. *History & Policy website*, Policy Paper. Accessed 2 June 2016. www.historyandpolicy.org/papers/policy-paper-133.html.

Lee, M. (2006) *The Race for the 2012 Olympics: The Inside Story of How London Won the Bid*. London: Virgin Books.

Macfarlane, N. and Herd, M. (1996) *Sport and Politics: A World Divided*. London: Willow Books.

McMaster, A. and Bairner, A. (2012) Junior Ministers in the UK: the Role of the Minister for Sport. *Parliamentary Affairs*, 65: 214–237.

Major, J. (1999) *The Autobiography*. London: HarperCollins.

Pickup, D. (1996) *Not Another Messiah: An Account of the Sports Council 1988–93*. Bishop Auckland: Pentland Press.

Sarantakes, N. (2011) *Dropping the Torch. Jimmy Carter, The Olympic Boycott, and the Cold War*. Cambridge: Cambridge University Press.

Seldon, A. (1997) *Major. A Political Life*. London: Weidenfeld & Nicolson.

Sports Council. (1969) *The Sports Council. A Review 1966–69*. London: CCPR.

Thomson, I. (2010) Sport in the devolved system: the Scottish experience. In M. Collins (ed.) *Examining Sport Development*. Abingdon: Routledge.

Wilson, H. (1971) *The Labour government 1964–1970: A Personal Record*. London: Weidenfeld & Nicolson.

18

SPORT, THE 2014 COMMONWEALTH GAMES AND THE SCOTTISH REFERENDUM

Grant Jarvie

The existence of a close relationship between sport, nations and nationalism was clearly illustrated before and during the 2014 Commonwealth Games in Glasgow, Scotland, revealing how sport was used to both promote and challenge Scotland's status as a nation within the United Kingdom (UK) and its potential status as an independent nation-state. The involvement of sport in the 2014 Scottish Referendum campaign was essentially limited to four broad areas: (1) endorsements from sports people for both the yes and the no camps; (2) the production of a series of documents and in particular the Scottish Government's White Paper on *Scotland's Future* and the *McLeish Report* into sport in an independent Scotland; (3) the hosting of and participating in major sporting events in the belief that they would influence the outcome of the Referendum; and finally (4) answers to an extremely limited number of survey questions about sport in Scotland.

All of the above will be drawn upon in assessing the role that sport had to play in the campaign. More specifically, the chapter considers the following questions:

- Is the use of sport in Scottish nationalist politics new?
- What part did sport play in the 2014 Referendum campaign?
- To what extent did Glasgow hosting the 2014 Commonwealth Games influence the outcome of the Scottish Referendum?

To answer such questions, this chapter is divided into four sections: first, it provides an introduction to sport in the context of Scotland and the campaign for independence. Second it reminds us of sport's association with Britishness, Scottishness and the break-up of Britain. Third, it considers key documents where sport figured in the debates. Fourth, it considers the role of sporting celebrities and major sporting events that were prominent during the 2014 Referendum Campaign.

The politics of sport, Scotland and the 2014 Referendum

Few, if any, studies have focused on the role of sport in Referendum politics and this, together with Whigham's chapter in this volume, is perhaps the first study to explore the role of sport in the 2014 Scottish and UK Referendum Campaign. O'Donnell, when asked about the link between sporting and political success or failure asserted 'I can't think of a single case where it has really made a difference' (James 2014: 1). Others point to the role that sport played in the downfall of apartheid South Africa, or the messages attached to the actions of athletes such as Jesse Owens (1936), Tommie Smith (1968), Cathy Freeman (2000) and many others who all helped to convey political messages at different Olympic Games.

There is a cross-disciplinary corpus of research that could contribute to a discussion on the role of sport in Referendum politics from diverse fields such as political science, nationalism, social movements and European integration and from the closely connected examples of studies on sport in Quebec (Harvey 1999), Catalunya (Hargreaves 2000) and the Basque Country (Walton 2011) (all discussed in this volume too). It is wise to caution against the acceptance of any rigid universalism or thinking that perpetually links a particular sport to a particular nation. The relationship between sport x and nation y is not fixed in terms of content, time or place. Many sporting heroes or heroines have helped to keep alive the idea of what a certain nation is, was or should be. For example, the idea of any fixed national identity being attached to or supported by Scottish sporting heroes and heroines should be challenged, for in the 1920s the situation was different from that of the 1940s or the 1990s or from the 2014 campaign for independence. The idea of Scotland championed by the likes of footballer Denis Law in the 1960s was different from the idea of Scotland championed by footballer Michael Stewart during the 2014 Referendum 'Yes' campaign.

As ex-club players, Denis Law and Michael Stewart were both associated with Manchester United, as was Sir Alex Ferguson who accused Alex Salmond of trying to silence Scots who lived in the rest of the UK after the First Minister called for severe restrictions on the sums of cash that they could donate to the independence Referendum (Ferguson 2012). The pro-independence 'Yes' Scotland campaign had imposed a £500 per person limit on donations from outside Scotland. Ferguson handed a symbolic sum of £501 to the *Better Together* pro-Union camp to highlight what he claimed was the injustice of the cap. Furthermore he added:

> It is quite wrong of the man who is supposed to be leader of Scotland to try and silence people like this. I played for Scotland and managed the Scotland team. No-one should question my Scottishness just because I live south of the Border.
>
> *(Ferguson 2012)*

On 18 September 2014, the Scottish electorate voted by 55 per cent to 45 per cent to remain part of the United Kingdom and say no to independence. Scottish voters were asked to vote yes or no to the question, Should Scotland be an independent country? Yet it was never entirely clear what yes or no meant exactly (Jeffrey 2014: 1). The Scottish National Party that had formed the majority government at the time of the campaign dominated the Yes camp. The UK Government and the three pro-unionist parties, Labour, the Conservatives and the Liberal Democrats formed a somewhat uncomfortable coalition as partners in *The Better Together Campaign*. The former Chancellor of the Exchequer Alistair Darling MP led the latter, while Nicola Sturgeon MSP, then Deputy Leader of the Scottish National Party, led the former.

The Referendum campaign lasted for more than two years and during that time more than 100 opinion polls monitored voting intentions on whether Scotland would be an independent country. Given that gambling and online betting is one of the greatest contemporary challenges facing not just Scottish or British, but world sport, it might be assumed that those placing a bet on sport might have been better informed about the outcome of the Referendum. Bell (2014) points out, on the Scotland decision the bookmakers got it right and the opinion polls got it wrong. The politics of sport during the campaign was marginal in comparison to the core ideological battlegrounds of the economy and calls for constitutional change. The No campaign focused primarily upon the economic benefits and risks of remaining outside of the United Kingdom while the Yes campaign argued that Scotland could only flourish if it had full control over its own affairs.

With the exception of high-performance sport, partly funded through UK Sport's high-performance programmes and centres and UK lottery funding, sport in Scotland has been a devolved area of Scottish affairs since 1999 when the Scottish parliament was re-convened. A prominent supporter of the Yes camp was Jim Sillars, former SNP deputy leader and Scottish Labour and Heart of Midlothian Football Club supporter. Sillars had chastised the Scottish electorate shortly after the 1992 General Election results saying 'The great problem is that Scotland has too many ninety minute patriots whose nationalist outpourings are expressed only at major sporting events' (Jim Sillars, *The Herald* 24 April 1992: 1). On the contrary, the politics of sport was not simply limited to 90-minute footballing nationalists, such as the previously mentioned Michael Stewart, the former Manchester United, Hearts and Scotland player, who fronted the Yes sport camp. Swimmers, cyclists, tennis players and rugby players all of whom participate in sports that take more or less than 90 minutes also expressed views.

The views of sporting celebrities on both sides of the campaign may help to bury the historical and mythical thesis that sport itself is not conducive to any form of political consciousness. Andy Murray and others faced a backlash for supporting the Yes campaign after tweeting on the day of the Referendum vote 'Huge day for Scotland today! No campaign negativity last few days totally swayed my view on it, excited to see the outcome, let's do this' (Murray 2014). Murray's older brother Jamie, a former Wimbledon mixed doubles champion, had already voiced his support for an independent Scotland while Sir Chris Hoy, Scottish Olympian and Olympic gold medalist was subject to a barrage of internet abuse by nationalists for warning that independence could harm Scottish sport. That athletes on both sides of the campaign voiced opinions is in itself to be welcomed for we need socially and politically committed voices in and from sport, people brave enough to speak up on the issues of the day and not totally ruled by the PR machines that advise today's sporting celebrities.

As well as Murray, athletes such as David Wilkie (swimming) and Eve Muirhead (curling) were criticised for taking a side during the 2014 Scottish Referendum campaign. Yet athletes such as Kareem Abdul-Jabbar who led the Milwaukee Bucks to five National Basketball Association (NBA) championships, and who converted to Islam and played for the Los Angeles Lakers, has openly encouraged sports stars to find their social and political voice (Broadbent 2015: 60). Hence he was pleased when basketball greats such as Kobe Bryant wore 'I can't breathe' T-shirts, which echoed the last words of Eric Garner, the black man killed after being placed in a chokehold by a New York police officer (Broadbent 2015: 60). He wrote an article for *Times Magazine*, pointing out that when the Ku Klux Klan burn a cross in a black family's yard, prominent Christians are not required or forced to explain how these are not Christian acts (Broadbent 2015: 60).

When Joey Barton of Queens Park Rangers appears on the BBC's *Question Time* and gets mocked for 'stepping out of his box', or Andy Murray gets criticised for tweeting about the Referendum, it is a reminder that we need more socially and politically motivated sports stars to continually challenge the myth that sport and playing sport are not conducive to any form of political consciousness. What all of these athletes had in common was that they spoke their political and social minds, lived with the consequences and provided different forms of leadership both within and through sport.

Nationalism, Scotland, and glamour of backwardness

The association between sport, nationalism, Britishness and threats to the Union are not new. Sport has figured in the works of many of Scotland's leading literary and political figures including Nairn (1979) and Jenkins (1983). For John Murdoch, who campaigned for the Highland Land Law Reform Association in 1883, the politics of land reform, nationalism and shinty were inextricably linked. Neil Gunn (1931) questioned the use of the Highlands as a sporting playground for the nouveaux rich but also abhorred the professional athlete picking up the winnings on the Highland Games circuit of the 1930s and 1940s. This he saw as symptomatic of a changing way of life that had little respect for local customs and traditional culture.

Just as Scottish writers have used sport to comment about the politics of place, nation and/or identity, then Scottish sports men and women have added their own commentary. For footballer Denis Law, Scottishness was crucial. Following Scotland's 1967 victory over England, one year after England's 1966 FIFA World Cup victory, a certain logic prompted Law to enthuse that Scotland were now World Champions. Yet for Law the dual nationality of Scottishness and Britishness was rarely questioned. It is doubtful if Law would have accepted Nairn's (1979) argument that the enemy was Britain and not England. He felt acutely embarrassed about committing a foul in front of the Royal Box in the 1967 Wembley game. Following her gold medal victory in the 1986 Edinburgh Commonwealth Games 10,000 metres Liz Lynch proclaimed, 'I did it for Scotland' and the popular press found an instant national heroine (see Jarvie and Walker 1994: 23). Following on from the curling bronze medal at the 2014 Sochi Winter Olympic Games, the Skipper of the Great Britain team Eve Muirhead, entered into the row over independence when she admitted it was more special representing Great Britain than Scotland (Ward 2014: 3). Curling is one of the few sports where the UK team is usually entirely Scottish in make-up. Alex Salmond pointed out that a breakaway Scotland would apply to the International Olympic Committee to send a team to future Games under the Saltire (Salmond 2014).

At different times different Scottish sports have carried messages about Scottish and British politics. Leading up to the 1992 General Election it was not football that seemed to reflect the feelings of the Scottish electorate, but rugby union and in particular the clash between Scotland and England at Murrayfield, the national rugby union stadium (Jarvie and Walker 1994). Those on the terraces were caught up in expressions of nationalism and patriotism. Perhaps idealistically, some political commentators of the time suggested that the game itself had taken on a much greater importance. In the words of one correspondent:

> The message of Murrayfield this weekend was bigger than scrimmaging techniques and line-out skills. It seemed etched on the emotions of the players as they sang Flower of Scotland. It boiled constantly around the arena. Sometimes events happening send a clearer signal than a thousand pieces of newspaper. Murrayfield was a message of Scottish identity and nationhood.
>
> (The Guardian *28 October 1991: 24*)

Sport may not provide the strongest foundation upon which to mobilise a campaign for national separatism, but sport is affected by its social and political surroundings. It carries social and political messages. To illustrate the general point that is being made, one additional example is noted. Much was made of remarks made by the Queen on 14 September 2014, just before the Scottish Referendum vote. She made a rare intervention on the political stage by stating that 'she hoped the voters would think very carefully about the future before voting' (*The Guardian*

14 September 2014: 1). The comments were made as she left Crathie Kirk near her Balmoral estate in Aberdeenshire (Scotland) following the Sunday morning service. Balmoral estate is historically the summer residence of the reigning monarch, and its close association with the Braemar Royal Highland Society Gathering and Games extends back to 1848. The reigning monarch is patron to the Gathering, an event that has been associated with royalism and referred to by Nairn (1988: 214) as helping to cement the glamour of backwardness. Nairn's main thesis relates to the process where ordinary folk's love of nation, crown and Union, cemented by popular events such as the Braemar Gathering, has helped to deflect from the decline of the nation itself into a condition of backwardness. The historical popularity of the Highlands as a sporting playground, the creation of a 'them and us together' or 'they're just like us' mentality was assisted by the creation of a British sporting calendar of events. This included the regular Braemar fixture that for Nairn (1988: 229) depicted the normality of the absurd. A love of crown, nation and 'Balmorality' through sport and other events facilitated not only the power of legitimation but also concealed, for Nairn, structural cracks in the make-up of the United Kingdom that would in turn lead to the break up of Britain.

Many other examples in which Scottish and British sport have been used could be cited in order to establish that the association of sport with Britishness, Scottishness and the *Break up of Britain* is not new. This is the backdrop to the most recent Scottish Referendum and the organisations and people associated with the Yes and No camps. It is evident that the nationalism and patriotism that had influenced so many sports men and women over the years was as similar as it was different but it is certainly not new. To draw again upon Nairn (2014: 416), a writer who has done more than most to challenge the perception of Great Britain as a multinational state, what Scotland was wrestling with in 2014 was a set of circumstances that this 'Auld Nation was ready for a New Age'. But was it?

Independent sport and the Scotland we can create

The Scottish Government's White Paper *Scotland's Future – Your Guide to an Independent Scotland* was published in November 2013. It ran to more than 649 pages of which four, in the section on Health and Well-Being and The Scotland We Can Create, were devoted to sport (Scottish Government 2013: 176–180). The White Paper was entirely positive in outlook other than where it spelled out, as seen at the time, the consequences of a No vote as viewed by an SNP government. These consequences were expressed primarily as opening the door to a new generation of nuclear weapons on the Scottish River Clyde, public spending cuts and a withdrawal from the European Union (EU). The commentary on sport asserted that Scots were passionate about sport and that Scotland had a long and proud sporting tradition (Scottish Government 2013: 177).

The White Paper gave a summary of investments in sport either spent or planned and aligned to the key political messages about the new Scotland that could be created. Since 2007 when the SNP government came to power, £73 million had been invested in sports facilities; 23 new football pitches and 12 new or upgraded swimming pools had been created; the development of new facilities for the Commonwealth Games in 2014; a £25 million National Performance Centre to be created at Heriot-Watt University; an £80 million investment in Active School sport co-ordinators; £8.5 million of funding to secure two hours of physical education delivered in schools; 114 Community Sports Hubs established; a £10 million active places fund to encourage more active participation in local communities; £24 million of cash back money (money retrieved from the proceeds of crime) to go to sport in the community and £5 million invested in club golf since 2003, which had provided 260,000 children with the opportunity to play golf.

A key priority for action arising out of the investments and aspirations listed above and set out in *Scotland's Future* was to set up a Working Group on Scottish Sport to consider its continuing development, including the impact of independence. Linked to this was the McLeish Report, published in May 2014. This placed an emphasis on physical activity for health but failed to address the role that sport plays in international or cultural relations and assumed rather than critically assessed the proposition that the solution was the transfer of further UK resources to Scotland despite sport having been devolved since 1999.

Around 11 per cent of the athletes on UK Sport's world-class programme, which distributes £350 million of Exchequer and Lottery funding every four years, are Scottish. Scottish athletes made a contribution to one in five of the 65 medals won in London by Team GB. Supporters of Scottish nationalism insisted that its share of the National Lottery investment in sport – estimated at around £37 million – should simply be transferred to SportScotland. But the UK government's position was that the entire basis of the National Lottery funding settlement would have to be revisited.

The 53-page McLeish Report was framed in part by pressures to pave the way for an independent Scotland to compete in the 2016 Rio Olympic Games. Commenting on the report, the then-Secretary for Sport Shona Robison said:

> The working group found that Scotland could compete as an independent country at the Rio Olympics in 2016 and there are no barriers to securing Olympic and Paralympic accreditation for an independent Scotland.
>
> *(The Scottish Government 2014a: 1)*

The question of Scotland's involvement in the 2016 Olympics and Paralympics was seen as a given on the basis that Montenegro and the Balkan States had received recognition within one year of independence and that Croatia and Serbia had been accredited in Olympic terms ahead of any United Nations membership. Yet such an assumption was challenged by one of the few Scots with a place on the International Olympic Committee, Sir Craig Reedie. As a Vice-President of the International Olympic Committee, he warned that athletes would 'follow funding and refuse to represent a newly independent nation' (Reedie 2014). UK Sport's chief executive, Liz Nicholl, commented that a yes vote would weaken the medal chances of both Scottish athletes and their British counterparts (Nicholl 2014). Reedie said he believed some athletes might choose to continue representing Team GB regardless of the outcome of the vote. No campaigners said that Scottish athletes who have already represented Great Britain would be free to choose. Scottish athletes benefit greatly from substantial funding through the UK Sport system and this, suggested Reedie, might mean that 'those who have received that may feel compelled to carry on representing Team GB' (Reedie 2014).

Imogen Bankier, who represented Scotland at the 2010 Commonwealth Games and Great Britain at the 2012 Olympics said that she 'preferred the status quo and was worried about sports funding in an independent Scotland'. She added, 'we can tap into the English system and be part of Team GB when it suits us and use it to our advantage . . . Independence would mean we would lose that'' (Slatter 2014). Lynsey Sharp, the Commonwealth and European silver medalist told BBC Scotland that she was worried about the implications of independence because she spent most of her time at Loughborough University, a place transformed by UK Sport money into a world-leading sports science centre. 'If Scotland is able to do that why hasn't it done it already?' asked Sharp (Slatter 2014).

The 2014 Glasgow Commonwealth Games and major sporting events

The ability of cities and countries to bid for and host major sporting events is uneven, in terms of both economic and human capacity and capability (Kidd 2011). The number of countries and cities wanting to host the Commonwealth Games has been problematic. In 2006 only Melbourne and Wellington initially expressed an interest. Wellington eventually withdrew, citing cost as the reason, leaving Melbourne to win by default. The situation was somewhat better in 2010, with both Hamilton in Canada and New Delhi tabling bids. There were head-to-head bids in 2014 and 2018 – Glasgow against Abuja in Nigeria; and Australia's Gold Coast against Hambantota in Sri Lanka.

There have been numerous studies outlining the advantages and disadvantages of hosting major sporting events (OECD 2008; Kuper and Szymanski 2014). Major sporting events are chased and secured in the belief that reputations can be enhanced and economies stimulated, yet few economic studies measure the 'feel-good' factor associated with major sporting events. 'Psychic income' takes many forms, including a sense of community and common purpose as well as sporting success. The OECD (2008) review identified direct benefits stemming from strategic alignment with plans for the city or nation; private–public investment partnerships; image and identity impact attracting population, investment and trade; environmental impacts upon built and natural environments and the potential for the expansion of infrastructure and the development of a more buoyant visitor economy. The indirect benefits include potential post-event use of land and buildings; infrastructure legacies; labour market impacts; property price increase and global positioning.

Having secured the right to host the Commonwealth Games in 2007, Glasgow proceeded to deliver an event that was presented as not only being good for Glasgow but good for the Commonwealth. The then-Commonwealth Games Federation Chief Executive, Mike Hooper described Glasgow as 'the standout Games in the history of the movement' (The 2014 Games Legacy, *Sunday Herald* 2015: 2). Some of the key factors that contributed to Glasgow being talked of in this way were as follows (Scottish Government 2014b):

- the Queen's baton relay covered 190,000 kilometres across 70 nations and territories representing a third of the world's population and making it the world's most engaging relay;
- 71 nations and over two billion citizens from the Commonwealth;
- 1.3 million tickets or 98 per cent of tickets were sold and 88 per cent of these were made available to the public;
- delivered within a budget of £575.6 million including a security budget of £90 million;
- 46 official Games sponsors;
- England topped the medal table and Scotland came fourth;
- Pride House was central to raising the profile of LGBT rights;
- the largest integrated Para-Sport programme of any Commonwealth Games;
- Glasgow saw an increase of shoppers of just under 22 per cent over the same period in 2013 and an increase of 36 per cent in the two weeks prior to the Games;
- the Athlete's Village legacy consisted of 700 new homes and a new 120-bed care home for the elderly.

Yet the evaluation report that accompanied the Scottish Government's pre-Games analysis highlighted seven lessons that were to be learned about the delivery and promise about what legacies can and cannot deliver. In many ways these were consistent with what was already known from research into legacies. Glasgow learned from the lessons. The lessons were (Scottish Government 2012):

- lack of robust evidence around long-term legacy gains;
- mixed evidence on economic growth and physical activity boosts;
- past events vary greatly in their explicit legacy plans;
- no automatic trickle-down effect upon positive legacy outcomes and any outcomes have to be planned for;
- importance of a long-term perspective, otherwise planned outcomes will not be achieved;
- importance of good institutional organisation;
- importance of community engagement, grass roots involvement and authority to make decisions.

That the Glasgow 2014 Commonwealth Games were a success is not in question, but what is in question is the extent to which they affected the Scottish Referendum result and the real politics of Glasgow 2014. The Scottish Government announced on 21 March 2013 that the Referendum would be held on 18 September 2014. Media reports at the time suggested that the date was chosen with 2014 being the 700-year anniversary of the Battle of Bannockburn (between Scotland and England) and the year that Scotland would be hosting two major sporting competitions – the 2014 Commonwealth Games and the 2014 Ryder Cup. It was asserted that this could influence the mood of the nation. Alex Salmond is on the record stating these events made 2014 a 'good year to hold a Referendum' (MacAskill 2014). Both events were couched in terms of Scotland being more active, celebrating a modern vibrant culture and illustrating that it could run major sporting events and, by implication, its own affairs. However the latter of these events took place after the independence vote and therefore could not be seen to directly affect political events to the same degree as the Commonwealth Games.

Throughout the build up to Glasgow 2014, coined as the 'friendly games', both the Yes and No camps strived for political advantage while not wanting to be seen to be overtly using the Games to deliver Referendum messages. Many asked if hosting the Games so close to the vote would affect the result (James 2014). Gerry Hassan (cited in James 2014) told the BBC documentary *The Games People Play*:

> of course the Commonwealth Games will have an effect on the Referendum – it couldn't be otherwise – and part of the independence argument is an argument about: whether Scots feel they have the confidence to do this.

So for supporters of independence such as Hassan, the Commonwealth Games were about mood creation and a feeling of optimism that Scotland could be independent.

The Survation survey for the *Mail on Sunday* of 1,000 adults, carried out between 30 July and 1 August 2014, included a question on whether the Commonwealth Games in Glasgow was likely to affect the independence Referendum vote. Eighty per cent said that the Games had made no difference to how they would vote. Twelve per cent said they had made them more inclined to vote yes, while 7 per cent said they had made them more inclined to vote no. Of those who were undecided, 14 per cent said that Scotland's organisation of and performance in the Games had made them more likely to vote yes, 4 per cent said no and 82 per cent said it would have no effect.

Blair McDougall, *Better Together* campaign director said:

> The Commonwealth Games were great for Glasgow and we all enjoyed cheering on Team Scotland to success, but the Games had nothing to do with the Referendum, which will be decided by the big issues like the economy.
>
> *(Ross 2014)*

Blair Jenkins, Yes Scotland chief executive, said:

> This is a very encouraging poll and confirms new research by Dr Arkadiusz Wisniowski of Southampton University for the Washington Post, which indicates that not only is the result too close to call, but that Yes can win.
>
> *(Ross 2014)*

There is no doubt that in the context of the Commonwealth as whole, sport is political and has an increasingly important international role in helping cities, the Commonwealth and countries talk to each other. As part of a soft power mix, sport can certainly persuade and influence and its popularity means it is a natural target for carrying messages. Just as the 2014 FIFA World Cup in Brazil carried messages about poverty, healthcare, education and the cost of the event, the opening ceremony of the Glasgow 2014 Commonwealth told us that these Games were about humanity, diversity and destiny. Billy Connolly evoked the memory of Nelson Mandela and reminded us of Glasgow and Scotland's support for the anti-apartheid movement. Sport played a big part in the apartheid struggle and perhaps unified the Commonwealth more than ever because it had a cause to rally around. Few if any of the Commonwealth leaders and sports ministers who flew into Glasgow expressed support for a Yes or No vote, despite the fact many of the countries and territories competing spawned independence movements.

For some the event may have provided a welcome break for voters from the onslaught of Referendum news and in this sense provided a cathartic function or a safety valve for heated emotions. Many felt that there was no need to talk about the Referendum during the Games and perhaps the real politics of Glasgow 2014 was that it helped promote the idea of the Commonwealth itself and in particular it bought more time for a Commonwealth Games Federation (CGF) that desperately needed Glasgow to be a success and restore faith in the event so that future cities and countries would continue to bid for the event.

There is ample evidence that Commonwealth Games carry political messages (Jarvie 2014; see also Whigham in this volume). Events, when they go well, as this one did, tend to create a feel-good factor, but it is a different thing to claim that this will translate into votes. It would be unfortunate and indeed somewhat contradictory to think that on the one hand Scottish voters had become politically informed or engaged by Referendum politics and on the other hand politically influenced by a medal table and the positive feeling created by sporting success. But sport is an effective medium for cities and countries to build stronger relationships and the social and political potential of sport to win friends or help the politics of humanity, diversity and destiny has still to be fully grasped.

So what of the future? What is the purpose of the Commonwealth Games in the twenty-firtst century and did Glasgow help? What does the CGF want sport to look like in the Commonwealth? Will it suffice to be the public face of the Commonwealth every four years or will the future of the event depend on more being done to deliver on the core Commonwealth values? At the Glasgow opening ceremony, the CGF told us the Games are about humanity, diversity and destiny. For the Games to continue to be held in only the safe, prosperous and secure cities would fly in the face of such values.

How should we balance the emphasis on a race for medals every four years with much more of a continued focus on the sport-for-development-and-peace initiatives that have been developing throughout the Commonwealth. In Rwanda and Sierra Leone, for example, sport has been used to restore normality in violent and war-torn communities. This was showcased during the Glasgow opening ceremony. The Commonwealth Games has never been just another international sporting event but an explicitly political and cultural exchange to affirm and strengthen values and communities.

Only a fraction of the public and private funds spent on sport in most Commonwealth countries goes to grassroots development and even less to initiatives such as major sporting events. This disconnect is exacerbated by the cost of the Games. Perhaps bid cities should ensure sustainable and measurable increases not only in sport and physical activity but involvement from the most marginal members of society. Perhaps the idea of joint bids should be revisited in order to ensure a more equitable hosting amongst the cities of the Commonwealth. It is not necessarily the case that campaigns led by international and local elites actually deliver for ordinary people.

What we can probably say about the politics of the Commonwealth Games is that Glasgow has bought the Games more time. Sport, as Glasgow reminded us, played an important part in the struggle for South Africa. Glasgow not only bought CGF time but also showed that effective cultural relations can be enhanced through sport. If the Commonwealth deeply believes in its values and wants to make the Games a sustainable resource for hope, it will have to think hard about where they go from here. Glasgow's Mandela moment is not a bad place to start. The realpolitik of Glasgow 2014 was not so much about local Referendum politics but saving the future of the Commonwealth Games.

In advancing a coherent consensus on the politics of sport that is good for sport and good for Scotland a framework for sport in Scotland is required. Unlike Canada, Scotland has no sports policy that it can call its own, but it urgently needs a framework and active set of governance tools to (a) bring this about and (b) deliver it on the ground in communities in ways that change behaviour, improve life chances and play a part in narrowing the gap between rich and poor. Canada Sports Policy 2012 may not be the solution but it provides a model framework that aims to forge excellence, enhance education and skill development, improve health and wellness, increase civic pride, engagement and cohesion, and increase economic development and prosperity.

Sport, soft power and winning friends

Sport is a culture that contributes to entire cultures; it is undoubtedly a site around which and through which many conversations take place. Imagined communities are presented through sport; business is conducted through sporting contacts and in and between cities; it is a language that helps nations, cities, communities and individuals to communicate; its popularity makes it a sought-after medium for carrying messages; nations build soft power strategies around sport; unions such as the European Union recognise that sport has a part in cultural relations; since 2003 the United Nations has increasingly used it as a development tool; sporting icons are sought after in terms of celebrity diplomacy and it provides a specific form of trade and labour migration as sports workers move from country to country. Those interested in Scottish cultural relations cannot afford to ignore anything that helps win friends, acts as soft power and helps countries and cities talk to each other.

Much of the existing body of research on the politics of sport makes a concerted plea that those studying politics, international relations and the politics of separation should not ignore the politics of sport. The relationship between social and political science should be mutual. They need each other in the sense that sports research needs social and political science, just as social and political science needs sport.

The general contention of this chapter is that a body of work on sport's contribution to Referendum politics is still in the making and that this study on the role of sport in the politics of the 2014 Scottish Referendum campaign provides but a small contribution to one of the silences within the politics of sport literature.

While some athletes and sports commentators past and present have made their voices heard, such interventions are to be welcomed for many reasons one of which is that they challenge the myth that athletes and sport rarely can be at the forefront of social and political campaigns. Perhaps this is more of a problem for mainstream politics or social and political scientists who continue to be blind to the social and political activism that is forged both in and through sport.

It is both argued and evidenced that during the Scottish Referendum campaign sport was neither a driver of cultural or political nationalism nor a hotly contested political issue. This is in the sense that it had no real political power in helping either the Yes or No campaign to achieve their political goals or influence Yes or No voters which way to vote.

However, the Referendum, while not affecting significant voting behaviour, may still have acted as a 'public policy catalyst'. This point was emphasised by the senior civil servant responsible for the delivery of the Commonwealth Games (field notes). While the 2014 Commonwealth Games might have been framed in terms of Scotland being more active, celebrating a modern vibrant culture and illustrating that Scotland could run major sporting events well, perhaps the realpolitik of Glasgow was more about the Commonwealth than Scotland or Glasgow.

Finally, there is Scotland itself and the way it thinks about its sportspeople and the invaluable contribution that those in sport can make to the social and political debate about Scottish culture. Far too often the popular language and culture of sport is forgotten when Scottish cultural critics meet to discuss important matters of the day and the role of culture in the shaping and making of nations. The role of arts, culture and identity in a changing Scotland was a common theme throughout 2014 and yet the silence on sporting matters within these very discussions was astonishing, not because the of the lack of socially or politically committed sportspeople, but because of the framing of cultural discussions in Scotland which are often blind to the fact that sport is culture and a useful vehicle for cultural relations. This too has to change.

References

Allison, L. (ed) (1993) *The Changing Politics of Sport*. Manchester: Manchester University Press.

Allison, L. (1998) Sport and civil society. *Political Studies*, (46): 709–726.

Bell, D. (2014) 'Scotland's decision: Bookies 1, opinion polls 0': The future of the UK and Scotland. Edinburgh: ESRC Research. Accessed 11 January 2015. www.futureukandscotland.ac.uk/blog/scotlands-decision-bookies-1-opinion-polls-0.

Broadbent, R. (2015) 'Kareem Abdul Jabbar still making his points'. *The Times*, 14 January, p. 60.

Cha, V. (2009) *Beyond the Final Score: The Politics of Sport in Asia*. New York: Columbia University Press.

Ferguson, A. (2012) Cited in United against Separatism. 15 December 2012. Accessed 17 January 2014. www.facebook.com/VoteNo2014/posts/45412663797965.

Grant, M. (2015) 'The state of Scottish football: part 1'. *The Herald Sport*, 3 March 2015, pp. 2–3.

Grix, J. (2014) 'Political science and sport'. In J. Maguire (ed.) *Social Sciences in Sport*. Champaign, IL: Human Kinetics, pp. 191–290.

Gunn, N. (1931) Highland Games. *Scots Magazine*, XV (6): 412–416.

Hargreaves, J. (2000) *Freedom for Catalonia? Catalan Nationalism, Spanish Identity and the Barcelona Olympic Games.* Cambridge: Cambridge University Press.

Harvey, J. (1999) 'Sport and Quebec nationalism'. In J. Sugden and A. Bairner (eds) *Sport in Divided Societies.* Aachen: Meyer and Meyer, pp. 31–50.

Harvey, J., Horne, J., Safai, P., Darnell, S, and O'Neil, S. (eds.) (2014) *Sport and Social Movements: From Local to Global.* London: Bloomsbury.

Holden, R. (2011) 'Never forget you're Welsh: the role of sport as a political device in post-devolution Wales'. *Sport in Society,* 14(2): 272–288.

Houlihan, B. and Zheng, J. (2014) 'Small states: sport and politics at the margin'. *International Journal of Sport Policy and Politics.* Published online 15 October. Accessed 18 January 2015. DOI: 10.1080/19406940.2014.959032.

James, A. (2014) 'Scottish independence: will Scotland's summer of sport affect the Referendum?' *BBC News Scotland's Politics Online.* 2 August 2014. Accessed 9 March 2015. www.bbc.co.uk/news/uk-scotland-scotland-politics-28510065.

Jarvie, G. (2014) 'Great but Games will not swing a single vote'. *Sunday Mail,* 27 July, p. 30.

Jarvie, G. and Walker, G. (1994) *Scottish Sport in the Making of the Nation: Ninety-Minute Patriots?* London: Leicester University Press.

Jeffrey, C. (2014) 'Focus: Scottish independence: the terms of the debate'. *Discover Society.* 1 April 2014, pp. 1–5.

Jenkins, R. (1983) *The Thistle and the Grail.* Glasgow: Macdonald and Co.

Kidd, B. (1996) *The Struggle for Canadian Sport.* Toronto: University of Toronto Press.

Kidd, B. (2008) 'A new social movement: sport for development and peace'. *Sport in Society,* 13(5): 901–910.

Kidd, B. (2011) 'The future of the Commonwealth Games'. *The Commonwealth Year Book.* London: Nexus Strategic Partnerships, pp. 139–145.

Kornbeck, J. (2014) 'Lisbonisation without regulation: engaging with sport policy to maximise its health impact'. *International Sports Law Journal,* 65. DO1 10.1007/s40318-014-0065-.

Kuper, S. and Symanski, S. (2014) *Soccernomics.* London: Harper Sport.

Linklater, E. (1959) *Magnus Merriemen.* Hammondsworth: Penguin.

MacAskill, M. (2014) 'Solo Scots athletes could miss Rio'. *The Sunday Times.* 10 August, p. 5.

Mackenzie, C. (1946) *The North Wind of Love.* London: Chatto and Windus.

Macpherson, G. (2015) 'The state of Scottish football: part 2'. *The Herald Sport.* 4 March 2015, pp. 2–3.

McLaughlin, M. (2014) 'Olympic hero Wilkie says SNP is hijacking Glasgow Games'. *The Scotsman.* 26 May 2014, p. 12.

McLeish, H. (2014) Working group on Scottish sport: the continuing development of Scottish sport- including the impact of independence. *Scottish Government.* Edinburgh. Accessed 6 January 2015. http://news.scotland.gov.uk/News/Scotland-s-Sporting-Future-c5f.aspx.

Murphy, D. (2014) *Schooling Scotland.* Edinburgh: Argyllshire Publishing.

Murray, A. (2014) 'Scottish Referendum: abuse directed at Andy Murray, vile'. *BBC News Scotland Online.* Accessed 6 January 2015. www.bbc.co.uk/news/uk-scotland-29249577.

Nairn, T. (1979) *The Break up of Britain.* London: Verso.

Nairn, T. (1988) *The Enchanted Glass.* London: Radius.

Nairn, T. (2014) 'Auld nation, new age'. In J. Maxwell and P. Ramand (eds) *Tom Nairn: Old Nations, Auld Enemies. New Times.* Edinburgh: Luath Press, pp. 416–419.

Nichol, L. (2014) Cited in Gibson, O. 'Sport's winners and losers beyond the great Scotland yes-no battle'. *The Guardian.* Accessed 8 January 2015. www.theguardian.com/sport/blog/2014/sep/06/sport-winners-losers-scotland-yes-no-battle.

OECD. (2008) *Local Development Benefits from staging Global events: Achieving a Local Development Legacy for London 2012.* London: OECD.

Parrish, R. (2007) 'Judicial intervention and sporting autonomy: defining the territories of European involvement in sport'. *European Sport Management Quarterly,* 2(4): 267–307.

Porro, N., Mussino, A. and De Nardis, P. (1997) *Sport: Social Problems and Social Movements.* Milan: Edizioni Seam.

Press Association. (2014) Vote intentions unaffected by Games. *Sunday Post.* 3 August 2014. Accessed 18 January 2015. www.sundaypost.com/news-views/politics/vote-intentions-unaffected-by-games-1.504483.

Reedie, C. (2014) cited in Gibson, O. 'Scotland team may miss Rio Olympics in event of vote for independence'. *The Guardian Online.* Accessed 8 January 2015. www.theguardian.com/sport/2014/sep/06/scotland-independence-rio-olympics-sir-craig-reedie.

Ross, J. (2014) 'Daily question: how will the Referendum result affect Scottish sport?' *BBC News Scotland Politics*. Accessed 18 January 2015. www.bbc.co.uk/news/uk-scotland-scotland-politics-29145436.

Salmond, A. (2014) 'Alex Salmond with Judy Murray. New Statesman Interview'. *New Statesman*. 6 March 2014, pp. 39–43.

Scottish Government. (2012) *Social Science: Commonwealth Games Legacy, Research Findings (1)*. Edinburgh: Scottish Government.

Scottish Government. (2013) *Scotland's Future: Your Guide to an Independent Scotland*. Edinburgh: Scottish Government.

Scottish Government. (2014a) 'Scottish Government response to the working group on Scottish sport'. Accessed 11 January 2015. http://news.scotland.gov.uk/News/Working-Group-on-Scottish-Sport-c62.aspx.

Scottish Government. (2014b) 'Glasgow 2014 XX Commonwealth Games highlights'. Edinburgh Scottish Government. Accessed 22 January 2015. www.scotland.gov.uk/Resource/0046/00463494.pdf.

Sillars, J. (1992) quoted in *The Herald*, 24 April 1992:1.

Sikes, M. and Jarvie, G. (2014) 'Women's running as freedom: development and choice'. *Sport in Society*, 17(4): 507–522.

Slatter, M. (2014) 'Scottish independence: what it might mean for sport?' *BBC Sport*. 17 September 2014. Accessed 9 February 2015. www.bbc.co.uk/sport/0/29234259.

Stewart, E. (2014) *The Economic Consequences of Scottish Separation*. Edinburgh: Scottish Research Society.

The 2014 Games Legacy (2015) *The Sunday Herald special supplement*. 8 March 2014.

The Guardian. (1991) 28 October, p. 24.

The Guardian. (2014) 14 September, p. 1.

UNESCO. (2010) *Reaching the Marginalised: Education for All*. Oxford: Oxford University Press.

Walton, J. (2011) 'Sport and the Basques: constructed and contested identities – 1876–1936'. *Historical Sociology*, 24(4): 451–471.

Ward, P. (2014) 'Time for a holiday, rink heroes return to Scotland'. *The Herald*. 26 February 2014, p. 3.

PART IV

Sport, corporate politics and the global community

This part discusses how sport has increasingly become an extension of the neo-liberal, nation-state economy, offering rich opportunities for advancing the commodification process (*in* sport and *with* sport). It does this by outlining sport's commodification as a spectacle, before presenting and discussing mega sports events such as the Olympic Games and the FIFA World Cup. The inner workings of FIFA are then critically discussed, revealing a crisis of confidence in those occupying top executive positions within world football and sport more broadly. Furthermore, this part illustrates how the neo-liberal politics of the nation-state have extended beyond the commodification of sporting spectacle into more diverse interest areas, including sport for diplomacy and international relations, and even to sport being used to present military interests and militarism itself as virtuous constitutive elements of major nation-states. Sport's propitious power in these regards is revealed.

The part begins with David Andrews' chapter, which analyses the political dimensions of contemporary sport culture as they relate to the relationship between sport spectacles, late capitalism and neoliberalism. The discussion highlights their political nature as sites of populist resonance with the values of the dominant late capitalist order. The relationship between late capitalism and neo-liberalism, as well as the precise nature of the latter, is examined, leading to an exploration of the neo-liberal politicisation of the late capitalist sport spectacle. The chapter discusses how sport spectacles are effective, if rarely overt, propagators of the prevailing neo-liberal consensus. This discussion identifies how within the context of the contemporary moment, popular sport spectacles are imbued with the largely corroborative expressions of the dominant late capitalist order, of which neo-liberalism is a constituent feature. The populist articulation of late capitalist sport spectacles positions them as agents of the prevailing neo-liberal political consensus, normalising corroborative subjectivities, ideologies and policies. Seemingly benign, these sport spectacles are, in actuality, potent expressions of neo-liberal public pedagogy, demarcating the permissible boundaries and limits in politics.

The second chapter by John Horne discusses the contemporary politics of both the Olympic Games and FIFA World Cups during the past fifty years. From the early 1960s onward both sports mega-events have been caught up in symbolic politics taking two main forms: the *promotional* opportunities offered by them to enhance reputations – by competing, winning and hosting them, as well as refusing to participate in them through different forms of boycott – and the opportunity to *protest* about a perceived social injustice by "seizing the platform". Housing evictions and other infringements of human rights are also part of the Olympic and FIFA Football World Cup "effect". Among the issues addressed are the gap between the rhetoric and reality of sports mega-event "legacies", the relationship between sports mega-events and social exclusion, and the global power shifts that hosting sports mega-events in emerging economies outside the global North reveals.

This leads into a critical discussion by Alan Tomlinson on the escalating "Crisis of Credibility" occurring within the world football governing body FIFA, bringing together some of the historic and more recent revelations about those top executives who run the sport. Tomlinson discusses how FIFA has managed to survive so many crises and has continued to operate according to an established *modus operandi* characterised by a lack of accountability, transparency and fair play, despite the scale of corruption that has been confirmed in the practices of numerous committee members, and some of its highest-level office-holders. The chapter considers recent cameos of people, events and responses, before reflecting on some social scientific theories, concepts and methods that may help us better understand the FIFA story. It does so by going back in time over some cases of leadership challenge, bidding outcomes, ethical processes, and internal conflicts and tensions. Challenges to the Havelange/Blatter dynasty are reviewed in the context of the May 2015 presidential election. The question of flexible ethics is also considered in the case of Russia's successful bid to stage the 2018 World Cup before a review of FIFA's internal investigation into the 2018 and 2022 World Cup-hosting decisions. Questions are raised in relation to allegations of Blatter's dishonesty and breach of trust to show how FIFA's corrupt practices were in place long before the U.S. authorities and specifically the FBI emerged on the scene to confirm the embeddedness of corruption within the operations of some of the most privileged networks of the FIFA-related hierarchy.

Thomas Zeiler then broadens the discussion out to international politics, security and diplomacy, showing how the intersection of sports and politics, connected by both states and transnational actors, illuminates regional, national, and individual relations in the world arena. This chapter builds on earlier chapters to illustrate how cultural, economic and political interactions have often been enmeshed in sporting events. While not often causative in terms of policy, sports do express ideologies, fears, desires, and policy preferences. This chapter shows how sports are now considered an element of soft power in world affairs.

The part concludes with John Kelly's chapter on Western militarism and the political utility of sport. This chapter illustrates how sport is incorporated into providing militarism with a platform enabling governments and militarists to "incorporate us by proxy" into supporting (or appearing to support) militaristic actions and related political frameworks. Sport is one of the primary sites involved in what has become a multi-agency web of inter-dependent and interactive figurations that facilitate and encourage us all to *support the troops*. This is shown to occur with sport people paying respect, injured military becoming athletes, sport uniforms becoming militarised and sponsors using sport to promote militarism. The ideological power of these inter-related actions can be compartmentalised into four representative categories – charity, invented traditions, necessary helpers and heroes/celebrities, each offering ideological representations that facilitate citizens being incorporated by proxy into supporting the military and its actions. The political results of this include sport being used for propaganda, the distinctions between soldier, hero and celebrity being blurred, and the normalising of everyday militarism and the surveillance state.

19

SPORT, SPECTACLE AND THE POLITICS OF LATE CAPITALISM

Articulating the neoliberal order

David Andrews

Introduction

With reference to the nature and influence of late capitalist sport, much of my previous work on the topic has focused on the centrality of culture to the workings of late capitalism (Andrews 2006, 2009). These Mandel (1998) and Jameson (1991, 1998) informed analyses tended to focus on the convergence of cultural and economic fields and forces, as manifest within and through the complexities of corporate sport. However, the logics of the late capitalist mode of production are not solely economic and cultural in nature, since it also incorporates political, social and/or technological dimensions according to the specificities of time and space (Hardt and Weeks 2000). Acknowledging this complex and conjunctural 'de-differentiation of fields' (Jameson 1998: 73), this chapter nonethelesss foregrounds the political dimensions of contemporary sport culture, particularly as they relate to the relationship between sport spectacles, late capitalism, and neoliberalism.

Broadly understood, the political system refers to the architecture of state governance, whereas politics encompasses the range of self-legitimising operations, ideologies, and effects of the said governmental system seeking to establish authority, influence, and thereby control over the populace. Unlike more authoritarian political regimes, late capitalist politics relies heavily on the mobilisation of the cultural sphere in looking to secure the active consent of the general public to the ascendant political-economic regime. Hence, late capitalism has to be understood as a complex assemblage of political-economic-cultural relations and effects. The argument espoused in this chapter thus focuses on the role of elite performance, mass-mediated, and corporately structured sport in both advancing and normalising the pseudo-democratic political system and politics of late capitalism (Wolin 2000, 2008). For, as Stuart Hall noted, there can be 'no separation' between popular cultural practices (such as corporate sport), and the conjunctural forces and relations operating at that given moment. Hall identified – in relation to early nineteenth-century Britain – that the 'most immediate forms of popular recreation' were 'saturated by popular imperialism' (Hall 1981: 229). Similarly, within the context of the contemporary moment, popular sport spectacles are imbued with the largely corroborative expressions of the dominant late capitalist order, of which neoliberalism is a constituent feature.

Late capitalism is by no means a universal monolith; the convergence of the cultural, economic, and political has manifested itself in varied socio-spatial settings over the past 80 years or so. This chapter focuses on the contemporary moment within late capitalist, putatively democratic societies re-fashioned by the 'long march of neoliberalism', and the role of the sport spectacle in normalising (and not infrequently celebrating) the ongoing, and seemingly relentless, neoliberal revolution (Hall 2011). Of course, neoliberalism is also far from a singular project. It is a flexible technology of governance appropriated in different ways, by different political formations, be they democratic, communist, or authoritarian (Ong 2006). Neoliberalism is therefore a complex and socio-historically contingent political and economic rationality (Ong 2006), creating an idealised (in political, economic, social, cultural and even biological terms), and thereby governable, citizen-subject attuned to the specificities of the local setting (Rose 1996, 2007).

This chapter offers a complex and composite model of contemporary sport spectacles, highlighting their political nature as sites of populist resonance with the values of the dominant late capitalist order. The relationship between late capitalism and neoliberalism, as well as the precise nature of the latter, is explored. This leads to an exploration of the neoliberal politicisation of the late capitalist sport spectacle which, *pace* Newman and Giardina, elucidates 'the cultural politics of neoliberalism' and 'how singular acts of consuming the sporting spectacle are complicated by cultural, political, and economic forces acting upon the seemingly banal sporting sphere' (Newman and Giardina 2011: 10). In short, the chapter attempts to demonstrate how sport spectacles are effective, if covert, propagators of the prevailing neoliberal consensus.

The complex composition of the late capitalist sport spectacle

Jameson (1991, 1998) offered a model of the social totality within which the commercial mass media occupies an unprecedented position and influence, in shaping the entangled social, cultural, political and economic spheres of late capitalist existence. Implicit within this understanding is the phenomenon of the mass-mediated spectacle, which – as famously conceptualised by French Situationist, Guy Debord – 'appears at once as society itself, as a part of society and as a means of unification' (Debord 1994 [1967]: 12). With regard to the late capitalist sport, there is a tendency to refer to spectacles solely in relation to global sport mega-events (specifically the Olympic Games, FIFA World Cup, and NFL Super Bowl). However, late capitalism's twinned processes of hyper-commercialisation and hyper-televisualisation have combined to spectacularise (Horne 2006; Miller; 1999) events and competitions with smaller spatial reaches and resonance (national, regional, and even metropolitan). The contemporary sport economy thus incorporates two, necessarily interdependent, orders of the spectacle: the upper-case or monumental Spectacle (the mass mediated event) and the lower-case or vernacular spectacle (the relentless outpourings of corroborating and/or parasitic cultural forms). As such, the 'mass multimedia spectacle' is the 'indispensable adjunct of the spectacle of the commodity' and vice versa, as the two combine to shape the structure and experience of the late capitalist condition (Roberts 2003: 65).

Debord's understanding of spectacular society, and its subsequent appropriation by numerous critical sport commentators, is certainly not without reproach (Tomlinson 2002; MacAloon 2006). According to Kellner, Debord offers 'a rather generalized and abstract' spectacle-based cosmology, whose sweeping generalisations point to the need for analyses that explicate how mass-mediated spectacles are 'produced, constructed, circulated, and function' within contemporary society (Kellner 2003: 2). In order to effect such empirically grounded analyses, the following offers a suggestive model of the late capitalist sport spectacle (adapted from

Andrews and Rick 2013). This unpacks the numerous seemingly discrete, yet mutually implicated, mediated sub-strands of the broader sport spectacle, thereby highlighting its complex and composite nature:

- *Performative spectacle:* The mediated representations of the athletic execution and outcomes that constitute the performative basis of the sporting event. These include the *a priori* narrative positioning and promotion of the event, live coverage of the event, and post-event analysis and reportage.

- *Embodied spectacle:* The accumulated understanding of, and familiarity with celebrated individuals (players, coaches, owners, or fans), and teams, associated with sporting events and contests. Involvement in the sporting event can either positively (augment) or negatively (diminish) celebrity identity.

- *Promotional spectacle:* The sanctioned and unsanctioned promotional mobilisation of various aspects of the sport-related spectacle (most frequently the event, involved teams, and/or individuals). These emotive cultural referents are used within advertising and marketing campaigns designed to enhance brand identity and market appeal of sport and non-sport related commodities.

- *Pernicious spectacle:* The outpourings of the sensationalist sectors of the mass culture industries, looking to further their readership/viewership through tabloid coverage of (sometimes tangential) sport themes and issues.

- *Delivery spectacle:* The processual, institutional, and infrastructural complexities responsible for the delivery of the sporting event, often reified in the popular media through the presence of high-profile figures, including owners, politicians, designers, architects, and administrators.

- *Spatial spectacle:* The contribution of the event location, landscape, and/or built environment to the constitution of the broader sport spectacle. Invokes different spatial scales based on the nature of the event, that is, nation-based FIFA World Cups; city/region-based Olympic Games; city/stadium-based teams.

- *Ceremonial spectacle:* The ritualistic and symbolic elements performed around the sporting event, that is, national anthems, anti-racism announcements, dignitary presentations, torch relays, opening and closing ceremonies, and award ceremonies.

- *Social spectacle:* The contributions from the various forms of new social media technologies, involving the contribution of disparately located, and differentially invested, individuals to the representation and experience of the sporting event.

These various sub-dimensions of the overarching sport spectacle have been differentiated for the purposes of analytical explication: the separations within this model of the sport spectacle are largely arbitrary and suggestive. Depending on the sporting event and socio-spatial location under scrutiny, differing permutations and intensities of these (and, indeed other) spectacular elements will be enacted. This points to what is the contingent and co-constitutive spectacular complexity of the late capitalist sport assemblage.

The political function of the spectacle – and that of late capitalist sport spectacles more pertinently – revolves around the reproduction of the status quo within the political-economic formation. According to a Debordian understanding, this political stasis is realised because, 'In form as in content the spectacle serves as total justification for the conditions and aims of the existing system' (Debord 1994 [1967]: 13). Hence, what Kellner (2012) referred to as the role of the spectacle in the pacifying and depoliticising of the consumptive masses. Accordingly, late capitalist sport spectacles act as virtual propaganda arms of the establishment: they are highly visible, and culturally cherished, platforms for the expression and reinforcement of societally dominant views and values.

Of particular relevance to forging an understanding of the political significance of the late capitalist sport spectacle is Debord's later notion of the 'integrated spectacle': a synthesis of his earlier understanding of concentrated and diffuse forms of 'spectacular power' (Debord 1990 [1988]: 8). The *concentrated* dimension of spectacular power understands the mass-mediated spectacle, or event, as a key vehicle of the technical apparatus through which the authority and influence of consumer capitalism is realised, not through authoritarian imposition, but through a process of mass seduction (to consumerist logics) and obfuscation (of the deprivations) (Best and Kellner 1997). This is because, as Debord noted, 'In all its specific forms, as information or propaganda, as advertisement or direct entertainment consumption, the spectacle is the present model of socially dominant life' (Debord 1994 [1967]: 6). Importantly, from a Debordian per-spective, late capitalist societies also exhibit the *diffuse* reach and effects of spectacular power, through the imprint, or integration, of the commodified 'spectacle' into 'almost the full range of socially produced behavior and objects' (Debord 1990 [1988]: 9). Hence, the diverse prac-tices of consumption, and the epoch-defining subjectivity of the consumer, become seductive agents of affirmation of, and political co-optation into, the integrated spectacular order at the basis of consumer society.

There is a tendency to view late capitalism's mass-mediated consensus – at least partly real-ised through the machinations of the economy of sport spectacles (Brohm 1978; Perelman 2012) – as being realised through direct conspiratorial relations between corporate and political interests. However, the manufacture of consent is less based on conspiratorial collusion, as it is the product of hegemonic forces and relations (Herman and Chomsky 1988). The managed consensus within spectacular societies derives from the inherent conservatism of the mainstream commercial media, whose overriding aim is to secure the largest possible mainstream audience share. Invoking Hall's (1981) understanding of the politics of popular commercial culture, the manufacturing of sport spectacles involves their reworking and reshaping in an attempt to reso-nate with the values of the dominant late capitalist (neoliberal) order. In this sense, there is 'no whole, authentic, autonomous "popular culture" which lies outside the field of force of the relations of cultural power and domination' (Hall 1981: 232).

Late capitalist spectacles are popular/populist entities created by the culture industries, not as political functionaries *per se*, but agents of political conformity as a function of the institutional rationalities that compel their yearning for a financially rewarding popular audience. The late capitalist sport spectacle thus represents a form of 'canned and neutralised demotic populism' (Hall 1981: 233) that, far from being overtly manipulative, covertly seduces the consuming audience to the state of play in political, economic, and social relations. Such, in mainstream terms, is the politically 'softening power of cultural influences and products' (Wolin 2008) within the late capitalist moment.

The neoliberal conjuncture

Before explicating more fully the political dimensions of late capitalist sport spectacles, it is first important to consider the specificities of the contemporary conjuncture. Specifically, one needs to consider the relationship between late capitalism and neoliberalism, and the very nature of neoliberalism itself. While appreciable overlap exists between the phenomena of late capitalism and neoliberalism, it would be imprecise to use them interchangeably, as is sometimes the case. In the broadest terms, *late capitalism* represents a mode of societal (re)production characterised by the de-differentiation (the collapsing of sectoral boundaries) between (amongst other things), the economic, cultural, and political spheres. By contrast, *neoliberalism* refers to a corroborating extension, or excrescence, of late capitalism. Characterised by new economic rationalities and associated political logics, the neoliberal conjuncture has re-written the social relationship between the state and its citizens, with significant effects on framing the nature and experience of the contemporary cultural landscape.

Neoliberalism is an interesting term, not least because routinely it is only used by the critics of this 'new planetary vulgate' (Bourdieu and Wacquant 2001: 2): its architects and exponents simply inhabit the neoliberal project's various political, economic, social, and cultural strands, advancing them as the way society could and, indeed, should be. A simultaneously economic, political, social, and cultural phenomenon neoliberalism is far from a singularity. There are, in fact, multiple iterations of the neoliberal project, as determined by spatial and temporal contingencies. Neoliberalism's various dimensions are mobilised, and in some cases resisted, in differing permutations, and to differing effects, depending upon the contingencies of the local context (Macdonald and Ruckert 2009). The conjunctural, plural, and multilayered nature of the neoliberal condition means that innumerable interpretive and disciplinary approaches – based on the intellectual predispositions of the inquirer – have been utilised in scrutinising its diversified nature and effects (c.f. Barnett 2010; Chomsky 1999; Comaroff and Comaroff 2001; Gane 2013; Giroux 2011; Hall *et al.* 2013; Harvey 2005; Ong 2006; Peck 2013; Roberts and Mahtani 2010). Lacking the space to consider the complexities of this literature, the current analysis adopts a general approach for deciphering the politics of the neoliberal sport spectacle, by highlighting some of the most commonly agreed dimensions of neoliberalism.

Neoliberal governmental orthodoxy did not spring forth fully formed. Rather, it evolved over decades into a comprehensive alternative to the social welfare consensus that dominated the socio-political organisation of many Western democracies, in the decades following the end of World War II. This period was characterised by the 'great reversal' (Palley 2005: 21), heralding the shift from Keynesian to neoliberal forms of macroeconomic policy informed by the workings of Chicago School economists (including Ludwig von Mises, Frederich Hayek, George Stigler, and Milton Friedman) (Gane 2013). Beginning in the 1970s, the Keynesian demand-side and socially redistributive economic approach, was systematically dismantled, and subsequently replaced by a monetarist supply-side approach, focused on stimulating the money supply within the economy. The alternative to Keynesian intervention was the nurturing of a largely unregulated – or ideally *self-regulating* –economy and competitive marketplace. According to neoliberal doctrine, the nurturing of free trade, and a concomitantly competitive market, would lead to greater economic efficiencies and innovations, and the consequent stimulation of the money supply within the economy (the money supply previously drained by the perceived excesses of Keynesian interventionism). A related component of neoliberal revisionism involved the creation of the legal, regulatory, and economic climate conducive to the interests of private capital. Crucially, such initiatives were often enabled and funded by the state's diminished fiscal obligation to interventionist social welfare and development, which allowed significant amounts of public monies to be diverted elsewhere. Hence, individual and corporate tax concessions, property and development tax initiatives, and financial industry deregulation – in addition to the concerted dismantling of labour unions – all combined to create the type of 'business-friendly climate' (Brodi 2015: 56) venerated by monetarists.

Importantly, neoliberalism rested on the (far from inalienable) assumption that creating corporate-friendly economic regulations and environments would advance society as a whole, and not simply the capitalist class:

> Continuous increases in productivity should then deliver higher living standards to everyone. Under the assumption that 'a rising tide lifts all boats', or of 'trickle down', neoliberal theory holds that the elimination of poverty (both domestically and world-wide) can best be secured through free markets and free trade.
>
> *(Harvey 2005: 64–65)*

Of course, some may question the persuasiveness of neoliberal assertions pertaining to the market-led recovery of societies en masse (and indeed global humanity). Nonetheless, there is little refuting the influence of this neoliberal credo in guiding government policy in attempts to shape societies, lives, and attitudes around the world. In numerous national settings, a situated neoliberal philosophy has justified the radical retrenchment of the state's social welfare and social redistributive obligations, and prompted the commercial privatisation (and profit-driven reorganisation) of many sectors and services previously under the express purview of the managerial state (Harvey 1989). Within the entrepreneurial neoliberal state, commercial corporate structures, rationalities, and efficiencies thus became the hegemonic form of social organisation; everything from the genesis of life itself, to the late capitalist way of death, succumbing to the entrepreneurial impulses of a society driven and defined by private capital accumulation.

The raft of neoliberal reforms leading to the retrenchment of state interventions in economic and social spheres (such as those designed to regulate unemployment levels, or provide a social safety net for the vulnerable), and the formation of an increasingly privatised and entrepreneurial society, has had a profound influence on re-working the relationship between the state and its citizenry (as well as waking established bonds of collection affiliation in favour of relations of self-interest and reliance). The 'epochal shift' from the managerial to entrepreneurial state has meant that rather than being realised in relation to the state, now individual 'citizenship is primarily realised through acts of *free but responsibilised choice* in a variety of private, corporate, and quasi-public practices from working to shopping' (Rose 1999: xxiii, italics added). Idealised neoliberal citizen-consumers are thus celebrated as rational, productive, and responsible entrepreneurs of the self (Foucault 2010), and play an important role in the normalising governance of the neoliberal masses (Larner 2000).

As Rottenberg (2014) noted:

> Neoliberalism, in other words, is a dominant political rationality that moves to and from the management of the state to the inner workings of the subject, normatively constructing and interpellating individuals as entrepreneurial actors.
>
> *(p. 420)*

Individualism is clearly a core dimension of neoliberalism: 'Neoliberal ideology rests upon a starkly utopian vision of market rule, rooted in an idealised conception of competitive individualism and a deep antipathy to forms of social and institutional solidarity' (Peck *et al.* 2009: 51). However, it is a competitive individualism prefigured on the responsibility of individuals to act, both rationally and competitively, in taking appropriate advantage of the freedoms they possess to craft their individual life chances and lives (freedoms afforded by the dismantling of the managerial state's greater involvement in the level of everyday experience). As well as being an entrepreneurial, the neoliberal citizen is also moral subject (Muehlebach 2012); the responsibilitising of the individual actor within, and through, involvement in the normalising free market being a central mechanism through which the practice of neoliberal governance is enacted. Within this conjuncture – in which all personal issues are presented as being remedied through an array of individualised market solutions – an inability to provide sufficiently for one's 'own needs . . . and ambitions' becomes a marker of a lack of moral responsibility, or a sign of pathological inferiority, rather than a statement on the inadequacies or inequalities implicit within the social formation (Brown 2006: 694).

Having provided a brief, yet hopefully informative, explication of the various components of the neoliberal formation, the following section highlights examples of the neoliberal politicisation of late capitalist sport spectacles.

Sporting neoliberalisms

Late capitalist sport spectacles are not consciously politicised as a result of some authorial intent. Rather, they are purposefully framed in populist terms and tones by: the audience-hungry prescriptions of the commercial media; and/or, by the popular support coveting promotional initiatives of event organisers or owners. The populist dictates of the contemporary culture industries – preoccupied with the desire to produce texts that resonate with, as opposed to controvert, mainstream views and values – generate popular representations of the sporting world that incorporate and covertly normalise various armatures of the neoliberal agenda. Hence, through their composite and conjunctural constitution, both the sport spectacle *in toto*, and its composite sub-strands (the performative, embodied, promotional, pernicious, delivery, spatial, ceremonial, and social spectacles) are efficient propagators of the prevailing neoliberal consensus. Critical analyses of the neoliberal sport spectacles have focused largely on privatisation, marketisation, and commercialisation processes, and their assumed role in increasing the money supply across all sectors of the economy (c.f. Andrews and Silk 2012; Chin 2011; Clift and Andrews 2012; Coakley 2011; Eick 2010; Friedman *et al.* 2013; Grix 2013; Jackson 2013; Newman and Giardina 2011; Polson and Whiteside 2013; Silk 2012). The economic logics and rationalities underpinning these neoliberal processes are core component parts of a truly transnational model of corporate sport, the ubiquity of which normalises the neoliberal order (Andrews 2006). While acknowledging these implicit elements of neoliberalism's core entrepreneurialism, this discussion focuses on the competitive individualism – the micropolitics of neoliberalism – that obscures the influence of the social system in reproducing inequalities, and thereby validates neoliberalism's regressive retrenchment macropolitics.

In their adroit analysis of the NASCAR (National Association for Stock Car Auto Racing) spectacle, Newman and Giardina (2011) have arguably wrought the most considered and wide-ranging analysis of the normalising cultural politics of sporting neoliberalism. They:

> pry . . . political regimes loose from both their discursive (sporting) veneer and stock car signifiers, and thereby illuminate and demystify the identities, practices, subjectivities, and hierarchies that are made 'normal' . . . through the spectacular machinations of NASCAR.
>
> *(Newman and Giardina 2011: 10)*

The sheer scope of this analysis is perhaps that which is most noteworthy, since Newman and Giardina provide multifarious examples of NASCAR's constitutive neoliberalism. As they identified, 'Although the term neoliberalism might not flow freely from the mouths of NASCAR Nation, the sport is both implicitly and explicitly bound to the fate of Hayek's and

Friedman's free market utopics' (Newman and Giardina 2011: 65). Space constraints preclude a longer examination of their rigorous and wide-ranging analysis, save their key recognition that NASCAR's neoliberal consuming masses are located within spaces of consumption in ways that remind them that through capital relations – and particularly those that give meaning to bodies and practices of the NASCAR spectacle – they are free to pursue individual (consumer) identities, interests, and politics (Newman and Giardina 2011: 84).

Whether consuming NASCAR – or, for that matter, the FIFA World Cup, the Olympic Games, English Premier League games, Indian Premier League games, or whichever corporate sport spectacle – one is confronted by a meticulously produced 'phantasmagoria of neoliberal commerce', whether real or virtual (Newman and Giardina 2011: 84). These are the branded sporting landscapes of the spectacular, through which the neoliberal citizen-consumer becomes individualised (by enacting normative, hence responsible, consumption choices), and in doing so affirms the legitimacy of the neoliberal order.

The mythos of neoliberalism is based on the assumption that consumptive freedoms and opportunities – through which the idealised neoliberal citizen-consumer becomes actualised – are readily accessible to all within consumer democracies. The reality is far from the case. Within the competitive market of labour and consumption, certain groupings (based on levels of inherited impoverishment, forms of discrimination, social marginalisation, and restricted economic opportunity) have little more than unfulfilled relations of longing with neoliberalism's consumer dreamscapes. This is precisely the case within the rapidly neoliberalising Indian context. Within this setting, an expanding range of late capitalist sport spectacles effectively legitimises broader neoliberal reforms to the entirety of the vast Indian populace, the majority of whom are economically and culturally excluded from these valorised expressions of neoliberal India (Ganguly-Scrase and Scrase 2009).

Contemporary Indian sport spectacles – such as the Indian Premier League (IPL), the 2010 Delhi Commonwealth Games (CWG), and the FIA Formula One Indian Grand Prix (IGP) (in addition to the less prominent Hero Indian Super League, the Pro Kabbadi League, and the Elite Football League of India) – are studious orchestrations bearing all the hallmarks of the global corporate sport model, simultaneously exuding locally expressive components and/or aesthetics. These glocal sport spectacles (Andrews and Ritzer 2007) are represented, within promotional and commercial media outlets, as celebrations of the cosmopolitan *and* traditional sensibilities associated with the new and vibrant neoliberalising India (Ganguly-Scrase and Scrase 2009), and the new Indian middle class at its economic, cultural, and political core (Brosius 2010; Fernandes 2004, 2006).

The IPL, CWG, and IGP are routinely presented as spectacular consumptive experiences, implicitly designed for the idealised consumer-citizen: the white-collar professional and consumption-oriented new Indian middle class (Andrews *et al.* 2014; Rajagopal 2011). As such, these Indian sport spectacles act both as agents of social inclusion/exclusion, and as authenticators of neoliberalising reforms and developments. The positioning of these sporting events as vibrant expressions of the 'great Indian (neoliberal) dream' (Friedman 2004 parenthesis added), idealises the new middle class subjectivity with which the spectacles are most readily associated. Consequently, as neoliberal sport spectacles gain ever more prominence within India, they normalise neoliberal values and initiatives: extolling the virtues of the productive, new Indian middle-class consumer-citizen targeted by their marketing initiatives. Those unable to afford access to these distinguishing 'consumption markers' of new Indian middle class (Donner *et al.* 2008: 327), are rendered visible as economically and culturally impoverished subjects, and 'rendered invisible and forgotten within the dominant national political culture' (Fernandes 2004: 241). Through their popular representation as spectacular signs of India's new-found economic and cultural vibrancy, the IPL, CWG, and IGP *et al.* become politicised in the service of India's neoliberal transformation. Their very presence tacitly reproduces attitudes and policies that celebrate and privilege the new Indian middle class for being productive citizens responsible for the rise of the new India, while nurturing a demonising and pathologising indifference towards poverty and the poor that justifies their continued economic, cultural, and political marginalisation (Fernandes 2004; Rizvi 2007).

Lastly within this section, the embodied nature of the performative spectacle, especially when allied to the contest-based nature of sporting, makes successful athletes almost unavoidably connected with the competitive individualism at the core of neoliberal thought. Although evident in the popular representation of Barcelona and Brazil footballer, Neymar da Silva Santos Júnior (henceforth Neymar), his populist neoliberalisation takes on an additional dimension as a function of his articulation to, and through, a particular moment in Brazilian sociopolitical history: a moment defined by the successive *Partido dos Trabalhadores* (the Workers' Party) administrations of Presidents Luiz Inácio Lula da Silva's (popularly referred to as Lula: 2003–2011) and Dilma Rousseff (2011–present), wherein 'Beneath the surface and behind the Workers' Party's populist rhetoric, the neoliberal agenda . . . remains functionally intact' (Chossudovsky 2013). A common feature of neoliberal projects, particularly those within democratic national settings, is the centrality of populist notions of individualism as the ideological cornerstone of neoliberal economic (re)formations. As Gilbert (2013) noted:

> neoliberalism understands individual interests to be largely mutually exclusive, self-interest to be the only motive force in human life and competition to be the most efficient and socially beneficial way for that force to express itself.
>
> *(p. 9)*

Heavily informed by this ideology of competitive individualism, popular and promotional discourse has fashioned the public representation (Marshall 1997; Miller 2007) of Neymar as a celebrated, and therefore idealised, neoliberal subject whose individual attributes (i.e. creativity, determination, fortitude, responsibility) provided him – regardless of his modest social origins – with access to the economic and consumerist benefits that demarcate individualised success within the consumerist culture of neoliberal Brazil.

Although by no means an overtly political figure, popular and commercial representations of Neymar routinely depict him (and in doing so covertly neoliberalise him) as a consummate competitive individual: a populist figure clearly benefitting from a steadfast commitment to his own self-interest and betterment as he crafts his career on and off the playing field. This is clearly illustrated in a Nike 'Bairro Brasil' campaign commercial, depicting Neymar's impromptu visit to a *bairro* (urban community/neighbourhood), where he is met with great enthusiasm. Here is the returning hero, seemingly revisiting his space and culture of origin, in a manner that celebrates both while furthering Neymar's popular aura as the exemplar of the rags-to-riches narrative that underpins neoliberalism's politics of individual hope. In this vein, Neymar – or more accurately his intertextuality and contextually constructed imaged identity – is both a compelling and influential representative subject of the neoliberal Brazilian conjuncture. In this way, as Helal *et al.* (2011) noted, Neymar's public representation naturalises and normalises neoliberal agendas and ideologies, allowing them to stealthily inhabit popular consciousness. The commercial celebration of Neymar's creative and competitive individualism is thus indivisible from the flexible technology of *Brazilian* neoliberal governance. Neymar is, at one and the same time, both the 'poster boy' of the *seleção* (Vickery 2014), and the 'human face' of Brazilian neoliberalism (Chossudovsky 2013).

Conclusion

The populist articulation of late capitalist sport spectacles positions them as agents of the prevailing neoliberal political consensus, normalising corroborative subjectivities, ideologies, and policies. Seemingly benign, these sport spectacles are, in actuality, potent expressions of neoliberal public pedagogy, stealthily demarcating the 'boundaries and limits of the tolerable in politics', that inhabit and frame the popular psyche (Hall 2010: 177). As such, late capitalist sport spectacles can be considered neoliberal Trojan Horses (Zirin 2014); practices of popular articulation have embedded the very essences of the neoliberal belief system (Bourdieu 1998) into sport spectacles, facilitating their infiltration into the popular experience and consciousness.

On the one hand, depending on one's political persuasion, the neoliberalised and neoliberalising dimensions of contemporary sport may or may not be deemed an issue of concern. Nevertheless, and as Brown (2006) identified, the process of neoliberalisation brings with it the 'nightmare' of de-democratisation. In Wolin's (2000: 20) terms, neoliberal sport spectacles – as the outgrowths of 'high-technology globalised capitalism' – incorporate norms (rampant individualism, consumption-based subjectivities, political illiteracy and indifference, a diminution of social affiliations and institutions, systemic inequality, the submissive deferral of political authority to the state) that are antithetical to the maintenance of an 'equalising, participatory, commonalising' substantive democracy. Hence, our enthusiastic – or even, for that matter, passive – consumption of late capitalist sport spectacles could feasibly contribute to neoliberal societies sleepwalking into a post-democratic state: a 'managed democracy . . . in which governments are legitimated' by elections and electorates 'that they have learned to control' (Wolin 2008).

That having been said, there are intimations that late capitalist sport spectacles can also be the site of resistance against the de-democratising neoliberal tide. For example, recent opposition against various aspects of spectacular sport: the rampant professionalisation of sport leagues; the exploitation of sport footwear and apparel workers, and migrant stadium labourers; the forced evictions precipitated by the building of major sport venues and facilities; and, the investment of public monies in hosting (or even the possibility thereof) sport mega-events, all incorporate discernible anti-neoliberal sentiments. Similarly, there is evidence within sport cultures of the self-same critical feelings toward neoliberalism, as those expressed by malcontents within wide society, actually coming to the fore: 'unfocused anger, a grudging, grumbling resentment at one's lot, and a troubled uncertainty about what to do next' (Hall and O'Shea 2013: 6). Therein lies *the* question for the future of neoliberal sport *and* society: What to do next?

References

Andrews, D.L. (2006) *Sport-Commerce-Culture: Essays on Sport in Late Capitalist America*. New York: Peter Lang.

Andrews, D.L. (2009) Sport, culture, and late capitalism. In B. Carrington and I. McDonald (eds.) *Marxism, Cultural Studies and Sport*. London: Routledge, 213–231.

Andrews, D.L. and Rick, O.J.C. (2013) Celebrity and the London 2012 spectacle. In V. Girginov (ed.) *The 2012 London Olympic and Paralympic Games*. London: Routledge, 193–211.

Andrews, D.L. and Ritzer, G. (2007) The grobal in the sporting glocal. *Global Networks*, 7: 135–153.

Andrews, D.L. and Silk, M.L. (eds.) (2012) *Sport and Neoliberalism: Politics, Consumption, and Culture*. Philadelphia, PA: Temple University Press.

Andrews, D.L., Batts, C., and Silk, M. (2014) Sport, glocalization and the new Indian middle class. *International Journal of Cultural Studies*, 17: 258–275.

Barnett, C. (2010) What's wrong with neoliberalism? In R. Pain, J.P. Jones, S.J. Smith, and S.A. Marston (eds.) *The SAGE Handbook of Social Geographies*. London: Sage, 269–296.

Best, S. and Kellner, D. (1997) *The Postmodern Turn*. New York: The Guilford Press.

Bourdieu, P. (1998) The essence of neoliberalism. *Le Monde Diplomatique* [Online]. Accessed 18 December 2015. http://mondediplo.com/1998/12/08bourdieu.

Bourdieu, P. and Wacquant, L. (2001) Neoliberal speak: Notes on the new planetary vulgate. *Radical Philosophy*, 105 (January/February): 2–5.

Brodie, J. (2015) Income inequality and the future of global governance. In S. Gill, (ed.) *Critical Perspectives on the Crisis of Global Governance: Reimagining the Future*. New York and Basingstoke: Palgrave Macmillan, pp. 45–65.

Brohm, J.M. (1978) *Sport: A Prison of Measured Time*. London: Pluto Press.

Brosius, C. (2010) *India's Middle Class: New Forms of Urban Leisure, Consumption and Prosperity*. London: Routledge.

Brown, W. (2006) American nightmare: Neoliberalism, neoconservatism, and de-democratization. *Political Theory*, 34: 690–714.

Chin, J.W. (2011) The new 'Superwoman': Intersections of fitness, physical culture and the female body in Romania. In E. Kennedy and P. Markula (eds) *Women and Exercise: The Body, Health and Consumerism*. London: Routledge, 229–246.

Chomsky, N. (1999) *Profit Over People: Neoliberalism and Global Order*. New York: Seven Stories Press.

Chossudovsky, M. (2013) Brazil: Neoliberalism with a 'Human Face'. *Global Research*. http://global research.ca/articles/CHO303C.html.

Clift, B.C. and Andrews, D.L. (2012) Living Lula's passion? The politics of Rio 2016. In H. Lenskyj and S. Wagg (eds) *The Handbook of Olympic Studies*. New York: Palgrave Macmillan, 210–229.

Coakley, J. (2011) Ideology just doesn't happen: Sports and neoliberalism. *Journal of ALESDE*, 1: 67–84.

Comaroff, J. and Comaroff, J.L. (eds) (2001) *Millenial Capitalism and the Culture of Neoliberalism*. Durham, NC: Duke University Press.

Debord, G. (1990) [1988] *Comments on the Society of the Spectacle*. London: Verso.

Debord, G. (1994) [1967] *The Society of the Spectacle*. New York: Zone Books.

Donner, J., Rangaswamy, N., Steenson, M.W., and Wei, C. (2008) 'Express yourself' and 'stay together': The middle-class Indian family'. In J.E. Katz, (ed.) *Handbook of Mobile Communication Studies*. Cambridge, MA: MIT Press, 325–338.

Eick, V. (2010) A neoliberal sports event? FIFA from the *Estadio Nacional* to the fan mile. *City: Analysis of Urban Trends, Culture, Theory, Policy, Action* (14): 278–297.

Fernandes, L. (2004) The politics of forgetting: Class politics, state power and the restructuring of urban space in India. *Urban Studies*, 41: 2415–2430.

Fernandes, L. (2006) *India's New Middle Class: Democratic Politics in an Era of Economic Reform*. Minneapolis, MA: University of Minnesota Press.

Foucault, M. (2010) *The Birth of Biopolitics: Lectures at the College de France, 1978–1979*. New York: Picador.

Friedman, M.T., Bustad, J.J., and Andrews, D.L. (2013) Feeding the downtown monster: (Re)developing Baltimore's 'tourist bubble'. *City, Culture and Society*, 3(3): 165–288.

Friedman, T.L. (2004) The great Indian dream. *The New York Times*. 11 March 2004.

Gane, N. (2013) The emergence of neoliberalism: Thinking through and beyond Michel Foucault's lectures on biopolitics. *Theory, Culture & Society*, 3(3): 3–27.

Ganguly-Scrase, R. and Scrase, T.J. (2009) *Globalisation and the Middle Classes in India: The Social and Cultural Impact of Neoliberal Reforms*. London: Routledge.

Gilbert, J. (2013) What kind of thing is 'neoliberalism'? *New Formations*, 80: 7–22.

Giroux, H. (2011) Neoliberalism and the death of the social state: Remembering Walter Benjamin's Angel of History. *Social Identities*, 17: 587–601.

Grix, J. (2013) Sport, politics and the Olympics. *Political Studies Review*, 11: 15–25.

Hall, S. (1981) Notes on deconstructing the 'popular'. In R. Samuel (ed.) *People's History and Socialist Theory*. London: Routledge and Kegan Paul, 227–240.

Hall, S. (2010) Life and times of the first new left. *New Left Review*, 61: 177–196.

Hall, S. (2011) The neoliberal revolution: Thatcher, Blair, Cameron – the long march of neoliberalism continues. *Soundings: A Journal of Politics and Culture*, 9–27.

Hall, S. and O'Shea, A. (2013) Common-sense neoliberalism. In S. Hall, D. Massey, and M. Rustin (eds.) *After Neoliberalism: The Kilburn Manifesto. Soundings: A Journal of Politics and Culture*. London: CBI Publishing, 1–18.

Hall, S., Massey, D., and Rustin, M. (eds.) (2013) *After Neoliberalism: The Kilburn Manifesto: Soundings: A Journal of Politics and Culture*. London: CBI Publishing.

Hardt, M. and Weeks, K. (2000) Introduction. In M. Hardt and K. Weeks (eds.) *The Jameson Reader*. Oxford: Blackwell, 1–29.

Harvey, D. (1989) From managerialism to entrepreneurialism: The transformation in urban governance in Late Capitalism. *Geografiska Annaler: Series B, Human Geography*, 71: 3–17.

Harvey, D. (2005) *A Brief History of Neoliberalism*. Oxford: Oxford University Press.

Helal, R.G., Cabo, A.D., Amaro, F., Pereira, C.A.A., and Teixira, J.P.V. (2011) A construção de um ídolo futebolístico na imprensa: estudo de caso (The construction of a soccer idol in the press: a case study). *Capa*, 8: 233–246.

Herman, E.S. and Chomsky, N. (1988) *Manufacturing Consent: The Political Economy of the Mass Media*. New York: Pantheon Books.

Horne, J. (2006) *Sport in Consumer Culture*. New York: Palgrave Macmillan.

Jackson, S. (2013) Rugby World Cup 2011: Sport mega-events between the global and the local. *Sport in Society*, 16: 847–852.

Jameson, F. (1991) *Postmodernism, or the Cultural Logic of Late Capitalism*. Durham, NC: Duke University Press.

Jameson, F. (1998) *The Cultural Turn: Selected Writings on the Postmodern 1983–1998*. London and New York: Verso.

Kellner, D. (2003) *Media Culture and the Triumph of the Spectacle: Media Spectacle*. London: Routledge.

Kellner, D. (2012) *Media Spectacle and Insurrection, 2011: From the Arab Uprisings to Occupy Everywhere*. London: Continuum.

Larner, W. (2000) Neo-liberalism: Policy, ideology, governmentality. *Studies in Political Economy*, 63: 5–25.

Macaloon, J.J. (2006) The theory of spectacle: Reviewing Olympic ethnography. In A. Tomlinson and C. Young (eds.) *National Identity and Global Sports Events: Culture, Politics, and Spectacle in the Olympics and the Football World Cup*. Albany, NY: State University of New York Press, 13–39.

Macdonald, L. and Ruckert, A. (eds.) (2009) *Post-Neoliberalism in the Americas*. Basingstoke: Palgrave Macmillan.

Mandel, E. (1998) *Late Capitalism*. London: Verso Classics.

Marshall, P.D. (1997) *Celebrity and Power: Fame in Contemporary Culture*. Minneapolis, MN: University of Minnesota Press.

Miller, T. (1999) Televisualization. *Journal of Sport and Social Issues*, 23: 123–125.

Miller, T. (2007) *Cultural Citizenship: Cosmopolitanism, Consumerism, and Television in a Neoliberal Age*. Phildelphia, PA: Temple University Press.

Muehlebach, A.K. (2012) *The Moral Neoliberal: Welfare and Citizenship in Italy*. Chicago, IL: University of Chicago Press.

Newman, J.I. and Giardina, M. (2011) *Sport, Spectacle, and NASCAR Nation: Consumption and the Cultural Politics of Neoliberalism*. London: Palgrave Macmillan.

Ong, A. (2006) *Neoliberalism as Exception: Mutations in Citizenship and Sovereignty*. Durham, NC: Duke University Press.

Palley, T.I. (2005) From Keynesianism to neoliberalism: Shifting paradigms. In A. Saad-Filho and D. Johnston (eds.) *Neoliberalism: A Critical Reader*. London: Pluto Press, 20–29.

Peck, J. (2013) Explaining (with) neoliberalism. *Territory, Politics, Governance*, 1: 132–157.

Peck, J., Theodore, N. and Brenner, N. (2009) Neoliberal urbanism: Models, moments, mutations. *SAIS Review*, XXIX: 49–66.

Perelman, M. (2012) *Barbaric Sport: A Global Plague*. London: Verso.

Polson, E. and Whiteside, E. (2013) Passing to India: A critique of American football's expansion. *Media, Culture and Society*, 36: 661–678.

Rajagopal, A. (2011) The emergency as prehistory of the new Indian middle class. *Modern Asian Studies*, 45: 1003–1049.

Rizvi, G. (2007) Emergent India: Globalization, democracy, and social justice. *International Journal*, 62: 753–768.

Roberts, D. (2003) Towards a genealogy and typology of spectacle: Some comments on Debord. *Thesis Eleven*, 75: 54–68.

Roberts, D.J. and Mahtani, M. (2010) Neoliberalizing race, racing neoliberalism: Placing 'race' in neoliberal discourses. *Antipode*, 42: 248–257.

Rose, N. (1996) Governing 'advanced' liberal democracies. In A. Barry, T. Osborne and N. Rose (eds.) *Foucault and Political Reason: Liberalism, Neo-Liberalism and Rationalities of Government*. London: University of Chicago Press, pp. 37–64.

Rose, N. (1999) *Governing the Soul: The Shaping of the Private Self*. London: Free Association Books.

Rose, N. (2007) *The Politics of Life Itself: Biomedicine, Power, and Subjectivity in the Twenty-First Century.* Princeton, NJ: Princeton University Press.

Rottenberg, C. (2014) The rise of neoliberal feminism. *Cultural Studies,* 28: 418–437.

Silk, M. (2012) *The Cultural Politics of Post-9/11 American Sport: Power, Pedagogy and the Popular.* New York: Routledge.

Tomlinson, A. (2002) Theorising spectacle: Beyond Debord. In J. Sugden and A. Tomlinson (eds) *Power Games: A Critical Sociology of Sport.* London: Routledge, 44–60.

Wolin, S.S. (2000) Political theory: From vocation to invocation. In J.A. Frank and J. Tambornino (eds) *Vocations of Political Theory.* Minneapolis, MN: University of Minnesota Press, 3–22.

Wolin, S.S. (2008) *Democracy Incorporated: Managed Democracy and the Specter of Inverted Totalitarianism.* Princeton, NJ: Princeton University Press.

Zirin, D. (2014) *Brazil's Dance with the Devil: The World Cup, the Olympics, and the Fight for Democracy.* Chicago, IL: Haymarket Books.

20

THE CONTEMPORARY POLITICS OF SPORTS MEGA-EVENTS

John Horne

Introduction

This chapter discusses the contemporary politics of sports mega-events, involving the Olympic Games and FIFA Men's Football World Cup Finals, as well as other lower 'order' sports megas (Black 2014). From the late 1960s onward – roughly from the Tokyo Summer Olympics of 1964 – sports mega-events have been caught up in symbolic politics, taking two main forms. First, there are the *promotional* opportunities offered by them to enhance reputations – by competing with other cities and nations, winning the right to stage them and actually hosting them. This form of politics is sometimes referred to as the exercise of 'soft power' (Nye 1990) or public diplomacy, as nations, and increasingly cities, have sought to develop their place in the modern world and establish what has been referred to as 'brand identity' (Anholt 2008; Grix and Houlihan 2014).

Second, there is the opportunity for non-state actors and social movements to *protest* about a perceived social injustice by 'seizing the platform' offered by sports mega-events watched by hundreds of millions of people and reported on by most of the world's media (Price 2008). The next Summer Olympics after Tokyo 1964, staged in Mexico City in 1968, saw the best example of this in the form of the famous 'salute' by John Carlos and Tommie Smith in support of the Olympic Project for Human Rights (Hartmann 2003; Henderson 2010). More recently evictions of low-income communities from housing to make way for mega-event-related projects and other infringements of human rights have also become part of the Olympic and FIFA Men's Football World Cup narrative (COHRE 2007).

This chapter considers: the gap between the rhetoric and reality of sports mega-event legacies; the relationship between sports mega-events and social exclusion; and the global power shifts involved in hosting sports mega-events in emerging economies outside the global North. It is structured in four sections: a brief discussion of the range and number of sports mega-events since 2000; an assessment of the contemporary politics of sports mega-events; a focus on three main sites of political contestation – rights, legacy and labour; and conclusions about future research into the politics of sports mega-events.

Defining the field

Definitions of mega-events vary across different theoretical understandings and disciplines, for example, geography, urban planning, political science and sociology (Müller 2015). In lieu of an agreed definition, Roche (2000) offers a way to understand the features of mega-events *sociologically* that has been adopted by many other writers – as 'large-scale cultural (including commercial and sporting) events, which have a dramatic character, mass popular appeal and international significance' (Roche 2000: 1). These characteristics go some way to explain the allure or attraction of sports mega-events to potential host cities or nations. For individuals, sports mega-events offer the promise of a festival of sport, with emotional moments, shaping personal (life) time horizons. Two features of contemporary sports mega-events are first then, that they are deemed to have highly significant social, political, economic and ideological consequences for the host city, region or nation in which they occur, and, second, that they will attract considerable media coverage. By this definition, therefore, an unmediated mega-event would be a contradiction in terms, and for this reason the globally mediated sports genre of mega-event has tended to supplant other forms of 'mega', such as World's Fairs or Expos, although the latter do continue to be enthusiastically hosted and attract substantial numbers of visitors.

Additionally we need to consider the existence of first, second, third and even lower orders or tiers of (sports) mega-events according to their reach and range, cost and size (Black 2014). For my purposes, in this chapter I will refer to the following as amongst the most significant sports mega-events: Tier 1 – Summer Olympic Games and FIFA Men's Football World Cup; Tier 2 – Winter Olympic Games and UEFA Men's EURO Football championship; Tier 3 – Commonwealth Games and Pan American Games (see Table 20.1).

Since 2000 there have been 23 editions of these six sports mega-events and there are 13 to come before 2024. Two hosts are still to be formally decided (at the time of writing in August 2015) and the Commonwealth Games and the Winter Olympics have been experiencing difficulties finding hosts recently. The deadline for submitting bids to the International Olympic Committee (IOC) for hosting the Winter Olympics in 2022 expired in November 2013, when six cities became official contenders. However, four European cities – Norway's Oslo, Poland's Krakow, Sweden's Stockholm and Ukraine's Lviv – withdrew and in July 2015 Beijing was selected ahead of the only remaining contender, Almaty (Kazakhstan).

With respect to the Commonwealth Games in 2022, Edmonton (Canada) withdrew in February 2015 leaving Durban (South Africa) the sole contender.

Nonetheless the Winter Olympics in 2010 attracted 2,600 competitors, the Commonwealth Games in Glasgow in 2014 featured 7,300 sports team members, and the Pan American Games in Toronto in 2015 featured over 6,100 competitors. Flyvbjerg (2014) suggests that, strictly speaking, we should distinguish between 'mega' (million), 'giga' (billion), and 'tera' (trillion) dollar (USD) projects depending on their scale. Certainly the biggest two sports mega-events routinely now cost several billions of dollars to stage and might justifiably be called 'giga' events. The sports mega-events staged by members of the BRICS alliance (Brazil, Russia, India, China and South Africa) since 2000 have also pushed the costs of staging events upwards.

Black (2014) argues convincingly that we should look at megas as a means to fund development processes and objectives. In doing so they will inevitably benefit certain interests, not all interests. With respect to 'second-order' megas, they are attractive to second-tier locales in the globalised world for two main reasons. First, the more 'relevance challenged' mega-events can offer the only realistic means of pursuing event-centred development for certain urban areas. Some places can never realistically aspire to host an Olympic Games or host the FIFA World Cup finals. This was found out by Birmingham and Manchester in England as three bids in the 1980s and 1990s failed to attract enough attention from IOC members. Today this also applies to cities such as Glasgow in Scotland, which hosted the Commonwealth Games in 2014, and Edmonton (Canada), which was in competition with Durban (South Africa) to host the 2022 edition of the Commonwealth Games until February 2015. Second, lower-order mega-events

Table 20.1 Sports Mega-Events in the twenty-first century: 2000–2023

Summer Olympics	Winter Olympics	FIFA World Cup	UEFA EURO	PAN AM Games	Commonwealth Games
2000 Sydney	2002 Salt Lake City	2002 Japan and South Korea	2000 Belgium and Netherlands	2003 Santo Domingo	2002 Manchester
2004 Athens	2006 Torino	2006 Germany	2004 Portugal	2007 Rio de Janeiro	2006 Melbourne
2008 Beijing	2010 Vancouver	2010 South Africa	2008 Austria and Switzerland	2011 Guadalajara	2010 Delhi
2012 London	2014 Sochi	2014 Brazil	2012 Poland and Ukraine	2015 Toronto	2014 Glasgow
2016 Rio de Janeiro	2018 Pyeongchang	2018 Russia	2016 France	2019 Lima	2018 Gold Coast
2020 Tokyo	2022 Beijing	2022 Qatar	2020 A 'Pan-Europe' competition staged in different countries: final at Wembley Stadium, London	2023 Possible Contenders: Santiago (Chile), Panama City, Miami (USA)	2022 Durban (SA)

can act as 'springboards' for cities to go on to bid to host first-order mega-events. This was the strategy that the municipality of Rio de Janeiro took, to first host a smaller-scale event (the Pan Americans in 2007) and then bid to host the summer Olympics. It is thought that if Durban is successful with its bid to host the Commonwealth Games in 2022, this might be used to launch a bid to host the Summer Olympics in 2024 or 2028. Thus it is that even the process of bidding to host a sports mega-event can be seen as full of political calculation.

There is a politics *in*, and a politics *of*, sports mega-events. The former focuses on the internal politics of the organising bodies, such as the IOC and FIFA. This form of politics is dealt with elsewhere (e.g. Tomlinson 2014) and in this collection, and hence there is no detailed discussion in this chapter about, for example, the controversy over potential corruption in the bidding process highlighted in the report into the selection of Qatar as host of the 2022 FIFA World Cup. The external politics of sports mega-events, which this chapter deals with, relates to corporate interests and global forces in combination with, or confrontation with, local interests, and it is to this that we now turn.

Contemporary politics

It is important to realise that the politics of each and every sports mega-event is conjunctural – that means that it will be affected by different political circumstances at local, national, regional and global scales at different times and places. Nonetheless since the 1970s there has been concern about 'gigantism' and 'white elephants' in the Olympics – the growth in scale of the events on one hand and the potential to build facilities and stadia that will be more costly to use and maintain than they are worth on the other. Economists and other social scientists have assessed sports mega-events in terms of their costs and benefits (Preuss 2004; Whitson and Horne 2006). Flyvbjerg (2014) suggests that an iron law of mega projects, including sports mega-events, is that they will be 'over budget, over time, over and over again'. Whether this is a constant or not it is certainly the case that most sports mega-events since the 1970s have attracted political controversy.

Horne (2007: 86–91) identified a number of 'known unknowns' with respect to sports mega-events that have remained part of the political debate about sports mega-events. These include: the emphasis on consumption-based development as opposed to social redistribution with respect to the goals of hosting sports mega-events; urban regeneration that often leads to 'gentrification' of specific areas being regenerated; the displacement (and subsequent 'replacement') of poor and less powerful communities of people; the use of (often quite extensive) public sector funds to enhance private corporate sector gain; the local host sites and spaces benefitting global flows of capital, trade and finance; the spatial concentration of the impact of the event; the impacts on employment of hosting sports mega-events – and the duration of the impacts; the impact on tourism flows never being near what is predicted by sports mega-event boosters, mainly because of the displacement of non-sport tourists by the sport-event tourists; the way in which boosters have to resort to the manufacturing of the consent of local and national publics to get them on their side about staging the event; and the growth of opposition event coalitions as a result of some or all of these developments.

As mentioned earlier symbolic politics – the promotional politics of promotional culture via public diplomacy, 'soft power' and/or propaganda – are fundamental features of the contemporary politics of sports mega-events. Whether competing with other cities or nations to host an event, winning the right to do so, or actually hosting an event, the potential for symbolic power plays, or pitfalls, are real. All such exercises in promotional politics – nation branding, city branding, image alteration – run the danger of heightening reputational risk to the bidders (and eventual hosts) involved. According to the 2014 Anholt-GfK survey of national image, rather than boost Brazil's reputation in the world, hosting the 2014 FIFA World Cup Finals saw the country lose ground in the rankings, whilst World Cup winners Germany knocked the USA off the top spot after five years (Anholt-GfK Roper 2014; Garcia 2014).

Another aspect of political controversy since '9/11' (in 2001), and that stretches further back to the 'Munich' terrorist attack (in 1972), has been the relationship between the staging of sports mega-events and the growth of the security state. Societies have seen a continuing transformation of surveillance capabilities as the supposed threat of terrorist attack has grown. Sports mega-events have offered opportunities for new security equipment and procedures and surveillance operations to be trialled. As these three features – costs, reputational risk and security – have developed, so too have other related sites of contestation.

Contentious politics: three sites

The next section briefly discusses the politics of rights, legacy and labour in relation to sports mega-events, which have been acknowledged by some but not given the focus that they deserve until now.

Rights

After Athens hosted the Summer Olympic Games in 2004, and with Beijing the next host, Jacques Rogge, then President of the IOC, made the comment that 'The IOC is always in favour of maximum application of human rights. . . . But it is not up to the IOC to monitor human rights' (Kelso 2004). Nonetheless the build up to Beijing 2008 over the next four years saw an unprecedented focus by campaigners on human rights. Seeking to use the first Olympics in China to highlight human rights abuses, the official torch relay was subverted and the Centre on Housing Rights and Evictions (COHRE) in Geneva published a dossier itemising the displacements of hundreds of thousands of people to make way for the Games (for details about the torch relay see Horne and Whannel 2010; Rowe and McKay 2012; on displacements see COHRE 2007).

Narratives associated with hosting mega-events, and the Summer Olympic Games in particular, in East Asia and developing economies have included the following: that it provides an opportunity to catch up or modernise, an opportunity to challenge (Western) modernity, and an opportunity to project distinctive forms of hybrid or hyper-modernity. Whether in the form of overt politics, protest or promotion, hosting a sports 'mega' provides an opportunity for power plays by states, civic authorities, and groups for and against the event. Commentators before and after the start of the Olympic torch relay warned that China would struggle to deal with the 'complex and contradictory circumstances of inviting world attention while also attempting to manage scrutiny and criticism both inside and outside the sporting arena' (Rowe and McKay 2012: 124). After the start it was exposed to several different anti-Chinese demonstrators, including Falun Gong and the Free Tibet movement. These attempts to hijack the torch relay actually provoked a nationalist response, including members of the Chinese diaspora communities turning out to support it, and a decision being taken not to take the relay though Taiwan. When previously the Olympics were being promoted as an internationalising event, the torch relay turned into a display of nationalism and anti-nationalism. Hence the Western media tended to portray the events of London, Paris and San Francisco as peaceful protests against a repressive regime and a military crackdown (Horne and Whannel 2010). The Chinese media eventually responded by considering the protests as violent acts against innocent people requiring the restoration of order and stability – especially when a disabled former athlete and supporter of the relay, Jin Jing, could be portrayed as the 'heroine' of Paris after she was filmed protecting the torch from pro-Tibet protesters (Spencer 2008). In this way, different actors sought to impose their frames of reference on the situation.

The prominence of rights discourse remains the case for other mega-events that have taken place since 2008 in different parts of the world. When thousands of Brazilians took to the streets during the Confederations Cup in June 2013, the then-FIFA President Sepp Blatter said on national television that 'I can understand people are not happy but they should not use football to make their demands heard' (Watts 2013). Yet symbolic transformations of urban environments to fit global expectations of modernity – expressing security, order, and economic success in vibrant, exciting, safe, places, 'open for business' – tend to impact on the quality of life of inhabitants and most negatively on poor and marginal populations (Broudehoux 2016). Ahead of the 2014 FIFA World Cup and the 2016 Olympic and Paralympic Games in Rio de Janeiro for example, campaigners have identified concerns over the rights of children, workers, women, the disabled, LGBT, marginal populations, the socially excluded and the environment (ANCOP 2014; also see the chapter by Horne and Silvestre in this volume). Issues surrounding rights of access to facilities built at public expense, the removal of poor communities from housing and evictions, have created struggles over who or what is (made) visible.

Legacy

The question of developing a legacy through hosting an Olympic Games or other sports mega-event was, until recently, a relatively low-order issue and one that was not seriously entertained until after an event had been concluded. While all cities had a general legacy vision, which was set out in bid books, no detailed operational plans were developed before the Games about how legacy would be implemented afterwards. Legacy plans were not seriously explored until after the Games had been staged, when there was a diminished interest in Olympic matters. The International Olympic Committee's (IOC) interest in an Olympic city largely ceased once the Games had been staged, so there was no monitoring or evaluation of post-Games legacy implementation.

From the 1990s to the present, the use of the concept 'legacy' in conjunction with sports mega-events has become more and more common and generalized. The concept appeared within sport management circles when questions about the costs and benefits of organizing them were first raised from not only financial and economic points of view but also with respect to social, cultural and environmental aspects. The word started to appear in mega-event organizers' and owners' discourse and literature – first with respect to the International Olympic Committee – and it gradually transferred to other mega-events, including the FIFA mens' football World Cup and the UEFA EURO competition.

Legacy remains 'essentially contested' as a concept and in practice. The key stakeholders – organizers, fans, governments and the general public – perceive mega-events in different ways according to their involvement and expectations of them. The various types of legacy associated with sports mega-events include: material – relating to urban and environmental legacies; symbolic – relating to cultural and political legacies; structural – relating to economic legacies; and phenomenological – relating to the social imaginaries and memories associated with legacies of major sports events. Hence it is much more appropriate to talk about *legacies* in the plural than the singular.

It is useful to consider two distinctions with respect to legacies when considering political implications – that they can be *tangible* and *intangible*, and also *universal* and *selective* (for further discussion see Horne 2015; Cashman and Horne 2013). It is well established that legacies related to sports mega-events can be tangible, that is related to, for example, changes in some way to the material infrastructure or economic performance of the city or nation, and intangible, that is related to, for example, emotional responses to a mega-event whether individual or collective (Preuss 2007). Tangible legacies refer to substantial and long-standing changes to the urban infrastructure – the building of iconic stadia being one of the most notable when it comes to sports mega-events. The intangible legacies of sports mega-events refer predominantly to popular memories, evocations and analyses of specific moments and incidents associated with an event.

A second distinction I want to suggest when thinking about legacy is that legacies can be *selective* and *universal*. By this distinction I mean the following. *Selective legacies* are particular, individualist and elitist, and tend to serve the interests of those dominating powerful political and economic positions in society. *Universal legacies* are communal, collectivist and inherently democratic, available to all by virtue of being made freely accessible. A problem for sports mega-events is that they largely generate *tangible legacies* that are *selective* and *intangible legacies* that are *universal*. *Selective legacies* are of benefit, enjoyed, and delivered to specific individuals or interests, rather than all, and exclude those considered not eligible to receive them. As Titmuss (1974: 39) suggested with respect to selectivism in social policy, selectivism also serves to facilitate the sovereignty of the market. *Universal legacies* on the other hand are those that affect, reach and are shared by all rather than specific individuals or communities. Legacies established universally to serve everybody might need to be financed by governments, philanthropic organisations or exceptionally private enterprises. Prioritising universal legacies would mean that organisers of sports mega-events would be obligated to deliver them to all without constraints. Rather than vague claims regarding legacy they would have to demonstrate a properly funded legacy management programme that continued for some years after the event. As Titmuss (1974: 39) suggested with respect to universalism in social policy, it is a re-distributive institutional approach; it considers welfare (that is, 'positive legacies') as a very important institution of society provided outside the market. For sports mega-events to live up to the promotional claims made for them, the legacies associated with them should follow the principle of universalism and this would require greater control and regulation over FIFA, the IOC and LOCs by non-market actors.

London's bid to stage the 2012 Summer Olympics was fashioned in the context of greater awareness of legacy (Davies 2012). In this respect London was the first true 'legacy' Olympics in so far as the IOC had not used the concept widely before and had only staged its first conference on legacy in 2002, just two years before London submitted its bid book. Since then it has become mandatory for a city to articulate at the bid stage both a vision of how the host city and country would benefit from the staging of the Games and how its operational plans about the realisation of legacy would be implemented. The same also applies now to other mega-events such as the Commonwealth Games and Pan American Games.

The United Kingdom government committed to five, and then six, legacy outcomes for the 2012 Games that collectively came to be referred to as the 'London 2012 Legacy Promises'. The sixth legacy promise was added in December 2009, belatedly mindful that 'London 2012' referred to both the Olympic and Paralympic Games (UEL/TGIfS 2010: 15):

1. To make the UK a world-class sports nation: elite success, mass participation and school sport.
2. To transform the heart of East London.
3. To inspire a new generation of young people to take part in local volunteering, cultural and physical activity.
4. To make the Olympic Park a blueprint for sustainable living.
5. To demonstrate that the UK is a creative, inclusive and welcoming place to live in, to visit and for business.
6. To develop the opportunities and choices for disabled people.

It has been suggested that one of the reasons why London won its bid in 2005 to stage the 2012 Olympic Games was that it had attractive legacy plans in the key areas of sport, youth and the regeneration of a part of east London. However the actual delivery of some of the six legacy promises is proving challenging. For example, one of the promises was to 'inspire a new generation of young people to take part in local volunteering, cultural and physical activity' (Horne and Houlihan 2014). Six of the local authorities closest to the Olympic site in east London were designated as 'Olympic Boroughs'. It was reported in November 2014 that two of them – Newham, the municipal authority containing Stratford, where most of the 2012 Olympics took place, and Dagenham and Redbridge – had the lowest physical activity rates in the whole of England. Over 39 per cent and 38 per cent respectively of people in these Boroughs were physically inactive (Campbell 2014). Three years after the Games and more, concerns have been expressed about the legacies associated with London 2012.

If the overall assessment of the legacy of the Games on sport participation immediately after the Games in 2013 was one of cautious optimism, by 2015 after two successive reporting periods when statistics showed a considerable fall in participation, it was declared a 'disaster' by the opposition (Labour) sports minister (Gibson 2015a). In June 2015 it was reported that the number of British people over 16 playing sport at least once a week had declined by 222,000 in six months. The figures also showed that the number of people playing no sport had increased by 1.2 million on the previous year. The trend was seen as firmly on a decline in participation with 391,000 fewer people swimming in the year from June 2014 (Gibson 2015a). Additionally, according to an Active People survey, there was another significant cause for concern, which was that the increases in participation were significantly skewed in favour of upper-income groups. Moreover, data from the previous Active People report (Sport England 2013) showed that while statistically significant increases in participation (2006–2012) were evidenced in the 26-year-plus age group, none were evident in the 16–25-year age group. A legacy, which relies on older and more affluent people for its delivery, would be, at best, only a partial success.

Disputes over the future use of the Olympic Stadium have also marred developments of an Olympic site legacy. While much of the construction work on the Olympic site has been seen as a triumph of engineering and organisation, questions have been raised about the planning for the post-Games legacy given the failure to secure a tenant for the Olympic Stadium. Initially the Olympic Stadium's future was to be as a scaled-down athletics venue. When that was judged economically uncertain, bids were invited from football clubs. West Ham United emerged as the preferred bidder, but both Tottenham Hotspur and Leyton Orient challenged the decision. With the legacy of London's Olympic Stadium heading for the law courts, the government decided to intervene, retain the stadium in public ownership, and lease the stadium to a bidder. The decision to allow West Ham to lease the stadium has left taxpayers to cover the cost of its conversion for football and stadium running costs after the Games. These costs have now increased to £272 million, taking the total cost of the stadium to more than £700 million, from an originally estimated total of £280 million (Gibson 2015b).

The politics of legacy associated with sports mega-events is quite well illustrated by three quotations from Lord Sebastian Coe (Table 20.2), the chair of the London Organising Committee of the Olympic and Paralympic Games (LOCOG) for London 2012.

Table 20.2 Lord Coe on the London 2012 legacy

Sebastian Coe, May 2006	'Legacy is absolutely epicentral to the plans for 2012. Legacy is probably nine-tenths of what this process is about, not just 16 days of Olympic sport' (Culf 2006).
Sebastian Coe, 2007	'50 per cent of the organising team are working on making sure that the Games are working functionally at Games time and the other 50 per cent spend every working hour worrying about what it is we are going to do with these facilities afterwards' (Cashman and Horne 2013: 55, quoting Shirai 2008).
Sebastian Coe, March 2012	'I don't want this to sound like this is not my job, but actually it isn't. We created the best platform in living memory to create the environment for that to happen. This begins after 2012. We finish and go off and do whatever we do' (Gibson 2012).

Over the six years that the build up to the London Games took place and the event itself approached there was a clear diminishing of focus on legacy and a distancing of responsibility from delivering on it.

Labour

The labour involved in putting on a sports mega-event includes paid and unpaid work; those on a living wage and those on or earning less than the minimum wage; and those who work on the supply chains providing equipment, clothing and footwear as well as merchandise associated with events. Few researchers have looked at this aspect of sports mega-events in detail, including the terms, conditions and safety record of the occupations required (although on London 2012 see Cohen 2013). In addition to paid workers, volunteers play a major role in the delivery of the events. Seventy thousand 'Games Makers' were trained for London 2012 (and the same number are required for Rio 2016). A total of 12,500 'Clydesiders' helped at the Glasgow 2014 Commonwealth Games, whilst others in Glasgow were trained in customer care based on the principles of the Disney Corporation (see BBC 2014).

Whilst London 2012 had an excellent safety record with respect to the building of the Olympic Park, in the build up to the 2014 World Cup in Brazil, at least ten construction workers died; and two drivers were killed when a flyover collapsed in Belo Horizonte just before a semi-final match in July 2014.

Since the decision to award the 2022 FIFA World Cup Finals to Qatar in 2010, concerns have been expressed about the 'kafala' sponsorship system that operates in Qatar and other Middle Eastern countries. The system requires that migrant workers surrender their passports to their sponsors, who effectively decide if they can leave employment or not. Investigative reporting has found that several hundred workers on World Cup-related projects have died since 2010 (Black *et al.* 2014). Sandra Burrow, International Trade Union Confederation (ITUC) Secretary General, stated in 2014 that 'FIFA, the athletics body IAAF, multinationals and others which are getting a free ride on the back of modern slavery in Qatar should be ashamed to be in league with a dictatorship like this' (Dorsey 2014).

The following two quotations, both from Sepp Blatter, the then-FIFA President, during a talk he gave at Oxford University in October 2013, allude to the work involved in putting on a World Cup, Olympics or other sports mega-event. On the one hand Blatter acknowledged that 'Football has the power to build a better future . . . [FIFA's job is] . . . helping communities in need through football' (Hyde 2013b). However when challenged about the working conditions of migrant workers in Qatar preparing the ground for the 2022 World Cup finals, he also stated that 'We are not the ones that can actually change it. . . . This is not FIFA's remit' (Hyde 2013b).

Timms (2012a, 2012b) discusses the way that the anti-sweat shop campaign 'Play Fair' uses the platform of the Olympics, how it has developed, and its form for 2012. Play Fair brings together a number of labour rights groups to 'use the hook, unashamedly, of the biggest sporting event in the world'. In using the Olympic Games as a platform for its protest, Play Fair is an example of how activists can mobilise or hijack for their own purposes a platform that has already been created (at great cost) by others. As pointed out by Price (2008: 86), this type of platform is a 'relatively unexplored vehicle for systematic communication', and the value and reach of the Olympic platform presents a very particular opportunity for those able to mobilise it. Whilst the Olympics have long been used to promote specific causes, Timms identifies three ways it can be useful for the issue of labour rights. First, the garment industry represents a significant proportion of the global labour market, with over 40 million workers;

including some of the poorest, least organised and protected workers, who are disproportionately women. Campaigners claim that employment can involve long hours, pressure to work at unrealistic speeds, low wages, dangerous conditions, intimidation, and little access to unions. Sporting goods are a high-profile part of this industry, and therefore the Olympics provides a platform to coordinate campaigns and to call for industry-wide improvements. Second, ethical campaigning on supply chains has had some success in establishing responsible governance as an issue that companies need to address. Major targets have been sports related, such as Adidas, Puma and Nike, many of whom are associated with the Olympics. This has allowed Play Fair to monitor the voluntary standards companies have agreed, drawing on the weight of Olympic bodies to add pressure. Third, key elements of the Olympic platform offer specific opportunities for Play Fair, and not only its global reach. Putting on an Olympic event involves systems of licensing – for merchandise, suppliers and sponsors, and Play Fair claim that Olympic officials could significantly impact working conditions if contracts were only granted to companies meeting internationally agreed labour standards. For example, merchandising for London 2012 involved 10,000 product lines from over 60 licensees. Then there is also the Olympic ethos, with the Olympic Charter promoting positive universal principles. This is used by Play Fair to argue that some Olympic suppliers violate the Charter, due to exploitative conditions.

Conclusions

Hosting the Olympic Games (and other mega-events) is a political act; public events and institutions involving decisions over the allocation of resources have political dimensions. They require consideration of the distribution of power, struggles and who gains from the situation. The increasingly corporate character of sports mega-events leads to various civic responses to their social impacts and legacies. Whilst security risk management differs between the World Cup and the Olympics, there are considerable opportunities for markets in security to develop around sports mega-events. This can have consequences for civil rights and concerns about the militarisation of urban locations. Hyde (2013a) asks:

> if hosting an Olympics or a World Cup were even remotely likely to advance the cause of human freedom in their countries, does anyone think the likes of China and Qatar would be as keen to host them as they are?

In response to her question she cited FIFA Secretary General, Jérôme Valcke, who commented: 'less democracy is sometimes better for organising a World Cup' (Hyde 2013a). Sports mega-events also tend to impact negatively on poor people – through pre-event construction and the post-event 'gentrification' of locations, the crowding out of other spending on welfare and the general redirection of scarce resources toward the priority of delivering a mega-event. The 2010 World Cup in South Africa presented several examples where the trade-off between housing projects for people in need and the building of a stadium went in favour of the latter. Profit and event delivery come before democracy and social justice, leading to a variety of responses and resistances. One of the unintended legacies of hosting a World Cup is that it can lead to social mobilisation – and sometimes confrontations – as was witnessed in Brazil in 2013 and 2014. Some organisers have attempted the integration and incorporation of NGOS and protest groups into the planning of events. But the mobilisation of people and communities affected remains one of the most unstable and unpredictable of the social legacies of the World Cup and other sports mega-events.

Flyvbjerg *et al.* (2012) argue that social scientists should investigate the 'tension points' in mega projects. We have tried to identify some of those involved with sports mega-events in this chapter. The contemporary politics of the sports mega-events is a continuing story. Given the increasing reluctance of urban populations in democracies to host sports mega-events, it appears that the analyses of earlier and more recent academic work on the politics of sports mega-events, informed by and informing the work of activists, is beginning to have some effect (Lenskyj 2008; Boykoff 2014). Lauermann (2015) thus identifies three recent 'trends in the urban politics of mega-events':

1. the professionalisation of a mega-event 'industry' in which consultancies, knowledge management systems and 'city-to-city policy transfer partnerships' have a key role;
2. the role of critics of mega-events who have attempted to counter bids and 'contest the ways in which the professionalisation of the industry impacts local decision-making';
3. the impact of questions raised by anti-bid activists, not just about the division of costs and benefits of mega-events, but also about 'the legitimacy of event-led development models' on cities contemplating bidding for them.

Other examples of 'seizing the platform' (Price 2008) will become available as protest and event coalitions and activism develop. It is important however to note that the mass media are of central importance in defining mega-events as important and giving them their political potency. Consumer culture and the expansion of the mediation of sport in the modern advanced world provide compelling opportunities to be noticed, and not just for advanced economies. Hosts' and potential hosts' interest in hosting vary according to local and national considerations – be they global cities, second-order cities, national projects, developing economies – but they are always involved in making political decisions.

References

ANCOP. (2014) *Megaeventos e Violações de Direitos Humanos no Brasil* ('Mega Events and Human Rights Violations in Brazil'). Rio de Janeiro: Articulação Nacional dos Comitês Populares da Copa (ANCOP).

Anholt, S. (2008) Place branding: is it marketing, or isn't it? *Place Branding and Public Diplomacy* 4(1): 1–6.

Anholt-G.fK. Roper (2014) Germany knocks USA off top spot for 'best nation' after 5 years. Accessed 1 December 2014. www.gfk.com/news-and-events/press-room/press-releases/pages/germany-knocks-usa-off-best-nation-top-spot.aspx [Brand index].

BBC. (2014) Back to Charm School, BBC Radio World Service. 15 July 2014. Accessed 2 December 2014. www.bbc.co.uk/programmes/p022f0m2.

Black, D. (2014) Megas for strivers: the politics of second-order events. In J. Grix (ed.) *Leveraging Legacies from Sports Mega-Events*. Basingstoke: Palgrave, pp. 13–23.

Black, I. Gibson, O. and Booth, R. (2014) Qatar promises to reform labour laws after outcry over 'World Cup slaves'. *The Guardian*. 14 May 2014. Accessed 2 December 2014. www.theguardian.com/world/2014/may/14/qatar-reform-labout-laws-outcry-world-cup-slaves.

Boykoff, J. (2014) *Activism and the Olympics: Dissent at the Games in Vancouver and London*. New Jersey: Rutgers University Press.

Broudehoux, A.M. (2016) Mega-events, urban image construction and the politics of exclusion. In R. Gruneau and J. Horne (eds) *Mega-Events and Globalization: Capital and Spectacle in a Changing World Order*. London: Routledge, pp. 113–130.

Campbell, D. (2014) London Olympics borough is the most physically inactive in England. *The Guardian*. 12 November 2014. Accessed 2 December 2014. www.theguardian.com/society/2014/nov/12/london-olympics-borough-most-physically-inactive-england.

Cashman, R. and Horne, J. (2013) Managing Olympic legacy. In S. Frawley and D. Adair (eds) *Managing the Olympics*. London: Palgrave, pp. 50–65.

Cohen, P. (2013) *On the Wrong Side of the Track? East London and the Post Olympics*. London: Lawrence & Wishart.

COHRE (2007) *Fair Play for Housing Rights: Megaevents, Olympic Games and Housing Rights.* Geneva: Centre on Housing Rights and Evictions.

Davies, L. (2012) Beyond the games: regeneration legacies and London 2012. *Leisure Studies*, 31(3): 309–337.

Dorsey, J. (2014) The turbulent world of Middle East soccer blog. Accessed 6 March 2016. http://mideastsoccer.blogspot.co.uk/2014/11/likely-qatar-deportation-of-striking.html.

Flyvbjerg, B. (2014) What you should know about megaprojects and why: an overview. *Project Management Journal*, 45(2): 6–19.

Flyvbjerg, B., Landman, T. and Schram, S. (eds) (2012) *Real Social Science: Applied Phronesis.* Cambridge: Cambridge University Press.

Garcia, G. (2014) Copa do Mundo não melhorou imagem do país no exterior, aponta índice britânico. *Brazilian News.* 18–24 November, p. 14.

Gibson, O. (2015a) Olympic legacy ends in lethargy and now anger. *The Guardian, Sport Section.* 12 June 2015, p. 1.

Gibson, O. (2015b) Final bill for revamped Olympic Stadium will exceed £700m. *The Guardian, Sport Section.* 20 June 2015, p. 9.

Grix, J. and Houlihan, B. (2014) Sports mega-events as part of a nation's soft power strategy: the cases of Germany (2006) and the UK (2012). *British Journal of Politics and International Relations*, 16(4): 572–596.

Hartmann, D. (2003) *Race, Culture, and the Revolt of the Black Athlete: The 1968 Olympic Protests and Their Aftermath.* Chicago, IL: University of Chicago Press.

Henderson, S. (2010) 'Nasty demonstrations by negroes': The place of the Smith–Carlos podium salute in the civil rights movement. In K. Brewster (ed.) *Reflections on Mexico '68.* London: Routledge, pp. 78–92.

Horne, J. (2015) Managing World Cup legacy. In S. Frawley and D. Adair (eds) *Managing the World Cup.* London: Palgrave, pp. 7–24.

Horne, J. (2007) The four knowns of sports mega-events. *Leisure Studies*, 26(1): 81–96.

Horne, J. and Houlihan, B. (2014) London 2012. In J. Grix (ed.) *Leveraging Legacies from Sports Mega-Events.* Basingstoke: Palgrave, pp. 107–117.

Horne, J. and Whannel, G. (2010) The 'caged torch procession': celebrities, protesters and the 2008 Olympic torch relay in London, Paris and San Francisco. *Sport in Society*, 13(5): 760–770.

Hyde, M. (2013a) The greatest trick FIFA ever pulled was to issue a Qatar weather warning. *The Guardian.* 4 October 2013.

Hyde, M. (2013b) Blatter must back up his World Cup blathering. *The Guardian.* 21 November 2013. Accessed 7 March 2016. www.theguardian.com/football/blog/2013/nov/20/sepp-blatter-world-cup-social-change.

Kelso, P. (2004) Human rights shadow over Beijing Games. *The Guardian.* 30 August 2004. Accessed 2 December 2015. www.theguardian.com/world/2004/aug/30/china.athensolympics2004.

Lauermann, J. (2015) Boston's Olympic bid and the evolving urban politics of event-led development. *Urban Geography, Online.* http://dx.doi.org/10.1080/02723638.2015.1072339.

Lenskyj, H. J. (2008) *Olympic Industry Resistance. Challenging Olympic Power and Propaganda.* Albany, NY: State University of New York Press.

Müller, M. (2015) What makes an event a mega-event? Definitions and sizes. *Leisure Studies Online.* Accessed 16 March 2015. www.tandfonline.com/doi/pdf/10.1080/02614367.2014.993333.

Nye Jnr., J. (1990) Soft Power. *Foreign Policy*, 80: 153–171.

Preuss, H. (2004) *The Economics of Staging the Olympics: A Comparison of the Games 1972–2008.* Cheltenham: Edward Elgar.

Preuss, H. (2007) The conceptualisation and measurement of mega sport event legacies. *Journal of Sport and Tourism*, 12: 207–228.

Price, M. (2008) On seizing the Olympic platform. In M. Price and D. Dayan (eds) *Owning the Olympics: Narratives of the New China.* Ann Arbor, MI: University of Michigan Press, pp. 86–114.

Roche, M. (2000) *Mega-Events and Modernity.* London: Routledge.

Rowe, D. and McKay, J. (2012) Torchlight temptations. Hosting the Olympics and the global gaze. In J. Sugden and A. Tomlinson (eds) *Watching the Olympics. Politics, Power and Representation.* London: Routledge, pp. 122–137.

Spencer, R. (2008) Disabled girl becomes China's Olympic heroine. *The Telegraph Online.* 12 April 2008. Accessed 18 August 2015. www.telegraph.co.uk/sport/2297096/Disabled-girl-becomes-Chinas-Olympic-heroine.html.

Sport England (2013) *Active People Survey 7 Q2.* London: Sport England.

Timms, J. (2012a) The Olympics as a platform for protest: a case study of the London 2012 'ethical' Games and the Play Fair campaign for workers' rights. *Leisure Studies*, 31(3): 355–372.

Timms, J. (2012b) Using sports mega-events to improve work in global supply chains: the Olympics, PlayFair 2012 and campaigns around corporate social responsibility. Accessed 2 December 2014. www.bl.uk/sportandsociety/exploresocsci/businesseconomics/business/articles/globalsupply.pdf.

Titmuss, R. (1974) *Social Policy*. London: Allen and Unwin.

Tomlinson, A. (2014). *FIFA (Fédération Internationale de Football Association): The Men, the Myths and the Money*. London: Routledge.

University of East London/Thames Gateway Institute for Sustainability. (2010) *Olympic Games Impact Study – London 2012 Pre-Games Report*, October 2010, Economic & Social Research Council. Accessed 5 March 2012. http://www.esrc.ac.uk/impacts-and-findings/features-casestudies/features/15278/early-impacts-for-london-2012-games.aspx.

Watts, J. (2013) Sepp Blatter urges Brazil protesters not to link grievances to football. *The Guardian*. 19 June 2013. Accessed 2 December 2014. www.theguardian.com/football/2013/jun/19/sepp-blatter-brazil-football-protests.

Whitson, D. and Horne, J. (2006) Underestimated costs and overestimated benefits? Comparing the impact of sports mega-events in Canada and Japan. In J. Horne and W. Manzenreiter (eds) *Sports Mega-Events: Social Scientific Analyses of a Global Phenomenon*. Oxford: Blackwell/ Sociological Review Monograph, pp. 73–89.

21

FIFA: "FOR THE GAME. FOR THE WORLD"?

The world governing body's escalating crisis of credibility

Alan Tomlinson

Introduction: background and problematic

FIFA (Fédération Internationale de Football Association) was founded in 1904. It was the initiative of seven European countries, mostly national associations, though some represented several sports and Spain was represented by a single football club. At that time there were no continental confederations (the South American one dates its foundation from 1916; the other five were founded in the 1950s and 1960s). The World Cup tournament was inaugurated in 1930 and was hosted and won by Uruguay. In its 112-year history, up to early 2016, FIFA had had eight presidents, all bar one (the Brazilian João Havelange) hailing from Europe. Havelange and his successor the Swiss Joseph 'Sepp' Blatter had, as this chapter was written, between them secured the presidency for 11 periods from 1974, Blatter having won his fifth term in a presidential election vote conducted on the last Friday in May at FIFA's 2015 Congress in Zurich. This electoral process had been marred two days before by the sensational arrest early on the Wednesday morning at an elite Zurich hotel of 14 people related to the football business of FIFA-affiliated confederations. Four of these had held positions as president of a confederation: Jeffrey Webb from the Cayman Islands was the incumbent president of CONCACAF, the central and north Americas and Caribbean confederation, and Trinidad and Tobago's Jack Warner had held that position before him; Uruguayan Eugenio Figueredo and Paraguay's Nicolás Leoz had been presidents of the South American confederation, CONMEBOL. These positions had carried with them a vice-presidential position on FIFA's Executive Committee (ExCo). A further ten individuals were arrested, four with strong FIFA connections: Costa Rica's Eduardo Li had been about to join the ExCo as a CONCACAF delegate; Julio Rocha of Nicaragua had held a position as a FIFA development officer, with a brief to introduce football projects around the world; and Rafael Esquivel and Jose Maria Marin are past presidents of, respectively, the Venezuelan and Brazilian football federations. The other six indicted individuals comprised British citizen Costa Takkas, personal attaché to Jeffrey Webb, and a former general secretary of the Cayman Islands' football federation; and five media/sport marketing executives (three Argentineans [one with dual Italian citizenship], one Brazilian and one US citizen). FIFA employs around 400 employees, and FIFA committees, commissions and bureaux were peopled by, in one 2011 count

(Tomlinson 2014: 35), 387 different individuals. FIFA supports an increasingly successful women's World Cup, age-banded tournaments around the world and innumerable development schemes for the majority of its member (national) associations/federations. But the indictment of the FIFA 14 brought into unprecedentedly sharp relief for the global audience the malpractices and endemic corruption of highly placed FIFA-related and connected personnel; the voices of those who could claim to be untainted were drowned out in a tsunami of negative coverage and general condemnation of the overall organisation. Some such individuals may believe, genuinely, that their endeavours are idealistically channelled 'for the game, for the world', as the FIFA slogan trills, but few were willing to listen to arguments about the injustice of condemning the many for the crimes of the few. In the medium term, an understanding of the politics of FIFA's flaws and failures will need to explore with forensic precision the conditions and circumstances whereby and when the relative innocence of collusion contributes to the consolidation of a culture of corruption. The 40-year career of Sepp Blatter at the heart of the FIFA organisation offers a case study of unparalleled richness for such an understanding.

In a blitz of global media coverage, following the indictment of the FIFA14, the world heard within three days from the victorious Blatter that he would not serve out his time in his fifth term; he would resign to allow a successor to be elected at a forthcoming extraordinary Congress, fixed later for February 2016. Blatter talked of his recognition that his victory did not represent a mandate to speak for the whole of the football world, though he pledged to stimulate the necessary reforms that might regain FIFA some credibility after the move by the FBI, the U.S. attorney general and the U.S. revenue services to move in the dramatic dawn raid of 27 May. They redefined FIFA as a RICO (Racketeering Influenced Corrupt Organisation) operated by some of its members as an "enterprise" serving their own and co-conspirators' interests rather than the stated goals of the organisation itself. In paragraph 265 of the indictment presented to the world, the suspects were charged with, over a period from 1991 to the present, "knowingly and intentionally" conspiring "to violate Title 18, United States Code, Section 1962(c)", that is:

> To conduct and participate, directly and indirectly, in the conduct of the affairs of such enterprise through a pattern of racketeering activity, as defined in Title 18, United States Code, Sections 1961 (1) and 1961 (5).

Blatter won the 29 May vote, as the majority of loyal national associations that had brought him to power as president in 1998 continued to give him their support. But his reign was clearly close to the end, his absolute domination curtailed. Outside totalitarian dynasties, political dictatorships, or monarchies that have found a niche in democratic nation-states, these elongated spells of power have little parallel. It is only in FIFA's earlier history, when Jules Rimet held the presidency from 1921 to 1954, or in comparable sports organisations such as the IOC (International Olympic Committee), when long-term presidents included French founder Pierre de Coubertin (1896–1925), Avery Brundage of the USA (president from 1952 to 1972), and Spaniard Juan Antonio Samaranch (1980–2000), that a concentration and longevity of power has characterised the leadership of purportedly representative bodies. The IOC, embroiled in bribery scandals linked to its committee members in the 1990s, has since reformed some of its core practices, and presidents must retire after two terms. FIFA, during Blatter's tenure from 1998, has survived numerous scandals and controversies, but though Blatter was moved to accept the introduction of an ethics committee in 2004, little reform has been implemented. What is seen as the biggest scandal of all, the awarding of the men's

World Cups of 2018 and 2022 to the Russian Federation and Qatar successively at a single FIFA Congress meeting in December 2010, is seen by activists, analysts and many in the media as the beginning of the end-game for FIFA in its current form. In January 2015, in Brussels, British Member of Parliament Damian Collins, in cooperation with European Parliament personnel, stimulated a "summit" meeting, to consider "FIFA's Future". Collins called supporters, fans and administrators from around the world "to speak out . . . and finally be heard": "Supporters", he went on, "want a new FIFA", replacing "FIFA's mismanagement". He added that "millions . . . around the world have had enough and they want change at the top". That initiative, labelled NewFIFANow, and other explicit challenges to Blatter's grip on the presidential position, will be considered in more detail in the following section, after further reflections on the broader context of Blatter's FIFA power base, in particular the profile and popularity of the men's World Cup.

Blatter's power has been rooted in, has indeed shaped, the history of FIFA over the last 40 years. Whilst allegations have swirled and revelations of maladminstration and corruption escalated, the men's World Cup itself, and associated FIFA events, have become increasingly embedded in the global media calendar. Despite protest and dissent at the Confederations Cup in Brazil in 2013, in the following year the World Cup in Brazil in 2014 was seen by many millions around the world as a huge success, the first one to be staged in South America since 1986, as the event meanwhile had toured North America (USA, 1994), Asia (Korea and Japan, 2002), and Africa (South Africa, 2010) as well as being staged in Europe (Italy, 1990; France, 1998; Germany, 2006). Popular protest in Brazil – over inequalities within the society, the expenditure on the World Cup and the soon-to-follow Rio Olympics in 2016, and drawing too on the simmering allegations of corruption over the allocation of the successive tournaments – certainly used the event to mobilise widespread dissatisfaction throughout the vast country. But the games happened; the tournament sparkled, even as the myth of Brazilian football excellence was demolished in Germany's ruthless 7–1 victory in the quarter-final game against the hosts. We need to recognise what FIFA accomplishes as well as the often dubious ways in which these accomplishments are achieved; the *problematique* – open-ended questions related to a particular political, historical and cultural question – that we need to frame for understanding the contemporary FIFA phenomenon is no longer a question of whether there is corruption within its bureaucratic and organisational layers, embedded malpractice within its corridors and cabals of higher power; it is, rather, to ask *how* such practices have been sustained over this remarkable dynastic period of the Havelange/Blatter presidencies.

The situation in Brazil of popular carnival pirouetting with popular protest created an intriguing scenario. As the tournament began, Blatter could hide away in his luxury suite at the far end of Ipanema, well away from the fans and the crowds at the FanFest on the Copacabana beach, keeping a low profile even on excursions to meet with the high and mighty of the football world at the Copacabana Palace. This move from popular protest to popular passion and pleasure is typical of sport's rhythms in popular culture, as the cultural politics of protest are balanced with the popular passions that are fuelled by the theatre of sporting competition and the rivalries of nations. Widely challenged, even ridiculed, in the weeks before the start of the tournament, Blatter could find a place to hide, emerging to hand over the trophy to the German captain at the Maracanã a month later, though accompanied by few VIPs, all now reluctant to share the stage with a man fast becoming a toxic brand, the focus of booing and jeering whenever appearing in an uncontrolled environment.

It is impossible, though, in a single overview chapter, to fully unravel the complexities of this socio-cultural chemistry whereby flawed leadership is sustained and the continuing success of the sporting spectacle reaffirmed, and so in what follows I offer snapshots and vignettes of how FIFA has managed to survive so many crises and continued to operate in an established *modus operandi* characterised by a lack of accountability, transparency and, to echo its own rhetoric, fair play; and despite too the scale of corruption that has been confirmed in the practices of numerous of its committee members, and some of its highest-level office-holders. To do this, the chapter considers recent cameos of people, events, and responses, before reflecting on some social scientific theories, concepts and methods that may help us better understand the FIFA story. It does so by going back in time over some cases of leadership challenge, bidding outcomes, ethical processes, and internal conflicts and tensions. First, in the following section, challengers to the Havelange/Blatter dynasty are reviewed in the context of the May 2015 presidential election. Second, the question of flexible ethics is considered in the case of Russia's successful bid to stage the 2018 World Cup. Third, FIFA's internal investigation into the 2018 and 2022 World Cup-hosting decisions is reviewed. Fourth, the muted rebellion of 2002 is revisited, when almost half the executive committee mobilised with the then-General Secretary to submit a criminal complaint to the Public Prosecutor's office in Zurich, against Blatter, "concerning 'Suspicion of breach of trust' and 'Dishonest management'", criminal elements as identified within the Swiss Criminal Code. Methodologically, this is to move from the present to the past, to show how FIFA's corrupt practices were in place long before the U.S. legal and tax-checking authorities and the FBI emerged on the scene to confirm the embeddedness of corruption within the operations of some of the most privileged networks of the FIFA-related hierarchy.

Alternatives/challenges?[1]

Relations with the People's Republic of China; Latvian art; forthcoming meetings on regulation of the fruit and vegetable sector; milk quotas; digital surveillance and intrusion in the third world – just another day of activity and planning at the European Parliament in Brussels in mid-January 2015. Except, an alliance of British Westminster parliamentarian Damian Collins and a couple of Members of the European Parliament was also in town, the catalyst for the launch of NewFIFANow, a self-labelled 'Brussels Coalition . . . on FIFA reform'. Art and vegetables could take backstage as a line up of British and Euro politicians, industry lobbyists and international football activists debated the primary proposition from the group: 'FIFA is one of the most discredited organisations in the world with serial allegations of corruption plaguing almost its every move off-the-field in terms of management and governance'. Bold headlining and privileged networking attracted around 100+ media and related professionals. At least things would be more interesting than putting questions to the clown candidate, former French footballing pin-up David Ginola (£250,000 better off for his efforts) or his Paddy Power pranksters that provided the backing for the stunt.

Debate in the morning included tales from insiders and whistleblowers who may have written this all before but themselves had not emerged unscathed from FIFA's own notorious summary of its investigations into the awarding of the Russia 2018 and Qatar 2022 World Cups. This added edge to reform as a revenge narrative, in the English and Australian voices of Lord (David) Triesman and Bonita Mersiades respectively on their experience of those bids. Former FIFA insider and senior bureaucrat Jérôme Champagne – the man with the knowledge from his 11 years inside that might topple his former boss Blatter, and a former member of Blatter's F-Crew (*Führensgruppe*), established in 2001 as a personal advisory body unaccountable to anyone but the FIFA president himself (Sugden and Tomlinson 2003; Tomlinson 2014: 75, 85) – spoke of the global inequalities fostered by FIFA and the need for fair redistribution of monies and resources. But when I reminded him that he was close to the top for much of Blatter's presidential reign, he conceded with the rueful smile of the veteran diplomat that though he'd talked about corruption issues at the time, as much as he could: "I tried my best but I lost the battle". Champagne failed to muster the support of sufficient national football associations to back his candidature for the presidency, persuading just three, and reporting that other national associations would have backed him but for their fear of reprisals from the FIFA establishment.

A second potential challenger was at the event. Former president of the Chilean football federation Harold Mayne-Nicholls, who'd also led the bid inspection process for the 2018 and 2022 World Cups, shed little light on that process and offered an idealistic, good old-fashioned speech on fair play and football as a form of global communication and citizenship. His was an interesting take, perhaps a long-shot pitch for the mid-term after Blatter finally goes. But before the deadline for declaration of candidates at the end of the month, Mayne-Nicholls had withdrawn, ceding to the profile of late challenger Luís Figo, 2001 FIFA Footballer of the Year and Portuguese superstar driven by his declared desire to "give something back to the game". Figo's glossy manifesto was infused with passion: "Football runs through my veins. I am a man of Football, inside and out and I am ready to bring about real change and usher in a far more positive era for FIFA and every one of its National Associations". "For Football" was his accompanying slogan, and Figo confirmed his candidacy with the backing of the national associations of Denmark, Luxembourg, Macedonia, Montenegro, and Poland (an all-European card). Michael van Praag, Dutch FA president, also entered the fray, backed by Belgium, the Faroe Islands, Romania, Scotland and Sweden (another all-European card); van Praag called for a "normalisation" programme to restore FIFA's reputation: "Normalization, that's the key word. The organisation must go back to being plain normal". One wonders, though, which FIFA he has in mind as a model for such a restoration project. The English FA (The Football Association) wasn't in town at Brussels, and waited until the closing day to announce its nomination of Jordan's 39 year-old "HRH Prince Ali Bin Hussein", as he is titled by FIFA as one of its seven Executive Committee Vice-Presidents. Bin Hussein, also a vice-president of the Asian Football Confederation (AFC), is a scion of the monarchical dynasty, a graduate of the UK military academy at Sandhurst, a serious-minded contender from the senior FIFA committee, youthful, smooth and charming, and untainted by internal FIFA scandals. He had politely sent his apologies to the Summit. But he was mounting a spirited challenge, calling for substantial, committed organisational reform, adding too, in a brave and revealing comment, that his candidature would certainly not be hampered by the culture of intimidation that is inbuilt within Blatter's FIFA. Suave and confident, Bin Hussein – "Prince Ali" as he was soon labelled – looked to be a serious candidate and boasted nominations from national associations from across three confederations, the USA from CONCACAF, Jordan from the AFC, and England, Malta, Georgia and Belarus from UEFA. But Bin Hussein was not sponsored by his own confederation, the AFC – he was from it but in this presidential race he was not of it – and he entered the fray in many respects as a rival to the incumbent AFC president, Shaikh Salman Bin Ebrahim Al Khalifa from Bahrain, who had assumed that office in May 2013. Intra-political rivalries certainly outweigh superficial contiguities in this case, and whilst Bin Hussein could mount an effective charm offensive, and eventually muster 73 votes, his elite dynastic pedigree in an at best fledgling democracy was hardly a convincing platform for the democratising reformer. Fourteen of these nominating countries were from within UEFA, and it was striking that the confederations beyond Europe looked to muster little nominating support for Blatter's challengers.

The manifesto of NewFIFANow was solid predictable campaigning stuff, classic rhetoric for a change agenda mixed with doses of power-broking realism. Ten guiding principles enshrined a commitment to democracy, transparency and accountability, with some big-change detail such as re-designating FIFA as a "public international organisation" in line with "OECD policy on Combating Bribery in International Transactions".

Blatter would have been smiling in his Zurich bunker as the nominations came in, watching the opposition votes split. The Brussels Summit was markedly dark-suited and fair-skinned, hardly a global coalition. Blatter gained power defeating Swede Lennart Johansson, UEFA president, in 1998, then Cameroon's Issa Hayatou, president of the African confederation, in 2002. He was unopposed in 2007 and 2011, though in 2011 it was the Asian confederation president, Qatar's Mohammed Bin Hammam, who had planned to oppose him before being disgraced in his own presidential challenge and suspended by FIFA from all football activities, having been caught red-handed distributing bribes to voters from the North American, Caribbean and Central Americas confederation. Blatter's a masterly survivor, outmanoevring over the years Europe, Africa and Asia's top men, increasing his majority in the Congress in 2002 and sustaining the power base that got him there for a further decade and more. Blatter has always understood, following Machiavelli's advice to princes in 1513, that it is "much safer to be feared than loved" (Machiavelli 2005: 91) and ruling by fear has enabled him to ride out numerous scandals, controversies and corruption allegations. Even after the indictment of the FIFA 14, Blatter polled 133 votes, 60 more than Prince Ali's respectable protest vote of 73.

Who next? As Blatter continued to occupy his presidential position and office at the home of FIFA, heavyweight candidates were emerging in mid-2015. These included UEFA president and former French football superstar Michel Platini, reportedly supported by four of the six confederations, and possibly former AFC president Chung Jon Moon, who would be unlikely to confirm participation in a contest that he was unlikely to win. The deadline for candidates to declare themselves with the necessary nominations was 26 October 2015 and the new FIFA president would be elected in February 2016, at the same sessions of Congress that would receive the Reform Committee's recommendations. If this schedule and its timings could be confirmed, Blatter had demonstrated to the last his capacity for scheming and his lust for control. He would leave the FIFA presidency of his own accord, anoint the winner of the election as his successor, and hand the new President a framework for reform that he could claim as his lasting contribution.

Putin's placeman[2]

Qatar has dominated the headlines in the corruption debate since the 2010 decision to award two World Cups at once, to Russia for 2018 and to Qatar for 2022. Human rights issues, labour exploitation, the absurdity of the careless consideration of the bids, in terms of infrastructure and climate; all these have made Qatar an easy target. But let's ask a little more about the World Cup that is a mere three years away from the time of writing. A first World Cup finals tournament in the world's largest country, and its ninth most populous, for the first generation of its post-communist transformation, fits the FIFA globalising mission of spreading the infrastructure of the game, confirming the reach of the game across the globe. "We go to new lands" as Blatter put it, "Never has the World Cup been in Russia and Eastern Europe, and the Middle East and Arabic world has been waiting a long time. So I'm a happy president when we talk about the development of football". Blatter was talking to Reuters following the announcement of the decision in Zurich in December 2010. The Qatar decision soon dominated the headlines, but there was an air of inevitability about the Russian success, and the country's president, Vladimir Putin, was speedily *en route* to Switzerland to anoint the outcome. In the celebrating party he would reunite with Vitaly Mutko, the Russian Federation's Minister of Sport, Tourism and Youth Policy from 2008, and Roman Abramovich, owner of Chelsea Football Club in London. They looked like they were certain winners from early on in the process, and winning the 2018 event was a form of coronation, an affirmation of all the background work undertaken over the previous few years. This had included the rapid career advancement of Mutko, and his simultaneous entry onto FIFA's global stage. Whilst many have questioned the processes whereby Qatar secured the vote to host the 2022 event, less attention has been paid to the Russian triumph in the lobbying stakes. It is, therefore, interesting and revealing to look more closely at the contribution of Vitaly Mutko to this triumph, and at the way in which his career has intertwined the politics of the Russian Federation and the politics of FIFA.

Mutko was born in 1958 in the Krasnodar Territory in the extreme west of the country close to the Black Sea. He attended the Water Transport Institute in Leningrad, and graduated from the River Vocational College, taking too a qualification by correspondence from the Law Department of Leningrad State University. He worked as a technician on shipping vessels, and moved into politics as chairman of the trades union committee of the River College, moving into public administration from 1983 to 1991 as "instructor, section head, secretary, chairman of the Kirov regional Council of People's Deputies", becoming head of the region's administration. This proved an effective platform for political elevation, particularly in the transformative phase of the cooling of the Cold War, and from 1992 to 1996, he was Deputy Mayor of St Petersburg, and chairman of the city Committee on Social Issues. Mutko had also moved into the football world, as president, from 1993, of Zenit St Petersburg Football Club, winning the national cup trophy and coming third in the national championship. His career horizons were now about to broaden, and his summative biography as published by the Russian government leaps to the formation of the Russian Football Premier League in 2001:

> at the initiative of Mutko, who is a member of the Executive Committee of the Russian Football Union, President of the Russian Football premier League and Vice President of the Football Federation of St Petersburg and North-West Russia.
> *(Government of the Russian Federation 2012)*

A year on, he diversified into committee work on Russia's Paralympic Committee, from 2002 – and up to the time of writing – chairing committees and charities dedicated to helping people with mental disabilities. He made the leap, too, in 2003 onto the Federation Council of Russia's Federal Assembly, representing the St Petersburg government. On this national basis, in 2008 he was appointed Russia's Minister of Sport, Tourism and Youth Policy; and in May 2012, reappointed "Minister of Sport of the Russian Federation by a presidential decree". What this potted history of Mutko's career does not include are several crucial facts.

First, in 2009 Mutko became a member of FIFA's Executive Committee (ExCo). The following year, he could participate in the run-in of the Russian bid and its presentation to FIFA in December 2010, when the hosting rights for World Cup 2018 were won. The Russian Minister could back his country's bid, participate in the bidding process, celebrate with Putin, in between times casting his vote as an ExCo member for whichever bid he considered to be the most deserving choice. A year and a half on from the FIFA vote his president's decree would confirm him in his ministerial position, focusing exclusively on sport. This has been an important time for Russian sport, staging too the Sochi Winter Olympics in January 2014, also a convenient launch pad and veil for Putin's militaristic adventures in the Crimea and the Ukraine. Later in that year Mutko, by now also chairman of the Russia 2018 Local Organising Committee, could announce to the world that the 2018 World Cup logo was inspired by "Russia's rich artistic tradition and its history of bold achievement and innovation" (http://rt.com/news/200231-russia-world-cup-logo/). FIFA president Blatter was there of course, adding that the logo reflected the "heart and soul" of the country. Mutko was captioned, for the national and global audience anticipated for this launch at the country's International Space Station, projected onto the Bolshoi Theatre during primetime evening television, as a FIFA ExCo member, not a Russian government minister.

Second, as president of the Zenit St Petersburg Football Club from 1993, Mutko was an agent of not just the rise to sporting prominence of the club, but of its economic transformation. In 1999, Gazprom, the largest natural gas extractor in the world, and in many respects international business arm of the Russian state, became the official sponsor of the club, completing a financial takeover of the club in 2005; in 2012, Gazprom became both a sponsor of Roman Abramovich's Chelsea Football Club in London, and an official partner of the UEFA Champions League (in 2005, Abramovich had received $13 billion for his Sibneft oil shares from Gazprom); from 2015, for an initial three years preceding and including the Russia 2018 World Cup, Gazprom is an official FIFA partner. The FIFA-Gazprom deal was signed on 14 September 2013. At the signing ceremony, FIFA president Blatter and Gazprom chair Alexei Miller were seated, looking down studiously at the historic paperwork; behind them were Vladimir Putin, president of the Russian Federation, and his sport minister Vitaly Mutko, the latter presumably in his capacity as a Minister of State of the country, rather than that of representative of UEFA on the FIFA ExCo. Putin had informed FIFA that he would not attend the presentation, so allowing the FIFA ExCo to make its decisions calmly without pressure; but his Minister of Sport, Tourism and Youth Policy was a voting member of FIFA's decision-making committee! Might the question of ethical accountability, or the issue of conflict of interests, have been raised as Mutko worked the national and international networks of football in the years building up to the December 2010 decision, supported as he was at the highest level by a figure whose practice and demeanour are those of a ruthless dictator rather than an elected public official? There is no trace of such conscience-threatening reflections. When Mutko became a member of FIFA's executive committee, he could have put the FIFA ethics policy and procedures on the table and declared his intent to avoid any conflict of interest between his political priorities, his loyalty to Putin and his role as sport administrator and FIFA committee member. He could have used what FIFA recognises as the "recusal" option to step back from the vote, given that his explicit high-profile political position in the upper echelons of the Russian state more than suggested that he was in breach of FIFA's ethical practices and out of line with FIFA's code of conduct.

In the 2009–10 edition of FIFA's Code of Ethics the ethical consequences of undeclared interests are plainly laid out. The preamble is unequivocal: "FIFA is constantly striving to protect the image of football, and especially that of FIFA, from jeopardy or harm as a result of immoral or unethical methods and practices" (FIFA 2009: 3). Below is an extract from section 5 on conflicts of interest:

1.   Before being elected or appointed, officials shall disclose any personal interests that could be linked with their prospective function.
2.   While performing their duties, officials shall avoid any situation that could lead to conflicts of interest. Conflicts of interest arise if officials have, or appear to have, private or personal interests that detract from their ability to perform their duties

as officials with integrity in an independent and purposeful manner. Private or personal interests include gaining any possible advantage for himself, his family, relatives, friends and acquaintances.

3. Officials may not perform their duties in cases with an existing or potential conflict of interest. Any such conflict shall be immediately disclosed and notified to the organisation for which the official performs his duties.

4. If an objection is made concerning an official's existing or potential conflict of interest, it shall be reported immediately to the organisation for which the official performs his duties.

5. The deciding authority of the relevant organisation shall decide on such conflicts of interest.

(FIFA 2009: 6)

As Mutko looked timidly on while Putin no doubt commended him on his good work in getting Gazprom into one of the most prized sponsorship deals in world sport, perhaps his mind turned away from the ethics of personal conflictual interests, and towards the sixth section of FIFA's code, in which you are asked to think about your conduct towards government and private organisations:

In dealings with government institutions, national and international organisations, associations and groupings, officials shall . . . remain politically neutral, in accordance with the principles and objectives of FIFA, the confederations, associations, leagues and clubs, and generally act in a manner compatible with their function and integrity.

(FIFA 2009: 6)

Mutko's dealings as a Russian politician, on his journey towards his membership of the FIFA ExCo, have been as far removed from political neutrality as one could imagine.

Gazprom chief Miller observes, "Gazprom is not only the largest gas company in the world, but also one of those most passionate about football." So passionate that on the back of the winning bid for the 2018 World Cup, Gazprom would be building a brand new stadium for Mutko's old club Zenit, also the football club of the city of Putin's origins. In these patterns of interlocking interests we can begin to understand Gazprom's "passion", fuelled by the links at local, regional, national and international level that it can secure through the networks and deal-making facilitated by the likes of the Russian president and his placeman, and the ethical neutrality and neglect of the latter's peers in the FIFA hierarchy.

Redacteur(s) at work: FIFA's ethical procedures and processes

On 13 November 2014 the Chairman of the Adjudicatory Chamber of FIFA's Ethics Committee published a statement relating to the *Report on the Inquiry into the 2018/2022 FIFA World Cup™ Bidding Process prepared by the Investigatory Chamber of the FIFA Ethics Committee.* Before going any further, it is worth clarifying the context here. FIFA's Investigatory Chamber investigates, and reports; its Adjudicatory Chamber makes judgements about what to do in response to the findings of the investigation. In this particular cast of characters Michael J. Garcia, a former U.S. attorney, was Chairman of the Investigatory Chamber; Hans Joachim Eckert, a German lawyer, was the Chairman of the Adjudicatory Chamber. The Garcia investigation took more than 18 months, cost an estimated $7 million, and, under lock and key and confidential to reputedly very few FIFA insiders, amounts to a reputed 450 pages; the Eckert statement on the Garcia report runs to a little under 42 pages. Eckert concluded, in his section 8.4 on "Findings", that the evaluation of the bidding process "is closed for the FIFA Ethics Committee"; that the investigation into the bidding process was fully in line with the FIFA Code of Ethics; that he himself, Eckert, supported recommendations "made by the Chairmen of the Investigatory Chamber"; and that his Adjudicatory Chamber could examine "specific cases if the Investigatory Chamber opens Ethics proceedings against officials based on information obtained during the FIFA World Cup™ investigation". Garcia responded with a strong condemnation of Eckert's version of things, referring to "numerous materially incomplete and erroneous representations of the facts and conclusions detailed in the investigatory chamber's report", excluding, for instance, criticisms of the practices and culture of many of the members of the FIFA ExCo.

Eckert claims to have focused upon not the high-profile individuals central to the process, but rather the activities and conduct of the bid teams looking to host the 2018 and 2022 finals tournaments. The short Eckert summary began to be referred to as a classic case of cover-up under the veil of the editorial process; from the French, the *redacteur* is the editor, and redaction has become a euphemism for the process of cutting or censoring a source or a text. Eckert's 42-page summary, based on selections, cuts and interpretations as he saw fit, sought to defuse the controversy surrounding the December 2010 situation. Garcia resigned his position as chair of the investigatory chamber in December 2014, lambasting FIFA's "lack of leadership" and calling Eckert's judgements into question: "No principled approach", Garcia wrote, could justify Eckert's "edits, omissions and additions".

The structure and language of the Eckert statement repays close scrutiny. Almost a half of the report is devoted to a summary of FIFA decision-making processes, ethics procedures and a history and description of bidding processes. In his "main findings", Eckert presents comments bidder by bidder: Australia, Belgium/Holland, England, Japan, Korea, Qatar, Russia, the USA. The most controversial cases – Qatar and Russia – were buried in the body of the report, a convenient perk of the alphabet one might think, as Australia (a little over two pages) and England (a little over three pages) were reprimanded, Australia for inappropriate use of consultants and payments to Jack Warner the then-CONCACAF president, as well as money for "football development" in the countries of some ExCo members; and England for looking to gain the support of a FIFA vice president, Jack Warner again, and proffering "football development funds" to Oceania's then president, Reynald Temarii. Eckert added that "England 2018 accommodated, or at least attempted to satisfy, the improper requests" of ExCo members, "thereby jeopardising the integrity of the bidding process" (6.3.5: 24) though "to a rather limited extent". Eckert devotes a little over four pages to the Qatar case, confirming massive financial machinations between Qatari Mohamed Bin Hammam and two named figures, Jack Warner and Reynald Temarii. But it is noted by Eckert that Bin Hammam "did not have a formal role with any bid" (6.6.6: 28), however much he might have paid out to ensure that, for instance, Temarii remained ineligible to cast his ExCo vote, being already suspended for a year by the FIFA Ethics Committee. Eckert adds that even if Temarii had been able to cast his Oceania confederation's vote for England (2018) and Australia (2022) this would have made little difference, so "the occurrences presently relevant did not affect the outcome of the FIFA World Cup™ 2018/2022 bidding process as a whole" (6.6.6: 29). Meanwhile, Bin Hammam has been widely recognised for 20 years as one of the most effective deal-makers in world football (Sugden and Tomlinson 2003), the man who led "the most corrupt World Cup bidding contest in history" and brought the world's biggest single-sport event to his desert nation as he moved "through the corridors of world football greasing palms and striking deals; revealing the ugly venality of the men who control the beautiful game" (Blake and Calvert 2015: 3). Sworn to silence by his superiors in his political class within Qatar, Bin Hammam's isolated existence in Doha is a silently echoing testimony to the corruption and betrayals of trust that Eckert's evasive and timid report seeks to deflect.

In a summarising comment in an earlier report on FIFA culpability in relation to financial scandals concerning ISL and unofficial payments to then president Havelange, Judge Eckert concluded that the "conduct of President Blatter may have been clumsy because there could be an internal need for clarification, but this does not lead to any criminal or ethical misconduct" (statement dated 29 April 2013, section II: 5). Clumsy Blatter then, but not culpable; nor, one might add, particularly capable. Eighteen months later in his statement on Garcia's report on the Qatar/Russia World Cup decisions, Judge Eckert himself was looking clumsy in defence of the indefensible. Actions can be seen in numerous cases, he reported – with the innocent exception of the Belgium/Netherlands bid – to have jeopardized, damaged or undermined the credibility and integrity of the bidding process; but only to some or a limited extent, and none serious enough that they could be seen as "suited to compromise the integrity of the FIFA World Cup™ 2018/2022 bidding process as a whole" (6.8.5: 34), Eckert's mantra for letting any suspected nation off the hook. Letting all of the bidding nations off with a slap on the wrists – but not even a slap for Russia in response to its declared prompt efficiency in disposing of paperwork and leased computers said then to have been destroyed by their owners, and claiming to have unsuccessfully approached Google for access to email accounts – he could comment in his "overall assessment of the findings" contained in the Garcia report that:

> As regards the procedural framework for conducting bidding procedures related to awarding the hosts of the final competitions of FIFA World Cups™, the Investigatory Chamber of the FIFA Ethics Committee did not find any violations or breaches of the relevant rules and regulations. The Chairman of the Adjudicatory Chamber of the FIFA Ethics Committee fully concurs with this finding.
>
> *(8.2: 40 of Eckert statement, November 13 2014)*

A concurrence that was not reciprocated by a furious and soon-to-resign Garcia. And as this chapter was being written, it was widely believed in the networks of the football business that a dedicated team within the home of FIFA was hard at work redacting the Garcia report in minute detail, ready for its "full" publication. The internal FIFA processes that generated the Garcia report and the Eckert whitewash are yet another example of the toothlessness or inherent collusiveness of FIFA's ethical processes. Eckert even credited (p. 34) Blatter with enabling the Ethics Committee's Investigatory Chamber, in 2012 reforms, to conduct the inquiry; and is praised for FIFA's cooperation throughout the investigation. Eckert concludes that "it must be made clear that President Blatter did not violate the FCE [FIFA Code of Ethics]" (p. 34). The bidding processes should be improved, he added, guaranteeing more transparency based in term limits for ExCo members, recusal of ExCo members in votes for their own nations, a rotation system, independent expert bid evaluation and enhanced reporting requirements. This is quite a list for reform of the process; Blatter was, as "the leader of FIFA", called upon to address these recommendations. But, though Eckert implied that the chair of the ExCo should have made ExCo members' obligations "more explicit", Blatter was presented as essentially blameless for any flaws and failings in the process.

The ExCo move against Blatter[3]

Thirteen years before the FBI swoop to round up the FIFA 14 at their luxury hotel in Zurich, 11 complainants (almost half of the 24 members of the FIFA Executive Committee) looked to start legal proceedings against Blatter. In May 2002, signing up to documentation delivered to the Public Prosecutor's office in Zurich by lawyer Professor Dr Rainer Schumacher, they generated a document, dated 10 May, that amounted to an accusation of extensive criminal conduct by Blatter in relation to his position as FIFA president. The complainants included Swedish UEFA president Lennart Johansson, AFC president Dr Mong Joon Chung from Korea, and Cameroonian Issa Hayatou, the president of CAF – the presidents of the three largest continental confederations, all three holding Vice-Presidential positions on the ExCo. So the senior figures in this group of 11 represented, in their positions within FIFA and the confederations, close to 150 of the national associations constituting the membership of FIFA, considerably more than the two-thirds (130) of the electorate that would be required to oust a FIFA president in a vote in Congress. The signatories included two further Vice-Presidents of the Committee, lawyer David Will from Scotland, and industrialist Antonio Matarrese from Rome, Italy. This group granted powers of attorney to Schumacher to "file the present criminal complaint". Schumacher also noted that the basement of FIFA's Pilatus Building in Zurich, where the organisation's "archive is to be found", had recently been rendered inaccessible by the instructions of FIFA's Finance Director Urs Linsi to change the locks, "so that the files are not currently accessible".

The ISL/ISMM Group, based in the canton of Zug, had gone bankrupt in May 2001; and the Kirch Group, Munich, had collapsed earlier in 2002. These circumstances, the complaint claims, rendered FIFA's financial situation "totally impenetrable". They were the companies that were handling the marketing rights for the 2002 and 2006 World Cups. In what is called the "initial situation", "the Accused [Blatter] was practising favouritism with FIFA assets in order to build up an autocratic power base (which is contrary to the Statutes) and in order to secure his re-election on 29 May 2002". FIFA was hovering on the edge of bankruptcy and the "FIFA Executive Committee's requests for information were either ignored or put off or fobbed off with global statements to the effect that FIFA was in perfect financial health".

Blatter, the case argues with detailed reference to FIFA's statutes, "cannot take any presidential decisions. Under the FIFA Statutes, he does not possess any presidential decision-making powers". Such powers lie, "to a very great extent", with the ExCo, "the executive body of FIFA; and the Congress (comprising a representative of each member national association) is the 'supreme authority' of the organisation, also having 'financial sovereignty'".

Having described the initial situation, the document proceeded to document Blatter's weaving elusiveness when asked by the ExCo to account for the financial situation. "Constant stalling and vanishing tactics" increased "the mistrust of numerous members of the Executive Committee," and initially 13 of its members resolved to act, calling for an extraordinary meeting of the committee in order to appoint an ad hoc committee "to audit FIFA's financial situation". Blatter, with no right so to do, ordered the "suspension of this internal audit committee (IAC)" in April 2002. That committee had been planning to interview, as part of the audit, both Linsi the financial director, and Zen Ruffinen the general secretary. Blatter's illegitimate move to "suspend" the work of the IAC therefore had, it was alleged, "the aim of *keeping secret* the financial situation of FIFA and his own financial machinations".

The Criminal Complaint went on to catalogue a range of financial irregularities and structural dysfunctions (Tomlinson 2014: 139): payment to individuals for bogus services for vague and unspecified work; the buying of information that could compromise critics or opponents;

support for lobbying of national associations or campaigning for FIFA elections; contracts gifted to FIFA committee members or favoured partners; debt clearance for some confederations and individuals; and payments without explanation or rationale to national associations. Three weeks later, Blatter was re-elected, 139 votes to 56, an increase on his majority in 1998 when he gained 111 to Johansson's 80. The Criminal Complaint was supported by documentation including a report, by the then-General Secretary Michel Zen-Ruffinen, that had been presented to the FIFA ExCo. In essence, the documentation accused FIFA's president of dishonest management and breach of trust, citing appropriate articles/clauses of the Swiss Criminal Code. In paragraph 25 of the documentation, the general case against Blatter is clearly stated:

> On the basis of the available information and documents, there is a pressing suspicion that the Accused misused FIFA assets entrusted to his care for the benefit of third parties and thereby for his own benefit, in order to consolidate his personal position of power. The Accused is campaigning for re-election as FIFA President. Considerable financial emoluments are associated with this position, so that the unlawful enrichment of third parties also directly served the unlawful enrichment of the Accused himself.

In a nutshell, then, the Criminal Complaint states the case against Blatter. This was in May 2002, when FIFA finances looked to be on the verge of bankruptcy, when KPMG auditors had actually questioned the veracity of financial reporting on income and assets, when Blatter had not yet seen through the first cycle of his presidential tenures. Criminal mismanagement of another's resources; unlawful use and/or misappropriation of another's assets; the Criminal Complaint brought the weight of the Swiss Criminal Code to bear in the case against Blatter. But at the FIFA Congress in Seoul, South Korea, at the end of that month, the FIFA Congress re-elected Blatter as President, when he gained 139 votes against the 56 votes received by CAF's candidate Issa Hayatou. Blatter deflected the biggest systematic internal challenge to his authority, confirming the magic formula of power-broking and power-keeping in FIFA: keep your core constituency – for Blatter, in particular the national associations far from the heart of UEFA's power in Western Europe happy in one-to-one relationships of patronage and mutual flattery, and the internecine conflicts of central FIFA committees could remain a mere sideshow. General Secretray Zen-Ruffinen, who had drawn up much of the evidence for the Criminal Complaint, was soon off the FIFA payroll, consigned to paid-off silence and an uncertain professional future.

Concluding thoughts: making sense of the FIFA story

Backpedalling through the contemporary history of FIFA politics in the four analytical vignettes above confirms the hold that the Havelange/Blatter dynasty has had on the governing body of world football. In 2015 Blatter had never been so vulnerable but he nevertheless mustered the loyal votes that would win the presidential election. The Eckert report on the 2018 and 2022 hosting decisions was released at the end of 2014, and wholly cleared Blatter of the responsibility for malpractices in or maladministration of the bidding process for World Cups. The malleability of the ethics processes could also be seen in the astounding silences surrounding the place of ExCo member Vitaly Mutko in the successful Russian bid. And back in 2002 we'd seen how Blatter could deflect an opposition that started out as a majority of the ExCo, simultaneously mobilising his worldwide powerbase to retain the presidency.

At the end of Blatter's career, though, the watching and waiting world was debating the key question of whether FIFA could accomplish meaningful reform from within or whether its future credibility rested on the reform of the organisation by an external body. Transparency International called, in a press release dated 6 August 2015, for the formation of an Independent Reform Commission (IRC) chaired by "a person of high standing such as a former leader of an international organization or a judicial figure of repute". This chair and his/her commission would be tasked to review FIFA's governance structure, "review and develop the Statutes and Codes of FIFA", propose anti-corruption measures, and review the criteria for the bidding, awarding and hosting processes for major FIFA events. A few days later, on 11 August, FIFA announced the membership of its "2016 Reform Committee". To be chaired by Dr François Carrard, who had coordinated the IOC 2000 Reform Commission, it comprised two members from each of the six confederations, and two representatives of FIFA's commercial partners. Carrard planned too to add an advisory board of representatives from outside football "to sup-port the work of the committee and provide an additional layer of independent expertise". NewFIFANow labeled this, the following day, "a busted flush before it meets", just another group of "sporting insiders"; it re-iterated its call for a wholly independent reform process with no "FIFA, football and sports insiders", for independent governance reform by "the European Parliament, the International Trade Union Federation, Transparency International, Avaaz and three of FIFA's sponsors, Coca-Cola, VISA and McDonald's". The credibility of FIFA might just be restored by far-reaching internal reform and transparency, though FIFA and comparable bodies have shown on many occasions how they can survive the storms of external critique. Much would depend on whether any further time-bomb such as the indictment of the FIFA14 in May 2015 would disrupt the plans and processes put in place for both reform and the final departure of Blatter himself.

Illuminating and revelatory studies of the nature of FIFA's operation by investigative and specialist journalists (Jennings 2006; Yallop 1999; Vecsey 2014; Blake and Calvert 2015) and critical, analytical and sometimes investigative social scientists (Pielke 2013; Sugden and Tomlinson 1998, 1999 and 2003; Tomlinson 2014) have shown the ways in which the FIFA of Havelange and Blatter has been flawed, exploited for personal gain, and institutionally cor-rupted. Zimbalist (2015) has reaffirmed the economic idiocies underlying the plans of those looking to do much of FIFA's work for it, in staging the events. It remains remarkable that in this context Blatter could still, in mid-2015, be at the helm of the organisation, navigating an exit strategy designed to leave FIFA on his own terms, in the same year that the FIFA Museum in Zurich would open, no doubt a vanity project for the celebration of his own career contri-bution from 1975 to 2016.

To understand FIFA we must look closely at what it is, where it has come from, who is in it or wants to be in it and who controls its practices and processes; as we follow up such ques-tions we can produce illuminating knowledge on previously neglected institutions, practices and sets of cultural and ideological dynamics and relationships. There are other, theory-led approaches: these include locating FIFA in the globalizing process; assessing its contributions to international relations or global public diplomacy; considering it as a network of stakeholders; examining FIFA as a form of commodification of the popular; and interrogating FIFA's influ-ence as a non-state, supra-national body in relation to national governments and states. But first and foremost, FIFA is peopled, it is a constellation of human actors. Seeing who these actors are, how they operate within institutions and networks, is a critical starting point for understand-ing the internal politics of FIFA, and the contribution of FIFA to a wider politics of sport in a globalising world.

Acknowledgements

I am grateful to have had opportunities to present some of the material used in this chapter in presentations at SOAS, University of London, and in publications in *When Saturday Comes*.

Notes on sources

This chapter is based upon analysis of some documents that are not in the public domain, and upon extensive personal observation of FIFA's workings and processes over a period of 30 years. It is not, therefore, an orthodox academic analysis in terms of sources and citation. The Internet has made it increasingly possible to access FIFA documentation, but the sources informing this chapter may not be universally available. I have chosen therefore to describe such sources within the text, rather than list them definitively as references.

Notes

1 This section draws upon Alan Tomlinson, in *When Saturday Comes*.
2 This section is a reworked version of a blog essay.
3 This section draws upon Tomlinson 2014.

References

Blake, H. and Calvert, J. (2015) *The Ugly Game: The Qatari Plot to Buy the World Cup*. London: Simon and Schuster UK Ltd.

FIFA. (2009) Code of Ethics (http://law.marquette.edu/assets/sports-law/pdf/2012-conf-fifa-ethics.pdf). Accessed 8 March 2016.

Government of the Russian Federation. (2012) *Vitaly Mutko* (http://government.ru/en/gov/persons/17/events/). Accessed 8 March 2016.

Jennings, A. (2006) *Foul! The Secret World of FIFA: Bribes, Vote Rigging and Ticket Scandals*. London: Harper Sport.

Machiavelli, N. (2005) *The Prince* (ed. W. J. Connell). Boston, MA: Bedford/St Martin's. (First distributed in 1513 but not officially published until 1532, five years after Machiavelli's death).

Pielke, R. (2013) How can FIFA be held accountable? *Sport Management Review*, 16(3): 255–267.

Sugden, J. and Tomlinson, A. (1998) *FIFA and the Contest for World Football: Who Rules the Peoples' Game?* Cambridge: Polity Press.

Sugden, J. and Tomlinson, A. (1999) *Great Balls of Fire: How Big Money is Hijacking World Football*. London and Edinburgh: Mainstream Publishing.

Sugden, J. and Tomlinson, A. (2003) *Badfellas: FIFA Family at War*. London and Edinburgh: Mainstream Publishing.

Tomlinson, A. (2014) *FIFA: The Men, the Myths and the Money*. Abingdon: Routledge.

Vecsey, G. (2014) *Eight World Cups: My Journey Through the Beauty and Dark Side of Soccer*. New York: Times Books/Henry Holt and Company.

Yallop, D. (1999) *How They Stole the Game*. London: Poetic Publishing.

Zimbalist, A. (2015) *Circus Maximus: The Gamble Behind Hosting the Olympics and the World Cup*. Washington, DC: Brookings Institution Press.

22

POLITICAL ISSUES IN INTERNATIONAL SPORT

Thomas Zeiler

One need only consider the Olympic Games to recognise the importance of the intimate links between sport and international politics (including diplomacy) over the past three-quarters of a century. The Berlin Games of 1936 featured controversy over race politics and strident Nazi propaganda (Keys 2006). Less remembered episodes that exemplify the Olympics as a stage for political expression include the 1992 Barcelona Games, when Spanish Basque separatists threatened violence, or when Aborigines peacefully demonstrated against discrimination at Sydney in 2000. The Athens Games of 2004 witnessed protests at the U.S. embassy against the war in Iraq, and the Beijing Olympics dealt with human rights complaints against bad working conditions in China, degradation of the environment, and treatment of political prisoners. When the torch was carried around the globe, activists campaigned against Chinese policies in Tibet and the arming of Sudanese government troops. Sadly, the spectre of international terrorism will likely hover over security preparations for Olympics for years to come, although these violent methods against the state have been around sports for decades (Houlihan 1994; Wedemeyer 1999). Just as infamously, Cold War tensions limited athletic competitions in 1980 and 1984. Terrorism rocked the 1972 spectacle in Munich, while civil rights came to the fore with the surfacing of Black Power salutes in Mexico City in 1968 (not to mention the decades-long ban on South African participation due to apartheid). Hovering over the Sochi Winter Games of 2014 was the invisible strong hand of Russian President Vladimir Putin and his seizure of Crimea, just after the event ended.

These Olympics' examples amply show that sport addresses even bigger themes of international politics, security, and diplomacy; scholars have used these intersections to illuminate regional, national, and global relations in the world arena (Andrews and Carrington 2013; Beacom 2012; Levermore and Budd 2004). Commentators have mined a rich trove of archives that reveal the linkages. And historians, having spent a few decades delving into the importance of the pluralism garnered by transnational actors – people, movements, firms, and non-governmental organisations – in shaping the global political environment, have also drawn on sport and sporting events as they analyse high politics, as well as the cultural, economic, and political interactions behind the headlines. The ample literature on sport and international politics also illustrates a reciprocal relationship, one that makes it hard to decipher the extent to which sport influences politics and vice versa.

The more significant point is that sport has been embraced by scholars as an expression of ideology, fears, desires, and policy preferences. International relations, in particular, can benefit from using sport as an empirical basis for testing theories that have been traditional foundations of the field. For instance, along the lines of idealist or realist paradigms, does sport serve the objectives of peace and reconciliation by engaging societies in either visionary hopes, or pragmatic processes, of promoting social justice and human rights? In short, sport is now considered an element of soft power that was, and is, reflective of – and, at times, even instrumental in – world affairs. Soft power implies that actors other than states determine policies; thus, does sport also relate to international relations theories of pluralism, in which transnationals, as well as governments, orchestrate decisions in global affairs? This is not to argue that sport has prompted international political policies, or that international politics depended on athletics to deal with incidents and tensions. Rather, sport serves as a window in which to view global politics, and, at times, exemplifies sentiments surrounding certain relations or circumstances between nations and blocs.

Politicisation of international sport

In fact, sport itself, particularly during the Cold War, reached its height of politicisation. Athletes and events were used by politicians to shape public opinion (both at home and abroad). The superpowers drew on sport as a means of public diplomacy and propaganda, that is, as a non-military cultural combat zone for their competing ideologies (Wagg and Andres 2007). Sport, then, serves as the terrain for expressing realist policy preferences, for testing the limits of rational but self-interested objectives in which winning (or putting on a good show) is equated with the successful wielding of power. Again, the Olympics serve as a good example, as attested to by the dramatic 1980 win by the American hockey team or the mutual boycotts of Olympic Games, first by the United States and a handful of other countries in the Moscow Summer Games of 1980, and the Soviets return of the favour in Los Angeles in 1984. Sport is certainly a brand of "soft power," but it had a powerful, nationalistic message, one hardened by politics and one reaching beyond a concern with ethics and cooperation, during the post-World War II era (Osgood 2006).

Although the linkage of sport to world politics can be overplayed in the media (the Chinese authorities, for instance, acted with impunity against potential human rights protests by arresting demonstrators but with feeble world outcry), the embedded tool of the Games as both a positive and negative agent in politics is clear. Lest the Olympics be deemed to have an adversarial role in diplomacy, the opening of United States–China relations through ping-pong competition is just one example of sport's salutary effect on international relations. Thus, liberalism (or idealism) applies to these instances. Sport has also led to economic development, while it has shone a spotlight on the universally constructive aspects of people-to-people and nation-to-nation contacts, although Marxist IR theory emphasises the exploitative and class-based pursuit of profit and hegemony inherent in these relationships. Note, for instance, the phenomenon of basketball star Michael Jordan's reach overseas in selling the Nike brand, as well as that of the Chicago Bulls and the National Basketball Association (LaFeber 1999). Solutions to deep-seated problems have been broached also by touring athletes and teams and investment abroad in sport development, to name just two aspects of sport as a mediation and promotional tool.

Indeed, while nations have interacted, transnational sport actors have intersected with global politics as carriers of national interests, though not always for good. That is, a pluralistic mix of official and non-state actors most often populate the ranks of decision makers in sports diplomacy. Former American professional basketball star Dennis Rodman was a case in point. Engaging in what some called basketball diplomacy, he visited the Democratic

People's Republic of Korea in February 2013, and then again in early 2014 with additional retired National Basketball Association players. The goal was seemingly to improve relations between the dictatorship and the outside world. His first visit occurred just weeks after North Korea tested its nuclear weaponry; the United States and the United Nations strongly condemned Pyongyang for such militarism. Rodman appeared with the new Supreme Leader, Kim Jong-Un, who embraced his effort to seek world acceptance of the rogue state. But when the unlikely sport diplomatic emissary agreed, at least initially, with North Korea that a detained American citizen was guilty of crimes against the state, and when he not only hugged Kim but also uttered several offensive and bizarre remarks, the mission collapsed. Nonetheless, Rodman was one in a long line of transnationals who leveraged sport in the political arena (Dichter and Johns 2014; Allison 1993).

Such personal contacts through a pluralistic policy structure have made sport a target of public diplomacy. The U.S. Department of State, as well as other nations' diplomatic agencies, has used sport figures as a means of facilitating an international political agenda. For example, the administration of President George W. Bush selected sports stars from baseball, basketball, and figure skating to serve as public diplomacy "envoys" to the world. This was one of just hundreds of instances in which, since World War II, athletes engaged in goodwill tours around the globe. Between 1945 and 1968, there were more than 500 such tours alone, which provide ample fodder for researching the connections between sports, politics, ideas, and societies. In addition, European nations engaged in football (soccer) or rugby matches to facilitate peaceful international relations (Beck 1999) to show sport's positive impact. Even enemy soldiers in World War I called a rather perverse truce from trench warfare to play a soccer game before the generals became concerned and ordered the men back to battle. Sport has been used more to try to avoid or ease conflict.

Sometimes, this effort to inject sports into politics has had salutary effects, other times not, as realists argue. Thus, it has called attention to South African apartheid, or in facilitating good relations – in a leftist application of realism – as in the case of the Chinese player losing purposely in badminton to an Indonesian in 1963 in order to encourage emerging nations (Downes 2014; Hong and Lu 2014). But the relationship of sports to global politics is more frequently decried than celebrated. Critics question whether sport benefits politics, and vice versa. Such a relationship is not often to our liking, for sport is viewed as a pleasurable aside to the real world. The negative manifestations are, nonetheless, prevalent enough even to violate the spirit of sport (Dichter 2014: 20). The relationship of the athletic field to national values and international machinations is often fraught with bad feelings and outcomes, the Olympics oftentimes having been the site of violence, big power politics, and political symbolism. Hard realism prevails. Thus, Dr Eric Williams, the Prime Minister of Trinidad, spoke volumes when he announced that "I do not like political interference in sport" (Downes 2014).

The clash of history and sport

Irrespective of opinions, politics do interfere in sport. After World War I, sport emerged as a means of expressing national values and policies in the international arena, and even as a way to trumpet political ideologies (Arnaud and Riordan 1998). Hitler's Berlin Olympics of 1936 offers a prime example of national manoeuvring. The liberal democratic United States and Great Britain pondered the dilemma of participating in Games in which fascist and communist dictatorships were present, as well as the problem of sending athletes to a blatantly politicised event. The Americans and the British pushed ideals of equality; the Nazis did not believe in such a universalistic principle but preferred to promote their own brand of racial superiority in which supposedly "inferior" Jews and blacks (both represented on the American team) were decidedly unwanted in Berlin. As both Germany and Italy advanced in their aggression in Europe and Africa in 1935–1936, vigorous debate ensued about whether democracies should forego the Olympics as a form of protest. Both nations staged boycott campaigns (more strident in the US than in Britain) and other protests, and some athletes attended the alternate liberal-leftist Olimpiada games in Barcelona, Spain. But the United States and Great Britain ultimately attended the Berlin Olympics, even though both knew that the event would be used to advance German political propaganda. Hitler managed to stay largely aloof at the Games, after some appearances, and the general lack of discrimination, the great feats of black athletes like Jesse Owens, and the magnificent facilities enhanced Germany's global image. As far as international propaganda, the Nazis came out looking supportive of the Olympic ideas; there was little Nazification of the Games, which most observers believed had embraced global rather than national values. Germany also emerged as a strong and dynamic nation, one that the democratic nations would continue to appease in the larger European political arena (Guttmann 1998; Holt 1998; Keys 2006).

As far as an ideological battleground, the 1936 Olympics showed the weakness of democracy, and the strength of fascism and communism. The British, in particular, were eager to avoid confrontation with Germany (and Italy); that would complicate running their far-flung empire in Asia. Appeasement was the rule, although as a founder of modern sport, they also made a valiant effort to uphold their principle of sportsmanship. For the Soviet Union, a country that disavowed both nationalism and competitiveness and which boycotted the 1936 Games but attended those in Barcelona, Hitler's Olympics provided an opportunity to issue calls for worker unity throughout Europe and the world against fascist tyranny. Thus, it was Moscow, ironically, that defended democracy in the face of Nazism and Italian fascism. But the Soviets also assaulted bourgeois liberalism as weak and backed the leftist Popular Front governments as the means of halting the spread of class enemies (Riordan and Kruger 1999; Parks 2007). The communist press led the charge in accusing Hitler of using the Olympics for propaganda purposes, a view espoused by many in France as well (Arnaud 1998). Germany effectively countered the charge. Peace and fulfillment of Olympic ideals, propagated by Leni Riefenstahl's famous film of the Games, rendered Nazi ideology as acceptable to the mainstream politicians and the Olympic movement itself.

The Nuremberg racial laws, World War II, and the Final Solution would, of course, give the lie to that false image, but sport provided a benign grandstand for the Nazis to regale the international community with their values of superiority (Kruger 1998). Yet so would the heavyweight boxing rematch between American champion Joe Louis and German Max Schmeling in 1938, a quick knockout victory for Louis. Still, Schmeling had issued Louis his first defeat, in 1936, just two months before the opening of the Berlin Summer Olympics. Americans, including President Franklin Roosevelt, fixated on the rematch. In what many viewed as a resounding victory not only for people of colour but for democracy, the second contest became legendary, even though Schmeling himself was never a Nazi (Erenberg 2006).

Cold War competition

The Olympics remained a focal point of international politics throughout the postwar period to the present, as well, and scholars have added in new elements into the discourse, such as concerns with race and gender. The superpower confrontation proved to be a catalyst to expressions of nationalism and ideologies, as the systems of the United States and Soviet Union were antithetical – or that is what propaganda on both sides claimed as both divided up the world. But importantly, and unlike in World War II, the Cold War did not engage these superpowers in direct, conventional battle; their surrogates did that in Korea, Vietnam, Afghanistan, and elsewhere. And sport, among other means of propaganda and diplomacy, served as a low-intensity (though emotional) means of manoeuvring, wrangling, and competing. In short, this was, in the words of George Orwell, "war minus the shooting" (Wagg and Andrews 2007: 1). A military conflict on the periphery, at its core the Cold War represented a realist ideological and cultural contest, a struggle between good and evil, and between capitalism and communism. With sport enjoying an international structure coming out of the World War – with the likes of the Olympics, FIFA's World Cup, and assorted world championships in various events – the superpowers (and their allies) would compete in highly symbolic, politically fraught competitions.

The symbolism could occur as much within each political bloc as between the two superpowers. For instance, France tried to maintain its grip on its empire after World War II by launching associative organisations to counter African independence movements. The All-African Games was one manifestation, designed to show the French bloc nations that they were part of a unified system that should not be completely autonomous (Charitas 2014). The Latin American pursuit of independence from the "colossus of the North," the United States, also used sport as a means of exhibiting its freedom and global stature. Thus, the Argentines under Juan Peron tried to attract the 1956 Olympics to Buenos Aires, recognising that he could project Argentina's image, through sport diplomacy, to its people and foreigners. The effort failed, but when his country beat the United States team in world basketball, he rejoiced that the victory did the work of one hundred ambassadors in showing his country's self-determination within the American security and economic system. In addition, Puerto Rico operated within the US political regime to carve out an identity, through the Central American and Caribbean Games of 1966, for its unique political system and to legitimise its own national role in the international sporting community (Sotomayor 2014). And when Cuba entered the Olympics, over the vehement opposition of Washington, DC, it thumbed its nose at the superpower, as well as striking a minor victory for communism.

Rivalry between supposed friendly, allied nations reached a peak (of brutality, for sure) in October 1956, when the USSR invaded Hungary to quell, quite savagely, a nationalist revolution against its rule. The next month, the Melbourne Olympics began, and the Hungarian team called attention to Soviet aggression. Once again, an Olympics venue showed the link between politics and sport, and between the realist assertion of interests and the field of play. In support, six nations eventually withdrew from the Games, while Hungarian athletes arriving in Australia were greeted by cheers from 500 expats (many of them former fascists who had fled Europe after the war) who denounced communism. Some athletes had actually fought against the Soviet incursion, while others wore black ribbons on their tracksuits. Some thought of defecting to the West. The water polo team famously decided to compete to defend its 1952 Olympic gold medal. The revolutionary fervor, and campaign of protest, carried over into the swimming pool as the team took on the Soviets in the finals round. Some 5,500 expats jammed the arena; signs urged the swimmers to remain in Australia. Within a minute of the opening whistle, a Russian viciously grabbed a Hungarian swimmer and went to the penalty box among catcalls from the crowd. Hungarian spectators and officials yelled abuse at the Russians throughout the contest, which was also accompanied by fistfights. Athletes focused on the opposition rather than the ball. Blood flowed in the pool, and the partisan crowd so worried officials that police were called to counter a possible riot. The game ended in victory for Hungary, and Olympic authorities played down the grudge match as an aberration to the overall positive spirit of the Games. But nobody could ignore the fact that some 200 athletes from Hungary,

Czechoslovakia, and Yugoslavia decided to defect to the West, including eight of the eleven members of the water polo team. As historian Robert Rinehart has explained, the victory served as a potent symbolic gesture for a nation being crushed by the militarily superior Soviet Union, a sign – a cultural icon referred to in decades to come – of grassroots resistance within the communist bloc to callousness and anti-democratic force (Rinehart 2007).

Of course, the water polo incident was not the only moment of Cold War representation in international sport in general. Basketball rivalry between the Soviets and Americans became intense, especially after the controversial Soviet victory in the gold-medal game in 1976. Ice hockey matches took on a new intensity, and not only between Americans and Soviets (the 1980 "miracle on ice" ramped up American nationalist pride). When Canadians and Russians squared off in the fierce 1972 Summit Series – according to Canada, a contest between capitalist democracy and communist totalitarians – the Canadians sought not to define their role in the Cold War but to shape their very national identity through the sport they invented (Scherer *et al.* 2007; McDonald 2007). Thus, Cold War ideology and conflict surfaced in events beyond bilateral, US–USSR matches. The British, for one, saw their history of imperial strength and notion of athletic amateurism fall to the wayside in the face of American and Soviet determination to dominate the Olympics through scientific training and an ethic of winning at all cost. Communist bloc athletes became notorious for drug use to the extent that there was a "muscle gap" to go with the supposed "missile gap" of the late 1950s that seemed to signal Soviet ascendance at the expense of American weakness (Montez de Oca 2007). Still, all nations, including the United States and Britain, resorted to steroids for their athletes. There was no clear moral champion in the Cold War-era Olympics.

Liberal idealism did not lose out across the board, however. No doubt, facilitated by sport, positive progress occurred in international relations during the period. In Asia, sport was a venue for diplomats to signal intentions. So-called "ping-pong diplomacy" was one notable case, in which the Chinese team invited the American squad to Beijing for a friendly tournament that indicated the Communist Party's willingness to engage in détente with Washington after over two decades of hostility between the two nations. The Olympic movement also served as a forum for complex negotiations between the Republic of China and the communist People's Republic of China (PRC) after the former nationalist government had fled to Taiwan. Both sides could "talk" to each other at the Olympics, even though both were sworn to silence and hatred. And when recognition of "Red" China finally ended the two-China policy in the 1970s, the Olympics became a venue to debate the identity of both nations (PRC and Chinese Taipei). Undoubtedly, Olympic officials tried to whitewash the effort by insisting that the Games did not mix with politics, but, in this case, at least the two sides used the quadrennial event to come to an understanding on names (Brownell 2007). Additional examples of affirmative politics through sport included FIFA officials, who, like Olympic authorities, frowned on mixing sport and politics. Despite such official opposition, the emergence of independent Asian and African nations in the 1950s and 1960s formed a bloc of opinion on issues ranging from South African apartheid to addressing the place of Israel in the Middle East that, at least, provoked dialogue among the press and publics worldwide (Murray 1999).

Soft power

The interaction of sport and politics on the international scene is also not limited to Big Power diplomatic relations but encompasses societal identities, pressures, and contacts as well. Religious views and values have been at the centre of India–Pakistan cricket matches, but cricket diplomacy has also been used by leaders of both countries (such as visits to India by Pakistani General

Zia Ul-Haq in 1987 and General Pervez Musharraf in 2005) to smooth relations and ease a half-century of hostility (though not always with success). The infamous "soccer war" between Honduras and El Salvador in 1969 was the culmination of bilateral tensions, but also spurred by transnational migration across the borders by workers seeking employment that prompted the entry of immigration into politics.

Gender and sexuality are cases that have also given rise to substantial scholarship, and especially the application of feminist theory to sport. Gender disputes, and the issue of homosexuality, have entered the sporting arenas in nations as well as globally (Muller 1999; Kruger 1999). Regarding gender, cultural norms and societal customs have run up against traditional notions of women, across all regions, that have a bearing on politics. For instance, in the 2012 London Olympics, five Muslim women competed, and Saudi Arabia, Qatar, and Brunei entered female athletes for the first time in history. Talk of headscarves injected political, social, and cultural norms into the Games, and certainly had an impact on cultural relations between nations in the Middle East region, not to mention reshaping perceptions in the West. After all, just eight years before, at the Athens Summer Olympics, over twenty countries sent no female athletes, of which about half were Muslim countries. Surely, women's issues and the diversity in the treatment of women across cultures affect the status of certain countries in the grand enterprise of modernisation, and even the aid given to them by the rich powers. That is, gender shapes political discourse that is then reflected abroad. Society matters in international relations, even if such debates over male domination and female subordination remain rather ritualised. International leadership for women depends, in part, on sport (among other institutions) to provide positions for females that will possibly ease discrimination, patriarchy, violence, and poverty worldwide.

The issue of gender speaks to the "soft power" of sport to address, and in cases, transform international politics. Race is often cited by liberal pluralists as a major factor at world sporting events, and as the battle over apartheid revealed (as well as the black nationalist movement of the 1960s), racial politics shaped public perceptions of the Olympics, and still does. The topic has flourished, as scholars increasingly view sport in terms of Western multiculturalism and politics at the international level, and highlight, for instance, the cultural politics involved in the so-called black diaspora of the past century (Carrington 2010). Pressure through sport on the racial divide did affect the Games; for instance, the Soviet Union tried to add African nations to the International Olympic Committee in the 1960s but failed due to the resistance of Secretary Avery Brundage. American racial discrimination was also contested on global playing fields, but perhaps more important was the perception of racism from abroad that prompted Cold War presidents to show that the United States was working on the problem. Thus, goodwill tours by black athletes were prevalent, even as conservatives confiscated passports of militants and the government denounced black nationalists and the Muslim Brotherhood (Thomas 2007; Parks 2014).

In addition, the history of the United States also reveals that race in sport illuminates the intersections of domestic and international politics. That is, because athletics reaches deeply into national cultures and transcends international boundaries, they can transcend mere sport, acting as a gauge of domestic society and global affairs. A prime example arises with Jackie Robinson, the baseball player who broke the colour barrier in America's so-called national pastime in 1947. Robinson was already a famed college and amateur athlete and had served in the U.S. Army in World War II, but when race combined with politics and foreign policy to shape the postwar era of baseball – itself steeped in the Cold War – he achieved iconic status. One of the interconnections was his appearance before the House of Representatives' Committee on Un-American Activities (HUAC) to counter the pro-communist remarks of the famous black singer and leftwing activist, Paul Robeson. It is a revealing example involving race, United States' domestic politics, and the Cold War (and also addresses the aforementioned ideological contest between the superpowers), whereby a baseball figure is used as a means of challenging the dangers of communism, linking the national pastime to international politics.

In July 1949, the famous Robeson questioned whether blacks would participate in a war against the Soviet Union. Robeson was a high-profile spokesman for human rights who had stridently condemned imperialism in Africa and the profound segregationist policies of his own nation during the 1920s and 1930s (and who also supported Robinson's efforts to integrate baseball). Robeson's embrace of Moscow during the height of the Cold War converted him from being a crusader against fascism to a prime suspect of HUAC. His unrestrained statements in praise of the Soviet Union, condemnation of American racial policies, and belief that pressure from abroad would help end Jim Crow at home merged in a speech in Paris, in April 1949, before 2,000 delegates to the Congress of World Partisans of Peace, remarks remarkable for their strident tone, and the publicity they provoked. HUAC, which had long investigated communist subversives and spies in American society and government, called upon the pillar of the black community, Jackie Robinson, for a rebuttal. He had broken the colour barrier in the national pastime with dignity (thus he was acceptable to white America) and was a relatively conservative, religious, married black man with a military record. Robinson, therefore, was a perfect representative of the "American way of life" and of the success of democracy in the country during the ideologically charged early Cold War, a conflict that had become ever more tense due to the Berlin airlift and a divided Germany, the creation of the NATO alliance, and, just after his appearance before HUAC, the exploding of a Soviet atomic bomb and communist victory in China.

The Cold War was an ideological as much as security battle, and baseball played its part. The Soviets, for instance, claimed that American players had no rights and could be bought and sold like slaves, in the capitalist marketplace of the Major Leagues. Americans countered that baseball helped combat socialistic ideology and indoctrinated young men in the American way of life. That went for watching baseball, as well as playing it, especially in Little League (which, with its Pledge to trust in God and country, displayed the ideals of Americanism for the world to see). The Robinson–Robeson episode is also instructive for revealing the complexities of race in the United States and beyond. Black opinion was complicated by the Left's support for African American economic and civil rights throughout the 1930s, and beyond. For instance, while some African Americans welcomed efforts by the American Communist Party on civil rights and economic aid, the same people were also not necessarily opposed to capitalism or patriotism. By the time of Robinson's HUAC appearance, the Cold War had magnified the supposed heresies of the Left, thus compelling blacks, like other citizens, to take sides in the ideological struggle between capitalism and Marxism. Anti-communist "Red Scare" hysteria and red-baiting had polarised Americans, but also marginalised those who seemed to undermine Americanism. Radicalism was suppressed, and Robinson made it clear in carefully scripted remarks that appeared on the front page of the *New York Times* on 19 July 1949 that he favoured moderation. The episode was another instance of the importance of the domestic roots of foreign policy, a topic of great interest to scholars of sport.

This was by no means the only time baseball functioned as both a conduit of foreign policy and a reflection of American values abroad, a fact that makes the sport a key candidate for exploring international politics. For instance, baseball has engaged in a robust regime of world tours going back to 1874 (to England), 1889 (around the globe), and to Asia (1913) that carried American messages abroad. In the 1889 world tour – a precursor to informal empire – American players and executives perceived racial and ethnic linkages between themselves and Australians, helped ease nineteenth-century Anglophobia by playing matches throughout Great Britain to wide acclaim, and learned of the poverty wrought by British and French imperialism in the Middle East (Zeiler 2006). Some have argued that baseball actually abetted imperialism, and most recently represented U.S. national security policy, by promoting the American dream and way abroad through its intimate relationship with conservative, nationalistic dogma (Elias 2010). Baseball toed (and still does) the government line of jingoistic patriotism, get-tough foreign policies, the self-interested commodification of the sport, and the hegemonic lure of the best foreign players to American shores. Some scholars have linked the game to the Cold War by showing how it was followed by the U.S. Armed Forces around the world on radio, as it remained a source of American identity (Tygiel 2000). Baseball and diplomacy merged also in the goodwill missions that have continued every other year to Japan, and have been reciprocated by Japanese college teams ever since the early twentieth century. That country actually has been a target of American cultural commingling; Japan's nineteenth-century modernisation project was aided by baseball contacts with Americans, who brought with them new ideas and practices. Baseball was also a source of post-World War II reconciliation between two enemies (Guthrie-Shimizu 2012).

The focus on baseball should not detract from the notion that many sports were politicised in the international arena in some way, at some point. Scholars have opened up a host of topics that previously lay buried under a static foreign policy research agenda (or fixation on sports heroics and games themselves) that did not include sport as an important element in international politics and security. It is clear, however, that the intersection of sport and diplomacy has long existed, and furthermore, that linkage reflects on theories of pluralism, idealism, and realism (among other IR models). While sport might not cause international tensions, it has been a forum for playing out diplomatic issues in cooperative or conflicting ways. This will remain the case in the current century as it was in previous ones; researchers will discover new linkages of sport to the many aspects of international relations, including security, culture, politics, and economics. And spectators will note that the meetings of athletes around the world, on fields and in arenas, are tied to the policies of nations and organisations, which themselves possess larger global political purposes.

References

Allison, L. (1993) (ed) *The Changing Politics of Sport*. Manchester: Manchester University Press.

Andrews, D.L. and Carrington, B. (2013) (eds.) *A Companion to Sport*. Malden, MA: Wiley-Blackwell.

Arnaud, P. (1998) 'French sport and the emergence of authoritarian regimes, 1919–1939'. In P. Arnaud and J. Riordan (eds) *Sport and International Politics*. London: Taylor and Francis, pp. 114–146.

Arnaud, P. and Riordan, J. (eds) (1998) *Sport and International Politics*. London: Taylor and Francis.

Beacom, A. (2012) *International Diplomacy and the Olympic Movement: The New Mediators*. New York: Palgrave Macmillan.

Beck, P. (1999) *Scoring for Britain: International Football and International Politics, 1900–1939*. London: Frank Cass.

Brownell, S. (2007) '"Sport and politics don't mix": China's relationship with the IOC during the Cold War'. In S. Wagg and D.L. Andrews (eds) *East Plays West*. London: Routledge, pp. 253–271.

Carrington, B. (2010) *Race, Sport, and Politics: The Sporting Black Diaspora*. Thousand Oaks, CA: SAGE Publications.

Charitas, P. (2014) 'A postcolonial sport as French international diplomacy (1945–1966)'. In H.L. Dichter and A.L. Johns (eds) *Diplomatic Games: Sport, Statecraft, and International Relations Since 1945*. Lexington, KY: University of Kentucky Press, pp. 183–214.

Dichter, H.L. (2014) '"A game of political ice hockey": NATO restrictions on east German sport travel in the aftermath of the Berlin Wall'. In H.L. Dichter and A.L. Johns (eds) *Diplomatic Games: Sport, Statecraft, and International Relations Since 1945*. Lexington, KY: University of Kentucky Press, pp. 19–51.

Dichter, L. and Johns, A.L. (eds) *Diplomatic Games: Sport, Statecraft, and International Relations Since 1945*. Lexington, KY: University of Kentucky Press.

Downes, A.D. (2014) 'Forging Africa-Caribbean solidarity within the Commonwealth?: Sport and diplomacy during the anti-apartheid campaign'. In H.L. Dichter and A.L. Johns (eds.) *Diplomatic Games: Sport, Statecraft, and International Relations Since 1945*. Lexington, KY: University of Kentucky Press, pp. 117–149.

Elias, R. (2010) *The Empire Strikes Out: How Baseball Sold U.S. Foreign Policy and Promoted the American Was Abroad*. New York: The New Press.

Erenberg, L. (2006) *The Greatest Fight of Our Generation: Louis vs. Schmeling*. New York: Oxford University Press.

Guthrie-Shimizu, S. (2012) *Transpacific Field of Dreams: How Baseball Linked the United States and Japan in Peace and War*. Chapel Hill, NC: University of North Carolina Press.

Guttmann, A. (1998) 'The "Nazi Olympics" and the American Boycott Controversy'. In P. Arnaud and J. Riordan (eds) *Sport and International Politics*. London and New York: Routledge, pp. 31–50.

Holt, R. (1998) 'The Foreign Office and the Football Association: British sport and appeasement'. In Pierre Arnaud and J. Riordan (eds.) *Sport and International Politics*. London and New York: Routledge, pp. 51–66.

Hong, F. and Lu, Z. (2014) 'Politics first, competition second: Sport and China's foreign diplomacy in the 1960s and 1970s'. In A.L. Johns (eds) *Diplomatic Games: Sport, Statecraft, and International Relations Since 1945*. Lexington, KY: University of Kentucky Press, pp. 385–407.

Houlihan, B. (1994) *Sport and International Politics*. New York: Harvester Wheatsheaf.

Keys, B. (2006) *Globalizing Sport: National Rivalry and International Community in the 1930s*. Cambridge, MA: Harvard University Press.

Kruger, A. (1998) 'The role of sport in German international politics, 1918–1945'. In P. Arnaud and J. Riordan (eds) *Sport and International Politics*. London: Taylor and Francis, pp. 79–96.

Kruger, A. (1999) 'The homosexual and homoerotic in sport'. In J. Riordan and A. Kruger (eds) *The International Politics of Sport in the Twentieth Century*. London: E and FN Spon, pp. 191–216.

LaFeber, W. (1999) *Michael Jordan and the New Global Capitalism*. New York: W.W. Norton.

Levermore, R. and Budd, A. (eds) (2004) *Sport and International Relations: An Emerging Relationship*. London: Routledge.

McDonald, M.G. (2007) '"Miraculous" masculinity meets militarization: Narrating the 1980 USSR-US men's Olympic ice hockey match and Cold War politics'. In S. Wagg and D.L Andrews (eds) *East Plays West*. London: Routledge, pp. 222–234.

Montez de Oca, J. (2007) 'The "muscle gap": Physical education and US fears of a depleted masculinity, 1954-1963'. In S. Wagg and D.L Andrews (eds) *East Plays West*. London: Routledge, pp. 123–148.

Muller, A. (1999) 'Women in sport and society'. In J. Riordan and A. Kruger (eds) *The International Politics of Sport*. London: E and FN Spon, pp. 121–149.

Murray, B. (1999) 'FIFA'. In J. Riordan and A. Kruger (eds.) *The International Politics of Sport*. London: E and FN Spon, pp. 28–47.

Osgood, K. (2006) *Total Cold War: Eisenhower's Secret Propaganda Battle at Home and Abroad*. Lawrence, KS: University Press of Kansas.

Parks, J. (2007) 'Verbal gymnastics: Sports, bureaucracy, and the Soviet Union's entrance into the Olympic Games, 1946–1952'. In S. Wagg and D.L Andrews (eds) *East Plays West*. London: Routledge, pp. 27–44.

Parks, J. (2014) 'Welcoming the "Third World": Soviet sports diplomacy, developing nations and the Olympic Games'. In H.L. Dichter and A.L. Johns (eds) *Diplomatic Games: Sport, Statecraft, and International Relations Since 1945*. Lexington, KY: University of Kentucky Press, pp. 85–114.

Rinehart, R.E. (2007) 'Exploiting a new generation: Corporate branding and the co-optation of action sport'. In Michael D. Guardian and Michele K. Donnelly, (eds) *Youth Culture and Sport: Identity, Power, and Politics*. New York: Routledge, pp. 71–90.

Riordan, J. and Kruger, A. (1999) (eds) *The International Politics of Sport in the Twentieth Century*. London: E and FN Spon.

Scherer, J., Duquette, G.H. and Mason, D.S. (2007) 'The Cold War and the (re)articulation of Canadian national identity: The 1972 Canada-USSR summit series'. In S. Wagg and D.L. Andrews (eds) *East Plays West*. London: Routledge, pp. 163–186.

Sotomayor, A. (2014) 'The Cold War Games of a colonial Latin American nation: San Juan, Puerto Rico, 1966'. In H.L. Dichter and A.L. Johns (eds) *Diplomatic Games: Sport, Statecraft, and International Relations Since 1945*. Lexington, KY: University of Kentucky Press, pp. 217–249.

Thomas, D.L. (2007) 'Playing the "race card": US foreign policy and the integration of sports'. In S. Wagg and D.L Andrews (eds) *East Plays West*. London: Routledge, pp. 207–221.

Tygiel, J. (2000) *Past Time: Baseball as History*. New York: Oxford University Press.

Wagg, S. and Andrews, D.L. (2007) (eds) *East Plays West: Sport and the Cold War*. London: Routledge.

Wedemeyer, B. (1999) 'Sport and terrorism'. In J. Riordan and A. Kruger (eds) *The International Politics of Sport in the Twentieth Century*. London: E and FN Spon, pp. 217–233.

Zeiler, T.W. (2006) *Ambassadors in Pinstripes: The Spalding World Baseball Tour and the Birth of the American Empire*. Lanham, MD: Rowman and Littlefield.

23

WESTERN MILITARISM AND THE POLITICAL UTILITY OF SPORT

John Kelly

Introduction

The historical connections between sport and the military are well established (Mangan 1981, 1998; Holt 1995; Mason and Rieda 2010) with self-defence (and physical attack) and military preparedness featuring in the formation or development of numerous sports: archery, biathlon, boxing, cross-country skiing, martial arts and shooting being obvious examples. Additionally, the inculcation of militaristic values in state schools through the teaching of physical training and subsequently physical education in various parts of the world has been charted (Hargreaves 1986; Mason 1988; Holt 1989) along with the intersection of military and sporting metaphors in media commentary (King 2008; Jenkins 2013). While these aspects of the sport–military nexus are fascinating and significant, revealing the often banal and latent military values embedded in culture and individuals through sport (as well as *in* sport) – such as sacrifice, duty, physical action, competitiveness, nationalism and sex segregation – this chapter focuses on military–civil relations and sport rather than the militarism of sports per se. It illustrates how sport has become one of a multitude of cultural practices employed in normalising, legitimising, endorsing and venerating militarism in general and Western state militarism in particular. It is argued that in so doing, the ideological and political justifications/excuses for acts of military violence are irrevocably mired in the sacred traditions of nations, with sport representing one of the most prominent and potent sites for performing such ideological work given its dual role as a floating signifier of national sentiment and an apolitical arena of untainted, virtuous commodified spectacle. This potent combination helps neuter political opposition to Western militaristic violence while appearing, on the surface at least, to reinforce some degree of apparent public support.[1]

Using sport for such propagandising is hardly a recent phenomenon of course. When I ask students to select examples of sport being used as a tool for political propaganda they often begin with Hitler and the 1936 Berlin Games. Sometimes they mention the old Soviet bloc's use of sport to promote communism. When Britain, the United States or one of their allies is acknowledged acting politically, it is often more virtuous[2] forms of political action such as in relation to Mexico 1968 or Moscow 1980 that are noted. The (real or perceived) deviant political use of sport by the national-political *other* is effortlessly illustrated in comparison to the apparently more permissible examples from the West. This chapter turns attention to the

277

West, specifically Anglo-American countries, focusing on military–civil relations and sport in the broader political context of the post-2001 American-led "war on terror".

Military–civil relations and sport

An established body of work exists detailing the increasing connections between the military and civil society (Denzin 2004; Giroux 2004, 2008; Woodward 2005; Gee 2014; Basham *et al.* 2015; Danilova 2015) and a growing number of authors are discussing sport's increasing presence within this conjunction (Jansen and Sabo 1994; Silk and Falcous 2005; Butterworth 2005, 2008, 2010, forthcoming; Stempel 2006; King 2008; Scherer and Koch 2010; Kelly 2012; Jenkins 2013). What is apparent is that since the post-September 11 2001 invasions/liberations of Afghanistan and Iraq and the subsequent American-led "war on terror", various Western allied countries have witnessed a multi-agency series of events placing nation-state and Western militarism at the centre of cultural and civic society in ways that enable and encourage public engagement and national support of both nation-state and state militarism.

The chapter articulates the convergence of the political system (state governance, policy, legal framework) and politics (seeking to establish ideological authority) with civil society and the manufacturing of public consent. In particular, it discusses how this political work is often done in the cultural sphere (as Andrews also demonstrates in this collection). The chapter is necessarily limited in scope, given that a variety of theoretical topics could be discussed in relation to the sport–military nexus. For instance, social class, gender and sexuality all promise potentially rich, important and overlapping insights.[3] But this chapter places primacy on the issue of ideological support for actors who conduct violence, rendering issues such as whether or not the actor is working class, female or gay discussions for elsewhere. The chapter illustrates how, in conjunction with a number of other highly valued cultural activities and symbolic goods, sport is incorporated into providing militarism with a platform enabling governments and militarists to "incorporate us by proxy" (Kelly 2012) into supporting (or appearing to support) their militaristic actions and related political frameworks. When broadened out further, these political frameworks encompass, to varying degrees, self/state surveillance, self/state censorship and the surrendering of individual freedoms to an overarching state authority. Sport is one of the primary sites involved in what has become a multi-agency web of inter-dependent and inter-active figurations involving governments, media, sporting governing bodies, sports organisations, grassroots charities, state sponsored charities and individual citizens that facilitate and encourage us all to *support the troops*.

This multi-agency figuration includes the setting up of government military propaganda departments which have been instrumental in directing many of these ideological activities and in inventing new traditions, many of which have been adopted by allied countries. For example, the United States' state department's "Operation Tribute to Freedom" emerged in 2003 stating on its website that it:

> identifies media opportunities . . . for returning Soldiers [sic] to share their experience with their local communities in an effort to *ensure the public maintains a direct connection to today's army.*
>
> *(OTF 2010: my emphasis)*

Similarly, a short time after this, "Operation Connection" became a Canadian government department with similar aims and activities focused on manufacturing consent for their military operations. Operation Connection seeks to raise the military's profile and invites young

Canadians to "fight with the Canadian Forces" through various community-based activities designed to bolster recruitment (see Scherer and Koch 2010). Many of the activities and aims associated with these departments have been replicated in Britain and Australia. In 2012 Australia's "Soldier On" initiative emerged, stating on its website that it:

> works to create opportunities for those affected by their [military] service to participate in a range of challenging cultural and adventurous activities that will inspire themselves and their communities.
>
> *(Soldier On 2016)*

In Britain, Army chief, General Dannatt, complained that the British public did not support the troops enough (see BBC 2007). Around this time, a whole host of support the troops initiatives emerged, many of which are almost identical to those the government propaganda departments of the United States and Canada championed. For instance, two new British charities, Help for Heroes and Tickets for Troops formed, both bearing remarkable similarity to the American Department of Defense's Welcome Back Veterans and the Canadian Defense Department's Tickets for Troops initiatives.

The full range of popular cultural activities that have been incorporated into supporting the troops is extraordinarily broad, revealing the wider cultural context in which the sport–military nexus exists. The list is far too long to detail fully, but ranges from serving soldiers becoming contestants in international "beauty contests",[4] military personnel (and their partners) releasing music albums, prime time television celebrity game shows hosting military personnel as "celebrity" guests, the production of military-supporting food products (hero sauce, hero cheese, military eggs) to posters in cinema toilets urging moviegoers to text a phone number to "buy a hero a drink". Although the array of support the troops initiatives is too vast to detail exhaustively, for analytical purposes, they can be categorised into four broad (albeit overlapping) areas of intersection between sport and militarism in Western countries:

1. sports people paying respect to the military;
2. injured military personnel becoming athletes;
3. sports uniforms becoming militarised;
4. sponsors using sport to support the military.

It is to these four areas that the chapter turns to offer more detailed discussion of initiatives that facilitate the support the troops ideology governments desire. Once these four areas of support the troops intersections are explained, they are then contextualised by outlining their ideological power, with four particular ideological representations illustrated (charity; invented traditions; necessary helpers; heroes and celebrities).

Sports people paying respect

One of these areas of intersection involves sports people paying respect to military personnel. This includes sports clubs, athletes (and ex-athletes), sport officials, governing bodies, sport journalists and media-sport presenters. For example, since 2008, most British football clubs in the top divisions in Scotland and England have worn an Earl Haig Poppy on club shirts in the lead up to the annual Remembrance Sunday commemorations. Both the Scottish and English Football Associations released specially made poppy shirts with national flags and patriotic slogans explicitly connecting armistice remembrance to current wars and government justification for contemporary British military violence (see New kits 2008). Canadian National Hockey League team Winnipeg Jets also used their sport kit to support the military by adopting a new Royal Canadian Air Force inspired badge in 2011. In 2009, the English Football League teamed up with new military charity Help for Heroes to facilitate a season-long "sponsorship"[5] deal involving each of the seventy-two football clubs staging a designated Football for Heroes match, complete with promotional photos featuring players with Help for Heroes banners and balls. Stars of American sport, including Larry Fitzgerald (Arizona Cardinals) Jared Allen (Minnesota Vikings) Danny Clark (New York Giants), Will Witherspoon (St Louis Rams) accompanied by the NFL commissioner Roger Goodell, joined numerous television and music celebrities in visiting oversees American soldiers, spending ten days in Iraq and Kuwait in 2009. In 2010 ex-England football captain and global sporting icon, David Beckham made a similar visit to Afghanistan, being photographed in various militarised poses including behind the barrel of a heavy machine gun, British military uniform worn for dramatic effect. In 2010, British princes William (vice-patron of the Welsh Rugby Union) and Harry (vice-patron of the [English] Rugby Football Union) greeted injured military personnel as the guests of honour onto the field of play at the annual Six Nations rugby union fixture between England and Wales. In 2014 NASCAR, driver, Kurt Busch paid his respects by announcing "I'm driving for the military". The same year, one of Canada's most prominent sports presenters, Don Cherry used the popular sport television show *Hockey Night* (in Canada) to urge viewers to support the troops (financially and morally) in a homily style address. In the lead up to the 2015 World Cup Final, ex-Australian rugby union player, Peter Fitzsimons called on both teams (Australia and New Zealand) to use the occasion to "pay special tribute to the Anzacs" (Fitzsimons 2015). These examples combine to illustrate the spectrum of sports people showing appreciation and support for Western militarism.

Injured military personnel become athletes

A second area of intersection in the sport–military nexus occurs with injured military personnel becoming athletes. There has been the formation and establishment of military focused Games such as the World Military Games (1995), the United States' Warrior Games (2010) and the British Invictus Games (2014), whose purpose includes providing sporting platforms for injured personnel to compete and, in doing so, elicit support from a grateful and appreciative public. Sport undoubtedly offers rich transformative opportunities to permanently wounded military veterans and, recognising this, Paralympic teams including those of the United States and Britain have also embedded veterans into their teams, the former having twenty veterans competing and additional military personnel as key backroom members at London 2012. Additionally, these Games witnessed close links being established between wounded military personnel and the event in broader cultural contexts. For example, in the lead up to the Games, the Paralympic flame was paraded through the streets by a British army unit, it was carried by a soldier who had lost both legs and an arm in Helmand and was then used to showcase one of Britain's largest military "shows" (see BBC online 2012a). The British government website reported the opening ceremonial aspects of the Paralympic Games, noting:

> the iconic Flame arrived in Whitehall, where former soldiers picked by Prince Harry from the Walking With The Wounded charity carried it past Horse Guards, the Ministry of Defence's Main Building and the Cenotaph. At the opening ceremony, after Her Majesty The Queen took her seat following a fanfare, nine servicemen and

women from the Royal Navy, Army and RAF raised a large Union Flag and marched past as a choir sang the national anthem.

(Gov.UK 2012)

Such militaristic iconography connecting past wars, past victories and past glories to current "wars", serving military personnel (including a serving royal family soldier) and the nation's military headquarters, national anthem and head of state illustrate the ideological utility of sport in the most emotive and nostalgic terms, exposing the transformation of a disability sporting competition and its disabled athletes into a military-focused procession honouring wounded military veterans as national, brave and heroic patriots. It is within this broader ideological context that official pronouncements of the significance and meaning of Paralympic sport should be judged. When the focus is on the ceremonial aspects of Paralympic sporting competition, the military are still often among the most visible and venerated contributors and when sport is secondary (or even absent) from the primary event (like a military parade and "show"), it is still incorporated into showing support and appreciation for Western military and their endeavours. Transforming injured military personnel into athletes and involving injured veterans in ceremonial aspects of Paralympic sport combine here in politically propitious ways.

Sports uniforms becoming militarised

The ceremonial inclusion of military paraphernalia is not limited to one-off events nor does it even require military participation. Militaristic iconography is increasingly afforded prominence on sports uniforms, many of which incorporate sport–military hybrid designs enabling sports teams to show appreciation and support for the military. In the United States, basketball, football and baseball have each witnessed the adoption of military-inspired playing uniforms with military camouflage, military-inspired logos and patriotic phrases incorporated into designs. These are seen in professional and college teams, including the San Antonio Spurs, the University of Maryland, Boston College and the San Diego Padres, the latter re-designing their uniform in 2011 to include more "marine-inspired camouflage" and a new military inspired logo (see Jenkins 2013). In Canada, the Toronto Raptors and hockey teams the Maple Leafs and Montreal Canadiens are among those adopting special military camouflage uniforms. In Britain, various football clubs including Bolton Wanderers, Millwall and Raith Rovers have adapted playing uniforms to incorporate military camouflage in honour of the military. One of the most high-profile intersections of military–sport uniform design occurred at the London 2012 Olympic Games when the United States' Ralph Lauren designed uniform clearly resembled a military uniform (see Achter 2012 for some critical comments on this). Thus, the patriotic representation of military-styled uniforms in the sporting environment compounds its representation in the military environment to facilitate the normalisation and universalism of militarism in wider civil society.

Sponsors using sport to support the military

The final area of sport and support the troops intersection involves sponsors using sport to support the military. This ranges from products interweaving elements of militarism with sport to league sponsors (including charities) ensuring that the public shows support for the military. Illustrating the former was Pepsi's "are you fan enough?" campaign replete with wholesome American iconography including family, teenage love, inter-generational and inter-racial support for the NFL, and uniformed military in a far-off desert landscape playing and watching football all linked by a common love of Pepsi. Illustrating the latter was the United Services Automobile Association (USAA), using its NFL sponsor status to oversee the NFL's "Salute to Service" which sought to ensure that "every NFL game features elements inspired by the military". The Salute to Service website states:

> USAA teams up with NFL teams to elevate military appreciation on and off the field. Learn more about how USAA provides once-in-a-lifetime experiences for current and former military.
>
> *(Salute to Service 2015)*

Charity sponsors have ensured that the fans can play their part and are seen to be involved. In North America and Britain, there have been a series of successful charity events involving Tickets for Troops resulting in sports fans donating their pre-paid seats to military men and women who get a free seat and also the adulation, recognition and support that usually accompanies these specially orchestrated occasions. These occasions show that sponsors are using sport to pay for the right to drive an ideological agenda that is highly politicised, morally debatable and, in some cases at least, unrelated to their primary business product for which presumably they are sponsors in the first place. An American insurance company ensuring that the American military are venerated at NFL matches illustrates this clearly.

These examples indicate the intersection of sport, business and charity in facilitating support the troops initiatives. Furthermore, recent freedom of information requests have disclosed that the American government paid numerous sports organisations monies totalling millions of dollars in return for supporting, hosting and advertising military parades at their stadiums on match days. This raises serious questions about sport's political use when a government using taxpayers' money buys public support for national militarism through the culturally valued pursuit of sport. For instance, if the military already has overwhelming and genuine grassroots public support, why would a government (not least during times of extraordinary financial pressure) spend millions of dollars of taxpayers' money to pay sports organisations for this already existing support? It is reasonable to consider a non-military equivalent: if consumers nationwide bought products completely voluntarily and unprompted, then advertising and marketing companies would rapidly disappear. While these events give the impression that the public is a keen and willing partner offering its unsolicited thanks and appreciation at grassroots level, the official and governmental involvement blurs the line between what is spontaneous grassroots appreciation and what is orchestrated (and publicly paid for) propaganda. The success that such propaganda elicits is undoubted and is, in large part, due to sport's position in Western society as a sacred site of national pride, national expression and national identity, reasons why sport is used for such purposes in the first place. The success is also due to the understandable human empathy people have with fellow citizens who are returning severely disfigured, emotionally unstable and often financially and educationally lacking, and who owe much of their misfortune to fighting for "our freedom" on "our behalf". This all contributes to exposing the political use of sport for highly contested ideological purposes and problematises sport's role in enabling governments to relinquish their moral duty to protect the very people they have sent to risk life and limb (and take life and limb) on the officially proclaimed behalf of its citizens.

Ideological power of the sport–military nexus

This tension between spontaneous support and government propaganda is further problematised when we consider the ideological power of the sport and military nexus, particularly when delineating the boundaries between support for soldiers, endorsement of invasions/liberations, defending deaths and life-changing injuries and believing the destruction of other people's towns and cities is more defensible than non-violent alternatives. The wide range of support the troops initiatives and actions discussed is therefore further classified as representing and supporting the military in four overarching and overlapping ideological ways, each of which simultaneously utilises sport while being situated in broader cultural and political contexts beyond it. These ideological representations are:

1. charity
2. invented traditions
3. necessary helpers
4. heroes and celebrities.

The remainder of the chapter, therefore, first sketches these four key ideological representations of nation-state militarism that have been commonly articulated in Western countries since 2001. This leads into the closing discussion of the *corporate culpability paradox* in which the relationship between military-related *ideology-actor-action-outcome of action* is shown to be articulated differently depending on whether they are viewed as applying to "our troops" or the "terrorist other" uncovering further the political significance of the post-2001 sport–military nexus.

Charity

The sport–military nexus has seen charity playing an instrumental role in the support the troops strategy. Bolstering the plethora of non-sport specific annual remembrance and military "appreciation" events like Remembrance Day and Armed Forces Day in Britain, Anzac Day in Australia and New Zealand and Veterans' Day and Memorial Day in the United States, the sport-related charity initiatives range from Tickets for Troops and Help for Heroes to Walking With the Wounded. These charities (and related events) generally have two primary purposes – financial and ideological support. As well as seeking money, they articulate for the public what their financial support represents ideologically, with official reminders such as: "we seek to convey the gratitude of the public for the work of the Armed Forces and the sacrifices they make" and "these brave men and women have done their duty. Now we need to do our duty to them".[6] Perhaps one of the clearest exemplars of this articulation is the charity Help for Heroes, with its ideological framing of injured military veterans as "heroes" in its title (discussed below in the section on heroes). This strategy keeps the military omnipresent and in public consciousness providing platforms for militarists to remind us what their official purpose is and how they wish "us" to frame our remembrance and charitable donations. At a national level, for example, when asked about the 2014 Earl Haig charity poppy display at London Tower, British Prime Minister David Cameron unequivocally connected the traditional armistice remembrance of two World Wars to current military violence/activity by explicitly discussing military appreciation in the present tense with accompanying ideological rhetoric framing the display as a reminder to "the nation" of those "fighting for our freedom and way of life" (responding in Parliament at Prime Minister's questions 29 October 2014).

Invented traditions

Many of these charities have extended into the next category of invented tradition, becoming part of the national fabric of remembrance and support the troops articulations. New sport-specific traditions like the aforementioned Warrior Games, Invictus Games and World Military Games have materialized, placing military personnel in the sporting spotlight and making them part of the sporting calendar alongside civilian sports events. These complement both the established and newly invented non-sport military traditions such as the aforementioned Veterans' Day, Armed Forces Day, Anzac Day and Remembrance Day. It is also commonplace to see sports teams being shown participating in such national events, exhibiting appropriate demeanor of bowing heads and solemnly observing public silences or showing due deference by gratefully thanking and appreciating military people and causes. A crucial point here is that even when sport is not central to an activity, sports people, sports events and sports venues are often consciously and strategically incorporated into the event, showing once again the ideological value and cultural reach that sports have (or are believed to have by militarists and political actors). A further example of this involves Andy Murray, in conjunction with the Wimbledon tournament, advertising the British Armed Forces Day.[7] This event – sponsored by one of the world's largest weapons companies, BAE Systems – was advertised as a "family day out" and a "cultural event" rendering its political and militaristic content and contexts inconspicuous. This context included a 2012 visit to British military personnel in the Gulf region by Prime Minister Cameron who combined it with a visit to Saudi Arabia to lobby for business including weapons sales on behalf of BAE (BBC 2012b). In January 2016, Saudi Arabia was widely condemned for the execution of forty-seven alleged "terrorist" sympathisers considered by many non-Saudis to be political activists, with Amnesty reporting the killings in unequivocal terms:

> [T]hey [Saudi authorities] are also using the death penalty in the name of counter-terror to settle scores and crush dissidents. . . . Carrying out a death sentence when there are serious questions about the fairness of the trial is a monstrous and irreversible injustice.
>
> *(Philip Luther, Director of the Middle East and*
> *North Africa Programme at Amnesty International 2 January 2016)*

In the days leading up to these executions and almost a year to the day since they announced a $1.3 billion weapons sale to Saudi Arabia, the United States announced another multi-million dollar weapons sale to the undemocratic state. BAE, one of the world's largest weapons sellers and a company which profits from arming Saudi Arabia (among others) is joined by Andy Murray, the Lawn Tennis Association and Wimbledon, to encourage British citizens to "show their appreciation for the armed forces" who are framed as fighting a war on terror on behalf of a nation and democracy more broadly.

Necessary helpers

The volume and reach of ideological practices in the sport–military nexus helps with the normalising of militarism, with sport featuring as an everyday (nay essential) part of its fabric. Yet, this is only half of this particular symbiotic relationship. The opposite also occurs. Military personnel are also framed as an everyday part of the fabric of sport in the form of necessary helpers. Like the previous examples, this category includes sport- and non-sport-specific illustrations, each compounded to provide a key ideological message – this time, that the military are necessary and helpful. This occurs with three inter-related roles, each one allowing the military to occupy one or more of them in the sporting environment: *surveillance and safety; embedded facilitators; state representatives*. These three roles of necessary helper could form an extended discussion on their own, each offering particular insights into how sport and military relations have become normalised, but, for brevity, their overlapping elements are merely sketched here to illustrate the ideological force of military personnel being represented as necessary helpers.

Surveillance and safety checks have become routine elements of major sports events globally and have helped normalise and institutionalise everyday state militarism and surveillance. From cordoned-off streets guarded by armed soldiers in the vicinity of sporting events/arenas, sniffer dogs roaming stadiums for bombs, bag searches and x-ray body scanners being used on fans entering sports arenas to anti-aircraft artillery located on apartment roofs during major sporting occasions (London 2012), numerous sports events and their arenas are now heavily militarised and surveilled environments. Further illustrating the political utility of sport as part of the sport–military nexus are claims that weapons sales were boosted by missile deployment during the 2012 London Olympics, with Beckett suggesting that an arms sale benefited from such advertising:

> [T]he brand of missiles deployed around the [London 2012] site . . . was a factor in the sale, and is still contributing to "interest" in the missiles from countries in the Middle East and Asia.
>
> *(Beckett 2013)*

While the Olympic Games allegedly bolstering weapons sales is troublesome, and while the increased visibility of military hardware and personnel on the streets could be viewed as intrusive and disruptive, the military's associated status as embedded facilitators helps diffuse and off-set potential negativity or dissent, with military personnel being seen to be helping. Although the embedded facilitator work sometimes overlaps with safety and surveillance work, it usually extends beyond what the state considers necessary military work of surveillance and safety. Thus, the roles of embedded facilitators include carrying or accompanying the Olympic torch, presenting cups and even providing the backdrop for sporting occasions. For example, in 2011, a serving soldier was given the honour of presenting the English FA Cup to the winning football team and, in the United States, Fox broadcast their weekend sports programme from the battleship *Missouri Memorial* in December 2015 to coincide with the seventy-fourth anniversary of Pearl Harbour. Thus, military personnel and military hardware are embedded into the sporting event in ways that allow them to be seen as enabling and facilitating the actual event itself. The final level of necessary helper is the level of state representatives and includes military personnel holding and carrying national flags at sport events, ceremonially guarding cups and medals and conducting the singing of national anthems before sports events, each allowing military personnel to be key visible representatives of the nation-state at local, national and international sporting events.

Heroes and celebrities

The final ideological representation involves the double bind articulation of military personnel as heroes/celebrities[8] and sporting heroes/celebrities exalting military, with both articulations serving to "appreciate and support" the military while effectively blurring the boundaries between military personnel and hero/celebrity. There are numerous examples of military personnel being framed as hero/celebrity. The aforementioned charity Help for Heroes is an obvious illustration, conferring hero status on military personnel requiring charitable help. Hero status is also, of course, conferred on dead military personnel, with the

United States procession route in which dead American military are driven for repatriation, being named the "Highway for Heroes". Similarly, in Britain, the country's most popular tabloid newspaper (*The Sun*) led a campaign to give Britain's equivalent route the same title. The British example was part of a broader campaign to honour the town of Wooten Basset, which became the focus of British military repatriation. In addition to this media campaign there were attempts by the British government to capitalise on what appeared originally to be local people showing genuine respect and sorrow towards the dead men and women being driven through their town. Despite many residents not wanting "'pomp" or "militarisation'" (Gee 2014: 31), the town had royal status conferred on it, a royal visit and an accompanying RAF fly-past (Gee 2014).[9] Other non-sport examples of military personnel being framed as hero/celebrity include The Military Wives Choir and The Soldiers releasing respective albums (in Britain), serving soldier Johnson Beharry appearing as a series-long "celebrity" on British television's *Dancing on Ice* programme (with his profession noted as "hero") and a similar example in the United States where double amputee Iraq veteran Noah Galloway starred in *Dancing with the Stars*. These contextualise the emotive wider environment in which sporting examples are situated. Returning to sport specifically, the newly created sporting events for military veterans like The Invictus Games and The Warrior Games each receiving high status and media coverage, enable both high visibility and appreciation of the military to occur and military personnel to be presented as celebrity stars and heroic athletes overcoming debilitating injuries.

In addition to military personnel being represented as heroes/celebrities, the double bind in this ideological representation sees the previously discussed point of sports heroes/celebrities glorifying and appreciating military and militarism. As noted, athletes have engaged in propaganda activities involving sports people visiting Iraq/Afghanistan and have promoted military events such as Armed Forces Day. Like other examples, a key feature of this double bind is that even when the ideological activities do not include sport as a key part of the story, sports people are still incorporated into the narrative. For example, the previously noted Don Cherry plea while presenting a Hockey programme is a clear illustration, as is the British example of the 2014 British remembrance ceremony; the centenary commemoration involved widespread media coverage of a specially selected thirteen-year-old army cadet in military uniform placing the final red poppy at the London remembrance instillation. In carefully timed synchronicity, this poignant moment was accompanied by television pictures cutting to the England football team ceremonially pausing during training and the Scotland rugby union team taking an active part in a remembrance service replete with a player shown doing a reading (see *Sky News* report 11 November 2014).

The next example offers an excellent illustration of this double-bind articulation of military personnel as heroes/celebrities and sporting heroes/celebrities acclaiming military. In the United States, athlete-turned-soldier and eventual military martyr Pat Tillman, who died at the hands of "friendly fire" in 2004, had a foundation named after him and has been widely valorised as a heroic symbol of American nationhood, military heroism and sporting virtue. The political capital of this hero-fying process can be summarised by Gee's observations of what he calls the "heroic quest" (2014):

> Our own culture romances war, fantasizing about it in gushing hyperbole that is anything but rational or reasonable. It is not dispassionate reason that leads mainstream media to call soldiers "heroes" for no other reason than that they are soldiers, George W. Bush to characterize the war in Afghanistan as a "crusade", or Tony Blair to "feel a most urgent sense of mission about today's world" after the invasion of

Iraq. . . . Language like this shows how the psyche, and thus our culture, are wont to stylize war as an heroic quest. The terms used – crusade, mission, hero, urgent, menace – recast war as an idealized, romantic story that valorizes violence as righteous and even appealing.

(pp. 42–43)

These ideological representations see sport being incorporated alongside other sacred cultural goods in the pursuit of showing appreciation and support for the military, and their cumulative political power is beyond doubt.

The corporate culpability paradox[10]

Since 2001, the sport–military nexus has witnessed an orchestrated shift towards forging closer connections between the military and civil society. Yet, when it comes to bearing responsibility for military violence and its outcomes, there is an apparent paradox in much of the preferred narratives of Western governments and media. This has three related elements to it. First, the official stance often taken and encouraged by Western governments is that irrespective of the political/ideological (lack of) justification for military violence, the public should support the troops, thus detaching the actors from the ideology, action and outcomes of their action. Correspondingly the public is told that sport is (and should be) non-political. Therefore, sports stars, sports events, sports sponsors and governing bodies combine to support the troops in ways that are encouraged to be viewed as politically neutral – evident in soundbites such as "we support the troops not the war". Second, when it comes to the terrorist other, s/he is usually represented in the opposite manner – that unless there is complete and total revulsion and rejection of the terrorist, there is a danger of being framed as endorsing or sympathising with the terrorist causes, terrorists, terrorist activities and atrocities (the ideology, actor, action and outcome of action). Third, this contradiction is further compounded by the fact that despite the rhetoric of support the troops while detaching selves from the ideology, action, outcome of action being applied to Western military, the true purpose of sport and wider cultural goods in supporting the cause as well as the actors is exposed by the public being incorporated by proxy into the wider political cause. These unequivocal ideological aims of governments sometimes emerge during official pronouncements. For example, in 2009, the British Chief of Defence Staff, Jock Stirrup, complained that the Taliban's bombs were less threatening to British troops' morale than "declining will" among the public to see the war won (Gee 2014: 29). Unambiguously connecting the military actor, action, and outcome of action with ideological cause, he further added, "support for our servicemen and women is indivisible from support for this mission" (cited in Gee 2014: 29). Consequently, according to this senior military official, the British public *cannot* support the troops without inadvertently supporting the mission – the cause, the actions and the outcomes of such action. Moreover, such is the importance of public support, the Chief of Defence considers it higher in value than avoiding Taliban bombs. Two years previously, British Prime Minister, Tony Blair made similar political connections unambiguous, stressing "the armed forces want public opinion not just behind them but behind their mission; [we should] understand their value not just their courage" (cited in Gee 2014: 29). The umbilical connection between ideology-actor-action-outcome of action exposing the incorporation by proxy of citizens into supporting the political and ideological causes of a nation-state (and wider "war on terror") is difficult to deny when expressed in such clear terms by senior servants of the nation-state such as a Chief of Defence and a Prime Minister. Additionally, key British public figures have made these connections explicit. British Prime Minister David Cameron discussing Armed Forces Day incorporated British citizens by proxy into supporting the military by stating:

> these initiatives have the full support of the nation . . . [Armed Forces Day is] an opportunity for the nation to pay respect to those fighting for our freedom and way of life.
>
> *(Sky News 2013)*

Returning to sport, in describing the Football League and Help for Heroes Partnership in 2010, Football League chairman Lord Mawhinney also incorporated Britain's football supporting public, informing the nation that:

> [t]he contribution being made by our armed forces around the world is truly humbling. The football for heroes week will provide an excellent opportunity for supporters to show their appreciation for the outstanding work being done.
>
> *(Sun Online 2010)*

In a similar vein, in the United States, numerous football teams endorse American military actions with comments of support often including phrases such as "without your sacrifices, we wouldn't be free to enjoy football" (see Salute to Service 2015 for examples). And in Australia, the founder of the new charity Soldier On incorporated Australians by proxy when explaining the purpose of the charity as being:

> about helping wounded soldiers reconnect with the community so that they see they have not hit the scrapheap of society – their contribution and sacrifice are appreciated by their fellow Australians.
>
> *(Interviewed in Gadd 2013)*

Thus, clear connection is continually made between a contested political/ideological cause (fighting for freedom) and the outcomes of current military violence. Furthermore, this violence is articulated as virtuous sacrifice that has universal citizen support. These comments unequivocally frame Western troops as fighting "terror" (a "just war"), defending our freedom and engaging in humbling and outstanding work that is fully supported by the nation. Placed in these discursive contexts, sport and other popular culture activities provide Western governments with rich propaganda potential and this is the political context in which the sport–military nexus should be placed for analyses to take place and judgements made.

This chapter has articulated the convergence of the political system and politics with public support for militarism, revealing the central role sacred cultural activities play in political public relations. In particular, it has shown how military–civil relations have utilised sport to support the troops. This has occurred with sport people paying respect, injured military becoming athletes, sport uniforms becoming militarised and sponsors using sport to promote militarism. The ideological power of these inter-related actions can be categorised into four representative categories – charity, invented traditions, necessary helpers and heroes/celebrities, each offering ideological representations that facilitate citizens being incorporated by proxy into supporting the military and its actions. The political results of this include sport being used for propaganda, the distinctions between soldier, hero and celebrity being blurred, and the normalising of everyday militarism and the surveillance state.

Western countries have increasingly incorporated their citizens by proxy into supporting their military and sport has played one of the most prominent roles in this. The sport–military nexus forms one part of a multi-agency strategy that utilises the cultural machinery of Western countries. As such, sport is undoubtedly entangled in the war on terror at the cultural level at least. In Boston in 2013, this war embroiled sport beyond the cultural level leaving the city's marathon devastated by violence and killings. More recently, in Paris on 13 November 2015, sport, along with a whole range of other cultural activities, experienced the material and human effects of the war on terror, with danger, violent attacks, death and destruction occurring in the name of someone else's ideological cause. If we are to fully understand the terrorist, we first have to understand our own protagonists of violence, not least because, unlike the terrorist who acts with no democratic mandate, Western military are acting on behalf of nation-state populations as propaganda initiatives, using sport, routinely remind us.

Notes

1 This "support" ranges from implicit disinterest on one end of the spectrum through to tacit acceptance and ultimately to enthusiastic glorification and hero-fication at the opposite end of the spectrum.
2 Virtuous at least in how official histories in the West are likely to view them, with Mexico 1968 and Moscow 1980 commonly seen to be worthwhile political expressions in support of Western versions of "democracy".
3 For example, in 2013 a British House of Commons Select Committee reported the average reading age of British soldiers was eleven; Britain has allowed non-heterosexuals to join the services since 2000 and is planning to put women in frontline "combat" roles from 2016 onwards; the United States permitted women to fight on the frontline in 2015 and allowed non-heterosexuals in the military to "come out" from 2011. Australia and Canada have allowed non-heterosexuals to join up since 1991 and 1992.
4 Katrina Hodge (nicknamed "Combat Barbie") replaced the ousted Miss England in 2009 and, upon being crowned, in her interview repeated the claim that the British public does not appreciate the army enough (see *Daily Telegraph* 2009).
5 The issue of a charity sponsoring a sports league is itself worthy of further analysis given that it is usually charities that are the beneficiary of sponsorship. It does raise questions about the nature and status of charities and their relationship with business.
6 An example of the breadth and volume of military-related charity activities, in one three-month period, I received three military charity leaflets through the door of my home (Combat Stress; The British Forces Foundation, ABF The Soldiers' Charity) and witnessed two additional military charities collecting at Scotland's two busiest train stations (Glasgow Central and Edinburgh Waverley). The cited statements appear in the leaflets that were delivered unsolicited to my home.
7 Andy Murray has been used to advertise and publicise a number of recent Armed Forces Days in Britain.
8 There are analytical distinctions to be made between hero and celebrity, but for this chapter's purpose and scope, it is reasonable to discuss them without going into detail of these distinctions; not least because with the examples discussed here, both hero and celebrity compound one another with military celebrities enabling hero-fication of militarism to occur.
9 Gee further highlights a leaked British government report that "warned that repatriation ceremonies (at Wooten Basset) were making the public 'risk averse' and recommended reducing their public profile" (p. 31).
10 This corporate culpability paradox is discussed in more detail in Kelly (forthcoming).

References

Achter, P. (2012) Is Team USA's militaristic uniform a problem? *CNN International Edition Online*. 28 July 2012. Accessed 7 January 2016. http://edition.cnn.com/2012/07/27/opinion/achter-olympic-uniforms/.

Basham, V.M., Belkin, A. and Gifkins, J. (2015) What is critical military studies? *Critical Military Studies*, 1(1): 1–2.

BBC. (2007) Army chief warns of social gulf, *BBC Online*. 22 September 2007. Accessed 23 September 2007. http://news.bbc.co.uk/1/hi/uk/7006720.stm.

BBC. (2012a) Paralympic flame at Preston military show. 26 August 2012. Accessed 3 January 2016. www.bbc.co.uk/news/uk-england-lancashire-19387068.

BBC. (2012b) David Cameron in the Gulf: Defence sales legitimate. 5 November 2012. Accessed 4 January 2016. www.bbc.co.uk/news/uk-politics-20202058.

Beckett, A. (2013) Is Britain's arms trade making a killing? *The Guardian Online.* 18 February 2013. Accessed 7 January 2016. www.theguardian.com/world/2013/feb/18/britains-arms-trade-making-killing.

Butterworth, M. (2005) Ritual in the "Church of baseball": Suppressing the discourse of democracy after 9/11. *Communication and Critical/Cultural Studies,* 2(2): 107–129.

Butterworth, M. (2008) Fox Sports, Super Bowl XLII, and the affirmation of American civil religion. *Journal of Sport and Social Issues,* 32(3): 318–323.

Butterworth, M. (2010) "Major league baseball welcomes back veterans, and the rhetoric of 'support the troops'". In R. Briley (ed.) *The Politics of Baseball: Essays on the Pastime and Power at Home and Abroad.* Jefferson, NC: McFarland, pp. 226–240.

Butterworth, M. (forthcoming) (ed.) *Global Sport and Militarism.* London: Routledge.

Danilova, N. (2015) *The Politics of War Commemoration in the UK and Russia.* Basingstoke: Palgrave Macmillan.

Daily Telegraph (2009) "Combat Barbie": Miss England Katrina Hodge launches Miss World 2009. 9 November. Accessed 9 November 2009. www.telegraph.co.uk/news/newstopics/politics/defence/6529042/Combat-Barbie-Miss-England-Katrina-Hodge-launches-Miss-World-2009.html.

Denzin, N. (2004) The war on culture, the war on truth. *Cultural Studies-Critical Methodologies,* 4(2): 137–142.

Fitzsimons, P. (2015) Wallabies and All Blacks should pay special tribute to the Anzacs before World Cup decider. Rugby Heaven online. Accessed 7 January 2016. www.stuff.co.nz/sport/rugby/opinion/73472128/Peter-FitzSimons-Wallabies-and-All-Blacks-should-pay-special-tribute-to-the-Anzacs-before-World-Cup-decider.

Gadd, J. (2013) Q&A: non-profit group Soldier On helping Australia's wounded. *Lifeplus Online Magazine.* 7 December 2013. Accessed 7 January 2016. www.australianunity.com.au/lifeplus/community/2013/december/soldier-on-helping-australian-wounded#sthash.fh2IOMg0.dpuf.

Gee, D. (2014) *Spectacle, Reality, Resistance: Confronting a Culture of Militarism.* London: Forces Watch Press.

Giroux, H. (2004) *The Terror of Neoliberalism: Authoritarianism and the Eclipse of Democracy.* Boulder, CO: Paradigm.

Giroux, H. (2008) Beyond the biopolitics of disposability: Rethinking neoliberalism in the new gilded age. *Social Identities,* 14(5): 587–620.

Gov.UK. (2012) Serving soldiers in GB Paralympics team. *Ministry of Defence Announcement, Gov.UK online.* Accessed 8 January 2016. www.gov.uk/government/news/serving-soldiers-in-gb-paralympics-team.

Hargreaves (1986) *Sport, Power and Culture.* Cambridge: Polity Press.

Holt (1989) *Sport and the British: A Modern History.* Oxford: Clarendon Press.

Holt, R. (1995) Contrasting nationalisms: sport, militarism and the unitary state in Britain and France before 1914. *International Journal of the History of Sport,* 12(2): 39–54.

Jansen, S.C. and Sabo, D. (1994) The sport/war metaphor: Hegemonic masculinity, the Persian Gulf War, and the new world order. *Sociology of Sport Journal,* 11(1): 1–17.

Jenkins, T. (2013) The militarization of American professional sports. *Journal of Sport & Social Issues,* 37(3): 245–260.

Kelly, J. (2012) Popular culture, sport and the "hero"-fication of British militarism. *Sociology,* 47(4): 722–738.

Kelly, J. (forthcoming) "The paradox of militaristic remembrance in British sport and popular culture". In M. Butterworth (ed.) *Global Sport and Militarism.* London: Routledge.

King, A. (2008) Offensive lines: sport–state synergy in an era of perpetual war. *Cultural Studies – Critical Methodologies,* 8(4): 527–39.

Luther, P. (2016) Shia cleric among 47 executed by Saudi Arabia in a single day. *Amnesty International Online.* 2 January 2016. Accessed 7 January 2016. www.amnesty.org/en/latest/news/2016/01/shia-cleric-among-47-executed-by-saudi-arabia-in-a-single-day/.

Mangan, J.A. (1981) *Athleticism in the Victorian and Edwardian Public School: The Emergence and Consolidation of an Educational Ideology.* Cambridge: Cambridge University Press.

Mangan, J.A. (1998) *"Benefits Bestowed": Education and British Imperialism.* Manchester: Manchester University Press.

Mason, T. (1988) *Sport in Britain.* London: Faber & Faber.

Mason, T. and Rieda, E. (2010) *Sport and the Military: The British Armed Forces 1880–1960*. Cambridge: Cambridge University Press.

New kits (2008) *New Football Kits* website. Accessed 5 January 2016. www.newkits.co.uk/scotland-poppy-football-kit-79.html.

OTF (2010) Operation Tribute to Freedom *USA Government Website*. Accessed 5 November 2011. www4.army.mil/otf/.

Salute to Service (2015) Accessed 7 January 2016. http://salutetoservice.com/?utm_source=NFL.com%2FSalute&utm_medium=Website%20Linkout&utm_term=OMAS&utm_content=Website&utm_campaign=Salute%20To%20Service.

Scherer, J. and Koch, J. (2010) Living with war: Sport, citizenship and the cultural politics of post-9/11 Canadian identity. *Sociology of Sport Journal*, 27: 1–29.

Silk, M. and Falcous, M. (2005) One day in September/A week in February: Mobilizing American (sporting) nationalism. *Sociology of Sport Journal*, 22: 447–71.

Sky News (2013) Armed Forces Day sees parades and fly-pasts. 29 June 2013. Accessed 14 November 2014. http://news.sky.com/story/1109432/armed-forces-day-sees-parades-and-fly-pasts.

Soldier On (2016) Soldier On: *Helping Our Wounded Warriors*. Accessed 23 December 2015. www.soldieron.org.au.

Sun Online (2010) Footie clubs unite for heroes. 2 March 2010. Accessed 3 June 2011. www.thesun.co.uk/sol/homepage/news/campaigns/our_boys/2874672/Footie-clubs-unite-for-heroes.html.

Stempel, C. (2006) Televised sports, masculine moral capital, and support for the US invasion of Iraq. *Journal of Sport and Social Issues*, 30(1): 79–106.

Woodward, R. (2005) From military geography to militarism's geographies: disciplinary engagements with the geographies of militarism and military activities. *Progress in Human Geography*, 29(6): 718–40.

PART V

Sport, political activism and social justice

The interaction between sport, political activism and social justice has been one of the emerging sport- and politics-related relationships in recent years. This part discusses this relationship by introducing a number of overlapping topics ranging from sport and peace, sexuality and gender, "race", indigenous culture and knowledge, the environment, sustainability, countercultural sport and the so-called Big Society's role in relation to sport. The first three chapters combine the topics of sexuality, gender and sport for development and peace. Naish focuses on sport for development and peace with specific attention paid to alignment, administration and power, while Chawansky and Kipnis extend the discussion by situating Sport for Development and Peace (SDP) within a gender politics context. These two chapters are separated by Jarvis's discussion on the politics of sexuality and sport. This section is completed by the three final chapters that each consider, in contrasting ways, grassroots involvement in sport. Totten looks at supporter/fan activism. In contrast, Gilchrist focuses on activist players reclaiming civic space, while Reid shifts the discussion away from players and fans to discuss less autonomous, civic activism in relation to the British neo-liberal concept of "the Big Society".

Jacob Naish utilises governmentality as a lens through which to view relations within Sport for Development and Peace (SDP). He discusses two specific tendencies in alignment within the SDP sector. The first is the private – in this case companies – aligned as socially responsible; the second is the corporatisation of the civic – in this case the SDP NGOs. Adopting a Foucauldian notion of power, Naish argues that governmentality is an appealing yet borderless system of ideas and concepts, practices and techniques.

Nigel Jarvis argues that LGBTQI sport spaces, such as the Gay Games, potentially represent a significant transgressive and alternative space in the world of sport. Recent positive developments, however, have been accompanied by a number of contested and highly political issues. Jarvis focuses on the politics associated with the socio-historical growth of gay sport, and recent popular media accounts of gay sexuality.

Megan Chawansky and Hilary Kipnis suggest that transnational organisations utilising sport for SDP objectives often emphasise the positive possibilities of sport. This understanding of sport, they argue, lacks a critical perspective on the ways in which sporting institutions and practices can encourage divisions on the basis of gender, class, race, ability, sexuality and nationality.

Kevin Hylton and Alexandra Rankin-Wright explore the place of "race" in sport and politics. They critique the politics of racialised terminology and their relevance to sport and the state, while juxtaposing the tensions within. The chapter focuses on two cases where "race", sport and politics coalesce. One is a current study of the "race" equality landscape in sport where they illustrate the political and organisational tensions and issues that national governing bodies (NGBs) and key sport organisations have in confronting the problem of the under-representation of Black and minority ethnic (BME) coaches. The authors illustrate how racialised outcomes in sport can be discerned and associated with influential hierarchies that perpetuate power relations and patterns of inclusion.

Bevan Erueti examines the implementation of mātauranga Māori, a Māori (indigenous person of Aotearoa New Zealand) term that encompasses Māori knowledge and cultural practices within Aotearoa New Zealand[1] elite level sport environs. It is argued that a unique combination of traditional qualities of mātauranga Māori in elite-level sport can result in the creation of a distinctive sense of identity at both a personal and national level for all involved athletes. However, even though Māori feature prominently in sport at the elite level, mātauranga Māori does very little to raise Māori politicisation in sport in present-day Aotearoa New Zealand.

Will Atkinson considers the growing issue of the environment and sustainability in sport. A feature of this has been the emergence of controlled environments in sport, offering a departure from the more natural environment. This is in part the result of commercial pressures to provide a certain "product" yet it sometimes results in a tension between "natural" (desirable) and "unnatural" (undesirable) aspects of the sporting encounter. Such a relationship can be understood as being problematic for the sustainability credentials of sports environments, not only because of the energy needed to control environmental conditions, but also because of the way in which they exemplify human dominance of the environment over nature.

Mick Totten's chapter on sport activism and protest dispels the myth that sport and politics do not mix. Discussing a range of sport activism examples, including historically iconic protests and radical activism, Totten examines sport activism and distinguishes it from more specific acts of protest. The chapter concludes offering a "framework of sport activism and protest" to accommodate its diverse nature and identify variables in the sport activism process.

Paul Gilchrist highlights how "counter-culture" is frequently applied to describe a distinctive feature of the history, politics, style and organisation of sport, yet as an analytical category it remains elusive. The idea of "counter-culture" or a "counter-cultural" legacy is perpetuated in studies of youth subcultures and lifestyle sport, in an often simplistic and a priori fashion. Gilchrist argues that "counter-culture" has tended to be deployed as a political trope, applied selectively in interpretations of lived practices and popular cultural forms. There is a need to better understand its conceptual parameters and analytical significance to the study of sport cultures. Gilchrist looks at the origins of the concept in sociological and political thought from the 1950s and details socio-historical contexts where the concept has been most pronounced. He concludes by reappraising "counter-culture" in relation to new or hybrid sport forms in the city, through the examples of pillow fighting and urban golf, which prefigure new political relationships within evolving "counter-cultural spaces."

The part concludes with Gavin Reid critically examining the currently fashionable but under-examined link between sport and social enterprise with specific focus on Britain. With local governments facing budget cuts and voluntary sports clubs struggling to develop sustainable positions in an increasingly competitive leisure market, some argue that innovative social business models will deliver increased sports participation and fundamental social change. This chapter draws on critical theories of social capital and research on a local sport social enterprise to highlight antagonistic "silent narratives" hidden behind the depoliticising positive grand narrative of social enterprise. Reid argues that dominant "fairy-tale" narratives of heroic (male) social entrepreneurs embracing "Robin Hood" business models that take from the rich and give to the poor, not only ignore the role of women in these political interventions, but also downplay the influence of social class and the state in undermining radical social change. The chapter suggests that sport social enterprises could address the conditions, rather than the symptoms, of poverty.

Note

1 Aotearoa is the Māori name for New Zealand, translated as "Land of the Long White Cloud". For this book chapter the unified term "Aotearoa New Zealand" is used.

24

SPORT FOR DEVELOPMENT AND PEACE

Alignment, administration, power

Jacob Naish

Introduction

For decades now the modern liberal state has justified investment in sport from public funds based upon a construction of the idea of sport as a public 'good'. For example, the UK government invests in grassroots participation in sport through the agency 'Sport England', to increase participation. It does this, it states, to create 'sporting habits for life'; the more people that play sport, the better (Sport England 2014). At the same time, the scale and scope of charities (both international and domestic) grew exponentially in the last two decades of the twentieth century. The Sport for Development and Peace (SDP) sector evolved as a hybrid of these two broad tendencies, overlapping as it does, where social and economic development meets the use of sport as a vehicle for desirable social and behavioural changes.

Academics now seriously consider the use of sport for social change. Coalter (2007, 2009), Kidd (2008), Levermore (2010), Giulianotti (2004, 2005, 2010, 2011), Hayhurst (2009, 2011) and Darnell (2007, 2010, 2012a, 2012b) all provide scholarly examples. The crucial debates now centre on the degree to which conditions of neoliberalism limit human agency. In other words, are the subjects of SDP really offering a critical challenge to dominant modes of thought and action, or reproducing it? This is perhaps most notable in a debate between Lindsey and Grattan (2012), who argue for greater attention to agency in the Global South on the one hand, and Darnell and Hayhurst (2012), who highlight neoliberal frameworks of thought as the context for understanding such action, on the other. This chapter compliments these debates by briefly discussing the interconnections between forms of actor in SDP, and making preliminary arguments about the nature of power as it flows between them; overviewing the actors that populate SDP and illuminating some interconnections and interrelations. This establishes an understanding of the constellations and networks of ideas and actors that deploy various techniques in the 'day-to-day' of SDP.

Adopting a Foucauldian (2004, 2008, 2009) notion of power, I argue that power is visible in SDP in its function. Summarizing from my doctoral research, I use empirical observations of behaviour within the constellation of actors in SDP to show discursive alignments between various types of actor in the SDP sector, and the usage of monitoring and evaluation processes within SDP to provide logical justifications for consistency in discourse between seemingly disparate types of organisational behaviour. These rationally underpin claims for various acts to be considered as coherent, and provide the connections between different actors.

The chapter begins by theoretically underpinning the ideas that follow, cementing governmentality as a lens through which to view relations within SDP. The main discussion draws on my doctoral primary data and discusses two specific tendencies in alignment within the SDP sector. The first is the private – in this case companies – aligned as socially responsible; the second is the corporatisation of a space in civil society – in this case the SDP NGOs.

Power and governmentality in SDP

Elements of Michel Foucault's work have been critical in understanding power in SDP. Foucault's functional and nodal understanding of power dictates the need to analyse relations between actors and individuals (Foucault 2004: 29). For Foucault, the state (civil society and class relations) are just locations in which we might empirically observe functions of power. Acceptance of this necessitates rejecting arguments that place certain forms of practice, agency or structure, as more powerful than others. What we should instead invest our efforts in is knowledges, administrative and technical apparatus. Therefore, what people 'say', 'write' and 'do' with each other in SDP becomes the crucially important terrain of enquiry for scholarly work.

In a world where FIFA, the UN and the IOC are purveyors of capital, culture and knowledge, the temptation to scrutinise closely the flows from 'the centre' of the SDP system, is one that should be cautioned against. Foucault's conception of power rather, is 'nodal', visible at peripheries in an interconnected system. Therefore we should focus empirically on micro levels: on what people do day-to-day in various contexts and where discourses and practices are reproduced. The term 'governmentality' is vital to Foucauldians in understanding how power functions. In a series of lectures in his later career, Foucault came to know governmentality as the single most important operationalisation of power under the conditions of postmodern liberalism; indeed it was the defining characteristic of it. He defined it thus:

> First . . . I understand the ensemble formed by institutions, procedures, analyses and reflections, calculations, and tactics that allow the exercise of this very specific, albeit very complex, power that has the population as its target, political economy as its major form of knowledge, and apparatuses of security as its essential technical instrument. Second, by 'governmentality' I understand the tendency, the line of force, that for a long time, and throughout the West, has constantly led towards the pre-eminence over all other types of power – sovereignty, discipline, and so on – of the type of power that we can call 'government' and which has led to the development of a series of specific governmental apparatuses (appareils) on the one hand [and, on the other] to the development of a series of knowledges (savoirs). Finally, by 'governmentality' I think we should understand the process, or rather, the result of the process by which the state of justice of the Middle Ages became the administrative state in the fifteenth and sixteenth centuries and was gradually 'governmentalized'.
>
> *(2009: 108–109)*

Foucault's work on governmentality offers a lens for seeing apparently coherent systems of thought in historical moments in a nuanced way (Rose 1999). 'Strategies' are the theoretical and methodological rationalities for why a given thing would be done in a certain way; for example, a 'best practice' document, a 'policy framework', a logical or 'outcomes framework' for monitoring and evaluating (M&E) projects. Claims to 'consistency' in strategy and apparatuses give political rationalities a social form in the creation, discipline and surveillance of practice (Rose 1999: 24–26). This gives rise to understanding a set of practices as *technologies* of governmentality. 'Microtechniques' are constituents of technologies which are used to govern certain spaces, rendering them knowable. Examples of such microtechniques can be surveys, reports, studies, registers, guidelines, etc. These are techniques that create rational bases for knowledge, and increasingly we see them digitised in terms of the space in which they happen (registers moving online for example, events recorded on social media).

SDP literature has not been immune to such critical considerations. Darnell (2010) operational-ised Foucault's work on biopower (a particular form of political power codifying the human being as a biological subject upon which rules, laws and methods can be exacted) within SDP. Hayhurst on the other hand took policy texts between and within international organisations, and unset-tled discourse around the idea of 'partnership' as a relation of power, using postcolonial theory (Hayhurst 2009). Hayhurst (2011) in later work, took on Global Corporate Social Engagement (GCSE) – what some have called Corporate Social Responsibility (CSR) – as a technology of governmentality in the work of SDP organisations. This rationality takes the form of 'expertise' given from corporate organisations to SDP NGOs, informing practice and discourse at the local level exposing the corporate infiltration of 'private sector expertise' into social spaces such as SDP.

In summary, power is visible in its function, and in its relations between actors in networks; it is nodal, and must be considered at the local level, as well as in relation to any identifiable 'core'; con-nections between actors in their relations are important because this tells us something about where/how power is functioning; and finally, governmentality is a perspective through which to view the attempts to gain rational coherence between a set of ideas logically, and through which to see govern-ance in relays of power. It is to the actors within the constellation of SDP that the chapter now turns.

Constellation of actors in SDP

The objective of this section is to provide an overview of the spatial dimensions of SDP, illustrating the constellation of actors as they relate to each other territorially and sectorally. Subdividing the constellation of actors in SDP allows us to focus on actors within the domains they identify with, even if segmentations may be only superficial and often transcended. Placing actors in relation to one another does not indicate hierarchy. Instead, this allows us to see if pretensions to coher-ent systems of thought and practice emerge. Giulianotti typifies such attempts in revealing three models of SDP organisation: 'technical', 'dialogical' and 'critical' (Giulianotti 2010: 211–214). In this chapter the goals are limited to providing the spatial context for SDP in order to illustrate how various actors within the SDP system codify and represent their behaviour. While there are inevitable overlaps, for analytical purposes these are divided into *private*, *not-for-profit* and *public*.

Private

These are organisations that distinguish themselves by directing their behaviours to commercial ends. In the global variant, huge multinational corporations (MNCs) are the only real organi-sations we find in this category, and predominantly interact with SDP by funding SDP pro-grammes via CSR/GCSE foundations. Specific companies of note are Barclays (see 'Spaces for Sport') and Standard Chartered, who in 2014 funded the Goal programme with Women Win. Increasingly MNC funding is allied to the engagement of corporate employees in SDP organi-sations, usually on a voluntary basis. Funded projects tend to be wrapped up with evaluations or research projects, by either private research consultancies or universities. These can occasionally produce printed or online reports, some of which explicitly refer to SDP programmes whilst others package this up in wider CSR programme reporting (see for example Barclays 2015).

MNCs are significant in that they are still one of the largest sources of revenue for SDP NGOs. Corporations such as Nike, Sony, Barclays, Hyundai and Adidas have all contributed funds to interventions using sport via their CSR programmes (see Figure 24.1).

	Global	Transnational	National	Local	Main form of interaction with SDP	Examples of actors
Private	Professional Sports People →				Ambassadorial	Birgit Prinz, Didier Drogba, Natascha Badmann, Sean Fitzpatrick, Marcel Desailly, Ben Ainslie
			Professional Sports teams →		Funding to SDP programmes, in-kind support	Manchester United FC, Manchester City FC, Chelsea FC, Hapoel Tel Aviv FC
				Fans	Interacting with content on SDP programmes	Cityzens (Manchester City FC fans), Brighton It Hove Albion FC fans
			Leagues		Funding to SDP programmes, in-kind support	English Premier League, Eredivisie, National Basketball Association, National Football League
	Multinational Corporations →				Funding to SDP programmes, in-kind support, knowledge production	Barclays, Standard Chartered, Richemont
				Firms	Funding to SDP programmes, in-kind support	Small to Medium sized Enterprises
	Research Consultancies →				Service provider to SDP programmes or funders, knowledge production	Ecorys, Substance, InFocus
			Universities →		Service provider to SDP programmes or funders, knowledge production	University of Brighton, Southampton Solent University, Swiss Academy for Development
Not-for-profit	Trusts Foundations →				Funding to SDP programmes	Comic Relief, Big Lottery Fund, Bill Melinda Gates Foundation, Laureus Sport for Good Foundation
	SDP Implementing NGOs →				Delivery of SDP programmes, knowledge production	Grassroot Soccer, Coaching for Hope, Albion in the Community, Women Win, Peace Players International, The Manchester United Foundation

Category		Activity	Examples
TANs	SDP participants	Participation in SDP programmes, monitoring thereof	SDP players, participants, volunteers
	SDP practitioners	Employment or volunteering in SDP programmes	Employees of SDP Implementing NGOS, employed on SDP programmes, volunteers, employees of private firms engaged in SDP, employees of SDP funders
		Advocacy on behalf of SDP programmes, knowledge production	streetfootballworld, SCORT, European Football for Development Network, International Platform for Sport It Development
	Confederations	Funding to SDP programmes, in-kind support	UEFA, AFC, CONMEBOL, CONCACAF, OFC, CAF
	International Federations at BINGOs	Funding to SDP programmes, in-kind support	FIFA, IOC, IAAF
	Bilateral Aid Agencies	Funding to SDP programmes, knowledge production	NORAD, USAID, British Council, DFID
	Multilateral Aid Agencies and International Organisations	Funding to SDP programmes, knowledge production	United Nations, World Banks, IMF
Public	National Federations	Funding to SDP programmes, training of staff knowledge production	The FA
	National Government	Funding to SDP programmes, training of staff knowledge production	Sport England, UK Sport, NIF
	Local Government	Funding to SDP programmes, knowledge production	Local Authorities

Figure 24.1 Cross-referenced territorial and sectoral categories in the constellation of SDP actors

Transnationally, private actors behave territorially in situations where private commercial gain is a factor, tending to do so across only one or two states at the same time. They may be based in one place but project activity across borders for fixed periods of time.

Within SDP, two very different identifiable types of actor generally fall into this category: *professional sports people* and *research consultancies*. The professional sports world is made up of thousands of individuals, some of whom engage in forms of charitable activity. Not all of this activity could be called SDP, but some is understood as such. Engagement and involvement varies widely. For heavily engaged professionals, a good example is Craig Bellamy who, whilst a Manchester City footballer in 2007, invested in a football and education project in Sierra Leone (Craig Bellamy Foundation 2015). For ex-professionals, perhaps there is no more high-profile example than the 'academy' of ex-professional sports people involved with Laureus via the Laureus Sport for Good Foundation; a CSR foundation of the Swiss-based conglomerate Richemont Group, founders of the Laureus World Sports awards. Primarily, athletes' engagement involves visits to projects that the Foundation resources, providing positive media coverage that accompanies their presence. SDP NGOs tend to hold professional sports people in high regard, and will recruit them as patrons, supporters, and funders. SDP is especially vulnerable to being 'spun' in this way, as professional sports people can and do provide an easy route for PR messaging (Levermore 2010).

An alternative type of transnational private actor can be found in the example of the Research Consultancy: private companies – occasionally legally constituted as not-for-profits – which win contracts from SDP NGOs or funders to research the effectiveness of programmes. Examples include the Walker Research Group, Substance, or Ecorys. However, the interrelationship between research consultancies and SDP organisations is not limited to these individual cases of studying a particular project or intervention. Research consultancies now produce 'platforms': data recording mechanisms for SDP projects. These pieces of software are virtual data-banks for participants in SDP programmes. Staff on SDP projects gather and upload data on participants, where reports can be collated about projects or individuals, and shared with funders.

National examples involve actors with commercial interests driven on a scale beyond the local and regional. While there are companies that operate on this scale and in this way, only a small percentage will reach this scale and explicitly invest in SDP. One type of private enterprise that can invest in SDP – and, if not, may be lobbied intensively by SDP actors do so – is the national professional league. It seems an obvious CSR win for a league to invest in community initiatives that use their sport, but whether or not they do seems to depend on the commercial success of the league and the sport. Examples of leagues that do engage with SDP are the National Football League (NFL) in the US, and the Football League (England). Possibly the most famous example of engagement with SDP is the Premier League's Charitable Fund that is primarily aimed at Club Community Organisations (CCOs) of Premier League football clubs.

Local private examples involve small- to medium-sized enterprises, focused largely on local production of goods and services. Companies may provide employees to volunteer on SDP programmes, or small amounts of sponsorship or 'restricted' funding. Whilst the overall levels of engagement in this way may be relatively small, they can represent significant investments for the companies involved and are important for smaller SDP organisations.

Not-for-profit

International federations and confederations make up the best known actors in the not-for-profit category. This category suggests non-commercial activities but this is not always the case, as FIFA and its confederations illustrate. International federations play particular roles in the world of sport. Broadly speaking their role is to advocate for the development of their sport at elite and grassroots levels, and commercially. How federations behave in relation to SDP is complicated, however.

FIFA has been one of the largest global supporters of Football for Development and Peace (FDP) organisations. It does this via a fund called Football for Hope (FFH). FIFA's FFH fund was originally codified in 2007 with the streetfootballworld network (see below on Transnational Not-for-Profits) and was born of the first FFH Festival in 2006. This fund supplies organisations with funding to spend on football-based social change programmes. This CSR exercise helps justify FIFA's lead in the implementation of World Cups: an event that has been argued to have profound negative consequences for social justice (see Gibson and Watts 2013). A total of $1.5 million invested in 26 FDP projects in Brazil in 2013/14, compared to 108 organisations receiving $3.1 million globally during the same period (FIFA 2015) might be considered in the context of these struggles for fairness.

International confederations coalesce around continental spatio-juridical realms (for example UEFA as the European football confederation), and display varying degrees of interaction with SDP. The European Handball Federation for example, does not make large investments of time and capital in SDP, whereas UEFA does. This has an impact, one could argue, on the types of SDP interventions that SDP organisations make. For example, it would be quite difficult to find SDP NGOs that use handball. But for football it would be far easier. UEFA has funded conventionally defined SDP organisations, where it is only organisations that use sport as an intervention for some kind of desired 'positive' change in society at a grassroots level, whilst also funding organisations that produce knowledge for SDP and advocate for it, such as the United Nations Office for Sport Development and Peace.

A vast number of organisations now operate in a Not-for-Profit transnational space (see Figure 24.1). During the course of my doctoral research, a number of the contributing respondents have been practitioners for, employees of, volunteers in or contributors to Transnational Not-for-Profits. A central mechanism in SDP for this happening is the Transnational Advocacy Network (TAN) (Keck and Sikkink 2002). These organisations are perhaps some of the most interesting in the world of SDP, cohering diverse sets of campaigns, NGOs and individuals around apparently shared interests, and collectively applying pressure on governments, companies and international organisations. Three interesting and differing examples can be found in the streetfootballworld network, the International Platform for Sport and Development and the European Football for Development Network (EFDN).

The Berlin-based streetfootballworld is focused on FDP organisations and also forms the secretariat of a collective bargaining network with over 100 FDP NGOs worldwide (representing 66 countries). This network's stated aim is for the advancement of the world through football. They advise FIFA on how to distribute almost $1.5 million of funding (streetfootballworld 2015), and most of it goes to streetfootballworld network members. EFDN is a different type of network. As its name suggests, it works on a European level to bolster the collective bargaining of the CSR departments, trusts and foundations within professional clubs. The International Platform for Sport and Development is again very different. This is a virtual network of SDP organisations where actors within the sector can share information, find resources for best practice, seek new careers, and advocate for sport as a tool for development. Over time, the platform has become more robust and has published debates that engage critically with SDP. However, it is still overwhelmingly a place to find support for sport and its use.

Funding is incredibly important to SDP organisations. A relatively stable source of this funding over the years has been trusts and foundations. These tend to be NGOS which are independently constituted organisations (such as a UK Registered Charity), and frequently they have their own fundraising campaign activities which generate the funds that they distribute to other NGOs upon receipt of successful applications. Occasionally, these foundations are attached to corporations (for example the Vodafone Foundation), and sometimes they are resourced via the wealth of philanthropists (for example the Gates Foundation). Comic Relief is one particularly successful and well-known British foundation that has, since at least 2007, been involved in funding SDP interventions. Perhaps the most common form of Transnational Not-for-Profit is the implementing NGO, because they are the deliverers of SDP projects. SDP implementing NGOs do not yet have the scale that some development NGOs have achieved – there are none on the scale of Oxfam (turnover of circa £700 million) for example – the largest SDP NGO appearing to be Grassroot Soccer ($5.5 million in 2013).

There is perhaps a greater *methodological* difference though between the organisations that make up the SDP implementing NGOs and the larger group of organisations that implement development projects (though there can be overlap between them). In terms of how their praxis is structured, development organisations tend to be understood as centred on an issue – for example rights, or sexual health. Whilst SDP implementing NGOs often start with one or more issues, they tend to communicate their identity not as the issue but as their solution to it: the use of sport.

Some SDP organisations operate nationally, though interact transnationally. Some well-known examples of these are Street Games and Street League (Britain), Sport Dans La Ville (France) and Kickfair (Germany). Actors of interest in the local not-for-profit are individuals at the micro level. SDP participants and SDP practitioners can act in spaces spanning from the transnational to the local, and in one-to-one interactions between SDP practitioners and participants. SDP practitioners are a diverse set of individuals who are concerned with the *delivery* of SDP programmes. Practitioners includes coaches, educators and volunteers 'at the coalface' as it were, and managers, fundraisers, trainers, directors and evaluators in bureaucratic positions. As with many of the other categories of actors in this chapter, many actors transcend the boundaries drawn here and find themselves with dual or multiple roles, acting locally, nationally and transnationally simultaneously: bipartisan researchers may find themselves embedded within SDP organisations, perhaps guiding praxis in action research; funders, especially corporates, may send employees to volunteer on SDP programmes and beneficiaries of programmes 'graduate' to become practitioners.

Perhaps the most important actors in SDP are the participants. Sometimes these individuals and communities are referred to as 'beneficiaries'. Their 'journey' through interventions, before them, and their verifiable 'changes' after, are increasingly the most important justifications for SDP programmes. They form the rational and logical basis for programme interventions and they give the rational explanation for questions of why *this* or *that* intervention.

Public

The World Bank and International Monetary Fund are perhaps two of the most prominent global multilateral and international organisations which act as consortia of state representatives. The UN office for Sport, Development and Peace (UNOSDP) has been strategically funding five SDP projects over the last five years and runs a series of youth leadership camps for SDP participants in various regions (United Nations 2015), but other organisations have now entered this space, including the European Union.

Bilateral aid agencies are state agencies that distribute funding to programmes via bilateral agreements between donor and recipient countries. Strategic agreements usually exist between two states and involve a number of measures for aid and trade. SDP, in the early part of the twenty-first century, began to appear more in the portfolios of these wider agreements. One agency, that has for some time supported SDP as a development intervention, is the Norwegian Agency for Development Cooperation (NORAD) in Zimbabwe, funding the Kicking AIDS Out Network as part of a wider package of interventions in its strategic agreement with Zimbabwe between 2006 and 2015 (NORAD 2015: iii–5). The President's Emergency Plan for AIDS Relief (PEPFAR) founded by the Bush administration, has supported efforts to stem the HIV/AIDS epidemic, including those efforts that use sport. In 2009 Grassroot Soccer received a grant from PEPFAR for its work in South Africa on prevention (Grassroot Soccer 2009). National governing bodies and national federations – usually members of transnational confederations – are the organisations that are primarily responsible for the development of their respective sports at both the elite and grassroots level. They usually administer the national team for each national sport they represent also. The Football Association (England) has a long-standing relationship with SDP organisations, for example.

Local authorities, in the UK but also, no doubt, elsewhere, have been commissioning services to local providers as the state becomes ever more privatised. SDP has been a recipient of some of these funds. Health services provide a certain discursive fit with SDP NGOs, particularly because they market themselves as being involved in the 'production' of healthy people, via their base in sport and physical activity. Sport in and of itself is often deemed to be a healthy activity.

Power, interconnections and alignments

How then, do these actors connect to one another in the constellation of SDP? There is clearly a temptation to view the flow of money as an indication of how power functions in SDP: the rich and powerful set the agenda for the powerless, who desire access to capital. Indeed money and 'funding' were frequently referred to by my doctoral research respondents. However, we should see flows of capital as a strategic means, and not an end. As Foucault argued, political economy is the major form of knowledge in governmentality, and not its *raison d'être* (2009: 108–109). Capital and its flow through the system of SDP rests upon the inter-exchange of ideas throughout widely arrayed systems. These ideas are 'knowledges': 'common-sense' understandings of the world and how things work within it. They fundamentally configure behaviour of actors and crucially they change the way people talk and write. In the case of SDP, this can be the understanding of what organisations should be, and how they should make change, in order to create 'better' human beings (Darnell 2010). These *rationalities*, by which I mean sets of incoherent or semi-coherent "common-sense" understandings, given a name or an overarching concept, are, in short, ways and means of rationally justifying, or appealing to, the connections between illogical collections of ideas (Rose 1999).

Though CSR/GCSE has been an incredibly effective vehicle for the transmission of certain ideas between different parts of the system (Hayhurst 2011), we should look deeper into CSR, beyond seeing it as simply a technology of governmentality in a hierarchical system of control of the relatively powerless. Instead, CSR is one way that SDP actors connect logically with dominant rationalities using their banks of data about the work they do, and the participants in their programmes. My research indicates that SDP actors use logical bases in a techno-strategic project to align to rational understandings of desirable organisational qualities.

Two discursive alignments emerge. In the first instance, we see a discursive alignment of the *company as 'socially responsible'*. In the second instance, we see an *alignment of the praxis of SDP organisations*, their internal administration and management, their strategies, the discourse of CSR, and a discourse of corporate strategy and business practice, presented as a coherent rationality. The logical basis of 'quality' *monitoring and evaluation* and data logically underpins these two alignments: the way in which individuals and groups are given order through administrative techniques. These micro techniques – which can be as simple as an attendance register, a best-practice guide, or a multi-million dollar participant database – incorporate people into systems, standardising praxis, capturing biological and behavioural data about people, and are the fundamental technology of governmentality in SDP, and the fundamental apparatuses of the biopolitical society that Foucault described (2008).

Company aligned as socially responsible

The idea of corporations aligning strategically to socially responsible aims is not new and can be partly related to customers; perceptions changed and social media empowered customers/critics and 'a dynamic and growing space between charities and businesses to work together' (Keale, interview 2013).

Aspiration for the values of 'doing good' to be embedded within the genetics of an organisation is a response heard regularly. The implication is that this reconstruction of what the company *is* should seep into its aspirations for itself (see Prescott and Phelan 2008). One participant in the research shared a speech with me made at a CSR conference, which stated that:

> the difference between sponsorship and CSR is largely one of intent, and essentially, (in one word): ownership. If I sponsor an individual or another organisation to do something, it is really down to them. If, as a CEO of an organisation, I create (or participate in the creation of) an agenda for change, and I am prepared to use all my resources: my employees, my technical capabilities, my brand, and my money. And I am prepared to set targets for success, even though I may work with other organisations, then that is looking rather more like a CSR agenda.
>
> *(Grant's speech 2013)*[1]

The creation of change agendas by the company, and not the charity raises questions about what the company identity must *be* in its authentication to employees and consumers. Company values and 'strategic fit' are important factors:

> When a business is seeking to pursue its CSR agenda through a specific charity, there does have to be a snug fit between the charity and the business – there has to be an alignment of values and cause. It doesn't matter where the synergy comes from but it does have to be powerful and clearly articulated.
>
> *(Grant's speech 2013)*

MNCs use their company values to connect to socially justifiable aims. Values, seen as transcending business objectives and presented as omnipresent, are held up as the very essence of corporate identity. Those with experience of CSR relationships based upon engagement with the charitable activities of the NGO talk about how values externalise in a company's strategy for 'giving':

> What they've done is basically impose their international and national philanthropy strategy that's based around their employees and their customers, and they will only get involved with programmes that compliment these objectives; otherwise they will work with us to look at ways we can *adapt* [my emphasis] our projects in order to fall into line with this.
>
> *(Graham, interview 2013)*

On the one hand, it is definitely about power and legitimacy, because if you look at what happened since the crash, and the fact that I guess that many people would think that CSR is about propping up the existing order, because you know for business to kind of continue being seen as legitimate in the eyes of most people, it needs to be able to show it's also a force for good rather than just a force for destabilising the economy . . . for many people CSR is sort of the saviour, it's sort of trying to stabilise the whole existing order.

(Keale, interview 2013)

Meanwhile, from an MNC perspective, the following quote captured a common view:

We don't care about the size of the NGO. But it must be innovative. [SDP NGO name] worked with us on training [young professional people] on social issues that affected them, and on improving communications. The content was used to lobby government. . . . Collaborations with NGOs can lead to market insight and innovation; ideas and such about consumers and markets. This is highly valuable and you can put a number on that.

(Hone, presentation 2013)

Whilst this political work undermines the aims of not-for-profits, this tendency by companies gives something to connect their work to; a problem to solve through sport. The knowledge objects of the de-unified, the uneducated, and the culturally disparate become therefore the issues to be solved. These are powerful connecting forces for SDP NGOs to appeal to. In so doing, they cohere to the discourse of the company as socially responsible in solving these and creating the agendas for their change. For companies, it is a dynamic whereby the 'social' work they undertake in their CSR mission justifies the identification of the problems that work is trying to solve; their machinations to do good invent and re-invent the problems they are trying to solve.

Practice, administration, strategy; corporatisation/ professionalisation alignment

SDP NGOs see 'socially responsible' companies, and they interpret the way the company sees itself. But they also design their own strategies based upon common-sense understandings of what effective administration is. It appears that the prevailing ideas of how to 'do business' within SDP NGOs imitate those commonly associated with corporations, presumably under an assumption that this increases the chances of finding corporate allies. The goals for communities and the challenges to be addressed by SDP programming have begun to be interpreted and represented by SDP practitioners in corporate terms. Practice and administration appears configured towards a 'different' way of doing things in NGOs. This involves the emergence of a more corporate administration within not-for-profits, where there is an equivocation of 'commercialisation', with 'efficiency', and 'accuracy'. The following respondent offers an excellent illustration:

The corporatisation of [Foundation], as a charity, was something I started to see ten years ago when I was working for them. They started to really look into efficiency, and much more corporate values. And the culture changed; the appointments changed: the backgrounds of people at a senior level. . . . They started bringing in people from places like [MNC] in their marketing departments and fundraising departments, to raise more corporate money, because they had a more effective way of raising more money for a charitable purpose.

(Harry, interview 2013)

What an SDP NGO can 'learn' from the corporate world is seen as important (Hayhurst 2010), tethering the two worlds via SDP NGOs justifying their own strategies, tactics, techniques, discourses and behaviours under a *rationality* of the logic of corporate practice and administration. The perception therefore of a viable organisation becomes one (social and otherwise) that is administrated commercially. The consequence of this for company and NGO, as well as a change in practice, is a change in the way people talk about themselves and others. For example another respondent noted:

> I think the language that we use, and the language that the [SDP] sector uses has got a lot of influence from Corporate Social Responsibility language. I don't know if that is a positive thing or not, but it just seems to be going that way. . . . So for example a key thing around the word 'sustainability' is that it's become quite prominent in our sector, in that it's originally an 'environment' word, and now it was adopted by businesses and now in Sport for Development.
>
> *(Masters, interview 2013)*

The influence of CSR in the change from the common-sense understanding of 'sustainability' is telling. The idea seemed to be that being 'business minded' had advantages for SDP organisations. Of the utmost import is to 'talk the language' of corporates, and to demonstrate behaviours in a certain way. Organisational practice is realigned to an appeal to the corporate/professional. By implication, the identity of the SDP organisation is fixed at a starting place that is 'unprofessional'; framed as a fault to be fixed:

> I think there is a lot of pressure . . . even on us as an organisation to be more business minded in our approach and in how we work. Because we think businesses are efficient, highly successful . . . but over the last few years of course they haven't proven themselves to be as efficient or successful.
>
> *(Masters, interview 2013)*

The logic is that more commercially minded SDP actors will deliver more effectively. This suggests an alignment between SDP administration and common-sense understandings of corporate practice.

Verifying; monitoring and evaluation: the logical basis

In line with a corporate business-focused approach, monitoring and evaluation of programmes appear to be increasingly central features of SDP. This was evident in programmes being considered good if they had *measurable* benefits and met a *demonstrable need* in the community. Raising questions of how legitimacy is gained, successive respondents indicated processes of evaluation of SDP programmes. 'Measuring' and 'demonstrating' are embedded in partnerships at the outset. These become the logical basis for connection to both corporations' pretensions to social responsibility, and corporate/professional aspirations of SDP NGOs. It is the rational justification for the alignments between each set of actors.

The appeal to the language of business encodes the attempt to connect with a set of seemingly logical discourses. Appeals for support are then framed in terms the corporate can connect with. The implication is that SDP NGOs must be verifiable to be fundable. Informed by this logic, they can connect with this discourse via a technical appeal from the *datarisation* of their work. By the objective demonstration that their work has made a 'positive' change, they can appeal to a rational discourse of what it is to be a commercially data-driven entity; to be informed, and 'in-the-know'. And in networks of SDP organisations this idea of sharing and commonality beyond funding was revealed by a number of respondents. There is a culture of finding consistency and coherence between different organisations, methods and discourses that seem to be shared by various people within the sector, at various different levels. Where organisations want to be part of something, they must demonstrate how they are similar in approach rather than demonstrate how they are different. Processes must be put into place; processes that sort the networked from the excluded. There is a perception amongst SDP practitioners that this logic of inclusion and exclusion is based upon shared objective notions of quality. So again, some dominant ideas and knowledges are circulated, connecting not just between donor and recipient actors, but in recipient-to-recipient relations also.

The impacts SDP programmes have are verifiable desired changes in behaviour and characteristics amongst participants (see for example, Coalter 2009: 4). For example, UK Sport's international wing, UK Sport International has invested in a research programme alongside Comic Relief, to look at two changes in 'personal development' amongst participants in six SDP programmes (Coalter and Taylor 2010: 18–19). In the case of SDP organisations that focus on HIV/AIDS, a change in participants' practices regarding safe sex, or getting tested may be assessed; or it may be that organisations encouraging work readiness amongst unemployed young people demonstrate a change in skills for the job market. Monitoring change involves the tricky practice of 'tracking' (maintaining contact or surveillance of a participant or group over a period of time in order to survey changes). In this way groups of participants' experiences are codified into data that spreads out over a predefined space in order to ascertain who changed, and who did not. Partnerships with private sector organisations are sought in order to enact the required technologies for measurement. As one research participant told me, charities are now working with companies to develop new systems of surveillance:

> that will enable them to track their impact on [participants] way more effectively. So you see at that level, what you've got is a transfer of IP [Intellectual Property] and technical know-how from the business into the charity that translates into them actually getting a lot more savvy and data driven in terms of how they measure their effect on the people they exist to serve, which will then filter into more innovation, more learning, and better practices.
>
> *(Keale, interview 2013)*

Conclusion: governmentality and power in SDP

Power is not something that some have and others are subject to. It is exercised in networks, between actors, and individuals (Foucault 2004). Power is not:

> A phenomenon of mass and homogenous domination – the domination of one individual over others, of one group over others, or of one class over others. . . . Power must, I think, be analysed as something that circulates, or rather as something that

functions only when it is part of a chain. . . . Power is exercised through networks, and individuals do not simply circulate in those networks; they are in a position to both submit to and exercise this power. They are never the inert or consenting targets of power; they are always its relays. In other words, power passes through individuals. It is not applied to them.

(Foucault 2004: 29)

Foucault understood *biopolitics* as the political power exercised over every aspect of human life, its production and reproduction (2009: 359–366). Whilst monetary policy of any government is deployed to this end, it is not the monetary system that empowers the politics of society. Instead the quest to realign the services of society to the problematic faced – the 'faults' within society – which the services are intended to remedy (Foucault 2008: 25–51).

Services in SDP have been configured to a rational and corporate understanding of how to administer the doing of good. What I have called 'alignments' of the actors analysed in this chapter, are first a common-sense understanding of aligning the activities of corporations as socially responsible, and second, of 'professionalisation' or 'corporatisation', where SDP NGOs align praxis with perceptions of effective corporate administration, internally within their own organisations and externally in communications. Lastly, monitoring and evaluation processes 'verify' the alignments, and provide the logical basis for appeals to connect with what Foucault called a *Regime of Truth* (2008: 1–25).

In Foucault's analysis, it was not that madness, sickness and sexuality became problems toward which various services, tactics and techniques were directed in remedy; rather, the services, tactics and techniques allowed the system of knowledges and common-sense understandings of those very faults (madness, sickness, sexuality, etc.) that made them knowledge objects (ibid.). In this chapter, we have seen that NGO practice is aligned with corporate administration to solving the issues posed by SDP, and justified rationally. A system of services, tactics and techniques deployed around an alignment of resources, discourses, ideas and praxis to solve problems identified by the same interventions meant to solve them. The responses seem to invent the 'social problems' to which the techniques and technologies of governmentality are aimed. This is not what power *is*, but it is *where* it is and how it *functions*. These are the capillaries of power in SDP. This chapter argues that a technology of governmentality is an appealing yet borderless system of ideas and concepts; practices and techniques, and it is to the minutiae of these machinations that research should now be orientated.

Note

1 Unless stated, the quotes originated from my doctoral research and include interviews with SDP practitioners and conference materials.

References

Barclays. (2015) Key facts and figures: Progress update. *Barclays Online.* Accessed 25 October 2015. www.home.barclays/citizenship/our-approach/key-facts-and-figures.html.

Coalter, F. (2007) *A Wider Social Role for Sport: Who's Keeping the Score?* London: Routledge.

Coalter, F. (2009) Sport-in-development: A monitoring and evaluation manual. *The International Platform for Sport and Development Online.* Accessed 5 May 2014. www.sportanddev.org/toolkit/?uNewsID=17.

Coalter, F. and Taylor, J. (2010) Sport-for-Development impact study, *UK Sport* [online]. Accessed 17 December 2011. www.uksport.gov.uk/docLib/MISC/FullReport.pdf.

Craig Bellamy Foundation. (2015) About us. *Craig Bellamy Foundation Online.* Accessed 12 April 2015. http://craigbellamyfoundation.org/about-us.

Darnell, S.C. (2007) Playing with race: *Right to play* and the production of whiteness in 'development through sport'. *Sport in Society*, 10(4): 560–579.

Darnell, S.C. (2010) Sport, race and bio-politics: Encounters with difference in 'Sport for Peace' internships. *Journal of Sport and Social Issues*, 34(4): 396–417.

Darnell, S.C. (2012a) Olympism in action, Olympic hosting and the politics of 'Sport for Development and Peace': Investigating the development discourses of Rio 2016. *Sport in Society*, 15(6): 869–887.

Darnell, S.C. (2012b) *Sport for Development and Peace: A Critical Sociology.* London: Bloomsbury Academic.

Darnell, S.C. and Hayhurst, L. (2012) Hegemony, postcolonialism and sport for development: A response to Lindsey and Grattan. *International Journal of Sport Policy and Politics*, 4(1): 111–124.

FIFA. (2015) Football for hope. *FIFA Online.* Accessed 22 March 2015. www.fifa.com/aboutfifa/socialresponsibility/footballforhope/.

Foucault, M. (2004) *Society Must Be Defended: Lectures at the Collège de France 1975–1976.* M. Bertani, F. Ewald and A. Fontana (eds). Translated by D. Macey. London: Penguin.

Foucault, M. (2008) *The Birth of Biopolitics: Lectures at the Collège de France 1978–1979.* M. Senellart, F. Ewald, A. Fontana and F. Davidson (eds). Translated by G. Burchell. Basingstoke: Palgrave Macmillan.

Foucault, M. (2009) *Security, Territory, Population: Lectures at the Collège de France 1977–1978.* M. Senellart, F. Ewald, A. Fontana and F. Davidson (eds). Translated by G. Burchell. Basingstoke: Palgrave Macmillan.

Gibson, O. and Watts, J. (2013) World Cup: Rio favelas being 'socially cleansed' in run-up to sporting events. *The Guardian.* Accessed 22 March 2015. http://www.theguardian.com/world/2013/dec/05/world-cup-favelas-socially-cleansed-olympics.

Giulianotti, R. (2004) Human rights, globalization and sentimental education: The case of sport. *Sport in Society*, 7(3): 355–369.

Giulianotti, R. (2005) *Sport: A Critical Sociology.* Cambridge: Polity.

Giulianotti, R. (2010) Sport, peacemaking and conflict resolution: A contextual analysis and modeling of the sport, development and peace sector. *Ethnic and Racial Studies*, 34(2): 207–228.

Giulianotti, R. (2011) Sport, transnational peacemaking, and global civil society: exploring the reflective discourses of 'sport, development, and peace' project officials. *Journal of Sport and Social Issues*, 35(1): 50–71.

Grant. (2013) Speech (supplied). 24 October 2013.

Grassroot Soccer. (2009) GRS named new PEPFAR partner. *Grassroot Soccer.* Accessed 29 March 2015. http://www.grassrootsoccer.org/2009/01/14/grs-named-new-pepfar-partner-2/.

Hayhurst, L.M.C. (2009) The power to shape policy: Charting sport for development and peace policy discourses. *International Journal of Sport Policy and Politics*, 1(2): 203–227.

Hayhurst, L.M.C. (2011) Corporatising sport, gender and development: Postcolonial IR feminisms, transnational private governance and global corporate social engagement. *Third World Quarterly*, 32(3): 531–549.

Hone. (2013) Conference Presentation. 25 June 2013.

International Platform on Sport and Development [sportanddev.org]. (2015) About this platform. *sportanddev.org Online.* Accessed 29 March 2015. www.sportanddev.org/en/about_this_platform/.

Keale. (2013) Interview (recorded). 1 October 2013.

Kidd, B. (2008) A new social movement: sport for development and peace. *Sport in Society*, 11(4): 370–380.

Keck, M.E. and Sikkink, K. (2002) Transnational advocacy networks in international and regional politics. *International Social Science Journal*, 51(159): 89–101.

Laureus Sport for Good Foundation and Ecorys. (2013) Sport scores: The costs and benefits of sport for crime reduction. Executive Summary. *Laureus Online.* Accessed 11 May 2014. http://www.laureus.com/sites/default/files/publications/laureusecoryssportscores211112.pdf.

Levermore, R. (2010) CSR for development through sport: Examining its potential and limitations. *Third World Quarterly*, 31(2): 223–241.

Lindsey, I. and Grattan, A. (2012) An 'international movement'? Decentring sport-for-development within Zambian communities. *International Journal of Sport Policy and Politics*, 4(1): 91–110.

Naish, J. (unpublished) PhD Thesis. University of Brighton, England.

Norwegian Agency for Development Cooperation (NORAD). (2011) Evaluation of the strategy for Norway's culture and sports cooperation countries in the south; case country Zimbabwe. *NORAD*

Online. Accessed 29 March 2015. www.norad.no/globalassets/import-2162015-80434-am/www. norad.no-ny/filarkiv/vedlegg-til-publikasjoner/report_3_2011_zimbabwe_web.pdf.

Prescott, D. and Phelan, J. (2008) Shared goals through sport: getting a sustainable return for companies and communities. *International Business Leaders Forum.* Accessed 27 December 2011. www.iblf.org/sport.

President's Emergency Plan for AIDS Relief (PEPFAR). (2007) Monitoring and evaluation systems strengthening tool. *PEPFAR Online.* Accessed 10 May 2014. www.pepfar.gov/documents/organization/79624.pdf.

Rose, N. (1999) *Powers of Freedom: Reframing Political Thought.* Cambridge: Cambridge University Press.

Sport England. (2014) What we do. *Sport England Online.* Accessed 4 August 2014. www.sportengland.org/about-us/.

streetfootballworld. (2015) Football for hope programme support. *streetfootballworld Online.* Accessed 29 March 2015. http://streetfootballworld.org/project/football-hope-programme-support.

UEFA. (2013) Football and social responsibility report 2012/13. *UEFA Online.* Accessed 29 March 2015. www.uefa.org/MultimediaFiles/Download/uefaorg/General/02/10/87/68/2108768_DOWNLOAD.pdf.

United Nations. (2015) Sport for development and peace: the UN system in action. *United Nations Online.* Accessed 22 March 2015. www.un.org/wcm/content/site/sport/home/unplayers/unoffice.

25

THE POLITICS OF SEXUALITY AND SPORT

Nigel Jarvis

Introduction

Annually I teach a group of final year undergraduate physical education students about issues related to sexuality and sport. The lecture starts with the students traditionally being asked to mention the first things that come to their minds when they think about lesbians and gay men and sport. After some initial trepidation, students consistently comment gay men like individual or 'feminine' sports like swimming or dance, while they perceive a lot of lesbians take part in soccer, field hockey or rugby. Normally these stereotypes generate quite a bit of laughter in the room. Further, after presenting them the history of the global growth of gay sport networks, one female student stated recently:

> I don't understand the big deal. Everyone gets along and young people here don't care if you're gay or straight. I don't understand why there is a need for gay sport clubs or the Gay Games . . . people should just openly play in a club or in the Olympics.

While this may indicate what McCormack (2012) considers as diminished cultural homophobia, the student demonstrates naiveté regarding the complex nature and politics surrounding sexuality and sport. She may not be considering her place of study being privileged. Her university and department, teaching physical education, which has a long history of feminism and being tolerant of sexualities, is located in the south of England, near a city (Brighton) known for being liberal and gay-friendly. Therefore her world view is biased, insulated perhaps by her environment (academia), and does not consider a perspective from more conservative parts of the country. This would include, for example, the debated challenges associated with being 'out' in rural areas or less developed nations (see Leedy and Connolly 2007; Weinke and Hill 2013). Additionally, she and her fellow colleagues had difficulty in identifying famous gay athletes, further showing that considerable work remains to be done despite her comments that people should play openly, regardless of sexuality. Further, as highlighted later, recent developments regarding (homo)sexuality and mainstream sport have attracted some significant (sport) media attention. Thus, this provides an opportune time to revisit the topic of sexuality and sport and delve into some current and key, but not exhaustive, political and ideological tensions associated with lesbian and gay sport.

In addition to a review of the literature and theoretical debates associated with sexuality and sport, this chapter is underpinned by a qualitative approach. A number of interviews were carried out with stakeholders at the most recent 2014 Gay Games in Cleveland/Akron. The author's experience and research at four past Gay Games (Sydney, Chicago, Cologne, and Cleveland/Akron), and considerable sport participation in both grassroots straight and gay clubs in Canada and the United Kingdom, helps provide a critical insight into some current political issues. Some may consider this insider view as subjective and potentially a source of bias; however, I argue this approach provided an in-depth understanding into key political issues.

While major themes related to the sociological and cultural analysis of modern sport have long focused on issues of gender, race, and class, only more recently since the 1990s has the topic of sexuality and sport strongly emerged (see for example Caudwell 2006; Connell 1990; Messner 1992; Pronger 1990; Theberge 1995). Like gender scholars, most sexuality researchers consider sexualities as ongoing and fluid constructions rather than stable identities around which action is organised (Butler 1990; Laurendeau 2004). Hence this chapter inter-changes and uses various terms to be inclusive of a range of sexual identities. The term gay is employed at times to encompass lesbians, gay men, bisexuals, transgendered persons, queer, questioning and/or intersex (LGBTQI). Many sport clubs around the globe simply use the term gay, whilst others incorporate lesbian/gay in their name to identify they are catering to sexual minorities.

Sexuality and sport falls under the wider analytical area of gender issues because sport is one of the cultural spheres that most explicitly generates, reproduces and publicly displays gender identities and difference, and justifies the existing hierarchical gender order (Connell 1995; McKay *et al.* 2000; Theberge 2000). Indeed, sport appears to be historically slower than other areas in society, like the workplace, politics and the military/police in welcoming or addressing issues related to women and/or LGBTQI persons. More on how the generally conservative sporting arenas attempt to preserve a masculine space is discussed later; however, it is initially important to keep in mind that gender and sexuality clearly intersect. The histori-cal roots of gay sport and recent popular media accounts of (homo)sexuality and sport are first discussed to set the scene before some key theoretical implications are reviewed and debated.

Historical roots of gay/LGBTQI sport

Formal organised gay sport clubs, networks and related events are a fairly recent global phe-nomenon. Messner (1992) noted since the outset of the gay liberation movement in the early 1970s, sport has become an integral part of the growth of lesbian and gay communities. As gay men and lesbians emerged from underground bars and other covert sites in Western industri-alised nations, sport became a new place where they could be more visible and socialise. Thus, gay athletes began an appropriation of spaces (Williams 1961), playing sport in public parks and venues, which were traditionally occupied by mainstream sporting groups and an ideology that favours and promotes heterosexuality (Krane 2001; Wright and Clarke 1999).

Lesbian and gay men in the 1970s began to organise clubs because mainstream sports were not comfortable spaces for them. With the establishment of gay sports leagues in many cities across North America (largely centred on softball, volleyball, tennis, bowling and swimming) and in Europe (mainly volleyball, tennis, badminton, soccer and swimming) the founders began to form annual tournaments that attracted teams from many places. The need to arrange and administer these national and international sporting events required further coordination, and thus many formal sport associations were established during the late 1970s and 1980s. These included the

North American Gay Amateur Athletic Alliance (established 1977), the San Francisco Arts and Athletic (1981), which eventually became the Federation of Gay Games (FGG) (1989), which manages the Gay Games movement, and the European Gay and Lesbian Sport Federation (1989), responsible for the EuroGames. Thus organised gay sport occurs within an increasingly sophisticated network of individuals, teams and leagues operating on local, national and/or international levels. For example, the Gay and Lesbian Tennis Alliance (2014), founded in 1991, has grown into a global group that has around 10,000 members, with some 70 tournaments per year in cities like Bangkok, Dallas, Katowice, Denpasar and Rome.

Since gay men and lesbians tend to migrate to urban areas, the vast majority of their sport involvement takes place in cities. Most larger cities in Europe, North America, Japan and Australia tend to have some type of visible gay sporting group. Although a vast array of organised sporting opportunities exist, it is important to recognise that there are obviously LGBTQI persons who participate in sport outside the formalised gay sport networks. A cursory internet review reveals an array of opportunities, with clubs offering golf, running/walking, surfing, darts, snowboarding, basketball, sailing, rodeo, dancing, ice hockey, curling and wrestling. Since the millennium, the growth and visibility of gay sport clubs and events has moved beyond the more developed nations to cities in developing countries such as Buenos Aires, Mexico City and Cape Town. These places, not traditionally known as gay friendly, are fast attracting local residents as well as international gay sport tourists as societal attitudes change. For example, the BBC (2012) reported that Kathmandu, Nepal hosted South Asia's first gay sports tournament in 2012 with more than 300 participants from 30 countries.

The Gay Games, held every four years like the Olympics, is arguably the most popular and recognised sport event for the LGBTQI community. The mission of the FGG (2014a), much like any gay sport group, is 'to promote equality through the organisation of the premiere international LGBT and gay-friendly sports and cultural event known as the Gay Games. They are built upon the principles of participation, inclusion and personal best'. Gay sports groups have gone out of their way to stress inclusiveness, regardless of skill, age, gender, disability, race, class, HIV status, geographic origin and sexual orientation. Less known is that straight athletes and allies can also participate in the event, a phenomenon known as 'inverse integration' (Elling *et al.* 2003).

A political conflict has emerged as it appears the Gay Games stress friendship over the sexuality of the event. Thus this could be seen as the erasure of lesbian and gay difference in the pursuit of sporting legitimation as Pronger (2000: 232) argued: 'gay sports proves the normality of lesbians and gay men'. While he believes gay sport groups are inclusive of gay identities, he is critical because they are attempting to remove homosexuality and sexual desire from the discussion. Miller (2001) disagrees and contends that sports are clearly undergoing immense change, with sex at the centre.

The opening and closing ceremonies of the Games are highly political events, with increasingly prominent celebrities and politicians taking part, reminding athletes of past and present struggles. The 2014 Cleveland/Akron opening ceremonies included a 90-second video from President Barack Obama, enthusiastically cheered by the audience. Obama said:

> we have come a long way in our commitment to the equal rights of LGBT people here and around the world. I am proud of my administration's record and of the citizens who've helped to push for justice. I know some of you have come from places where it requires courage, even defiance to come out, sometimes at great personal risk. You should know the United States stands with you and for your human rights, just as our athletes stand with you on the field at these Games.

Athletes can also apply for financial support, as part of the FGG's human rights campaign, to help subsidise the cost of travelling to and taking part in the Games. They have been granted to athletes coming from developing nations in Africa, Asia and South America, as well as parts of Eastern Europe. Many of these athletes become activists and travel back to their own host nations to further promote the development of gay sport. Some Russian athletes were honoured by the FGG to travel and participate in the 2014 Cleveland/Akron Gay Games, to highlight the oppression of gay rights under the leadership of Vladimir Putin.

Athlete figures at gay competitions tend to vary by source and can be disputed. According to the FGG (2014b) the number of participants in the Gay Games has grown from an initial 1,300 athletes in San Francisco in 1982 to a peak of 13,000 in Amsterdam in 1998. Cologne attracted 10,000 in 2010, whereas just under 8,000 attended Cleveland/Akron in 2014. Critics may point to this as a diminished demand although there are some more simple explanations for the declining numbers. Cleveland/Akron, may possess less tourism appeal among potential participants within the US and globally (Gilbert 2014) compared to previous host cities like New York or Vancouver. However, further scrutiny reveals some more complex political issues at play. There was a split within the Gay Games movement with the awarding of the event to Montréal in 2006. The Federation pulled support for the Canadian hosts over concerns about the size and lack of financial transparency and gave Chicago the Games (Jarvis 2013a). From the ashes of Montréal a new global gay sport event emerged, namely the World/OutGames, overseen by the Gay and Lesbian International Sport Association. This spread and diluted the demand for an iconic global event, as more were occurring not just every four years. There have been discussions to reconcile the schism between the two competing groups to pave the way forward for one global unified games; however, at the time of writing, recent talks failed. Participation numbers from previous World OutGames in Montréal, Copenhagen and Antwerp are difficult to verify although *The Guardian* (2009) claimed that 5,500 attended the Danish event in 2009.

In addition to the multitude of annual local sport festivals, travelling to compete in multi-day events is expensive and many gay athletes, especially women, those from ethnic minorities or developing nations, find it difficult to take part. Executive Director Phyllis Harris (2014) of the LGBT Community Center of Greater Cleveland expressed concern about the lack of African-American, Hispanic and youth participants in the Games. Indeed, much like the mainstream arena (King *et al.* 2007; Theberge 2000), the organisation and participation of gay sport tends to be dominated by a privileged white male middle class (Davidson 2013). Recent Games numbers are likely to have been affected by the global financial crisis and recession (2007–12). A litmus test may be seen at the next Gay Games, which are to take place in Paris in 2018. The French organisers plan to attract 15,000, which would make it the largest gay sport event ever. Certainly its geographic position, high tourist amenities and appealing sport venues, such as Roland Garros for tennis, may make the targeted number achievable, as participants choose this event over others on the gay sporting calendar.

Many of the sports participated in by lesbian and gay athletes reflect what Messner (1992) and Pronger (2000) identify as a value system and vision based on feminist and gay liberationist ideals of equality and universal participation. This is defined by allowing a range of people to participate, regardless of sexuality and/or skill level. Sport for gay people is seen as part of a general celebration and display of gay culture with a marked focus on making conspicuous lifestyle statements (Hargreaves 2000). They also constitute a powerful and public reaction to homophobic discrimination and oppression in sport, and provide a safe space for participants. On this level then, participation in gay sport can be seen as having emancipatory power. The global growth and development of gay sports networks and events, like the Gay Games, have transformed the way gay athletes experience and understand sport (Pronger 2000; Symons 2010). While this paints a positive picture and signifies progress for sexual minorities in the arena of physical activity, there exists a series of issues with wider implications that have accompanied the development.

The Gay Games/OutGames and smaller tournaments may be significant and meaningful for those that take part, in addition to the considerable economic and tourism impacts for the destinations, but they gain little attention from the wider national and global mainstream media. Some television reporting was noted on local stations where Gay Games have taken place. Major newspapers in host cities, such as the *Sydney Morning Herald, Chicago Tribune, Kölner Stadt-Anzeiger,* and *Cleveland Plain Dealer,* devoted extensive daily front page news coverage of the Gay Games, but significantly only in the news section, and not in the sports pages. Whether this helps validate or undermine the legitimacy of the event as a sport spectacle is worthy of future scrutiny.

Much of gay sport, especially at the grassroots level, tends to take place away from the public gaze. Whether this represents a local gay tennis club playing on some courts, badminton in an indoor community centre, or softball teams competing on a diamond in a public park, few people walking by would likely stop to notice LGBTQI persons playing sport. Certainly larger events, like the Gay Games, receive some local media attention, but how challenging can they be if wider society is limited in their awareness? Messner (1992) suggested the Gay Games represent a radical break from past conceptions of the role of sport in society, they do not represent a major challenge to sport as an institution. This is because they still do not necessarily confront or change the dominant structure of sport because they largely occur in spaces outside of the dominant mainstream settings. Hargreaves (2000) furthered this point by observing that gay sport tends to take place in insular, ghettoised spaces and that gay sports liberation is partial and conditional – it has only come with separation and not with integration. The contestation and clash around space and meaning, and the aspiration to provide space for new types and different forms of sporting cultural expression, such as the OutGames and Gay Games, is a key issue. Thus while opening and closing ceremonies of the Gay Games held in public hypermasculine spaces like Soldier Field, home of the National Football League's Chicago Bears, Amsterdam Arena (Ajax football club), or Quicken Loans Arena (National Basketball Association's Cleveland Cavaliers), can be seen as somewhat challenging, it is not until these events and their political ambitions become even more widely reported among more (sporting) media outlets, that gay sport will further challenge traditionally conservative sport institutions.

However, some noteworthy movements and integration between mainstream and the gay sporting spaces offers some potential. The traditional locations of where LGBTQI athletes can take part is seen conceptually as in binary opposition – see Figure 25.1 (modified from Jarvis 2013b). The more conservative mainstream sites are considered as professional leagues, schools, adult/youth voluntary, private and grassroots clubs. Here, it is assumed that the vast majority of participants are heterosexual although closeted or openly gay athletes may also take part. According to Jarvis (2006) some gay women and men leave mainstream sport sites for a multitude of reasons, move into gay sport clubs, and remain for the rest of their sporting careers. This is represented by a smaller circle because of the fact there are less of them available compared to mainstream spaces.

Elling *et al.* (2003) and Wellard (2002) argue that the reality of gay sport clubs can be full of tensions and contradictions. On the one hand they are created to offer a setting away from the oppressive compulsory heterosexuality in mainstream sites; on the other, they tend to be based on conventional sporting values that promote competition and winning. Some gay

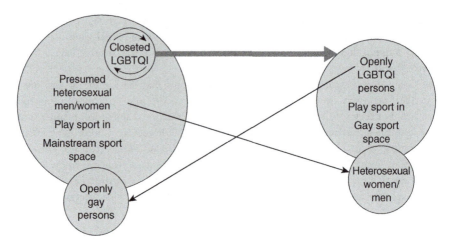

Figure 25.1 The binary of mainstream and gay sport space

athletes may gain sporting capital within these sites and progress back into mainstream sites and participate openly as gay. The Brighton gay tennis club in England openly competes within the mainstream parks league and is accepted regardless of sexuality. Many gay clubs like rowing or curling also compete directly with straight mainstream clubs simply because of the lack of numbers and/or competition. To add complexity and fluidity to the model, some heterosexual men and women move from mainstream spaces into gay clubs, for example because of siblings or friends, or a lack of available offerings (Jarvis 2013b), previously noted as reverse integration (Elling *et al.* 2003). Thus the traditional binary is becoming more blurred. This does offer some further political intrigue. While some critics (Davidson 2014; Pronger 2000) may argue that gay sport is not challenging traditional dominant notions of sport, the increasing transgressive movement of athletes, regardless of sexuality, between the two binaries, mainly at the grassroots level, but also within elite and professional sites, shows some opportunity to break down the conservative nature of sport as an institution. The next section continues with other disruptive developments related to popular media accounts of the contested integration and prominence around sexuality and sport discourse.

The political implications of sexuality and sport accounts in the media

Recent developments regarding (homo)sexuality and mainstream sport have attracted some significant media attention. There are strong reasons why academics should now pay attention to how traditional mainstream and increasingly web-based and social media talk about sport, including that it is inescapable and mediasport's global reach means messages reach billions of people (Bruce 2012). Earlier media accounts of gay athletes were reported generally in a negative fashion, such as the 'tragic' life of English professional football player Justin Fashanu, who hung himself in 1998 after being accused of sexually assaulting a 17-year-old youth in the USA. The tabloids, and especially the (black) football media, were particularly harsh (see Caudwell 2011). However, more positive perspectives are now commonly provided. *The Sporting News* (2014) reported that the Women's National Basketball Association became the first professional sports league to specifically recruit gay fans to its games. Various sport media outlets and official team websites show a number of professional franchises in the US and Canada, and now host 'pride events' for LGBT people, recognising their diverse fan base. Some may argue that this is simply a marketing exercise to fill empty seats.

The 'It Gets Better Project', an anti-bullying campaign created by syndicated columnist and author Dan Savage in the US, attracted many high-profile professional teams and athletes to video post their support for LGBT youth. High-profile professional (and self-identified hetero-sexual) athletes have become political allies, supporting gay rights and equality, not only within sport spheres, but also related to wider societal issues such as gay bullying and same sex marriage. Griffin (2011) comments that these developments seem like progress although she states 'more is required of straight "allies" in the campaign against homophobia and discrimination toward the LGBT community'.

The former German footballer Thomas Hitzlsperger came out in 2014, which attracted significant news attention in Germany, and the UK. Chancellor Angela Merkel's spokesperson praised the news as reported in mainstream sources like *Die Zeit* (Caspari and Fritsch 2014). Previous athletes, like former National Basketball Association (NBA) player John Amaechi in 2007, have typically revealed their sexuality after their playing careers were finished, because they reveal it likely would have affected their earning potential. However, Hitzlsperger stated, 'for me it would have been almost impossible had I still been playing – not because of the fans or the other players, but because of the media' (Gallagher 2014). Australian swimmer and Olympic medallist Ian Thorpe, who finally came out in 2014 at the age of 31 on a popular television show, indicated that he wanted to as early as the year 2000 but was warned of the financial consequences (McClymont and Bagshaw 2014). More encouraging are recent developments of current athletes declaring their homosexuality while still in the midst of their careers, albeit some toward the end of their peak. The 'coming outs' of Welsh rugby star Gareth Thomas and Irish Hurler Donál Óg Cusack both in 2009, the English cricketer Steven Davies, and Swedish footballer Anton Hysén both in 2011, and Robbie Rogers, an American soccer player in 2013, were reported in the British media. Orlando Cruz, from Puerto Rico, became the first openly gay and highly ranked professional boxer in 2012.

The acknowledgement of the NBA's Jason Collins' sexuality in 2013, the first openly active gay player in one of the four major professional leagues in North America, seems to be a watershed moment, generating front page mainstream and sport news coverage. Further, in 2014 Michael Sam became the first openly gay college American football player to be drafted by the National Football League. Both coming outs warranted the prestigious cover story for *Sports Illustrated* and provide further political intrigue because both athletes are also African-American. Sam's announcement, in 2014, along with British diver Tom Daley coming out at the age of 19 in 2013, are significant because they represent young athletes at the start or entering the prime of their careers, with less consideration for loss of potential earnings. Indeed, they may attract additional sponsorship opportunities specifically because they are gay. Nike reportedly wants to sponsor the first prominent professional gay athlete (Anderson-Minshall 2013), perhaps making it lucrative for someone to come out. Indeed mainstream corporate sponsors have increasingly associated themselves with the gay sport movement (Jarvis 2002), although Davidson (2014) is concerned with the commodification of the Gay Games, as some may argue that companies may just be trying to market to and exploit niche markets. Either way, attracting wider sponsorship can be seen as helping to legitimise gay sport (Suchman 1995).

For the most part, these coming outs were welcomed by the media, other players and management. Despite this, Kian *et al.* (2013) state that most American-based sport journalists are reluctant to report on athletes' non-normative sexual orientation. They further say that U.S. sport fans are ready for openly gay players in men's professional team sport but the locker room may be slower to adapt. However, athletes like Daley, Sam and Collins have suffered homophobic abuse on many mainstream sport media blog sites, with many comments asking why these stories are even newsworthy. An initial review of sport fan comments on *Sports Illustrated* or CBS Sports websites over the past couple of years show that negative homophobic remarks far outweigh positive support. This undermines the earlier comments made by some of my students, who were naive about sexuality and sport not being such a 'big deal'. This demonstrates that there is still considerable progress to be made, despite signs of diminished cultural homophobia.

The coming out of male athletes garners considerable media scrutiny, because sport is often viewed as a male, heterosexual and masculine pursuit and space (Allain 2008; Bruce 2012). Females who announce they are lesbian or bisexual merit less spotlight. However, this may also be due to the long-standing under-representation of women in the mainstream media (Bernstein 2002; Cooky *et al.* 2013) and/or their sexuality being less of a story, because in certain sports female athletes are expected to be gay (Krane 1996; Lenskyj 1991). While tennis players Martina Navratilova and Billie-Jean King attracted much, somewhat negative, coverage in the 1980s, female athletes who more recently acknowledged their sexuality have been less problematic or 'newsworthy'. A young Amélie Mauresmo came out in 1999 at the start of her tennis career. She did initially receive some negative comments from a couple of high-profile fellow female players although this issue seemed to disappear rather quickly after some apologies. Mauresmo became a popular player among fans, reporters, competitors and sponsors. The more recent announcements of athletes like Casey Stoney, England football captain, Brittney Griner, American basketball player, Ireen Wüst, Dutch Olympic medallist speed skater, and Casey Dellacqua, an Australian tennis player, received little attention. These quieter declarations raised some media interest and, along with the media frenzy associated with their male counterparts, serve more importantly as role models for many aspiring young LGBTQI athletes who may be questioning their sexuality, trying to compete at high levels, considering the potential loss of earnings and/or deciding whether to come out to fellow teammates, sponsors, coaches, management or the media.

These collective mainstream accounts indicate some significant positive changes in the attitudes towards homosexuality within the Western sporting world, or what Anderson (2009, 2011a, 2011b) considers to be diminished cultural homophobia. Further academic research helps support this trend, not only in wider society (McCormack 2012), but explicitly within sport, and contrary to popular assumptions about embedded negative attitudes toward homosexuality. For example, Adams and Anderson (2012) argue that athletes in a small Midwestern Catholic college soccer team were accepting of homosexuality. Cashmore and Cleland's (2012) research on fans and professionals found rapidly decreasing homophobia within the culture of football fandom in the UK.

However, negative attitudes about homosexuality remain strong in many parts of the world. Russian pole vaulter Yelena Isinbayeva, a gold medal winner in the 2013 World Athletic Championships in Moscow, defended her country's anti-gay propaganda laws, and disapproved of fellow athletes for showing solidarity for lesbians and gay men (Majendie 2013). A clearer example that garnered significant media coverage was the 2014 Winter Olympics held in Sochi, where Russian President Vladimir Putin controversially welcomed gay visitors to the Games but said 'they must leave children alone' (Walker 2014). Russia has been criticised for its treatment of LGBT people, along with a number of other human rights issues, with Amnesty International (2014) claiming that the legacy of the Sochi Games has been tarnished. Coincidentally several heads of states did not attend the opening ceremonies, likely in a thinly veiled protest, including those from Germany, the United Kingdom, France and the United States. Boren (2013) reported that President Obama instead sent two openly gay athletes to represent the American delegation, namely tennis legend Billie Jean-King and Caitlin Cahow, a two-time Olympic hockey medallist. This demonstrates the conventional understanding of the relationship between politics of sexuality and sport remains a complex and much-contested topic.

Theoretical frameworks for understanding sexuality and sport

This final section discusses the key theoretical debates related to sexuality and sport issues. Scholarship has long focused on how sport reproduces, legitimates and occasionally challenges ideologies of gender. Thus it has been framed by diverse methodological and theoretical approaches particularly exploring femininities and masculinities, and how gender is constructed. Sport has traditionally been seen as a mainly male and hegemonically masculine space (Bruce 2012). The aforementioned media accounts are largely written by men, for a male readership. News stories are normally about male athletes, teams owned by men or sporting institutions run by them. Sport, whether mediated or not, therefore tends to marginalise athletes who do not fall within this narrow domain, including women and people from sexual minorities. The notion of power is thus central to the topic of gender and sexuality (in)equality within sport. Women are simply under-represented in the sporting world, especially within leadership positions (Adriaanse and Claringbould 2014), even more so for lesbians and gay men. Several relevant critical concepts have been used to explore sport and sexuality and gender issues.

Historically, the most common theoretical framework for understanding the hierarchy of masculinities is Connell's concept of hegemonic masculinity (1995). For some academics (Hirose and Pih 2010; Jones and McCarthy 2010), Connell's framework provides a useful tool to theorise gendered power relations among men and understand the effectiveness of masculinities in the legitimation of the gender order within sport. However, this framework has been challenged from several directions in recent years (Anderson 2011a; Beasley 2008; Cashmore and Cleland 2012; Howson 2006; McCormack 2011).

For instance, Anderson (2009) argues that hegemonic theory was appropriate in the 1980s and 1990s when there were higher levels of homophobia in society, especially within sporting spheres. In times of decreased cultural homophobia, he argues for a rethinking of traditional theories to understand men and their masculinities. Anderson (2011b: 252) argues that hegemonic masculinity theory 'fails to accurately account for what occurs in a macro or even local culture of decreased cultural homophobia'. Instead, he claims 'inclusive masculinity' is a way forward to frame current research because 'multiple masculinities coexist harmoniously, but also fewer behaviours will be associated with homosexuality' (2011b: 254). Inclusive masculinity is a space for less oppressive masculinities to proliferate without social stigma as the hegemonic archetype of conservative masculinity fails to maintain its dominance (Adams and Anderson 2012). Clayton and Harris (2009) refer to the emergence of new types of sporting identities and masculinities, such as the metrosexual athlete David Beckham. Dashper (2012) draws on inclusive masculinity theory with her research on gay and straight men within equestrian sport, showing low levels of homophobia within once unreceptive locales.

At a symposium at Sussex University, Connell (2014) recently reflected on the origins and critics of her highly influential concept of hegemonic masculinity. She argued that in times of economic and social instability, the concept of a gender order does not necessarily work. She suggested that hegemonic masculinities are 'under construction', and are trying to stabilise themselves. She welcomed challenges to the idea of hegemonic masculinity, particularly studies exploring masculinities coming from the global peripheries, such as Africa and South America. Her keynote concluded by emphasising that scholars cannot remain in the conceptual world in which the field was constructed, and that methods also need to change in order to examine new configurations of masculinities, and new forms of contestations and transformations. Perhaps there remain possibilities for exploring and understanding masculinities in sport by combining elements of both hegemonic and inclusive masculinity frameworks, as homophobia has not diminished universally. As Caudwell (2011) comments, social power relations infuse and suffuse (sport) spaces, and the human body helps construct hegemonic but also counter-hegemonic identities and subjectivities. Besides, sport's gender politics are far from being totally dominated by a straight, orthodox masculinity; some athletes are marketed to niche groups, such as heterosexual women and gay men. Connell (2009) contends that researchers need to move away from a focus on gender differences to one on relationships between and among women and men, including the personal and institutional.

Queer theory has also been used as a framework in an attempt to critically explore the intersection of sexuality, gender and sport (Caudwell 2006). Queer theory has generally been mobilised in the service of non-normative sexualities and desires to destabilise and contest hegemonic structures, such as heteronormativity (Warner 2004). Therefore it can be considered to be a critical theory, which is about action and political involvement. The strength of queer theory is that it enables identity categories and binaries to be questioned. Caudwell's (2006) edited book shows how researchers documented the experiences of lesbian, gay, transgender and transexual athletes in sport in an attempt to move beyond traditional sex-gender distinctions found in sport institutions. Broad's (2001) research on women rugby players in the US demonstrated how they destabilised the heterosexual/homosexual binary through resisting gendered norms. Queer theorists such as Davidson (2014) argue that traditional conventional sport should be challenged and disrupted. However, queer advocates (Pronger 2000; Sykes 2006) do not offer clear new ways to reconfigure sport once the more conservative aspects are dismantled. Davidson's (2006) call for the Gay Games to become more radical and 'queer', such as athletes dressing up in wedding outfits and not awarding medals to winners, falls on many deaf ears. Jarvis (2013a) indicated this would not be popular among the athletes that take part, nor the organisers who want to maintain a commercially viable event.

Coming back to gay sport, the question remains as to whether LGBTQI athletes, clubs and global events are resisting or undermining traditional notions of a dominant masculinity when most of the play occurs solely within gay leagues and is minimally integrated within mainstream sport. Many gay athletes and clubs are not very political. They do not go out of their way to overtly challenge hegemonic practices found in mainstream sport as many have the same values of competition and winning (Wellard 2002; Jarvis 2006). Indeed the majority of lesbian and gay male participants exhibit many conventional forms of femininity and masculinity found in straight sport spaces. The vast majority of LGBTQI athletes want to show they like sport just like anyone else.

Progressing sexuality and sport research

The condition of LGBTQI athletes can offer important political insights into the contemporary and generally conservative, albeit evolving, world of sport. This section offers suggestions to progress the knowledge and debates related to political issues associated with sexuality and sport. More information on the stories and experiences among a diverse range of LGBTQI athletes is required, especially from developing nations or global peripheries. This will help extend how sporting femininities and masculinities are understood in an increasingly global world, as these constructs tend to be dominated by Western orthodoxy. In-depth ethnographic approaches are needed to provide detailed accounts of the lived experiences of gay athletes at either the elite or grassroots level. This is especially important within mainstream settings, as this will potentially offer more chances to challenge or disrupt conservative sporting institutions. These insights can allow the chance to reinterpret the athletic experience in ways that offer the potential to transform the heterosexist/heteronormative culture of sport. Does their participation allow for the possibility of new embodied masculine/feminine identification to emerge, not only among themselves but their fellow heterosexual colleagues? More data are needed on the transgressive movements of athletes crossing the increasingly blurred binary of mainstream and gay sport spaces.

The popular media accounts of gay athletes offers some exciting avenues. Does the (lack of) coverage help validate or undermine the legitimacy of gay sport events? Further, how does the television, print or social media contribute to undermining or maintaining the traditionally conservative masculine nature of sport as an institution? Do the stories of high-profile athletes help other elite or grassroots participants to acknowledge their own sexuality? The attraction and/or commodification of gay athletes or events by mainstream sponsors, and links again to legitimacy, are also worthy of more scrutiny.

It is crucial to continue to explore how contemporary forms of mainstream and/or LGBTQI sport reproduce or challenge traditional dominant notions of masculinity and femininity. What social conditions underlie this and enable it to occur? More empirical data are required to conceptualise how LGBTQI sport can potentially offer resistance to traditional hegemonic masculinity much in the way past feminist research on women and sport has explored and debated the same issue. Inclusive masculinity theory is an exciting development; however, more research is needed to support whether all types of sport sites are indeed evolving and changing for the better all around the world. Certainly there is diminished cultural homophobia, but this is not occurring at the same rate universally.

Gay sport provides opportunities for queer resistance, but this can also lead to increased opposition by the wider public instead of greater acceptance of the gay community. Some gay participants themselves are not very political and do not agree with the radical politics of queer, which calls for the dismantling of existing sport institutions. Therefore further insights are needed into how gay sport may be abandoning its queerness in order to seek acceptance and legitimisation by wider sport institutions. What can be done about queer participation in mainstream sports?

References

Adams, A. and Anderson, E. (2012) Exploring the relationship between homosexuality and sport among the teammates of a small, Midwestern Catholic college soccer team. *Sport, Education and Society*, 17(3): 347–363.

Adriaanse, J.A. and Claringbould, I. (2014) Gender equality in sport leadership: from the Brighton declaration to the Sydney scoreboard. *International Review for the Sociology of Sport*, 1–20. DOI: 10.1177/1012690214548493.

Allain, K.A. (2008) Real fast and tough: the construction of Canadian hockey masculinity. *Sociology of Sport Journal*, 25(4): 462–481.

Amnesty International. (2014) Russia: legacy of Olympic Games tarnished by arrests. Accessed 22 July 2014. www.amnesty.org/en/news/russia-legacy-olympic-games-tarnished-arrests-2014-02-22.

Anderson, E. (2009) *Inclusive Masculinity: The Changing Nature of Masculinities*. New York: Routledge.

Anderson, E. (2011a) Masculinities and sexualities in sport and physical cultures: three decades of evolving research. *Journal of Homosexuality*, 58: 565–575.

Anderson, E. (2011b) Gay athletes, straight teams, and coming out in educationally based sport teams. *Gender & Society*, 25(2): 250–268.

Anderson-Minshall, D. (2013) Nike wants to sponsor first major out pro athlete: who is going to lead the way? *The Advocate*. Accessed 2 October 2014. www.advocate.com/sports/2013/04/15/nike-wants-sponsor-first-major-out-pro-gay-athlete.

BBC. (2012) Nepal hosts South Asia's first gay sports tournament. Accessed 30 September 2014. www.bbc.co.uk/news/world-asia-19929010.

Beasley, C. (2008) Rethinking hegemonic masculinity in a globalizing world. *Men and Masculinities*, 11(1): 86–103.

Bernstein, A. (2002) Is it time for a victory lap? Changes in the media coverage of women in sport. *International Review for the Sociology of Sport*, 37(3–4): 415–428.

Boren, C. (2013) Obama names openly gay athletes to Sochi Olympic delegation. *The Washington Post*. Accessed 10 December 2014. http://www.washingtonpost.com/blogs/early-lead/wp/2013/12/18/obama-names-openly-gay-athletes-to-sochi-olympic-delegation/.

Broad, K.L. (2001) The gendered unapologetic: queer resistance in women's sport. *Sociology of Sport Journal*, 18(2): 181–204.

Bruce, T. (2012) Reflections on communication and sport: on women and femininities. *Communication & Sport*, 1(1/2): 125–137.

Butler, J. (1990) *Gender Trouble: Feminism and the Subversion of Identity*. London: Routledge.

Cashmore, E. and Cleland, J. (2012) Fans, homophobia and masculinities in association football: evidence of a more inclusive environment. *The British Journal of Sociology*, 63(2): 370–387.

Caspari, L. and Fritsch, O. (2014) Merkel lobt Hitzlspergers Coming-out. *Die Zeit*. Accessed 6 October 2014. www.zeit.de/gesellschaft/zeitgeschehen/2014-01/hitzlsperger-reaktionen-westerwelle-zwanziger.

Caudwell, J. (ed.) (2006) *Sport, Sexualities and Queer/Theory*. London: Routledge.

Caudwell, J. (2011) Does your boyfriend know you're here? The spatiality of homophobia in men's football culture in the UK. *Leisure Studies*, 30(2): 123–138.

Clayton, B. and Harris, J. (2009) Sport and metrosexual identity: sports media and emergent sexualities. In J. Harris and A. Parker (eds) *Sport and Social Identities*. Basingstoke: Palgrave Macmillan, pp. 132–149.

Connell R. (1990) An iron man: the body and some contradictions of hegemonic masculinity. In M. Messner and D. Sabo D (eds) *Sport, Men and the Gender Order*. Champaign, IL: Human Kinetics, pp. 83–114.

Connell, R. (1995) *Masculinities*. Berkeley, CA: University of California Press.

Connell, R. (2009) *Gender*. Cambridge: Polity Press.

Connell, R. (2014) Masculinity, coloniality, hegemony: trajectories of research and politics. Keynote Address. *Dislocating Masculinity Revisited Symposium*. School of Global Studies, University of Sussex. 4 July 2014.

Cooky, C., Messner, M.A. and Hextrum, R.H. (2013) Women play sport, but not on TV: a longitudinal study of televised news media. *Communication & Sport*, 1(3): 203–230.

Dashper, K. (2012) 'Dressage is full of queens!': masculinity, sexuality and equestrian sport. *Sociology*, 46(6): 1–16.

Davidson, J. (2006) The necessity of queer shame for gay pride: the Gay Games and cultural events. In J. Caudwell (ed.) *Sport, Sexualities and Queer/Theory*. London: Routledge, pp. 90–105.

Davidson, J. (2013) Sporting homonationalisms: sexual exceptionalism, queer privilege, and the 21st century international lesbian and gay sport movement. *Sociology of Sport Journal*, 30: 57–82.

Davidson, J. (2014) Racism against the abnormal? The twentieth century Gay Games, biopower and the emergence of homonational sport. *Leisure Studies*, 33(4): 357–378.

Elling A., Knoppers, A. and de Knop, P. (2003) Gay/lesbian sport clubs and events: places of homo-social bonding and cultural resistance? *International Review for the Sociology of Sport*, 38: 441–456.

FGG. (2014a) *Mission, vision and values*. Accessed 18 September 2014. www.gaygames.net/index.php?id=5.

FGG. (2014b) *History of the FGG and the Gay Games*. Accessed 18 September 2014. www.gaygames.net/index.php?id=28.

Gallagher, S. (2014) Thomas Hitzlsperger. *Daily Mail*. Accessed 30 September 2014. www.dailymail.co.uk/sport/football/article-2747813/Thomas-Hitzlsperger-It-impossible-come-gay-I-player-attention.html#ixzz3EnNxqb2p.

Gay and Lesbian Tennis Alliance. (2014) Accessed 30 September 2014. http://glta.net/general-info.

Gilbert, D. (2014) Interview with David Gilbert, President and CEO of Positively Cleveland (Cleveland Convention and Visitor Bureau). 14 August 2014.

Griffin, P. (2011) Some thoughts on straight allies in sport. Accessed 13 June 2011. http://ittakesateam.blogspot.com/2011/06/some-thoughts-on-straight-allies-in.html.

Hargreaves, J.A. (2000) *Heroines of Sport: The Politics of Difference and Identity*. London: Routledge.

Harris, P. (2014) Interview with Phyllis Harris, Executive Director, The LGBT Community Center of Greater Cleveland. 6 August 2014.

Hirose, A. and Pih, KK-h. (2010) Men who strike and men who submit: hegemonic and marginalized masculinities in mixed martial arts. *Men and Masculinities*, 13(2): 190–209.

Howson, R. (2006) *Challenging Hegemonic Masculinity*. London: Routledge.

Jarvis, N. (2002) Sponsorship and gay sport: a case study of the 2000 Gay Softball World Series. *International Journal of Sports Marketing and Sponsorship*, 4(3): 205–230.

Jarvis, N. (2006) *The Meaning of Sport in the Lives of Gay Men*. PhD Thesis, University of Brighton, UK.

Jarvis, N. (2013a) A short selective history of the Gay Games: conflicts, clashes and controversies. In U. Merkel (ed.) *Power, Politics and International Events: Socio-Cultural Analyses of Festivals and Spectacles*. Routledge Advances in Event Research Series. Abingdon: Routledge, pp. 85–102.

Jarvis, N. (2013b) The inclusive masculinities of heterosexual men within UK gay sport clubs. *International Review for the Sociology of Sport*, DOI: 10.1177/1012690213482481.

Jones, L. and McCarthy, M. (2010) Mapping the landscape of gay men's football. *Leisure Studies*, 29(2): 161–173.

Kian, E.M., Anderson, E., Vincent, J. and Murray, M. (2013) Sport journalists' views on gay men in sport, society and within sport media. *International Review for the Sociology of Sport*, 1–17. DOI: 10.1177/1012690213504101.

King, C.R., Leonard, D.J. and Kusz, K.W. (2007) White power and sport: an introduction. *Journal of Sport and Social Issues*, 31(3): 3–1.

Krane, V. (1996) Sport psychology lesbians in sport: toward acknowledgement, understanding and theory. *Journal of Sport and Exercise Psychology*, 18(3): 237–246.

Krane, V. (2001) We can be athletic and feminine, but do we want to? Challenging hegemonic femininity in women's sport. *Quest*, 53(1): 115–133.

Laurendeau, J. (2004) The Crack Choir and the Cock Chorus: the intersection of gender and sexuality in skydiving texts. *Sociology of Sport Journal*, 21(4): 397–417.

Leedy, G. and Connolly, C. (2007) Out in the cowboy state: a look at lesbian and gay lives in Wyoming. *Journal of Gay and Lesbian Social Services*, 19: 19–34.

Lenskyj, H. (1991) Combating homophobia in sport and physical education. *Sociology of Sport Journal*, 8(1): 61–69.

Majendie, M. (2013) 'We are normal Russians': pole vaulter, Yelena Isinbayeva defends anti-gay laws. *The Independent*. Accessed 10 December 2014. www.independent.co.uk/news/world/europe/we-are-normal-russians-pole-vaulter-yelena-isinbayeva-defends-antigay-laws-8764393.html.

McCormack, M. (2011) Hierarchy without hegemony: locating boys in an inclusive masculinity setting. *Sociological Perspectives*, 54(1): 83–101.

McCormack, M. (2012) *The Declining Significance of Homophobia*. Oxford: Oxford University Press.

McClymont, K. and Bagshaw, E. (2014) Ian Thorpe. Accessed 30 September 2014. www.watoday.com.au/sport/swimming/ian-thorpe-considered-coming-out-before-2000-olympics-20140713-zt65z.html.

McKay, J., Messner, M. and Sabo, D. (eds.) (2000) *Masculinities, Gender Relations, and Sport*. London: Sage.

Messner, M. (1992) *Power at Play: Sports and the Problem of Masculinity*. Boston, MA: Beacon Press.

Miller, T. (2001) *Sportsex*. Philadelphia, PA: Temple University Press.

Pronger, B. (1990) *The Arena of Masculinity*. Toronto: University of Toronto Press.

Pronger, B. (2000) Homosexuality and sport: who's winning? In J. McKay, M. Messner and D. Sabo (eds) *Masculinities, Gender Relations, and Sport*. London: Sage, pp. 222–244.

Suchman, M.C. (1995) Managing legitimacy: strategic and institutional approaches. *Academy of Management Review*, 20(3): 571–610.

Sykes, H. (2006) Queering theories of sexuality in sport studies. In J. Caudwell (ed.) *Sport, Sexualities and Queer/Theory*. London: Routledge, pp. 13–32.

Symons, C. (2010) *The Gay Games: A History*. London: Routledge.

Theberge, N. (1995) Gender, sport and the construction of community. *Sociology of Sport Journal*, 12(4): 389–402.

Theberge, N. (2000) Gender and sport. In J. Coakley and E. Dunning (eds) *Handbook of Sports Studies*. London: Sage, pp: 322–333.

The Guardian. (2009) World Outgames 2009. Accessed 30 September 2014. www.theguardian.com/world/gallery/2009/jul/27/gay-rights-denmark.

The Sporting News (2014) WNBA to recruit gay fans to games, market to LGBT community. Accessed 2 October 2014. www.sportingnews.com/nba/story/2014-05-21/wnba-gay-community-campaign-bisexual-homosexual-lgbt-effort-marketing-fans-brittney-griner-players-teams.

Walker, S. (2014) Vladimir Putin: gay people at Winter Olympics must leave children alone. *The Guardian*. Accessed 10 December 2014. www.theguardian.com/world/2014/jan/17/vladimir-putin-gay-winter-olympics-children.

Warner, D.N. (2004) Towards a queer research methodology. *Qualitative Research in Psychology*, 1(4): 321–337.

Weinke, C. and Hill, G.J. (2013) Does place of residence matter? Rural–urban differences and the well-being of gay men and lesbians. *Journal of Homosexuality*, 60(9): 1256–1279.

Wellard, I. (2002) Men, sport, body performance and the maintenance of 'exclusive masculinity'. *Leisure Studies*, 21: 235–247.

Williams, R. (1961) *The Long Revolution*. Harmondsworth: Penguin.

Wright, J. and Clarke, G. (1999) Sport, the media and the construction of compulsory heterosexuality: a case study of women's rugby union. *International Review for the Sociology of Sport*, 34(3): 227–243.

26

GENDER POLITICS IN SPORT FOR DEVELOPMENT AND PEACE

Megan Chawansky and Hillary Kipnis

Introduction

The sport for development and peace (SDP) sector receives considerable attention in research devoted to sport and the arena of international politics (e.g. Darnell 2010; Coalter 2007; Schulenkorf and Adair 2014). From its loose beginnings in the early to mid-1990s (Kidd 2008) the SDP sector now warrants serious attention from a variety of multilateral institutions. Kidd (2008) suggests that the current SDP *movement* reflects a long-standing interest in the use of sport for social change, but he argues that it is unique from other one-off endeavours because of:

> the rapid explosion of the agencies and organization that are involved . . . the financial support it enjoys from the powerful international sports federations, and the extent to which it has been championed by the United Nations, its agencies and significant partners.
>
> *(p. 371)*

The SDP sector consists of a host of transnational NGOs, official government development agencies, multinational corporations (MNCs), sport governing bodies, universities, coaches, athletes, and volunteers who seek to utilise sport to address a range of issues to youth living primarily in 'developing' or post-conflict contexts (Kidd 2008; Levermore and Beacom 2009; Black 2010). While it proves feasible to identify some of the key players in the SDP movement, it is continuously growing and difficult to precisely quantify. Writing in 2010, Hayhurst and Frisby (2010) suggested that 'over 400 sport for development non-governmental organizations (NGOs) . . . operat[e] in more than 125 countries globally' (p. 75), and there have been various attempts to map the field and research of SDP (Levermore and Beacom 2009; Cronin 2011; Hillyer *et al.* 2011; Van Eekeren *et al.* 2013; Schulenkorf *et al.* in press).

In part, the SDP sector proves difficult to quantify or contain because of its ambitious aims and broad claims. In sum, the transnational SDP movement seeks to consider the utility of sport as a tool through which lessons on (for example) teamwork, communication, empowerment, and conflict resolution can be delivered. Of interest for this chapter is the increased focus on SDP programming which seeks to empower or target girls or young women.

As noted above, it is difficult to ascertain definitive numbers, but a 2008 attempt to measure the existence of girl-centred SDP programming listed on the International Platform on Sport and Development (www.sportanddev.org) found that 'only 30 of the 264 total projects documented as somehow dealing with gender, and only 34 of the 264 as having some component targeted specifically towards girls and women' (Saavedra 2009: 137). In 2013, a more extensive search of four internet databases related to SDP projects by Hancock *et al.* (2013) 'yielded 1,033 sport for development programmes' with '440 programmes, or 42.5% of all programmes, specifically targeting girls and women' (p. 18). We would suggest that the increased opportunities for girls' and women's participation signal a shift in the 'gender politics' of the SDP sector and we use this chapter to further explore the broad notion of gender politics within SDP. In using the term 'gender politics' we suggest that gender matters at all levels of the SDP sector, from decisions related to programming design and research to how power, access, and opportunities in SDP relate and refer back to girls, boys, women, and men. To begin this analysis, we provide a brief review of the existing literature on SDP with a particular focus on if and how gender is invoked. Through this process, we identified a significant lacuna in terms of how gender is conceptualised, especially in research related to sport and peace. When gender is considered, it usually refers to discussions of girls and women and their gendered experience of SDP; it is rare to have research which pointedly considers the gendered nature of SDP for male participants. To align with this mentality, we borrow insights from the academic field of peace and conflict studies to offer future considerations on the gender politics within research on girls' and women's SDP experiences.

Review of literature

This section reviews the existing literature on gender within the SDP sector. In particular, it considers the absence and presence of gender, girls and women within this literature to be a part of the analysis of the gender politics of SDP. Though it attempts to be comprehensive, it is not exhaustive or systematic. It considers the key themes in both the sport for development and the sport for peace domains when examined through a lens of gender. While the work on the ground in the name of 'sport for development' and 'sport for peace' can frequently overlap, we can discern a clear demarcation between research studies that attempt to address development issues and those interested in sport for reconciliation or peace. We begin with the sport for development literature.

In our cursory review of the literature on gender within sport for development, we identified three categories: overviews of the field that attempted to advocate for or document girls' participation in SDP; studies of or about individual projects; and research that critiqued the corporatised or heteronormative space of SDP. It was rare to locate research which attempted to theorise masculinity or explicitly foregrounded men's experiences (as men) in SDP; Evers (2010) and Forde (2013) would be exceptions and serve as examples of research that does interrogate masculinity within the site of sport for development.

In the first category, examples of research which attempts to document or advocate for girls' experiences can be found (Brady 1998, 2005; Brady and Khan 2002; Saavedra 2009; Chawansky 2011; Hancock *et al.* 2013). Largely, these studies focus on the possibility of SDP initiatives for girls (Brady 1998), on the limited existence of girl-focused programmes (Saavedra 2009) or critique the movement for failing to adequately theorise gender in SDP (Chawansky 2011). Examples of the second theme involve focused studies on Moving the Goalpost-Kenya (Forde 2008); on female role models in Zambia (Meier and Saavedra 2009); on female footballers in Zambia (Jeanes and Magee 2014); on a girls' martial arts project in Uganda (Hayhurst 2013);

within a girls' programme in Namibia (Friesen 2013); and with Indigenous girls in Canada (Hayhurst *et al.* 2015). While the analysis within each of the above allows for a consideration of issues beyond gender, it is noteworthy that they each foreground the gendered dimension of their studies at the start. This simultaneously contextualises and perhaps limits the perceived transferability of their findings onto contexts which do not focus on girls' experiences. In other words, we would suggest that these particular studies tend to position themselves in ways that make their work to be about challenges for girls in SDP or about girls' participation in SDP, whereas other research in the sector can be understood to be *just* about SDP.

The final category of existing research considers more expansive ideas which begin with gender and girls' and young women's experiences but ultimately moves beyond a girl-centred frame. For instance, Hayhurst (2011) critiques the corporatised 'sport, gender and development' (SGD) sector through an analysis of the Girl Effect, whereas Carney and Chawansky (2014) and Chawansky (2014) identify the heteronormative framing of the SDP sector and its impact on female SDP workers, not just programme beneficiaries. These works tend to afford more complex considerations of the gender politics of the SDP sector whilst simultaneously maintaining a focus on girls or young women. In sum, the majority of the existing literature on sport for development and gender tends to focus on girls as recipients of programming and also foregrounds its research as being about girls with the implication that the findings are limited to comparable girl-centred programmes. While outliers to our system of categorisation exist (e.g. Kay and Spaaij 2012) and calls have been issued to engage in studies of gender as relational, the attempts of this form of analysis are not yet readily visible in the SDP literature.

While there is a discernable focus on the gendered experiences of girls and young women within sport for development research, the same cannot be said for research which examines sport for peace initiatives. One of the first edited collections to consider sport in divided societies (Sugden and Bairner 1999) largely considers the sporting experience of boys and men, but it does not significantly consider gender, or denote these experiences as being of or about men. Instead, the collection focuses on divisions mostly related to race, ethnicity, caste, or religion. An assortment of other more recent contributions (e.g. Armstrong 2004; Martin 2009; Gasser and Levinsen 2004) deals with the theme of sport for peace or the use of sport in post-conflict settings and follows the tendency to overlook any sort of analysis of gender. An exception to this is Caudwell's (2007) reflection on gender and girls' experiences within the Football 4 Peace (F4P) project wherein she succinctly highlights a number of challenges for the F4P project as they pertain to girls' involvement. An additional recognition of the importance of gender occurs when Giulianotti and Armstrong (2011) note that those involved in sport-orientated peacebuilding activities must ensure that:

> gender relations within the host setting to be fully understood. In many settings peace-building officials will have to engage with distinctive, deep-seated cultural values, which may proscribe forms of inter-gender social relations; they will also have to understand the different traumas and tragedies faced by women during recent conflicts, such as the loss of family members, mass rape, and other forms of sexual, physical and emotional abuse. The planning of sport-based interventions will have to take stock of the extent to which cross-gender social interaction is tolerated culturally.
>
> *(p. 389)*

While this acknowledgement is significant in terms of the dearth of writing on gender in sport for peace work, it does not go into great depth or offer specific suggestions of how to interrogate these areas. In what follows, we build on Giulianotti and Armstrong (2011) to offer further ideas and direction for considerations of gender politics within the next phase of SDP research and programming.

Gender politics in peace and conflict studies

This section provides an overview of current issues and discussions on the experiences of girls and women in peace and conflict studies. As such, it explains why a gendered approach to conflict and sport for peace is imperative in light of the changing face of war (or 'new wars'), the widespread use of gender-based violence (GBV) in conflict settings, and the presence of female child soldiers. It also briefly explains new developments in international law that helped shift the traditional view of war as a male domain to one that considers the impact war has on women and the role of women in the post-conflict reconstruction of society. We use this overview to comment briefly on two SDP projects currently underway and dealing with the effects of conflict: Kids Break the Ice (Ukraine) and Capoeira4Refugees (Palestine and Syria).

Serious consideration is now being given to the role of gender in war and in the post-conflict reconstruction process. This can be seen in the rise of discussions taking place in mainstream academic, government, international legal, and policy circles and also from the newly created policies and laws by the UN to address gender in war. One of the biggest challenges is altering deeply ingrained gender stereotypes about women and myths about war which send out the message that gender issues and concerns are of secondary importance in wartime. Traditional approaches to gender and war portrayed women in war as vulnerable victims and without agency. While this may be the case in certain instances, it oversimplifies the role of women in conflict societies. In addition to being victims, women have been known to fight alongside men, work, and make vital contributions to their households during conflicts and to play an active role in resolving conflicts.

New wars

Unlike during the Cold War period where inter-state wars were common, the majority of contemporary wars are intra-state wars or part of the 'War on Terror' (WOT) and involve state, non-state actors, and international forces fighting one another. The 'new wars', according to Chinkin and Kaldor (2013) have a different 'logic from old wars, stemming from differences in the types of actors, the goals, the tactics, and the forms of finance' and 'they tend to be persistent and more difficult to end' (p. 169). Causes that lead to these seemingly intractable wars can be one or a combination of factors, such as: scarce resources, territories, ethnicity, minority rights, religion, land, and terrorism (Jansen 2006).

New wars present more risks to non-combatant women and children. This pertains to the reality that war is no longer fought on distant battlefields but instead wars are hitting close to home. The danger to civilians can be seen in light of the fact that in World War I 15 per cent of casualties were civilians, compared to today where the rate has risen to 90 per cent (Jansen 2006: 136). Additionally, wars carried out in civilian areas often destroy important infrastructure (e.g. roads, electricity grids, water sanitation), hospitals and schools, and lead to a decline in socio-economic conditions. Lastly, through force or by fear, wars have displaced millions of people from their homes into refugee camps within the state or in neighbouring countries.

While no one can escape the negative consequences of war, a gendered analysis of war helps to isolate and project the way in which women are uniquely impacted by war. For instance, lack of access to medical services in conflict zones means lack of maternal care and therefore places pregnant women and their unborn children's lives in jeopardy. Furthermore, in many societies, losing a male family member means loss of income and support for the household. Finally, there is evidence to support that women and children become more vulnerable to gender-based violence (GBV) when they are fleeing from violence and living in refugee camps (Vickers 1993).

Gender-based violence (GBV): women's bodies as battlefields

The United Nations Security Council Report of the Secretary-General includes in its definition of conflict-related sexual violence:

> rape, sexual slavery, forced prostitution, forced pregnancy, forced sterilization and any other form of sexual violence of comparable gravity perpetrated against women, men or children with a direct or indirect (temporal, geographical or casual) link to a conflict.
>
> *(UN Security Council Report 2014)*

Judging by wars taking place since the 1990s in Rwanda, Bosnia, and Hertzegovina and the current civil war in Syria, it is evident that conflict-related sexual violence is on the rise and that men, women, and children are all at risk. The 'strategies' and uses of GBV are varied and context specific. In the case of ethnic civil wars, warring ethnic groups rape and seek to forcefully impregnate women with the hope of diluting the others' ethnic population. In societies such as Syria, wherein a woman's honour is especially culturally significant, rape not only violates a woman, but it also humiliates men by exposing them as weak and incapable of defending 'their' women. In some cases, women who are raped are killed for dishonouring their families. These deaths are commonly referred to as 'honour killings'. Finally, it is known that during conflict, women are often targeted by armed groups, forced into sexual servitude and then trafficked. Human trafficking is a lucrative business, and, for some armed groups, human trafficking is a means of funding their acquisition of weapons. The above examples offer three reasons why a gendered analysis of the use of sexual violence in war is necessary.

That said, in the 2014 report, *Conflict-Related Sexual Violence*, the UN Secretary-General discussed some of challenges that the UN and member states face in protecting women, children, and men. According to the report, sexual violence frequently remains under-reported by victims. This may be due to socio-cultural factors and the overall breakdown of functioning governments and health care services in war and the aftermath of wars. Indeed, in Syria's ongoing civil war, the International Federation for Human Rights (FIDH 2014) and the Arab Women Organisation (AWO) have compiled evidence which they present in their report, *Violence Against Women in Syria: Breaking the Silence*, on the Syrian government's and militias' widespread use of rape. In Syrian society, like many honour-shame societies, the majority of the population considers sexual violence as a socio-cultural and religious taboo, and female survivors of sexual violence risk being blamed for bringing shame and humiliation to their families.

As a consequence, women are often forced into, a 'culture of silence' which prohibits them from discussing rape. In return, women are denied the medical and psychological treatment to address the trauma of their experiences, and without the freedom to discuss and identify rape, rapists remain free to commit more crimes. The widespread use of rape in the Syrian conflict has been linked to the rise in the number of child brides. Young women who have become pregnant because of rape and families of young women who are not pregnant but have been raped are covering up the shame and attempting to protect young women's honour by marrying them to older men.

Though rape has been a part of war since ancient times (O'Connor 2012), the Geneva Convention is credited as the first international law for acknowledging the war crime of rape. Until now, few perpetrators have been prosecuted for committing the war crime of rape. The lack of prosecutions can be partially attributed to the legal definition of rape which, under international law, has classified it as a lesser crime. For instance, the Geneva Convention has defined the crime of rape as an honour crime. In other words, the focus of the law is on the impact rape has on bringing shame to the male kin, thus ignoring the impact it has on the female victim. Put differently, if the law is applied it would protect a husband, brother, father, uncle and not the 'rape victims'. For this reason, the Geneva Convention has been a weak, underused and ineffectual law for protecting rape victims and prosecuting perpetrators for the criminal act of rape during war.

In light of recent prosecutions and changes to the criminal legal definition of rape, now more than ever before, the war crime of rape is being taken more seriously in the international community. The shift began after the International Criminal Tribunal for the former Yugoslavia (ICTY) and the International Criminal Tribunal for Rwanda (ICTR) became the 'first international courts to prosecute rape as an international crime in armed conflict' (O'Connor 2012). Moreover, the Statute of the International Criminal Court has explicitly stated that rape is a war crime and has defined rape in a 'victim-sensitive' manner as opposed to its previous 'honour crime' classification (O'Connor 2012). These recent changes in the law are positive developments that work towards strengthening and protecting women.

Female fighters and child soldiers

While contemporary warfare has become more deadly and dangerous for non-combatant women, this is not to imply that all women are victims. Women make numerous contributions in conflict, as noted by their active participation in conflict as armed combatants and as peace-makers. A newer development has been the rise in the number of female child soldiers. Contrary to the traditional views of war and guerrilla warfare, which maintains the view that men are armed combatants, there are many instances in which women fight side by side with men. Sajjad (2004) investigated whether women fighting alongside men had an impact on their role in society after war. She concludes that even when women demonstrate they can fight as equals with men, this does not guarantee that they will treated as equals in a post-conflict society. She draws this conclusion from a comparison of the roles of women guerrilla fighters in El Salvador, Iran, Sri Lanka, and Algeria, in which all case studies reflected the following result: instead of finding prominent roles in society after fighting side by side with men, the majority returned to their homes following the resolution of the conflict.

A notable and disturbing development in contemporary wars has been the rise in the number of female child soldiers[1] who are forcibly recruited by non-state armed groups engaged in conflict (Ravizza 2012). Having been orphaned or simply left vulnerable due to the perils of conflict, young girls are frequently abducted by armed groups. Girls are often forced into sexual servitude where they are subjected to rape and other forms of sexual violence. Some girls are forced to become the 'wife' of a military commando or find themselves part of the modern-day slave trade, or as human trafficking victims, where they become the armed groups' commodity and sold to earn money. The armed group Boko Haram, operating in Nigeria, is using girls, some as young as ten years old, to carry out suicide bombings. There is recognition of this problem in the UN Security Council Resolution 1325 and the UN-based programmes for child soldiers or disarmament, rehabilitation, and reintegration (DDR), both of which are new developments in international law and policy. However, there is limited or no knowledge about if and how sport operates in some of these contexts – in 'new wars' – or in working with survivors of GBV or female child soldiers (Ravizza 2012). We would suggest that exploring these areas will offer new insights into the gender politics of sport for peace and sport in conflict/post-conflict settings.

Conclusion

This chapter examined the various understandings of gender politics in the domain of SDP, with a focus on the use of sport in conflict or post-conflict settings. In adopting an intentionally broad understanding of the term 'gender politics', we sought to highlight the multiple ways to interpret and consider the concept within the delivery and research of SDP. A review of the SDP literature demonstrated that there is scope for additional considerations of gender politics, and, as such, we offered suggestions about future considerations that can take place. This is especially the case in the realm of sport for peace, where more careful considerations of new wars, of GBV and of female soldiers are encouraged. Two current SDP initiatives that show promise for attending to the gender politics of sport are 'Kids Break the Ice', a project in Ukraine that uses table hockey to help rehabilitate children displaced by the current conflict (Canever 2015) and Capoiera4Refugees, an initiative in Palestine and Syria, that provides psychosocial support to youth through the use of the Brazilian artform, Capoeira (Prytherch and Kraft 2015). The former is still in its beginnings, and it seeks to work with internally displaced youth in Ukraine to offer a sense of normalcy within an active conflict setting. Capoiera4Refugees (formerly Bidna Capoeira) began its work in the Middle East in 2007, and recent research demonstrates how the activity assists children in the (re-)development of 'playfulness, emotional stability, friendship, tolerance and inner strength' (Prytherch and Kraft 2015: 7). Importantly for this chapter, Prytherch and Kraft (2015) explored the unique pressures faced by girls and boys in light of socially sanctioned gender roles; girls often felt torn between their interest in Capoeira and their expected contributions to housework and childcare whereas boys felt the strain of helping to (financially) support their families and to becoming the 'men of the house' (pp. 24–25). Though these findings do not immediately refer back to some of the aforementioned issues we hope that future SDP research will consider, we believe it is a good sign that this particular research engaged the concept of gender in its analysis. We would suggest that our suggestions will further enable new considerations and understandings of gender politics in SDP by organisations such as Capoeira4Refugees and Kids Break the Ice moving forward.

Note

1 For our purposes here, a child is anyone under 18 years of age.

References

Armstrong, G. (2004) The lords of misrule: Football and the rights of the child in Liberia, West Africa. *Sport in Society*, 7(3): 473–502.

Black, D.R. (2010) The ambiguities of development: implications for 'development through sport'. *Sport in Society*, 13(1): 121–129.

Brady, M. (1998) Laying the foundation for girls' healthy futures. Can sports play a role? *Studies in Family Planning*, 29(1): 79–82.

Brady, M. (2005) Creating safe spaces and building social assets for young women in the developing world: a new role for sports. *Women's Studies Quarterly*, 33: 35–49.

Brady, M., and Khan, B. (2002) *Letting Girls Play: Mathare Youth Sports Association's Girls' Football Program*. New York: Population Council.

Canever, B. (2015) Pucks for peace in Ukraine. 4 August 2015. Accessed 9 October 2015. www.insightonconflict.org/2015/08/pucks-peace-ukraine/.

Carney, A. and Chawansky, M. (2014) Taking sex off the sidelines: challenging heteronormativity within 'Sport in Development' research. *International Review for the Sociology of Sport*. DOI: 10.1177/1012690214521616.

Caudwell, J. (2007) On shifting sands: the complexities of women's and girls' involvement in Football for Peace. In J. Sugden and J. Wallis (eds) *Football for Peace: The Challenges of Using Sport for Co-Existence in Israel*. Oxford: Meyer and Meyer Sport, pp. 97–112.

Chawansky, M. (2011) New social movements, old gender games?: Locating girls in the sport for development and peace movement. *Research in Social Movements, Conflicts and Change*, 32: 123–136.

Chawansky, M. (2014) You're juicy: autoethnography as evidence in sport for development and peace (SDP) research. *Qualitative Research in Sport, Exercise and Health*, DOI: 10.1080/2159676X.2014.893900.

Chinkin, C. and Kaldor, M. (2013) Gender and new wars. *Journal of International Affairs*, 67(1): 167–187.

Coalter, F. (2007) *A Wider Social Role for Sport*. London: Routledge.

Cronin, O. (2011) *Comic Relief Review: Mapping the Research on the Impact of Sport and Development Interventions*. Manchester: Comic Relief.

Darnell, S. (2010) Power, politics and 'Sport for Development and Peace': investigating the utility of sport for international development. *Sociology of Sport Journal*, 27: 54–75.

Evers, C. (2010) Intimacy, sport and young refugee men. *Emotion, Space and Society*, xxx: 1–6.

Forde, S. (2008) *Playing by Their Rules. Kenya: Moving the Goalposts*. Self published.

Forde, S.D. (2013) Fear and loathing in Lesotho: an autoethnographic analysis of sport for development and peace. *International Review for the Sociology of Sport*, DOI: 10.1177/1012690213501916.

Friesen, V.R. (2013) Discourses of agency and gender in girls' conversations on sport in Windhoek, Namibia. *Girlhood Studies*, 6(1): 98–116.

Gasser, P. and Levinsen, A. (2004) Breaking post-war ice: open fun football schools in Bosnia and Herzegovina. *Sport in Society*, 7(3): 457–472.

Giulianotti, R. and Armstrong, G. (2011) Sport, the military and peacemaking: history and possibilities. *Third World Quarterly*, 32(2): 379–394.

Hancock, M., Lyras, A., and Ha, J.P. (2013) Sport for Development programmes for girls and women: a global assessment. *Journal of Sport for Development*, 1(1): 15–24.

Hayhurst, L.M.C. (2011) Corporatising sport, gender and development: postcolonial IR feminisms, transnational private governance and global corporate social engagement. *Third World Quarterly*, 32(3): 531–549.

Hayhurst, L.M.C. (2013) Girls as the 'new' agents of social change? Exploring the 'girl effect' through sport, gender and development programs in Uganda. *Sociological Research Online (Special Issue: Modern Girlhoods)*, 18(2).

Hayhurst, L.M.C. and Frisby, W. (2010) Inevitable tensions: Swiss and Canadian sport for development NGO perspectives on partnerships with high performance sport. *European Sport Management Quarterly*, 10(1): 75–96.

Hayhurst, L.M.C., Giles, A.R., Radforth, W.M., and The Vancouver Aboriginal Friendship Centre Society. (2015) 'I want to come here to prove them wrong': using a Postcolonial Feminist Participatory Action Research (PFPAR) approach to studying sport, gender and development programs for urban Indigenous young women. *Sport in Society*, 18(8): 952–967.

Hillyer, S., Zahorsky, M., Munroe, A., and Moran, S. (2011) *Sport & Peace: Mapping the Field*. Accessed 2 June 2016. http://idrottsforum.org/wp-content/uploads/2013/11/Sport-Peace-Mapping-the-Field-2.pdf.

International Federation for Human Rights (FIDH). (2014) Violence against women in Syria: breaking the silence. Accessed 2 June 2016. www.fidh.org/IMG/pdf/syria_sexual_violence-web.pdf.

Jansen, G.. (2006) Gender and war: the effects of armed conflict on women's health and mental health. *Journal of Women and Social Work*, 21(2): 134–145.

Jeanes, R. and Magee, J. (2014) 'Promoting gender empowerment through sport? Exploring the experi-ences of Zambian female footballers'. In N. Schulenkorf and D. Adair (eds) *Global Sport for Development: Critical Perspectives*. London: Palgrave Macmillan, pp. 134–154.

Kay, T. and Spaaij, R. (2012) The mediating effects of family on sport in international development con-texts. *International Review of the Sociology of Sport*, 47(1): 77–94.

Kidd, B. (2008) A new social movement: Sport for development and peace. *Sport in Society*, 11(4): 370–380.

Levermore, R. and Beacom, A. (2009) Sport and development: mapping the field. In R. Levermore and A. Beacom (eds) *Sport and International Development*. Hampshire, England: Palgrave Macmillan, pp. 1–25.

Martin, P. (2009) Some thoughts on the meaning of sport in war zones. *European Journal for Sport and Society*, 6(2): 135–145.

Meier, M. and Saavedra, M. (2009) Esther Phiri and the Moutawakel effect in Zambia: an analysis of the use of female role models in sport-for-development. *Sport in Society*, 12(9): 1158–1176.

O'Connor, V. (2012) Prosecution of rape as a war crime. *International Network to Promote the Rule of Law Research Memorandum*. Accessed 2 June 2016. http://inprol.org/sites/default/files/publications/2012/prosecution_of_rape_as_a_war_crime_07_2012_final.pdf.

Prytherch, H. and Kraft, K. (2015) *The Psychosocial Impact of Capoeira for Refugee Children and Youth*. London: Capoeira4Refugees.

Ravizza, D.M. (2012) We don't play war anymore. In K. Gilbert and W. Bennett (eds) *Sport, Peace and Development*. Champaign, IL: Common Ground, pp. 61–70.

Saavedra, M. (2009) Dilemmas and opportunities in gender and sport-in-development. In R. Levermore and A. Beacom (eds) *Sport and International Development*. New York: Palgrave Macmillan, pp. 124–155.

Sajjad, T. (2004) Women guerillas: marching toward true freedom? An analysis of women's experiences in the frontlines of guerrilla warfare and in the post-war period. *Agenda: Empowering Women for Gender Equality*, 59: 4–16.

Schulenkorf, N. and Adair, D. (eds.) (2014) *Global Sport-for-Development: Critical Perspectives*. London: Palgrave Macmillan.

Schulenkorf, N., Sherry, E., and Rowe, K. (in press) Sport-for-Development: an integrated literature review. *Journal of Sport Management*, DOI: http://dx.doi.org/10.1123/jsm.2014-0263.

Sugden, J. and Bairner, A. (eds) (1999) *Sport in Divided Societies*. Aachen: Meyer and Meyer.

United Nations Security Council. (2014) Conflict-related sexual violence. *Report of the Secretary-General*, 13 March 2014. Accessed 2 June 2016. http://reliefweb.int/sites/reliefweb.int/files/resources/N1426364.pdf.

Van Eekeren, F., ter Horst, K., and Fictorie, D. (2013) *Sport for Development: The Potential Value and Next Steps Review of Policy, Programs and Academic Research 1998–2013*. Arnhem: Foundation LM Publishers.

Vickers, J. (1993) *Women and War*. London: Zed Books.

27

"RACE", SPORT AND POLITICS

Kevin Hylton and Alexandra J. Rankin-Wright

> Sport is meant to foster social cohesion, bring different cultures together in a celebration of healthy competition, and to overcome the diffidence and even contempt that all too often divide countries and communities in the political and social arenas.
>
> *(UN Human Rights Chief, Navi Pillay UN 2013)*

When the United Nations make statements about the presence of racism in sport it should be clear that "race", sport and politics are not only linked, but inextricably so. There are numerous instances through history where "race", sport and politics have taken centre stage as a form of resistance, or more broadly as a cultural tool. The nature of politics is such that, depending on perspective, these events have shown sport as not always a vehicle for good, yet it remains a tool for the expression and reinforcement of values for the broadest spectrum of actors and political issues. Many commentators have identified sport and "race" as triggers for social and political events. The image of Martin Luther King Jr explaining to his daughter why she could not go to a public amusement park because it was closed to Black children offers us further insight into sport and recreation as spaces for social control, subordination, oppression and dysfunction (Wolcott 2012). Further, King's "I have a dream" speech that followed this shameful event is brought into sharper relief, as his personal and political lives are further focused in what some would paradoxically describe as the benign fields of sport and recreation. This state-sponsored support of racism through the systematic defence of individual and institutional actions against minoritised Americans reinforced racial hierarchies in a plethora of ways. The social relations in sport and recreation not only reflected the broader travails of the racial and political landscape of the 1960s; it also symbolised a "frontline" arena for the state of the nation (Hylton 2014).

In this chapter we broadly explore the place of "race" in sport and politics. We do this by critiquing the politics of racialised terminology and their relevance to sport and the state, while juxtaposing the tensions within. The chapter moves on to focus on two cases where "race" sport and politics coalesce. One is a current study of the "race" equality landscape in sport, where we illustrate the political and organisational tensions and issues that national governing bodies (NGBs) and key sport organisations have in confronting the problem of the under-representation of Black and minority ethnic (BME) coaches. With a backdrop of the broader public sector equality duties and compliance mechanisms, this study emphasises the influence of everyday individual acts, the rhetoric and realities of provision. Following this, we discuss the racialised outcomes of unconscious bias in the USA and the implications of the Rooney Rule for sport elsewhere.

According to Houlihan's (2008: 39) three definitions of politics, the implications for "race", in regards to sport and politics is that resource allocation decisions are subject to a range of influences. He argues, first, that in the public domain there are official actors that must manage their everyday environment and contingencies. Second, there are those influences that are sometimes *ad hoc* and/or not always formally or publically agreed. Thus stakeholders at a number of levels can effect influence on policy in a range of fashions. They can also interpret policy in practice and thus make decisions as "proximate policy-makers". Beyond the formal state institutions there is that third element of politics that can occur anywhere where there are disputes over goals, or challenges that require resolution. Houlihan (2008) suggests that these manifestations of power are even more nuanced, ambiguous and slippery to identify. He goes on to argue that:

> Politics is seen as a pervasive feature of modern life, inherent in all organisations whether public or private and common to all areas of human activity, including sport.
>
> *(2008: 37)*

As a result we should consider that any examination of "race", sport and politics could feasibly incorporate a broad range of issues in vastly differing contexts. For example, the independent UK-based organisation the Sports People's Think Tank (SPTT), established in 2014 by ex-professional footballers Jason Roberts (Blackburn), Darren Moore (West Bromwich Albion) and Michael Johnson (Birmingham), has heavily influenced debates concerning the lack of Black and minority ethnic football coaches and managers (Sports Peoples Think Tank 2014). Their collective profile and commissioned research have made many stakeholders in professional football take note of what they are saying. The SPTT was set up because Black sports people felt excluded from industry discussions and wanted to contribute to conversations that they felt required resolution. The SPTT clearly understands that the nature of politics is multifaceted and that actors can influence important decisions where they can effect leverage directly/indirectly, formally or through "back channels".

Globally, others in sport operate different versions of politics in regards to "race", dependent on context, history and culture. These stakeholders can effect a variety of influence formally, informally, directly or otherwise while residing inside or outside of sport. Houlihan (2008) describes these forms of political power as (1) confined to the state, (2) an aspect of all institutions, and (3) ubiquitous and inherent in all social activity. While conflict and resolution are often central to discussions of "race", sport and politics, other policy implementation discussions recognise that where resources are at stake and therefore finite, those contesting "conversations" will intuitively know there will also be winners and losers. Many of the conversations concerning "race", and the variety of political discussions in sport are often concerned with the way Black and minoritised groups are regularly excluded or subject to racialised barriers and patterns of inequality compared to their White counterparts. Sport as a racially contested arena and site of politics, oppression and subjugation is the conclusion of many such discussions on this topic.

The politics of "race" and racism

In Mason's (2013: xi) *Encyclopedia of Race and Racism* "Race" is defined as,

> Social groups partially and inconsistently defined by differences in observable physical characteristics such as skin colour and hair, but it also signifies ethnic, cultural, linguistic, and religious differences that animate persistent conflict between social groups.

"Race", sport and politics have an uneasy relationship, because the presence of the discourse of "race" itself signifies that some people are systematically differentiated not by the substance of their character, but by biology and culture (Guinier and Torres 2003). The racialisation of people is well documented, though the outcomes of this process lead to forms of racism that are complex and requiring of interventions to reduce their impact on those affected. State and international conglomerations have taken time to implement statutory instruments to curtail the worst excesses of these oppressive processes that range from the abolition of slavery, abolition of apartheid, and the inception of racial discrimination and anti-xenophobia acts and cross-continental sanctions.

We must consider the politics of "race" and ethnicity in sport and politics at a time when many would argue that we live in a state of *post-raciality*. By "post-race" it is argued by some social commentators that "race" was significant before but it is less so now. Post-"race" arguments are thought-provoking and paradoxical in any discussion of sport and politics because they deny the presence of something that did not exist in science in the first place. Nevertheless, what differentiates those who agree with this position, or otherwise, is not that racialisation and racism are unproblematic, but their disagreement on the nature and extent of racism. We are careful not to deny the impact of racisms when arguing that "race" is a social construction used to differentiate groups of people into crude categories that change over time. These categories reflect any number of cultural, national, geographical, religious, physiognomic and biologically perceived characteristics that between them distinguish groups of people into "races". To destabilise this view, it is important to recognise the unfixedness of "race" as a subjective, recursive, pseudo-scientific phenomenon. For us the most significant point to emphasise about "race" is that it does not exist in science but is replete with meaning from history, through discrimination, xenophobia, and forms of oppression and subordination. It therefore conspires to make these realities "lived".

The politics of "race" is such that there is often a pragmatic incorporation of the notion of ethnicity *because* of how "race" is used unproblematically in the everyday. Both "race" and ethnicity are used to demarcate individual and group identities, mark boundaries, include and exclude, and are situated. Often ethnicity is said to be freely chosen, yet such labels are still socially constructed, limited and changeable over time and space. We all experience the racialisation of people, places, even spaces and sports. However, many nation-states argue that it is necessary to employ racial and ethnic labels if they are to pursue the interests of all their constituents. By reinforcing racial and ethnic categories, whether they are endorsed by a census or otherwise, institutions such as the state perpetuate racialised discourses and ideologies with a view to prosecuting and promulgating their duties. This discourse of "race" is significant because it does a number of conflicting and confusing things, it (1) validates the everyday use of racialised terminology, (2) reinforces Black/White binaries, (3) centres "White" as the norm, (4) leaves biological arguments unfettered, (5) retains racial hierarchies through descriptive statistics, and (6) significantly, even in a neo-liberal society, recognises that where individuals and communities identify with racial and ethnic categories there are many serious disparities in facilities and services that require correction.

State and institutional preoccupations with "race" and ethnicity revolve around recognition of systemic conscious and unwitting barriers that operate at a societal level. It is custom and practice at the highest levels of public policy-making for a degree of regulation and management of these disparities to enable a healthy cohesive society (Cantle 2002; Hylton 2010b). As part of this policy exercise, the UK Equality Act 2010 makes a number of stipulations that those in receipt of public funds have a duty to eliminate unlawful discrimination, harassment, and victimisation and other conducts prohibited by the Act; advance equality of opportunity between people who share a protected characteristic and those who do not; foster good relations between people who share a protected characteristic and those who do not. This process is most significant in the way the state manages social relations using "race" and ethnicity as organising categories that reify and fix the way social groups are mediated, signified, represented and resourced. Departments of immigration, employment, education, crime, health and sport have all relied upon racial and ethnic categories and the consequent racialised statistics collected to inform policy agendas (Long and Hylton 2014).

The presence of "race" talk and racialised discourses indicate the presence of racism as their more pernicious end product (Guinier and Torres 2003; Long and Spracklen 2011; Hylton 2015). Racism has been described as endemic and a permanent aspect of modern societies (Bell 1992). It has become embedded in value systems, institutions and structures while manifesting in ways that challenge those in sport to be reflexive and critical. The use of the term *racism(s)* is often used to illustrate the plethora of layers to what is often simplistically referred to as racism. Racism(s) has been defined as,

> Racialised . . . Modes of exclusion, inferiorization, subordination and exploitation that present specific and different characters in different social and historical contexts.
>
> *(Anthias and Yuval-Davis 1993: 2)*

Anthias and Yuval Davis' (1993) summation of the complexity of racialised processes and barriers emphasise the challenges that require a critical approach to managing the politics of "race" and racism in any sport setting. So, institutional providers, conscious of historical inequalities, barriers and disparities, are likely to recognise a need to use their resources in a way that may seem inequitable to the whole community. Small (1994) uses the term "racialised barriers" to denote the outcomes of the material distribution of racialised property, privilege and power. These dimensions facilitate the racialised processes that lead to the inequalities we see in sport that Rankin (2014) explores in her work on national governing bodies (NGBs).

The following section is taken from the first stage of an ongoing larger study by Rankin (2014) aimed at gaining an understanding of the policy and provision landscape for racial equality and diversity in sport organisations and NGBs. In this study, equality and coaching lead officers (6 NGBs and 5 National Sport Organisations) considered the under-representation of Black and minority ethnic coaches in the upper echelons of each organisation, and sport in general. The study sheds light on the politics of "race" in NGBs and the subsequent tensions of managing "race" equality and diversity across sport's vast landscape. Rankin reveals an overview of the politics within and across these NGBs and sport organisations in how they manage "race" and racialised gender equality in the everyday. Her conclusions fall under three main themes: (1) locating "race" and ethnicity in the equalities agenda, (2) denying inequalities and racism, and (3) rationalising inequalities and racism.

Locating "race" and ethnicity in the equalities agenda

A prominent finding from Rankin's interviews was that "race" and ethnicity were seemingly absent from the sport stakeholders' discourse and as a result were often unwittingly overlooked within their equalities agenda. This absence of "race" and ethnicity can be explained as a result of the colour-blindness embedded within the sporting organisations and NGBs. These colour-blind ideologies serve to normalise and privilege the centrality of whiteness whilst subordinating the issues of those excluded from this dominant group (Burdsey 2007). NGBs were much more proactive around the inclusion of women and disability groups, which was attributed to the prioritisation of the high-performance discourse in sport. Yet the funding for this high-performance discourse does not explicitly focus on "race" and ethnicity, which reflects its lower profile in the equalities and sporting agendas. The Head of Consultancy at race equality in sport organisations, Sporting Equals,[1] explains this here:

> There's a louder political voice around disability and gender in comparison to the ethnic [sic] voice . . . because you have a pathway for disability sport, so if you've got a disability [it's] got its own pathway and similar with gender, you've got a women's arm of governing bodies and you've got separate structures. I think governing bodies as a whole find the issues around ethnicity and faith and race [– they are] not sure how it fits in and therefore there's almost some danger of it's in the "too difficult to do" tray.

This was evidenced where those interviewed omitted "race" and ethnicity when discussing the equality characteristics and under-represented groups within their organisations. Alternatively, they expressed a degree of anxiety and were vague when discussing "race" and ethnicity issues. Bonilla-Silva (2002: 62), argues that such a colour-blind narrative that results in an increased degree of anxiety and rhetorical incoherence when discussing "race" and racial equality issues is often reflected in predominantly White institutions where "race" matters least. This omission to analyse their own whiteness and its related processes in sport is based upon the explicit recognition of whiteness as normal, "race-less" and invisible (Massao and Fasting 2010; Hylton 2009; Hylton and Lawrence 2014; Long and Hylton 2002). It also offers some insight into the biographies of the actors making the decisions that maintain these customs and practices. So the politics of "race" in sport does not exist in a vacuum. Strategic and resource allocation discussions are affected by the invisible hand of institutional and individual values.

Thus, it is apparent that the colour-blind ideologies used within these sporting organisations and NGBs inhibit discussions around "race" and racial equality and directly affect resource allocation activities (Burke 2012). This "colour-blind package of racial understandings", in which "race" is no longer "seen" and thus no longer matters, falsely allows social structures to be viewed as meritocratic, equal and impartial in their day-to-day functioning (Doane and Bonilla-Silva 2003: 12). Such an approach is argued by Rollock and Gillborn (2011) to sustain racial inequality, sport organisations and NGBs included.

Denying inequalities . . . denying racism

Framing the institutional politics of the sport organisations and NGBs in Rankin's study was the powerful discourse of meritocracy and equality of opportunity that positioned access to, and progression in, sport and coaching qualifications as a "level-playing field" (Burdsey 2011a;

Burdsey 2011b; Hylton and Morpeth 2012). This discourse was illustrated by the normative expectation and embedded belief that the sporting arena is a space in which individuals from different social backgrounds could enter and progress without the constraints of racial or gender conflicts and division (Brown *et al.* 2003). Within this narrative of meritocracy, a number of the participants' responses for the espoused value of racial equality endorsed a denial of racial inequities and/or racism (Hoeber 2007). This denial of racism and systematic inequalities coupled with a lack of knowledge of the intersecting barriers that may impact upon aspiring coaches from BME backgrounds is exemplified here:

> I've never really . . . umm perceived it as being an issue that we don't have a diverse group of coaches or that we discriminate in any way or that the same opportunities aren't available to everybody. I think the barriers that would prevent people from progressing in their coaching apply to everybody regardless of their background, so whether that's cost or you know, time commitments or whatever else I don't think they are specific to any particular group.
>
> *(Coaching Lead)*

Burdsey (2007) states that this sense of denial derives from a dominant sport culture that discourages speaking out about racism and has consistently failed to acknowledge and challenge the shift from overt and explicit racial encounters to more subtle institutional and insidious practices. An adherence to the ideology that NGBs are bastions of equality and that sport is free from racialised barriers ignores the salience of "race" and racialised inequalities. Such ideologies serve to obscure and defend any processes that lead to racialised disparities that function as a way to maintain current resource allocations, opportunities, interests and privileges of the dominant groups in sport (Hoeber 2007). Burdsey (2007) argues that this reluctance to acknowledge racial inequalities and the denial of its existence in sport means that NGBs are less inclined to recognise or challenge racism. Ultimately, this serves to obstruct the efforts of organisations to effectively discuss or work towards racial equality (Acker 2009; Burke 2012; Duru 2011).

Rationalising inequalities . . . rationalising racism

The colour-blind ideologies evident in the stakeholder responses were further underpinned by a rationale that the under-representation of Black and minority coaches is a result of individual agency. By justifying the inequalities as a matter of *their* unwillingness to engage in sport coaching, the sport organisations and NGBs not only position BME groups as the problem but also dissociate any responsibility for the construction and maintenance of racial inequalities and exclusion (Burdsey 2007). This transfer of blame is exemplified here:

> We get a bit of heat and grief in terms of we don't have representative black and ethnic minority tutors to deliver our courses, so sending in a white middle class male tutor makes it un-relatable to the coaching community. . . . Which on the one hand I can see but on the other hand whenever we've advertised we don't have people with that background applying to become tutors, so it's like how you attract those people to role model what you are moving forward . . . do you know what I mean?
>
> *(Coaching Lead)*

Through framing this as a "cultural issue", the NGBs struggle to dissociate any responsibility for the lack of engagement by Black and minority ethnic groups without appearing to be racist (Bonilla-Silva 2006/2010). Ultimately this distancing of responsibility serves to reinforce current practice while deflecting attention away from possible systemic racialised and sexist discrimination. The onus placed on BME individuals to "possess" the correct motivation, drive and competency to engage and progress further represents a disengagement from a responsibility to be proactive. Further, the reality of intersecting racialised and gendered barriers facing aspiring Black men and women coaches is ignored. Here, notions of pluralism and meritocracy are unwittingly used to defend White privilege within sport coaching, and rationalise the under-representation of BME coaches.

Unconscious bias, Rooney and realities

The politics of "race" permeate sporting organisations and institutions in a variegated fashion. For example, unconscious racial bias has been described as the social networking systems and stereotypical perceptions held by those in authoritative positions that reinforce traditional power structures by excluding Black coaches from recruitment practices (Conway 2015; Collins 2007; Bradbury *et al.* 2015). In some cases positive change can be made much simpler where success has occurred in another organisation that has positive implications for the way they do business. This is currently the case for many who have seen the symbolic shifts in the ethnic diversity of managers in the National Football League (NFL) since the inception in 2003 of the Rooney Rule. Duru's (2011) analysis of the way closed social networks in American Football mitigate against diversity and equal opportunities in senior hiring practices is reflective of many inward-looking professions. Yet the realisation by lawyers, Cyrus Mehri and Johnnie L. Cochran Jr, that these practices needed to shift to change the unequal hiring patterns of NFL clubs still required the support of significant others; an example of how good ideas only become so with the institutional support that follows. Mehri and Cochran Jr's observation of the differences in hiring for African Americans wishing to become players compared with the glass ceiling stopping them from occupying positions of leadership concluded that the best of a few rather than the best of rest were being given a chance to progress beyond their playing years and into management. Previous assessments of such practices would surmise that racial processes were apparent in the making of these racialised outcomes. Some of these behaviours have been explained through debates on stereotyping and racial reductionism that leave some players with higher levels of physical characteristics and lower levels of intellectual characteristics, which make them less suited to positions of senior leadership (Carrington and Mcdonald 2001; Spracklen 2008; Fitzpatrick and Santamaría 2015; Hylton 2009). The ultimate result of such social relations, for the NFL, whether deliberate or otherwise required a shift in approach to how they conducted business. In the case of the NFL, a sporting institution driven toward achieving excellence on the field and in business it seems as though this problem eventually became beyond dispute with their acceptance of the need for the Rooney Rule. It is a rule that accepts the realism of past NFL inequalities, behaviours and cultural norms with a view to correcting them. A rule that required the equivalent of a seismic shift of ideas on recruitment for NFL front-of-house roles, such as managers and coaches, ensures at the very least that a suitably qualified minority ethnic [*sic*] candidate be interviewed where in the past they would have been overlooked.

Ingle's observation that we had never seen two Black managers/head coaches shake hands at the Wembley national stadium in London until Mike Tomlin of the Pittsburgh Steelers led his team out to play Leslie Frazier's Minnesota Vikings should have been a wake up call for British football (Ingle 2013). Alas, leadership in this matter is still lacking, though there have been some signs of movement with the English Football League announcing their intention to implement a version of the rule in 2016–17 (Conway 2015). According to Bridgewater's (2014) report into how football managers are appointed, British football suffers from a lack of transparency in its recruitment processes, the advertising of roles, elitist networks and a distinct patronage culture. This patronage culture is exemplified by connections and influential others in positions to endorse the abilities of potential applicants while remaining silent on those outside of their patronage. This is further illustrated by Bradbury *et al.*'s (2015) metaphor of the glass ceiling to illustrate the under-representation of visible minorities and women across European football; Black and minority ethnic women falling even further back as a result. In addition to "closed mechanisms" and "patronage", gendered and racial stereotypes are framed by entrenched historical inequalities. This is exacerbated by a general lack of understanding of how these inequalities persist, and where there is some awareness of these issues there is often an unwillingness to implement the changes that might disturb the hierarchies in place. An example of this resistance to change is exemplified in the lack of consensus of Rooney Rule-type initiatives or even more radical redistributive approaches. Bradbury *et al.* (2015: 8) state that part of the problem relates to:

> Conscious and unconscious racial bias and stereotypes in the coaching workplace and negative perceptions of key decision makers regarding the attitudes, behaviours, abilities and authority of "visible" minority coaches.

Though many believe in the meritocratic "level playing field" notions of sport, they are rarely skilled enough to recognise what has been described as unconscious bias. An unconscious bias that Collins (2007) argues the Rooney Rule goes some way to address. Yet, the notion of unconscious bias itself is not absent from criticism as it has been described as a more acceptable way of conjuring up the significance of racial inequalities while *mis-describing* the real *substantive racial inequalities* (see Hylton and Morpeth 2014), and instead focusing on *the hidden bad attitudes of individuals* (Banks and Ford 2009: 1121). Though the Rooney Rule in the NFL and European sport has drawn many plaudits, it remains contested. A critical politics of "race" and race equality challenges ideas such as "unconscious bias" and the Rooney Rule and suggests that they are used under advisement in contemplation, pre-implementation (What do you wish to achieve and how does this fit a race equality strategy?) and during implementation (Is it working and does it support related institutional initiatives?), on the journey to race equality. Though "sport for all" is a common mantra inside and outside of the industry, sport can be accused of offering piecemeal and *ad hoc* approaches to these important issues (Spracklen *et al.* 2006; Long *et al.* 2009; Hylton 2010a).

Conclusion

With a background of tensions around resourcing, Rankin's observations of blind strategies to "treat everybody equally", coupled with the failure to recognise the multiple intersecting issues for Black and minority ethnic coaches (men and women) demonstrates how a dominant racialised hegemony can be reinforced. Here, the male-centric nature of key sport organisations, combined with the dominance of whiteness illustrates that the coaching profession is both a gendered and "raced" arena. This White, male-centric knowledge, and the resulting practices, went unquestioned and unchallenged and thus reinforced a taken-for-granted, "common-sense" environment that upheld the existing order/inequalities characterised by asymmetrical power relations (Hoeber 2007), a state of affairs in the US that forced the NFL to accept the consequences of a new Rooney Rule. We can evidence that the necessity of underpinning race equality work with policies and practices linked to strategies can be a step too far for some in sport. In many ways this approach is one that some organisations accept, while others reject and therefore remain static.

We hint at the promise of progress in Rankin's study of the race equality landscape of sport where the under-representation of Black and minority ethnic coaches is the result of denial and misdirected ideologies of merit and opportunity. We illustrate how racialised outcomes in sport can be discerned and associated with influential hierarchies that perpetuate power relations and patterns of inclusion. They are subtle and seemingly unconscious, thus making any challenge to them a complicated project (Bonilla-Silva 2006/2010). However, the politics of "race" and sport is multifaceted complex and a subtle lived reality (Carrington 2010; Long and Hylton 2014). Systemic tensions concerning individual and institutionalised processes lead to decisions that can constrain and disempower, while we must be alive to the prospect that, conversely, opportunities exist for them to be disrupted (Hylton and Morpeth 2012).

Note

1 Pseudonyms were used for NGBs only.

References

Acker, J. (2009) From glass ceiling to inequality regimes. *Sociologie du travail*, 51: 199–217.

Anthias, F. and Yuval-Davis, N. (1993) *Racialized Boundaries*. London: Routledge.

Banks, R. and Ford, R. (2009) (How) does unconscious bias matter? Law politics and racial inequality. *Emory Law Journal*, 58: 1053–1122.

Bell, D. (1992) *Faces at the Bottom of the Well: The Permanence of Racism*. New York: Basic Books.

Bonilla-Silva, E. (2002) The linguistics of color blind racism: how to talk nasty about blacks without sounding "racist". *Critical Sociology*, 28: 41–64.

Bonilla-Silva, E. (2006/2010) *Racism Without Racists: Color-Blind Racism and the Persistence of Racial Inequality in the United States*. Lanham, MD and Oxford: Rowman and Littlefield Publishers.

Bradbury, S., van Sterkenburg, J. and Mignon, P. (2015) The glass ceiling in European football: levels of representation of visible ethnic minorities and women in leadership positions, and the experiences of elite level ethnic minority coaches. FARE, pp. 1-20. Accessed 2 June 2016. www.Farenet.org.

Bridgewater, S. (2014) How are football coaches appointed? *League Managers' Association*. Accessed 2 June 2016. www.Farenet.org.

Brown, T.N., Jackson, J.S., and Brown, K.T. (2003) "There's no race on the playing field": Perceptions of racial discrimination among white and black athletes. *Journal of Sport & Social Issues*, 27: 162–183.

Burdsey, D. (2007) *British Asians and Football: Culture, Identity, Exclusion*. London: Routledge.

Burdsey, D. (2011a) Applying a CRT lens to sport in the UK: the case of professional football. In K. Hylton, A.P.W. Pilkington, P. Warmington and S. Housee (eds) *Atlantic Crossings: International Dialogues on Critical Race Theory*. Birmingham: The Higher Education Academy Network.

Burdsey, D. (2011b) That joke isn't funny anymore: Racial microaggressions, colour-blind ideology and the mitigation of racism in English men's first class cricket. *Sociology of Sport Journal*, 28: 261–283.

Burke, M.A. (2012) *Racial Ambivalence in Diverse Communities: Whiteness and the Power of Color-Blind Ideologies*. Plymouth: Lexington Books.

Cantle, T. (2002) *Community Cohesion: A Report of the Independent Review Team*. London: Home Office.

Carrington, B. (2010) *Race, Sport and Politics*. London: Sage.

Carrington, B. and Mcdonald, I. (2001) *"Race", Sport and British Society*. London: Routledge.

Collins, B. (2007) Tackling unconscious bias in hiring practices: The plight of the Rooney Rule. *NYU Law Review*, 82: 870–912.

Conway, R. (2015) *Gordon Taylor: "Hidden" Resistance to Hiring Black Managers*. Accessed 2 June 2016. www.bbc.co.uk/sport/0/football/29333826.

Doane, A.W. and Bonilla-Silva, E. (2003) *White Out: The Continuing Significance of Racism*. London: Routledge.

Duru, J.N. (2011) *Advancing the Ball: Race, Reformation and the Quest for Equal Opportunity in the NFL*. New York: Oxford University Press.

Fitzpatrick, K. and Santamaría, L.J. (2015) Disrupting racialization: Considering critical leadership in the field of physical education. *Physical Education and Sport Pedagogy*, 20(5): 532–546.

Guinier, L. and Torres, G. (2003) *The Miner's Canary: Enlisting Race, Resisting Power, Transforming Democracy*. Cambridge, MA: Harvard University Press.

Hoeber, L. (2007) Exploring the gaps between meanings and practices of gender equity in a sport organization. *Gender, Work & Organization*, 14: 259–280.

Houlihan, B. (2008) *Sport and Society*. London: Sage.

Hylton, K. (2009) *"Race" and Sport: Critical Race Theory*. London: Routledge.

Hylton, K. (2010a) How a turn to critical race theory can contribute to our understanding of "race", racism and anti-racism in sport. *International Review for the Sociology of Sport*, 45: 335–334.

Hylton, K. (2010b) Social integration through sport. In B. Houlihan and M. Green (eds.) *Routledge International Handbook of Sports Development*. London: Routledge, pp. 100–113.

Hylton, K. (2014) Victoria Wolcott, race, riots and roller coasters: the struggle over segregated recreation in America. *Urban History*, 41: 559–560.

Hylton, K. (2015) "Race" talk! Tensions and contradictions in sport and PE. *Physical Education and Sport Pedagogy*, 20(5): 503–516.

Hylton, K. and Lawrence, S. (2014) Reading Ronaldo: contingent whiteness in the football media. *Soccer and Society*, 16(5/6): 765–782.

Hylton, K. and Morpeth, N.D. (2012) London 2012: "race" matters, and the east end. *International Journal of Sport Policy and Politics*, 4: 1–18.

Hylton, K. and Morpeth, N.D. (2014) "Race" matters, and the east end. In D. Bloyce and A. Smith (eds) *The "Olympic and Paralympic" Effect on Public Policy*. London: Routledge.

Ingle, S. (2013) NFL is proving that the Rooney Rule works, so why won't we give it a try? *The Guardian. Com*. 29 September 2013. Accessed 2 June 2016. www.theguardian.com/sport/blog/2013/sep/29/nfl-rooney-rule-premier-league.

Long, J. and Hylton, K. (2002) Shades of white: An examination of whiteness in sport. *Leisure Studies*, 21: 87–103.

Long, J. and Hylton, K. (2014) Reviewing research evidence and the case of participation in sport and physical recreation by black and minority ethnic communities. *Leisure Studies*, 33: 379–399.

Long, J. and Spracklen, K. (2011) *Sport and Challenges to Racism*. London: Routledge.

Long, J., Hylton, K., Spracklen, K. and Bailey, S. (2009) *A Systematic Review of of the Literature on Black and Minority Ethnic Communities in Sport and Physical Recreation*. Sport England: Birmingham.

Mason, P. (2013) *Encyclopedia of "Race" and Racism*. Detroit: MacMillan Reference.

Massao, P.B. and Fasting, K. (2010) Race and racism: Experiences of black Norwegian athletes. *International Review for the Sociology of Sport*, 45: 147–162.

Rankin, A.J. (2014) Stage one data analysis: the broad picture of racial and gender equality, diversity and inclusion: Policy and practice for sport coaching. *Carnegie Faculty*. Leeds: Leeds Beckett University.

Rollock, N. and Gillborn, D. (2011) Critical Race Theory (CRT). Accessed 24 October 2014. www.bera.ac.uk/files/2011/10/Critical-Race-Theory.pdf.

Small, S. (1994) *Racialised Barriers: The Black Experience in the United States and England in the 1980s*. London: Routledge.

Sports Peoples Think Tank. (2014) Ethnic minorities and coaching in elite level football in England: a call to action. The Sports Peoples Think Tank and FARE. Accessed 24 October 2014. www.sptt.com.

Spracklen, K. (2008) The holy blood and the holy grail: myths of scientific racism and the pursuit of excellence in sport. *Leisure Studies*, 27: 221–227.

Spracklen, K., Hylton, K., and Long, J. (2006) Managing and monitoring equality and diversity in UK sport: an evaluation of the Sporting Equals Racial Equality Standard and its impact on organisational change. *Journal of Sport and Social Issues*, 30: 289–305.

UN. (2013) *UN and Antiracism in Sport*. Accessed 24 October 2014. www.ohchr.org/EN/NewsEvents/IDERD/Pages/EliminationRacialDiscrimination.aspx.

Wolcott, V.W. (2012) *Race, Riots and Roller Coasters: The Struggle Over Segregated Recreation in America*. Pennsylvania, PA: University of Pennsylvania Press.

28

THE IMPLEMENTATION OF INDIGENOUS KNOWLEDGE AND CULTURAL PRACTICES WITHIN ELITE-LEVEL SPORT

Bevan Erueti

Introduction

Inquiry within the field of sport sociology provides the space to explore and interpret the interactions that exist between the domain of sport and the reality of human experience. In Aotearoa New Zealand, the discipline of sport sociology naturally encompasses the relationship between sport and Māori, the indigenous people of Aotearoa New Zealand. Although *te Ao Māori* (the Māori world) deteriorated due to the harmful influences of colonisation, assimilation and urbanisation, sport has provided a space where *te Ao Māori* recuperation can occur. This has most certainly been evident through the implementation of Māori knowledge and cultural practices, *mātauranga Māori* in elite-level sport environs (see Erueti and Palmer 2013; Hippolite and Bruce 2013).

Mātauranga Māori (Māori knowledge and cultural practices) is a compound concept that comprises 'Māori knowledge . . . in its widest and broadest terms' (Mead 2012: 9–11). Mead's (2012) expansive definition embraces a philosophical stance that considers the intentions of those who wish to 'recreate the old world and reinstall old customs', and those who feel that it 'is neither achievable nor wanted' (p. 12). Recently, the application and integration of mātauranga Māori 'in its widest and broadest terms' has shifted towards the development of Māori autonomy and sovereignty to nurture Māori revitalisation (Mead 2012; Smith 2012). The interpretation given by Mead therefore also challenges the notion that Māori knowledge involves cultural practices that belong in the era prior to colonisation.

Mātauranga Māori has various guises. In this chapter, I thematise them into two main categories: intangible assets such as *te reo me ngā tikanga*, Māori language and customs (see Wyeth *et al.* 2010) and tangible or material aspects such as Māori artwork. Intangible aspects incorporate customs such as *powhiri* (ceremonial welcome), *karakia* (blessing/prayer), *waiata* (songs), *mihimihi* (oral introductions) and *haka* (dance, for instance *Ka Mate*). Intangible aspects also include conceptual ideas inherent in Māori episteme, such as *kotahitanga* (unity), *whānaungatanga* (relationships) and *tiakitanga* (guardianship). Conversely, tangible features include for example, *pou* (standing posts), *taonga* (gift/jewellery) and *kakahu/korowai* (cloak). These examples (although not limited to) are 'a rich source of knowledge that can be unpacked to connect with ngā taonga tuku iho a ngā tūpuna (treasures passed down to us by our ancestors) – our timeless epistemological truths' (Edwards 2012: 45). Although tangible and intangible forms of mātauranga Māori are largely taken for granted qualities in mainstream Aotearoa New Zealand, modified forms of mātauranga Māori have been reinterpreted for the context of sport.

Historicity and political beginnings of Māori

Māori oral histories describe the discovery of Aotearoa New Zealand in 750 AD by the Polynesian explorer Kupe. Since his discovery through to 1350 AD, Māori narratives depict the voyages of seven *waka* (canoes) from the warmer climes of the Pacific heralding the creation of a new language and culture that, 'to a large degree, still held the history, genealogy, beliefs and values of its ancient Polynesian past' (Anaru 2011: 15). The foundation of Māori life was based on the familial societal structure of the *whānau* (family) nuclei, with many *whānau* contributing amongst one another to form *hapū* (extended family/sub tribe). The process of reciprocity between communal *hapū* formed *iwi* (tribe) resulting in 'complex lineages woven together by intermarriage [and] political alliance' (Andres 2011: 51) particularly functional during periods of warfare or expansion (Best 1925; Buck 1958).

The European discovery of New Zealand dates to the Dutch explorer Abel Tasman in 1642, however, he was not able to make a successful landing. It was not until 1769 when British sailors led by Captain James Cook actually landed on New Zealand soil that initiated contact with Europeans from a British penal colony at Port Jackson, Sydney in 1788. As European settlers began to make serious claims to Māori land in the late 1830s, conflict between settlers and Māori became more prominent. To ease tensions, representatives of the Crown created a treaty of cession in 1840 called *Te Tiriti o Waitangi* (Māori version) or the Treaty of Waitangi (English version) that contained a dual political purpose; 'provision for British settlement on one hand, and protection of Māori interests on the other' (Wyeth *et al.* 2010: 305). The English version of the treaty expressed:

1. Article I: Māori cede sovereignty of New Zealand to the British Crown.
2. Article II: In return, Māori are guaranteed full exclusive rights of ownership and use of their lands, forests, fisheries and other possessions, but if they wish to sell any of these, it must be to the Crown.
3. Article III: Māori enjoy the same rights and privileges as British citizens.

(Orange 2001)

Anomalies between the English and Māori texts of the treaty exist, consequently both parties have different perceptions and expectations of the treaty. However, the three articles of the Māori version respectively are manifested by the terms:

kāwanatanga (governorship), the Crown has the right to govern; rangatiratanga (chieftainship), Māori kin groups have the right to own and manage collective assets; and ōritetanga (equality), Māori individuals have the same rights and responsibilities as non-Māori New Zealanders.

(Wyeth et al. 2010: 305)

In regards to sport in Aotearoa New Zealand, the application of *rangatiratanga* (chieftainship) is particularly pertinent in this chapter given that the implementation of mātauranga Māori pro-actively entails the security and safety of tangible and intangible assets such as *te reo me ngā tikanga*: Māori language and customs.

Defining mātauranga Māori

Royal (2004) defines *mātauranga* as a term that refers 'to a body of knowledge' (p. 2), and the ethnic appellation *Māori* signifies that this 'body of knowledge' was 'brought to these Islands by Polynesian ancestors of present day Māori (p. 2). As such, mātauranga Māori incorporates 'things Māori . . . Māori tradition and history, Māori experience of history . . . Māori intellectual tradition' (Wiri 2011: 25) that were 'handed down from the past' (Andres 2011: 86). The symbolic construction and formation of this knowledge founded upon the understandings of our 'Polynesian ancestors' bestowed individual and collective identity factors and group membership through 'prescribed sets of standards, values and rules for living' (Friedman 1994: 243). Although these classifications have provided an appropriate understanding from a perspective of long-established customary practices, the revival and restoration of mātauranga Māori apparent in more recent times is a result of a progressive evolutionary pragmatism that is increasingly 'inclusive and allows for innovative ideas and practices' (Mead 2012: 14). Wiri (2011) further articulated that mātauranga Māori refers to:

> Māori epistemology, the Māori way, the Māori worldview, the Māori style of thought, Māori ideology, Māori knowledge base, Māori perspective, to understand or to be acquainted with the Māori world, to be knowledgeable in things Māori, to be a graduate of the Māori schools of learning, Māori tradition and history, Māori experience of history, Māori enlightenment, Māori scholarship, Māori intellectual tradition.
>
> *(p. 25)*

It is obvious that Wiri's description can be summarised as 'a Māori worldview owned by Māori' (Waitangi Tribunal 2011: 17). Additionally, Edwards (2012) complimented these definitions when he said that:

> mātauranga Māori is unashamedly a Māori-centric space, focused on Māori. It does not rely on seeking validity or approval from other worldviews, and it is not couched in the epistemes of others.
>
> *(p. 44)*

The understandings and associated explanations mentioned have guided in the formulation of a definition of mātauranga Māori for this chapter as *Māori knowledge and cultural practices*. The suffix *and cultural practices* is pertinent, as it is inclusive of both the tangible and intangible elements mentioned previously.

A brief historical analysis highlights that mātauranga Māori in the form of the *haka 'Ka Mate'*, was first observed in a sporting context when the New Zealand Natives, the inaugural representative national rugby team, toured Australia and England in 1888 (Mulholland 2009). During the tours, the players performed *Ka Mate* as a pre-game celebration of Māori culture. While the *haka* would continue to be considerably displayed in subsequent tours, the 1905/06 tour of the New Zealand Originals Team that visited the British Isles and France would unfortunately minimalise *haka* to a form of entertainment rather than a valued expression of Māori knowledge (Mulholland 2009). For 80 years the meaning of the *haka* as an aspect of mātauranga Māori would be diminished until 1985 where All Black team members Hika Reid and Buck

Shelford ensured for the first time that the whole team understood the words and could correctly perform the actions. Although Shelford's success as a Māori athlete is well-known in New Zealand's Rugby history, he has been recorded as declaring that the major triumph he is most proud of during his captaincy is the way he 'helped save the All Blacks haka'. He continued that 'haka is about respect; respecting Māori; respecting ourselves' (*Sunday News* 2008). The development of *haka* as a pre-game tradition in the All Black rugby team is a living example that demonstrates how mātauranga Māori has adapted as a mechanism to create and establish a distinct Aotearoa New Zealand national identity.

However, while the New Zealand Rugby Union (NZRU) are happy to use or appropriate decontextualised elements of Māori culture such as *haka* to mark a national identity, Māori are denied very little further decision making in Rugby at international level. For instance, the New Zealand Rugby Union board comprises of a solitary Māori representative of a board of nine members, despite Māori athletes being well represented and integrated at the higher echelons of elite or professional Rugby Union (Jackson and Hokowhitu 2002; Hippolite 2008; Palmer 2009).

A New Zealand Māori Rugby Board exists, but its perfunctory role is to act as a subsidiary committee to the New Zealand Rugby Union and does not select nor assemble the Māori All Blacks national team. The All Blacks *haka 'Ka mate'* while acting as a positive example of the implementation of mātauranga Māori, implicitly reveals that the *haka* better serves the interest of the dominant culture in maintaining a nationalistic identity rather than raising the profile of Māori as a social group or to revitalise Māori knowledge and customary practices.

Regardless, the examples provided in this chapter demonstrate how mātauranga Māori 'is inclusive and allows for innovative ideas and practices' (Mead 2012: 14) to be enjoyed today by Māori and non-Māori in the context of elite-level sport. By providing an insight into the strategies employed by sport organisations at the elite level that have adapted and incorporated portions of traditional Māori knowledge systems, the principle of *rangatiratanga* (chieftainship) is examined. Specifically, I discuss the integration of *powhiri* (ceremonial welcome), *waiata* (songs), and *haka* (dance), complimented by *pou* (standing posts), *taonga* (gift/jewellery) and *kakahu/korowai* (cloak) to promote *kotahitanga* (unity) and *whānaungatanga* (relationships). The narratives and experiences of athletes and coaching/management personnel highlight that mātauranga Māori, when applied in sport is a central and defining feature that unites athletes inspiring a unique sense of national identity.

The implementation of mātauranga Māori

National sport organisations

The extent to which National Sporting Organisations (NSO's) implement mātauranga Māori is varied. The following narratives demonstrate the experiences of athletes whom highlight the methods in which specific national sporting bodies have integrated mātauranga Māori. For the New Zealand women's (field) Hockey team (known as the Blacksticks) implementing Māori cultural knowledge started very simply with the execution of the New Zealand national anthem being sung in *te reo* Māori (Māori language).[1] An athlete explains:

> One of the big shifts that came with being in hockey was the use of the Māori national anthem and this was widely supported by all the players regardless of being Māori or non-Māori. It wasn't an easy process; the girls struggled with learning the words but it was awesome to see their perseverance and to finally be proud to say that we could sing both versions of our national anthem equally and together.

The athlete continues to affirm that the journey of incorporating mātauranga Māori evolved to incorporate *waiata* (songs) as several athletes 'contained a good level of understanding of things Māori especially *waiata* and so they taught us the songs and the meaning'. She continues by adding that 'it felt like it was the right thing to do . . . it just allowed our team to express our support and gratitude in a unique way, in our way . . . and of course it was really cool'. The knowledge that was shared regarding the 'meaning' and the 'reasons' not only gave an appropriate validation for the use of *waiata* but also gave an insight into Māori knowledge and protocol for all those involved. Certainly learning *waiata* had a profound impact on the hockey athletes who provide this narrative to the extent that when *waiata* was applied in the context of sport 'it felt like it was the right thing to do'. Reflecting positively about the use of *waiata*, athletes conveyed that mātauranga Māori is 'unique to New Zealand and that is our connection . . . it certainly brought us closer together', signifying that mātauranga Māori does encourage and promote a sense of national identity and team unity.

Similarly, within the sporting organisation of Netball New Zealand, an athlete described the positive influence of *waiata* in their team, stating that:

> Whenever we would go anywhere and [our captain] would speak we could actually stand as a whānau and support her with our unique waiata as is the norm in the Māori world. That makes it quite special when we were either welcoming new girls into the team or when we had visitors and so the team is treated like a whānau; it's just a different type of whānau.

The concept of *whānau* (family) as it exists within the traditional realm of *te Ao Māori* (the Māori world) generally refers to membership based on *whakapapa* (geneology/ancestry). Yet, the *whānau* concept in this chapter and as it applies to high-performance sport describes the distinct sense of belonging and unity that considers going beyond genealogical boundaries. In a contemporary view Te Rito (2006) declared that the concept of *whānau* in the sporting context can be denoted as 'a number of people with complementary skills who are committed to a common purpose and share sets of performance goals' (p. 14). As such Te Rito's definition compliments how mātauranga Māori has aided in a contemporary perception of *whānau* that incorporates the creation of mutual personal connections and inter-relationships between athletes, coaching and management staff.

Netball New Zealand continues to be proactive in implementing Māori knowledge and cultural practices as a means to encourage mutual personal connections and inter-relationships by employing *haka*. Seeking the aid of a spokesman from the *iwi* (tribe) Ngāti Toa that has cultural proprietorship of the haka *Ka mate* (explained earlier, see endnote 3), national netball athletes were afforded the opportunity to learn the historical analysis of the *haka* as understood from the oral accounts provided by the spokesman. An athlete narrative adds that they were educated on the correct 'edition of the haka and its associated meaning'. They were later taught the actions and words, but not prior to the information previously discussed. Her narrative describes a progressive attitude that certainly sustains the principle of *rangatiratanga* (chieftainship) by showing the proper 'respect' to the *haka* by seeking the advice of an expert acknowledging mātauranga Māori as *taonga* (treasure, prized possession).

Several national sporting organisations in New Zealand have been increasingly pro-active in implementing mātauranga Māori in the form of *haka*. More recently Basketball New Zealand, Swimming New Zealand and New Zealand Football are examples of national sport associations that have had *haka* composed specifically for their teams when representing New Zealand in global events. In regards to basketball, this was evident at the 2014 Men's Basketball World

Championships held in Spain where the New Zealand team referred to as the Tall Blacks performed their pre-game *haka* named '*Tu Kaha o Pango Te Kahikitia*'.[2] The assistant coach Paul Henare stated that 'the Tall Blacks have been educated in the meaning of their new haka, and as a result feel a lot more connected to it' (Hinton 2014). Henare continued that:

> sometimes the Tall Blacks over the years have been guilty of just doing the haka just to do the haka [but] this has brought so much meaning back into doing the haka, and also a little bit of ownership and pride, and why we're doing it and what it means . . . it's unique to us.
>
> *(Hinton 2014)*

Given its recent reintroduction on the global basketball stage, the *haka* received a mixed reception. For instance, the Tall Blacks' first opponents, Turkey, returned to their team bench while the *haka* was being performed. While the significance of *haka* embraces the concept of 'challenge', the Turkish team were completely ignorant that it was also an act of admiration, esteem and respect to them. Such reactions highlight the challenges that exist when employing mātauranga Māori in sporting contexts that are quite unfamiliar to indigenous displays of culture. However, team USA coach Mike Krzyzewski articulated that 'we actually were going to shake hands with them afterwards because we knew that was a really neat thing to do and it's part of their tradition, and we admire that' (news.com.au 2014). Krzyzewski's explicit admiration for the *haka* indicates openness and sincerity and are sufficient traits for indigenous knowledge to be appreciated and accepted for its cultural significance.

The athlete narratives from New Zealand Hockey, Netball New Zealand and Basketball New Zealand, highlight that the Māori version of the New Zealand national anthem, *waiata* and *haka* can encourage an environment that promotes a contemporary feeling of unity, belonging and team and national identity. Such unifying structures and group dynamics are complimentary elements for an environment conducive for athletes performing to the best of their abilities. Additionally, these sporting organisations exemplify that the implementation of Māori knowledge and cultural practices requires an appropriate approach that recognises and maintains the understanding and the meaning associated with Māori modes of knowledge such as *waiata* and *haka*. For this reason, sensitivity and consideration of the use of Māori knowledge and cultural practices are required in order to encourage and protect the indigenous value of the knowledge being applied. The interpretations and experiences aforementioned will act as a 'blueprint' for other sporting organisations intending to create a similar national identity distinction.

The New Zealand Olympic/Commonwealth teams

The circumstances of the Olympic/Commonwealth Games provides a challenging environment in which 'a powerful single team entity' (Hodge and Hermansson 2007) can be nurtured. Yet with fervent support and agreement from the Chef de Mission, the New Zealand Olympic Committee (NZOC) response was to implement mātauranga Māori, and has done so since the 2000 Olympic Games in Sydney. This was followed by an initiative referred to as the 'One Team-One Spirit' (New Zealand Olympic Committee 2004) campaign that described the implementation of mātauranga Māori during the 2004 Olympic Games in Athens.

To ensure the appropriate integration of and the protection, security and safety of mātauranga Māori, two cultural advisors travelled with the New Zealand Olympic/Commonwealth Games teams demonstrating exemplary application of the principle of *rangatiratanga* (chieftainship) as espoused by *Te tiriti o Waitangi*/the treaty of Waitangi. The cultural advisors consisted of an ex-Olympian athlete of Māori descent and a respected kaumātua (elder) carefully selected by a cultural advisory council that directed the New Zealand Olympic Committee (NZOC) in matters pertinent to Māori development in high-performance sport. The cultural advisors identified that the Māori concepts of *whānau* (family), *whānaungatanga* (developing family ties), and *kotahitanga* (community or unified vision) were specific concepts chosen to create a sense of intra-personal connection and to develop an understanding of what it means to represent Aotearoa New Zealand at the Olympic Games. Through the appropriate integration of both intangible and tangible methods, a powerful foundation of identity, meaning, belonging and cohesion was established.

Examples include the erection of a *waharoa* (gateway) for the entrance to the New Zealand location at the Sydney Olympic village and *pou* (vertical standing posts) at the location of the New Zealand Commonwealth Games village in Delhi 2010. Mead (2003) explicitly testifies that the employment of *waharoa* and *pou* from a Māori perspective symbolises 'a change in state . . . a threshold', that is, a metaphysical 'change' occurs that allows those people passing through a *waharoa* to be cleansed of the 'profane' (Barlow 2001: 179). When athletes arrive at the Commonwealth/Olympic Games, they too begin a process of preparation (psycho-physical and for some metaphysical) for their sporting event. As such 'the observance of tikanga [traditional rituals and cultural practices] of creative work actually enhances . . . gives significance . . . and elevates . . . something special and highly valued' (Mead 2003: 265). *Waharoa* and *pou* are tangible examples of *taonga* (highly prized possessions) that provide learning opportunities for athletes to amalgamate participation in sport at the elite level and indigenous knowledge of Aotearoa New Zealand.

Additional *taonga* included a ceremonial cloak or *kākahu* to be worn by the flag bearer, the *Mauri* stone (greenstone/touchstone) that has travelled to every Commonwealth/Olympic Games since Sydney in 2004, and *pounamu* (greenstone pendant) for each athlete. One of the cultural advisors clarifies that:

> All these things symbolise the gifting process, the act of giving and representing the essence of pounamu, that strength can come from small things as represented in the whakataukī 'ahakoa he iti he pounamu'. So pendants are gifted to the athletes and it is a hugely personal and special thing.

The mauri-stone/touchstone and *pounamu* are gifted as part of the reciprocal agreement that the New Zealand Olympic Committee (NZOC) has with *Kai Tahu* (a tribe located in the South Island) whom are the *kaitiakitanga* (guardians) of the largest repositories of *pounamu* in Aotearoa New Zealand. This agreement exemplifies the optimistic political agenda of the NZOC and the cultural sensitivities necessary in developing a bicultural partnership in sport at the elite level. These forms of tangible *taonga* provide learning opportunities and are culturally responsive strategies in formulating connectivity between athletes and Aotearoa New Zealand. Moreover, the mauri-stone/touchstone encouraged the intangible concepts of *whānaungatanga* (relationships) and *kotahitanga* (unity) to connect athletes to reaffirm a unique national New Zealand identity.

To further encourage a unified identity and belonging, the implementation of several specific Māori cultural practices was employed, namely, *powhiri* (welcoming ceremony), *mihimihi* (greeting formalities) and *haka* (dance). Athlete narratives from those who participated at the Olympic Games in Athens testify to the impact of incorporating Māori knowledge and cultural practices to inspire athletes and enhance team environment. Dean Kent (swimmer) commented that:

It just gives you a sense of home, a sense of pride . . . just that little inner feeling that this is what it means to be an elite athlete representing your country representing everyone that's gone before you . . . you know . . . your history and culture.

Kent identifies that for him the implementation of mātauranga Māori aroused deep emotional attachments that exposed the personal links he internalised as an athlete and as a New Zealander. In two more examples, gold medallists Sarah Ulmer (cycling, women's individual pursuit) and Hamish Carter (triathlon) openly express their feelings of receiving a *haka* when they returned to the Olympic village after being awarded their medals. Ulmer describes that:

I get bloody goose bumps now from it just thinking about [the haka] . . . to me that was way cooler than shaking a stranger's hand and having a medal put around my neck . . . to me that was just everything . . . that was winning at the Olympics.

Carter adds:

Winning the gold medal was great and it was the most fantastic feeling, but the things like the haka and the spirit in the team made it even sweeter because . . . there were your peers and fellow athletes who had worked just as hard as you had and had put just as much into the build-up as you had and they were bestowing this honour upon you I guess, it was just so moving and so fantastic. I'll never forget it.

The narratives of Olympic athletes who participated at the Athens Olympic Games demonstrate that the use of mātauranga Māori was perceived as an appropriate method to mark a 'unified national identity' (McCreanor *et al.* 2012: 241). Hodge and Hermansson (2007) as sport psychologists to the Athens and the Torino Winter Olympic Games 2006 respectively, highlighted that the application of mātauranga Māori in those Games resulted in:

a clear and solid sense of team unity and togetherness . . . positive social interaction and communication, obvious team stability and acceptance of role responsibilities and a commitment to shared group norms. A heightened sense of trust and security with each other has developed . . . a commitment to and enjoyment from being part of a unified team.

A more recent example of where an amalgamation of Māori knowledge and cultural practices of *powhiri* (welcoming ceremony), *mihimihi* (oral introductions) and *haka* were brought together occurred when the New Zealand Winter Olympic Team were competing at the Winter Olympic Games in Vancouver in 2010. The cultural advisor for the NZOC deemed it important to create a relationship with *tāngata whenua* (hosts), the indigenous first nation's people of Vancouver. There are some obvious similarities between the indigenous epistemes of first nation's people and Māori and these became more evident when the New Zealand Winter Olympic team were invited to a formal welcome referred to as a Squamish blanketing ceremony. It involved the didactic interaction between selected tribal speakers called 'blanketed speakers', in which the cultural advisor was afforded the honour to be the 'blanketed speaker' for the New Zealand Olympic team. Furthermore the gifting of *taonga* took place in the form of traditional first nations blankets for each athlete and personnel of the New Zealand team. Given the emotions that were shared, the cultural advisor decided that the team should honour their hosts with an impromptu *haka*. This is a prime illustration of the global application of mātauranga Māori because it realises that a Māori approach was a necessity when it came to acknowledge the indigenous peoples of the Winter Olympic Games' hosting nation.

The examples of athlete, cultural advisor and sport psychologist narratives emphasise that expressions of specific Māori knowledge and cultural practices have allowed an opportunity for a distinct unification of indigenous knowledge and elite-level sport. Indeed, one of the cultural advisors for the New Zealand Olympic/Commonwealth Games teams concluded that mātauranga Māori:

> as proposed by our ancestors is a wonderful blueprint for achieving [and] creating relationships not only with people but with their whenua [land]. These concepts are as relevant today as they ever were . . . [It] reminds [athletes] of who they are and where they are from and who they are doing this for. [Māori] culture provides that vehicle; it aids them in thinking past the physical.

Certainly, the implementation of mātauranga Māori establishes an emotional belonging and sense of home by forging a connection to the physical environment of Aotearoa New Zealand. Tangible forms of *taonga* (pendants/jewellery) and the mauri-stone/touchstone and the intangible aspects – *powhiri*, *waiata* and *haka*, encouraged concepts such as *whānaungatanga* (relationships) and *kotahitanga* (unity) assisting in the merging of athletes into the wider New Zealand team relationship. The narratives also suggest that the actions and symbols of mātauranga Māori may contain a direct or indirect potential message of relevance to the identity/performance equation. The cultural advisor to the Olympic/Commonwealth Games teams expresses:

> I believe that while our athletes are 98 to 99% physically and mentally attuned to what they have to achieve to compete and go into battle on the world stage I see my role as making up that last one or 2%.

Commensurate with these thoughts expressed by the cultural advisor, Rob Waddell, the Chef de Mission for the New Zealand Commonwealth Games team at Glasgow 2014 was recorded as saying that at 'pinnacle events . . . 1% of preparation can lead to 100% of difference' (Hermansson 2014). Emphasising that the convergence of indigenous knowledge and elite-level sport affords opportunities where the insights and methods of one can in fact enhance the other. Consequently, mātauranga Māori continues to be employed and enjoyed within the context of the New Zealand Olympic/Commonwealth Games teams.

The Super XV rugby union competition: the Waikato Chiefs

The Super XV Rugby competition is a Southern Hemisphere Rugby Union premier transnational club competition involving teams from Australia, New Zealand and South Africa. For sponsorship reasons, this competition is known as Asteron Life Super Rugby in Australia, Investec Super Rugby in New Zealand and Vodacom Super Rugby in South Africa. Including its past incarnations as Super 12 and Super 14, 2014 heralded its nineteenth season and comprised of 15 teams; 5 teams from each of the three countries involved (SANZAR Rugby 2014). The Waikato Chiefs, a New Zealand team based in the city of Hamilton that represents the combined provincial Rugby Unions of the Bay of Plenty, Counties Manukau, King Country, Thames Valley, Waikato and Taranaki, incorporates mātauranga Māori in various forms as part of their organisations' identity.

Foremostly, the team name is taken from a *whakataukī* (proverbial saying) about the Waikato area *He piko, he taniwha* that translates literally to 'around every bend [of the Waikato river] there is a *taniwha*' (a mythical creature). Yet, in the context of which it is conveyed in the Māori world, the word *taniwha* is symbolic of the status given to a 'chief'. As such the *whakataukī* articulates that 'around every bend [of the Waikato river] there are numerous chiefs'(Hapeta and Palmer 2014). Hapeta and Palmer (2014) continue to explain that:

> A chief also refers to a person of tremendous influence, and this expression under-lines the mana [integrity, charisma, prestige] of the Waikato people. From the team's perspective, this whakataukī reflects their link to the region, to their supporters, and would also have meaning for the team internally. Perhaps this meaning suggests that every player has, enhancing mātauranga Māori and the ability and responsibility to influence the team in a positive way.
>
> *(pp. 110–111)*

The integration of this *whakataukī* is displayed in the Chiefs' logo design that features a male figure clasping a *patu* (club-like weapon) (Hokowhitu *et al.* 2008). The proverbial saying is also incorpo-rated into a specifically composed haka. The creation of the *haka* was co-constructed with a teacher from a full-immersion Māori language school, *Te Wharekura o Rākaumanga* situated in the town of Huntly in the Waikato province (Elliott 2012). By employing the skills of the teacher, the Waikato Chiefs' franchise management exemplify the principle of *rangatiratanga* (chieftainship) by ensuring the protection and security of specific Māori knowledge exclusive to the Waikato area. The Chiefs' *haka* went 'viral' (Lynch 2013) after being displayed following the Chiefs' second Super XV title win over Australian opponents the Brumbies in 2013. It caught the attention of *Huffington Post*[3] reporter Dominique Mosbergen, who described the haka as 'a jaw-dropping coordinated perfor-mance' and 'one of the coolest rituals in today's world of sports' (Lynch 2013).

Head coach Dave Rennie (2012) acknowledges that he was inspired by Māori heritage and set about incorporating specific Māori knowledge that was unique to the region the team rep-resents. In describing the integration of mātauranga Māori, he expresses that:

> The integration of things Māori has been really good. A lot of those elements have gone a long way to creating the sort of culture we want here. The boys have bought into it and enjoyed it and it's helped us to grow Chiefs' mana.

Intriguingly, ever since Rennie began as the head coach and subsequently the introduction of the integration of mātauranga Māori in 2012, the Waikato Chiefs moved from ninth place in 2011 to claim back-to-back Super XV tournament title wins in 2012 and 2013 (ESPN Staff, 17 February 2014) and finished a reputable fifth in 2014. Assistant Coach Wayne Smith (cited in Hapeta and Palmer 2014) concurred that:

> We wanted more than just cultural change . . . essentially creating a champion team is a spiritual act. Not everyone's cup-of-tea, but definitely ours! We sought an identity and have ended up honouring it. We wanted our behaviours to be specifically identifi-able and upheld.
>
> *(p. 108)*

The Waikato Chiefs' organisation exemplify that mātauranga Māori and elite-level Rugby Union provides a positive space to reinvigorate knowledge and cultural practices with 'deeper understanding and application of the core elements' (Edwards 2012: 58) of Māori knowledge and cultural practices. Certainly, the team's contemporary employment of mātauranga Māori has enabled them to define and establish their own team culture founded on collective aspirations – undoubtedly that has been demonstrated both on and off the field.

Conclusion

The inventiveness of particular national sporting organisations, the New Zealand Olympic/ Commonwealth Games teams and the Waikato Chiefs Rugby Union organisation demonstrate that an integration of mātauranga Māori has stimulated a unified sense of identity that is unique to the sporting context of Aotearoa New Zealand. The Honourable Dr Pita Sharples (Minister of Māori Affairs) described the influence mātauranga Māori can have in developing a national identity by stating that mātauranga Māori is 'not something that divide[s] us' but gives opportunity to bring 'our entire nation together and focus us on the challenges ahead' (Sharples 2012). Additionally Sharples (2012) declared that:

> Our athletes know that traditions like haka and karakia . . . link us back to our people, our homeland, our heritage, our courage, our culture, our ability to unite – many people's as one. This is our unique edge we have over the rest of the world. This is who we are. This is what a New Zealander is.

While there is a general consensus that the utilisation of mātauranga Māori in sport at the elite level may bring Māori and non-Māori together in sport at the elite level, it does not automatically lead to the adoption of tolerant attitudes. It is clear that the application of mātauranga Māori does very little to raise Māori politicisation, even though Māori feature prominently in sport at the elite level. In this respect mātauranga Māori contributes no more than to provide an impetus for nationalistic semblance and perhaps even distracts and avoids the paramount debate of the relatively low representation of Māori participation in sport at the elite level in areas of leadership, management and governance. The rhetoric that sport is an epoch of Aotearoa New Zealand society unfettered by politics, race and other social barriers and is often portrayed as an even playing field is therefore debunked.

Nonetheless, the examples given throughout this chapter have exposed how the treaty principle of *rangatiratanga* (chieftainship) has been maintained to uphold the 'humanitarian interests' (Wyeth *et al.* 2010: 305) of Māori. Moreover, mātauranga Māori consists of dynamic components that have become an integral source of energy to the demands of competition, without detracting from the high-performance environment in operation. It ensures an enjoyable backdrop that encourages an essence of measured optimism, realistic self-belief, well-grounded affirmations and motivational desire, for athletes personally and nationalistically. Māori knowledge and cultural practices can inspire a consciousness where all involved, athletes and support staff, can procure strength and meaning from knowing who they are and where they come from, crucial elements that heighten the athlete experience.

Notes

1 The New Zealand national anthem 'God Defend New Zealand' was first written in 1876. The Māori version (translation) followed in 1878.
2 The *Tū Kaha o Pango Te Kahikitia haka* was first introduced in 2007 by then Tall Black member Paora Winitana. The Kahikitia is a native tree that is known for its foundation; hence the *haka* is symbolic of

the strength of the tree's intricate root system. While this particular *haka* faded soon after, Mika Vukona, a current member of the national team, requested its reintroduction.

3 An American online news aggregator and blog formed in 2005. The headline to her column reads 'Haka victory dance performed by New Zealand rugby team is just too awesome for words.'

References

Anaru, N.A. (2011) A critical analysis of the impact of colonisation on the Māori language through an examination of political theory. *A thesis submitted for the degree of Master of Arts in Māori Development.* Auckland University of Technology.

Andres, U.P. (2011) Return migration and Māori identity in a Northland community. *A thesis submitted in fulfilment of the requirements for the degree of Doctor of Philosophy.* The University of Auckland.

Barlow, C. (2001) *Tikanga Whakaaro: Key Concepts in Māori Culture.* Auckland, NZ: Oxford University Press.

Best, E. (1925) *Games and pastimes of the Māori: an account of the various exercises, games and pastimes of the natives of New Zealand, as practised in former times, including some information concerning their vocal and instrumental music.* Wellington, New Zealand: The Board of Māori ethnological research, for the Dominion Museum.

Buck, P. (1958) *The Coming of Māori.* Christchurch, NZ: Whitcombe and Tombs.

Edwards, S. (2012) Na te Mātauranga Māori, Ka ora tonu te ao Māori. In T. Black, D. Bean, W. Collings and W. Nuku (eds) *Conversations on Mātauranga Māori.* Wellington, NZ: New Zealand Qualifications Authority (NZQA).

Elliott, H. (2012) Chiefs inspired by Māori warrior heritage. *3News Online.* Accessed 26 September 2014. www.3news.co.nz/sport/chiefs-inspired-by-Māori-warrior-heritage-2013020619#axzz3Ncp6067q].

Erueti, B. and Palmer, F. (2013) Te Whariki Tuakiri (the identity mat): Māori elite athletes and the expression of ethno-cultural identity in global sport. *Sport in Society: Cultures, Commerce, Media, Politics,* pp. 1–15. doi:10.1080/17430437.2013.838351.

ESPN Staff (2014) Dave Rennie hails Chiefs' Māori heritage. 17 February. Accessed 2 January 2015. www.espnscrum.com/super-rugby-2014/rugby/story/215001.html.

Friedman, J. (1994) *Cultural Identity and Global Process.* London: Sage Publications.

Hapeta, J. and Palmer, F. (2014) Māori culture counts: A case study of the Waikato Chiefs. In T. Black, H. Murphy, C. Buchanan, W. Nuku, and B. Ngaia, B. (eds) *Enhancing Mātauranga Māori and Global Indigenous Knowledge.* Wellington, NZ: Haemata Ltd/New Zealand Qualifications Authority (NZQA).

Hermansson, G. (2014). *Massey University Blues Sports Awards Address.* 26 October 2014.

Hinton, M. (2014) Tall Blacks to unleash new haka at World Cup. *stuff.co.nz.* Accessed 26 September 2014. www.stuff.co.nz/sport/basketball/10443197/Tall-Blacks-to-unleash-new-haka-at-World-Cup.

Hippolite, H.R. (2008) Towards an equal playing field: Racism and Māori women in Sport. *MAI Review,* 3(1): 1–12.

Hippolite, H.R. and Bruce, T. (2013) Towards cultural competence: How incorporting Māori values could benefit New Zealand sport. In C. Hallinan and B. Judd, (eds) *Native Games: Indigenous Peoples and Sport in the Post-Colonial World.* Bingley, WA: Emerald Group Publishing Ltd, pp. 85–106.

Hodge, K. and Hermansson, G. (2007) Psychological preparation of athletes for the Olympic context: The New Zealand Summer and Winter Olympic teams. *Athletic Insight. The Online Journal of Sport Psychology,* 9. Accessed 18 July 2009. www.athleticinsight.com/Vol9Iss4/NewZealand.htm - OneTeam.

Hokowhitu, B., Sullivan, S.J. and Williams, L.T. (2008) Rugby culture, ethnicity and concussion. *MAI Review,* 3.

Jackson, S.J. and Hokowhitu, B. (2002) Sport, tribes, and technology: The New Zealand All Blacks' Haka and the politics of identity. *Journal of Sport and Social Issues,* 26: 125.

Lynch, J. (2013) Chiefs' haka goes viral. Accessed 27 October 2014. www.stuff.co.nz/waikato-times/sport/9024117/Chiefs-haka-goes-viral.

McCreanor, T., Rankine, J., Moewaka Barnes, A., Borell, B., Nairn, R., Gregory, M., and Kaiwai, H. (2012) Māori sport and Māori in sport: Mass media representations and Pakeha discourse. *AlterNative: An International Journal of Indigenous Peoples,* 6: 235–247.

Mead, H.M. (2003) *Tikanga Māori: Living by Māori Values.* Wellington, NZ: Huia Publishing.

Mead, H.M. (2012) Understanding Mātauranga Māori. In T. Black, D. Bean, W. Collings, and W. Nuku (eds) *Conversations on Mātauranga Māori*. Wellington, NZ: New Zealand Qualifications Authority (NZQA).

Mulholland, M. (2009) *Beneath the Māori Moon: An Illustrated History of Māori Rugby*. Wellington, NZ: Huia Publishers.

NEWS.com.au. (2014). *New Zealand haka mesmerises USA's NBA stars at Basketball World Cup*. Accessed 26 September 2014. www.news.com.au/sport/basketball/new-zealand-haka-mesmerises-usas-nba-stars-at-basketball-world-cup/story-fndkzqrr-1227045949263.

New Zealand Olympic Committee (2004) NZ Olympic team – One team one spirit Athens 2004. Accessed 26 September 2014. www.youtube.com/watch?v=qYXwqlsTYDc.

Orange, C. (2001) *The Treaty of Waitangi*. (Reprint edition). Wellington, NZ: Bridget Williams Books.

Palmer, F. (2009) *Tino rangatiratanga in sport*. Accessed 16 August 2012. http://tur-media-db1.massey.ac.nz/mediasite/Viewer/?peid=d99e4492285a4bbb94ce4c7eb664e7c8.

Rennie, D. (2012) Interviewed on the Chiefs' television channel. Accessed 26 September 2014. http://chiefs.onsport.co.nz/chiefs-head-coach-dave-rennie.

Royal, C. (2004) *Mātauranga Māori and museum practice: A discussion*. Wellington, NZ: Te Papa National Services – Te Paerangi.

Sanzar Rugby. (2014) Super rugby conferences. *Sanzar Rugby Online*. Accessed 26 September 2014. www.sanzarrugby.com/superrugby/.

Sharples, P. (2012) Olympic cultural event. A public address retrieved. Accessed 9 April 2014. www.beehive.govt.nz/speech/olympic-cultural-event.

Smith, G.H. (2012) Interview-Kaupapa Māori: The dangers of domestication. *New Zealand Journal of Educational Studies*, 47: 10–20.

Sunday News (2008) Buck put bang back into haka. *Sunday News*. Accessed 24 September 2014. www.stuff.co.nz/sunday-news/latest-edition/699767/Buck-put-bang-back-into-haka.

Te Rito, P. (2006) Leadership in Māori, European cultures and in the world of sport. *MAI Review*, 1: 1–19. Accessed 2 June 2016. www.review.mai.ac.nz/index.php/MR/article/view/17/17.

Waitangi Tribunal (2011) Ko Aotearoa Tēnei: A report into claims concerning New Zealand law and policy affecting Māori culture and identity. *Waitangi Tribunal Report* (Wai 262). Accessed 2 June 2016. www.waitangitribunal.govt.nz.

Wiri, R. (2011) The prophecies of the Great Canyon of Toi: A history of Te Whaiti-nui-ā-Toi in the western Urewera mountains of New Zealand. Unpublished Doctoral Thesis. University of Auckland.

Wyeth, E., Derrett, S., Hokowhitu, B., Hall, C., and Langley, J. (2010) Rangatiratanga and Ōritetanga: Responses to the treaty of Waitangi in a New Zealand study. *Ethnicity and Health*, 15: 303–316.

29

SPORT AND SUSTAINABILITY

Will Atkinson

The politics of sustainability

Sustainability and environmentalism have become increasingly prevalent terms in many aspects of society. We are increasingly made aware of the importance of sustainable transport and reducing energy use, we are informed of the provenance and 'air miles' of our food and the 'carbon footprint' of our activities, and governments aim to create 'green jobs'. In 2010, British Prime Minister David Cameron stated that the coalition government would become the 'greenest government ever', which indicates how the values of environmentalism are now part of mainstream politics.

It is the spectre of climate change, however, that has dominated the discourse of environmentalism and sustainability so far this century, taking over from concerns over global warming in the 1990s. Despite the breadth of the values of the sustainability movement and the innumerable ways in which these can impact on our lives, climate change, the importance of sustainable transport and green jobs, for example, are invariably framed in terms of how to mitigate the risks of or adapt to climate change. This is also reflected in the media profile of the UN Climate Change Conferences, where leaders from around the world 'thrash out deals', aiming to reduce the use of fossil fuels. In terms of responses or 'solutions' to climate change and many other environmental concerns, technology is often seen to be the answer. Hi-tech solar panels and wind farms are more commonly seen to be environmentally friendly solutions to energy demands than changing consumers' habits and 'geoengineering' or 'climate modification' interventions such as reflecting sunlight back into space and seeding the atmosphere with non-greenhouse gases.

Media focus on sustainability issues may focus primarily on climate change, but the difficulties of reaching a consensus at the UN Climate Change Conferences does show how difficult these issues are to 'solve' because of the geographical, temporal and political breadth of the discourse surrounding sustainability. Actions, reactions and solutions are global and local; coal-fired power stations in the UK may impact on sea levels in the Seychelles in three generations' time. It is therefore evident how a focus on climate change can lead to a loss of perspective on how environmental issues can be more local and immediate, and perhaps also a loss of perspective on how actions on a non-global scale can point towards a more sustainable future.

This chapter therefore aims to draw attention to immediate, local environmental issues of sport, most centrally how the nature of sporting environments can impact on the sustainability credentials of the sports industry, with a focus on the 'technologisation' of once 'natural' sporting environments: geoengineering solutions to climate change may sound imposing and extreme, but we have been modifying our immediate and indoor climates for centuries through heating and cooling systems, and sport environments are no different.

The specific activities carried out by humans are influenced by the environments in which they exist, and environments are, in turn, influenced by the activities we wish to take part in. With regard to sport and physical activity, for example, we can run on a treadmill in a gym, run on roads and pavements, run on an artificial running track and run up and down the fells. How 'natural' or 'manufactured' do we perceive these environments as being? Are there trends in the ways that sporting environments are being organised? What are the environmental impacts of environments that are built solely for sport? Can these environments influence individuals or institutions to act in line with sustainability agendas? These questions will be explored through a case study of the redeveloped Centre Court at Wimbledon, which was opened in 2009 with a retractable roof and an air management system to ensure that play can continue in all weather conditions on the famous living, natural grass courts.

Humans and nature

As alluded to above, an aspect of sustainability thought is the interaction between humans and nature. How do societies influence nature? How does it influence us? Writing in the mid-1990s and influenced by Beck's (1992) 'reflexive modernity' thesis – one that is particularly prominent in contemporary sustainability thought – Lash and Urry (1994: 297) argue that 'humans are increasingly viewed culturally as part of nature rather than distinct from and opposed to it. As such it is thought less appropriate for humans to simply "conquer" nature since they are part of it'. On the other hand, Brennan's (2007) philosophical approach claims that the West is still in the 'humanistic mastery' stage of relations with nature, with much of society yet to see itself as 'cooperative equals' with the natural world. Looking to the future, Brennan (2007: 514) wonders whether continuing to 'dominate nature will make life less worth living' and therefore believes that with this growing reflexivity, 'many people are beginning to find the attitude of domination unsatisfying' (2007: 517). Brennan understands that a number of stumbling blocks must be overcome in order to reach the 'desirable' stage of humans being a 'cooperative equal' with nature. He views our relationship with nature as not being a reciprocal one, due to nature not being able to return our respect. This is not necessarily indicative of how all humans interact with their environments, but it certainly reflects a pervasive contemporary understanding of human/nature relationships within our society, so asking people within 'Western' societies to engage in a reciprocal relationship with the environment is perhaps unrealistic. Brennan also uses the example of our love for chimpanzees and dolphins as indicative of how we show more care to something that we share levels of consciousness with, emphasising that we cannot relate to the atmosphere or the weather in this way. Brennan's (2007: 525) conclusion to this dilemma is challenging and enlightening in equal measure:

> Viewing oneself as completely unified with nature is arguably a failing of ecological consciousness. What makes respect for other persons morally interesting is that this respect involves *recognising* the boundaries and differences between others and us (original emphasis).

This suggests that a *consciousness* of the environments that we find ourselves in – and, by extension, a *consciousness* of our place in 'nature' – is the most productive way to work towards a 'cooperative equal' relationship with nature. Bixler and Floyd (1997: 462) who, in their study of negative perceptions towards wildland environments, found that 'respondents with high disgust sensitivity and desire for modern comforts expressed lower preferences for wildlands and wildland activities and *greater preference for indoor environments*' (emphasis added) and 'human modified environments' such as manicured park paths. This, read alongside Brennan's (2007) perspective, points towards a vicious circle where someone who does not enjoy the vagaries and 'discomforts'of the outdoors prefers sanitised spaces, and someone who is less likely to engage with the 'discomforts' present in the outdoor environment is less likely to have a consciousness of their place in nature. Is commercialised sport moving away from being carried out in more 'natural' surroundings? If so, could this be problematic in terms of the sustainability credentials of the sports industry on a deeper, longer-term level than is often considered?

Controlling sport environments: a social perspective

John Bale is one of the few academics to have written on the 'geography of sport' and his writing and theoretical positions are therefore conscious of how the practice of sport influences and is influenced by 'natural' and '(hu)man-made' spaces. Bale (1994: 39) believes that due to its 'inherent character', sport is 'at root . . . anti-nature' and Galtung (1984: 14), quoted in Bale (1994), understands that:

> sporting events decreasingly take place in natural surroundings, and increasingly in special places made for the purpose, with an overwhelming amount of concrete rather than just pure, uncontaminated, unmanipulated nature. The sports palace and the stadium, Olympic or not, are anti-nature and have to be because they are near-laboratory settings in which the undimensionality of competitive sports can unfold itself under controlled conditions. Pure nature has too much variation in it, too much 'noise'. . . . Although the human body is nature and nature is also the human body, the distance between sport and nature in itself seems to be ever increasing.

Bale (1994: 39–40) conceptualises this trend as the:

> emergence of *sportscape* – a manifestation of sport's fixation with neutralising or altering the effects of the physical environment . . . producing a landscape given over solely to sport.
>
> *(original emphasis)*

Following on from Eichberg (1989, 1993), Bale (1994) notes that 'fitness sport' and 'body experience sport' (more recreational sporting activities) are likely to have a relatively strong connection to nature, and are therefore more likely to consider the environmental impact of their activities.[1] On the other hand, 'achievement sport' – sporting activities where performing to the optimum is the central aim – is considered to have a more dominating relationship on the natural environment. In achievement sport, for example, 'win at all costs' is an oft-repeated phrase, as well as coaching philosophies such as 'the aggregation of marginal gains', 'no excuses' and the Olympic motto *citius, altius, fortius* – faster, higher, stronger. These phrases and philosophies are taken for granted in achievement sport, yet they have clear repercussions on 'sustainability'. If, for example, having new kit for every rugby game and even changing at half time improves performance, it will be provided for the players: it is an unquestioned assumption in achievement sport that athletes should, if possible, be given the optimum conditions in which to perform.

Peyker (1993: 73) recognises how the 'nature' of the natural human body and the 'nature' of the 'natural' environment are modified in order to fulfil the ideology of sport:

> The 'correcting' of nature is justified according to requirements of sport, confirmed by the general ideology of growth and progress. . . . [The] elements of uncertainty of man or nature have to be extinguished to attain the scientifically calculated goal.

Bale's (1994: 168) prediction that *sportscapes* would become 'increasingly technologised' has been duly realised, with, for example, nothing less than billiard table-smooth 'reinforced' natural turf now acceptable in top-level football and rugby.

Using Yi-Fi Tuan's metaphor of a garden, however, Bale (1999: 50) recognises that humans do not simply dominate *sportscapes* but that this domination is counterpoised by a 'desire to civilise [nature]' and by the great affection felt for sport and the places in which it takes place. Bale (1999: 51) therefore sees 'the sports landscape . . . like the modern garden, [as a landscape] of "playful domination"'. This metaphor serves to blur the division between (damaging, dominant) culture, and (powerless, dominated) nature, and also informs Bale's conclusion that it is not just a one-way street in terms of sport moving further away from the natural environment as a hegemonic trend (dominating the natural environment, for example) generates counter-hegemonic 'green wave' movements with a closer relationship to nature. There has been recent concern, for example, within the football industry regarding the quality of fully artificial pitches, and controversy within the women's game that 2015 FIFA Women's World Cup will only be played on such surfaces.

Controlling the vagaries of 'nature', and as such controlling weather is a central element to Bale's *sportscape* thesis. Importantly for this chapter's case study of the controlling of conditions within Wimbledon's Centre Court, Kay and Vamplew (2006) discuss how variable weather is an integral part of the sporting environment that is celebrated by many participants and spectators, yet organisers simultaneously try to 'neutralise its effects' (Bale, 1994: 46).

> [Spectators] sometimes fail to see bad weather as a wrecker of good quality sport but view it instead as part of the experience and as a leveller for competitors. . . . This attitude seems to be summed up by a correspondent . . . reporting on plans for the Millennium Stadium in Cardiff, the new home for Welsh national rugby. 'Sadly', he mused, 'when the new stand is built, it will have a retractable roof for bad weather, which will take away half the fun.' . . . Sport itself and the spectacle it presents for fans will be the losers because one of the truly unpredictable factors will be removed from the sporting equation . . . the intervention of the weather is seen as enhancing the excitement and the uncertainty.
>
> *(Kay and Vamplew 2006: 102)*

Sporting occasions are not just made memorable by unsurpassed ultimate performance (Usain Bolt's numerous sprint world records on the grandest stage of the Olympics or Arsenal's unbeaten 'Invincibles' team of 2003–2004) – they are also made memorable by the performers overcoming seemingly insurmountable external factors, upsets against all odds and the uncertainty of the outcome. Top performers in many sports need to deal with the vagaries of environments in order to be seen as true greats. Aryton Senna and Michael Schumacher were seen to be the finest drivers of their generations in Formula 1, not only because they won world championships but also because they dominated the sport in wet weather and could adapt to all conditions. Similarly, the drama of the famous rugby union international between Scotland and England in 2000 was created by the torrential rain and the England team's inability to adapt to the conditions, something that would not now happen under the roof at the Millennium Stadium in Cardiff. The uncertainty of the outcome of sporting occasions may not always generate the most interest in an event, but perhaps such uncertainty is more important in continuing to add to sporting folklore. There is, however, a fine line between difficult conditions adding to the uncertainty of outcome and the events being ruined for paying spectators. As such, Kay and Vamplew (2006: 98) note the interrelated media and economic factors that increasingly impact on twenty-first-century sport, factors which have had a particularly pronounced impact on Wimbledon's Centre Court:

> Wimbledon, the sole grass court Grand Slam tennis tournament, has been severely affected by rain . . . [which has cost] Wimbledon money. Episodes like these, together with pressure from television companies, has finally persuaded the All-England Club to incorporate a sliding roof into plans for redevelopment of the Centre Court in order 'to safeguard the commercial viability of the tournament'.

The architects of Wimbledon's Centre Court also speak of the pressure to install the roof from 'digital television, which pays handsomely for the live coverage of international tennis' and from 'other international tennis venues, which had already installed roofs to ensure that play continues during bad weather' (Sheard *et al.* 2005: 76). The installation of the roof over Centre Court, however, led many to question the *sporting* value of the roof. Kay and Vamplew (2006: 103) note that 'the idea of a retractable roof at Wimbledon has regularly brought forth observations that no-one is a champion unless they have dealt with the weather'.

Dominating nature by controlling conditions

The way in which Bale understands achievement sport dominating nature is important to note in terms of sport's sustainability credentials. As Bale (1994: 41) contends, 'once nature is separated from self the stage is set for nature's exploitation'. Lash and Urry (1994: 293) explain that despite human beings being a part of nature, it appears that in much mainstream debate there are two autonomous spheres of 'nature' and 'society', a view which stems from the

> long process of modernization since the seventeenth century [during which] nature came to be seen as something outside society, as a machine rather than an organism . . . modernity involved the belief that human progress should be measured and evaluated in terms of the human domination of nature.

Katz (2002: 173) recognises that technology is heavily implicated in this ethno-centric view of nature, as humans search for a 'technological fix . . . [meaning] that natural processes are to be "improved" to maximise human satisfaction and good'. This view of humanity's use of technology to dominate nature is understood to be a condition of and to be at the root of many environmental problems (Feenberg 2003, 2009; Vitousek *et al.* 1997). Ritzer (1993) conceptualised this 'modern' condition in his 'McDonaldization' thesis, identifying four defining components of this rational, modern society: efficiency, calculability, standardisation and technological control. According to Feenberg (2003: 73–74), this technical rationality and increase in efficiency 'impoverishes our relation with the world . . . [yet] gives power over nature'.

Sustainability and sport

Despite the increasing integration of 'sustainability' into many aspects of society, it still seems unusual to consider the potential environmental impacts of elite sport and the commercial world within which it takes place. Nonetheless, there are examples of the modern commercialised sports industry taking steps to become more 'sustainable'. The most well-publicised of these have been linked with sporting 'mega-events' such as the FIFA World Cup and the Olympic Games. The relatively high recognition of these issues is understandable given the conspicuous construction, development of infrastructure and global and local travel needed for these events. In response to these concerns, The London 2012 Olympics, for example, aimed to 'hold the world's first truly sustainable Olympic and Paralympic Games', with sustainable building design, travel, food and waste policies (London 2012a, 2012b).

Formula 1 is a sport that is rooted in the consumption of fossil fuels and extensive worldwide travel, yet in recent years it has responded to environmental concerns by introducing technology and rule changes which aim to reduce the fuel consumption of the vehicles. In 2014, for example, engine sizes were reduced from 2.4 litres to 1.6 litres, reducing fuel consumption across the whole season by around 40 per cent, and the principles behind energy recovery systems such as KERS which were developed in Formula 1 are now being used outside the sport. The development of this technology, however, must be understood alongside the steady increase in the number of races in the Formula 1 calendar, along with the associated environmental costs of transporting the teams and equipment to all corners of the globe. Formula 1 is also perhaps the sport that is most openly linked to the pressures of sponsors, and it is widely accepted that these sustainable change developments to the sport's technology have been largely driven by the threat of sponsors pulling out of an environmentally damaging sport rather than an intrinsic desire from within the sport for sustainable change.

Global sportswear manufacturers are also working towards becoming more 'sustainable', with a number of Nike's football shirts being manufactured from recycled plastic bottles and Puma bringing compostable trainers to market. Ecotricity founder and Forest Green Rovers owner Dale Vince aims to make Forest Green Rovers 'the most sustainable football club in Britain, probably the world' (Forest Green Rovers 2012) through a host of initiatives which include solar panels on the stadium's roof, a Soil Association-certified organic pitch and a ban on selling meat at the stadium. These initiatives at Forest Green, alongside the launch of the British Association for Sustainability in Sport (BASiS) in October 2011 and debates regarding the environmental 'legacy' of the London 2012 Olympics, suggest that interest in sustainable practices in sport is set to rise, despite sport being 'maybe ten years behind business when it comes to implementing sustainability practices' (BASiS 2012).

This increasing interest in sustainability in the sports industry is an interesting trend, but sustainability still seems an afterthought in commercialised sport, and the values of sustainability and environmentalism are some way off being congruent with those of elite, commercialised sport. The sponsorship of London 2012's recycling bins by Coca-Cola, for example, illustrates the contradictions and challenges of working towards 'sustainability' in a heavily commercialised industry, as well as illustrating the malleability of a sustainability agenda.[2]

Despite 'the movement of sporting bodies through space and time . . . deeply affect[ing] the environment', environmental issues are rarely discussed in sport and academia (Mincyte *et al.* 2009: 105). Existing literature covers issues such as the environmental impact of mega-events

(Lenskyj 1998; Magdalinski 2004) and other more local sporting practices (Mincyte *et al.* 2009; Tranter and Lowes 2009), corporate social responsibility in sports clubs (Jenkins 2012), and the ability of sports clubs (Baldwin 2010) and sporting activities (Horton 2006) to inspire pro-environmental behaviour. These have been followed by the first collection of academic work on the topic, 'Sustainability and Sport' (Savery and Gilbert 2011).

Rather than studying higher-profile sustainability 'solutions' or detailing the current state of play in the sports industry, the case study of Wimbledon's Centre Court will aim to examine how and why a number of inherent assumptions in the modern professional sports industry result in the industry's quest for sustainable practices being full of unique challenges.

Case study: Wimbledon's Centre Court

In 2009 the redeveloped Centre Court at Wimbledon was opened, complete with a retractable roof to allow tennis to be played during rain. There is an air management system which not only creates suitable conditions for play to continue on grass when the roof is shut but also is designed to be as close to a warm British summer's day (outside) as possible (see AELTC 2012). This makes Centre Court a particularly interesting case study as the difference between inside ('manufactured') and outside ('natural') environments is meant to be minimal; the constructed indoor environment is meant to be inconspicuous, unnoticed, and even perhaps seem 'natural'. In terms of constructing sporting environments, it could be argued that the constructed climate is no different to constructing indoor ski slopes in Dubai or climatic atmosphere, in that it could be argued that the act of constructing an indoor environment in Centre Court is, in essence, the same as constructing indoor ski slopes in Dubai. Elizabeth Shrove, a leading academic on human behaviour and sustainability, states that:

> the capacity to manipulate indoor climates at will generates a number of still dis-quieting questions about the relation between nature and civilization. Manufactured weather is a key ingredient in utopian visions of the future . . . but at what price do we cut ourselves off from nature? It is one thing to modify the elements but when buildings are constructed as climactic fortresses, the symbolic division between a man-aged interior and an unruly and unpredictable world outside is ever more strongly pronounced.

As there are very specific requirements for the temperature and movement of the air in indoor sport environments, 'a huge amount of energy will be consumed to control the environment of such a large space, even if adequate precautions have been taken' (Nishioka *et al.* 2000: 217). In an analysis of the Shanghai International Gymnastic Stadium's indoor thermal environment, for example, Huang *et al.* (2007) detailed the 240,000 m³ per hour of cooled air needed for air conditioning with a total of 4750 kW of the cooling load provided by three screw chillers, which kept the temperature fluctuation to 2.4°C and the humidity fluctuation to 4 per cent. The air conditioning was needed all day in the summer and 'intermittently' in the winter. As with the associated services energy use for the MCG, Nishioka *et al.* (2000) recognise that the amount of energy needed for heating and cooling a large multi-use domed stadium's arena is minimal in comparison with the energy needs of the rest of the building. Of the total energy needed to heat and cool the building throughout the year (53,906 gigajoules [GJ]), 'only' 5,952 GJ were needed for the arena. However, a useful conceptualisation in order to appreciate this energy use is that burning one barrel of oil produces six GJ of energy (Energy Choices 2012). The energy for the heating and cooling of the arena alone therefore required energy equivalent to nearly 1,000 barrels of oil. It is therefore undeniable that it requires a lot of energy to control conditions.

The virtues of the retractable roof and air management system within Centre Court at Wimbledon are often detailed in highly technologised ways. It takes ten minutes to close the 1,000 tonne, 5,200 m² retractable roof and the structure is shut when there is rain, a risk of rain or when a game cannot continue because of bad light. In order to 'provide appropriate playing conditions when the roof is deployed in adverse summer weather conditions', the 'bespoke design sports lighting system' of 130 'sports luminaries' is activated:

> The air management system control[s] and then stabilise[s] the internal bowl environment at the specified levels (24 degrees C +/− 2 degrees C, with 50% +/− 10% relative humidity) . . . to prevent condensation on the inside of the roof or sweating of the grass, and to provide a fresh air allowance into bowl of eight litres/second/person − a total of 143,000 litres per second.
>
> *(All information and quotes from AELTC 2012)*

In terms of energy use, no data are available. It can, however, be assumed that all these measures (closing the roof, illuminating the lights, controlling and stabilising the environment) require a large amount of energy, whereas the pre-2009 'outdoor' Centre Court needed no energy whatsoever for any of the above operations.

The framing of the environment under the roof in such a clinical, scientific and technologised way fails to recognise the *social* aspect of the sporting environments − a particularly important viewpoint in sport stadiums, as they are places where different aspects of the sporting environment (including the elements) elicit strong emotions. Framing Centre Court in this way also reflects the dominant discourse of promoting technology rather than societal solutions to climate or weather problems, as alluded to at the beginning of this chapter. The air management system, according to chief architect Rod Sheard, 'is all about the grass, not the crowds', as

> grass is much more delicate than human beings. We can take off our coats or jumpers to cool down. Grass can't, so if we just put the roof over, it would sweat and turn the court into a skating rink.
>
> *(Stanford 2012)*

Alongside the technological framing of the redeveloped Centre Court detailed above, the following paragraphs will aim to understand other ways in which the redevelopment has been framed.

> The All England Club . . . has to be seen to be moving with the times. The Australian Open has a covered surface and organisers at Roland Garros are also considering installing a roof.
>
> *(BBC Sport 2004)*

'In a tournament of this stature the facilities here are expected to be world class' (Ian Ritchie, then the chief executive of the All England Club, Wimbledon, quoted in Melik and Webber 2009). These quotes show how Centre Court's roof and air management system is a sign of development, progress and modernity which can be used as a commercial tool. In an industry based on novelty, competition and the quest for ultimate performance, sport environments must be of the highest quality; rain delays may have been acceptable in the 1990s, but now the industry is highly and increasing commercialised, this is no longer the case. Due to the roof, Wimbledon can now offer guaranteed live tennis for broadcasters and can enjoy the commercial benefits of such a development. This desire for constant development, however, is on an exponential curve. How much have sporting environments 'progressed' in the last twenty years? Where will, or can, this development end? What are the environmental and societal implications of this constant quest for modernity? Following the success of the roof over Centre Court, Wimbledon has already put plans into motion for a roof over its second show court, Court No. 1.

Although perhaps a cold phrase to describe sports spectatorship, the roof is also seen as an 'efficiency tool' that can help spectators make the most of their time and money. Fans make sacrifices to travel to Wimbledon, with many taking days off work, travelling from overseas and spending large amounts of money to enjoy the tennis. The roof over Centre Court – and soon over Court No. 1 – means that if it rains, those who have tickets for Centre Court are guaranteed to be able to watch live tennis, and those who have ground passes can watch on the big screens around the site. There are many perceived time pressures in modern society, and technology affords a 'rationalisation' of our time, which allows people to 'make the most' of their time, but also perhaps 'impoverishes out relation with the world' (Feenberg 2003: 73–74) due to a focus on efficiency, predictability and control – just like the *sportscapes* imaged by Bale.

> If the weather makes tennis unpredictable, why not shut it out? Indoor tournaments eliminate both the risks of bad weather and general atmospheric influence on the game. Indoor courts allow for a 'true' game of tennis. . . . If all tennis were to be played indoors we would have a more standardised game. Every tournament on the world circuit would be similar; the weather conditions give tennis its character. A compromise would seem to be courts which have roofs which can be closed.
>
> *(BBC Weather 2010)*

> If anything [the conditions under the roof are] almost too perfect. There's no wind, no sun, no elements to contend with. It's different grass-court tennis. [My opponent] was able to hit a lot of huge forehands, which it's normally harder to do when it's a little bit breezy outside.
>
> *(Andy Murray quoted in* The Telegraph *2011)*

> Alan Mills, tournament referee for 22 years before his retirement, thinks that the roof is 'killing some of the spirit of Wimbledon'.
>
> *(Stanford 2012)*

> The fabric is . . . translucent, so that Centre Court should have an 'open' feel even when the roof is close.
>
> *(BBC Sport 2004)*

How much environmental 'noise' should there be in sporting environments? The above quotes illustrate how there is a sliding scale of what is deemed to be an acceptable controlling of conditions. Some of the finer, adaptive skills are taken out of sport when conditions become predictable and constant, but at least the roof allows the performers to showcase their skills when it is raining outside. Wimbledon is an important part of the British summer, and a connection with the weather and images of garden parties, lawns and nature is, in turn, an important part of the British summer, but maintaining these images should not be at the cost of people being able to enjoy their leisure time. The fact that the constructed atmosphere inside Centre Court is made to feel as close as possible to a warm summer's day perhaps indicates why this controlling of conditions is not deemed to be too much of a cause for concern or too strange, as compared to the construction of ski slopes in Dubai or air-conditioned football stadiums in Qatar. In the constructed atmospheres in Wimbledon, there is not too much discordance with the natural spaces outside, even though the energy demands of maintaining such an atmosphere are still huge.

Conclusions

This chapter is most centrally concerned with the interrelated 'sustainability' and societal impacts of choosing, altering, constructing and controlling conditions (or 'nature') in sports environments, but *sustainability* has been left as a term open for interpretation throughout.[3] Hulme's (2009) claims regarding climate change can also translate to issues concerning sustainability, where climate change (or, in this case, sustainability):

> should be seen as an intellectual resource around which our collective and personal identities and projects can form and take shape. We need to ask not what we can do for climate change [sustainability], but to ask what climate change [sustainability] can do for us.
>
> *(Hulme 2009: 326)*

Hulme (2009: 239) further asserts that 'because the idea of climate change [sustainability] is so plastic, it can be deployed across many of our human projects and can serve many of our psychological, ethical, and spiritual needs'. What shape and role can and should sport take when we advocate for sustainability and in what ways do we want 'sustainability' to be made manifest in our society? In terms of the elite, professionalised, commercialised sports industry, the outlook does not therefore seem positive as far as dominating nature is concerned. As technology advances and becomes more 'efficient', Bale's *sportscape* thesis is undoubtedly being realised at Wimbledon and in other developments in the sports industry, due to the significant commercial pressure from the media and sponsors, and the need for constant improvement in all aspects of sport: *citius, altius, fortius*. Sport must sustain itself and also sustain its values.

What about the future of sportscapes? Cost is undoubtedly the main factor preventing the further proliferation of retractable-roofed stadiums where climates are controlled. It has been suggested that the redevelopment of Centre Court at Wimbledon cost £80 to £100 million, yet the long-term profits amassed as a result of the benefits of retractable-roofed structures mean that they can often be justified financially. Also, for some stadium development projects such as the planned construction of stadiums for the 2022 FIFA World Cup to be held in the heat of Qatar, money seems to be no object. It had been discussed that – if the tournament should take place in the region's hottest months when temperatures can reach over 41°C – stadiums should be cooled to under 27°C in order to allow the competition to continue, using a combination of shading from roofs and solar-powered air conditioning systems. These extreme developments could give a glimpse of the sporting future as various globalised sports expand beyond their traditional landscapes and climates towards specialised, sanitised environments.

It becomes technologically possible to control, construct and ultimately choose natural elements that are desirable and undesirable, confusing further the already indistinct boundaries between 'natural' and 'unnatural', 'indoors' and 'outdoors', and 'nature' and 'culture'. This blurring of the boundaries is particularly interesting in the case of the Centre Court roof, as it aims to eliminate the *undesirable* element of the rain but keep the *desirable* summer outdoor conditions. In order to have the best of both worlds, the summer conditions are completely (re)constructed and become distinctly, yet in some cases unnoticeably, 'unnatural'. Being so selective with nature has obvious implications in terms of energy consumption, and finer control is exacted on the undesirable and desirable elements alike. The implications of this in terms of our relationship with nature – and our desire to be 'sustainable' – is worrying and fascinating in equal measure. Bearing in mind the Brundtland definition of sustainable development (see endnote 3), do we want to *sustain* a close relationship with nature? Is this a 'need' of the present, and a 'need' of future generations? In terms of common definitions of sustainability, how can we best work towards 'supporting the long term ecological balance'? Perhaps working towards becoming a 'cooperative equal' with nature as explicated by Brennan (2007) is a significant and often overlooked way to achieve this, but this would be a particularly significant challenge in the increasingly commercialised sports industry. Contending that all sports stadiums should be designed to be completely open to the elements, for example, would be naïve in the extreme. The commercial and *citius, altius, fortius* ideologies, alongside the expectations of fans, are surely too ingrained in elite, commercialised sport. It is interesting in this regard that the 'outside' courts at Wimbledon, populated by athletes lower down the tennis food chain, will still be more constantly and directly connected to and affected by nature and the weather.

If decision-makers in sport truly want to work towards being sustainable, they must themselves reflect on what 'brand' of sustainability they want to promote. Do they want to continue to promote technologised responses to natural problems and sustainability that dominates the discourse of environmental decision-making in sport in the context of climate change being the most pressing environmental issue? If so, they should be wary of the scale and geography of these interventions in order to avoid the scepticism that surrounds geoengineering and ski slopes in Dubai.

Could elite sports organisations instead turn their attention to those who are influenced by 'achievement sport', blurring the lines between 'fitness sport', 'body experience' and 'achievement sport' movement cultures (Eichberg 1989), and encouraging the general public to be engaged with sport in more 'found' or 'natural' and less specialised, exclusive environments, something that is often promoted in 'developing' countries? This may be difficult to achieve with grass-court tennis, but it is certainly possible with a road closed to traffic, rackets, balls, chalk and a net.

Such developments are already happening in some sports, with fell-running and open-water swimming under the organisational umbrellas of the UK's athletics and swimming associations respectively, developments which give optimism for a 'green wave' in sport activities that Bale (1994) so hopes for. With these positive potentials, we can in fact imagine and realise a world in which participation in sport facilitates in our relationship with our (natural) surroundings simply through our extended engagement with these environments. As such, sport has the potential to directly enhance our ability to become 'cooperative equals' with our natural environments, subsequently imploring us to hold greater respect for the world around us and thus, to have a greater consciousness for sustainability.

Notes

1 This is evident with the 'Surfers against Sewage' campaign by British suffers, a campaign critically analysed in Wheaton (2007).
2 See http://www.coca-cola.co.uk/environment/helping-london-recycle-for-the-2012-olympics.html for Coca-Cola's information on their recycling practices. In contrast, a number of scholars have questioned the sustainability of Coca-Cola's practices (see Burnett and Welford 2007; Hills and Welford 2005).
3 Definitions of 'sustainable development' (meeting the needs of the present without compromising the ability of future generations to meet their own needs, according to the UN's Brundtland Report 1987) and 'sustainability' (the quality of not being harmful to the environment or depleting natural resources, and thereby supporting long-term ecological balance according to Dictionary Reference 2012) are undoubtedly open for interpretation, too.

References

All England Lawn Tennis Club (AELTC). (2012) *The Long Term Plan.* Accessed 27 April 2012. http://aeltc2011.wimbledon.com/footer/press-and-media/long-term-plan.html.

Baldwin, R. (2010) Football and climate change: Strange bedfellows or a means of going beyond the usual suspects in encouraging pro-environmental behaviour change? *Local Environment,* 15(9–10): 851–866.

Bale, J. (1994) *Landscapes of Modern Sport.* Leicester: Leicester University Press.

Bale, J. (1999) Parks and gardens: Metaphors for the modern places of sport. In D. Crouch (ed.) *Leisure/Tourism Geographies: Practices and Geographical Knowledge.* London: Routledge, pp. 46–58.

BASiS. (2012) The British Association for Sustainability in Sport. Accessed 21 July 2012. www.basis.org.uk/.

BBC Sport. (2004) Wimbledon's roof: The lowdown. Accessed 6 June 2012. http://news.bbc.co.uk/sport1/hi/tennis/3371835.stm.

BBC Weather. (2010) Tennis and the weather. Accessed 6 June 2012. http://news.bbc.co.uk/weather/hi/weatherwise/newsid_8483000/8483698.stm.

Beck, U. (1992) *Risk Society: Towards a New Modernity.* London: Sage.

Bixler, R. and Floyd, R. (1997) Nature is scary, disgusting, and uncomfortable. *Environment and Behaviour,* 29(4): 443–467.

Brennan, J. (2007) Dominating nature. *Environmental Values,* 16: 513–528.

Burnett, M. and Welford, R. (2007) Case study: Coca-Cola and water in India: Episode 2. *Corporate Social Responsibility and Environmental Management,* 14(5): 298–304.

Eichberg, H. (1989) Body culture as paradigm: The Danish sociology of sport. *International Review for the Sociology of Sport,* 24(1): 43–60.

Eichberg, H. (1993) New spatial configurations of sport? Experiences from Danish alternative planning. *International Review for the Sociology of Sport,* 28(2/3): 245–263.

Energy Choices. (2012) Why do my energy bills keep rising? Accessed 6 June 2012. www.energychoices.co.uk/ask-our-expert/why-do-my-energy-bills-keep-rising-ask-our-expert.htmlv.

Feenberg, A. (2003) *Modernity and Technology.* Cambridge, MA: The MIT Press.

Feenberg, A. (2009) Critical theory of technology: An overview. In J. Buschman and G. Leckie (eds) *Information Technology in Librarianship.* London: Libraries Unlimited, pp. 31–46.

Forest Green Rovers. (2012) Greening up football. Accessed 25 July 2012. www.forestgreenroversfc.com/about-forest-green-rovers/ecotricity-and-forest-green-rovers/greening-up-football.

Galtung, J. (1984) Sport and international understanding: Sport as a carrier of deep culture and structure. In M. Ilmarinen (ed.) *Sport and International Understanding.* Berlin: Springer-Verlag, pp. 12–19.

Hills, J. and Welford, R. (2005) Case study: Coca-Cola and water in India. *Corporate Social Responsibility and Environmental Management,* 12(3): 168–177.

Horton, D. (2006) Environmentalism and the bicycle. *Environmental Politics,* 15(1): 41–58.

Huang, C., Zou, Z., Li, M., Wang, X., Li, W., Huang, W., Yang, J., and Xiao, X. (2007) Measurements of indoor thermal environment and energy analysis in a large space building in typical seasons. *Building and Environment,* 42: 1869–1877.

Hulme, M. (2009) *Why We Disagree About Climate Change.* Cambridge: Cambridge University Press.

Katz, E. (2002) The call of the wild. In D. Schmidtz and E. Willott (eds) *Environmental Ethics.* Oxford: Oxford University Press, pp. 172–177.

Kay, J. and Vamplew, W. (2006) Under the weather: Combating the climate in British sport. *Sport in Society: Cultures, Commerce, Media, Politics*, 9(1): 94–107.

Lash, S. and Urry, J. (1994) *Economies of Signs and Space*. London: Sage.

Lenskyj, H. (1998) Sport and corporate environmentalism: The case of the Sydney 2000 Olympics. *International Review for the Sociology of Sport*, 33(4): 341–354.

London 2012. (2012a) Velodrome. Accessed 6 May 2012. www.london2012.com/venue/velodrome.

London 2012. (2012b) Sustainability. Accessed 25 July 2012. www.london2012.com/about-us/sustainability/.

Magdalinski, T. (2004) Homebush: Site of the clean/sed and natural Australian athlete. In P. Vertinsky and J. Bale (eds) *Sites of Sport: Space, Place, Experience*. London: Routledge, pp. 101–114.

Melik, J. and Webber, M. (2009) Wimbledon still serving up profits. Accessed 6 June 2012. http://news.bbc.co.uk/1/hi/business/8118258.stm.

Mincyte, D., Casper, M., and Cole, C. (2009) Sports, environmentalism, land use, and urban development. *Journal of Sport and Social Issues*, 33(2): 103–110.

Nishioka, T., Ohtaka, K., Hashimoto, N., and Onojima, H. (2000) Measurement and evaluation of the indoor thermal environment in a large domed stadium. *Energy and Buildings*, 32: 217–223.

Peyker, I. (1993) Sport and ecology. In S. Riiskjaer (ed.) *Sport and Space*. Council of Europe: Copenhagen, pp. 71–77.

Ritzer, G. (1993) *The McDonaldization of Society*. London: Sage.

Sheard, R., Bingham-Hall, P., and Powell, R. (2005) *The Stadium: Architecture for the New Global Culture*. North Clarendon, VT: Tuttle Publishing.

Savery, J. and Gilbert, K. (eds) (2011) *Sustainability and Sport*. Champaign, IL: Common Ground.

Stanford, P. (2012) Is the centre court roof the real star of Wimbledon 2012? *The Telegraph* (online) 7 July. Accessed 7 July 2012. www.telegraph.co.uk/sport/tennis/wimbledon/9381145/Is-the-Centre-Court-roof-the-real-star-of-Wimbledon-2012.html.

The Telegraph. (2011) Wimbledon 2011: Andy Murray says All England club's retractable roof makes conditions 'too perfect'. *The Telegraph* (online) 21 June 2011. Accessed 26 April 2012. www.telegraph.co.uk/sport/tennis/wimbledon/8588441/Wimbledon-2011-Andy-Murray-says-All-England-clubs-retractable-roof-makes-conditions-too-perfect.html.

Tranter, P. and Lowes, M. (2009) Life in the fast lane: Environmental, economic, and public health outcomes of motorsport spectacles in Australia. *Journal of Sport and Social Issues*, 33: 150–168.

Vitousek, P., Mooney, H., Lubchenco, J., and Melillo, J. (1997) Human domination of earth's ecosystems. *Science*, 277(5325): 494–499.

Wheaton, B. (2007) Identity, politics and the beach: Environmental activism in surfers against sewage. *Leisure Studies*, 26(3): 279–302.

30

SPORT ACTIVISM AND PROTEST

Mick Totten

Introduction

Even though many powerful stakeholders and mass consumers of sport still claim to believe that sport and politics do not mix, sport has proved fertile ground for activism and protest, its history littered with many forms of both. There are iconic examples such as John Carlos and Tommie Smith's Black Power salute at the 1968 Mexico Olympics and the Black September group kidnapping and killing of eleven Israeli athletes, coaches and officials at the 1972 Olympics. More recently Ultras Ahlawy fans joined the Arab Spring protests in 2011, fighting street battles in Cairo to help seize control of Tahrir Square, while in 2014 members of Pussy Riot were whipped and tear-gassed when attempting to sing at the Sochi Winter Olympics, and millions of Brazilian people took to the streets in multiple protests against hosting the FIFA World Cup with many facing percussion grenades and tear gas. Despite the diverse nature of these and numerous other protests, of who is protesting on what issues, how and why, they are all forms of sport activism. They are also connected by political praxis, a compelling rationale for why doing nothing in the face of perceived injustice cannot be considered, and why political action and protest is required.

Kaufman and Wolf (2013) identify athlete activists pursuing progressive social change while Zirin (2005) recounts the dramatic history of sport activism in the United States as well as the power of sport in more contemporary activism (Zirin 2013). In addition, Kuhn (2011) has compiled a history of how football has agitated for activism against the state, which includes distinctions between fan and grassroots club activism. Others have focused more specifically on fans, for example Merkel (2012) in Germany, Numerato (2015) in Italy, and Brimson (2006) in England, and Kennedy (2013) describes the growth of left-wing fan activism. Few football fans encapsulate sport activism as well as those of FC Sankt Pauli in Germany, whose exploits have attracted the attention of many including Kuhn (2011), Davidson (2014), and Totten (2015a, 2015b, 2015c).

There are also examples of growing grassroots sport club networks engaged in radical sport activism worldwide, with Kennedy and Kennedy (2015a) highlighting DIY alternatives which emerge as counter-cultural resistance. Kennedy and Kennedy (2015b) describe this type of resistance as resoundingly anti-capitalist. These and other studies reveal sport activism and protest to be in buoyant health and establish this growing phenomenon as an intriguing area of study.

This chapter focuses on sport activism beginning by contextualising sport as a contested cultural practice offering a theatre of opportunity ripe for activism. It then conceptualises sport activism broadly and distinguishes it from more specific acts of protest. The significance of praxis and critical consciousness are examined as drivers for activism and influences upon activists' aims for change. Having established its conceptual grounding, sport activism is then explored in practice drawing on a range of examples to illustrate who is protesting, which issues they are protesting about, how activism is carried out, and the ethics of engagement utilising different methods. These examples include familiar iconic protests but also, and importantly, less well-known ones as Ledwith (2011) contends that authentic stories previously under the radar of popular exposure must be at the heart of a theory for change. In particular, innovative and sustained radical sport activism from the sub-cultural shadows is illuminated to reveal alternative ways of being, and emancipatory praxis. Continuing in this vein there is a more in-depth case study of FC Sankt Pauli fans who offer a vision of radical integrity and sustainability that might inspire other sport activists. The chapter concludes by offering a 'framework of sport activism and protest' which flexibly accommodates its diverse nature and consolidates an overview of understanding.

Activist praxis and aims

Sport as contested cultural practice and theatre of opportunity

Sport and society are in symbiosis whereby social inequities and intolerances are manifested resulting in discrimination, power differentials and social exclusion. But sport is not simply a passive reflector of reactionary prejudices. It can also be an active inculcator and breeding ground for intolerance, and is therefore too easily perceived as a conservative rather than a transformative phenomenon. Some believe sport is unsurpassed in its divisiveness and is irredeemable (Perelman 2012). But sport is contested ideological terrain on which there is a polarisation between activists who reject sport as a cynical form of manipulation or distraction and those who seek to reclaim it, believing it ripe with possibilities to reawaken consciousness and empower (Dart 2012). Sport can liberate or constrain and thus represents a dichotomy whereby it can act simultaneously as a tool for empowerment but also as an opiate which nullifies political consciousness.

Sport often serves the interests of dominant groups and institutions, and elite sport is conspicuous for its rapacious commercialism often constructed and promoted as a product for relatively passive consumption (Carrington and McDonald 2009; Coakley and Dunning 2000). Kennedy (2013) describes how sport fans can be co-opted and commodified as part of the spectacle, but also acknowledges that sport only exerts relative commercial power as there is also capacity for resistance not least around the strong sense of community it can foster. Sport has a long history of community ownership and can be fertile ground for sport activists seeking effective bottom-up community empowerment. Thus, sport inhabits a hegemonic context, which includes incomplete attempts by dominant cultural groups to control potential opposition as well as resistance from that opposition (Williams 1977).

Resistance is as much a part of hegemony, as control and hegemonic processes reflect ongoing power struggles. These hegemonic dynamics are perpetual, all-encompassing, never completed and continually assembled and re-assembled, reproduced and secured (and reversed!) (Bennett 1981). For example, sport is often perceived as a site for the segmentation and cultivation of hyper-masculine or traditional feminine values, yet it is also an arena in which such stereotypes can be contested and some empowered to recapture previously alien cultural terrain

(Scraton and Flintoff 2002). Sport can be an attractive and exciting vehicle to rally around politically and it offers a distinct theatre of opportunity for activism and protest, whether through the gaze of popular and alternative social media or at the sub-cultural grassroots, or local knowledge of community activism levels.

Although sport has the potential to act as part of a wider social movement, engage in resistance, and enable challenges to dominant structures of power, the significance of sport itself is ambiguous. Sport activists can project activity onto a bigger canvas where the importance of playing sport becomes less and less significant.

Sport activism

Despite the mainstream tendency of sport to be mediated and ideologically sanitised according to a prevailing functionalist orthodoxy, sport is undeniably political. All sports policy and practice from elite to grassroots needs to be understood as inhabiting broader political processes of how ideas are translated into actions and of who has the power to affect that. Sport activism represents a challenge not only to those who uncritically assert that sport is non-political and think that politics should be kept out of sport, but also to blinkered sport evangelists who believe that sport is always a benign force for social good – a 'cultural glue' which helps to hold society together. As such, activism contests the conservative and functionalist social values that permeate sport and the global neo-liberal economic context within which sport is practiced.

Sport activism often represents an intervention which is politicised against, rather than on behalf of the status quo and emphasises a challenge to conventional social and political values (Totten 2015b). It advocates or acts for social or political change in sport or through sport and for many it is also a radical activity politicised against the dominant hegemony or status quo in sport or broader society. Sport activism engenders a sense of critical consciousness and praxis that prompts advocacy and action on behalf or in pursuit of a cause. Such resistance can be acted out in different realms of sport – ideologically, economically, politically, socially and culturally – and sometimes through sport towards external targets as well.

There are great variations in the practice of sport activism including the type of change that is sought. But there are important distinctions to be made between activism and protest. Sport activism should be thought of as an all-encompassing process which identifies issues, proposes solutions, and undertakes to attempt change, whereas protest should be considered an aspect of activism and a more specific subset of activity or events. Protest is most often an organised expression of disapproval, opposition or dissent, utilising specific methods. It can accommodate discrete activity and temporary involvement from some citizens, opting in or out at their discretion, as part of a broader campaign. But activism can be a process with or without protest, as there are important aspects of activism which cannot neatly be considered as protest. Though not exhaustive, this includes the important day-to-day experiential practice of activists, their lived experience, discursive activity, informal education, the cultivation of awareness, as well as organisational activity addressing issues and participating in community activity. For some, activism is a state of being, a full-time preoccupation, and protests are merely significant events which punctuate their vocation.

Activist praxis: why protest?

There are many issues that may irk those involved in sport. For many these may be tiresome frustrations that invoke stoicism but elicit no real appetite for action. But for sport activists, discontent reaches a tipping point and translates into an imperative for action due to praxis. Praxis can be viewed as the symbiosis of outlook and action, the application of a critical perspective to a social context with the intention of transforming it for the better.

The all-pervasive envelopment of sport within a neo-liberal global economy cannot be ignored and neither can the impotence of most political leaders to imagine or create alternatives. Neo-liberal ideology largely reigns supreme in a global marketplace where everything has a price and sport can be bought and sold like any other commodity. Most governments and powerful economies perpetuate these commercial imperatives which, alongside authoritarian governance in sport, mean that corporate and statutory agencies can seldom be trusted to deliver genuine empowerment. However, prolific sport activism and praxis has given birth to community organisation, networks of resistance, community action and empowerment.

For many sport activists the very act of resistance, the struggle, can be empowering in its own right as empowerment is 'a continuous process that enables people to understand, upgrade and use their capacity to better control and gain power over their own lives' (Schuftan 1996: 260). Empowerment can act against injustice, enhance democracy, and help to develop cooperative local economies and healthy communities. However, Ledwith (2011: 78) cautions that this is not enough and that there is a difference between good activity, which may improve the quality of life in communities, and transformative activity that aims to tackle the unequal power relations that perpetuate inequality. She bemoans 'action-less thought' founded on rhetoric not reality, and 'thoughtless action'; doing, at the expense of thinking, lacking critical reflection. 'Thoughtful action' necessitates critical consciousness to challenge 'accepted' practice and dominant power relations, changing power structures that affect lives (SCCD 2001). Sport activism and praxis entail translating radical ideas into coherent actions.

Activist awakening: critical consciousness and political imagination

One consequence of the wholesale permeation of neo-liberal ideology is that certain values are mediated to dominate everyday life. Ideological work is carried out to portray these values as inevitable, common sense, and 'normal'. Chomsky (2002) conceives of this as propaganda ultimately controlled by government, business and media through which necessary illusions replace truth. In effect this amounts to a form of thought control, even in democratic societies, as ideas are narrowly filtered and opinions manipulated in order to manufacture consent. Sport can become a currency of propaganda, complicit in indoctrinating neo-liberal values whereby these become the norm and appear to shape and create expectations across sport as a whole. McSweeny (2014) asserts that neo-liberalism's greatest achievement has been to persuade us that there is no alternative! In such circumstances sport can come to represent 'bread and circuses', or an 'opium of the people', as its consumers are encouraged to become experts on trivia rather than to think critically.

However, sport activism encourages critical thinking to connect deeply personal experiences to the profoundly political structures which shape them, thereby 'challenging the reigning ideological system and seeking to create constructive alternatives of thought, action and institutions' (Chomsky 2003: 236). Insights into other ways of thinking require critical consciousness to challenge orthodox norms and deconstruct prevailing ideologies, to think more freely and consider alternatives. Increasingly, sport activists question convention and take action to organise, participate in protests and pursue more community-centred activity, building resistance to dominant hegemony through grassroots activism.

A heightened sense of critical consciousness enhances political imagination. While the sociological imagination enables a deeper insight into society, the political imagination reveals personal daily life as deeply political and sport profoundly so. Thoughtful reflection encourages a depth of understanding to contest mainstream thinking, challenge ideas and pursue emancipation. Political imagination promotes greater democracy of values from which to explore and celebrate alternative activities and approaches to sport. Unlike neo-liberal hegemony, it often encourages a greater focus on collective welfare, shared needs, and redistribution of opportunity. It also encourages more libertarian thinking, promoting democracy, valuing diversity, putting people and planet before profit to pursue freedom. Through political imagination, sport can be promoted as a site of struggle and resistance, and can illuminate issues connected to their broader structural causes.

Activist aims

Sport activism begins as an act of conscience that may require a leap of faith to translate into projected outcomes and, although all sport activism targets some form of change, the type of change sought may vary. Different degrees of desired change can be plotted as aims on a spectrum from conservation to reform to transformation to outright revolution. And although sport activists' aims may change over time, and it is difficult to establish exact boundaries between them, these distinct aims can be considered separately (see Figure 30.1 'A spectrum of activism').

Sport activists pursuing conservation are attempting to hold on to something that is perceived to be in jeopardy. But even for conservationists, understanding power dynamics and politics is core to affecting sport policy. Conservation may preserve an established form of provision, maintain a traditional way of doing things, protect the balance of power in an established relationship, or sustain more recent change that has subsequently provoked a backlash. However, much more sport activism seeks to reform, improve and enhance current provision and sometimes this can encompass adjusting or amending relatively mainstream sport development policy. Activists campaign to alter arrangements, draw attention to a previously neglected issue, or provoke a response to accommodate a new issue which has arisen for sport. Trusting that reform can deliver desired change, activists retain a belief that the status quo is inherently adaptable and acts ultimately in sympathy with the common interest.

Radical sport activists seek more than mere reform, embrace a more overarching ideological commitment to political change and seek transformation. Conventional sport policy tends to reflect the prevailing interests of the most powerful, who seldom represent the best interests of others with an investment in sport. But as Sugden and Tomlinson (2002) note, sport has the potential power to transform circumstances. Ledwith (2011: 14) insists that 'collective action for change has to follow through from local to structural levels in order to make a sustainable difference. Anything less is ameliorative'. For sport activists pursuing transformation, potential change is contingent on movements to generate resistance and challenge dominant structures of power which can involve vibrant local activism linked, beyond purely local issues, to strategic networks and alliances, and this collective power can be harnessed as social capital which 'comprises both the network and the assets that may be mobilized through that network' (Nahapiet and Ghoshal 1998: 247). Although some sport activists may proclaim their causes loud and proud, others (working within mainstream organisations) may operate more covertly for fear of repercussions (Totten 2015b).

There are also sport activists with even more ambitious aims beyond transformation who seek revolution. Although it is somewhat difficult to discern the exact distinction between

⇐ Conservation ⇔ Reform ⇔ Transformation ⇔ Revolution ⇒

Figure 30.1 A spectrum of activism

transformation and revolution, some activists are clear about revolutionary aims in their stated intent (Kelly 1984). Such radicalism may be well hidden in sport or simply obscure but it exists and is evidenced by the infiltration of organisations by practitioners with radical political motivations (Totten 2015b). Subversion by these sport activists against dominant organisational ideology in favour of community activism implies political projects to undermine or circumvent dominant hegemonic institutional organisations and resist culturally conservative practices inherent in much sport. But there are also grassroots sport clubs and fan groups spread worldwide that are driven by more radical political agendas engaged in sport activism whose experiential practice reflects their alternative political and organisational culture. Despite increasing publicised awareness of these clubs, their very nature means many activities are desirably covert and necessarily avoid the limelight of sustained public exposure (Wilson 2011; Tucker 2011, 2015; Simpson and McMahon 2012; Simpson 2015; Dolk and Kuhn 2015).

Sport activism in practice

Sport activists: who protests?

The range of those involved in sport activism is vast and encompasses those directly involved in sport, but also interlopers from elsewhere who seize an opportunity to use sport as a means towards an extrinsic end. All can be considered to be engaged in counter-hegemonic struggles to gain influence. Williams (1977) identifies different hegemonic positions and processes that ebb and flow over time. These include broad traditions, formal institutions and smaller cultural formations which may be considered dominant, residual or more emergent in nature. In sport, traditions represent established ways of doing things, institutions represent large stakeholders, and formations include smaller groups and campaigns. Each vies for hegemonic power and jostles for influence between those with dominant sway, those receding residually, and those with emerging prominence, so that complete control of or a monopoly over reason are never assured in sport.

Sport traditions encompass cultural variations but broadly include longstanding hegemonic ideas about rules, customs and practice, sexual separation and fair play, all underpinned by functionalist and patriarchal values. In addition, newer ideas such as winning at all costs, hyper-masculinity, and hyper-commercialisation are supported by more individualistic neo-liberal values. Any of these may be subject to the scrutiny of activists but none can be considered activism in themselves. Hegemonic institutions involved in sport activism include large top-down organisations such as governments promoting boycotts of events as Grix (2016) describes how sport has been used in foreign policy as a form of soft power. Other institutional governing bodies, including the Olympic movement and FIFA, pressurise host nations to impose restrictive commercial and anti-democratic policies. The Rugby Football League in England, however, has created equality and diversity policies based on a sense of corporate responsibility and core beliefs and values of care, share, fair and dare (Hylton and Totten 2013). Large institutional corporate sponsors also put pressure on organisations, such as FIFA, to reform their governance but often only to protect global brand image.

Sometimes activism by mainstream organisations reflects an undertow of activism by smaller cultural formations. Bottom-up resistance and campaigning is conducted by ordinary citizens and community organisations, protesting in, or through, sport. Indeed, community sport initiatives have proved a popular site for activists who engage in praxis by being critically conscious and reflective. Community sport activists employ innovative and unconventional methods to bypass conventional restrictions and can apply political imagination to transform structures by empowering local control. Examples illustrate the potential for sport activism in opposition to the dominant hegemonic order, but they also highlight the difficulties of resisting assimilation and avoiding marginalisation or expulsion as professional sport activists may jeopardise their longevity if they raise their heads too high above the parapet.

Individual athletes participate in sport activism in different sports for different reasons. Four hundres metre winner Kathy Freeman brandished an aboriginal flag at the 2000 Sydney Olympics to draw attention to indigenous land and human rights, and test cricketers, Andy Flower and Henry Olonga, wore black armbands in 2003 to protest at the 'death of democracy' in Zimbabwe. Mohammed Ali revealed his critical consciousness very publically in 1967, repeatedly demanding his Islamic name from his opponent whilst winning the 1967 boxing heavyweight championship, then refusing the draft to serve in the US Army comparing the treatment of Vietnamese to that of black Americans by white slave masters. Many specific campaign groups have sprung up in sport, amongst them the Brazilian citizens opposed to the 2014 FIFA World Cup, the Green and Gold protests against club ownership initiated by Manchester United supporters from 2010, and Liverpool and other fan groups against high ticket prices in 2016.

Sport fans are increasingly engaged in sport activism, especially in football because, as Merkel (2012: 373) asserts, contemporary football culture is 'constructed both by commercial interests and by defiant and rebellious reactions to them' giving rise to a new breed of sport activists. Fans have challenged power and oppression, cultivated critical consciousness, promoted leftist libertarian thought, and become part of a broader politicised fan base. Maguire (2005: 41) describes how some Charlton fans 'were transformed from passive spectators into social activists' in response to ill treatment during their successful campaign over plans for stadium renewal. Furthermore, many fans increasingly believe that they have to take more control over their own circumstances and circumvent the authorities to solve their own problems. In 2005, some fans of Manchester United FC were sufficiently agitated to form their own breakaway community club, FC United of Manchester. Radical left-wing football supporters' networks worldwide share ideas about how to foster the political imagination and confront oppression. The Alerta network declares, 'We are awake: We fight against the repression that tries to destroy our culture. See you on the barricades or on the terraces' (Alerta 2012). These groups form alliances that have the potential to become movements (Ledwith 2011). Thus, international political links and strong allegiances between different networks leads to hundreds of teams of ultras, fans, immigrant groups, and activists coming together through events such as the annual Mondiali Antirazzisti (Anti-Racist World Cup).

Finally, individual alternative grassroots sports clubs, including Los Autonomous in San Paulo, the Easton Cowboys and Cowgirls in Bristol (England) and Republica Internationale in Leeds (England), are heavily involved in sport activism and radical political activity (Totten 2015b). Collectively, they and others pursue 'freedom through football' utilising the emancipatory potential of sub-cultural activity to challenge dominant norms and structures. They are anti-capitalist organisations that provide 'a breeding ground for the political left through the plethora of opportunities to engage in radical community development, enhancement of social cohesion and development of social inclusion' (Tucker 2011: 152). All these examples of traditions, institutions and formations represented in sport activism possess relative power in their different settings of engagement and their hegemonic prominence varies between dominant, residual and emergent in pursuing different causes in context.

Resistance through sport: which issues?

If the range of those involved in sport activism is broad then the range of issues they represent is even more so. It is impossible to consider all of these adequately here but an attempt is made to discern different types of issues and their conceptual nature. Broadly, they are all reactions either to perceived injustice, unfairness or inequality. All can also be understood as forms of resistance to dominant hegemony in sport or broader society and the extent of that resistance may vary in relation to the degree of change that activists seek. Distinctions can be made between ideological, political, economic, socio-cultural and environmental resistance, but an absolute division between these realms is impossible as a single issue may encompass more than one form of resistance.

To an extent all resistance is ideological, but more radical sport activists are overtly conscious of undertaking ideological resistance towards neo-liberalism, even capitalism. Republica Internationale FC in Leeds utilises sport as a vehicle to nourish socialist enquiry and explore and express socialist ideas and actions (Totten 2015b). In pursuit of an integrity of praxis, some of the previously cited activists express overtly anarchist inclinations; these include grassroots clubs such as Autonomous FC and the Easton Cowboys and Cowgirls as well as some supporters of elite clubs such as Ultras Ahlawy in Egypt and many within the Alerta network.

Ideological resistance through sport is sometimes fostered by alliances of anti-capitalist, socialist, anarchist, feminist and gay rights sport activists. Initiatives such as the freedom through football, cricket and basketball tours to troubled political hot-spots including Chiapas in Mexico and the West Bank in Palestine (including the first ever involvement of women) have been organised autonomously outside the gaze of sport and political authorities. Teams act as human rights activists, expressing solidarity with indigenous struggles, with games being played in the Mexican jungle while being buzzed by military helicopter surveillance overhead and in Palestinian villages with Israeli army sentries looking on from gun towers.

Political resistance is forged through challenging powerful established authorities and vested interest. Sport governance is increasingly scrutinised amid scandals and accusations of authoritarianism, cronyism and corruption. Institutional doping scandals mire sport, while the sponsoring of senior athletics officials by global sport brands casts a shadow over the hosting rights of world championships. Senior FIFA officials are arrested on bribery charges. The list is vast. Meanwhile, campaigners rally to promote workers' rights in the construction of sports stadia and infrastructure for mega-events such as the World Cup in Qatar, and defend local land rights for those oppressed during the construction of Donald Trump's luxury Aberdeenshire golf course, which was shrouded by backdoor political dealing.

Political subservience is rejected in favour of DIY empowerment as sport activists contest the institutional control of sport. Although the ownership of iconic sport teams has become a hyper-commercialised playground for oligarchs, corporate entities and mass media commodification, autonomous fan organisations can cultivate empowerment informally and engender it implicitly through involvement in action for change. Democratic processes can embed autonomous community control by enabling fans to participate in decision-making and gain greater long-term control over their circumstances. With reference to the relatively fan-friendly arrangements for football in Germany, Merkel (2012: 372) notes that this is not due to the 'altruism, generosity and compassion of the football establishment in Germany, but is largely a result of the fans' opposition, which has a rebellious and subversive quality'.

Economic resistance is also exhibited by sport activists disillusioned with corporate ownership and commercial imperatives. Commercial mission creep has alienated many traditional sport fans as a sense of community is increasingly being replaced by a passive consumer spectacle which activists reject in favour of a more authentic and democratic grassroots culture (Totten 2015a). Fan activists protest about travel and ticketing costs and campaign for community-led provision. There are also ethical and human rights concerns about the dubious transnational trading and ownership of young sporting talent from struggling economies.

Sport activists campaign for fair trade in the production of sport goods and against low wages and appalling conditions in sport garment factories in the developing world. The campaign for a living wage has been extended to scrutiny of professional sports teams and the divide between millionaire athletes and support staff struggling against poverty. Campaigns for ethical consumption encourage a less materialistic culture than the planned obsolescence and disposability of sports goods. Although there have always been concerns related to the economy of sport, these are heightened in times of uncertainty, the politics of austerity and increasing inequality. Community facilities and services are strained under spending cuts, and local sport activists are engaged in campaigns to retain community provision.

Socio-cultural resistance by sport activists can be viewed as a response to the scale of funding and numbers participating (or not), but also in terms of discriminatory experiences in sport. Socio-cultural resistance covers an extensive remit in relation to inequalities, opportunity and discrimination including social class, culture, ethnicity, gender, sexuality, age, ability and disability. Historically sport has produced iconic activists campaigning against discrimination who could be considered as pioneers of future resistance.

Women have only relatively recently secured full membership of the Marylebone Cricket Club at Lords and the Royal and Ancient at St Andrews, the historic rulers of cricket and golf respectively. The Justin campaign continues to highlight homophobia in football, and Kick It Out and Football Against Racism in Europe pursue ongoing challenges to racism. Sport activism is channelled through challenges to oppressive conservative social norms, an ongoing process of struggle over values, including how the media portray sport, and its participants, judgementally and stereotypically in terms of culture and identity. At a grassroots level the female freedom through football tourists to Palestine addressed specific discrimination against Islamic female footballers as well as Palestinians generally. Republica Internationale has carefully considered how to include transgender footballers, despite opposition from the FA, and has planned trans-football matches outside the gaze of the authorities (Totten 2015b).

Environmental resistance in sport is reflected in green issues and campaigns against animal cruelty and for better animals rights in sport. Already mega-sport events are increasingly criticised for their destructive preparation, carbon footprint, impact on flora and fauna, for land and human rights issues, and the resulting ravages of social cleansing and homelessness. Additionally, Erickson (2011) describes how environmental concerns are leading to forms of recreational activism emerging from participation in outdoor pursuits. Although not yet as substantively documented as other forms of resistance, growing global concern for the environment suggests that this will become a more prominent motivation for future sport activism.

Methodology of dissidence: how to protest?

An incredible range of protest methods are used by sport activists from the more conventional to the highly creative. Activism employs a methodology of dissidence from a versatile toolkit of methods. This is comparable to the methodological notion of bricolage, whereby strategy and methods are shaped to capitalise on the options available and the circumstances encountered (Levi-Strauss 1966; Kincheloe and McLaren 2005). This also relates to praxis and political imagination, since bricolage is not limited to an interest in method but extends to understanding how knowledge is produced as it 'addresses the plurality and complex political dimensions' (Rogers 2012: 14).

Choice and combinations of method from the activist's toolkit are influenced by the nature of activism, who may be protesting, what issue is under consideration, what segment of the realm of sport provides the context, what the activists are hoping to achieve and how activist praxis disposes orientation to all of this. All protests are acts of conscience, some entirely within the law but others straying into the greyer area of civil disobedience. Lawful methods of protest may not be questioned beyond whether there is support for the issue or not or, at worst, whether activists are perceived as 'spoil-sports' (a status sometimes considered worse than cheating!). But for some sport activists, the ethics of their praxis may legitimate forms of protest beyond what others consider lawful. Civil disobedience may be justified on the grounds that the law itself is immoral, unjust, and perpetuates other injustices, with protest justified therefore as being in the broader public interest. Open civil disobedience aims to attract attention, place issues in the public domain, appeal to others' sense of moral justice, and garner support to change public policy. Civil disobedience can sometimes result in forms of direct action that intentionally break the law, usually peacefully but sometimes condoning material damage or violence through commitment to a broader sense of moral justice.

A relatively peaceful aspect of sport activism can be when the very act of participation in sport is itself provocative; 'resistance by existence'. This includes manifestations of identity politics by individual athletes and teams and the organisation of politicised sport events, tournaments, and tours. In rugby union this might include athletes (former Welsh captain Gareth Thomas) or officials (referee Nigel Owens) 'coming out' as gay. Such resistance is also exemplified by the growing emergence of women's rugby teams, invading and culturally challenging what was once exclusively male territory (Hylton and Totten 2013). In football, there has also been the formation of breakaway clubs by fans exasperated by established club ownership; these include AFC Wimbledon in 2002, FC United in 2005, and Ebbsfleet United FC, which became a fully fan-owned club in 2008.

Sport activism can utilise the emancipatory potential of sub-cultural activity to challenge dominant norms and structures, and promote radical action (Totten 2015c). This approach is more likely to focus on grassroots and recreational sport, encouraging alternative sub-cultural activity including sport events. The freedom through football tournaments cultivate activity in which politics are manifest, the organic intellectual cherished and participants empowered through a process of informal education engendering a critical consciousness and praxis (Totten 2011). Sterchele and Saint-Blancat (2013) contend that the liminality of these alternative festivals de-structures 'normality' and offers creative potential to explore anti-discrimination in a more liberated way.

Many campaigns employ conventional media, including newspaper and fanzine articles, advertisements, flyers and film documentary, with Sport England's award winning media 'This Girl Can' campaign exemplifying an apparent success (Rumsby 2016). Sometimes campaigns are accompanied by celebrity or athlete endorsement such as prominent American football and basketball players wearing 'I Can't Breathe' t-shirts in protest against racist police brutality (Littlefield 2014). Nelson Mandela publicly promoted the notion of a rainbow nation during mass media coverage of the rugby union World Cup in South Africa in 1995. The British graffiti artist Banksy participated in an Easton Cowboys' football tour to the indigenous Zapatista communities in 1999 and contributed a legacy of emblematic political artwork (Simpson and McMahon 2012). Sport can sometimes even become a humorous playground for activists who employ ridicule, parody and satire. Performance art and symbolism are particularly common, especially that involving fans using the choreography of chants and banners.

Petitions are also used to good effect, such as that by swimmers from Bramley, Leeds, who in the face of austerity and funding cuts campaigned to keep their local pool open and assumed community ownership in 2013. Sport activists also employ community organisation and action both as volunteers and as professional community mobilisers. Some campaigns involve whistle blowing, shareholder acquisition, legal action or sanctions, amongst them the plea-bargained recruitment of Chuck Blazer to expose FIFA corruption, the growth of supporter trusts to pursue football club takeovers or the Gleneagles Agreement of 1977, which used sport to isolate the apartheid regime in South Africa. Significantly, those campaigning on behalf of Liverpool FC fans killed in the 1989 disaster at Hillsborough gained some justice by winning legal disclosures and recourse for investigation into misconduct by public authorities.

Increasingly sport activists utilise social media, including blogs and discussion forums. Clicktivism means surveys and petitions can be created more easily and distributed more widely, and online videos can go globally viral. More sophisticated use of technology has led to guerrilla media whereby activists produce sources of information to counter mainstream outlets. Some activists are even able to subvert, flood or hack mainstream sources. The Spirit of Shankly Liverpool fans' protest group was so effective from 2008 at targeting financial institutions that it led to the club being portrayed as a risky investment, and to the owner referring to the 'militant role (of) internet terrorists' who helped force the club's sale (Millward 2012: 643).

More radical sport activists are likelier than others to resort to direct action, foregoing negotiation in favour of the immediate effective stoppage of that which offends. Lone wolf activist Trenton Oldfield, motivated by the politics of class war, risked injury and imprisonment halting the elite Oxford and Cambridge university boat race in London 2012 by swimming across the Thames river amongst the boats. Non-violent resistance includes aspects of non-cooperation including working to rule and player strikes. Sport activists have organised strikes, boycotts, demonstrations, marches, flash mobs, sit-ins, squatting, occupation, and blockades and fan groups have used their presence at or absence from stadia to draw attention to their causes.

Resistance from the early 1990s by Brighton and Hove Albion fans against potential ground relocation which eventually deposed the club chairman was described as 'effective guerrilla warfare' (North and Hodson 1997) and some activities can be considered as guerrilla sport activism. The necessarily secretive freedom through football political tours to Palestine and Mexico utilised subterfuge to circumvent travel restrictions to oppressed communities, including posing as tourists, and walking secretively through mountains overnight to avoid military checkpoints (Totten 2011). Occasionally protest has included property damage, vandalism, sabotage and violence. This ranges from purist climbers sabotaging unnatural bolts and aids, to fans fighting police, to the Black September kidnaps and murders at the 1972 Munich Olympics. Last but not least, Newsome Sport and Bowling Club members gained unlikely notoriety in Yorkshire 2015 by using an angle grinder to break through the landlord's steel gate to their club and then playing a celebratory match.

Case study of sport activism: FC Sankt Pauli fans

There are few better examples of radical sport activism sustained over time than FC Sankt Pauli fans from Hamburg in Germany. Since the mid-1980s these fan activists have maintained an alternative football culture influenced by street politics and the punk movement offering inspiration for other fans throughout Europe (Sanderson 2009). The fans are organised autonomously, bottom-up, non-hierarchically and informally, which has empowered them to create an authentic vibrant democratic culture which exerts great influence over their club. This gives rise to prolific community action and empowers individuals, the fan body itself and broader communities in a sustainable way.

Sankt Pauli fans have advocated and acted vigorously for social and political change in football, and they have also utilised football to advocate and act for social and political change elsewhere. They are knowingly engaged in political and cultural struggle, having fought long and hard to achieve their unique status and maintain it. Effective sport activism and praxis are allied to a heightened sense of critical consciousness, and fan culture is flexible enough to offer different opportunities for immersion in activism. Fan activists engage in 'thoughtful action' (Ledwith 2011) by organising, supporting, acting, campaigning and protesting prolifically, and core fans also link their politics to action, distinguishing between being '*politically minded*' and '*politically active*' (Totten 2015c).

Fans feel a sense of potential threat to their do-it-yourself, left-wing culture from the commercialisation of the club. Thus, the protection of political integrity is more important than compromise in pursuit of playing success for fans who feel a need for eternal vigilance over the club. The fans' relationship to the club is not one of unconditional positive regard as they are not blinded by romanticism, and they sometimes treat the club with disdain due to the perceived commercialising tendencies the club embraces (Totten 2015c). They use football as a form of political praxis whereby their 'thoughtful action' galvanises radical ideas and emancipatory practice. This, and unshakable conviction, have led to fearless confrontation of issues and political action.

Fans have campaigned for rights in relation to stewarding, overzealous security, surveillance, and the criminalisation of protest (Totten 2011). But perhaps the concerns of the local district have become the main focus of the fans, who emphasise that social problems are accentuated against a backdrop of creeping gentrification. Their campaigns have taken account of poverty, unemployment, homelessness, low educational attainment, intergenerational issues, oppression by the state and police against alternative lifestyles, squatters' rights, immigrants' rights and in support of the 'working girls' who ply their trade in the red-light district (Totten 2015c).

Sport activists are prominent on the Sankt Pauli board and fan groups coordinate activity through the Fanclubsprecherrat which incorporates delegates from individual fan clubs and democratically identifies which issues to support and positions to be taken as well as initiatives and campaign planning (Totten 2015c). Fans have built a foundation for personal and community empowerment through an infrastructure of community organisation, democratic participation and involvement, leading to positive social and political action and community projects including youth work and computer literacy (Totten 2015a). Fans have also set up social housing projects, and squats have been utilised as nightclubs and fan group clubhouses. Fans have close relations with the squatting movement and have inherited its tradition of direct action. Fan activism has sustained conscious acts of '*resistance*' against powerful institutions including civil disobedience through protests and demonstrations, which sometimes lead to conflict with the police and, in 2011, fans even went as far as to acquire their own authentic second-hand water cannon to parody and rival those of the police (Totten 2011).

Sankt Pauli fans keep the commercialising tendencies of their own club in check sustaining an authentic grassroots fan culture in the process. Fans are intrusive and effective in influencing the running of the club and scathing about any dilution of political ideals.

But this is a hard-fought struggle. The club is caught between the commercial inducements and 'imperatives' of professional football, and the political integrity of the fans, and these tensions are held in some form of equilibrium. Sankt Pauli fans were pioneers in German and world football in combating fascism, racism, and homophobia, and demanding the football authorities to do likewise; many of their ideas have now become mainstream (Totten 2015a). They have challenged the hegemony of passive consumption, resisted commercialisation and created a radical do-it-yourself culture. They have created a participatory democracy which demonstrates transformational potential.

Sankt Pauli fans offer a vision for sport activism and for sport more generally to realise its transformative potential. The fans successfully utilise their support of a football club as a springboard for political activity. Activists show unambiguously that professional sport can be reclaimed as a site for resistance through the propagation of leftist libertarian ideas and culture. They guard against complacency by defending the idea that they are supporting a cause, not just a football club. Although by no means the only fans engaged in this struggle, Sankt Pauli acts as a beacon of hope for many fellow travellers across the world, a Mecca for some who visit this iconic phenomenon and share alternative ideals for football and politics. Sankt Pauli fans also reach out to others offering solidarity and messages of support. Sankt Pauli represents a buoyant hotbed of sport activism, exemplifying a never surrender attitude to the inducements of the neo-liberal commodification of sport.

Conclusion

Sport activism and protest have deep historical roots but appear to be increasingly manifest in contemporary times, arguably as a backlash against the consequences of neo-liberalism. Sport activism and protest sometimes receive high-profile recognition but often occur more locally and sub-culturally. Activism is sometimes employed top-down by large institutions but more often bottom-up and more radically by community organisers and lay-activists. Sport activism incorporates discrete campaigning and protest, but also broader community organisation, and more immersed preoccupations reflecting ideological convictions. Activism can be directed through sport towards targets both inside and outside sport by those with an investment in sport or, more opportunistically, by external interlopers.

As sport is contested cultural practice, it can be a site of oppressive hegemonic control but because power is a relational dynamic, ordinary people also possess the potential to transform their circumstances. Sport offers a site for resistance as a strategic response. Most, if not all, of what transpires can be understood within a 'framework of sport activism and protest' (see Figure 30.2), which identifies related variables that shape the process of sport activism. Distinct instances of sport activism can be deconstructed to reveal how individual variables can fluctuate and collectively generate the determination of different outcomes.

In practice, sport activism is driven by praxis and political imagination, ideological dispositions whose integrity awakens critical consciousness. This, in turn, emboldens action aimed at addressing issues and enables connections to broader structural causes that define the degrees of change to be pursued across a spectrum ranging from conservation to reform to transformation and even revolution. Sport activism is further shaped by the identity of activists, and the theatre of opportunity that they inhabit, accommodating a range of contributors from large institutions to, much more commonly, grassroots community organisations, clubs, fan groups and individuals. A plethora of issues inspire sport activists and provide different incentives for action to organise, campaign and protest, and

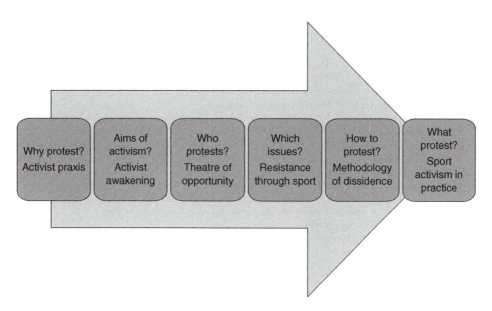

Figure 30.2   A framework of sport activism and protest

these acts of counter-hegemonic resistance occur ideologically, politically economically, socio-culturally and environmentally. The nature of specific activism and protest draws on a methodology of dissidence, with choices being made from a toolkit of options. Sport activism has drawn on both lawful means and civil disobedience, and has utilised both conventional and new media, the identity politics of resistance by existence, alternative cultural activities, direct action and even guerilla sport. Effective sport activism and protest dispel the myth that sport and politics do not mix and offer a degree of optimism that oppressions can be challenged and a fairer world envisaged. Sport activism entails an aspirational outlook, an empowering commitment to change and an enthusiastic imagination of the power of sport.

References

Alerta. (2012) About Alerta. Accessed 25 February 2016. www.alerta-network.org/about.

Bennett, T. (1981) *Popular Culture: History and Theory, Popular Culture: Themes and Issues 2*. Milton Keynes: Open University.

Brimson, D. (2006) *Rebellion: The Inside Story of Football's Protest Movement*. London: John Blake.

Carrington, B. and McDonald, I. (eds) (2009) *Marxism, Cultural Studies and Sport*. London: Routledge.

Chomsky, N. (2002) *Media Control: The Spectacular Achievements of Propaganda* (second edition). New York: Seven Stories Press.

Chomsky, N. (2003) *Hegemony or Survival: America's Quest for Global Dominance*. New York: Metropolitan.

Coakley, J. and Dunning, E. (eds) (2000) *Handbook of Sports Studies*. London: Sage.

Dart, J. (2012) Representations of sport in the revolutionary socialist press in Britain, 1988–2012. *International Review for the Sociology of Sport*. DOI: 10.1177/1012690213497352.

Davidson, N. (2014) *Pirates, Punks and Politics*. York: Sportbooks.

Dolk, K. and Kuhn, G. (2015): Stockholm's 17 SK: A case study in community football. *Sport in Society: Cultures, Commerce, Media, Politics*, 18(4): 440–445.

Erickson, B. (2011) Recreational activism: Politics, nature and the rise of neo-liberalism. *Leisure Studies*, 30(4): 477–494.

Grix, G. (2016) *Sport Politics: An Introduction*. London: Palgrave.

Hylton, K. and Totten, M. (2013) Developing sport for all? Addressing inequality in sport. In K. Hylton (ed.) *Sport Development: Policy, Process and Practice*. Abingdon: Routledge, pp: 37–79.

Kelly, O. (1984) *Community, Art and the State*. London: Comedia

Kaufman, P. and Wolf, E. (2013) Playing and protesting: Sport as a vehicle for social change. *Journal of Sport and Social Issues*, 34: 154, DOI: 10.1177/0193723509360218.

Kennedy, P. (2013) Left wing supporter movements and the political economy of football. *Soccer and Society*, 14(2). DOI:10.1080/14660970.2013.776462.

Kennedy, P. and Kennedy, D. (2015a) DIY football: The cultural politics of community based football clubs – introduction. *Sport in Society: Cultures, Commerce, Media, Politics*, 18(4): 403–409.

Kennedy, D. and Kennedy, P. (2015b) Grass-roots football, autonomous activity and the forging of new social relationships. *Sport in Society: Cultures, Commerce, Media, Politics*, 18(4): 497–513.

Kincheloe, J. and McLaren, P. (2005) Rethinking critical theory and qualitative research. In N. Denzin and Y. Lincoln (eds) *The Sage Handbook of Qualitative Research*. London: Sage, pp. 303–342.

Kuhn, G. (2011) *Soccer Versus the State*. Oakland, CA: PM Press.

Ledwith, M. (2011) *Community Development: A Critical Approach*. Bristol: Polity Press.

Levi-Strauss, C. (1966) *The Savage Mind*. Chicago, IL: University of Chicago Press.

Littlefield, B. (2014) 'I can't breathe' protests reach pro sports. *WBUR, Only a Game*. 13 December 2014. Accessed 2 June 2016. http://onlyagame.wbur.org/2014/12/13/nba-protest-brown-garner.

Maguire, J. (2005) Back to the valley. In J. Maguire (ed.) *Power and Global Sport*. Abingdon: Routledge, pp. 41–60.

McSweeny, J. (2014) The absence of class: Critical development, NGOs and the misuse of Gramsci's concepts of counter-hegemony. *Progress in Development Studies*, 14(3): 275–285.

Merkel, U. (2012) Football fans and clubs in Germany: Conflicts, crises and compromises. *Soccer and Society*, 13(3): 359–376.

Millward, P. (2012). Reclaiming the Kop? Analysing Liverpool supporters' 21st century mobilisations. *Sociology*, 46(4): 633–648.

Nahapiet, J. and Ghoshal, S. (1998) Social capital, intellectual capital, and the organizational advantage. *The Academy of Management Review*, 23(2): 242–267.

North, S. and Hodson, P. (1997) *Build a Bonfire: How Football Fans United to Save Brighton and Hove Albion*. Edinburgh: Mainstream Publishing.

Numerato, D. (2015) Who says no to modern football? Italian supporters, reflexivity, and neo-liberalism. *Journal of Sport and Social Issues*, 39(2): 120–138.

Perelman, M. (2012) *Barbaric Sport; A Global Plague*. London: Verso.

Rogers, M. (2012) Contextualizing theories and practices of bricolage research. *The Qualitative Report*, 17(7): 1–17.

Rumsby, B. (2016) 'This Girl Can' campaign inspires almost 150,000 women to take up sport. *Daily Telegraph*, 23 January 2016. Accessed June 2016. www.telegraph.co.uk/sport/telegraphsportnews/12044946/This-Girl-Can-campaign-inspires-almost-150000-women-to-take-up-sport.html.

Sanderson, C. (2009) 'Nie wieder Faschismus, Nie wieder Krieg, Nie wieder 3. Liga!'; A social history of FC St. Pauli, 1986–1991. Accessed June 2016. www.playleftwing.org.

SCCD (2001) *Strategic framework for community development*. Standing Conference for Community Development. Sheffield.

Schuftan, C. (1996) The community development dilemma: What is really empowering? *Community Development Journal*, 31(3): 260–264.

Scraton, S. and Flintoff, A. (2002) Sport feminism: The contribution of feminist thought to our understanding of gender and sport. In S. Scraton and A. Flintoff, (eds) *Gender and Sport: A Reader*. London: Routledge, pp. 30–45.

Simpson, W. (2015) Easton Cowboys and Cowgirls: A 'political' sports club that is not political and 'anarchist' sports club that is not actually anarchist. *Sport in Society: Cultures, Commerce, Media, Politics*, 18(4): 466–476.

Simpson, W. and McMahon, M. (2012). *Freedom Through Football*. Bristol: Tangent.

Sterchele, D. and Saint-Blancat, C. (2013) Keeping it liminal. The Mondiali Antirazzisti (Anti-racist World Cup) as a multifocal interaction ritual. *Leisure Studies*, DOI: 10/1080/02614367.2013.855937.

Sugden, J. and Tomlinson, A. (2002) *Power Games; A Critical Sociology of Sport*. London: Routledge.

Totten, M. (2011) Freedom through football: A tale of football, community, activism and resistance. In A. Ratna and B. Lashua (eds) *Community and Inclusion in Leisure Research and Sport Development*. Eastbourne: Leisure Studies Association, pp. 155–168.

Totten, M. (2015a) Football and community empowerment: How FC Sankt Pauli fans organise to influence. *Soccer and Society*. DOI: 10.1080/14660970.2015.1100436.

Totten, M. (2015b) Playing left wing: From Sunday League socialism to international solidarity. A social history of the development of Republica Internationale FC. *Sport in Society: Cultures, Commerce, Media, Politics*, 16(4): 453–468.

Totten, M. (2015c) Sport activism and political praxis within the FC Sankt Pauli fan subculture. *Soccer and Society*, (4): 453–468.

Tucker, L. (2011) Forza, Forza Republic: A case study of politics and socialist culture in a Sunday league football club. In A. Ratna and B. Lashua (eds) *Community and Inclusion in Leisure Research and Sport Development*. Eastbourne: Leisure Studies Association, pp. 143–154.

Tucker, L. (2015) 'It's not just about the football': Leading social change in a Sunday league football team. *Sport in Society: Cultures, Commerce, Media, Politics*, 18(4): 410–424.

Williams, R. (1977) *Marxism and Literature*. Oxford: Oxford University Press.

Wilson, R. (2011) The Easton Cowboys and girls' sports and social club. In G. Kuhn *Soccer Versus the State*. Oakland, CA: PM Press.

Zirin, D. (2005) *What's My Name, Fool? Sports and Resistance in the United States*. Chicago, IL: Haymarket.

Zirin, D. (2013) *Game Over: How Politics Has Turned the Sports World Upside Down*. New York: The New Press.

31

'COUNTERCULTURAL' SPORT

Paul Gilchrist

The term 'counterculture' is frequently applied to describe a distinctive feature of the history, politics, style and organisation of sport. As an analytical category it is elusive. The term is commonly wheeled out to pad discussions of subculture (Beal 1995; Midol 1993; Rinehart 2000; Stranger 2011; Wheaton 2013), without ever being sufficiently developed in its own right to lead or frame an analysis. To coin an idiom, counterculture is somehow always the bridesmaid, never the bride. Den Tandt, commenting on cultural studies more widely, has speculated that this state of affairs is a product of academic caution and unease over endorsing a broader project of progressive social transformation. He argues that the study of subculture involves immersion into the way of life of a social group and the researcher does not necessarily have to agree with its ideals and values when they expose its cultures and practices (2014: 82). On the other hand, the study of counterculture is envisaged as breaking academic conventions of cool detachment and studied disinterest, as it is seen to require the researcher to adopt a cause, to work to undermine dominant ideologies, even to exercise a revolutionary praxis. To write sympathetically about counterculture is therefore to cross a threshold of scientific neutrality, where the researcher can become a covert champion of a revolutionary agenda without subjecting it to rational scrutiny (Den Tandt 2014: 82).

Nevertheless, Andy Bennett (2014: 25) writes that:

> despite the theoretical arguments that can be raised against the sociological value of counterculture as a meaningful term for categorising social action, like the term 'subculture', it lives on as a concept in social and cultural theory . . . to become part of a received, mediated memory.

While this statement may hold true in the fields of music and popular culture studied by Bennett, the concept is deployed in sport studies in a simplistic fashion, deployed without a sense of its parameters, or its exegetical heritage. In spite of this situation, counterculture has been used in various ways by the sport studies community: to comment on oppositions between a mainstream sporting culture and a dissenting one (Beal 1995; Wheaton 2013); the colonising tendencies of capitalist consumer culture over youth sport subcultures (Rinehart 2000; Stranger 2011; Walters 2008); the influence of Californian sport culture in the development of lifestyle sport (Griggs 2012; Midol 1993; Midol and Broyer 1995); social protest and student activism in U.S. college sport (Zang 2001; Oriard 2009; Wiggins 1988; Henderson 2009); underground or alternative clubs and leagues (Kuhn 2011); the establishment of new sporting space by urban hipsters (Gilchrist and Ravenscroft 2012); and prophecies of sporting futures through the development of new movement cultures (Renson 2001) and digital sporting competitions (Jonasson and Thiborg 2010).

The aim of this chapter is to advance the political understanding of sport through a fuller consideration of the concept of counterculture. Counterculture is revisited and reappraised here as it has significance to the analysis of sport politics; important to understanding the ways in which sport cultures evolve as well as understanding some of the legacies of the sixties, and in helping to document and analyse forms of cultural resistance and social action in more contemporary contexts. In taking this approach, I concur with George McKay's uncovering and tracing of continuities between sixties counterculture and subsequent cultures of resistance and his aim 'to reclaim the power of the notion of counterculture, partly to show that the utopian project of the sixties is still with us' (1996: 6). The chapter considers the conceptual evolution of 'counterculture', returns to the sixties to reveal some significant cultural changes that occurred in the sports world, and provides more recent examples of 'spectacles of rebellion' which affirm the need for a more developed notion of 'counterculture' in accounting for social and political change in and through sport. The concept is reappraised in the concluding section.

The concept of counterculture

The concept of counterculture has its origins in the work of post-war sociologists and political scientists who sought to account for deviance from dominant norms and values within a social and political system. The American political scientist H.D. Lasswell, drawing on Freud's discussions of the *super-ego, ego* and *id*, discussed 'counter-mores' as culturally expected patterns of conduct that deviate from mores, or socially acquired inhibitions (1950: 49). Talcott Parsons in *The Social System* (1951: 521) makes passing mention of 'counter-culture' as a consequence of 'alienative motivational orientations' that arise in opposition to an institutionalised order. Parsons argues that subcultures lend coherence to countercultural orientations; however, he notes that they are in process of seeking wider ideological justification and they face a 'dilemma of institutionalisation' as the requirements of power necessitate a process of institutionalisation which may come at the cost of the utopian purity of countercultural movements (Parsons 1951: 522–526). This is a tension which bedevils social change and can lead to feelings of missed chances and rued opportunities.

Counterculture entered wider academic discourse through an article written by J. Milton Yinger in 1960. Yinger sought conceptual clarification for the concept of subculture in the hope of a more accurate analysis of empirical cases. He distinguished subculture from 'contraculture'. Both are on a spectrum to denote groups whose norms set them apart from a larger society, though 'contraculture' was developed by Yinger to emphasise a theme of conflict with wider social values. Where subcultures could be studied *sui generis*, Yinger argues that countercultures relate to a dominant culture as they directly oppose dominant norms and values. Youth delinquency, gang cultures, the study of lower-class society, and jazz musicianship were suggested as fruitful areas for the application of the concept.

Theodore Roszak helped to popularise 'counterculture'. *The Making of a Counter Culture* was published with serendipitous fortune just three weeks after the Woodstock Festival in 1969 and helped to identify what was at stake. The book followed the Summer of Love in 1967 and the year of student dissent, and came in the year of mankind's greatest technological achievement:

placing man on the moon. Roszak used 'counterculture' to underline a generational schism and an alliance of college students and young people across hippie and New Left movements, opposed to American 'technocracy'. Roszak observes:

> By way of a dialectic Marx could never have imagined, technocratic America produces a potentially revolutionary element amongst its own youth. The bourgeoisie, instead of discovering the class enemy in its factories, finds it across the breakfast table in the person of its own pampered children.
>
> *(1969: 34)*

Counterculture rejected the corporate and technological expertise that dominates industrial society. Born from a post-war disenchantment with Enlightenment conceptions of science, technology and truth – where the 'habitual mode of contact with the world is a cool curiosity untouched by love, tenderness, or passionate wonder' (1969: 218–219) – young people confronted the span of 'technocracy', from the military–industrial complex and consumer materialism to the stifling conformity of organisational man.

The demand for social and psychological transformation was loudest on college campuses. These were the nurseries of new political energy, sites of radical dissent and cultural innovation. Here, young people could find freedom and pleasure, fun and games, and dream of (and sometimes, if temporarily, create) meaningful communities and dissenting lifestyles. The image of the hippie epitomised a countercultural aesthetic, which embraced sensuous, joyful and humanistic experiences wrought by psychedelic music, consciousness-altering drugs, and sexual revolution. These aspects of the counterculture hit a nerve with those young people seeking escape from a lifetime of playing 'the system'. New forms of wisdom and subjectivity were explored through Eastern and Zen philosophies, which were being popularised throughout California through self-expressive therapies. Theoretical validation was found in the work of influential theorists Herbert Marcuse and Norman O. Brown, who translated the radical social critiques of Freud and Marx and explored possibilities for social and psychic revolution, and in the visionary sociology of Paul Goodman, founder of Gestalt Therapy, whose popular book *Growing Up Absurd: The Problems of Youth in the Organised System* (1960), was a commentary of an affluent society which can fulfil needs, but not satisfy deeper wants.

Whilst holding out hope for the Great Refusal and a post-technocratic age, Roszak remained critical of counterculture. He accused faux-intellectual hipsters of superficial dalliances with Eastern ideas and philosophies and accused users of psychedelic drugs of wilful distraction from political consciousness. Roszak was concerned whether the counterculture amounted to a superficial gesture rather than a radical moment; an idea that continues to reverberate. All too readily, he felt, could the energies of youth collapse into inanity and parodies of freedom and fulfilment that spoke more of enduring social control than social and psychic liberation. He wrote:

> If the counter culture should bog down in a colourful morass of unexamined symbols, gestures, fashions of dress, and slogans, then it will provide little that can be turned into a lifelong commitment. . . . It will finish as a temporary style, continually sloughed off and left behind for the next wave of adolescents: a hopeful beginning that never becomes more than a beginning.
>
> *(1969: 72)*

The Making of a Counter Culture still resonates. It helps us to think about aspirations and dreams that exist beyond the mainstream, the personal as political, capacities for cultural and political change from youth cultures and movements, and the importance of spirituality and personal forms of transcendence in discussions of self and environment. With hindsight, several authors have sought to expand the agents of counterculture beyond white, middle-class hippies or student radicals, by viewing counterculture as an aggregate movement of progressive causes, including environmentalists, the civil rights movement, pacifists, feminists, gay liberationists and other minority crusades against a hegemonic mainstream (Clecak, 1983; Eyerman and Jamison 1998). Doug Rossinow (1997: 79) explains that:

> this category has always been a heuristic device . . . used to group together values, visual styles, social practices, and institutions that were widely disparate but considered by most to be unified in their rebellion against the dominant culture.

This more expansive notion of counterculture has attracted social movement scholars to consider the coalescence and contribution of small alternative subgroups within and along-side new social movements in processes of political change (see Haenfler 2013). McKay has suggested that the concept continues to be useful when applied to cases of radical political action enacted by small, autonomous groups, as it enables us to consider forms of prefigura-tive politics, cultures of resistance, social actions and tactical innovations pioneered by new social movements in opposition to hegemonic forms of power, on unpopular public policies (McKay 1996). New concepts such as 'social movement scenes', have been added to the literature in ways that engage with the original conceptual uses of counterculture, through analyses of fluid and non-organisational networks of like-minded individuals based in certain locations, brought together through shared lifestyle orientations, dress and aesthetic tastes as well as political concerns (Haunss and Leach 2007). As Roszak and others signalled in their commentaries on sixties counterculture, the centre of attention for countercultural studies is a politics that exists outside of formal arenas and institutions of government and which is given energy through forms of political *enactment*; demonstrations, events, and counter-institutions which attempt to prefigure a desired society through embodying oppositional and alternative values in practice (Breines 1982: 6). Political enactment involves a shift from a 'politics of demand' to a 'politics of the act' (Day 2004). Whereas the former works with state mecha-nisms and procedures to deliver social change, the latter is about an inventive and participa-tory politics, fundamentally about 'doing it' – creating and performing an alternate vision for society (Sharpe 2008; Duncombe 2007).

A countercultural 'politics of the act' or, as McKay terms them, 'spectacles of rebellion' are also fundamentally spatial, involving the creation of countercultural zones of resist-ance (McKay 1996: 9). Whilst the notion of 'spectacle of rebellion' is informed by artistic traditions, especially situationist-inspired performative interventions, which aim to change social life – particularly in urban environments – by disrupting the everyday flows of public space and provoking discussions and confrontations over use (see Martin 2002), a range of possible acts should be noted, from formal experiments in alternate living and com-munity building (Farber 2013), to 'temporary pockets of sovereignty' (Riley *et al.* 2010: 48) which produce alternative spatial meanings as individuals and communities gather to make meaningful their political values through behaviours and practices that often stress the values of sociality, community and belonging. The latter in particular chimes with Hakim Bey's (1991) notion of 'temporary autonomous zones', spaces that are temporarily liberated then disappear when the state is 'forced' to intervene to reclaim the space. 'Spectacles of rebellion' draw on the contradictions of space, identified by Henri Lefebvre, who cogently observes:

Socio-political contradictions are realized spatially. The contradictions of space thus make the contradictions of social relations operative. In other words, spatial contradictions 'express' conflicts between socio-political interests and forces; it is only *in* space that such conflicts come effectively into play, and in so doing they become contradictions of space.

(Lefebvre 1991: 365)

As this discussion has shown, the concept of 'counterculture' lives on not only through the vast literatures of youth and popular music studies, where it is readily applied alongside 'subculture' to help us understand the shaping of individual and alternative cultures and lifestyles (see Bennett 2014; Whiteley and Sklower 2014), but in the political analysis of oppositional norms, values, styles and identities, and the occasional moments of confrontation with institutional authority and dominant cultures (cf. Klein 1999).

Countercultural sport and the 'spirit of the sixties'

George Lipsitz (1994: 208) claims that 'any retrospective account of the sixties inevitably runs up against our collective societal capacities for remembering and forgetting'. Indeed, our remembering of the past is crucial to how we analyse cultural currents and social conditions present in any age. Frederic Jameson (1984) noted in an essay on 'Periodizing the 60s', that the process of cultural periodisation can invite homogeneity and forwards a selective historical narrative that solidifies historically dominant trends and tendencies at a particular time, at the expense of 'residual' or 'emergent' tendencies within a culture (Williams 1977). These problems are ones faced too in the application of 'counterculture' in the telling of the historical origins of alternative sport. Sport sociologists have used 'counterculture' to highlight the presence of an alternative sport culture, one that is culturally different or oppositional to mainstream sport cultures through its rules and practices. A typical example is that of ultimate Frisbee, where it is frequently asserted that the origins of the game lie in the American countercultural values of the 1960s (Griggs 2011: 102; see also Walters 2008). Whilst this alternative activity – and we can add surfing and skateboarding too (cf. Beal 1995; Wheaton 2013) – has developed sporting frameworks, competitions, governing bodies and professional athletes, the hippie roots and origins of ultimate Frisbee are retold as a dominant narrative of the sport's history, underlining its non-conformist values and anti-establishment ethos. However, the public meanings and collective stories of these alternative sports invoke the spirit of the sixties, but the analysis is centred upon the processes of commodification and commercialisation and their social and cultural consequences to new (or redefined) sport cultures. Used this way, 'counterculture' tends to be deployed as a trope, applied selectively in interpretations of lived practices and popular cultural forms as a compression of collective understanding (see Townsley 2001). As Braunstein and Doyle (2002: 6) observe:

that's the inexorable fate of easy terms like 'counterculture' or, for that matter, 'Generation X': they inevitably lose their original historical mooring, become shorthand references, then shortcuts to thinking, and finally Pepsi commercial soundbites.

Counterculture is employed by sport sociologists to explain the development of alternative lifestyles and communities. Arguably, the prime focus is a politics of dichotomies – capitalist and anti-capitalist, authentic and phony, insider and outsider, mainstream and non-mainstream (Rinehart 2000; Stranger 2011; Wheaton 2013), at the expense of an analysis of the wider political imaginaries and forms of explicit social action suggested in the concept's oppositional imaginary. As Bennett (2014: 25) acknowledges:

> counterculture connotes something larger in scale – a movement or series of movements directed towards and orientated to address large, globally dispersed socioeconomic problems and issues.

Similarly, Haenfler (2013: 2) has noted that subcultures 'tend to be more narrowly focused on style, leisure, and youth', whilst counterculture addresses counter-hegemonic organisation and action. This is a position that echoes Langman's notion of counterculture as seeking 'a fundamental transvaluation of ethics, alternate life styles, and transformations of consciousness' (Langman 1971: 82). What I'm suggesting is that the historical picture is much more complex beyond the shorthand use of the term. In this section I wish to briefly consider some examples of cultural and ideological struggles, 'countercultural' moments of the 1960s and 1970s which, while interesting in their own right, suggest important historical legacies that continue to resonate.

In *Sports Wars: Athletes in the Age of Aquarius*, sportswriter David Zang (2001) has shown how the norms and social rules of sport were under pressure from cultural changes in American society throughout the 1960s and into the 1970s. The challenge came both from within and without. Former players-turned-sportswriters began to question the dominant values underpinning team sport. Dave Meggyesy in *Out of Their League* exposed American football as brutal, militaristic and dehumanising; sport serving as an easy allegory for the style of war being practised in Vietnam. Others shone a light on demeaning practices exerted by coaches in locker rooms and training sessions (Shaw 1972); while classics like Paul Hoch's *Rip Off the Big Game* was followed by landmark texts of New Left critique, such as Bero Rigauer's (1981) *Sport and Work* and Jean-Marie Brohm's (1978) *Sport: A Prison of Measured Time*, in condemning the capitalist and imperialistic values inherent in big time sport. The critique of sport straddled the idea of mass spectator sport as an opiate of the masses; to a ridiculing of sport as either too trivial or too serious and thus a threat to a natural play instinct (Zang 2001: 81–82).

The sense of radical possibility and disruption to the old ways of doing things was also witnessed through changes in fashion and personal identity. At a superficial level, athletes began to use fashion and style to claim agency and subvert disciplinary codes. Through lengthening hair, the wearing of sideburns and casual attire, athletes helped to undermine the demand for conformity. The image of the well-groomed and clean-cut sportsman, a sign of team discipline and unity, was challenged by some athletes whose look owed more to hippie culture. While some coaches relaxed their requirements for marine-style grooming (Oriard 2009: 50), others were pro-active in upholding the sartorial management of the sportsman's body. The NCAA Wrestling Rules Committee opposed long hair and sideburn growth on health grounds, and by the 1971–1972 season, wrestling referees were empowered to measure and trim hair before a match (Zang 2001: 13–15). Fans could be active too in policing hippies from the sport sanctuary. Peter Cetera, the lead singer of Chicago, was beaten up at a Chicago Cubs–LA Dodgers baseball game in May 1969, his jaw broken in three places by four Marines who objected to his long hair (Zang 2001: 16).

For sports historian Michael Oriard, the sixties was the culmination of an impulse, an explosion of a playfulness which 'came close to overwhelming society' as it subverted the dominant middle-class work culture (1991: 442). This was not just a case of theoretical abstraction. Experimentation with anarchic styles of play continued into the 1970s. The New

Games Movement of the early 1970s promoted free, non-competitive play events where people were encouraged to 'Play Hard. Play Fair. Nobody Hurt' (DeKoven 1978). The Movement still upheld the principle of 'intense physical interaction between players', but according to Stewart Brand, one of its founders (Fluegelman and Tembeck 1976: 7–8), play became the focus for social interaction and subjective experience. Mass team games like 'Slaughter' and 'Mother Earth' were invented, based on simple rules, where the aim was not to win, but simply to play. Slaughter involved forty players entering a large wrestling arena, on their knees and barefoot, and whilst a rock band set an energetic tempo, four moving balls and two moving baskets circulated the players, and anyone could be eliminated by being thrown from the wrestling mat. 'The game was intense and energetic, with much body contact and almost no injury' (ibid.: 8). Mother Earth involved hundreds of participants moving a large rubber pushball, the Earthball, towards goals at each end of the field, but when the ball approached the goal, players defected in support of the losing side and so the movement continued, with much pushing and cheering. The first New Games Tournament was held in October 1973 at the Gerbode Preserve, near San Francisco. The 6,000 participants took part in a series of games designed to be inclusive of people with different abilities, cooperative and based on principles of trust (see Pearce *et al.* 2007). New Games, according to Bernie DeKoven, a key figure within the movement:

> were really less about games than they were about playing. One of the best examples I can think of is how we played Tug of War. Here is a highly strenuous clearly competitive game. But because it was clear that playing was more important than winning, when people noticed that their side was 'winning' they tended to (without prompting from any of the New Games 'referees') abandon their side and join the other.
>
> *(Pearce* et al. *2007: 264–265)*

Through these examples, popularised in a series of subsequent books which extended the forms and types of game (Fluegelman and Tembeck 1976; Fluegelman 1981; Le Fevre 1988; DeKoven 2004), can be witnessed the creation of an alternate way of being, an attempt to create a change in consciousness and subjectivity, of the parameters of sport, in ways that resist the dominant values of competition, winning and elitism. Experimentation was valued, codes made up as play developed, and people were embraced as equal participants engaged in creating a play community (DeKoven 1976). The ingenuity of the New Games Movement lay in creating different spaces and practices and corresponds with Dawney's notions of 'communing', the process of making new worlds together and the sense of feeling part of something new, even if the actions and stakes are relatively small in the wider political game (Dawney 2014). The New Games Movement had shown the possibilities for challenging the conventions, styles and forms of sport, and the enjoyments to be had in creating new movement cultures. In the following section I provide some recent examples which suggest a continued legacy.

Countercultural sport and the 'spectacle of rebellion'

Whereas DeKoven has maintained that the New Games Movement is historically and political contingent to American society in the late 1960s and early 1970s (Pearce *et al.* 2007: 266), the spirit of the Movement is manifest in more recent examples. The presence of countercultural leisure practices, through rave scenes and music cultures (Riley *et al.* 2010) to guerrilla gardening (McKay 2011; Adams and Hardman 2014), has been observed in different urban contexts, though there are few examples from sport (for an exception, see Gilchrist and Ravenscroft 2012). While a full survey is not possible here, and other examples might include the social actions of groups like Reclaim the Streets or Critical Mass, whose uses of bicycles has posited a challenge to the 'right to the city' (Boykoff 2014: 122–123; Spinney 2010; Stevens 2007), I wish to provide two small and more contemporary examples of 'countercultural' sport: pillow fight club and urban golf.

Pillow fight club

Pillow fights performed in public spaces are a social phenomenon linked to the rise of flash mobs. Promoted via social media, these events, which take their name from Chuck Palahniuk's popular film *Fight Club* (where anyone could join and fight as long as they obeyed the rules), have become popular in towns and cities around the world, especially in North America and Europe. Participants learn about the fights via new media technologies, such as smartphones, and gather at both appointed times and at very short notice. Pillow fights have tended to mirror other flash mob pranks in their spontaneity, interactivity and humour (see Molnár 2014). The organisation of the event is largely through decentralised and anonymous networks. Hundreds of strangers assemble in streets or squares and when a whistle blows previously concealed pillows emerge and a good-natured fight ensues. The fights can last from a few minutes to several hours. Video recordings and photographs appear on social media websites such as Facebook and YouTube documenting the battles and showing public space transformed into a sea of feathers. International Pillow Fight Day was established in the mid-2000s and according to the *Wall Street Journal*, more than 5,000 people participated at the New York event in March 2008 (Athavaley 2008).[1] Pillow Fight Club is a natural heir to the New Games Movement, in particular the 'softwar' concept pioneered by Stewart Brand, in its promotion of free and fun mass participatory events centred on an intense, energetic, though pacified release of aggression and use of cushioned weapons (Fluegelman and Tembeck 1976: 9). As with other forms of urban play, bystanders are encouraged to play and the event becomes one of active public engagement as strangers escape normal social behaviours and routines and join in (Stevens 2007).

Some have claimed that this type of collective action lacks a political component (Molnár 2014); though in some cities there is an explicit attempt to claim a political agenda. The Urban Playground Movement, which originated in San Francisco, has adopted the 'Right to the City' (Harvey 2008), with its call to democratise the power to shape the urban experience, as its inspiration (Berton 2007; Plyushteva 2009). Its stated aim is:

> [T]o make these unique happenings in public space become a significant part of popular culture, partially replacing passive, non-social, branded consumption experiences like watching television, and consciously rejecting the blight in our cities.
>
> *(Urban Playground Movement, cited in*
> *Plyushteva 2009: 91)*

As such, Pillow Fight Club is positioned as a creative, non-instrumental and participative activity that challenges symbolic boundaries and the spatial differentiation of pleasure, blurring the acceptable, regulated and socially sanctioned uses of space for work, travel and consumption. Play becomes a form of praxis, deployed to critique, appropriate and expand the social meanings grafted onto urban space (Stevens 2007).

Urban golf

The routine of metropolitan life has also been disrupted by urban golf. In an affront to the traditional game, with its exclusive country clubs, expensive green fees, and strict dress codes, urban golf (or street golf) involves players using golf equipment in a city environment to create fun and engaging challenges. Clubs have formed in major cities, events held, and national associations have been established. A World Urban Golf Day was held in Portland, Oregon, in 2007 (Intini 2004; Lennard 2013). The popularity of this countercultural sport owes much to the invention of Cross Golf, created by German designer Torsten Schilling, who developed the sport in homage to the French/Belgian game of *jeu de crosse*, and which borrows from this game a spatial promiscuity. Cross Golf can be played across a diversity of locations – abandoned buildings, industrial ruins, inner-city streets, storm drains, from rooftops, in areas awaiting development – but the primary objective is fun. Fire hydrants, parked vehicles and office buildings are substitutes for water hazards, whilst drains, abandoned containers, garbage bins, open windows and doorways, become makeshift holes. Schilling formed Natural Born Golfers in 1992, which boasts a membership of 150,000, and organises events across various cities, from Paris to Kuala Lumpur (Lennard 2013). The sport has been taken up by organisations in the UK, such as StreetGames, as a way to encourage informal physical activity as barriers to participation are removed (StreetGames 2013), and companies like Microsoft, IBM and AmEX have included urban golf in a roster of corporate events. Schilling has claimed that urban golf appeals primarily to hipsters from the media and cultural industries. In France the sport is considered more of an underground activity, whilst in the UK it has had a firm presence in hipster enclaves in East London. The Shoreditch Urban Open was established in 2004; a more mainstream event, it attracts hundreds of applicants for its 64 places and includes stroke play scoring (Lennard 2013).

Whilst codification, regulation and commercial appropriation have crept into the urban golf movement, the sport has been seized upon by anarchist groups as a means of unsettling, or confusing, the normative socio-legal relationships that govern public space. The Space Hijackers, a self-proclaimed group of 'anarchitects' and culture jammers, operating in London since 1999, have deployed urban golf within their evolving catalogue of performative subversions (see Gilchrist and Ravenscroft 2012). The Space Hijackers engage in 'humor-based, antistate subversion that aims to refashion space for political purposes' (Boykoff 2014: 119). Their brand of clandestine rebellious spectacle involves 'projects' undertaken by 'agents', which are a form of 'psychological reclaiming' of use of public space, converting it from a space of economic functionality to one of social exchange (Engwitch 1999). The most famous 'projects' have been subterranean. The Circle Line parties on the London Underground, for instance, at their height involved 3,000 clubbers taking over a tube train on the network and fixing lights and sound systems to reproduce for free the atmosphere of a dance club. However, it is significant that many of the 'projects' undertaken by the Space Hijackers involve the street. Their interventions have been highly visible, with strangers invited to engage with the activity.

On 1 April 2006 the Space Hijackers hosted the Brighton to London Crazy Golf Tournament (www.spacehijackers.org). Its aim was 'to re-explore and re-imagine our surroundings via a different set of rules to the ones we usually live by'. The participants explored the landscape of the built environment, playing through and across streets. They blissfully ignored by-laws which prohibited ball games in Brighton's conservation areas and played through spaces primarily defined for retail and tourism. The spectacle involved thirty-five 'agents' equipped with costumes of finest Argyll and golf clubs of various shape and weight procured from charity shops.

The tournament was conducted with aero-balls rather than real golf balls in order to minimise the prospect of damage. Following the principles of Cross Golf, holes were improvised and the play coursed from pub to pub and rules were hastily produced to avoid the prospect of balls being crushed by passing buses. A police 'tail' directed them away from busy streets and the play took to the back streets and dog-legged around the lanes of Brighton. Returning to London, the action was completed in the evening when the winner of the competition was declared to be the first 'agent' to land a ball from Parliament Square over the fence and into the grounds of Parliament.

This example of urban golf is akin to Pillow Fight Club in the grafting of a sportscape onto the city environment as an act of subversion of the norms and regulations governing the use of public space. The politics is deliberately playful rather than revolutionary, with 'agents' exercising collective responsibility and care in their choice of locations, creation of informal rules and avoidance of confrontation with police. In the use of found objects it borrows too from later iterations of the New Games Movement, particularly DeKoven's 'Junkyard Sports', through its design of an informal cooperative game born from the imaginative possibilities of discarded objects and the materialities of the street (DeKoven 2004). In this regard, like the Pillow Fight Club, there is a repurposing of city streets for outdoor recreation (Wilson *et al.* 2012), though a subtle environmental politics is present too as the game establishes – even if only temporarily – new values related to sustainability alongside the social and pleasurable outcomes of participation.

Conclusion: 'counterculture' reappraised

This chapter has sought to detail cases of an alternative culture of sport, a 'countercultural' sport. The examples of pillow fighting and urban golf, and the games developed by the New Games Movement in the 1970s, suggest there is a rich vein of physical cultural practices which contrasts with high-achievement sport and prefigures a progressive politics of a 'right to the city', sustainability, pacifism, anti-materialism and anti-consumerism. And yet, as Ian McDonald (2009: 44) argues, such examples pose a problem for critical social scientists who live in hope that progressive ideals can translate into practical social change. The 'spectacles of rebellion' disrupt and provoke, but organisational and structural power is left unchanged. 'Countercultural' sport finds a cul-de-sac, too, in the wide variety of lifestyle sport where history has shown that the swift appropriation by media, cultural and sports industries nulli-fies their original radical potential, becoming incorporated into dominant ideological frame-works (ibid.). Although some participants are conscious of these processes and work through mainstream and outsider statuses, to suggest a continuation of 'countercultural' values and identities in more 'authentic' practices (Beal 1995), whether countercultural sport makes a genuine political contribution is a question that looms over any assessment of its radical potentiality.

Is Roszak therefore correct in acknowledging that the political prospects of counterculture equate to no more than a superficial gesture? This critique was updated by the philosopher Murray Bookchin (1995) in his concept of 'lifestyle anarchism', which identifies an 'introspec-tive personalism' geared more toward self-realisation than social change and a 'recycled situ-ationism' which displays a prelapsarian return to a 'petulantly infantile ego' (Bookchin 1995: 10–11). For Bookchin, the types of 'spectacles of rebellion' mentioned above would be no more than trendy posturing, which is antithetical to a radical politics and programmatic relevance. They serve instead as a safety valve for discontent that celebrates transience and, like other coun-tercultural forms of resistance, are liable to be incorporated and commodified.

However, Bookchin's critique of 'lifestyle anarchists' can be read as a denial of the productive nature of countercultural sport. It is important to resist the urge to dismiss these examples as frivolous and therefore of little political consequence, because they have meaning and import to organisers and participants on the grounds that they articulate utopian hopes and political futures, however incoherent and idealised they may be. Historians of sixties counterculture have begun to write more fully about the difficulties of creating intentional spaces and community-building from dreams of doing something alternative to a mainstream (Farber 2013). The power of counterculture as a concept here is to alert us to processes of 'communing' (Dawney 2014) or materialising 'everyday utopias' (Cooper 2012) through collective organisation and creation of new leisure spaces, while holding onto the idea that the possibilities of creating 'other' worlds may be nourishing to the people involved. Observing the 'politics of the act' present in countercultures of resistance means we attend to the ways in which people connect and play together, and the forms of personal and social transformation that may transpire (see Moore *et al.* 2014).

There is undoubtedly further work to be done on alternative sport cultures and the concept of counterculture is an important heuristic device to scholarship in this area. It alerts us to causes, values, ideals, visual styles, social actions, and cultures of resistance, present within sport and found in spaces where the challenge to 'the man' continues. Revealing and documenting examples of 'countercultural' sport will be key for furthering our understandings of the forms of political agency enacted through sport, as well as how some sporting participants seek to actualise utopian futures. A revolution in sport may not come through pillow fights in Trafalgar Square, but in these times of heightened security, licencing of spaces of protest, and feelings of disconnect between government and the people, deviation from expected patterns of conduct still mounts a cultural challenge to authority which can unsettle and unnerve the powerful.

Note

1 Pillow Fight Club has raised the attention of viral marketers and has been used by charities to help raise money and profile. There are some examples of mass pillow fights being called off over police fears for public safety. See Plyushteva (2009).

References

Adams, D. and Hardman, M. (2014) Observing guerrillas in the wild: Reinterpreting practices of urban guerrilla gardening. *Urban Studies*, 51(6): 1103-1119.
Athavaley, A. (2008) Students unleash a pillow fight on Manhattan. *Wall Street Journal*, 15 April. Accessed 15 December 2014. www.wsj.com/articles/SB120814163599712081.
Beal, B. (1995) Disqualifying the official: An exploration of social resistance through the subculture of skateboarding. *Sociology of Sport Journal*, 12(3): 252-267.
Bennett, A. (2014) Reappraising 'counterculture'. In S. Whiteley and J. Sklower (eds) *Countercultures and Popular Music*. Farnham: Ashgate, pp. 17-26.
Berton, J. (2007) Flash mob 2.0: Urban Playground Movement invites participation, *San Francisco Chronicle*, 10 November. Accessed 15 December 2014. www.sfgate.com/cgi-bin/article.cgi?f=/c/a/2007/11/09/MNMVT8UM9.DTL.
Bey, H. (1991) *TAZ, The Temporary Autonomous Zone, Ontological Anarchy, Poetic Terrorism*. New York: Autonomedia.
Bookchin, M. (1995) *Social Anarchism or Lifestyle Anarchism*. Stirling: AK Press.
Boykoff, J. (2014) *Activism and the Olympics: Dissent at the Games in Vancouver and London*. New Brunswick, NJ: Rutgers University Press.
Braunstein, P. and Doyle, M.W. (2002) Historicizing the American counterculture of the 1960s and '70s. In P. Braunstein and M.W. Doyle (eds) (2002) *Imagine Nation: The American Counterculture of the 1960s & '70s*. New York: Routledge, pp. 5-14.

Breines, W. (1982) *Community and Organisation in the New Left, 1962–1968: The Great Refusal.* New York: Praeger.

Brohm, J.-M. (1978) *Sport: A Prison of Measured Time.* London: Ink Links.

Clecak, P. (1983) *America's Quest for the Ideal Self: Dissent and Fulfillment in the 60s and 70s.* Oxford: Oxford University Press.

Cooper, D. (2012) *Everyday Utopias: The Conceptual Life of Promising Spaces.* Durham, NC: Duke University Press.

Dawney, L. (2014) Commoning: The production of common worlds. *Lo Squaderno,* 30: 33–55.

Day, R. (2004) From hegemony to affinity. *Cultural Studies,* 18(5): 716–748.

DeKoven, B. (1976) Creating the play community. In A. Fluegelman and S. Tembeck. (eds) *The New Games Book.* New York: A Headlands Press Book, Dolphin/Doubleday, pp. 41–42.

DeKoven, B. (1978) *The Well-Played Game: A Playful Path to Wholeness.* New York: Dolphin/Doubleday.

DeKoven, B. (2004) *Junkyard Sports.* Chicago, IL: Human Kinetics.

Den Tandt, C. (2014) The rock counterculture from modernist utopianism to the development of an alternative music scene. In S. Whiteley and J. Sklower (eds) *Countercultures and Popular Music.* Farnham: Ashford, pp. 81–94.

Duncombe, S. (2007) *Dream: Re-Imagining Progress Politics in an Age of Fantasy.* New York/London: The New Press.

Engwitch, D. (1999) *Street Reclaiming: Creating Liveable Streets and Vibrant Communities.* Gabriola Island, BC: New Society Publishers.

Eyerman, R. and Jamison, A. (1998) *Music and Social Movements.* Cambridge: Cambridge University Press.

Farber, D. (2013) Building the counterculture, creating right livelihoods: The counterculture at work. *The Sixties,* 6(1): 1–24.

Fluegelman, A. (1981) *More New Games.* New York: Doubleday.

Fluegelman, A. and Tembeck, S. (eds.) (1976) *The New Games Book.* New York: A Headlands Press Book, Dolphin/Doubleday.

Gilchrist, P. and Ravenscroft, N. (2012) Space hijacking and the anarcho-politics of leisure. *Leisure Studies,* 32(1): 49–68.

Goodman, P. (1960) *Growing up Absurd: Problems of Youth in the Organised Society.* New York: Random House.

Griggs, G. (2011) 'This must be the only sport in the world where most of the players don't know the rules': Operationalising self-refereeing in UK Ultimate Frisbee. *Sport in Society,* 14(1): 97–110.

Griggs, G. (2012) Why have alternative sports grown in popularity in the UK? *Annals of Leisure Research,* 15(2): 180–187.

Haenfler, R. (2013) Countercultures. In *The Wiley-Blackwell Encyclopedia of Social and Political Movements.* DOI: 10.1002/9781405198431.wbespm056.

Harvey, D. (2008) The right to the city. *New Left Review,* 53: 24–40.

Haunns, S. and Leach, D.K. (2007) Social movements and scenes: Infrastructures of opposition in civil society. In D. Purdue (ed.) *Civil Societies and Social Movements. Potentials and Problems.* London: Routledge, pp. 71–87.

Henderson, S. (2009) Crossing the line: Sport and the limits of civil rights protest. *International Journal of the History of Sport,* 26(1): 101–121.

Intini, J. (2004) Street tigers. *Maclean's,* 117(31): 82–83.

Jameson, F. (1984) Periodizing the 60s. In S. Sayres, A. Stephanson, S. Aronowitz and F. Jameson (eds.) *The 60s Without Apology.* Minneapolis, MN: University of Minnesota Press, pp. 178–209.

Jonasson, K. and Thiborg, J. (2010) Electronic sport and its impact on future sport. *Sport in Society,* 13(2): 287–299.

Klein, N. (1999) *No Logo.* London: Harper Collins.

Kuhn, G. (2011) *Soccer vs. the State: Tackling Football and Radical Politics.* Oakland, CA: PM Press.

Langman, L. (1971) Dionysus – child of tomorrow: Notes on post-industrial youth. *Youth and Society,* 3(1): 80–99.

Lasswell, H.D. (1950) *Power and Society: A Framework for Political Inquiry.* New Haven, CT: Yale University Press.

Le Fevre, D.N. (1988) *New Games for the Whole Family.* New York: Perigee Books.

Lefebvre, H. (1991) *The Production of Space.* Trans. D. Nicholson-Smith. Oxford: Blackwell.

Lennard, D. (2013) *Extreme Golf.* Chicago, IL: Sourcebooks.

Lipsitz, G. (1994) 'Who'll stop the rain?': Youth culture, rock 'n' roll, and social crises. In D. Farber (ed.) *The Sixties: From Memory to History.* Chapel Hill, NC: University of North Carolina Press, pp. 206–234.

Martin, G. (2002) Conceptualizing cultural politics in subcultural and social movement studies. *Social Movement Studies*, 1(1): 73–88.

McDonald, I. (2009) One-dimensional sport: Revolutionary Marxism and the critique of sport. In B. Carrington and I. McDonald (eds) *Marxism, Cultural Studies and Sport*. London: Routledge, pp. 32–48.

McKay, G. (1996) *Senseless Acts of Beauty. Cultures of Resistance since the Sixties*. London: Verso.

McKay, G. (2011) *Radical Gardening. Politics, Idealism and Rebellion in the Garden*. London: Frances Lincoln.

Midol, N. (1993) Cultural dissents and technological innovations in the 'whiz' sports. *International Review for the Sociology of Sport*, 28(1): 23–32.

Midol, N. and Broyer, G. (1995) Towards an anthropological analysis of new sport cultures: The case for 'whiz' sports in France. *Sociology of Sport Journal*, 12: 204–212.

Molnár, V. (2014) Reframing public space through digital mobilization: Flash mobs and contemporary urban youth culture. *Space and Culture*, 17(1): 43–58.

Moore, N., Church, A., Gabb, J., Holmes, C., Lee, A. and Ravenscroft, N. (2014) Growing intimate privatepublics: Everyday utopia in the naturecultures of a young lesbian and bisexual women's allotment. *Feminist Theory*, 15(3): 327–343.

Oriard, M. (1991) *Sporting with the Gods: The Rhetoric of Play and Game in American Literature*. Cambridge: Cambridge University Press.

Oriard, M. (2009) *Bowled Over: Big-Time College Football from the Sixties to the BCS Era*. Chapel Hill, NC: University of North Carolina Press.

Parsons, T. (1951) *The Social System*. New York: Free Press.

Pearce, C., Fullerton, T., Fron, J. and Morie, J.F. (2007) Sustainable play: Toward a New Game Movement for the digital age. *Games and Culture*, 2(3): 261–278.

Plyushteva, A. (2009) The right to the city and struggles over urban citizenship: Exploring the links. *Amsterdam Social Science*, 1(3): 81–97.

Renson, R. (2001) Messages from the future: Significance of sport and exercise in the third millennium. *European Journal of Sport Science*, 1(1): 1–17.

Rigaeur, B. (1981) *Sport and Work*. New York: Columbia University Press.

Riley, S., Morey, Y. and Griffin, C. (2010) The 'pleasure citizen': Analysing partying as a form of social and political participation. *Young*, 18(1): 33–54.

Rinehart, R. (2000) Emerging arriving sport: Alternatives to formal sport. In J. Coakley and E. Dunning (eds) *Handbook of Sport Studies*. London: Sage, pp. 504–519.

Rossinow, D. (1997) The New Left in the counterculture: Hypotheses and evidence. *Radical History Review*, 67: 79–120.

Roszak, T. (1969) *The Making of a Counter Culture*. Garden City, NY: Doubleday.

Sharpe, E.K. (2008) Festivals and social change: Intersections of pleasure and politics at a community music festival. *Leisure Sciences*, 30(3): 217–234.

Shaw, G. (1972) *Meat on the Hoof: The Hidden World of Texas Football*. New York: St Martin's Press.

Spinney, J. (2010) Rereading practices of urban cycling on London's South Bank. *Environment and Planning A*, 42: 2914–2937.

Stevens, Q. (2007) *The Ludic City: Exploring the Potential of Public Spaces*. London: Routledge.

Stranger, M. (2011) *Surfing Life: Surface, Substructure and the Commodification of the Sublime*. Farnham: Ashgate.

StreetGames (2013) *Street Golf in the StreetGames Network*. London: StreetGames.

Townsley, E. (2001) The 'sixties' trope. *Theory, Culture & Society*, 18(6): 99–123.

Walters, K. (2008) Ultimate spin: Contesting the rhetoric, countercultural ethos and commodification of the ultimate 'frisbee' sport, 1968–2000. Unpublished PhD dissertation, University of Iowa.

Wheaton. B. (2013) *The Cultural Politics of Lifestyle Sport*. London: Routledge.

Whiteley, S. and Sklower, J. (eds) (2014) *Countercultures and Popular Music*. Farnham: Ashford.

Wiggins, D.K. (1988) 'The future of college athletics is at stake': Black athletes and racial turmoil on three predominantly white university campuses, 1968–72. *Journal of Sport History*, 15(3): 304–333.

Williams, R. (1977) *Marxism and Literature*. Oxford: Oxford University Press.

Wilson, J.D., Tierney, P., Mi-Sook, K. and Zieff, S. (2012) Temporary parks? Sunday streets, serving the need for urban outdoor recreation. *Journal of Park and Recreation Administration*, 30(4): 38–52.

Yinger, J.M. (1960) Contraculture and subculture. *American Sociological Review*, 25(5): 625–635.

Zang, D. (2001) *Sports Wars: Athletes in the Age of Aquarius*. Fayetteville, AR: University of Arkansas Press.

32

THE POLITICS OF SPORT AND SOCIAL ENTERPRISE

Gavin Reid

This chapter examines the politics of the under-examined link between sport and social enterprise. Some argue that, with the current global dominance of neo-liberalism, we see sport's 'deep politics' come to the fore, through sweatshop labour practices, zero hours contracts, dominance of sponsors' rights over democratic freedoms, and the undermining of football club traditions by billionaire owners (Collins 2013). The aforementioned author argues that, while the exploitative relationship between sport and capitalism has never been so visible, sport supports the neo-liberal hegemony by offering an escape from poverty and opportunities for joyful self-expression and personal identification. As he argues, 'little wonder that corporate giants and local businesses alike seek to profit from such a potent cocktail' (p. 12). The fear of this is captured by Jarvie's (2003: 150) comment that 'if the public domain of Scottish sport is . . . invaded by the market domain of buying and selling, the primordial democratic promise of equal citizenship and sporting equity . . . will be negated'. However, social enterprise supporters embrace a more positive view of business arguing that, in the hands of social entrepreneurs, it can be harnessed for fundamental social change. They believe that innovative business models that see profit as a vehicle for the common good, not unlimited private or shareholder gain, generate levels of social capital not found in outdated business, charity and public sector models (Thorp 2015a, 2015b).

With much sport policy class-blind (Coalter 2013), there is a case for social business models operating in the margins of the public, private and voluntary sectors delivering a 'de-traditionalisation of sport' (Westerbeek 2010a). This is reinforced by Theeboom et al. (2010: 298) who state, 'there is increasing evidence that a commercial approach to delivering sport (products) to so called lower-chance communities . . . can bring excellent outcomes for producers and consumers', and we should not ignore 'the latent potential of sport as a source of social business ventures that may solve problems regarding self-sustainability'. Westerbeek (2010b: 1415) draws on the thoughts of one of the world's foremost social entrepreneurs (Muhammed Yunus) to state that, while sport business has witnessed 'a money grab by a wealthy few . . . it could shift some practices to social business activities'. With traditional voluntary sport clubs unable or unwilling to meet wider social goals, as dwindling volunteer numbers and administrative burdens focus minds on their core sport product, Theeboom et al. (2010: 1415) believe 'it will be up to the creativity and ingenuity of social entrepreneurs to come up with social sports business plans that successfully tackle social issues'. These social entrepreneurs have the passion, knowledge, experience and networks to develop under-used resources, attract funding and create partnerships of concerned people to meet the needs of the disadvantaged (Gilmore *et al.* 2011).

Scotland provides an interesting setting for this study, as it has an international reputation for being at the forefront of the social enterprise movement, building on long-standing links between business and society (Social Value Lab 2015a). One of the earliest social entrepreneurs (Robert Owen) demonstrated, in the early 1800s, a different (utopian socialist) relationship between business and society at New Lanark, where a compassionate regime attempted to improve individual character and deliver greater profits (Herman 2007; Paterson 2002). Currently, the Scottish National Party (SNP) Scottish government give political and economic support for the field, believing it furthers their aim of a fairer and more inclusive Scotland (Armour 2015). The country has a long tradition of instigating new types of businesses, mutuals, co-operatives and social enterprises that demonstrate the Scots' concern for a more egalitarian society where business is a 'means to this end not an end in itself' (Social Value Lab 2015b). However, such egalitarianism may be more myth than reality, with recent reports – *Elitist Scotland?* and *Is Scotland Fairer?* – highlighting the role of class, gender, disability and ethnic divisions within Scottish society (Social Mobility and Child Poverty Commission 2015; Equality and Human Rights Commission 2016).

Some argue that the relationship between business and society was undermined by the deadening hand of post-World War II state socialism, as its collectivist consensus produced a 'cradle to the grave' government dependency that reduced the Scots' capacity for innovation and entrepreneurship (Herman 2007; Monteith 2008) and restricted the business sector's contribution to society to charitable donations (Hamil and Morrow 2011). Negative perceptions of enterprise deepened from the 1980s because the entrepreneurial culture espoused by Margaret Thatcher was associated with greed and indifference to human suffering, encapsulated by her much-quoted view that there was 'no such thing as society', which contributed to the Conservative Party's 'toxic' brand in Scotland (Torrance 2009).

An often-quoted 'official' definition describes social enterprise as 'a business with primarily social objectives whose surpluses are principally reinvested for that purpose in the business or in the community, rather than being driven by the need to maximise profit for shareholders' (Department of Trade and Industry 2002: 1). While adopted in Scotland, Scottish stakeholders argued that it was not invested with sufficient authority to be effective and, with an English lobby seeking to keep definitions vague, it allowed private businesses with some emphasis on corporate social responsibility to masquerade as social enterprises diluting the brand. In response to the misuse of the term by: private companies seeking market opportunities; local authorities labelling their externalised – but council controlled – leisure trusts as social enterprises; and third sector charitable organisations with minimal social and trading objectives, Scottish stakeholders documented 'values and behaviours' through which organisations could identify each other and others identify them. It was hoped that, as mandatory rules encourage 'dispute and division', this voluntary code of practice (The Code) provided conditions for a self-regulating community. Key characteristics of a Scottish social enterprise are: it cannot be a subsidiary of a public sector body; it is driven by values in its mission and business approaches; it trades in a marketplace with the primary objective of social or environmental benefit; it is a trading business that seeks financial independence; and has an asset lock on its trading surplus and residual assets (Social Value Lab 2015a). Central to the Scottish narration of social enterprise is the asset lock, which guarantees that organisations do not distribute dividends – with 100 per cent of profits reinvested in their social or environmental mission – and, on dissolution, assets are reinvested in an organisation with similar objectives. To supporters this positions social enterprises as having a fundamental goal of shifting how society operates, with business working for the common good not the unlimited gain of a few (Social Value Lab 2015a, 2015b). Scotland's social enterprise narrative also embraces the social democratic phrase 'more than profit', with its positive initial emphasis highlighting that, while profit is crucial, its goal is social change (Jones and Keogh 2006).

Having met many representatives of sport social enterprises, I am struck by their innovative approaches to addressing unmet sporting and social needs and genuine passion for their local geographical and/or sporting communities. I have listened to uplifting stories of young people's lives turned around by sport and practitioners' incredible commitment in exceptionally difficult circumstances. However, I believe that political analysis, which asks the critical questions 'who gets what, when and how', combined with sociological analysis, which acknowledges the role of structural processes on individual values and behaviours, shows disputes and divisions hidden within this 'Scottish approach' to doing business. While heart-warming stories from social enterprises make conversations about limitations and failure problematic (Ziegler 2009), these 'silent narratives' provide a necessary counter to the sector's depoliticising grand narrative – its 'image of goodness' (Scott and Teasdale 2012) – and one-sided, quasi-religious 'individualised, messianic script that incorporates a model of harmonious social change' (Nicholls and Cho 2006: 87). Without this, as the aforementioned authors argue, social entrepreneurship mirrors the problem with entrepreneurship studies more generally, notably 'the urge to de-politicise, trivialise and individualise complex social processes' (ibid.: 99). My chapter therefore reflects Grix's (2010) argument that the academic study of sport and politics should shift from its 'hobby' status amongst political scientists to the mainstream, as sport is 'a microcosm of wider political life' and acts as a 'lens for understanding wider politics and policy'. To illustrate this, it first highlights key issues within academic writings on the related concepts of social enterprise, social entrepreneurship and social entrepreneurs. It then critically reflects on these debates through a case study of ongoing research on a previously local government-run sport centre now operated by a local basketball consortium operating as a social enterprise.

Social enterprise

The popularity of social entrepreneurship as a solution to deep-rooted social problems is underpinned by the belief that somehow social and business goals can be successfully combined (Teasdale 2012) for an altruistic capitalism (Tan *et al.* 2005). My interest in this 'inherently political activity' (Cho 2006: 38) began in the late 1990s when left-leaning think tanks identified social enterprises as the organisational vehicle of New Labour's 'third way' ideology (Teasdale 2010, 2011), with Leadbetter's (1997) influential *The Rise of the Social Entrepreneur* drawing on the manager within the Youth Charter for Sport to illuminate the concept. To Leadbetter, a bureaucratic and unresponsive welfare state could not respond to joblessness, illiteracy, family break-up and drug and alcohol problems, with the solution being an active, problem-solving welfare system that facilitates social capital by 'encouraging people to take control over their lives' (ibid.: 12). The necessary social innovation would be delivered by social enterprises existing between the family and the state, initiated by driven, ambitious and charismatic social entrepreneurs with the 'ability to identify under-utilised resources – people, buildings, equipment – and find ways of putting them to use to satisfy unmet social needs' (ibid.: 12). However, with Scottish Labour's 'Old Labour' values linking New Labour 'enterprise' with the despised Thatcherite ideology, this reduced the traction of social enterprise in Scotland until its recent embrace by the SNP (Roy *et al.* 2014).

In theory, the traditional conservatism of the voluntary and public sectors could be offset by social entrepreneurs' outward-looking attempts 'to discover, define and exploit opportunities . . . to enhance social wealth by creating new ventures or managing existing organisations in an innovative manner' (Zahra *et al.* 2009: 519). Social entrepreneurs assume risk from the significant culture change needed to develop a business-like focus, and demonstrate innovative thinking via a greater focus on the external environment and stakeholder concerns (Walsham *et al.* 2008). Supporters champion their ability to address 'wicked problems' in deprived areas better than public and private sectors, through a deep appreciation of, and passion for, their client groups and integration of stakeholders in their governance arrangements (HM Treasury 1999). However critics argue that the messianic image around social entrepreneurship, which postulates that social change can be delivered by 'white, male heroes' without tension (Ogbor 2000) silences the role of structural factors and the state in this political process of narration (Dey and Steyaert 2010, 2012).

Sport social enterprises: delivering sustainable community sport?

An interesting example of a sport social enterprise in Edinburgh is the Crags Community Sport Centre. The facility is located in the Dumbiedykes estate, which has high levels of unemployment and income deprivation, with hospital admissions for drugs and alcohol misuse among locals well above the national average (Scottish Neighbourhood Statistics 2011). The area took its name from an Academy for Deaf and Dumb people, built in 1760, and known locally as 'Dummie Hoose'. The facility only lasted until 1783 but, by then, the area's name 'Dummiedykes' had been established locally. However, highlighting the impact of social class on ways of speaking (Bourdieu 1984), middle-class outsiders pronounce the area Dum – bie – dykes – overcoming the lack of political correctness within the working-class habitus. In the early to mid-twentieth century the area was home to printers, biscuit factories and breweries and a community spirit, which existed despite severe overcrowding and poverty in its slum housing. The collapse of one of the area's tenement flats precipitated Edinburgh Council's slum clearance programme and the creation of a 'new Dumbiedykes' in the early 1960s. Some locals talk of a period of stability between 1960 and 1980, disrupted by the election of the Thatcher government in 1979 whose neo-liberal ideology championed a 'right to buy' policy and private home ownership over council housing. This saw the least disadvantaged purchase their home and then, with subsequent New Labour administrations not building more social housing, the remaining stock was given to those most in need; notably single parents with dependent children and those released from institutions (Jones 2011). Some locals also chose to let their property, with the result being a transitory population who often did not look after their homes, in contrast to the women who polished the stairs of the former tenements. Neo-liberal housing policy, designed to undermine and divide working-class identity, meant this estate became a social dumping ground, leaving the Crags to address social problems that were politically made (ibid.). In Edinburgh, the continued ideological dominance of Thatcherite neo-liberalism has widened social inequality (Connell 2015) and justified a class-inspired vilification of Dumbiedykes' 'undeserving poor', accentuated by the latter's housing having stunning views of the city's Salisbury Crags. Dominant groups within the city, what Bourdieu terms the cultural arbitrary, have given Dumbiedykes' residents a public reputation for 'self-inflicted' problems of 'Chav' violence, drugs and worklessness, with this demonisation (ibid.) making Edinburgh's increasing social inequality more palatable to its middle classes.

Locals are critical of Edinburgh University's role in the area's decline, highlighting that, since the 1960s, its purchase of land and demolition of local amenities – to build accommodation blocks for affluent international students – had ripped the heart out of the community. Some argued that university senior management were 'acting like capitalists' by creating a 'student community' which limited affordable homes for locals. One local talked of a 'student ghetto' where, compared with previous years when students developed sports clubs for local youngsters, students now contributed little to the community. This questions whether an apparent decline in student altruism stems from a 'me first' Thatcherite-inspired individualism and/or the need to pay off tuition fees initiated by a neo-liberal corporate university (Giroux 2012).

Highlighting the importance of looking beyond dominant narratives of heroic male social entrepreneurs (Ogbor 2000) the 20-year campaign for a sport centre was led by two working-class older women who used connections with those from the Dumbiedykes/ Southside area – who had achieved success in sport or business – to raise £200,000 for the facility. The women also received support from the supporter networks of the city's two professional football teams (Heart of Midlothian and Hibernian) as both had roots in the Southside. Another £1 million was provided by sportscotland – the national agency for sport in Scotland – and an independent grant-making body (The Robertson Trust). The latter was established in 1961 by the Robertson sisters, who donated shares in their family's whisky business to fund charitable organisations delivering positive change in Scottish communities. The Crags' attempts to reduce local social problems thus depends (in part) on the profits of a global company's alcohol sales. However, while successful in getting a facility built, the elderly working-class management group struggled to move from a campaigning mind-set to one capable of developing a sustainable business model in a deprived area. It was perceived that the community-led facility 'failed' because its open membership structure – reflective of community sport's bottom-up democratic ethos (Hylton 2013) – produced a 'business run by committee', when what was required was a new business model led by a small team of trustees with the knowledge, contacts and skills needed for sustainability. The community management group prioritised activities valued by the local working class community – such as football and trampolining – but they lacked access to social capital networks within surrounding middle-class areas to provide financial sustainability. A local Member of Parliament tried to overcome this by cultivating partnerships with Edinburgh University and local financial institutions, believing that this would transform the centre's fortunes. However these attempts were unsuccessful, with a perception from some locals that the university was using sport to market itself to financially lucrative overseas students. With the university championing its Global Academy of Social Justice, this should not deflect from its potential role in local community injustices. Indeed, its use of privately educated Olympic medal winning alumni (e.g. Sir Chris Hoy) in its marketing may help legitimate a system contributing much to societal inequality. From the above we can see that, while the grand narrative of social enterprise is overwhelmingly positive (Nicholls and Cho 2006), the context within which it originates is antagonistic and linked to politics and power.

Facing financial difficulties, Crags' supporters persuaded Edinburgh Council to add it, in 2010, to Edinburgh Leisure's facility portfolio. Edinburgh Leisure is a trust set up to manage the city's sport and leisure facilities on behalf of the council. However, it was perceived that the city-wide nature of Edinburgh Leisure could not address specific local concerns, while staff employed – on relatively low pay – lacked the motivation to engage with 'troublesome' youth. The effect of the latter was seen when local youths invaded the gym and hurled abuse at customers. Interestingly, Edinburgh Leisure defines itself as a social enterprise – which balances the heart and the pound – but this is disputed by those in the social enterprise community, who point to its continued reliance on council funding and councillor representation on its board as undermining the independence required of social enterprises. While Simmons (2008) argued that leisure trusts harnessed the power of social enterprise to deliver greater innovation, dynamism and a different attitude towards risk than when under council control, many local actors felt that trust staff were wedded to bureaucratic processes that minimised risk and hindered innovation. With Edinburgh Council needing to make £126 million of savings in response to government austerity measures, Edinburgh Leisure faced funding cuts in 2010 of £347,000, on top of the previous year cut of £349,000. As a result the Crags, with its low usage levels, was earmarked for closure. While the local community may not use public sports facilities, attempts to close them can meet fierce local resistance (Pringle and Cruttenden 2001; Reid 2014). Thus, with outright closure politically unacceptable, a procurement process was initiated for an asset transfer to an alternative delivery partner. The facility was closed in 2010 and boarded up for a year. As the process was a reactive one, which lacked attempts at building the capacity of local disadvantaged groups to bid, it was aligned towards affluent professionals with the time and skills to develop an acceptable business plan. A small group of parents from a local basketball club met round a kitchen table to develop a new business model for the Crags. This needed, they argued, to contrast significantly from Edinburgh Leisure's failed model and embrace key skill sets of the group (e.g. architect, fundraising consultant, chief executive, facility manager) who would become, as one supporter commented, the 'dream team' of 'smart people' who became the new trustees. The group created an innovative partnership between Boroughmuir Blaze basketball club, the sport's governing body (Basketball Scotland) and Castle Rock Edinvar Housing Association – operating as a Scottish Charitable Incorporated Organisation – which won the procurement process and took over the facility under a 25-year lease from the council at £1 a year.

The initial aim was to create a 'home' for the basketball club and overcome problems in obtaining affordable access to local government sport facilities. However, to supporters it had grown into something much more and was now about, as one commented, 'the development of people to give them a step-up'. Given that community sport is characterised by 'egos, vested interests and power struggles' (Oakley and Green 2001) the partnership between the governing body and social enterprise was initially controversial, with another basketball club critical of the former's apparent favouritism towards the latter. The benefits of being small, in terms of responding quickly to changing societal trends, was complemented by the partnership with the local housing association, whose large size gave the Crags economies of scale in maintenance costs crucial to financial sustainability. However, partnerships that did not happen were more important than those that did. With the local government spending a small amount on merely re-commissioning the building, rather than enabling local poorer groups to take advantage of empowerment opportunities from asset transfer, the Crags' initial operation predominantly benefitted affluent groups. Taking a more co-production approach to service delivery (King 2013, 2014) the council could have used savings from asset transfer – and economies of scale in energy costs – to aid the centre's initial income flow. Without this, it initially prioritised financial sustainability over social concerns. A co-production model would also have maintained links to council sport staff who, embracing ideas of civic professionalism (Houlihan 2001), sought to use their knowledge and networks to give identity and dignified representation to local poorer groups. Not having this meant that Edinburgh Leisure's inclusive youth work programme (Open All Hours), which ran at the centre on a Friday and Saturday night, was discontinued and transferred to one of their nearby facilities.

Much of the Crags' success was rightfully attributed to the passion and expertise of the social entrepreneur driving the process. However, such positive language ignores feelings of isolation and stress felt by someone who, as the only staff member, performed functions previously done by a local authority centre manager – deemed 'solidly non developmental' (Houlihan and White 2001) – and development officer. While studies highlight how sport staff with social democratic values struggle when working within contemporary organisations prioritising neo-liberal financial concerns (Cureton and Frisby 2011), here the clash of ideologies is played out in the mind of the social entrepreneur. Lacking local government support, the social entrepreneur needed to develop expertise in boiler maintenance and other facility management concerns before social issues could be addressed. Given his passion towards 'sport for development', this initial relegation of social goals was stressful. Supporters argued that the social entrepreneur's passion for business and 'sport for development' delivered quality levels beyond that possible under the bureaucratic local government business model, where staff merely delivered 'a job' within a subsidised facility. However, having left a relatively secure job within mainstream sport, the manager faced greater financial risk, and risk to his standing in the local sporting community, if the organisation faltered. Positive language surrounding social enterprise also ignores its vulnerability should the practitioner leave or fall ill, and the impact of the inevitable long working hours on family and friends.

In the beginning, the social entrepreneur did not recognise the organisation as a social enterprise, perceiving it as 'just a project with no guiding philosophy but the more I got into it the more comfortable I've become with the label'. However the weak political position of sport organisations means they are 'policy takers not makers' (Houlihan and White 2001) keen to adopt fashionable concepts – like social capital and social enterprise – without appreciating that the political and social processes aiding their comfort increase others' discomfort. It was felt that basketball had to become more entrepreneurial as UK Sport's 'no compromise' funding regime, which saw money follow medals (Grix 2009), disadvantaged team sports while favouring middle-/upper-class individual sports like equestrianism that lacked basketball's mass participation base and ability to reach inner-city black and ethnic minority youth. There was frustration that, with the UK Government's welfare reform policies cutting benefits for the poor, 'sport for development' was subservient to a 'sport for sport's sake' agenda, with the latter's hidden and questionable assumptions surrounding often privately educated Olympic medalists encouraging mass participation (Outram 2015) bolstered by articulate individuals like Lord Sebastian Coe.

Reflecting cultural factors influencing social enterprises, the social entrepreneur was aided by his Kiwi 'do-it–yourself' mentality as the isolation of New Zealand fostered an innovative small business mind-set (Grant 2008). The social entrepreneur was also aided by the 'latent value' of his local sport contacts, his Business degree and practical experience in his father's business. Many local actors contrasted his entrepreneurial outlook with Scottish sport development staff whose reliance on government funding delivered less innovative provision. However, highlighting another hidden tension within social enterprise, the social entrepreneur stated that, having this mind-set within a dominant public sector orientation caused him trouble in the past as the two cultures clashed. This may occur in the future as, with the Crags achieving visibility as a successful asset transfer, it received calls for advice from those seeking to go down this increasingly popular route. In what could be seen as an innovative step, it created a consultancy to financially gain from knowledge accumulated on asset transfers. While Thompson (2008: 160) argues that social entrepreneurs' commendable desire to give free advice to others undermines focus and damages their enterprise, others may argue that this generates trust, which will be reciprocated to aid their enterprise.

Without local government support, the facility's start-up phase was entrepreneurial in selling parking spaces to local businesses, attracting non-sport funding to transform its basketball court and lighting, and in establishing partnerships with local schools to deliver PE and

Active Schools' sessions to drive revenue during critical day periods. Entrepreneurial behaviour also involved creating a sustainable niche in the local sporting market through an innovative programme – with basketball as the anchor tenant – and targeted partnerships with under-served market segments (e.g. hip hop, roller derby and aeriel yoga clubs) deemed on the margins of mainstream provision. This fitted their vision of a social enterprise taking an alternative and fresh approach to community sport. However, within this, tensions exist, with studies on roller derby highlighting its potential inaccessibility to disadvantaged groups (Breeze 2013), while – like the centre's focus on pole dancing – feminists question if it is empowering or disempowering women (Carlson 2010; Finley 2010).

While Coalter (1999) stressed that sport providers are successful when they 'flow with the flow' of wider social trends, notably by shifting towards a gym culture to reflect greater societal individualism and a postmodern emphasis on 'the look', the Crags saw Edinburgh Leisure's gym model as financially unsustainable. To reduce staff costs, a keyholder system allowed the clubs to use the facility in the evenings and weekends when it was closed to the public. By reducing costs, management could charge cheaper prices than local competitors and give clubs a level of ownership and trust crucial to community sports development (Jarvie 2003). Supporters argued that the keyholder system would be impossible within risk-averse local government, where clubs are mere recipients of a space from those delivering a 'job'. Here, customers became volunteers and were integrated within the sustainable business model. Linked to the keyholder system was the creation of a 'welcoming' reception space with the aim of developing social capital in and amongst clubs using the facility. It was argued that the 'simple provision of tea and coffee' within this space before and after club sessions 'enabled conversations amongst parents and coaches' that delivered bonding and bridging social capital within and between clubs. However, the domination of sports clubs by more affluent groups (Reid 2012) reduces their likelihood of developing social capital for all (Morgan 2013), as conversations undertaken and space created may align with middle-class norms that exclude lower socioeconomic groups. As Skille (2011) argues, sports clubs can be 'specialised in interest and reach' and may develop social capital for small groups with certain interests, not the wider community.

While Putnam's positive and democratic conceptualisation of social capital – that networks have value for all (Field 2003) – was embraced by Crags' supporters, Bourdieu's more critical reading of social capital and social class offers insights into the facility's winners and losers. With the Crags facing fierce local competition from Edinburgh Leisure and Edinburgh University sports facilities, and being located on a postcode not deprived enough to access significant social funding, their initial operations mirrored Macmillan's (2011: 110) view that voluntary sector organisations

> may be interested (and/or compelled by competitive pressures) to secure and retain the involvement of people who can bring particular kinds of resources/forms of capital (such as knowledge, technical expertise, connections and capabilities). In so doing they may simultaneously side-line or frustrate the involvement of those who might not be able to contribute as much, or who might disrupt or compromise their activities.

Securing the involvement of a fundraising consultant was crucially important, as she had the cultural capital to 'play the funding game' beyond limited sports funding. It was felt that, while including local disadvantaged people as trustees was more democratic, the 'failure' of the initial community-led model justified the closed governance arrangement. However, while one local actor stated that 'it depends how success is evaluated', it also depends how failure is evaluated. The lack of capacity building by Edinburgh Council for the working-class community model was ignored in the organisation's dominant political narrative, with the possibility that working class 'failure' is influenced by unacknowledged middle-class prejudices also ignored.

The lack of local state support and the non-deprived postcode meant that the Crags' initial two years was dominated by financial objectives, with bookings paying commercial rates prioritised over those potentially delivering social impact. Its location at the enterprise end of the social enterprise spectrum reflected Macmillan's (2011: 111) comments that, facing competitive funding regimes, voluntary organisations are pressurised towards 'high volume "quick wins"' . . . and may prioritise work with service users that are in some sense "easy to help" and thereby push the "hardest to help" further back in the queue'. However, having obtained a level of financial sustainability, staff now sought to develop their social programme which involves low cost drop-in basketball sessions for local youth in-between club bookings, free use of the 'kick-pitch' to the rear of the building for mentored youth work and self-organised sessions, and free use of a traverse climbing wall on the outside of the facility. However, despite his best efforts, there was only so much one social entrepreneur could do in terms of community engagement, particularly when also facing demands from articulate middle-class sports club members. The introduction of Friday afternoon football on the kick-pitch was deemed an opportunity to prevent, or at least delay, the alcohol consumption of local disadvantaged school children, who could otherwise misuse Edinburgh's half-day Friday school opening policy. Another initiative involved a young leaders project for 12 young people (aged 15–18) who, over nine months, would work with business mentors to develop and implement ideas for new facility projects. It was advertised that this would provide resources (e.g. a certificate and written feedback) useful in young people's further education/work applications. The programme cost was £180. The business partner provided a scholarship fund for those needing support, with the website advertising that 'Any family in this position is strongly encouraged to have a confidential conversation' with the Development Manager. It would be interesting to examine if the cultural capital benefits of this reactive process are accumulated by more affluent youngsters, encouraged by their 'sharp elbowed' middle-class parents who seek to differentiate their children from others within their class and from the working class. The above parallels Coakley's (2011) comment that, for those in poverty, the 'development' in youth sport development may revolve around social control while, for affluent youth, it links to achievement and upward mobility. It also questions whether this sport-based intervention is part of the city's social control policies (Spaaij 2009) and thus geared towards males over females and the young over the elderly.

While those running the Crags had a 'social conscience to deliver social objectives', adopting Bourdieu's critical reading of social capital – which appreciates the role of social structure under-played in Putnam's conceptualisation (Field 2003) – highlights hidden and unconscious processes potentially maintaining middle-class advantage. While Putnam's functional and democratic reading stresses the extensiveness of bonds and bridges between individuals and communities, Bourdieu emphasises the aforementioned status of connections within networks, and how particular socioeconomic conditions create differing habitus for social classes that produce differing ways of acting, speaking and attitudes to the body (Molnar and Kelly 2013; Hastings and Matthews 2015). Such socialised norms direct behaviour and thoughts and – in the quest for distinction – facilitate social closure over social connections (Bourdieu 1984). To Bourdieu, the distribution of social capital is therefore class-related and can be used to reproduce class advantage (Blackshaw and Long 2005). Thus, while Crags' supporters felt that having basketball as the 'anchor tenant' aided financial sustainability, this non-contact and facility-based sport is anchored within a middle-class habitus,which may exclude local working-class youth unless it moves in a more 'street' direction. The provision of aerial yoga may also chime with a middle-class (aesthetic) attitude to the body, accentuated by its location within a 'studio' rather than gym.

Highlighting the source of hidden narratives within the positive social enterprise grand narrative, Bourdieu demonstrates how middle-class advantage flows from unconscious processes that occur as 'the system is allowed to take its course' (Hastings and Matthews 2015). Without the local state building decision-making capacity amongst deprived groups, or offering ongoing support for the Crags after asset transfer, the SNP's Community Empowerment legislation may undermine social capital within and between communities and 'valorise Bourdieusian forms which emphasise connectivity to power and influence' (Hastings and Matthews 2015: 555). As the aforementioned authors argue, without this the local context advantages those who can play the game, or have links to those who can play it for them. Bourdieu's theories critique the 'more than profit' language of Scottish social enterprise. The positive narrative of using financial profit for social change ignores how the 'profits of membership' of networks are not available to everyone, with all capitals – social, physical, cultural or symbolic – resources to be collected and exploited. It is their exclusivity in the ongoing battle for distinction from other classes – to thwart not encourage social change – that underpins their importance (Blackshaw and Long 2005).

Bourdieu's sociology contrasts middle-class concerns about the violent conduct of local working class youth – when they invaded the facility when run by Edinburgh Leisure – with the silence ('doxa') over the 'symbolic violence' of dominant groups over the disadvantaged as the unequal social system is allowed to take its course within the facility's new space. While much is made of the club keyholder system generating trust and ownership, the fact that keys are not given to local disadvantaged groups suggests a symbolic violence that 'normalises the marginality of the poor who are denied the kind of trust that they could manage public resources for themselves' (Blackshaw and Long 2005: 252). Thus, rather than conceptualise social enterprises as radical and progressive business models delivering social change without tension (Dey and Steyaert 2010), they encapsulate 'a competitive struggle between social agents who embody class-based power asymmetries' (Hastings and Matthews 2015: 548). While Crags' trustees have a social conscience to use sport for social change, Bourdieu (1984) highlights how cultural alignment and empathy between practitioners and users may give advantages to middle classes that exist 'below the level of consciousness', as the space created comfortably fits forms of capital and habitus enjoyed by them. Such processes are not acknowledged by politicians who often conceptualise sport as a photo opportunity and 'good news' story. Highlighting this, the SNP's Minister for Local Government and Community Empowerment visited the Crags – in the week the Community Empowerment Bill was passed – to state that, while there was still a role for local government in providing services, the keyholder system provided a trust-based approach that 'encourages a sense of shared ownership and brings clubs together with the common interest of having the best centre possible'. To him it showed what was possible when 'ordinary people pitch-in and get the facilities they want by doing it themselves'. However, Bourdieu's theories highlight exclusionary processes behind the 'new energy' unleashed when local communities control local facilities. The positive emphasis on trust emanating from the keyholder system ignores how, drawing on Bourdieu, in our class system trust 'will inevitably be exploited for gain in the practice of symbolic power (including symbolic violence) and symbolic exchange' (Blackshaw and Long 2005: 18). By not requiring local government to promote the participation of disadvantaged groups – and by adopting a homogenous view of 'the community' – the SNP's Community Empowerment Bill ignores inequalities between communities, which could widen socioeconomic inequalities (Hastings 2015).

Conclusion

The above discussion questions the positive grand narrative of social enterprise, which sees it as a progressive business blueprint for fundamental social change without tension (Dey and Steyaert 2010). The passion and expertise of people linked to the Crags created a vibrant space that, without their efforts, would have been lost to the community. However, fairy tale narratives of a heroic (male) social entrepreneur with a 'Robin Hood' business model taking from the rich and giving to the poor not only ignores the role of women as activists, philanthropists and trustees, but also the divisive role of social class and the state in mitigating radical change (Ziegler 2009). The positive 'win-win' language of social enterprise supporters rests on Putnam's overly democratic and functional view of social capital and sport's contribution to it. Drawing on Bourdieu's more critical theories of social capital and social class exposes the silences (doxa) towards how dominant groups (the cultural arbitrary) define: the neighbourhood's 'self-inflicted' reputation for violence; what is a 'progressive' and 'failed' business model; and who should be keyholders and trustees and who should not. Highlighting the violence of local deprived youngsters encourages a fear, not understanding, of the local working class, while attributing it to Edinburgh Leisure's bureaucratic business model ignores how the loss of local industries and dignified work may encourage local youth to seek 'cool respect' via spectacular violence (Blackshaw and Long 2005; Coalter 2013). Further research is needed with local people to examine whether being linked to a 'chav' estate (Jones 2011) and 'failed' business model, while not being accepted as trustees or keyholders, exacerbates feelings of inadequacy: what Sennett and Cobb (1973) term *The Hidden Injuries of Class*.

The above symbolic violence was enabled by the local government as, by limiting support to re-commissioning the building over developing decision-making capacities of the locally deprived, the system was 'allowed to take its course', facilitating the comfortable integration of middle-class cultural capital and habitus (Hastings and Matthews 2015) to this sport social enterprise field. However, we must also question why the SNP government does not compel local authorities to undertake such capacity building and whether this, together with its homogenous view of 'community', encourages photo opportunities with 'apolitical' sport social enterprises to deflect from socially unjust outcomes of its Community Empowerment Act and cost cutting neo-liberalism (Mooney and Poole 2004; Mooney *et al.* 2008).

The positive emphasis on 'more than profit' within the Scottish social enterprise narration ignores how 'profits of membership' of sports clubs and social networks are not available to everyone, and can aid social closure not fundamental social change (Blackshaw and Long 2005). While social enterprise representatives exhibited a social conscience towards poorer groups, without alterations to the wider system – requiring politics and appreciation of power not innovative business models – unconscious processes of cultural alignment and empathy between them and middle-class local professionals and users (Hastings and Matthews 2015) may disadvantage poorer groups. There is a danger that if 'can do' social entrepreneurs let their passion for social change deflect from the damaging role of social structure and neo-liberal politics on the social problems they seek to address – perceiving social enterprise to be rewarding and empowering (Amin 2009) – they take responsibility for the divisive values and behaviour stemming from our very British class war (Jones 2011), creating stress for them and their families (Dempsey and

Saunders 2010). The denigrating of 'risk-averse' local government by social enterprises ignores the more fundamental risk that they deepen the role of business in society and encourage an exaggerated focus on a few 'easier to reach' deprived youngsters, silencing a socialist vision of bettering conditions for the working-class community.

Following Coalter (2013), if the arguments in Wilkinson and Pickett's (2009) seminal book *The Spirit Level: Why Equal Societies Almost Always Do Better* are right, they highlight major weaknesses in the Crags' attempts to address local social problems. Its asociological focus ignores how widening inequality harms social relations, undermines trust, limits cooperation, and creates a divisive focus on status competition linked to feelings of superiority and inferiority and self-blame for not achieving in supposedly meritocratic societies. These socio-psychological consequences of inequality were hidden by the Crags' political narration emphasising (1) an absence of skill sets within the 'failed' working-class business model, and (2) Edinburgh Leisure's bureaucratic business model, which encouraged youth violence. To fully appreciate the politics of this social enterprise, further research will examine the changing nature of the local working-class community to see if the decline in manufacturing employment and shifting government housing policy lessened community belonging and trust. It will assess whether an understanding of the locally deprived has been hindered by middle-class fears of the Dumbiedykes 'estate' and negative media representations of the working class in 'poverty porn' television programmes. This will review Coalter's (2013) argument that, with social mobility defined in terms of embracing middle-class lifestyles, this downplays working-class cultures and, with the system preventing mobility and encouraging a demonisation of the poor to justify widening inequality, it points to 'a possible fundamental contradiction between such dominant socio-cultural values, attitudes and experiences and those policies aimed at ill-defined "inclusion" or increased sports participation based on rather managerialist analyses of "constraints"' (ibid.: 17).

However, as Blackshaw and Long (2005) argue, Bourdieu's sociology highlights a politics that could confront the conditions of poverty through (middle-class) new cultural intermediaries (Bourdieu 1984) – seen here as sport social entrepreneurs embracing community development approaches – whose 'cool' sporting brand, use of working-class cultural capital, articulate spokespersons, business acumen, empathy with the deprived, and access to affluent sporting and social networks could facilitate communication and mutual respect between their organisations and 'hard to reach' individuals while maintaining the necessary 'cool distance'. This may provide a counter-culture to what, for deprived youth, are hostile 'Establishment' services (e.g. social work), who (they believe) seek to remove them from their families. If delivered through a sport that connects to a working class habitus (e.g. football, boxing or street basketball) then social mobility for some may occur. To extend this 'ripple effect' of social enterprise (Schwartz 2012), Edinburgh University academics could publicise sport social entrepreneurs' 'happening world' (Featherstone 1991: 44) to local working-class people through free courses, and to our local, national and international contacts encouraging fundamental change (Tucker 2013). This could legitimate the academic study of social business within sociologically dominated Leisure Studies.

Without this, academic discussion will remain led by uncritical management and business schools (Dey and Steyaert 2012) and a focus on the politically safe terrain of social enterprise definitions and conceptual debate. Universities must act as forums to debate and resolve the inevitable tensions that surface when attempting fundamental social change. The Scottish preference for powerful individuals documenting social enterprise 'values and behaviours' for a voluntary code of conduct and self-regulating community avoids such disputes, potentially contributing to a neo-liberal ideology so all pervasive as to be virtually invisible (Davidson *et al.* 2010).

References

Amin, A. (2009) Extraordinary ordinary: Working in the social economy. *Social Enterprise Journal*, 5(1): 30–49.

Armour, R. (2015) Revealed: Scots social enterprise leads the world. *Third Force News*, 2 September 2015.

Blackshaw, T. and Long, J. (2005) What's the Big Idea? A critical exploration of the concept of social capital and its incorporation into leisure policy discourse. *Leisure Studies*, 24(3): 239–258.

Bourdieu, P. (1984) *Distinction: A Social Critique of the Judgement of Taste*. London: RKP.

Breeze, M. (2013) Analysing 'seriousness' in roller derby: Speaking critically with the serious leisure perspective. *Sociological Research Online*, 18(4): 1–13.

Carlson, J. (2010) The female significant in all-women's amateur roller derby. *Sociology of Sport Journal*, 27(4): 428–447.

Cho, A.H. (2006) Politics, values and social entrepreneurship: A critical appraisal. In J. Mair, J. Robinson and K. Hockerts (eds) *Social Entrepreneurship*. London: Palgrave Macmillan, pp. 34–56.

Coakley, J. (2011) Youth sports: What counts as 'positive development'? *Sport and Social Issues*, 35(3): 306–324.

Coalter, F. (1999) Sport and recreation in the United Kingdom: Flow with the flow or buck the trends? *Managing Leisure*, 4(1): 24–39.

Coalter, F. (2013) Game plan and the spirit level: The class ceiling and the limits of sports policy? *International Journal of Sport Policy and Politics*, 5(1): 3–19.

Collins, T. (2013) *Sport in a Capitalist Society: A Short History*. London: Routledge.

Connell, J. (2015) Edinburgh's shame: One in five kids live in poverty. *Edinburgh Evening News*, 2 October 2015.

Cureton, K. and Frisby, W. (2011) Staff perspectives on how social liberal and neo-liberal values influence the implementation of leisure access policy. *International Journal of Sport Policy and Politics*, 3(1): 3–22.

Davidson, N., McCafferty, P. and Miller, D. (2010) *Neoliberal Scotland: Class and Society in a Stateless Nation*. Newcastle: Cambridge Scholars Publishing.

Dempsey, S.E. and Saunders, M.L. (2010) Meaningful work? Nonprofit marketization and work/life imbalance in popular autobiographies of social entrepreneurship. *Organization*, 17(4): 437–459.

Department of Trade & Industry (2002) *Social Enterprise: A Strategy for Success*. London: DTI.

Dey, P. and Steyaert, C. (2010) The politics of narrating social entrepreneurship. *Journal of Enterprising Communities People and Places in the Global Economy*, 4(1): 85–108.

Dey, P. and Steyaert, C. (2012) Social entrepreneurship: Critique and the radical enactment of the social. *Social Enterprise Journal*, 8(12): 90–107.

Equality and Human Rights Commission (2016) *Is Scotland Fairer? The State of Equality and Human Rights 2015*. London: OGL.

Featherstone, M. (1991) *Consumer Culture and Postmodernism*. London: Sage.

Field, J. (2003) *Social Capital*. London: Routledge.

Finley, N.J. (2010) Skating femininity: Gender maneuvering in women's roller derby. *Journal of Contemporary Ethnography*, 39(4): 359–387.

Gilmore, A., Gallagher, D. and O'Dwyer, M. (2011) Is social entrepreneurship an untapped marketing resource? A commentary on its potential for small sports clubs. *Journal of Small Business and Entrepreneurship*, 24(1): 11–15.

Giroux, H. (2012) *Education and the Crisis of Public Values: Challenging the Assault on Teachers, Students and Public Education*. Oxford: Peter Lang.

Grant, S. (2008) Contextualising social enterprise in New Zealand. *Social Enterprise Journal*, 4(1): 9–23.

Grix, J. (2009) The impact of UK sport policy on the governance of athletics. *International Journal of Sport Policy and Politics*, 1(1): 31–49.

Grix, J. (2010) From hobbyhorse to mainstream: Using sport to understand British Politics. *British Politics*, 5: 114–129.

Hamil, S. and Morrow, S. (2011) Corporate social responsibility in the Scottish Premier League: Context and motivation. *European Sport Management Quarterly*, 11(2): 143–170.

Hastings, A. (2015) *Written evidence on the provision of the Community Empowerment (Scotland) Bill*. Submission 67, Edinburgh: Scottish Parliament.

Hastings, A. and Matthews, P. (2015) Bourdieu and the Big Society: Empowering the powerful in public service provision? *Policy and Politics*, 43(4): 545–560.

Herman, A. (2007) *The Scottish Enlightenment: The Scots' Invention of the Modern World*. London: HarperCollins.

HM Treasury (1999) *Enterprise and Social Exclusion*. London: HM Treasury.

Houlihan, B. (2001) Citizenship, civil society and the sport and recreation professions. *Managing Leisure*, 6(1): 1–14.

Houlihan, B. and White, A. (2001) *The Politics of Sports Development*. London: Routledge.

Hylton, K. (2013) *Sport Development: Policy, Process and Practice*. Abingdon: Routledge.

Jarvie, G. (2003) Communitarianism, sport and social capital: Neighbourly insights into Scottish sport. *International Review for the Sociology of Sport*, 38(2): 139–153.

Jones, O. (2011) *Chavs: The Demonization of the Working Class*. London: Verso.

Jones, D. and Keogh, W. (2006) Social enterprise: A case of terminological ambiguity and complexity. *Social Enterprise Journal*, 2(1), pp. 11–26.

King, N. (2013) 'Sport for All' in a financial crisis: Survival and adaptation in competing organisational models of local authority sport services. *World Leisure Journal*, 55(3): 215–228.

King, N. (2014) Local authority sport services under the UK coalition government: Retention, revision or curtailment? *International Journal of Sport Policy and Politics*, 6(3): 349–369.

Leadbetter, C. (1997) *The Rise of the Social Entrepreneur*. Demos: London.

Macmillan, R. (2011) The Big Society and participation failure. *People, Place and Policy Online*, 5(2): 107–114.

Molnar, G. and Kelly, J. (2013) *Sport, Exercise and Social Theory: An Introduction*. Abingdon: Routledge.

Monteith, B. (2008) *Paying the Piper: From a Taxing Lament to a Rewarding Jig*. London: Birlinn Ltd.

Mooney, G. and Poole, L. (2004) A land of milk and honey? Social policy in Scotland after Devolution. *Critical Social Policy*, 24(4): 458–483.

Mooney, G., Scott, G. and Mulvey, G. (2008) The 'Celtic Lion' and social policy: Some thoughts on the SNP and social welfare. *Critical Social Policy*, 28(3): 378–394.

Morgan, H. (2013) Sport volunteering, active citizenship and social capital enhancement: What role in the 'Big Society'? *International Journal of Sport Policy and Politics*, 5(3): 381–395.

Nicholls, A. and Cho, A.H. (2006) Social entrepreneurship: The structuration of a field. In A. Nicholls (ed.) *Social Entrepreneurship: New Models of Sustainable Social Change*. Oxford University Press.

Oakley, B. and Green, M. (2001) The selective reinvestment in British sport, 1995–2000. *Managing Leisure*, 6: 74–94.

Ogbor, J.O. (2000) Mythicising and reification in entrepreneurial discourse: Ideology-critique of entrepreneurial studies. *Journal of Management Studies*, 37(5): 605–635.

Outram, S.M. (2015) Protecting sport from itself: A critical analysis of the 2013 Australian Crime Commission's Report into Crime and Drugs in Sport. *International Journal of Sport Policy & Politics*, (4): 605–622.

Paterson, L. (2002) Civic democracy. In G. Hassan and C. Warhurst (eds) *Anatomy of the New Scotland*. Edinburgh: Mainstream, pp. 56–64.

Pringle, A. and Cruttenden, T. (2001) *Sport and Local Government in the New Scotland*. Edinburgh: Sportscotland.

Reid, F. (2012) Increasing sports participation in Scotland: Are voluntary sports clubs the answer? *International Journal of Sport Policy and Politics*, 4(2): 221–241.

Reid, G. (2014) Save Meadowbank stadium: The politics of local stadium closure. *International Journal of Sport Policy and Politics*, 6(1): 37–54.

Roy, M.J., MacLeod, R., Baglioni, S. and Sinclair, S. (2014) *Social Enterprise, Social Innovation and Social Entrepreneurship in Scotland: A National Report*. Glasgow Caledonian University: EFESEIIS.

Schwartz, B. (2012) *Rippling: How Social Entrepreneurs Spread Innovation Throughout the World*. New York: Jossey-Bass.

Scott, D. and Teasdale, S. (2012) Whose failure? Learning from the financial collapse of a social enterprise in 'Steeltown'. *Voluntary Sector Review*, 3(2): 139–155.

(Scottish Neighbourhood Statistics, 2011.

Sennett, R. and Cobb, J. (1973) *The Hidden Injuries of Class*. New York: Random House.

Simmons, R. (2008) Harnessing social enterprise for local public services: The case of new leisure trusts in the United Kingdom. *Public Policy and Administration*, 23(3): 278–301.

Skille, E.A. (2011) The conventions of sports clubs: Enabling and constraining the implementation of social goods through sport. *Sport, Education and Society*, 16(2): 253–265.

Social Mobility and Child Poverty Commission (2015) *Elitist Scotland?* Edinburgh: David Hume Institute.

Social Value Lab (2015a) *Scotland's Vision for Social Enterprise 2025: Moving Social Enterprise in from the Margins to the Mainstream*. Edinburgh: Social Value Lab.

Social Value Lab (2015b) *Social Enterprise in Scotland: Census 2015*. Edinburgh: Social Value Lab.

Spaaij, R. (2009) Sport as a vehicle for social mobility and regulation of disadvantaged urban youth: Lessons from Rotterdam. *International Review for the Sociology of Sport*, 44(2–3): 247–264.

Tan, W.L., Williams, J. and Tam, T.M. (2005) Defining the 'social' in 'social entrepreneurship': Altruism and entrepreneurship. *The International Entrepreneurship and Management Journal*, 1(3): 353–365.

Teasdale, S. (2010) How can social enterprise address disadvantage? Evidence from an inner city community. *Journal of Nonprofit and Public Sector Marketing*, 22: 89–107.

Teasdale, S. (2011) What's in a name? Making sense of social enterprise discourses. *Public Policy and Administration*, 27(2): 99–119.

Teasdale, S. (2012) Negotiating tensions: How do social enterprises in the homelessness field balance social and commercial considerations? *Housing Studies*, 27(4): 514–532.

Theeboom, M., Haudenhuyse, R. and De Knop, P. (2010) Community sports development for socially deprived groups: A wider role for the commercial sports sector? A look at the Flemish situation. *Sport in Society: Cultures, Commerce, Media, Politics*, 13(9): 1392–1410.

Thompson (2008) Social entrepreneurship and social enterprise where have we reached? *Social Enterprise Journal*, 4(2): 149–161.

Thorp, D. (2015a) Mutual benefits of social cooperation. *The Scotsman*, 20 August 2015.

Thorp, D. (2015b) Census reveals full impact of social enterprise. *The Scotsman*, 13 October 2015.

Torrance, D. (2009) *We in Scotland: Thatcherism in a Cold Climate*. London: Berlinn Ltd.

Tucker, L. (2013) Politics, policy and sport development. In S. Robson, K. Simpson, and L. Tucker (eds) *Strategic Sports Development*. Abingdon: Routledge.

Walsham, M., Dingwall, C. and Hempseed, I. (2008) *Healthy Business: A Guide to Social Enterprise in Health and Social Care*. London: Social Enterprise Coalition.

Westerbeek, H. (2010a) Sport management and sport business: Two sides of the same coin? *Sport in Society*, 13(9): 1293–1299.

Westerbeek, H. (2010b) Commercial sport and local communities: A market niche for social sport business? *Sport in Society*, 13(9): 1411–1415.

Wilkinson, R. and Pickett, K. (2009) *The Spirit Level: Why Equal Societies Almost Always Do Better*. London: Allen Lane.

Zahra, S.A., Gedajlovic, E., Neubaum, D.O. and Shulman, J.M. (2009) A typology of social entrepreneurs: Motives, search processes and ethical challenges. *Journal of Business Venturing*, 24: 519–532.

Ziegler, R. (2009) *An Introduction to Social Entrepreneurship: Voices, Preconditions, Contexts*. Cheltenham: Edward Elgar.

PART VI

Politics and sporting events

When considering the relationship between sport and politics, global sports mega-events, such as the Olympic Games and the FIFA World Cup, are worthy of close attention. From sending a national team to international competitions to hosting a mega sporting event, what seem to be relatively autonomous areas are in fact intricately connected to a government's political considerations. A sports mega-event has undeniably significant political implications for internal affairs and international relations of the nation-state. Whilst such sporting occasions are often presented as global festivals which are presumably intended to promote international friendship and fraternity, in reality, global sport arenas are the place where nationalistic pride and rivalry prevail. For newly established states, gaining recognition from international sport governing bodies and taking part in major international championships represent important political tactics for displaying to the world the legitimacy and sovereignty of their governments. For more established nation-states, winning medals at the Olympics and hosting premier global sporting events are closely associated with the governments' political strategy to show off their sporting, economic, and cultural prowess to international audiences. This implies that, with reference to international relation theories, while the rationales for organising sports mega-events, such as the *Fundamental Principles of Olympism* underpin political idealism's promise to build a harmonious and peaceful world, the actual delivery and operation of the competitions appear to be largely dominated by the political realist perspective, which highlights that securing power and promoting the self-interests of the state constitute the fundamental logic of the world politics.

A decision to host a mega sporting event is also complicatedly related to domestic political issues. State officials tend to exploit a global sporting competition as an instrument for materialising their political goals. It normally requires a minimum of seven years preparation to deliver the Olympic Games or the FIFA World Cup. During this preparation period, it is common to observe the government of the host country initiating a political campaign for social cohesion and national integration, claiming that the sporting occasion is of huge public interest. At the same time, in order to provide legal safeguards for the seamless delivery of the event, the ruling party (or parties) also attempts to introduce new rules that primarily aim to protect the interests of the established groups. Some of these laws involve introducing a more comprehensive surveillance system to public spaces including sport facilities and restricting the commercial and political use of symbols associated with the event in question. With these institutional mechanisms, the established social order and the neo-liberal market system can be maintained. Furthermore, hosting a sports mega-event often works as a catalyst for social change. Civic organisations and political activists try to use the sporting spectacle as a platform for demonstrating their cause to wider audiences. In particular, for those events awarded to countries where non-democratic regimes rule, pro-democratic protesters use the opportunity to negotiate with the government because the event cannot be enacted effectively without support from the people. When the international media begin to pay attention to these movements from below, the political elites come under more pressure to reform, and eventually, albeit reluctantly, they may accept some of civic groups' demands for the implementation of more democratic practices.

Hence, it may not be an exaggeration to say that a sport mega-event is yet another type of a political project through which both governmental and non-governmental organisations vie to win public support and consensus both nationally and internationally. In this section, contributors examine the political nature of sports mega-events held in different geopolitical locales in different historical periods. In the next chapter, Large and Large revisit arguably the most politicised Olympic Games ever, the 1936 Berlin Olympic Games. The authors identify the political legacies of Hitler's Games and look at their influence on future Olympics taking place in countries where non-democratic regimes are in power. Brewster and Brewster's chapter investigates the political protests which occurred before and during the 1968 Mexico Olympic Games and discusses how the authorities dealt with massive anti-government demonstrations. Gajek surveys the political meaning of sports mega-events held in the post-fascist period with reference to the cases of the Rome and Munich Olympic Games in 1960 and 1972 respectively. In the following chapter, Chepurnaya introduces the first Cold War Olympics, which took place in Moscow in 1980, highlighting the interface between the Soviet Union's internal politics and an ideologically divided international political structure. Dong looks at the political motivation of hosting the Olympic Games in China, and considers how the Chinese government responded to a range of political events taking place during and in relation to the Olympic Games. Lee examines the different political connotations assigned to three sports mega-events that South Korea has hosted since 1988. Horne and Silverstre's chapter provides a brief political history of sport in Brazil. The authors also discuss the contemporary aspects of mega-event bidding and hosting in the country. In the next chapter, Chen investigates the political character of sport in Taiwan with reference to the islanders' sensitive national identity politics represented in and through global sport. Whigham's chapter explores the historical and contemporary politics of the Commonwealth Games, and the relationship between the Games and the politics of the Commonwealth as an evolving geopolitical entity. Finally, Malcolm and Waldman explore the colonial/(post)colonial/and (neo)colonial relationships and tensions that have operated in, and continue to structure, the politics of international cricket.

33

THE BERLIN OLYMPICS, 1936

David Clay Large and Joshua J. H. Large

In the contention-ridden history of the modern Olympics, no single festival, summer or winter, has been more controversial than the Berlin Summer Games of 1936. Oddly enough, though, Berlin '36 also stands as one of the most formative and influential of the five-ringed Olympic circuses. In the end, no Olympiad has had a greater impact on the modern world – not just the sporting world – than the one hosted by Adolf Hitler in the German capital.

A boycott of Berlin?

On 29 April 1931, the International Olympic Committee (IOC) voted 43 to 16 to hold the Olympic Summer Games in Berlin, over runner-up Barcelona. At that time Germany was still a democracy, albeit a beleaguered one, and some of the IOC voters hoped that a Berlin Olympiad might help buttress the Weimar Republic. Alas, less than two years later the country was under the control of a Nazi-led government that stood as a mockery of the (purported) Olympic ideals of internationalism and peaceful competition among the peoples of the world, independent of religion, race, or ethnicity.

Before Hitler assumed power it seemed highly unlikely that a Nazi government, should one come to pass, would even want to host the Olympic Games. Various National Socialist leaders and sports commentators had shown nothing but contempt for the modern Olympic movement, and indeed for most international sporting events, calling instead for purely German competitions and fitness programs based on *Turnen*, or synchronised group gymnastics. In the early 1920s they had objected to Germans competing with athletes from the Allied countries, which had imposed the "Yoke of Versailles" on the Fatherland. They had also objected to "Aryans" competing with "racial inferiors," such as Slavs, blacks, and Jews (Haller 1933). Hitler himself called the Olympics "a plot against the Aryan race by Freemasons and Jews" (Hart-Davis 1986: 45).

The Nazi objection to competing with black athletes was especially relevant because having had a modest presence in the Summer Olympics of 1920 and 1924, black athletes performed well in the Los Angeles Summer Games of 1932. African-American runners Eddie Tolan and Ralph Metcalfe, labeled the "Sable Cyclones" in the American press, excelled in the sprints, with Tolan setting a world record in the 100-metre race and an Olympic record in the 200-metre event. For Nazi ideologues, it was a "disgrace" that white athletes, including a German runner named Arthur Jonath, had deigned to compete at all with the likes of Tolan and Metcalfe (Teichler 1991: 47). *Der Völkische Beobachter*, the Nazi house-journal, demanded in August 1932 that blacks be "excluded" from any German-hosted Olympic festival.

Hitler did not begin to view the Olympics more favourably until after he had assumed the chancellorship in January 1933. In March of that year one of the key members of the German Olympic Organizing Committee (GOOC), Theodor Lewald, who happened to be half-Jewish, argued in a meeting with the Führer that hosting the Games would provide an invaluable propaganda opportunity for Germany and undoubtedly constitute an economic windfall for the country (Lewald 1933). But what really seems to have transformed Hitler's initial skepticism was the prospect of building a grandiose stage for the Games in the Nazi capital, along with the prospect of demonstrating "Master Race" superiority on the athletic field. In May 1933 he therefore let it be known that his government would not only support the Olympic project, but would host the most magnificent Olympic festival ever.

Yet even while belatedly endorsing the Games, the Nazi government and German sporting associations pursued policies that clashed sharply with Olympic principles of openness and fair play in athletic competition. The Hitler government's programme of anti-Jewish persecution thoroughly embraced the world of sport, which was forced into conformity with Nazi dogma. In spring 1933 the German Swimming Association banned Jews from its member clubs. Germany's Davis Cup tennis team expelled one of its stars, Dr Daniel Prenn, because he was Jewish. The Nazi press called for the dismissal of Theodor Lewald on grounds of his part-Jewish ancestry, and he surely would have been pushed out had not the IOC warned that such a move might compromise Berlin's chances of holding on to the 1936 Games (Teichler 1991).

The retention of Lewald, however, was hardly enough to reassure a growing chorus of critics around the world who were beginning to insist that the Games be removed from Berlin, and to threaten a massive boycott of the Olympics if they transpired in the Nazi capital after all.

Interestingly, the protest movement had its origins and greatest resonance in America – a nation hardly without its own policies of racial discrimination in sport, and elsewhere. Early on, the American push to boycott a Nazi-hosted Olympiad was largely a Jewish affair, American Jews having reacted with alarm and outrage to the Hitler government's anti-Semitic pronouncements and measures. Various Jewish groups asked Avery Brundage, the president of the American Olympic Committee (AOC), to take a stand against holding the Games in the German capital. What the Jewish activists did not know was that Brundage was vehemently against moving the Games out of Germany, or boycotting the contest should it remain there. Time and again, he would justify this stance on the (specious) grounds that high-level "sports" and "politics" occupied independent realms, and that the Olympic movement could survive only if politics were kept out of it (Guttman 1984).

Brundage's position notwithstanding, the GOOC was deeply worried about the American protests. Hoping to stifle and inhibit the boycott movement, Theodor Lewald convinced the Hitler government to issue a statement promising to respect the Olympic charter and to welcome to Germany "competitors of all races." The regime added a significant caveat, however: the composition of Germany's own team was nobody else's business but Germany's. The Germans hoped the IOC would agree.

And in fact, for the most part the IOC did agree. IOC President Henri de Baillet-Latour, a Belgian aristocrat, held views similar to Brundage's in regard to the relationship between the Olympic movement and politics. He believed that the IOC should avoid taking any "political" positions except in the case of Communist penetration of the Games, which he felt must be avoided at all costs. Thus he issued a statement saying the IOC would hold to its 1931 decision for Berlin as long as Germany imposed no racial or religious restrictions on foreign participation.

The stance of the IOC guaranteed that the Games would stay in Berlin, but not that they would go un-boycotted. In fact, Jewish groups in America now openly called for a U.S. boycott unless the Germans opened their own Olympic programme to qualified competitors regardless of religion or ethnicity. Jewish groups also threatened to withhold financial contributions to the American Olympic programme should the AOC decide to send a team to Berlin (Gottlieb 1972).

Genuinely afraid that American Jews could help effect a U.S. boycott of Berlin, the Germans decided to concede more ground, in principle at least. In June 1933 they promised not only to observe all Olympic regulations but also that "Jews would not be excluded from membership in German teams [for Berlin or the Winter Games in Garmisch-Partenkirchen]" (Teichler 1989: 47–48).

The reality, however, was that Jewish athletes, of which Germany had a sizeable number, were not considered for membership on the German Olympic teams. Most notably, a German-Jewish female high-jumper named Gretl Bergmann was denied the chance to compete in the qualifying rounds for Berlin, despite having won the German national championship in 1935. Moreover, anti-Semitic policies in other dimensions of public life in Nazi Germany continued unabated.

Against this backdrop of persistent government-backed racism in Germany, the American boycott movement expanded beyond its original Jewish base to include Catholic and Protestant organisations, labour groups, and the American Civil Liberties Union. On 7 March 1934, a mass rally was held in New York's Madison Square Garden to protest against Nazi racial policies and to threaten boycotts of German goods along with the Olympics if these policies persisted.

In response to the growing boycott movement, Avery Brundage undertook a "fact-finding" trip to Germany in the fall of 1934, promising to investigate the sporting scene in the Third Reich. He interviewed a few German-Jewish athletic officials, albeit only in the presence of uniformed SS officers. At one point he put his Nazi hosts at ease by pointing out that his own men's club in Chicago excluded Jews and blacks. Upon his return to America he gave the Germans a clean bill of health, saying he saw no evidence of racism and echoing German assurances that there would be no discrimination against any of the foreign athletes competing in Berlin (*New York Times* 1934).

Undeterred by Brundage's "whitewash" of Nazi Germany, the American boycott-Berlin movement continued to expand. In yet another effort to undercut domestic protest sentiment, Charles Sherrill, one of three American IOC members and, like Brundage, a strong proponent of keeping the Games in Berlin, travelled to Germany in summer 1935 with the goal of persuading Hitler to include at least one Jew in its Olympic team, a gesture he privately equated with the American tradition of the "token Negro". Sherrill warned Hitler that unless this happened, Berlin advocates like himself and Brundage might not be able to prevent a U.S. boycott in 1936 (Aufzeichnung [Sherrill] 1934).

Hitler personally rebuffed Sherrill, even threatening to call off the Olympics entirely and to substitute "purely German" games in place of the international festival. Yet this was a bluff: Hitler knew that German-only games would be useless in terms of propaganda, and would not facilitate the desired generation of foreign currency. In the end, he acquiesced with a gesture of tokenistic compromise worked out between Sherrill and the GOOC. The Germans agreed to name a half-Jewish fencer named Helene Mayer to their team for Berlin. For the Nazis, this decision was made more palatable by the fact that Mayer was an excellent fencer with medal prospects for Germany, looked the part of a perfect Aryan Valkyrie, and was careful not to criticise Hitler's regime in any way (Large 2007).

The Mayer concession weakened the American boycott effort, which was further undermined by a lack of public support from President Franklin Roosevelt, who kept silent on the issue despite calls from the U.S. consular staff in Germany to signal his disapproval of Hitler via an American no-show in Berlin (Large 2007). At a crucial AOC meeting in December 1935, Brundage was able to outmanoeuvre his opponents and, by a very close vote, secure an endorsement of U.S. participation in the Berlin Games.

America's decision to go to Berlin significantly undercut boycott efforts elsewhere in the democratic West, from Canada to Switzerland. No nations ended up boycotting "Hitler's Games", although Spain failed to send a team due to the outbreak of its civil war in July. The willingness of national Olympic committees to overcome whatever scruples they might have had regarding participation in Hitler's spectacle did not stop some prominent individual athletes from staging personal boycotts of Berlin (Large 2007).

Innovations

The Berlin Olympic festival was the first of the modern Games to generate a large-scale (and nearly successful) boycott movement, but that was hardly the only way in which this Olympiad was innovative. Hitler's enormous financial and organisational support for Berlin (and Garmisch) was the first, but by no means the last, instance in which a national government provided extensive backing for a project officially managed by the host cities. The Berlin spectacle was also the first Olympics to be broadcast worldwide by radio and, more notably, by television (even though viewers could barely make out what was going on). Berlin inaugurated the now-traditional, opening-day release of doves. The track and field competitions at Berlin featured a display of African-American talent far surpassing earlier achievements and heralding the later domination by blacks of many Olympic events. America's Jesse Owens, the undisputed star of Berlin 1936, unwittingly ushered in the age of commercial endorsements by Olympic athletes when he donned a pair of running shoes given him by the Bavarian-based Gebrüder Dassler Company (forerunner of Adidas and Puma). Dassler was the tip of the iceberg at Berlin, which encouraged corporate advertising to an unprecedented degree. Among the sponsors were Mercedes, Lufthansa, and Atlanta's Coca-Cola Company, which ran a photo of Hermann Göring drinking a bottle of its product. With its combination of embryonic television and extensive corporate advertising, Berlin 1936 heralded the current global Olympic experience, wherein the Games constitute the world's longest commercial (Boykoff and Tomlinson 2012). Also unprecedented, at least in scale, was Berlin's vast array of the now-ubiquitous ancillary events such as dress balls, banquets, art exhibitions, scholarly conferences, parades and concerts. Perhaps most importantly, and certainly most ominously, Berlin 1936 made "safety" for visitors, athletes, and VIP's a major priority, providing a security apparatus of a size and sophistication never before seen in the history of the modern Games.

While these innovations were adopted by subsequent nations and National Olympic Committees, Berlin's most notable (and perhaps least forgivable) contribution to the modern Olympic experience involves its introduction of the now-unavoidable Olympic torch relay from ancient Olympia to the host city. This epochal undertaking transpired within a broader promotional campaign for Berlin 1936 that was itself unprecedented in scope and ambition. To advertise the Games both at home and abroad, German organisers hired stunt flyers and enlisted the Reich's famed Zeppelins. They sponsored an "Olympic Train" that toured parts of the nation in what was clearly a propagandising pursuit. Yet these Barnumesque productions paled in comparison to the GOOC's pièce de résistance, a twelve-day, seven-nation-spanning relay run involving over 3,000 torchbearers (Large 2007).

Although the 1936 torch relay, which was documented by Leni Riefenstahl in her famous film *Olympia*, proved successful enough to launch a whole new Olympic "tradition", unlike most of its later emulators it was far more than Olympic romanticising: it was a slowly moving advertisement for Nazi Germany over a part of Europe that Hitler coveted – and would indeed soon seize via a faster-moving march travelling in the opposite direction. The underlying political and ideological implications of the torch relay became fairly obvious at various points along the route. Right at the beginning, during a kitsch-laden lighting of the Olympic torch by fifteen Greek virgins, Germany's ambassador to Athens apostrophised the sacred flame as a greeting across the ages from "our Führer Adolf Hitler and his entire German people". Relay organisers encouraged villagers to express their enthusiasm for the Olympic host nation by shouting "Hail Hitler" as the torch passed through their towns. When the torch (made by Krupp out of the best steel) reached Vienna, local Nazis exploited the occasion to demand Austria's incorporation into the Nazi Reich, a goal they would achieve two years later courtesy of the Austrian-born Führer. In the ethnic-German Sudeten region of Czechoslovakia, also soon to be part of Greater Germany, residents hailed the passing torch as a beacon from Berlin. By contrast, in the Slavic parts of the country torch bearers required police escorts to avoid being assaulted. If in more recent Olympic torch relays the bearers might be elderly, female, and/or handicapped, all the (German) participants in 1936 were expressly manly "Super-Aryans", perfect young embodiments of a physical ideal endlessly preached by Nazi leaders even if rarely realised in their own bloated or stunted physiognomies.

In addition to anticipating the Wehrmacht's romp through south-eastern Europe in World War II, the 1936 Olympic torch relay buttressed Hitler's imperial ambitions with an illustrious (albeit bogus) pedigree by positing a symbolic bridge between Nazi Germany and classical Greece. Carl Diem, general-secretary of the GOOC and mastermind of the relay, claimed that the Olympic flame was an ancient "symbol of purity" prefiguring the purity of the modern German nation. He touted the torch relay as a reawakening of the cult surrounding Prometheus, whose theft of fire from the gods for the betterment of mortals was honoured in antiquity by torchlight parades. The fact that the ancient Olympic Games had included no torchlight parades did not prevent Diem from seeing the "sacred flame" at Olympia as an anticipation of the blazes carried by Hitler's followers on the night of his inauguration as German chancellor. For Diem and other philhellenic Germans, including Hitler, the torch relay, and then the Berlin festival itself, with its neo-Doric stadium and exposition entitled "Sport in Hellenic Times," would remind the world that Nazi Germany was the true "blood" and spiritual heir of ancient Greece and the most worthy modern steward of the pagan values underlying the original Olympic Games (Large 2007).

"Darktown parade"

The ancient Greeks "would turn over in their graves if they knew what modern men were doing with their sacred national games", thundered the *Völkische Beobachter* (1932), with reference to the presence of black athletes in the Olympics. If one of the great ironies of Berlin 1936 is that an Olympiad originally awarded to buttress a struggling democracy ended up benefitting a profoundly anti-democratic regime, another is that a contest envisaged by the host nation to confirm a perennial and immortal athletically and intellectually superior "Master Race" ultimately helped to undermine that dogma, though in the shorter term, alas, merely brought refinements to it.

Berlin 1936, at least in the track and field competition, was largely an African-American show – a "Darktown Parade," as one American newspaper put it. Jesse Owens's four gold medals is the achievement that many appear to remember, but Owens's ten black teammates were successful in their own right: Ralph Metcalfe took gold in the 400-metre relay and silver in the 100-metre sprint; Mack Robinson (Jackie Robinson's brother) won silver in the 200-metre race; Archie Williams got gold in the 400-metre event; James LuValle took bronze in the 400 metres; John Woodruff won the 800 metre; Cornelius Johnson and David Albritton went one-two in the high jump; Fritz Pollard took bronze in the 110-metre hurdles. In total, America's black athletes accounted for 83 of its 107 points total in track and field. No other team, Germany included, came close.

Naturally, the huge success of America's "race boys" (another U.S. newspaper term) was much celebrated back home. Yet the importance of America's "Darktown Parade" resided not only in the medal haul but in the very presence of these black athletes in Berlin. There is considerable significance, too, in the ways in which the black triumph was interpreted by contemporaries, both in Germany and in America itself.

During America's boycott-Berlin debate some African-American organisations, most notably the National Association for the Advancement of Coloured People (NAACP), had insisted that blacks, including Jesse Owens, must shun "Hitler's Games" on the grounds that Nazi Germany was as hostile to blacks as to Jews. The NAACP warned that blacks might be mistreated if they dared show up in Berlin. Apparently accepting this argument, Jesse Owens initially declared that he would boycott Berlin should he be selected for the American team. Yet, ultimately Owens and the other black athletes selected for Berlin participated in the Games. Owens in particular hoped not only to showcase his brilliance on an international stage but to parlay expected Olympic gold into a remunerative post-Games professional career – something he notoriously failed to achieve in a persistently racist society.

Contrary to NAACP warnings, America's black Olympians received a very cordial welcome from the Berliners when they arrived in the Nazi capital. Owens, his earlier athletic feats well known to the Germans, was mobbed by autograph-seekers wherever he went. Young women pressed love letters into his hands. But what Owens and his black teammates did not know was that they were being closely monitored by the German police, who were determined to prevent any "unsuitable" contacts between the visitors and natives. Fearing possible acts of miscegenation between the black Americans and willing German women, the Gestapo issued fifty-two warning citations to female citizens "for approaching foreigners, especially coloured foreigners, in an unseemly manner" (Krüger 1972: 194).

Although the great athletic achievements of Owens and company were touted in the American press, newspapers in the South tended to record the victories without any commentary, and not a single southern paper printed a photograph of Owens. In Germany, on orders from Propaganda Minister Joseph Goebbels, newspapers avoided discussing "race" in connection with the African-American performances (Bohrmann 1936).

According to the American black-owned press, Hitler was so upset over Owens's victories that he refused to shake the athlete's hand. The charge of a Hitler "snub" was taken up by the mainstream press and has since become part of the popular lore about the Berlin Games. The snub story, however, remains spurious, since Hitler avoided the possibility of physical contact with Owens by promising IOC President Baillet-Latour after the first day of competition to eschew *any* public hand-shaking with athletes, a breach of Olympic protocol he had committed early on. Had he not made this pre-emptive promise, Hitler would undoubtedly have found some other way to avoid physical contact with Owens: "I would never shake the hand of a black man", he later told an aide (Schirach 1967: 217–218). It should be noted, too, that Owens himself did not, initially at least, claim to have been rebuffed by Hitler. On the contrary, upon returning from Berlin, he insisted that it was *President Roosevelt* who had acted ungraciously. "Hitler didn't snub me – it was our president who snubbed me. The president didn't even send me a telegram", Owens added (Olympic File, Box 384). Moreover, Owens professed admiration for the Nazi ruler, calling him a "man of civility" and "the man of the hour in Germany" – a leader who deserved much better treatment from the American press than he was getting (Baker 1986: 137).

Hitler's anger over the African-American victories is said to have played a role in another race-related story to emerge from Berlin – this one involving American Jews rather than blacks. Runners Marty Glickman and Sam Stoller, the only Jews on America's track team at Berlin, were originally scheduled to participate in the 4 × 100-metre relay but lost out at the last minute to make room for Owens and Metcalfe. Glickman claimed that Avery Brundage himself intervened with the American coaches to effect this change so as not to further offend Hitler, who would have seen Jewish triumphs on top of the black ones as adding insult to injury. Glickman's interpretation of his and Stoller's exclusion has since become widely accepted and may be correct. Yet there is no empirical evidence for a Brundage intervention, and in the end it seems equally plausible that the American coaches simply wanted to have the best possible team on the track, which is what they maintained all along (Large 2007).

Contrary to another tenacious element of Berlin Games lore, the victories by Owens and other African-American athletes in 1936 did not significantly challenge prevailing theories of white athletic supremacy in Hitler's Germany, or for that matter in FDR's America. Nazi pundits argued that America's black Olympians were little more than gifted freaks who owed their victories to their "jungle inheritance". Disgusted by America's reliance on "animals" to win medals, a German Foreign Office official proclaimed: "If Germany had had the bad sportsmanship to enter deer or another species of fleet-footed animal, it would have taken the honours from America in the track events" (Dodd 1939: 212). Germany won the largest number of medals overall in the Berlin Games, but finished a distant second to America in the track and field competition. Influential American commentators offered similar explanations for the black successes. Assistant track coach Dean Cromwell opined: "The Negro excels in the events he does because he is closer to the primitive than the white man. It was not long ago that his ability to spring and jump was a life and death matter to him" (Large 2007: 331). Owens's own coach, Larry Snyder, argued that his "boy" and other black sprinters owed their success to "the striation of their muscles and the cell structure of their nervous system" – not to mention their willingness to take orders from their white coaches (Large 2007: 331). Thus the black achievements at Berlin tended to refine earlier stereotypes regarding racial differentiation for both the Nazis and the Americans, whereby Negroes were said to possess biological advantages in certain sports like boxing, but owing to alleged character and intellectual shortcomings, could never surpass whites in contests requiring discipline, fortitude, stamina, strategy, and teamwork such as long-distance running and basketball. It was only later, during America's belated and tortured soul-searching regarding ongoing racism in sport and society that the great black athletic achievements in the Berlin Games took on the meaning they deserved.

Legacies

Today, much of the public perception about Berlin 1936 derives largely from Leni Riefenstahl's famed documentary, *Olympia*. Riefenstahl always claimed that her work was a purely non-political piece of cinematic art, but in actuality it is rife with Nazi ideological and aesthetic motives – probably the most effective advertisement for the Third Reich ever made. Yes, the film makes Owens one of its stars, but the other African-American achievements are largely ignored and there is a strong bias in favour of home-team athletes. The work's long prologue, ending with Myron's statue of an ancient Greek discus thrower morphing into an Aryan super-man, underscores the Nazi thesis that the classical Greeks were just modern Germans waiting to happen.

Leni Riefenstahl hoped to make a film about the second German-hosted Summer Olympics, the Munich Games of 1972, but the Munich organisers wanted no part of her. "Hitler's favourite filmmaker" was a living reminder of Berlin 1936, and the makers of Munich 1972 were determined to do everything they could to differentiate their Games from those of 1936. This second chance at Olympic-hosting would showcase a Germany (or at least a West Germany) that had thoroughly cast aside the bad old ways and become a paragon of democratic pluralism, openness, and amiability. Alas, the push to erase memories of the past embraced even the security arrangements for the festival, which were kept minimal and relaxed. Unquestionably, lax security at the Olympic Village was partly responsible for the greatest tragedy in modern Olympic history: the murder of eleven Israeli Olympians by Palestinian terrorists. The bitter irony of Munich 1972 is that its organisers, in trying so hard move beyond Berlin 1936, ended up re-awakening memories of the bad old days in the worst possible way (Large 2012).

Inevitably, memories of Germany's first Summer Olympic festival resurfaced with a ven-geance when Berlin itself, in the early 1990s, bid to replay its Olympic-hosting role – this time as the freshly minted capital of newly reunified Germany. Oddly, Berlin's bid for 2000 included using as its principal venue the very same stadium in which Hitler had stood in 1936. This breathtakingly insensitive proposal offended even many Germans, who complained that it rep-resented an insult to the memory of all those who had suffered under the Nazis. Many Berliners expressed relief when the 2000 Summer Games were awarded to Sydney.

Ghosts of Berlin 1936 have ended up haunting not only German turf but the Olympic landscape in general ever since the Games resumed after World War II. Undeterred by charges of having helped bolster an enemy of pluralistic (and Olympic) values with its Berlin decision (or, for that matter by giving the war-cancelled 1940 and 1944 Games to militaristic Tokyo and fascist Rome, respectively), the IOC would award Olympic-hosting honours to several other authoritarian venues, most notably Moscow (1980), Beijing (2008), and Sochi (2014). Echoing its attempts to justify staying with Nazi Berlin in 1936, during every subsequent venue controversy the IOC claimed that the process of organising the Games would help foster "liberalising" tendencies in oppressive host nations. Of course, just the opposite occurred.

Equally predictably, opponents of these controversial venue decisions cited Berlin 1936 in their condemnations of IOC behaviour – and, in the case of Moscow 1980, to justify boycotts of those Games. Of the Beijing selection in 2001 a French politician, François Londe, warned:

> The decision of the IOC goes toward justifying a repressive political system that each day flouts freedom and violates human rights. Following the example of Nazi Germany in 1936 and the Soviet Union in 1980, Communist China will use [the Games] as a powerful propaganda instrument destined to consolidate its hold on power.
>
> *(CNN 2001)*

Some twelve years later, American presidential candidate Mitt Romney invoked the Berlin Games to chastise the IOC for awarding the 2014 Winter Games to Sochi, thus affording Stalinesque strongman Vladimir Putin a huge advertisement for authoritarian Russia – and for himself. For his part, as if to prove Romney right, Putin jailed a Moscow journalist for comparing Sochi 2014 to Berlin 1936. Putin unwittingly emulated the Nazis also in making some token pre-Olympics concessions, such as freeing the jailed "Pussy Riot" protestors in order to pacify foreign critics and prevent any shunning of his Games. Meanwhile, the German Olympians at Sochi may have had not just Russian homophobia in mind but also their own dark past when they showed up in rainbow-coloured outfits that looked like an advertisement for Gay rights.

If the examples of Beijing and Sochi offer the most obvious recent parallels to 1936, the upcoming 2016 Summer Games in Rio de Janeiro beg the fundamental question of whether Berlin's ghosts do not merely haunt the Olympic regime but constitute it. Rio, after all, is supposed to open a new and splendid chapter for the Games – just as Berlin 1936 was meant to showcase the modern Games at their finest (something Avery Brundage insisted they had actually done). Rio will indeed be, as Brazil's president Luiz Inácio Lula da Silva proudly pointed out when the city was selected in 2009, the first city in South America to host the Games (Clift and Andrews 2012). The host nation of Brazil, Lula also boasted, stood as a veritable poster child of economic progress and democracy in the "developing" world. In keeping with this democratic spirit, Rio's Olympic facilities would be the most "transparent" and "inclusive" in history.

Predictably, the real story behind Rio's Olympic build-up has proven to be more complicated. Municipal and state governments, as well as business elites, clearly view the Olympics as key to the physical reshaping of the city and its global rebranding for investment. Central to this undertaking is an alleged "public–private partnership" in the planning and financing of projects. "Legacy," "sustainability," and "transparency" are the favoured buzzwords.[1] Here we seem to have come a very long way from Berlin 1936, and yet the Nazis too were obsessed with making the Olympics a lasting part of their anticipated "1000-year" legacy – "sustainability" in spades.

The builders of Berlin 1936 cleared out a whole section of the city to make way for Hitler's grand Olympic stage. Potential "troublemakers," including Communists and Gypsies, were rounded up in advance and incarcerated in camps. In the case of Rio, a vast $1.7 billion "pacification" programme launched in 2007 began clearing away unsightly *favelas* and hunting down the gang lords who ran them (Baena 2011). Yet despite these efforts, violent crime has increased since 2012, while drug-trafficking has likely moved to parts of the city not yet "pacified" (Monteiro 2014).

The Olympic Games, Brazilian critics claim, do not merely inspire horrors like this but supply the exigent legal means whereby normal channels are circumvented or overwritten in the name of efficiency and patriotic necessity.[2] Tellingly, these critics have deployed the term "state of exception" to justify circumventions of established law by Brazil's Olympic planners, thus directly invoking the language the Third Reich's favourite legal philosopher, Carl Schmitt, used to describe the *Ausnahmefall* (Exceptional Situation) exploited by Hitler to rule dictatorially (Vainer 2011).

Emergency laws and police brutality notwithstanding, one might reasonably observe that the sort of anti-Olympic (and anti-World Cup) mass protests that Rio witnessed in recent years distinguish this case from Berlin (or Moscow, Beijing, or even Sochi), where no similar protests could have occurred. So too, one might note that the very embrace of "entrepreneurial" civic development and its attendant push to make the city safe for international capital betrays a markedly different set of priorities from those of Berlin. Undoubtedly the age of neoliberal globalisation has created a competitive market for international urban development on a wholly different scale from the 1930s. Even so, if the essential myths of the Olympic Games – that they are not political, that they celebrate the purity of amateur sport over professionalism, commercialism, and so forth – were laid bare by the "Nazi Games" as never before, then surely no modern Olympic festival can escape the ghosts of Berlin. For it is in that gilded gulf between concocted fantasy and reality that the Olympic Games trade. Were that gulf to close, what would be the point in bidding for them?

Notes

1 The words "transparency," "inclusivity," and "sustainability" are omnipresent in the Rio Candidature File.
2 Municipal Decree 30.379/2009, for instance, dictates that "all the necessary efforts" are made "to ensure that properties belonging to the municipal government are available for use if they are essential to the 2016 Rio Games, even if they are (currently) occupied by third parties." See "Mega-Events and Human Rights Violations in Brazil," Report from the National Coalition of Committees for a People's World Cup and Olympics, Executive Summary, June 2012, p. 5.

References

Aufzeichnung über den Empfang [Sherrills] (1934) Memo on the Meeting with Sherrill on 24 August, 1934, File 4508, Political Archive of the Foreign Office, Berlin.
Baena, V. (2011) Favelas in the Spotlight: Transforming the Slums of Rio de Janeiro. *Harvard International Review*, 33(1): 34–37.
Baker, W. J. (1986) *Jesse Owens: An American Life*. New York: Free Press.
Bohrmann, H. (ed.) (1936) *NS-Presseanweisungen der Vorkriegszeit*, Bd. 4/II (1936). Berlin: Ewart.
Boykoff, J. and Tomlinson, A. (2012) Olympian Arrogance. *New York Times*. 5 July 2012. Accessed 16 Feburary 2016. www.nytimes.com/2012/07/05/opinion/no-medal-for-the-international-olympic-committee.html?_r=0.
Clift, B.C. and Andrews, D. L. (2012) Living Lula's Passion?: The Politics of Rio 2016. In H. J. Lenskyj and S. Wagg (eds) *The Palgrave Handbook of Olympic Studies*. London: Palgrave, pp. 210–229.
CNN (2001) IOC Errors Again. *CNN.Com/World*, 14 July 2001.
Dodd, M. (1939) *Through Embassy Eyes*. New York: Harcourt Brace.
Gottlieb, M. (1972) The American Controversy over the Olympic Games. *American Jewish Historical Quarterly*, 61(3): 184–185.
Guttmann, A. (1984) *The Games Must Go On: Avery Brundage and the Olympic Movement*. New York: Columbia University Press.
Haller, G. (1933) Der Olympische Gedanke. *Nationalsozialistische Monatshefte*, 3: 388–396.
Hart-Davis, D. (1986) *Hitler's Games*. London: Century.
Krüger, A. (1972) *Die Olympischen Spiele 1936 und die Weltmeinung*. Berlin: Bartels & Wernitz.
Large, D.C. (2007) *Nazi Games: The Olympics of 1936*. New York: W.W. Norton.
Large, D.C. (2012) *Munich 1972: Tragedy, Terror, and Triumph at the Olympic Games*. Lanham: Rowman Littlefield.
Lewald, T. (1933) Letter to Lammers, 16.3.33, R8077, 46/173/612, Bundesarchiv Berlin.
Monteiro, J. (2014) Reversão dos Indicadores de Segurança do Rio de Janeiro. 10 May 2014. Accessed 16 February 2016. https://oagenteprincipal.wordpress.com/2014/05/10/reversaodos-indicadores-de-seguranca-do-rio-de-janeiro/.
New York Times. (1934) U.S. Will Compete in 1936 Olympics. *New York Times*, 27 November 1934.
Olympic File, NAACP, Box 384, Library of Congress.
Schirach, Baldur von (1967) *Ich glaubte an Hitler*. Hamburg: Mosaic Verlag.
Teichler, H. J. (1989) Zum Ausschluss der deutschen Juden von den Olympischen Spielen 1936. *Stadion*, 15(1): 47–48.
Teichler, H. J. (1991) *Internationale Sportpolitik im Dritten Reich*. Schlondorf: Verlag Karl Hofmann.
Vainer, C. (2011) Cidade de exceção: reflexões a partir do Rio de Janeiro. *Anais: encontros nacionais da anpur*, 14: 1–14.
Völkischer Beobachter (1932) Neger haben auf der Olympiade nichts zu suchen. *Völkischer Beobachter*, 19 August, 1932.

34

LATIN AMERICA'S FIRST OLYMPICS

Mexico 1968

Keith Brewster and Claire Brewster

With barely two years to go before the 2016 Olympics, unsubstantiated rumours were circulating the international media claiming that the International Olympic Committee (IOC) was perturbed by the 'state of unreadiness' in Rio de Janeiro. With only 10 per cent of the infrastructure completed, the IOC was apparently making 'informal, secretive enquiries' with a view to London taking on the Games if the Brazilians were unable to deliver (*Independent* 2014). While the rumours provoked strong denials and even stronger reassurances from the IOC, there may have been more than a few Mexicans who could be forgiven for offering a wry smile: they had heard it all before.

Despite the cyclical nature of mega-sports events and the predictability of the controversies they attract, organising committees are keen to emphasise features that make their Games different. In the case of the 1968 Olympics in Mexico City, several were easy to identify. This was the first time the Olympics had come to Latin America; indeed it was the first time a Spanish-speaking country had played host. It was the first time a nation from the euphemistically labelled 'developing world' had staged the Games. It was the first time a woman lit the Olympic flame, and the first time that televised images of the events were transmitted 'live' and in colour across the globe. It was also the first time that the Olympics and Football World Cup were held in the same country within two years; an occurrence that has seldom been repeated and would take until Brazil 2014 and 2016 for this to be achieved again in Latin America.

Mexico 1968 also set a series of precedents that its organisers neither planned nor celebrated. It was one of the first in which the spectre of a large-scale international boycott seriously threatened to jeopardise the Games. It was one of the first at which competing athletes used the global sporting arena to make political protests. It was also one of the first in which the host nation's sense of insecurity on the international stage led to heightened tensions at home. This produced a situation that would be witnessed in later Games: an international posture of inclusion and magnanimity existing simultaneously with domestic press censorship and containment of protests. An analysis of Mexico 1968, therefore, offers an opportunity to scrutinise a host nation under multiple and varied strains, to compare its differing reactions to local and foreign protests, and to assess the ways in which the IOC fed into the equation.

The international boycott challenge

The threat of international sporting boycotts reached its zenith in 1980, when many Western governments placed considerable pressure upon their athletes to withdraw from the Moscow Olympics. While such coercion met with varying levels of success, the absence of many world class athletes in Moscow, and again four years later in Los Angeles, emphatically refuted the IOC's insistence that politics had no place within the world of sport. In the same way that these Games would be violated by Cold War politics, Mexico 1968 had already been placed in jeopardy by developments beyond its own borders; namely, the rising assertiveness of a post-colonial African continent seeking to ostracise apartheid South Africa.

To appreciate fully the ways in which Mexicans dealt with this challenge, we need to understand Mexico's position on the world stage. When Mexico City won the bid to host the Olympics in October 1963, Mexico understandably took this as a vote of confidence in its economic growth and political stability.[1] Yet considerations beyond Mexico's borders were equally important factors. From one perspective, Mexico City was the best of a bad bunch: Eastern bloc countries were unlikely to vote for either Detroit or Lyon because in 1962, the United States and France had refused visas for East German athletes to compete in their countries. In the wake of Indonesian President Sukarno's decision to create an Asian Games beyond the reach of IOC jurisdiction, the IOC was under pressure to recognise the presence of the emerging world within the sporting arena. As such, in 1963 the Olympic Movement was more predisposed to entertain bids from developing nations than had been the case in the past. Coming just one year after the Cuban Missile Crisis, some IOC delegates may have perceived the need for the West to embrace Latin American countries in order to help prevent the spread of the Cuban model. While Buenos Aires would have been a worthy competitor to Mexico City in this respect, ongoing political instability in Argentina severely undermined its case. The apparently overwhelming endorsement for Mexico City, therefore, may not necessarily have been a vote of confidence in the Mexican nation, nor its people: Cold War politics and the need to be seen to embrace the developing world made Mexico City a rational option (Brewster and Brewster 2010: 43–51).

That international support for Mexico was less than resounding was evident almost as soon as the ballot was counted. Critics drew attention to Mexico City's high altitude and pollution, questioned Mexico's ability to afford the Games, and argued that its 'mañana' culture would bring chaos to all organisational aspects of the Olympics. Such scepticism immediately placed the Mexican Organising Committee (MOC) on the defensive. It would be amidst fears of half-built installations and oxygen-starved athletes fighting for their lives that the MOC was to face its most serious diplomatic challenge. Following a wave of de-colonisation, the Mexico Games were the first to which many of the newly formed African nations were invited. When the inclusion of South Africa threatened to foster a widespread boycott by other African nations, the Mexicans moved decisively. Reflecting the then-white, Western-dominated predisposition of the IOC, its president, Avery Brundage, forcefully argued that South Africa's right to participate was in accordance with the Olympic Charter. In response, the Mexicans risked isolation and further international criticism by opposing him: with staunch support from Mexico's president, Gustavo Díaz Ordaz, the MOC insisted on the withdrawal of South Africa's invitation.

While the threatened African boycott of the 1968 Olympics has been well documented, considerably less attention has been placed upon Mexico's early and adamant support for the African nations' position (Hill 1996: 207–217).[2] Mexico's motives are, however, worth considering because the controversy provides an example of a host nation adopting an alternative perspective on fundamental IOC principles. The MOC's public relations officer, Roberto Casellas, later reflected that Brundage had not been convinced that South Africa's presence in Mexico would provoke a mass boycott (Casellas 1992: 101–102). This, in itself, might explain why Brundage took this controversy to the wire. That the IOC president seriously miscalculated African and, indeed, Mexican resolve suggests a degree of complacency and a failure to recognise how the changing world would affect previous practices. Whether or not the Mexicans were displaying a greater degree of awareness of the global mood is a moot point. From a purely pragmatic point of view, the spectre of up to thirty-two African nations boycotting their first Olympic Games would have been a considerable blow to Mexico's reputation as host. An equally strong factor determining Mexico's stance, however, may have been its desire to prove itself on the international arena. At the time of the proposed boycott, criticisms of Mexico City's preparations were increasing in the Western media. As in the case of Brazil 2016, rumours circulated that an alternative venue was ready to step in should Mexico City default on its obligation to host the Games. More fundamental, per-haps, was the fact that U.S. sports administrators joined other English-speaking delegates to demand South Africa's inclusion and Lord Exeter, vice-president of the IOC, issued thinly veiled threats that should South Africa be excluded 'many other members of our Movement' might not wish to participate in what would then be deemed to be a 'political Games'.[3] As the nations of the IOC marshalled their forces on either side of the apartheid issue, Mexico remained firm. Reinforced by the support of other Latin American countries, the MOC was determined not to let Mexico 1968 be hijacked by international heavy-weights (Brewster 2001). The IOC eventually backed down and South Africa's invitation to attend the Games was withdrawn.

The significance of the threatened international boycott of Mexico 1968 lies predomi-nantly upon the posture of the IOC. Mexico could, with some justification, boast that it was free from the corrosive form of racism that maligned many Western nations during this period. As such, its insistence on South Africa's exclusion was consistent with its purported position on apartheid; this also upheld the Olympic Charter's aspiration that the Games should be free of political interference or prejudice. One might have expected the IOC to be fully supportive of such a stance: certainly in the case of Moscow, Los Angeles and, more recently, the Sochi Winter Olympics, the IOC has stood shoulder-to-shoulder with host nations in rebuking international calls for boycotts on such grounds. Yet in the case of Mexico 1968, the hosts and the IOC found themselves on opposing sides of a struggle between clashing principles. On one side was the imperative of racial equality within the sporting arena; on the other an insistence that domestic politics and global sport should not mix. Neither side wanted an international boycott to occur, but the differing perspectives of the host nation and the IOC resulted in conflicting views regarding which was the least damaging resolution to the dispute.

Domestic protest and its containment

For many observers, the tragic death of Israeli athletes in Munich 1972 marks the time when the Olympic Games lost its innocence. The increasing threat of international terrorism now means that security is a salient priority for any host nation. The safety of competitors and the public is an essential prerequisite for any mega-sports event and the presence of security forces has become a familiar sight. For British athlete Mary Peters, however, fresh from the highly militarised environment of late 1960s Northern Ireland, the sight of security forces on the streets of Mexico City and within the Olympic village caused concern:

> You saw these soldiers . . . not many of them, mostly unarmed. I suppose they took us by a quiet route. But you suddenly started to think about the troubles and you felt a bit scared. It suddenly hit you what you were doing. But once you were in the stadium, all these feelings disappeared.
>
> *(Samuel 1968)*

Yet the strong presence of Mexican security forces in 1968 was not to deter international terrorists. It was due to the fear of home-grown threats to disrupt the Games; a fear that would grow out of all proportion as the constant stream of international concerns regarding Mexico's ability to stage the Olympics made the Mexican government increasingly sensitive.

It has to be acknowledged that the Mexican political authorities were not adept at handling demonstrable expressions of opposition. Since the 1930s, political debates and dissent had effectively taken place within the ruling party, the Partido Nacional Revolucionario (PRI). The PRI had maintained power since 1929 with vote rigging and co-option ensuring the 'right' results in successive elections. National agrarian and labour movements operated within the system, and state patronage was variously deployed to soothe periodic tensions. Protests beyond the parameters of this tight framework were deemed to be a threat and often depicted as anti-patriotic. That the leaders of the 1958 railway workers' strike remained in prison a decade later, reveals much about the extent to which Mexico's democratic credentials as Olympic hosts were masking a different reality.

Indicative of a phenomenon that would be seen in later mega-sports events in developing nations, the Mexican authorities took decisive measures to eradicate all aspects of society that might corroborate foreign slurs on their nation. In August 1965, a national campaign to create an 'Olympic Conscience' among the lower classes began. That such emphasis was given 'to teach Mexicans how to behave' reveals both a determination to ensure that the Games were successful and the genuine concerns of certain sectors of Mexican society (in agreement with much of the developed world) that when faced with the pressure of being in a critical world spotlight, Mexico might indeed fail (Estrada Núñez 1965; Brewster 2010: 46–62). In the months leading up to the Games, hawkers, street sellers and slums were forcibly removed from areas of Mexico City likely to attract foreign visitors and relocated to less high-profile locations.

Within this socio-political environment channels for domestic criticism of Mexico's Olympic bid were limited. Although Mexico has no official censorship policy, in the 1960s and particularly during the presidency of Gustavo Díaz Ordaz (1964–70), the government strictly regulated the Mexican press. As the Olympic Games approached, journalists were further restricted by the MOC tactic of appealing to a sense of patriotic duty, fostering an atmosphere in which to oppose the Olympic effort was tantamount to betraying the country. Objections to hosting the Games were nonetheless voiced within Mexico and compelled the MOC to allay concerns raised. Criticisms about the cost of staging the Olympics, for example, were countered with details of the MOC's economic prudence and the immediate and long-term benefits to Mexican society that would spring from increased tourism, provision of sports facilities, and improved communications (*Excélsior* 1966).

Yet the greatest threat to national stability did not come from impoverished sectors of society but from the educated middle classes and the consequent response of the security forces themselves. During the mid-twentieth century vociferous and articulate sectors of the younger generation began to reject the paternalistic intervention of the state in their lives. University campuses, especially Mexico City's National University and Polytechnic, harboured a form of radicalism that frequently led to violent exchanges between students and authorities.

By the 1960s, student activism represented an increasing threat as students reached out to other disgruntled sectors of society.[4] On 22 July 1968, Mexican students, in common with their counterparts in several first-world countries, took to the streets of Mexico City to voice their discontent with a political system that no longer addressed their needs and concerns. Although some students criticised the use of public investment on Olympic sites to the detriment of social infrastructure projects, most of the students were not opposed to the Olympic Games. Indeed, many of them were working for the Olympic project as translators and guides. The Olympic stadium, situated within the University campus, was never a target for these rallies, and the nearby Olympic Village was never disturbed. Yet the authorities increasingly viewed the student protests as an attempt to disrupt the Games.[5] In their efforts to remove such 'unsightly objects' from the streets of Mexico City, many students were injured and arrested. On 18 September the National University campus was occupied by the army in an operation in which several students were killed.

The Mexican Student Movement ended in violent bloodshed on 2 October at Tlatelolco Square, Mexico City, just ten days before the Olympic Opening Ceremony. Although there is still considerable discrepancy regarding what actually happened, few would agree with the official version that students fired shots and that government forces responded in self-defence.[6] Survivors claim that, as the meeting came to a close, tanks sealed off the square and the army then opened fire into the crowd (Poniatowska 1971: 166–171; Benítez 1968: ii; Femat 1968). In the ensuing chaos a considerable number of people were killed and injured, and thousands were arrested. Official statistics finally listed 43 civilian deaths and 8 soldiers injured; other sources put the mortality figure at 500. The majority of victims were Mexican students.[7]

As journalist and author Elena Poniatowska (1993: 9) later reflected, 'the Tlatelolco massacre was practically silenced' in Mexican newspapers. A combination of intimidation, censorship, and perhaps an unwillingness to accept unconfirmed reports produced a compliant national press. Although some Mexican publications offered alternative versions on their inside pages, the main headlines were reserved for the forthcoming Olympics.[8] The international press had fewer constraints and indeed the events at Tlatelolco provided one last reason to question the wisdom of holding the Games in Mexico City. Avery Brundage faced a barrage of questions from international reporters regarding safety guarantees for participants and spectators, and consequent changes to the programme (IOC 1970). One of the more vociferous voices was that of John Rodda, sports correspondent for the UK *Guardian* newspaper, who had witnessed the massacre. Rodda's vivid testimony, in which he estimated the death toll to be 500, was published as a front-page spread on 4 October (Rodda 1968a). He attempted to speak to the IOC early in the morning of 3 October to explain the seriousness of what had happened, but met further hostility (Rodda 2010: 17). In his journal, Brundage recorded how 'a full avalanche of journalists' descended on the IOC office at 7 am to see if the Games had been cancelled. He described the reporters as having been so persistent that 'it took almost physical fighting to keep them out of the doors'. He continued, 'unfortunate as this incident was, the public opinion knew that the real objective was to frustrate the efforts of all Mexicans to stage the Games'. Such assurances were, of course, merely repeating the uncorroborated Mexican government line. With barely concealed annoyance, Brundage concluded that the massacre was 'an isolated incident regretfully covered by many journalists who have been welcome in the sincere belief that they were covering the sports events' (IOC 1970: 6–7). Hours later the IOC issued a reassuring press statement that the Games would go ahead as planned.

Rodda later reflected that Brundage had been correct to insist that the Olympics should go ahead:

Had the Games been cancelled then, they may not have survived – they would have been halted in Munich four years later [. . .] the Moscow Boycott 1980 would probably have succeeded, and that in Los Angeles four years later would have had greater impact. Its dogged resilience in the face of political interference, demonstration and intimidation is the bedrock of Olympic survival.

(Rodda 2010: 19)

Poniatowska, who had supported and has continued to work tirelessly for the student victims, would agree. She reported on the Games and celebrated Mexico's triumph. She explained, 'the lamentable acts of the last weeks [. . .] hurt all of us', but underlined that she was also tremendously proud that Mexico was staging the Games and was determined not to allow the brutal massacre to spoil the achievements of the country as a whole (1968: 5).

Yet most Mexicans' memories of 1968 can nonetheless be encapsulated in just one word – 'Tlatelolco'. They rarely reflect upon their successful Olympics. This is largely to do with the government's denial of any wrongdoing and the ongoing campaign led by the Mexican intelligentsia to clarify what happened and to apportion blame. Indeed, a veritable 'Tlatelolco' literature spawned in the decades that followed; one which promises to gain further momentum as the fiftieth anniversary approaches. In the international press, conversely, interest in the human rights of Mexicans quickly disappeared from the headlines. Once the Games began, attention turned to the sporting achievements. Following the Closing Ceremony, the Olympic caravan moved to Munich, where a different human tragedy would temporarily shake the confident stride of the Olympic movement. The most enduring foreign memory of the Mexico 1968 Games is not the massacre of protesters that took place on the streets of Mexico City, but an entirely different protest that took place within the Olympic Stadium: the so-called 'Black Power' salute.

Foreign protest in Mexican space

When the U.S. athletes Tommie Smith and John Carlos each put on a black glove and raised a fist during the medal ceremony for the 200 metres final, their gesture blended improvisation with conviction. While their accounts differ in the details, it appears that the decision to wear black socks and gloves and to remove their shoes was only formulated as they walked into the Olympic arena to receive their medals (Henderson 2010: 79–80). Yet the sentiments behind their protest were anything but spontaneous. Throughout the months leading up to the Olympics, an active campaign had been taking place on U.S. campuses and training camps which aimed to use the Mexico Olympics to draw attention to the civil rights struggle in the United States. Revisionist analysis of the podium protest convincingly argues that it would be wrong to describe it as a 'Black Power' salute. Rather, Smith and Carlos were acting under the badge of the Olympic Project for Human Rights (OPHR), a movement that had an undoubted racial egalitarian agenda, but that also attracted many white sympathisers from both within the U.S. Olympic team and the broader civil rights movement in the United States (Henderson 2010: 78–92). What would become an iconic gesture that defined the Mexico Games around the world, began as a U.S. domestic debate concerning whether attending or boycotting the Games would best serve the OPHR cause.

For those within the U.S. Olympic camp and those who appreciated the intensity of the OPHR debate within the United States, the Smith and Carlos podium protest caused a mixture of emotions: astonishment, admiration, fear, opposition. The IOC reaction was unequivocal: Avery Brundage demanded that the U.S. Olympic Committee should suspend the two athletes and expel them from the Olympic Village. He also instructed them to issue a formal apology to the IOC, the MOC, and 'to the people of Mexico for the discourtesy displayed by two members of its team' (IOC 1968). Yet there is no evidence that the MOC and Mexicans shared Brundage's indignation. Within the Olympic arena, the small audience that witnessed the protest displayed a mixture of bemusement and quiet respect for the U.S. national anthem. The immediate reaction in the Mexican press was merely to report it. Interestingly, more reflective pieces showed understanding and solidarity with Smith and Carlos (Aymami 1968; Nanclares 1968). The MOC kept a diplomatic silence at the time, but the inclusion of the protest in the official Olympics film indicates where sympathies lay. In August 1969 an incensed Brundage sent a sharp letter to the MOC president Pedro Ramírez Vázquez, copied to all IOC members, in which he stated the 'nasty demonstrations against the United States flag by negroes' had no place in the film (IOC 1969a). Ramírez Vázquez defended its insertion, arguing that to omit any important incident that had taken place within the Olympic arena 'would have been much more notorious' (IOC 1969b). Under pressure from Brundage, Ramírez Vázquez did remove the scene from the edition of the film sent to IOC members, but copies destined for commercial outlets had already been distributed.

The differing reactions to the podium protest deserve further analysis. Brundage was resolute in the IOC's stance: any political protest by athletes during the Olympics would result in immediate expulsion. That such a warning had been on the IOC agenda suggests that Brundage was not only aware of the OPHR debate within the United States but also of the likelihood that some manifestation of solidarity for the cause would arise in Mexico City (Brewster and Brewster 2010: 142). It would be fruitless to debate whether Brundage's uncompromising position was due to his imperative to protect the Olympic movement or, as his detractors contend, because he harboured racist tendencies.[9] The end result was the same: the IOC condemned using the sporting arena for political purposes. Yet had this view been shared by the hosts, one might have expected at least some sign of indignation that Mexican hospitality had been abused by the protest. Instead, the Mexican government, MOC and public opinion appeared to have been much more relaxed. After all, African American members of the U.S. team had not, in the end, boycotted the Games and as a result Mexico 1968 was treated to some of the most memorable feats of athleticism in Olympic history. While unrest within the U.S. team at the Olympic village was palpable, neither the podium protest nor any less overt forms of non-conformity adversely affected the smooth running of the Games. There may also have been some inward pleasure among Mexicans that the United States, whose press and officials had so vociferously questioned the wisdom of hosting the Games in Mexico, should have had its own dirty linen aired on Mexico's well-constructed global stage.[10]

Patterns of behaviour

An analysis of the 1968 Olympics reveals the ways in which diverse interested parties reacted to the challenges the hosts faced. From Mexico's perspective, there was a clear distinction between international protests and those of its own people. Mexico adopted a liberal, humanitarian approach towards international protests, one that was in keeping with its self-portrayal as a modern nation with good race relations, which respected human rights and the integrity of nation-states. Its strong support for African nations against the inclusion of apartheid South Africa was consistent with its failure to express indignation at Smith's and Carlos's podium protest. In both these cases, Mexico's stance was different from that of the IOC Executive board.

One might argue that Mexico's attitude was the more prescient in that the rise of Third World consciousness and civil rights agendas would soon cause significant changes in the culture of global sporting institutions.

At a domestic level, however, Mexico's press censorship and its brutal suppression of the Student Movement were far from liberal and contrary to the image that Mexico sought to create overseas. The explanation for this reveals the paradox within Mexican society in the 1960s. The Student Movement of 1968 was merely the latest, and admittedly the most public, display of a nation that was finding it hard to embrace new forms of political engagement.[11] Mexico was still led by politicians who had conveyed the country from economic and political instability into an era of prosperity and prolonged civilian government. That Mexico had bucked the Latin American trend of economic bankruptcy and military dictatorships was due to the strong, paternalistic hand that the ruling party laid upon the shoulders of its people. Hence, while the Mexican elite's craving for acceptance into the community of the developed world recognised the need for altruism at an international level, the foundations upon which such aspirations depended meant that it could not afford to loosen control of its own people. Compounded by increased international scrutiny over Mexico's ability to host the Games, national prestige demanded that the tried and tested solution to internal disturbances was deployed to maintain order: force.

Regarding the utility of the Mexico City Games for understanding more recent developments within the staging of mega sporting events, our thoughts are more tentative and await analysis of events that have yet to take place. Nonetheless, the ways in which domestic and international protests were manifest at Mexico 1968 offer interesting benchmarks for judging subsequent events. First, it is clear that Mexico 1968 heralded the era of threatened boycotts by individual or groups of nations. Reflecting the nature of global politics during the last fifty years, the impulse for later boycotts changed to Cold War ideologies and then reverted to human rights. There is little doubt that in 1968 the threat of a boycott was very real: African national Olympic committees simply would not have countenanced their athletes going to Mexico if South Africa was included. Similarly, in the case of U.S. athletes to Moscow or Soviet athletes to Los Angeles, an all-or-nothing approach was adopted. Yet increasingly in the contemporary sporting arena, demands for boycotts have not emanated from governments, but from various human rights organisations. In the case of the United States in the mid-1960s, sympathy for the OPHR's overall objectives was severely tempered, and eventually defeated by the ambitions of individual athletes. Some argued that the best way to showcase African American potential was to underline its prowess in the international sporting arena. Others believed that individual sacrifice of Olympic ambitions was too high a price to pay for a social ill that would be best remedied outside the world of sport. These same responses were seen in Beijing 2008 and Sochi 2014. Despite vociferous campaigns by international human rights and gay rights groups against a Russian law making the provision of information on homosexuality to under-eighteens a crime, there was no major boycott of the 2014 Winter Olympics. Foreign dignitaries may have stayed away out of conviction or for political posturing, but it was left to the consciences of individual athletes as to whether or not they should compete and how they could show solidarity with the issues raised by protesters.

In the case of Mexico 1968, individual athletes made a conspicuous stand in the most dramatic way. The podium protest arguably drew more attention to the plight of African Americans than any blanket boycott could have hoped to achieve. While sporting aficionados might continue to rue the absence of the world's elite at Moscow in 1980, a more casual observer of sport is much more likely to remember the raised fists of the two African

American athletes in 1968. Yet such action by individual athletes, or indeed groups of athletes, has not become a common occurrence in sporting events. Prior to the Sochi Winter Olympics there was much talk about how foreign athletes might compete in their events and then circumvent Russian restrictions to make high-profile protests in support of gay rights. In the event, no major protests took place and within days of the Closing Ceremony international focus on gay rights within Russia was distracted by the country's conflictive relationship with Ukraine.[12]

One aspect of the Mexico Games that can inform present debates concerning the staging of mega sports events is the connection between the relative wealth of a host nation, the nature of popular protest, and the ways in which authorities deal with such protests. While the vast expenditure on any Olympic Games sets off an internal debate based upon cost/benefit analysis, its intensity is far more deeply felt in countries with a great inequality of wealth. In the cases of Mexico 1968 and 1970 and Brazil 2014 and 2016, the host nations could argue that being selected to stage both the Olympics and the Football World Cup provided demonstrable international recognition of their economic strength and political stability. Certainly in the 1960s the international business community regarded Mexico in very much the same light as it currently views Brazil: a leading regional economic player that offers profitable business opportunities. Yet in the developing world, economic growth masks deep levels of inequality, as witnessed by the stark contrast between the ultramodern high-rise office buildings and the slum dwellings that are a common feature of Mexico City and Rio de Janeiro. As such, it should come as no surprise that many of the scenes that took place prior to Mexico 1968 are being replicated in Brazil: forceful clearance of slum areas, removal of street traders, protests against rising bus prices, and demands that government funding should be spent on deprived areas rather than Olympic projects. So too, the heavy-handed tactics deployed by Mexican security officials to quell disturbances are present in Brazil. Whereas visitors and athletes may have become accustomed to the high security measures that now accompany mega-sporting events, in the developing world these have long been the norm. The vital difference is that security measures in the developed world are to deter international terrorism, whereas security guards in Mexico City and Rio are to protect the competitors and spectators from perceived malefactors within the host population.

Staging a mega-sports event places any host country under exceptional international scrutiny. Yet would-be hosts assert confidence in their ability to fulfil their obligations and demonstrate their potential on the world stage. From the time a bid has triumphed until the closing ceremony, all aspects of organisation are focused on making these aspirations a reality. These preparations are much more intense in developing countries in which everyday reality is often far removed from the idealised version depicted by the bidding team. The need to conceal this gap places additional pressures on the hosting nation and becomes manifest in a variety of ways: crackdowns on dissenters, the removal of 'anti-social elements', and the over-elaborate renovation of public spaces. In doing so, blemishes appear in the smooth veneer that the host offers to the international community, as does an inner fear that the country's denigrators could be right. In the case of Mexico 1968, the imperative to maintain a façade of social harmony provoked a degree of repression that seriously jeopardised that very objective. Yet in the final analysis, as soon as the Olympic flame ignites the opening ceremony, local issues and concerns retreat into the shadows as others take the stage. And as the flame is extinguished, the critical world spotlight switches to the next host. For many international observers the legacy of any Olympic Games barely extends beyond the celebratory scenes immortalised in the official film.

Notes

1 The first round ballot was Mexico City 20 votes, Detroit 14, Lyon 12, Buenos Aires 2. The result was so emphatic that a second round was not necessary.
2 For Mexico's stance see Brewster and Brewster 2010: 68–73.
3 For details of the IOC correspondence and debate concerning the South Africa issue see: the Historical Archive of the International Olympic Committee (hereafter IOC/HA): file no. 0101561, Comites Nationaux Olympiques (Afrique du Sud 1968). Also see various correspondence relating to South Africa in the IOC/HA: Brundage Microfilm Collection Reel 103, Box 179.
4 In 1958, for example, students joined protesters demonstrating against rising bus fares in Mexico City. The ensuing demonstrations resulted in the destruction of buses and the violent intervention by security forces and the injury and/or imprisonment of protesters (Pensado, 2013: 129–131).
5 On 1 September Díaz Ordaz took a firm line against those who for 'ideological and political' ends were denigrating Mexico and 'perhaps sought to prevent the staging of the Olympic Games'.
6 For accounts in English see Poniatowska 1991; Adler Hellman 1983; Paz 1985; Mabry 1982; Brewster 2005.
7 It is claimed that most Mexicans believe that between 300 and 400 people died (Meyer et al. 2003: 70; Paz 1970: 38; Poniatowska 1971: 170; Rodda 1968a, 1968b; Ortiz Pinchetti: 11).
8 For a discussion of the part played by Excélsior and the weekly magazine Siempre in informing Mexicans about the massacre see Brewster 2002.
9 For an interesting contextual discussion regarding such accusations see Brichford 1998: 129–134.
10 While most focus has been placed on the podium protest of Smith and Carlos, it should be remembered that the Australian sprinter, Greg Norman, also showed his support by wearing an OPHR badge during the medal ceremony. Equally significant, the Czech gymnast, Vera Caslavska gained much sympathy from the Mexican public for her protest against the Soviet invasion of her country. Sharing gold medal position with the Soviet gymnast, Larisa Petrik, she turned and bowed her head away from the Soviet flag as it was being raised.
11 In this, we tend to agree with recent studies that reject the dominant narrative that presents the massacre as a watershed in Mexico's move towards democracy (Zolov 1999; Pensado 2013).
12 Two snowboarders Alexey Sobolev (Russia) and Cheryl Maas (Netherlands) did offer forms of visual protests: Sobolev carried a Pussy Riot design on his board and Maas raised a rainbow design glove to TV cameras.

References

Adler Hellman, J. (1983) Mexico in Crisis. New York: Holmes & Meier.
Aymami, J. (1968) En México se han Roto Récordes y Mitos. El Día. 24 October 1968.
Benítez, F. (1968) Los días de la ignominia. La Cultura en México. 23 October 1968, pp. ii–iii.
Brewster, C. (2002) The Student Movement of 1968 and the Mexican Press. Bulletin of Latin American Research, 21 (2): 171–190.
Brewster, C. (2005) Responding to Crisis in Contemporary Mexico. Tucson, AZ: University of Arizona Press.
Brewster, K. (2001) Interview with Pedro Ramírez Vázquez. Mexico City. 26 April 2001.
Brewster, K. (2010) Teaching Mexicans How to Behave: Public Education on the Eve of the Olympics. In K. Brewster (ed.) Reflections on Mexico '68. Oxford: Wiley Blackwell, pp. 46–62.
Brewster, C. and Brewster, K. (2010) Representing the Nation: Sport and Spectacle in Post-Revolutionary Mexico. Oxford and New York: Routledge.
Brichford, M. (1998) Avery Brundage and Racism. In Robert K. Barney (ed.) Global and Cultural Critique: Problematizing the Olympic Games, Proceedings 4th International Symposium for Olympic Research. Ontario: University of Western Ontario, pp. 129–134.
Casellas, R. (1992) México 68: Confidencias de una Olimpiada. Mexico City: Editorial Jus.
Estrada Núñez, Armando (1965) Campaña Nacional Para Crear una 'Conciencia Olímpica'. Excélsior. 29 August 1695.
Excélsior (1966) Nuestro Decoro Olímpico, 17 September 1966.
Femat, L. (1968) La noche de Tlatelolco. Siempre, 16 October 1968, pp. 12–13.
Henderson, S. (2010) "Nasty Demonstrations by Negroes": The Place of the Smith-Carlos Podium Protest in the Civil Rights Movement. In K. Brewster (ed.) Reflections on Mexico '68. Oxford: Wiley Blackwell, pp. 78–92.

Hill, C.R. (1996) *Olympic Politics: Athens to Atlanta 1896–1996*. Manchester: Manchester University Press.

Independent (2014) Game on: Could London really be asked to host the 2016 Olympics? 10 May 2014, p. 4.

IOC (1968) Commission, Executive Board, Mexico City: Annex V. *Historical Archive of the International Olympic Committee*. Lausanne: The International Olympic Committee.

IOC (1969a) Brundage Microfilm Collection: Reel 78. *Historical Archive of the International Olympic Committee*. Lausanne: The International Olympic Committee.

IOC (1969b) Brundage Microfilm Collection: Reel 102. *Historical Archive of the International Olympic Committee*. Lausanne: The International Olympic Committee.

IOC (1970) Brundage Microfilm Collection: Reel 46. *Historical Archive of the International Olympic Committee*. Lausanne: The International Olympic Committee.

Mabry, D.J. (1982) *The Mexican University and the State: Student Conflicts 1910–1971*. College Station: Texas A & M University Press.

Meyer, M., Sherman, W., and Deeds, S. (2003) *The Course of Mexican History*. Oxford: Oxford University Press.

Nanclares, F.C. (1968) Presencia del Tercer Mundo. *Excélsior*. 28 October 1968.

Ortiz Pinchetti, F. (1978) Políticamente, el movimiento triunfó. *Proceso*. 2 October 1978, pp. 6–12.

Paz, O. (1970) *Posdata*. Mexico City: Siglo Veintiuno Editores S.A.

Paz, O. (1985), *Posdata*, trans. Lysander Kemp. New York: Grove Press.

Pensado, J. (2013) *Rebel Mexico: Student Unrest and Authoritarian Political Culture during the Long Sixties*. Stanford, CT: Stanford University Press.

Poniatowska, E. (1968) Microcosmos: Mariana Yampolsky. *Novedades*. 17 October 1968, p. 5.

Poniatowska, E. (1971) *La noche de Tlatelolco*. Mexico City: Ediciones Era.

Poniatowska, E. (1991), *Massacre in Mexico*, trans. Helen Lane. Columbia: University of Missouri Press.

Poniatowska, E. (1993) La prensa en tiempos de Díaz Ordaz. *El Nacional*. 8 February 1993, p. 9.

Rodda, J. (1968a) Trapped at Gunpoint in the Middle of Fighting. *The Guardian*. 4 October 1968, pp. 1–2.

Rodda, J. (1968b) After the Games Are Over. *The Guardian*. 1 November 1968, p. 10.

Rodda, J. (2010) Prensa: A Journalist's Recollections on Mexico '68. In K. Brewster (ed.) *Reflections on Mexico '68*. Oxford: Wiley-Blackwell, pp. 11–22.

Samuel, J. (1968) The Ceremony of Relief. *The Guardian*. 14 October 1968, p. 17.

Zolov, E. (1999) *Refried Elvis: The Rise of the Mexican Counterculture*. Berkeley, CA: University of California Press.

35

THE ROME AND MUNICH OLYMPICS, 1960, 1972

Eva Maria Gajek

In 2014 the Winter Olympics took place in the subtropical seaside village of Sochi, Russia. According to *The Economist*, this hosting was the most expensive event in the history of the Olympic Games. Putin's vanity project cost approximately 50 billion dollars. The region underwent a process of complete restructuring. Stadiums were built where only recently refugee camps were located. In this context the question arises: What leads a country to spend so much money for this athletic mega-event? This question has a special significance if in the host countries there still exist numerous underdeveloped regions. In the Caucasus as well as in China and Brazil there is still a lot of poverty and even the simplest infrastructure is often missing.

The answer is simple, but nonetheless sustainable: it is about presenting one's own nation, it's about acceptance and recognition, and it's about working on one's own image. The opportunity to present oneself in front of the whole world still triggers a huge fascination and is a big motive for the candidacy. Still, the Danish Institute for Sport Studies has observed a geographical movement: while in the post-war period the Games mostly took place in Europe, and especially in democracies, today many authoritarian countries strive to host them. In the ranks of host countries London is almost an exception. At the moment the Olympic Games rather offer the BRICS-countries an opportunity to distinguish themselves as "new powers". The central argument of gaining national prestige has increasingly lost its significance for Western countries.

In the post-war period the situation was totally different: that argument was especially effective for the former Axis Powers of World War II. After fascism, holocaust, and dictatorships they attempted to integrate themselves into the international system and to propagate a new image of themselves. And this was to happen alongside perceptions regarding foreign policy strengthening new friendships and rebuilding old relationships were important guidelines in the cultural policy of the three countries. For such an image campaign, the Olympic Games set the perfect stage. Thus after 1945 all three countries got to prove themselves in short periods of time as hosts for the athletic mega-event. Only ten years after the end of World War II the commission of the International Olympic Committee (IOC) awarded the city of Rome with the holding of the XVII Olympic Games in 1960. Following these fourth Games after World War II were Tokyo in 1964 and Munich in 1972. The Axis Powers were also represented (prominently) at the holdings of the Winter Olympics in the post-war years with Cortina d'Ampezzo in 1956 and Sapporo in 1972.

Japanologist Christian Tagsold has already demonstrated for the Olympic Games in Tokyo in 1964 that the self-staging at the Games became an important means for the new definition of Japan's identity after 1945 (Tagsold 2002). Christopher Young and Kay Schiller (2010) concluded similar results for Munich. But in particular, the comparison promises important insights into hosting by former Axis Powers. It helps to sharpen the outline of the events and to classify them into an historical context as well as to find similarities, differences, and peculiarities. Moreover, the time lag between the Games makes it possible to answer questions about transfer and development processes. Therefore the question is in which different ways these "fractured societies" used the athletic event.

First I want to demonstrate the special potential of the Olympic Games for a post-fascist staging of the event. Second, I will highlight with various examples the different images and terms Italy and the Federal Republic of Germany used for their image campaigns. However, these outlined images should not be mistaken for actual states. Rather they must be seen as desired self-images, whose interpretations were negotiated by the public and which re-effected the social sphere as social constructs (Münkel and Seegers 2008). Therefore, third, a central goal is to focus especially on the role of the media. Because as Lu Seegers and Daniela Münkel stated (2008), image policy without mass media is not possible. Especially in the 1960s and 1970s a critical public solidified, following the rather consensus-oriented journalism of the 1950s. Mass media not only spread and distributed the image of the post-war republics, they were not only the "transmission belt between image policy and the audience", but they also themselves shaped the knowledge as well as the patterns of their meaning and interpretation (Münkel and Seegers 2008). Therefore I understand the media as consisting of independent protagonists, besides policy and sports officials, who played a central part in shaping the events and re-formulating a national identity.

The Olympic Games as a post-fascist stage

To tell the history of the holding of the Games by the former Axis Powers, one has to start prior to 1945 (actually a lot earlier, namely with their entrance into the Olympic movement, but that would go too far here). I will begin my historical review in the year 1936. The sixth Olympic Games fell into the laps of the National Socialists. The hosting of the Games was given to Germany prior to their seizure of power. But Berlin 1936 demonstrated to their Allies the enormous stage the Olympic Games provided for their self-portrayal. As a result, Mussolini, Hitler and the Japanese emperor agreed upon the so-called "Olympic plan": after Berlin in 1936, Tokyo was supposed to host the Games in 1940 and Rome in 1944. Mussolini already had the huge sport complex ForoItalicos built and compiled a concept, which emphasised the claim to power of the regime by ascribing it to Roman Antiquity (Caporilli and Simeoni 1990). The preparations in Tokyo also took shape. However, both projects failed due to different reasons, but eventually due to World War II (Carli 2008; Dogliani 2000; Guttmann 2006) Nonetheless, as mentioned before, all three countries were to prove themselves as hosts of the Olympics in the post-war period. But behind that was no arranged alliance of the former Allies, but rather a clear policy of the IOC in the post-war period.

Similarly to the procedure after World War I, as cities of the entente-countries were considered in dense sequence (Antwerp in 1920, Paris in 1924, Los Angeles in 1928), after 1945 the IOC assigned the Olympic Games purposefully to former Axis Powers. President Avery Brundage and his IOC-chancellor Otto Mayer specifically urged the three cities to present themselves as candidates (Gajek 2013). They did this not only to bring back harmony into their own ranks after the war's chaos, but also to contribute to the rehabilitation of the affected countries through global sports. The countries were offered a unique chance, which all three countries gladly took in spite of the high costs. Four reasons can be deduced as to why exactly the media event of the Olympic Games offered a unique stage for the post-fascist image campaign and therefore was worth the investment.

First, the diversity of athletics offered attracted worldwide attention like no other sports event. In the 1960s and 1970s the concentration in the press and in television, with its technical innovations like satellite and recording technology, led to a novel and hitherto unknown densification in communication (Fickers 2009). The Games of Rome and Munich frame the historical phase in which the relationship of TV with the Olympics was defined: Rome was characterised by the first attempts at TV coverage, and Munich celebrated its triumph. During 12 years, the number of accredited journalists tripled and the number of TV journalists increased tenfold (Rivenburgh 2010). This was caused by the fact that no longer did only 21 countries broadcast the Games as in Rome, but 95 TV stations did. In Rome, the TV rights were sold for the first time, while 12 years later in Munich the sale of TV rights for the first time surpassed the sale of tickets. Additionally, technological opportunities developed rapidly. While in Rome, in 16 days, a total of 102 hours was broadcast live in 18 countries on the European continent, the live offer in Munich rose to 40 to 50 hours a day (Wenn 1993, 1994). The increased international attention/publicity made it possible to communicate national self-images globally and to use the Olympic Games as "diplomatic territory" (Roche 2000).

Second, the "unifying" character and the "peacemaking" image of the Olympic Games offered the countries a fitting frame for a pacifist staging after fascism and the Holocaust. Italy, Japan, and Germany in the post-war period tried to demonstrate to the world their democratic system. In particular, the conception of the Olympic Village as a place for encounter offered the countries space for such a staging. They could use images and terms for their own staging. They could also design the local place of their nation as a place for peaceful and reconciled encounter between the different nations, almost a global community, and use these pictures against dominant pictures of wartime atrocities, although they could not rewrite these.

Third, the holding of the sports event involved a huge financial effort. Not only did stadia have to be built. The extension of the transportation system was also an essential part of the preparations. Images of economic power and technological innovation could be transmitted alongside images/conceptions of political sovereignty. Hosting the event could celebrate a comeback into the political sphere as a partner with equal rights, whose economic power did not stand behind those of its former wartime enemies (Modrey 2008).

Fourth, it was possible for Italy, Japan, and Germany to give the Games an individual note, due to particular conceptions. Thus, national historical images, a diagnosis of the present, or ideas for the future could be leading categories for this individuality, which had to be symbolically rooted, but also to be re-negotiated after 1945. After the dictatorships and the experiences of the war, all three countries suffered from a chronic "insecurity of their self-worth as a nation" (Elias 1998). In the post-war period they searched for appropriate self-representations between tradition and a new beginning and had to cope with the "odium of guilt" (Cornelißen *et al.* 2003). Italy, Japan, and Germany were shaped by a dynamic process of "invention of tradition" (Hobsbawm and Ranger 1983). The re-formulation of a national identity after 1945 was accompanied by public controversies and different offers for identification. But for the holding of the Olympic Games, the young nations were forced to formulate their self-image.

Terms and images of the post-fascist Games

The terms and images of the Games can be classified easily into the four categories outlined above, which the two European countries used very differently to set their own emphases.

In 1910, Pierre de Coubertin already found it absolutely necessary to keep the IOC out of the actual organisation of the Games. Therefore the preparations of the Games were (and still are) assigned to an organisational committee, which had the ultimate authority in developing the concept around the hosting of the event. This was despite intensive attempts by the IOC to influence the concept (Alkemeyer 1996). If one looks at the persons who were part of the organisational committees in Rome and Munich, it is striking to see that not only officials from the fields of sport, policy, culture and economy were important members, but also media officials. Thus, media and the organisers of the Olympics were not only two bodies that mutually observed themselves, but they were also institutionally linked with each other in multiple ways. They discussed the self-image with politicians and creative minds, took part in Olympic meetings to share their professional evaluation of the medial working conditions, advertised the event in their own media, and helped the organisers to establish international media contacts (Organizing Olympic Committee of the Games of the XVII Olympiad 1963). To both organisational committees it was obvious early on that international coverage would be essential for the image campaign. Therefore, journalists were to be kept happy. However it was not to be conceived that the media solely were exploited for advertising. Rather their relationship fluctuated between fraternisation for the Olympic idea and highlighting their autonomous role, in which they offered their readers critical background reports as a sort of know-it-all knowledge base and negotiated the designed image in public. Moreover, the Olympic Games became a reference opportunity for them, in which they presented their achievements to the international guild.

But what encompassed these "fractured societies'" contested self- and external images, which the organisational committee designed and afterwards emitted? Basically, the organisers of both Games used the earlier mentioned categories – past, present, and future – but focused on very different points.

Past

The past was an important reference for both countries, but in very different ways. First, Rome as well as Munich had highly influential Olympic predecessors. Even though Mussolini did not have the pleasure of becoming the patron of an Olympic hosting, already during fascism a committee developed an extensive concept, which, according to Pierre de Coubertin, planned for a combination of antique traditions and modern plans for the future. The Roman organisers took over this Olympic concept in nearly all its details. They also organised modern contests at historical sites like the Maxentius-Basilika and staged antique sports like chariot races anew (IOC 1957). Moreover, the contests took place in the sport complexes, which had been built for the Olympic Games in 1944. They did not even mind that these sport complexes were decorated with numerous dedications. However, this thoughtless takeover led to a debate in the media, political circles, and the public about the situation of the young republic 14 years after its formation. Here, architecture functioned as a symbol for the inner turmoil of the Italian government, but also as a trigger for an historical-political struggle over interpretation between communists, socialists, Christian democrats, and the multiple inner-party *correnti* of the Christian Democratic Party (Modrey 2009). Finally, Prime Minister Amintore Fanfani had some dedications eliminated before the Olympic Games commenced on 25 August 1960. Thereby he made a heavily discussed decision: dedications with "historical content" were to remain, while dedications with obviously "ideological content" were to be eliminated (*Il Messaggero* 1960). On 11 August 1960, the operations were halted due to protests at the ForoItalico. In the end, only two dedications were removed. The justification for this was that the remaining dedications were part of a concluded past (L'Unità 1960).

The Olympic predecessor of Munich in 1972 was Berlin in 1936. The sixth Olympic Games served the German organisers as a clear contrast. This becomes evident for example in the conception of architecture. Instead of the parade grounds of the Berlin Olympic Stadium, the organisers in Munich chose the lightness of a tent roof, green lawns and a lake (Koenig 1968). But this also becomes evident in the conception of the opening ceremony, in which marches were replaced by modern rhythms (Modrey 2010).

Thus, second, both Olympic predecessors illustrate the role played by the national past in the concepts of both host countries. In Rome, historicisation dominated. The media, organisers and the Lausanne Institution no longer differentiated between Roman and Greek Antiquity. A general historicisation in the middle of the 1950s also met the need for continuity and stability. First, the historicisation was an advantage for the IOC, which had been criticised in the 1950s. Historicisation became an opposite pole to commercialisation and technicality and thereby helped to brush up the IOC's image (*Chicago Daily Tribune* 1958). Second, the antique legacy was also important for the national identity of post-war Italy. The First Republic, which suffered from the low self-esteem of the nation after World War II, could present itself internationally with this historical recourse (Corriere della Sera 1960). The organisers did not mind that the antique Rome now only existed as a fascist representation. Mussolini had numerous historical sites excavated and recreated (Schieder 2006). Dealing with the legacy of fascism at the Games is also symbolic for Italy's dealing with its past. As recently as the 1990s, the public and politics dealt with war criminals and Italy's role in World War II.

Munich, however, demonstrated a different way of dealing with its past. "Munich wants to forget its past", was the headline of the *Sydney Sun Herald* on 22 August 1971. While Rome used its history for its self-expression, Munich made an effort to break off all lines of continuity with its own past. But the break did not mean silence. Press, radio and TV coverage internationally reminded people of Munich's, and Germany's, history. While the historical reference was used in the Eastern European sphere for revanchism, the Western allies used the reference to verify Germany's transformation (Gajek 2013). Western media demanded a "forgive and forget" attitude and described a success story. Local and Bavarian traditions were especially used for this, thus symbolising tranquillity and consistency. Bavarian comfort and cordiality were supposed to add an emotional component to technological power (Vermerk 1972). Thus, the organisers of Munich did not concentrate on national history, but rather referred to local traditions. Additionally the concept in Munich focused much more on ideas for the present and the future.

Present and future

The presentation of present and future in the image campaigns was, in contrast to the reference to the past, very similar. Both organisational committees used modern stadium architecture, infrastructure measures such as road construction and the extension of the transport system, and (media) technologies. However, the function that these visions for the future held for both countries differed. Germany saw it as proof of regaining its national prestige, Italy thereby demonstrated its arrival in the line of industrial countries. The construction of the airport, the Via Olympico and the four big buildings by Pier Luigi Nervi were representative of this. The sports facilities in particular combined tradition and a new beginning (Bauer 2009). Unlike the plan 12 years later in Munich, Nervi did not intend his Olympic buildings to signify "hard cuts and clean breaks" with fascist architectural traditions. Rather the old was supposed to become part of the new. New and democratic architectural approaches can be found especially in the roof construction of the small sports palace. As at the Munich Olympic Stadium, the use of certain materials diminished the sports complex's mightiness and opened a new view on the possibilities of architecture in the modern present.

The new, not least, symbolised newly achieved economic power. The buildings were supposed to help dissolve the stereotype of a poor, underdeveloped country and to demonstrate to the world the achievements and success of the economic miracle. Already for the candidacy, the representation of economic change had been a guiding idea. Onesti formulated it self-confidently: "We have the enthusiasm, we have the money to do it and we got the plans", which led the *Los Angeles Times* (1954) to write: "The sport-minded Italians are waging a campaign to stage the world's greatest amateur sports show with their pockets just bulging with money." In contrast to the preparations of the Games in 1908, which Rome had had to return in the end due to financial hardships and discrepancies, money was used as a display of power and competence. Thus, they emphasised a history of development, which effectively staged the achieved prosperity. This interpretation was also born by the majority of the Italian press, which offered their readers an overview of the expected costs by using lots of images and illustrations and which saw the potency of the Italian post-war society proven therein (Corriere della Sera 1960).

The reference to success was also an inner political strategy. While the economic miracle mobilised a mood of "we are somebody again" in Germany, Italy was far from being satisfied with its present (Woller 2010). Thus, the demonstration of economic power must be seen as an effort, which was not only supposed to influence Italy's image abroad but also had the goal of strengthening Italy's self-image.

But the display of financial liquidity also led the media to question the accurate and just economic focus of the Italian government. This critique was not only initiated by the Italian left liberal press, but also by international media (*Los Angeles Times* 1958; L'Avanti 1960). Italy's economic stability was regionally limited. The situation in south Italy was still dramatic. Although the Olympics were given to the southern Rome, the Olympic organisers' presented self-image was that of a rich, modernised north, which wanted to strengthen its stand within the industrial countries. The still mainly agricultural south did not play a part in this national representation. In particular, the American press repeatedly referred to this discrepancy. Consequently, in the middle of the 1950s old, pauperised references were still connected to Italy's image abroad. Similar interpretations can be found in the media south of Rome and in the media from the communist milieu. More and more, the two interpretations opposed each other: on the one hand, the economic achievements, on the other hand, the still existing gap between north and south were discussed (Gajek 2013).

Thus, the designed present and seminal self-image as a powerful nation ruptured at the image presented in the international coverage. Moreover the goal of the Roman organisers to appear as an equal partner on the international floor failed due to problems with construction and finally due to the increasing government crisis at the end of the 1950s. The Olympic Games became a place for political disagreements, for partisan intrigues and for *correnti*. Their fight over national representation at the Olympic Games was also often a fight over position within their party (Modrey 2009).

In Munich, the staging of economic potency was also not a targeted and homogeneous image policy. As mentioned earlier, Munich designed a completely new sports complex. But this was not meant to demonstrate a pacifist character to the international public, like the elevated, light tent roof, which had been planned in contrast to the Berlin Stadium. Rather, the organisers wanted to demonstrate their technological achievements with it. The media clearly supported this view and printed lots of numbers and statistics (*Der Spiegel* 1961). At the same time, the innovative and modern ideas led to numerous debates. In public it was heavily debated whether one could see this Olympic Stadium as representative. Two groups appeared in this discussion: traditionalists and reformers. While the traditionalists focused on reasonable arguments concerning costliness, the reformers emphasised the innovation and the symbolism of the concept. Thus, the tent roof was also seen as an aspect of progressiveness; "vision for the future" and "pioneering achievement" became heavily used terms. Such battles of opinion were present in all parts of the concept. For some, the font chosen by Otl Aicher was not German enough, while others saw it as fittingly modern. Some did not even look at the symbolic system, while others were fascinated by its cosmopolitanism (*Abendzeitung* 1971). The corona as symbol for the Games even led some readers of the tabloid *Bild* to design an alternative symbol: the Munich-Kindl, who lifted five rings (Organisationskomitee der Spiele der XX. Olympiade 1973). The foreign press also observed this discussion and interfered. For them, the tent roof became (other than was intended) a symbol of the fact that the Germans could not resist making a show of superlatives. This was, for example, shown in the headlines: "The Monster of Munich" (*The Province* 1972), "Munich thinks big for the Games" (*The Australian Women's Weekly* 1972) or "Big Talk at Munich is the Big Cost of Big Roof" (*New York Times* 1972). But in retrospect, the Olympic chroniclers rated the roof as very positive, representing the diligence and ability of German architects. In 2002, the roof was even appointed the most important building in Germany.

Perspective

An activity report of ARD and ZDF summarised the Games in 1972:

> The organizers have the most thankless task at the Olympic Games. Their gold medal is oblivion. They have worked well, if no one noticed them. Their task of housing thousands of people from all over the world, to transport them, to provide passes and clothing for them, to provide medical care and to entertain them, is a difficult task, whose highest praise is not to be mentioned, and whose failure rapidly, and certainly and most of all thoroughly threatens the success of a big event. The organizational committee had to bear the main burden.
>
> *(Bericht über die Tätigkeiten der Deutschen*
> *Rundfunkanstalten bei den Olympischen Spielen 1972)*

During the preparation of the Games in Rome and Munich, the organisers might often have asked themselves whether the efforts, the discussions, and the difficulties, which they had to face in the six years of preparation, would be worth it for the few days of the Games. However, the new efforts of cities for candidacy in 2011 demonstrate how effective the conceptions of the 1960s and 1970s still are. The slogan for Munich's candidacy for the Winter Olympics 2018 as the "friendly Games" inevitably remind one of the 1972 announced attribution of the "cheerful Games". For its candidacy for the Summer Olympics, Rome 2020 also recruited its predecessor of 1960. Of course, a Games hosting without reference to past hostings would be unimaginable. The current reports were shaped by many anecdotes. An Olympics nostalgia became apparent, in which subjective memories often overlaid the facts. The new organisers hoped to profit from this boom of memory. Unfortunately, the historical reference did not bring them a victorious candidacy. Munich's new efforts for candidacy for the Olympics in 2022 also polarises minds and oscillates between Olympics nostalgia and financial reservations. If one visualises that the estimated costs for Sochi are already 24 times higher than in Munich in 1972, meaning a calculation of 24 billion euros, the question remains, of how much the holding of Olympic Games, and with it the image-policy within the Olympic competition, may be worth. Where this journey will lead is still uncertain. And this not only concerns the costs for the Olympic Games, but also the future of the Olympic Idea.

References

Abendzeitung. Den Münchnern kommt das Spanisch vor. Olympische Bildzeichen regen zum Rätselraten an, 17.11.1971. In Bundesarchiv Koblenz, B 185/683: Presseausschnittssammlung; *Die Zeit*, Olympia graphisches Problem, 4.10.1968, p. 68.

Alkemeyer, T. (1996) *Körper, Kult und Politik. Von der "Muskelreligion" Pierre de Coubertins zur Inszenierung von Macht in den Olympischen Spielen 1936*. Frankfurt am Main/ New York: Campus Verlag, p. 141.

Australian Women's Weekly (1972) Munich thinks big for the Games, *Australian Women's Weekly*. 28 June.

Bauer, F. (2009) *Rom im 19. Und 20. Jahrhundert. Konstruktion eines Mythos*. Regensburg: Verlag Friedrich Pustet.

Bericht über die Tätigkeiten der Deutschen Rundfunkanstalten bei den Olympischen Spielen (1972) *Historisches Archiv des Bayrischen Rundfunks*, Sammlung Gerhard Borgner 1972–1974, Nr. SL 22.25.

Caporilli, M. and Simeoni, F. (eds) (1990) *Il Foro Italico e lostadio olimpico. Imaginidallastoria*. Rome: Tomo edizioni

Carli, M. (2008) Olimpionica Tra "fascistizzazione" e "italianizzazione" dello sport nella propaganda fascista dei tardi anni. Venti. MR, 16/27: 79–89

Cornelißen, C., Klinkhammer, L. and Schwentker, W. (2003) Nationale Erinnerungskulturen seit 1945 im Vergleich. In C. Cornelißen, L. Klinkhammer and W. Schwentker (eds), *Nationale Erinnerungskulturen. Deutschland, Italien und Japan seit 1945*. Frankfurt am Main: Fischer Taschenbuch Verlag, pp. 9–27.

Corriere della Sera (1960) Olimpiadi di Roma impegnod'onore. 18, p. 15.

Der Spiegel (1961) Zank ums Zelt. August, pp. 132–135.

Dogliani, P. (2000) Sport and fascism. *Journal of Modern Italian Studies*, 5(3): 326–343.

Elias, N. (1998) Der bundesdeutsche Terrorismus – Ausdruck eines sozialen Generationskonflikts. In N. Elias, *Studien über die Deutschen. Machtkämpfe und Habitusentwicklung im 19. und 20. Jahrhundert*. Frankfurt am Main: Suhrkamp, pp. 300–389.

Chicago Daily Tribune (1958) Remember Olympic spirit. 20 March, p. D1.

Fickers, A. (2009) Europäische Fernseh- und Mediengeschichte als Zeitgeschichte. *Archiv für Sozialgeschichte*, 49: 1–28.

Gajek, E. (2013) *Imagepolitik im olympischen Wettstreit: Die Spiele von Rom 1960 und München 1972*. Göttingen: Wallstein Verlag.

Guttmann, A. (2006) Berlin 1936: The most controversial Olympics. In A. Tomlinson and C. Young (eds), *National Identities and Global Sports Events: Culture, Politics and Spectacle in the Olympics and the Football World Cup*. New York: State University of New York Press, pp. 65–82.

Hobsbawm, E. and Ranger, T. (eds) (1983) *The Invention of Tradition*. Cambridge: Cambridge University Press.

Il Messaggero (1960) E proseguitaieri la cancellazione delle scrittefasciste al Foro Italico. 10 August, p. 4.

IOC (1957) *Bulletin Officiel 1*. In Archive of the International Olympic Committee, JO-1960s-COJO 1957–1959. Lausanne: the International Olympic Committee.

Koenig, W. (1968) Das Münchner Oberwiesenfeld wird Olympische Landschaft. *Olympisches Feuer*, 18(2): 1–7.

L'Avanti (1960) Tremilliardi e 700 millionispesioerilluminare la capitale. 13 August, p. 4.

Los Angeles Times (1954). Italy bid for Olympic Games in '60. 25 December, p. 4.

Los Angeles Times (1958) Rome Games in '60 Dream Trip. 13 July, p. C8.

L'Unità (1960) Imbarazzatosilenzio di Folchisullescrittefasciste del foro. 12 August, p. 2.

Modrey, E. (2008) Architecture as a mode of self-representation at the Olympic Games in Rome (1960) and Munich (1972). *European Historical Review*, 6: 691–706.

Modrey, E. (2009) Das Olympia-Kabinett. Die Olympischen Spiele 1960 und die Regierungskrise Italiens Ende der 1950er Jahre. In *Quellen und Forschungen aus Italienischen Archiven und Bibliotheken*, 89: 353–378.

Modrey, E. (2010) Das Publikum und die Medien. Die Eröffnungsfeier der Olympiade 1972. In F. Bösch and P. Schmidt (eds), *Medialisierte Ereignisse. Performanz, Inszenierung und Medien seit dem 18. Jahrhundert*. Frankfurt am Main/ New York: Campus Verlag, pp. 246–278.

Münkel, D. and Seegers, L. (2008) Einleitung. Medien und Imagepolitik im 20. Jahrhundert. In D. Münkel and L. Seegers (eds), *Medien und Imagepolitik im 20. Jahrhundert Deutschland, Europa und die USA*. Frankfurt: Campus Verlag.

New York Times (1972) Big Talk at Munich is the Big Cost of Big Roof. 3 September, p. S2.

Organisationskomitee der Spiele der XX. Olympiade (eds.) (1973) München, p. 270.

Organizing Olympic Committee of the Games of the XVII. Olympiad (1963), *The Games of the XVII. Olympiade: Rome 1960: The official report of the organizing committee*. Organizing Olympic Committee of the Games of the XVII. Olympiad: Rome.

Roche, M. (2000) *Mega-Events and Modernity: Olympics and Expos in the Growth of Global Culture*. London/ New York: Routledge.

Rivenburgh, N. (2010) In pursuit of a global image: media events as political communication. In N. Couldry, A. Hepp and F. Krotz (eds), *Media Events in a Global Age*. London: Routledge, pp. 187–202.

Schieder, W. (2006) Rom, die Repräsentation der Antike im Faschismus. In E. Stein-Hölkeskamp and K. Hölkeskamp (eds.), *Erinnerungsorte der Antike. Die römische Welt*. München: C. H. Beck, pp. 701–721.

Sydney Sun Herald (1971) Munich '72 wants to forget the past. 22 August.

Tagsold, C. (2002) *Die Inszenierung der kulturellen Identität in Japan. Das Beispiel der Olympischen Spiele in Tôkyô 1964*. Munich: Iudicium-Verlag.

The Province (1972) The Monster of Munich. 8 July.

Vermerk vom (1972) Betreff: Informationsmaterial, unterzeichnet von Pätzold. 3 August.

Wenn, S. R. (1993) Lights! Camera! Little Action: Television, Avery Brundage and the 1956 Melbourne Olympics. *ST*, 10, November: 38–53.

Wenn, S. R. (1994) An Olympic Squabble: The distribution of Olympic television revenues 1960–1966 *OIJOS*, 3: 2747.

Woller, H. (2010) *Geschichte Italiens im 20. Jahrhundert*. München: C. H. Beck.

Young, C. and Schiller, K. (2010) *The 1972 Munich Olympics and the Making of Modern Germany*. Berkeley, CA: University of California Press.

36

THE MOSCOW OLYMPICS, 1980

Competing in the context of the Cold War and state dirigisme

Olga Chepurnaya

At the seventy-fifth meeting of the International Olympic Committee (IOC) held in October 1974, the decision was made to select Moscow as the host city of the XXII Summer Olympic Games in 1980 (almost immediately the media reduced the full name down to Olympics-80). This event was preceded by a long history of relations between the USSR and the IOC, which emerged during the post-World War II period, when in the spring of 1951, the USSR became a member of the Olympic Movement. From 1952, the Soviet national team regularly took part in the Olympic Games.

It is also worth noting that by 1974, the significance of sports in the USSR had undergone considerable change. The role given to sports now went beyond being a tool of hegemonic control employed to address internal challenges (such as sustaining the health and working capacity of the population, distracting the public from problems, and enhancing discipline) to become a Cold War weapon. The militaristic language of Soviet sport in the 1920s to the 1930s continued into this new historical context (O'Mahony 2006).

For the USSR, the Moscow 1980 Olympic Games became the first event of such scale in Soviet history. Many years of preparation, mass media coverage, hundreds of thousands of visitors, unprecedented drama – all of these undoubtedly connect the Moscow Olympic Games to mega-events more generally (Roche 2000). More specifically, however, the Moscow Games provide an opportunity to examine sport mega-events in the context of the Cold War and the late Soviet period.

This chapter analyses the preparations for and the results of the Moscow 1980 Olympic Games. Empirical materials include official documents that were only declassified in recent years and partially published material such as resolutions of the Central Committee and reports and memoranda of the bodies involved in arranging the Olympic Games that offer substantial data for an analysis of this sort (Pyat' kolets 2011). The chapter focuses on certain issues related to preparing for and holding the Olympic Games in the light of international problems, boycott and the consequences of the event for the host country.

The historical context

The importance of the Moscow Olympic Games for the Soviet regime and the event's influence on the external and internal politics of the USSR are hard to assess without understanding the historical context. James Riordan's (1977) work provides a basis for identifying specific periods in the development of Soviet sport. The period of 'Soviet physical culture and sports'(1917–1928) was characterized by criticism of bourgeois sports and a quest for alternatives, by the principle of proletarian internationalism in international contacts, and by debates about the role of sports in creating 'the new Soviet person'. The period of the centralization of control over sport (1929–1938) was a time when sport associations were subordinated to the country's party leadership, and international contacts with clubs and sport associations of workers were established. The next is the war period (1939–1945) when sports functioned as a way of unifying the people and sustaining and demonstrating the soldierly spirit, then the Cold War period (1946–1991), when the USSR pursued international recognition, exported the Soviet sport model, and joined international sport organizations (becoming a member of thirty international sport organizations by 1958, and as many as forty-two by 1973). During this period, sport functioned as part of large-scale opposition to capitalist countries, with the main point of tension being between the USSR and the USA. During the period after 1991, it experienced the transition from socialist to market sport economics, whilst retaining some elements of the previous organizational structure.

Officially, sport was presented in the USSR as a branch of the public field which was not dependent on politics. This official position followed the Marxist approach to sport as being akin to religion – a means of subordination, sustaining class divisions and shaping the system of domination in capitalist society. In the early Soviet period, this attitude to sport was enshrined in practice. By the end of the 1920s there were heated discussions of the bourgeois nature of competitive sports alongside the emergence of ideas about sport for all, with its emphasis on participation rather than competition and audience appeal. Sport was considered to be an important means of emancipation, especially for women, and a means by which to produce a 'new Soviet person'. These were the aspects of large-scale involvement in the educative function of sport that were manifest in the multiple physical training movements and volunteer sport associations that emerged during that period (Guttmann 1988; O'Mahony 2006; Dubin 2006).

In the early post-revolution years, the centralized system of sport activities for Soviet citizens had not yet been established. Indeed, during the first decade, Komsomol, trade unions, and educational and military committees handled the formation of different sport associations, events and norms. However, by the beginning of the 1930s, sport management underwent a transformation with the control of sport becoming centralized and international connections with workers' sport clubs and associations being established.

The value of the USSR participation in the Olympic Movement before World War II was constantly in doubt. In 1920, Vsevobuch (the organization in charge of the system of the General Military Training from 1918 until 1923) intended to delegate Soviet sportsmen to the Antwerp Olympic Games, but was refused permission under the pretext of the Soviet powers refusing to accept the liabilities of the Russian Empire. In 1924, the Organising Committee of the Paris Olympic Games delivered an invitation to Soviet sportsmen through the agency of the French Workers' Sport and Gymnastic Union. However, the Soviet government refused to participate and protested against German athletes being banned from the Games (Pyat' kolets 2011: 6).

The fact that the USSR did not attempt to regain IOC recognition during the inter-war period points to a lack of government interest in participating in the Olympic Movement. During the years preceding World War II, Soviet sport organizations were searching instead for contacts with sport associations with similar proletarian origins as opposed to international organizations that they regarded as bourgeois and hostile.

Only in April 1951 was the Olympic Committee of the USSR (currently the Russian Olympic Committee) established. The following month, at the forty-sixth IOC session, the USSR was admitted to IOC membership. When discussing the USSR's request to join, issues on the agenda included the amateur status of Soviet athletes (this was considered to be more nominal than actual) and the independence of the USSR Olympic Committee from the Communist Party and government. Nevertheless, according to Riordan, at that time the IOC was facing many more problems due to the changed geopolitical situation after World War II, and the USSR was admitted in spite of evident non-compliance with admission conditions (Guttmann 1988; Demeter 2005; Riordan 1977).

As early as 1956, the Sportkomitet of the USSR (an official abbreviation of the Physical Culture and Sports Committee attached to the Council of Ministers of the USSR) submitted a bid to the Central Committee of the Communist Party of the Soviet Union (CPSU Central Committee) to host the 1964 Summer Olympic Games in Moscow. The idea of the proposal was initially approved, but in the course of detailed consideration and examination of the experience of other host countries as well as of IOC requirements, it became clear that it would not be possible to realize this in the near years. The lack of suitable sport facilities, low service standards and poor living conditions (hotels, restaurants, transport), apprehensions that Soviet citizens were not ready to resist the impact of the Western guests and, arguably, most important of all, an unwillingness to have contact with countries with which the USSR had no diplomatic relations, set back the fulfillment of the idea of 'the first Socialistic Olympic Games' for years. Sportkomitet re-submitted its bid in 1963 and in 1965 for the 1968 and 1972 Olympic Games (respectively), but found no support from the CPSU Central Committee. Prozumenschikov and other sports historians explain these decisions with reference to the personality of Nikita Khrushchev, who had little interest in sport. However, one cannot ignore internal problems and issues of foreign policy relations that played their roles as important deterrents (Pyat' kolets 2011: 15; Peppard and Riordan 1993).

When Leonid Brezhnev assumed the post of Secretary General, the Central Committee revisited the idea of holding the Summer Olympics in Moscow. A bid to host the 1976 Games was developed and submitted, but, despite optimism amongst the USSR's political elite, the bid lost during the final round of voting. The next bid was prepared more thoroughly by USSR representatives and was submitted nine years prior the 1980 Games. Active work had been conducted with IOC members, foreign mass media and representatives of international sport associations. All of this helped to result in the desired outcome in February 1975, when the resolution of the CPSU Central Committee 'Of Preparations for the XXII Summer Olympic Games in Moscow' was approved by the Organizing Committees for the Olympic Games and large-scale preparations for the event began.

According to documents relating to preparations for the 1980 Olympics, from the very beginning every element of the process, including construction, propaganda, counter-propaganda, the allocation of funds in rubles and foreign currency, international contacts and contracts, was strictly controlled at the level of the CPSU Central Committee. This is clear evidence of a state dirigisme strategy for hosting international events in the USSR, which remains an issue in contemporary Russia (Muller 2011).

A turning point in the preparations for the Games came in the winter of 1979/80, when the tensions intrinsic to the Cold War were exacerbated after Soviet troops were sent to Afghanistan and the international situation changed significantly. This is why it is important to see the history of preparations for the 1980 Olympic Games chronologically, i.e. before and after the crisis of 1979/80.

The ideological context

Ideology was undoubtedly one of the most important features of the Moscow Olympic Games from the moment that the bid was submitted to the IOC in 1971. The Olympic Games were planned as an event that would establish a basis upon which to propagandize the Soviet way of life and belief system both in countries of the socialistic bloc and in capitalist countries. In addition, a purportedly non-political headline event in the country fully fitted in with the general pattern of Soviet achievements, including space exploration and providing assistance to developing countries. By hosting a mega-event such as the Olympic Games, the USSR could considerably improve its international image on the one hand, and enhance patriotic feelings inside the country on the other.

Much effort was made to smooth over differences in both international and domestic politics. One significant issue which the Soviet leadership faced was the need to follow the IOC requirement to invite all recognized representatives of the Olympic Movement to the Olympic Games. The problem was that the USSR had strained relations with some countries and no diplomatic relations with others. A series of such issues can be traced in the published documents on the 1980 Olympic Games. For example, the report of the Organizing Committee of the 1980 Olympic Games, in disclosing analysis of Montreal's Olympic Games experience, states that it is important to summarize the materials and 'develop suggestions on awareness-raising campaigns and work with journalists' to avoid negative views in the press and 'moral damage' to the country (Pyat' kolets 2011: 114).

The 'Two Chinas' issue was also repeatedly mentioned in Organizing Committee memos and reports. On the one hand, the National Olympic Committee (NOC) of Taiwan was officially recognized by the IOC under the name of Republic of China, and the USSR was bound to invite them to take part in the Moscow Games. On the other hand, taking into account tensions in relations with the People's Republic of China and the fact that the PRC was not recognized by the IOC and did not participate in the Olympic Movement, Beijing was expected to react strongly should the Soviet Organizing Committee comply with IOC requirements. Having solicited the support of Lord Killanin, the IOC President, and representatives of socialist countries in the IOC, the Soviet representatives successfully came up with proposals to resolve the issue. As a result, in 1979, the eighty-first IOC session adopted the resolution of acknowledging the NOCs of both the PRC and Taiwan, to be followed by working out the issues of names, flags and anthems (Pyat' kolets 2011: 157). This middle ground was not fully satisfactory to all stakeholders, but at least resulted in the issue being officially resolved.

One more concern was the requirement to invite sport delegations, journalists and tourists from countries with which the USSR did not maintain relations for a variety of reasons. Until the middle of 1977, official reports consistently referred to the fact that, during IOC meetings and press conferences, the question of guaranteed participation of all national sport teams recognized by the IOC was regularly raised. The USSR representatives had to constantly confirm the readiness of the country's leadership to fulfil their obligations and invite all recognized members to take part in the Olympic Games. As early as September 1977 the CPSU Central Committee issued the decree that allowed the Organizing Committee to 'maintain required contacts with all IOC members and national Olympic Committee recognized by the IOC', to invite Olympic attachés of these countries to the USSR while minimizing contact with the NOCs of Taiwan, Chile and South Korea, as well as access to the country for their officials, journalists and tourists during the Olympic Games (Pyat' kolets 2011: 157). At the same time, Organizing Committee representatives constantly me with counterparts from socialist countries (the PRC, North Korea, East Germany, etc.) to persuade these allies that unwanted contact with the NOCs of certain countries was merely a matter of protocol and did not affect the USSR's official position regarding these countries in any way.

The Organizing Committee of the 1980 Olympic Games, the KGB (Committee for State Security) and the Press Agency 'Novosti' ('News') were continuously monitoring the Western press to discern changes in the attitude of capitalist countries towards the 1980 Olympic Games. Regular briefing notes indicate the main elements of criticism of the USSR and the Moscow Olympic Games: human rights violations, unsatisfactory level of services, censorship, KGB officers in Sportkomitet, Organizing Committee of the Olympic Games, and among athletes, passport regulations. Similar reports were submitted to the Central Committee on an incredibly regular basis, but initially the strongest apprehensions concerned 'slanderous' radio stations, Radio Free Europe and Europe, that were accredited for the Innsbruck and Montreal Olympic Games. Huge efforts were made to amend the media accreditation procedures of the IOC to avoid the need to invite these radio stations to Moscow. Moreover, as early as the summer of 1978, notes of the KGB and Novosti Press Agency were changed to include more detailed information about anti-Soviet organizations that were beginning to directly oppose the Moscow Olympic Games taking place. The rhetoric of these reports, especially those of the KGB, changed considerably – it began simply with such phrases as 'hostile intelligence agencies', 'enemy propaganda', and 'slanderous organizations of the enemy'. While initially the KGB let it be known that it was possible that members of anti-Soviet organisations (e.g. the National Alliance of Russian Solidarists) would attempt to be included in national delegations seeking to disrupt Olympic Games ceremonies, perform acts of terrorism, distribute anti-Soviet literature (Pyat' kolets 2011: 177), later they provided more detailed information about anti-Soviet operations that were already in progress. It becomes clear from these reports that even by the summer of 1978, long before Soviet troops went into Afghanistan, calls to boycott or move the 1980 Olympic Games from Moscow to another place had been articulated. The main reason related to human rights violations in the USSR. By summer 1979, the KGB reports suggested that, in many countries of Western Europe, different groups, sometimes linked to local parliaments, were openly taking a stand against holding the Olympic Games in Moscow (Pyat' kolets 2011: 235).

In response, the USSR adopted a variety of counter-propaganda measures including negotiating the establishment of information centres in Western countries to disseminate information about preparations for the 1980 Olympic Games. For example, a memo from the USSR embassy in the UK dated October 1976 refers to a meeting with K. Morgan, a 'famous press and advertising specialist', who suggested that a London Information Centre for the Moscow Olympic Games should be established to maintain direct liaison with Moscow. The suggestion caught the interest of the Soviet leadership not least because after the Olympic Games, information networks of this type could be used to achieve propaganda tasks abroad (Pyat' kolets 2011: 130–131). As criticism of the USSR grew, the country's leadership paid ever more attention to propaganda. Thus, it follows from a report of the Organizing Committee for the 1980 Olympic Games as of August 1978 that the awareness of the need for propaganda should consist of several dimensions: holding regular press conferences (38 were held) and meetings (800 held) with journalists, distributing Olimpiada-80 and Olimpiyskaya Panorama magazines and books, producing TV films of preparations for the Olympic Games in 30 countries, and arranging exhibitions. At the same time, the Organizing Committee pointed to the fact that related agencies did not fulfill the book publishing plans and failed to produce enough films, while international cultural and economic ties could have been used more intensively for propaganda purposes (Pyat' kolets 2011: 304).

Simultaneously, security measures were developed for Moscow, as well as for Tallinn, Leningrad, Kiev and Minsk, where certain Olympic Games competitions were to be held. In this context, 'safety' had a double meaning: on the one hand, it meant ensuring proper order and the personal safety of all participants during the Olympic Games, but on the other hand, 'ideological' safety was implied. While the first task was addressed by drawing on the experience of the Federal Republic of Germany, Canada and other countries that had already hosted similar mega-events, the second required new initiatives.

First, it was decided to end the academic year in Moscow universities and institutes earlier than usual to clear hostels and make sure that students left Moscow. Soviet students were sent to pass practical training sessions outside the city, while foreign students were provided with rest time in recreation and holiday centres at public expense. In addition, a resolution of the Secretariat of the CPSU Central Committee dated 24 July 1979, introduced temporary measures restricting entry to Moscow during the 1980 Olympic Games and sending Moscow citizens to construction force units, sport/pioneer camps, and other recreation facilities (Pyat' kolets 2011: 351–353). This is how Soviet citizens were to be safeguarded from the 'pernicious influence of the Western world'. Other resolutions of the KGB and the Ministry of Internal Affairs dealt with cleansing Moscow of dangerous criminals and mentally affected people who could potentially interfere with the Games (Pyat' kolets 2011: 635–637). Finally, all foreigners who entered the jurisdiction of the USSR were subject to strict security screening procedures and were escorted within the country.

During the Olympic Games, the Committee of Foreign Tourism issued a large number of reports, which contained a list of positive assessments from Olympiad members of official delegations and foreign tourists. These documents were often given the names of the respondents, and include quotations from conversations with them. These documents show that foreign visitors to Moscow Olympics were escorted not only to ensure the safety standards but also to collect information.

The economic context

Another important aspect of preparing for and holding the Moscow Olympic Games was the financial domain. Until 1984, the Olympic Games had little commercial significance; no profit was usually made as a result of hosting the event. However, some commercial practices to cover expenses had emerged. This consisted initially of selling broadcasting rights, with 50 per cent of the profits being transferred to the IOC. The production and sale of souvenir items, stamps, coins and lottery tickets also brought some income. Furthermore, since the Rome Olympic Games in 1960, sports equipment could be supplied for free in exchange for providing the providing companies with the 'official supplier' and 'official sponsor' status. The USSR tried to use all of these mechanisms to the maximum extent.

From 1971, Soviet sport managers started to gather and analyse information about how the Olympic Games had been prepared for and held in other countries. After Moscow had been approved as the host city, members of the Organizing Committee collected as much information as possible about the Olympic Games in Munich, Montreal and Innsbruck. According to reports of Organizing Committee delegates, in addition to entering into negotiations with foreign colleagues, they also met with representatives of TV companies, firms and companies that showed an interest in signing contracts with the Organizing Committee. The report of the Montreal trip in 1976 refers to Canadian colleagues' experience of issuing coins, holding a lottery, arranging medical services and so on. While in Canada, committee members also had negotiations with CBS and Coca Cola, and signed a contract with the French affiliate of Adidas. Proposals from IBM, Siemens and Phillips to supply hardware and software are also mentioned. Thus, a year before the 1980 Olympic Games, contracts for broadcasting rights had been signed with world-leading TV companies, and contracts were concluded with 54 foreign corporations, official suppliers and sponsors (Pyat' kolets 2011: 281, 307). Every proposal had to be discussed and approved by the CPSU Central Committee, while the documents themselves were assigned 'secret' status. It is evident that the 1980 Olympic Games had set unprecedented conditions for goods from capitalistic countries to penetrate beyond the 'iron curtain'.

The Organizing Committee also submitted requests for an allocation of foreign currency funds in order to buy press centre equipment, Mercedes cars for official entertainment purposes, and business trip expenses (Pyat' kolets 2011: 59, 281, 286–287). In addition, it took charge of the production and sale of souvenir products, gold and silver Olympic coins, and holding Sportloto and Sprint international lotteries (the latter being sold in the countries of the socialistic bloc, giving them status of the first ever designated international lotteries).

For many years, the total budget of the Moscow Olympic Games was not disclosed. However, the sum could have been estimated at least approximately from archival documents (although they contain only individual amounts allocated to finance different needs, such as the construction of sport facilities, building roads, and putting on cultural programmes). The important point is that the USSR agreed to sign a wide range of contracts with Western companies in order to minimize expenses associated with organizing the Olympic Games, thereby extending international economic cooperation.

What attracted attention in reports of Olympic Games progress was that the spending of budget funds was controlled, and in every case when work provided for in the plan was not carried out on time, the budget was not implemented to the full extent. This dealt with Olympic Games facilities construction, publication of awareness-building and propaganda materials, and many other aspects of preparation. Thus, in 1978–1979, there were many reports of delays in the construction of the Olympic Games facilities (stadia, hotels, restaurants, airports), but requests for additional financing were rarely submitted. Factors mentioned in relation to delays included project complexity, lack of personnel and equipment, late supplies or the low quality of construction materials, the large scale of work and the inadequate capacity of construction organizations. Occasionally, difficulties with implementing a certain project occurred, and requests to amend the projects were submitted to the Central Committee (Pyat' kolets 2011: 73, 77, 83, 304). All in all, the plan was to build or reconstruct 99 Olympic Games facilities, with 76 of them being located in Moscow. A creative solution to arranging the Olympic village in one of the new residential quarters of Moscow seems to have been found by chance. It was not included in the original project submitted to the IOC, but at a press conference held in May 1974, S. P. Pavlov, Chairman of Sportkomitet and head of the Steering Committee for the Moscow 1980 Olympic Games, first expressed the idea of using new housing developments for this purpose. Later, this idea was implemented with the residential quarters that included eighteen 16-storey buildings, with a directorate, restaurant, sports centre and other amenities being built in the south-western district of Moscow. As yet, no documents containing information about the distribution of this new housing stock amongst Moscow citizens after the Olympic Games have been located.

Alongside construction work, the Organizing Committee, jointly with international sport federations, also planned the detailed programme of sport competitions, conferences and meetings relating to certain kinds of sport, and a cultural programme for officials, sportsmen and tourists. A particular item to be discussed was arranging for religious services in the Olympic village. With specific reference to the experience of previous Olympic Games, it was decided to equip three premises – for Christians, Muslims and Jews (with Buddhists). The decision to provide such a service arose from the desire to refute Western press statements that the USSR did not guarantee freedom of religion (Pyat' kolets 2011: 409–415).

A considerable amount of attention was paid to service sector management (catering, transport, trade) because this aspect of Soviet life was also subject to criticism in the foreign mass media. The issues discussed included not only the construction of new restaurants and stores, but also additional training of personnel. Later, during and after the Olympic Games, Soviet civil servants and the press actively used interviews with foreign tourists to prove that the accusations of the Western press were unsubstantiated (Pyat' kolets 2011: 796–799).

The international relations context and the boycott

The crisis resulting from the invasion of Afghanistan by Soviet troops substantially altered the context in which preparations for the Moscow Olympics took place. By the end of 1979, progress reports prompted some anxiety, but generally speaking, both the IOC and the Soviet leadership were satisfied. However, events that occurred in the winter and spring of 1979/1980 brought many new problems. The Soviet invasion of Afghanistan which began on 27 December 1979 gave an additional impetus, or perhaps simply provided more ammunition for the government of the USA and some other countries to increase protests about holding the Olympic Games in Moscow. On 1 January 1980, at a meeting of NATO countries, the governments of the USA, the UK and Canada spoke in favour of boycotting the Moscow Games. This suggestion was sent to the IOC, while the USSR was delivered an ultimatum for immediate troop withdrawal from Afghanistan.

The situation was aggravated by the fact that these events took place before the opening of the Winter Olympic Games in Lake Placid, USA, and the USSR did not intend to forfeit its participation. At the eighty-second session of the IOC, the issue was put to a vote, and Moscow retained its right to hold the XXII Summer Olympic Games after a unanimous decision. Under pressure from U.S. President Carter, however, the American administration announced its refusal for the U.S. team to take part in the Games (Aronoff 2006). In March 1980, the USA suspended all trading transactions with the USSR, thus creating tremendous difficulties for the local Organizing Committee of the Olympics. Payments under contract with ABC and Coca Cola were suspended, other imported goods from the USA were not supplied to the host city, and the USA stopped selling tickets for events and souvenirs. With other countries joining the boycott, the USSR faced similar problems with them. The CPSU Central Committee made a series of decisions aimed at improving the situation; propaganda via embassies and other information channels was enhanced. Upon agreement with the IOC it was announced to all sportsmen that they were guaranteed the possibility of participating in the competitions, in circumvention of the boycott, under the Olympic flag instead of a national one. Furthermore, tourists from the USSR and other socialist countries were tempted with partial compensation for travel and accommodation expenses. According to all documents produced during this stage of preparation for the 1980 Olympic Games, the main task of the Central Committee was to prevent the USA and other countries that joined the boycott from fatally sabotaging all of the efforts that had already been made. The key idea to emerge from these documents was that the Olympic Games were certain to take place, and that everything must be taken to the highest level. It is most likely that, during this period, considerations of profit-making from holding the mega-event were no longer a focus of attention.

All efforts were put into counter-propaganda, in the course of which the reasons for boycott were replaced with the claim that the USSR was fighting for world peace, while the USA was pursuing an aggressive international policy aimed at ruining the first ever Soviet Olympic Games. New awareness-building and propaganda materials for Soviet and international audiences, including posters, films, cartoons and books, were created at an accelerated pace. Other activities that took place simultaneously included engaging the participation of athletes and spectators to the largest extent possible and explanatory work with the countries that were still uncertain about their attitude to the proposed boycott (Pyat' kolets 2011: 602–609, 614–619, 644, 647–656). In the end, the Moscow Olympic Games were boycotted by 65 countries, with 81 countries participating in the opening ceremony (Liberia refused to take part in the competitions but only joined the boycott after the opening the ceremony). In a very short time, the Organizing Committee managed to get spectators to the stadiums to replace the tourists who had failed to come from the boycotting countries. All competitions were held in accordance with the schedule, and the Olympic Games were considered to be successful by both the USSR government and the IOC.

Conclusion

So what were the possible profits and losses of the USSR hosting this mega-event? On the one hand, one can suggest that the fact that South Korea, Chile, Israel and some other countries joined the boycott turned out to be a relief for the CPSU Central Committee, as this meant that there was no need to invite representatives of these countries. However, in addition to the competitions as such, during the Olympic Games important meetings of the IOC and international sport federations were held, at which representatives of many of these countries wanted to be present. In addition, journalists from these countries also applied for accreditation, and in compliance with IOC rules, the USSR had no right to refuse them. Therefore, one can argue that the 1980 Olympic Games did not in any way improve, but on the contrary, aggravated the difficulties that the USSR faced in the international relations.

With the need to urgently resolve issues related to filling the stadium seats, the inadequate deliveries of products and equipment, breaches of contracts for broadcasting rights and so on, the costs of the Olympic Games increased. Necessary security measures resulted in the almost complete destruction of civil rights movements inside the country, which met the interests of the CPSU Central Committee but did not make the internal situation easier for the country's citizens.

One of the positive consequences of the Moscow Olympic Games one should mention is that the USSR, having shown steadiness and confidence in its own position, had not turned out to be a defeated party in the eyes of the international community. Anti-Soviet and anti-capitalist propagandas counter-balanced each other, and the opposing parties broke even, especially given that the USA also suffered economic losses.

In addition, an openness and willingness to cooperate in the course of preparing for and holding the Olympic Games had been demonstrated, which, for a short time, increased 'iron curtain' transparency at least by way of trade relations. Another notable enhancement was that in the infrastructure of Moscow (with smaller changes in Leningrad, Tallin, and other cities that hosted individual Olympic Games competitions) – repaired roads, new cafes and restaurants, and a new residential district emerged. The short-term effects of the Olympic Games also included service improvement and an increased product range in Moscow stores.

Due to active counter-propaganda and the policy of deliberately silencing unfavourable facts, the USSR had also updated the image of the foreign enemy, whilst an image of the Moscow Olympic Games as the most peaceful, safe and friendly Olympic Games was created. Today this image continues to dominate the construction of memories of the Soviet mega-event. These propaganda activities and the use of the Olympic Games' image persisted long after the Games were over, and to some extent still persist (Gonitel 1981; Kolodniy 1981; Guskov 1982; Samaranch 2001).

During the Cold War, capitalist and Soviet sport management systems were affected by each other, such that they increasingly acquired more common features. Analysis of sport and sport management, both in specific countries and in the overall international context, helps us to understand relations of power in the society since sport is a field of production, reproduction and transformation of cultural practice, ideology and religious faiths (Hargreaves 1982: 37). Mega-events such as the Olympic Games reveal a disposition of forces within the field of sports and, in the case of the subject under discussion, in the field of international politics in the second half of the twentieth century. The main participants in the Cold War, the USSR and the USA, accused each other of having ambitions of the world domination and hegemony. However, in terms of the political manoeuvring that took place around the 1980 Olympic Games in order to gain victory over the Cold War opponent, the match ended in a tie, despite the home-ground advantage of the USSR.

References

Aronoff, Y. S. (2006) In Like a Lamb, Out Like a Lion: The Political Conversion of Jimmy Carter. *Political Science Quarterly*, 121(3): 425–449.

Demeter, G. S. (2005) *Ocherki po Istorii Otechestvennoi Fizicheskoi Kultury I Olimpiiskogo Dvijeniya*. Moscow: Sovetskii sport.

Dubin, B. (2006) Sostyazatel'nost' I solidarnost'. Rojdenie sporta iz dukha obshchestva. *Otechestvennye zapiski*, 6 (33): pp. 100–120.

Gonitel, A. I. (1981) *Poka ne Ostyli Olimpiiskie Strasti*. Moskva: Znanie.

Gus'kov, S. I. (1982) *Olimpiada-80 Glazami Americancev*. Moskva: Fizkyltura I sport.

Guttmann, A. (1988) The Cold war and Olympics. *International Journal*, 43(4): 554–568.

Hargreaves, J. (1982) *Sport, Culture and Ideology*. London: Routledge and Kegan Paul.

Kolodnyi, A.G. (1981) *'Igry' vokrug igr*. Moskva: Sovetskaya Rossiya.

Muller, M. (2011) State Dirigisme in Mega Projects: Governing the 2014 Winter Olympics in Sochi. *Environment and Planning*, 43(9): 2091–2108.

O'Mahony, M. (2006) *Sport in the USSR: Physical Culture – Visual Culture*. London: Reaktion Books.

Peppard, V. and Riordan, J. (1993) *Playing Politics: Soviet Sport Diplomacy to 1992*. Greenwich: JAI Press.

Pyat' kolets pod kremlevskimi zvezdami: Documental'naya khronika olimpiady-80 d Moskve. (2011) Avtory-sostaviteli: Konova T.Yu, Prozumenshchikov M.Yu. Rdactor: Tomilina N.G. Moskva: MFDJames.

Riordan, J. (1977) *Sport in Soviet Society*. Cambridge: Cambridge University Press.

Roche, M. (2000) *Mega-Events and Modernity: Olympics and Expos in the Growth of Global Culture*. London: Routledge.

Samaranch Kh.A. (2001) *Ot Moskvy do Moskvy*. Moskva: Golden B.

37

POLITICS AND SPORTING EVENTS

Beijing Olympics, 2008

Dong Jinxia

The Olympic Games and politics have long been linked. This is especially true of the 2008 Olympic Games staged in Beijing, the capital city of People's Republic of China. The Games attracted over 10,000 athletes, over 50,000 media personnel, hundreds of thousands of tourists, a million volunteers and over four billion TV viewers across the world, which put China at the centre of world attention. The highlights of the successful bid, the eye-catching art airport terminal and stadiums, and the spectacular Opening and Closing ceremonies as well as the incidents during the Olympic torch relay on some European and North American legs made the Games one of the most politicized events in recent history. Arguably the Games might 'have far more influence than any other Games in history' (Penn 2008: 80–81).

Though the Games have been over for eight years, their impact is still felt in China and perhaps the world as well. In the past decade and more, a number of books and articles targeting Games-related issues such as national identity, foreign policy, media freedom, sports invest-ment and so on have been published. Although some works targeted the political aspects of the Games, such as *Beijing's Games: What the Olympics Mean to China*, by Brownell, S. (2008); *Beijing 2008: Preparing for Glory: Chinese Challenge in the 'Chinese Century'*, by J. A. Mangan and Dong Jinxia (2009); 'The Beijing Games in the Western Imagination of China: The Weak Power of Soft Power', by Wolfram Manzenreiter (2008), very few examined the Beijing Games from a comprehensively political and historic perspective and its impact on today's China. Some issues still need to be examined. What made the Games more of a political event? What is the complex inter-relationship between the Beijing Games, identity politics and the modernization drive of China? What impact did the Games have on China's rise and on world affairs? This chapter explores the interconnections of the Beijing Games, domestic and international politics and modernization drive; it analyses the impact of the 2008 Games on implementing China's grand strategy of modernizing the nation and reviving its influential status in the world, and foresee the future development of the Olympic Movement in China.

Awakening China: Olympic bids

In 1991, Beijing submitted its first application to the IOC for the 2000 Olympic Games. This event turned world attention towards China, the awakening East-Asian giant. Why did the Chinese want to host the Olympic Games? An immediate answer is to restore China's national grandeur, to erase past memories of defeat and to showcase to the world a new, vigorous image of an open, modernized, civilized and well-developed nation. What then is the past defeat? What changes have happened in Chinese society? Here it is necessary to add some historical context. Between 1840 and 1945 China suffered 'the century of shame and humiliation' after two Opium Wars between 1840 and 1898, which resulted in the granting of some 'concessions' – by Western powers such as Britain, the United States, France, Germany and Japan – to China and which resulted in unfair commercial privileges and the Japanese invasion and war (1931–1945) against China. All this dealt a heavy blow to China, which for centuries had seen itself as the centre of the world because of its sophisticated and advanced culture. By the end of the nineteenth century, China was in the throes of Western invasion and partial colonization and the country was labelled the 'sick man of East Asia'. To revive their ancient and humiliated nation, a National Reform Movement (Gray 1990) was initiated by radical Chinese intellectuals and officials in 1896. Various efforts, including sending students to Western countries to study, were made to modernize the country. After the 'May Fourth Movement'[1] in 1919, modernization became a keyword in newspapers and journals. Meanwhile, patriotic Chinese reformers believed that 'a strong nation must be built on a strong race and a strong race built on strong body' ('qiang guo bi xian qiang zhong, qiang zhong bi xian qiang shen'). Sport was thus encouraged. As early as 1908 Zhang Boling, a famous educationalist and the principal of Nankai High School in Tianjing, raised three questions in the Tianjin Youth magazine: When can China send an athlete to participate in the Olympic Games? When can China send a team to participate in the Olympic Games? When can China host an Olympic Games?

China, for the first time, sent just a single athlete to the Olympic Games in 1932. Four years later, 69 Chinese athletes participated in the Berlin Games and 36 athletes and coaches travelled to the 1948 Olympic Games in London. However, Chinese athletes did not win any Olympic medals. On 1 October 1949 Chairman Mao announced to the world: 'Chinese people have stood up!' This announcement marked the beginning of the PRC, a socialist country ruled by the Communist Party of China. Now the Chinese wanted a new global identity – one characterized by prestige, esteem and respect.

The goals of modernizing the nation and obtaining world recognition were put at the top of the new government's agenda. Sport was utilized as an effective tool to these political goals. With the establishment of a centralized sports system and professionalized coaching and training, sport developed quickly in the country in the 1950s. However, due to the dispute over the representation of China between PRC and Taiwan, PRC withdrew from the International Olympic Committee in 1958 and did not send athletes to the Olympic Games until 1979.

Sport is not isolated from politics. In the early 1950s, China and America were dragged into the Korean War and their relationship deteriorated. As a result, the United States and its allies blocked Chinese admission to the United Nations for two decades. This had a knock-on effect on the Chinese relationship with the IOC. While China remained distant from the USA and its West alliance, in the 1950s it developed a close 'brotherhood' relationship with the former Soviet Union, the first powerful socialist nation in the world. The Soviet Union was a model for China in virtually every field. Soviet experts from all walks of life were sent to China to assist Chinese reconstruction. Soviet influence was visible everywhere. However, this friendship turned sour in the 1960s, which resulted in the withdrawal of Soviet experts and technical aid (Lowenthal 1966). In the face of the potential threat from the USA and the Soviet Union the two superpowers in the world, China had to rely on itself. In 1964, it declared publically the goal of fulfilling the modernization of industry, agriculture, science and technology, and national defence by the turn of the century.[2] However, this modernization drive was not on track until the late 1970s.

Arguably, China's serious participation in the Olympic Movement 'has been part of its increasingly widening and deepening integration into world affairs, as well as its continuous modernization through a grand strategy of reform and opening-up' (Xu 2006). Immediately after China inaugurated the opening up and economic reform of the country in 1978, it re-entered the IOC. To attract foreign capital, investment, enterprise and technology four 'Specialised Economic Zones' (*jinji tequ*)[3] were established in 1980, the year China joined America and other Western countries to boycott the Moscow Summer Olympic Games over the presence of Soviet troops in Afghanistan. Chinese Olympic participation is embedded in international and domestic politics. That the pragmatic Chinese stood by Western countries was largely associated with considerations of modernization.

In 1984, China sent a big delegation to the Los Angeles Games and won 15 gold medals, which created unprecedented national pride among the Chinese at home and abroad. The ambitious Chinese were not content to win just a few gold medals. They wanted to match their huge size, big population and long history to further Olympic achievement and become an Olympic power; this became China's Olympic goal, and it resulted in the introduction of the Olympic Strategy in 1985 and later Olympic glory plans in the following three decades.

After a decade of economic reform and opening up, the Chinese economy improved significantly. The national gross product increased from 362.4 billion yuan in 1978 to 1,859.84 billion yuan in 1990. Meanwhile, Chinese trade and exchanges with foreign countries surged notably. More than 10,000 foreign joint ventures were established between 1978 and 1987, involving contracts of about $30 billion. Foreign loan contracts amounted to around $40 billion (Lee 1994). The increased economic power and improved international relationship provided a congenial climate for China to host sports mega-events.

The ability to host a big international sports competition was considered a symbol of Chinese political stabilization and economic prosperity (Kristof and Wudunn 1994; Zhang 1993). The 1990 Asian Games held in Beijing was the first international sports mega-event at which Chinese athletes achieved remarkable performances.[4] This event consolidated China's image as a major sports power, symbolic of power in general, in Asia. Through sport, China made a political statement (Jinxia 2003). However, the Chinese were not completely satisfied with what they achieved. They wanted more: to host the Olympic Games – the largest multi-sports event in the world – to raise Chinese standing in the world and to facilitate the social, economic and cultural development of the world's most populated country. Beijing publicly expressed its intention to host the 2000 Games in 1991. Sport is often used as an effective political instrument. As former President Jiang Zeming once stated: 'The bid was made to further China's domestic stability and economic prosperity. The quest for the Olympics was to raise national morale and strengthen the cohesion of the Chinese people both on the mainland and overseas' (Qu 1992: 36–37).

More specifically, the bid was expected to help break the post-1989 international political deadlock and build a new positive national image with a collective consciousness of national identity. To win the bid, Beijing built an extensive infrastructure, including an expressway from the airport to the city and a large railway station (Zhang 1993). The capital soon possessed 76 per cent of stadiums and gymnasiums necessary for the Olympic Games and organized various sport-related activities to support the bid. However, the bid for the 2000 Games failed.[5] In spite of various reasons, such as criticism over the Chinese human rights record and environmental problems, Huntington's claim that the new fault line in world politics falls between the West and the 'Rest' was surely relevant (Huntington 1996). Sport was inextricably entwined with international political struggle. In its bids for both the 2000 and 2008 Olympic Games, China argued that a truly international Olympic Movement would have to encompass the non-Western world (Xu 2006).

A year after Beijing submitted its Olympic host application in 1991, market economy was advocated in China, which brought about fundamental changes in Chinese society. Within the eight years between the first bid in 1993 and the second bid in 2001, China accomplished major achievements, from improved living standards and modernized communications to expanded higher education. Between 1993 and 2001, per capita annual disposable income for urban households increased from 2,577 yuan (US$452.1) to 6,860 yuan (US$830.5); the net income of rural households increased from 921.6 yuan (US$161.9) to 2,366.4 yuan (US$286.5); the number of motor vehicles owners increased dramatically; and the number of mobile phone users from 639,300 to 116 million. After the Internet appeared in 1995, its subscribers numbered 33,700,000 in 2001. Moreover, there were more university graduates, from 57.1 out of 10,000 people in 1993 to 103.6 in 2001, and students studying abroad rose significantly from 10,742 in 1993 to 83,973 in 2001. The rapid social and economic development laid a foundation for Beijing to host a mega-sports event. Beijing made its second bid for the Olympic Games in 1999. The bid slogan 'New Beijing, Great Olympics' reflected the Chinese wish to show the world its new image of contemporary China. Virtually all of China, from the government to its citizens, pledged all-out support for Beijing's bid to host the 2008 Olympic Games. Some 1,100 non-governmental groups from various fields including hi-technology, commerce, construction, sports, education, sanitation and the environment, wrote a letter to the IOC president Juan Samaranch in support of Beijing's bid. A public poll conducted by the Gallup Organization in Beijing in November 2000 showed that 94.9 per cent of residents in Beijing strongly supported the city's bid to host the 2008 Olympics and 62.4 per cent were fairly confident that Beijing would win (Lai 2001). Noticeably, Western opposition to the Chinese bid due to China's human rights records did not frighten the Chinese, but to some extent strengthened Chinese determination – home and abroad – to fight and win. As a result, Beijing won by 56 votes, leaving a large margin between rival cities. When Beijing was awarded the right to host the 2008 Olympic Games in 2001, the entire Chinese population, who were watching the live telecast of the voting, burst into thunderous cheers and applause. For the first time, public demonstration of national pride was witnessed on a scale rarely seen in Chinese history. In summary, China's persistent pursuit to host the Olympics was largely motivated by memories of past grandeur and humiliation and the keenness to build a new, vigorous, modern and strong nation in the world.

Rise of China: staging the Beijing Games

'While the award to host the Olympiad has certainly set the new impetus for China's modernization drive and international integration, it has also compelled China to carefully handle some intractable contradictions in the process of modernization'(Xu 2006). The aforementioned unprecedented level of support for the Beijing Games from the government to the public reflects Chinese determination to build its national identity in the world. Though the Games had always been used by host cities and countries to present or improve their international image, the efforts and attention of the Chinese government, as Manzenreiter (2008: 42) states, 'were overwhelmingly addressing domestic concerns and the need of educating the Chinese for the challenges of globalization and immediate encounters with the West'.

The infrastructural construction was under way immediately after Beijing won the right to stage the 2008 Games. To ensure that the Beijing Games was the best ever in Olympic history, China made a concerted effort. More than 290 billion yuan (US$40 billion) was invested in the Games in order to modernize Beijing's airport and other infrastructures, build the required 31 competition venues, and clean up its pollution and environmental hazards. In consequence, 'the eye-catching stadiums, the state-of-art airport terminal and modern subway lines, among other things, changed the outlook of Beijing, which reflected 'the country's effort to give shape to an emerging national identity' (Jinxia 2011).

Prior to the Games, many commentators were concerned about the possible collapse of the transport system during the event (Min and Ding 2006). To solve this problem, Beijing invested 90 billion yuan (about US$11.25 billion) in the construction of subways, light railways, express ways and airports. Eight new subway lines were constructed in the urban area and the number of public transit lines increased to over 650 by 2008. Two months prior to the Beijing Games, Beijing adopted a measure that vehicles were allowed on the roads every other day, depending on even or odd registration numbers.

Another compelling issue facing the organization committee of the Beijing Games was pollution. Environmental problems led to severe criticism and even opposition to the Chinese bid to host the Olympic Games. To tackle this problem, a 'Green Olympics' became one of the three core concepts of the Beijing Games (the other two were the People's Olympics and the Hi-tech Olympics):

> A series of measures including adjusting the industrial economic structure, controlling industrial pollution, suspending or closing seriously contaminated plants, removing the most 'purulent' plants from within the four ring-road systems, intensifying industrial pollution source management, publicizing clean manufacture and recycling, have all been taken.
>
> *(Jinxia and Mangan 2008)*

In addition, the emission of waste gases was reduced and environmentally friendly methods adopted in several renovation projects. For example, 60,000 taxis and buses were removed from the roads by the end of 2007 and 200 local factories, including the prominent Capital Steel Factory, were relocated. To reduce air pollution, another 40 factories in Tianjin and 300 factories in Tangshan, two cities close to the capital, were asked to suspend operations and 300,000 heavy polluting vehicles were banned in early July 2008. On 20 July, additional factories were shut.[6] Supermarkets and shops in China were forbidden to hand out free carrier bags after 1 June 2008 (China News 2008).

It should be noted that preparations for the Games stood against a background of rapid urbanization in China. The urban population was only 30.1 per cent of China's total population in 1999; by 2006 it had reached 43.92 per cent (China News 2007). Between 2001 and 2007 the industrial production of China rose by 80 per cent, while the number of privately owned cars increased from 1.5 million in 2001 to 11.49 million in 2006 (China Commodity Marketplace 2007). All this made environmental protection more difficult.

Another issue that should not be overlooked is security, which often keeps foreigners away. Because of the potential threat from Muslim extremists in China's western Xinjiang region, who claimed responsibility for bombings in cities including Shanghai, Wenzhou and Kuming (Hutzler 2008), heavy security was necessary to ensure a secure games. With the approach of the Games, razor-wire barriers and soldiers guarded the outskirts of the Olympic Green area, many nightspots near Olympic venues were closed and even ground-to-air missiles were installed near one Olympic venue to protect it from possible attacks.

Education of Olympic knowledge and of being civilized citizens was stressed and various educational activities were organized in the years of preparation for the Beijing Games. An Olympic Education Project was launched throughout the nation after 2002, involving 400 million students from 500,000 schools (Huang 2007). Guided by People's Olympics (the renwen aoyun), the Chinese were concerned with the modern civilized subject and harmonious coexistence. Thus, the education of a populace fit for the twenty-first century was incorporated into Olympic education. Lectures, seminars, TV programmes and newspaper special columns were devoted to Olympic-related topics. Not a single day in China passed without news of Beijing 2008. Photography, painting, poetry, calligraphy and foreign-language speech contests were all organized throughout the country. Various contests for the design of sports venues, for sculpture, for the motto, for the mascots and for the theme songs were also held at national and/or international level. Nothing in the history of the Olympic Movement came close to the Chinese coverage of the nature of Olympism. As a result, hosting the Olympics Games brought about not only the infrastructural and economic changes indicated earlier, but also changes in social values and norms.

One of the changes is the relaxed control over the media. Ensured by the 'Regulations on reporting activities in China by foreign journalists during the Beijing Olympic Games and the preparatory period', issued in late 2006, foreign reporters were allowed to travel anywhere in the country without prior permission from local authorities between 1 January 2007 and late October 2008 (Sparre 2006). This was a big step for China. Prior to January 2007, journalists were required to obtain prior approval to travel to certain parts of China and were frequently refused access. In spite of the limited time period, the Games helped accelerate the process of media freedom, which is still far from ideal. In consequence, the Beijing Games attracted the record number of media representatives: 21,600 accredited and 30,000 non-accredited media personnel. Presence of such large-scale international media in China itself illustrates the extent of the world's interest in the Beijing Games and China's relaxed control over the media.

While Olympic education was stressed, the traditional culture of China was not forgotten. With increased confidence, an overwhelming majority of Chinese feel proud of their long historical heritage and wish to revive it and retain it. One clear illustration of this was the emphasis on Chinese traditional culture via the symbols of the Beijing Games. The Olympic emblem, entitled 'Chinese Seal-Dancing Beijing' (*zhongguo yin, wudong de Beijing*), featured a single Chinese character on a traditional red Chinese seal with the words 'Beijing 2008' written in an *eastern-style* brush stroke. The official mascots of the 2008 Games consisted of five little children (*Fuwa*) embodying the natural characteristics of the Fish, the Panda, the (Tibetan) Antelope and the Swallow together with the Olympic Flame. The 5,000-year Chinese culture was vividly demonstrated through an impressive and applauded choreographic display in the Opening and Closing Ceremonies of Beijing 2008. Collectively and individually, they carried a Chinese message of friendship, peace and blessings to children all over the world.

Coincident with Beijing's successful Olympic bid was China's entrance into the World Trade Organization, which greatly facilitated Chinese integration into the global community. The Olympic Slogan: 'One World, One Dream' demonstrated Chinese eagerness to be part of the global community. To organize the Beijing Games successfully, a sizable number of foreign experts in design, security, environmental protection, News Service, competition administration and publicity were employed as Olympic advisors, consultants and evaluators. To ensure athletic achievement of Chinese athletes in Beijing, a number of foreign coaches were employed and Chinese coaches were sent abroad. In the Chinese delegation to the 2008 Games, there were 28 foreign coaches who were from 16 countries including America, Canada, Germany, France, Korea and even Japan. They worked on 17 sports, including archery, canoeing, handball, hockey and softball, basketball, synchronized swimming and fencing (Yang *et al.* 2008). Between 2003 and 2008, some 139 Chinese coaches were sent to the USA, Russia, Germany, Britain, France and Canada to attend coaching courses, seminars or workshop (Wang and Zhang 2009).

After decades of economic reforms and opening up to the world, China has been closely intertwined with the world. By 2003, China had earned about 7,148 billion yuan (US$851 billion) in exports and at the same time surpassed Germany as the world's third-largest market (Zedillo 2004). By 2008 real per capita income – both in cities and in rural areas – had multiplied more than five times. As a result, according to a survey in 2008, some 86 per cent of respondents were satisfied with China's current situation and 82 per cent were optimistic about China's economy, a much higher figure than in most other countries in the world (*Washington Post* 2008). With its rising economic strength, China has become an important player on the world stage. Hosting the Olympic Games is a demonstration of this influence. The fact that world leaders from over 80 countries attended the Opening Ceremony of the Games in 2008 speaks volumes about China's political influence in the world today.

On the other side, the world has also turned its attention to China with ever more intensive concentration. More non-Chinese are learning Mandarin. Publications on China flow off the world's presses. Increasingly, worldwide conferences, lectures and seminars cover China. The Games was an eye-opener to foreigners visiting China or watching China via the media.

However, organizing the Games was not smooth nor without any challenge. Less than a month before the Relay, there had been a violent riot in Lhasa, followed by widespread demonstrations in areas with significant Tibetan populations. This triggered Western sympathy to the Tibetans and criticism of the Chinese human rights record.

Bombarded with the extensive Olympic ideas such as peace and friendship, the majority of Chinese were quite positive about the international community before the Torch Relay was launched in April 2008. According to a survey of Chinese citizens in five big cities, including Beijing, Shanghai, Guangzhou, Chongqin and Wuhan in 2006, over 90 per cent of respondents were optimistic that with the increased strength of China, the future international environment would be in favour of it (*Global Daily* 2006). Thus, the Chinese designed the longest Olympic Torch Relay in Olympic history, which would travel through the six continents of the world and last for four months, with 21,880 torchbearers and 5,000 escort runners involved (IOC 2007). However, the so-called 'journey of harmony' was not harmonious at all. The Relay was assailed in both London and Paris, and dramatically re-routed in San Francisco. This dealt the optimistic Chinese a heavy blow and triggered a surge of nationalism in and outside China (Elegant 2008). Counter-protest action was taken by Chinese both at home and abroad to support the Olympics. They considered the Western media coverage to be biased and unfair (*People's Daily* 2008). The French nation was accused of pro-secessionist conspiracy and anti-Chinese racism. Chinese cities including Kunming, Hefei and Wuhan organized boycotts against the French-owned retail chain Carrefour (Sina 2008). This episode proves what Huntington (1996) claimed:

> In the post-Cold War world, culture is both a divisive and a unifying force. People separated by ideology but united by culture come together, as the two Germanys did and as the two Koreas and the several Chinas are beginning to.

This might be one of the reasons for the drop in China's positive ratings, from 45 per cent in early 2008 to 39 per cent in early 2009, surveyed by BBC World Service across 21 countries (BBC 2009).

In spite of the unpleasant incidents of the Torch Relay, in the context of globalization and modernization, the Chinese have become more globalized. They applauded excellent performances for both Chinese and foreign athletes. Actually, the most popular athletes in Beijing during the Games were Kobe Bryant,[7] Michael Phelps[8] and Usain Bolt.[9] 'Sometimes we feel we are better supported here than back at home', the American basketball point guard Chris Paul said (Wetzel 2008).

For many Chinese the 2008 Games, through the successful organization of the Games and remarkable athletic performances, helped advance the international image, esteem and dignity of China. According to a study of Chinese Image in the Eyes of Foreigners, conducted by Chinese Media University, the Beijing Games significantly upgraded the national image of China in the eyes of foreign respondents, and those who had direct contact with Chinese and were highly involved in the Olympics had a better impression of China as a whole (International Centre for Media and Public Agenda 2008). Nevertheless, some studies by Western scholars found that the Beijing Games had a weak impact on altering global perceptions of China (Manzenreiter 2008) and limited impacts on the city's brand (Zhang and Zhao 2008). Nevertheless, hosting the Games for the first time was a symbol of China's new power and place in the world. The Games marked the high point of China's modernization. It was a watershed of Chinese renaissance.

Future of China: post the Beijing Games

It was expected that the Beijing Olympics 'will power a national drive toward modernisation, provide a broad bridge to the West and pave the way for China to play a greater part in world affairs. Through the Games China will make the clearest of political statements' (Jinxia and Mangan 2008). Is this goal realized?

It is widely held in China that hosting the Olympic Games has brought about broader social and political impacts. First of all, the Beijing Games accelerated the process of China's rise in the twenty-first century. China surpassed Japan to become the world's second-largest economy in 2010. China's GDP increased from 300,670 billion yuan (about US$43,893 billion) in 2008 to 636,463 billion yuan (US$101,842 billion) in 2014 (Xin 2015). China has become an important player in the world economy and other affairs. Now virtually all the World Top 500 enterprises have invested in China.

Tourism is an industry that has developed very quickly in the twenty-first century. By 2014, foreign tourists reached 128 million, an increase over 2008. Chinese tourism overseas has also increased from 3.69 million in 2001 to 109 million in 2014. Chinese tourists spent US$164.8 billion abroad, US$113.6 billion more than that of foreign tourists in China (*SX Daily* 2015). This to a certain extent demonstrates Chinese integration with the world. China is predicted to be the world's leading economic power by 2025 (Hawksworth and Cookson 2008).

In addition, the Beijing Games has boosted Chinese confidence in their country, their culture and their future development. A survey found that 55.3 per cent of respondents claimed that 'after the Games they are confident in everything without fear' and 48.4 per cent thought they were rationally patriotic. Indeed, China has made steady progress in political, economic and social aspects after the Beijing Games. Society, culture and lifestyle in China have become more pluralistic, and people's awareness of their own interests and public good has increased. The Chinese embrace more extensively the universal values of human rights, curb malpractice, reduce corruption and limit exploitation.

The goal of tackling environmental problems has been pushed forward by the public. In spite of various efforts made, the environment in China is certainly still far from ideal. Worries about quality of air and water have been growing among ordinary citizens after the Beijing Games. Polluted air and water have become one of the major reasons for the increased incidents of lung cancer and some other health problems. Because of the pollution, increasing numbers of affluent families have migrated abroad. Beijing is faced with severe environmental challenges. The positive legacies of the Beijing Games in terms of environmental improvement appear minimal, but they helped the Chinese, to a degree, to become more conscious of the need to balance economic development and environmental protection. Three large state-funded programmes for research into and the development of environmentally friendly water technologies were approved by the State Council in 2008 (*China Daily* 2008). However, the lakes that are choked with pollution and over-exploited will not return to a pristine condition until 2030 (Graham-Harrison 2008). No doubt, China has a long way to go to turn the sky bluer and water cleaner.

Another indication of increased awareness of public interest is enthusiasm for sport for all. For decades, especially after the Olympic Strategy was issued in the mid-1980s, elite sport had been emphasized over sport for all. With improved living standards, increased leisure time, and rising awareness of their fitness and health, public need for sport as recreation has grown, but is not fully met due to limited access to sports facilities. In the face of requests voiced increasingly loudly in all sections of society to weaken performance-oriented sports policies and investment, the Chinese government has paid more attention to sport for all after the Beijing Games. The opening day of the Beijing Games, 8 August, was officially designated as National Fitness Day. From 2009 on, every year, all kinds of sports activities and demonstrations are organized in the National Sports Stadium and other places. Most of the stadia and sports facilities used for the Games have been open to the public for their fitness and recreational needs. Now a majority of the sports lottery revenue managed by the National Sports Associations goes to national fitness. In consequence, sports participation from schools to communities, from families to clubs, has reached an unprecedented height in China's recent history.

Change and continuity are a recurrent theme of global politics in the twenty-first century. With rapid economic growth and modernization, the Chinese have become more confident in dealing with the outside world and they require a higher level of respect from the international community (Zheng 1999). But the Chinese have to learn quickly how to negotiate both the legacy of traditional culture and the current practices of the global world.

China is a huge country, with obvious regional differences in terms of development and resources. Although Shanghai, Tianjin, Shengyang, Qinghuangdao, Qingdao and Hong Kong were invited to co-host some events of the 2008 Games, it is undeniable that Beijing benefitted more. The 2008 Olympic Games clearly demonstrates the significance of successfully hosting a mega-sports event for regional overall development. Two years after the Beijing Games, Shanghai hosted the World Exhibition Fair, Guangzhou hosted the Asian Games in 2010, Shenzhen hosted the World University Games in 2011 and Nanjing staged the Youth Olympic Games in 2014. Zhang Jiakou, a city less than 200 kilometres from Beijing, is bidding jointly with Beijing to host the 2022 Winter Olympic Games. Clearly, sports events have been, and will continue to be, utilized to facilitate the balanced regional development of the country and then collectively build it as a powerful nation in the world.

In terms of history, the Beijing Games was a festival that the Chinese had awaited for over a century. The Games was not just the dream fulfilled, but a future vision (Ren 2008). The Games sent a clear signal to the world: the revival of the Chinese nation has started (Fang 2008)

Conclusion

The Beijing Games helped restore China's national grandeur by bringing to an end the century of humiliation and subordination to the West and Japan (Garver 1993). It is the result of the century of struggle to put behind it the image of the 'Sick-man of East Asia' by modernizing the most populated country in the world. Through the Games, China showed the world not only that it was an economic power, but also that it was a nascent important global political power that would play a crucial part in shaping the new world order. China used the Games not only as a stage on which to display its staggering economic progress, but also as a launch pad to propel itself into the international diplomatic stratosphere (Ren 2008). China will exert more impact on world affairs – social, political, economic, cultural environmental and sporting. Is the world prepared for accepting Chinese influence? This is a question that is yet to be answered.

Notes

1 Some 3,000 students from Peking University and other schools demonstrated in Beijing on 4 May to protest the Chinese government's weak response to the Treaty of Versailles, especially the Shandong Problem. The May 4th Movement takes its name from the protest. The radical intellectuals blamed traditional culture for the dramatic and rapid fall of China into a subordinate international position and maintained that China's cultural values prevented China from matching the industrial and military development of Japan and the West.

2 At the first meeting of the Third National People's Congress in December 1964, Zhou Erlai put forward in the Governmental Work Report that by the end of the twentieth century, China should become a strong socialist country with modern agriculture, industry, national defence and technology.

3 Four special economic zones include Shenzhen, Zhuhai, Shantou and Xiamen. They are situated in the coast areas near Hong Kong and Taiwan, where joint venture companies and even foreign-owned enterprises exist. They have opened up new opportunities for many Chinese.

4 At the Games, Chinese athletes won 183 out of the 310 gold medals (60 per cent) in 29 sports, and broke several world records and over 100 Asian records.

5 In 1991, Beijing declared its intention to host the 2000 Olympic Games. Two years later China lost to Sydney by two votes.

6 Beijing motorists could drive on alternate days, depending on whether the last number on their license plate was odd or even. This policy was to reduce daily traffic by two million vehicles.

7 Kobe is an NBA All-Star shooting guard for the Los Angeles Lakers. Most Chinese young people wanted to go to the basketball stadium because of him. Therefore, it was extremely difficult to get a ticket for the matches between the American team and other teams.

8 American Swimmer Michael Phelps became the most successful and popular athlete in Beijing 2008 where he won eight gold medals in swimming.

9 Jamaican sprinter Bolt not only won three gold medals in athletics, but also became the first sprinter to set three world records in the same Olympics.

References

BBC (2009) Views of China and Russia decline in global poll. 6 February. Accessed 20 February 2010 www.bbc.co.uk/pressoffice/pressreleases/stories/2009/02_february/06/poll.shtml.

Brownell, S. (2008) *Beijing's Games: What the Olympics mean to China*. Lanham, MD: Rowman & Littlefield.

China Commodity Marketplace (2007) 2007–2010 nian zhongguo qiche fuwu ye shichang yuce yu touzi qianjing fenxi baogao [Report on the forecast of the automobile service market and its investment prospect between 2007 and 2010]. 8 November.

China Daily (2008) China to invest billions to deal with water pollution. 15 January. Accessed 20 February 2016. www.chinadaily.com.cn/bizchina/2008-01/15/content_6395700.htm.

China News (2007) Jianshe bu fu buzhang: 2015 nian zhongguo chengzheng renkou jiang tupo ba yi [The Deputy Minister of the Ministry of Construction: By 2015 the urban population in China will be more than 800 million]. 3 August.

China News (2008) Liu yue 1 ri qi quangguo jingzhi mianfei tigong suliao gouwu dai' [from June 1, providing plastic bags will be banned] 8 January.

Elegant, S. (2008) Why China's burning mad. *Time*. 24 April 2008. Accessed 20 February 2016. http://content.time.com/time/magazine/article/0,9171,1734821,00.html.

Fang, N. (2008) zhe yang de ao yun hui zhi neng chu xian zai zhong guo [Such an Olympics can only occur in China]. *zhong guo qing nian bao*. 26 August 2008.

Garver, J. W. (1993) *Foreign Policy of the People's Republic of China*. Englewood Cliffs, NJ: Prentice Hall.

Global Daily (2006) quan guo wu da cheng shi nian zhong min yi diao cha: zhongguo ren ru he kan hi jie [Poll of the nation's five big cities at the end of the year: how Chinese think about the world]. 31 December.

Graham-Harrison, E. (2008) China sets 2030 target to clean up lakes. *Reuters*. 22 January 2008. Accessed 20 February 2016. www.reuters.com/article/environment-china-environment-water-dc-idUSPEK62 58620080122.

Gray, J. (1990) *Rebellions and Revolutions: China from the 1800s to the 1980s*. Oxford: Oxford University Press.

Hawksworth, J. and Cookson, G. (2008) *The World in 2050 Beyond the BRIC Economies: A Broader Look at Emerging Market Growth Prospects*. London: PricewaterhouseCoopers LLP.

Huang, Y. (2007) zhongguo jiang zai gengduo de xuexiao zhong kaizhan aolinpike jiaoyu [China will promote Olympic education in more schools]. *Xinhua*. 18 September 2007.

Huntington, S. P. (1996) *The Clash of Civilizations and the Remaking of World Order*. London: Simon & Schuster.

Hutzler, C. (2008) Beijing cites numerous Olympic threats. *USA Today*. 28 July 2008. Accessed 20 February 2016. http://usatoday30.usatoday.com/sports/olympics/2008-07-28-3123605487_x. htm.

International Center for Media and the Public Agenda. (2008) Study: Global media coverage of Beijing Olympics avoids politics. *University of Maryland College News*. September 2008. Accessed 20 February 2016. http://merrill.umd.edu/2008/09/study-global-media-coverage-of-beijing-olympics-avoids-politics/.

IOC (2007) Beijing 2008: BOCOG launches torchbearer selection programme. 25 June. Accessed 20 February 2016. http://www.olympic.org/news/beijing-2008-bocog-launches-torchbearer-selection-programme/54866.

Jinxia, D. (2003) *Women, Sport and Society in the New China*. London: Cass Publisher.

Jinxia, D. (2011) National identity, Olympic victory and Chinese sportswomen in the global era. In W. W. Kelly and S. Brownell (eds) *The Olympics in East Asia: Nationalism, Regionalism, and Globalism on the Center Stage of World Sports*. New Haven, CT: Council on East Asian Studies at Yale University, pp. 161–184.

Jinxia, D. and Mangan, J. A. (2008) Beijing Olympics legacies: Certain intentions and certain and uncertain outcomes. *International Journal of the History of Sport*, 25(14): 188–209.

Kristof, N. D. and Wudunn, S. (1994) *China Wakes: The Struggle for the Soul of a Rising Power*. London: Nicholas Brealey Publishing Limited.

Lai, H. (2001) cong zi jing cheng wu men zou xiang 2008 [Moving towards 2000 from the Midday Gate of the Forbidden City]. China News. 1 August 2001. Accessed 10 December 2015. www.chinanews. com.cn/zhonghuawenzhai/2001-08-01/txt3/12.htm.

Lee, K. (1994) 'Making another East Asian success in China'. In Chung H. Lee and Helmut Recsen (eds) *From Reform to Growth: China and Other Countries in Transition in Asia and Central and Eastern Europe*. Paris: Organization for Economic Co-operation and Development, pp. 186–194.

Lowenthal, R. (1966) Diplomacy and revolution: The dialectics of a dispute. In Roderick Macfarquhar (ed.) *China under Mao: Politics Take Command*. Massachusetts: The M.I.T. Press, pp. 425–448.

Manzenreiter, W. (2008) The Beijing Games in the Western imagination of China: The weak power of soft power. *Communication and Critical/Cultural Studies*, 5(4): 29–48.

Min, J., and Ding, Y. (2006) diaocha faxian, shijie yulun pubian guanzhu Beijing aoyunhui saishizhi wai de shiqing [Surveys show that the world is concerned about the issues beyond the Olympic Games]. *guoji xianqu daobao*. 18 December 2006.

Penn, M. (2008) aoyun: rang shijie chongxin renshi 'zhongguo' pingpai [The Olympic Games: let the world know 'China' brand]. *Fortune China*, 1: 80–81.

People's Daily (2008) Overseas Chinese rally against biased media coverage, for Olympics. 20 April.

Qu, X. (1992) A new height in Beijing. *China Sport*, 10: 36–37.

Ren, Z. (2008) Beijing xin zheng tu de you yi ge qi dian – xie zai di 29 jie ao yun hui bi mu zhi ji [Beijing, another starting point of new journey: writing on the moment of the close if the 29th Olympiad]. *Beijing cheng bao*. 26 August 2008.

Sina (2008) kun ming wang you fa qi fan di zhi xing dong, jia le fu qian: guo qi du men shui ping za ren [Internet users in Kunming launched anti-boycott action, doors were stifled by national flags the and people were smashed by water bottles]. 17 April.

Sparre, K. (2006) China relaxes rules on foreign reporters in the run-up to the Olympics. *Play the Game*. 22 December 2006. Accessed 5 March 2014. www.playthegame.org/News/Up%20To%20Date/China_relaxes_rules_on_foreign_reporters_in_the_run_up_to_the_Olympics.aspx.

SX Daily (2015) nian zhongguo youke haiwai zhichu 1648 yi meiyuan [Chinese tourists spent 164.8 billion US dollars overseas]. 29 January. Accessed 20 February 2016. www.sxdaily.com.cn/n/2015/0129/c339-5614676.html.

Wang, F. and Zhang, R. (2009) tiyu rencai chujing peixun zhuangkuang diaoyan [Survey of the overseas training of sports talents]. *Sports Culture Herald*, 6: 1215.

Washington Post (2008) The joy luck country. 24 July.

Wetzel, D. (2008) China offers warm embrace for Team USA. *Yahoo Sport*. 10 August 2008. Accessed 20 February 2016. http://sports.yahoo.com/news/china-offers-warm-embrace-team-181800466--oly.html.

Xin, W. (2015) guojia tongji ju jieshao 2014 nian guomin jingji yunxing qingkuang [National statistics bureau introduces the situation of national economy in 2014]. China Gate. 20 January 2015. Accessed 10 March 2015. http://cn.chinagate.cn/news/2015-01/20/content_34604987_6.htm2015-01-20.

Xu, X. (2006) Modernizing China in the Olympic spotlight: China's national identity and the 2008 Beijing Olympiad. *The Sociological Review*, 54(2): 90–107.

Yang, M., Wang, J. and Li, L. (2008) zhong guo ao yun jun tuan cheng li shi shi, can sai gui mo jug e tuan zhi shou [Formation and oath of Chinese Olympic delegation with the largest participants in the world]. *Xinhua*. 25 July 2008.

Zedillo, E. (2004) Current events: On China's rise. *The Forbes*. 24 May 2004. Accessed 20 Feburary 2016. www.forbes.com/columnists/free_forbes/2004/0524/043.html.

Zhang, L. (1993) (ed.) Shiji qing - zhongguo yu aolinpike yundong [A century of contact: China and the Olympics]. Beijing: Renmin tiyu chuban she.

Zhang, L. and Zhao, S. X. (2008) City branding and the Olympic effect: A case study of Beijing. *Journal of Urban Affairs*, 30(2):175–190.

Zheng, Y. (1999) *Discovering Chinese Nationalism in China: Modernization, Identity and International Relations*. Cambridge: Cambridge University Press.

38

THE POLITICS OF SPORTS MEGA EVENTS IN SOUTH KOREA

A diachronic approach

Jung Woo Lee

Since the 1980s, South Korea has hosted a series of sports mega-events such as the Asian Games, the Olympics, and the FIFA World Cup Finals. While these are essentially sporting contests, the political implications that these sporting events had for the host country must not be underestimated. In fact, the decision to bid for hosting and eventually to deliver a large-scale sporting competition is often the outcome of strategic political calculation that reflects the goals of the domestic and foreign policy of the government (Cho and Bairner 2012; Lee 2010; Ha and Mangan 2002; Hill 1996). Hosting mega-events is often regarded as a useful opportunity to display the merits, image, and even the prowess of the host nation to both domestic and international audiences (Grix and Houlihan 2014; Nye 2004) and it is this representational nature of sports mega-events that the South Korean government attempts to utilise in order to realise its political aim (Cha 2009).

In addition to the instrumental use of sport by the government, political activist groups also involve themselves in sports mega-events as a way to express their political messages (Horne and Whannel 2012; Senn 1999). Examples of political protests can be found frequently in the history of the major sporting events, including the Munich massacre in 1972 and the Free Tibet movement in 2008. The case of South Korea is no exception. From the pro-democratic movement against the military regime in 1980s to the recent environmental protest campaign concerning the 2018 Winter Olympic Games, the mega-events held in South Korea have operated as public fora through which various individuals and organisations can demonstrate their political opinions.

This chapter investigates the political ramifications of a series of mega-sporting events awarded to South Korea over the last thirty-five years. More specifically, it is concerned with how each sporting occasion reflects the political and historical context in which the event is situated and how different political activist groups exploit it as an opportunity to publicise their political interests. By doing so, this chapter attempts to identify a conceptual framework by which the political nature of sports mega-events can be understood. Adopting a diachronic approach, I examine six sporting events awarded to South Korea in the 1980s, the 2000s, and the 2010s. These were the historical periods when significant political developments occurred, such as democratisation in the 1980s, reconciliation between South Korea and its political rivals in the 2000s and the South Korean government's aspiration to become a global core state in the 2010s. These political changes significantly influenced, and were facilitated by, the organisation of the six sports mega-events in question (two cases in each historical period). By looking at the implications of the six mega-events in the three different political contexts, the chapter aims to build theoretical concepts through which the political value of hosting international sporting competitions can be measured more intelligently than has sometimes happened in the past.

The mega-events of the 1980s

In the 1980s, the South Korean capital of Seoul hosted two international multi-sporting events: the Asian Games in 1986 and the Olympic Games in 1988. These were the first major international events that South Korea delivered and the country's willingness to host these sports mega-events was not unrelated to the political circumstances surrounding the Korean Peninsula at that time. Thus, it is necessary to consider three distinctive political and economic conditions that influenced politics in South Korea in order to grasp the political meanings of these two Games more accurately. These include the country's rapid economic growth, the Cold War political structure, and the repressive military regime.

South Korea's coming out party

South Korea enjoyed remarkable economic growth in the 1960s and the 1970s, and such development led to the rapid recovery from the post-Korean War devastation. In spite of this, South Korea was still largely regarded as a less-developed and marginalised nation in the world. Hence, it is not surprising that the South Korean government prioritised improving the image of the country and enhancing its status in the international community amongst its key diplomatic aims (Collins 2011). Since the 1960s, South Korean political elites had been aware of the role that sport plays in international relations in terms of the politics of recognition, especially in the context of the rivalry between North and South Korea (Ha and Mangan 2002). The South Korean government also witnessed how the successful delivery of the 1964 Olympic Games in Tokyo had resulted in the dissemination of new Japanese identity to the world audience (Larson and Park 1993). Based on this experience and observation, the South Korean government decided to host major international sporting contests in an attempt to show off its increasing economic power and its notable development to the world audience (Cha 2009).

When Seoul won the Olympics and Asian Games bid in the early 1980s, the outstanding preparation and organisation of the two events became the South Korean government's major political tasks. The government provided a diverse range of financial and administrative support to mega-event-related development projects such as the construction of sport facilities and other social infrastructure, and subsidised a number of civil organisations that engaged in social campaigns for the successful delivery of the Olympics and Asian Games (Larson and Park 1993). While the two events were awarded to the South Korean capital, and the most sporting competitions took place in the district of the metro Seoul area, the South Korean government presented the event organisation as a national project. The government implemented a nationwide redevelopment policy, which included the gentrification of urban areas, the sanitisation of rural regions, and the improvement of people's living standards in preparation for the sporting competitions (Koh 2005). These extensive mega-event-driven projects paid off. The Asian

Games and the Olympics were amongst the most successful competitions by that time and South Korea could effectively demonstrate its revamped image to the world through hosting sports mega-events (Bridges 2008; Collins 2011).

The Cold War and political rivalry

The complicated Cold War structure of international relations influenced the organisation and delivery of the 1986 Asian Games and the 1988 Olympic Games. In this respect, it is necessary to identify two different political mechanisms at work concerning the ideological conflict in this period. First, the world observed Perestroika in Moscow and the subsequent development of the mood of détente between the West and the East in Europe from the mid-1980s. This was also the time when the Eastern European communist countries were trying to open new economic ties with the West. In line with this newly emerging political order, South Korea introduced a new foreign policy called *Nordpolitik*. This was the country's initiative to reform its relationship with communist states (Chung 1991). In particular, this policy aimed to build a trade relation with the communist states and eventually to normalise diplomatic channels with them (Sanford 1993).

Second, the Korean Peninsula was seen as the East Asian frontier of the Cold War, and the relation between North and South Korea was somewhat insulated from the wind of change in Europe. The two Korean states were still vying for ideological supremacy over the other and neither recognised the political legitimacy of the other. In effect, military confrontation and mistrust dominated the political environment of the Northeast Asian region (Chung 1991). These two separate political developments characterised the political nature of the Asian Games and the Olympics in Seoul in the 1980s.

In terms of inter-Korean relations, the news that the two sporting mega-events were awarded the South Korean capital implied that the world now began to see the south as a more important political player in the East Asian region. Because both the Korean governments had utilised sport as part of their ideological struggle and propaganda, the North Korean regime perceived the successful South Korea's bidding campaigns for the Asian Games and the Olympics as a significant political challenge. In this respect, it was not surprising that communist Korea reacted negatively to the South Korean's delivery of the two sporting events.

Initially, the north sent a petition to the International Olympic Committee contesting its decision to select Seoul as the host of the 1988 Summer Olympics (Pound 1994). North Korea claimed that South Korea was an inappropriate country to deliver the Olympic Games because of the existence of the repressive military regime and its undemocratic political practices, which were in contradiction to the values that the Olympic Charter embraced. Yet, South Korea defended its position and the United States also backed its political ally's campaign (Hill 1996). Additionally, the then-president of the International Olympic Committee, Juan Antonio Samaranch, was on the South Korean side (Pound 1994). Subsequently, the sport governing body did not overturn its decision to award the Games to Seoul.

In addition, North Korea plotted terrorist attacks twice, in 1986 and 1987, in a deliberate attempt to interrupt the organisation of the large sporting competitions in the south (Lee 2010). A week before the commencement of the Asian Games, a bomb exploded at the Gimpo International Airport in Seoul, claiming the life of five civilians and injuring more than thirty people. Later, it was revealed that this incident was an act of terrorism carried out by agents acting on behalf of the North Korean government. In November 1987, North Korean agents destroyed a civilian aircraft en route to Seoul via Baghdad. The terrorists planted a bomb in an overhead storage locker and it detonated during the flight, killing 104 passengers and 11 crew members. Most victims were Korean.

When the two sporting competitions took place as scheduled without any delay or disruption in spite of the North Korea's continued intervention, the communist state boycotted them as a last resort. In 1986, most communist states in Asia with the exception of China followed suit in support of communist Korea's anti-South Korean campaign. In 1988, however, only Albania, Cuba, Madagascar, and Seychelles sided with North Korea while China, the Soviet Union and its satellite states all sent their delegates to Seoul. It is important to note the Chinese athletes' participation in these two international sporting occasions. Given that China was the closest ally of North Korea, the Chinese government's decision to participate in the Asian Games and the Olympics had meaningful implications for the power balance in the Northeast Asian region (Kim 2006). This could be read as a sign of improving diplomatic relations between South Korea and China, to which the emerging mood of détente and South's Korea's *Nordpolitik* gave rise. Opening official relations between North Korea's closest ally and its fiercest foe implied a significant decline of the political leverage that the communist Korean regime had enjoyed in the region. Similarly, the fact that the Soviet Union and most Eastern European communist states such as East Germany, Hungary, and Romania sent their delegates to Seoul was also indicative of the shift in power dynamics in Northeast Asian geopolitics in favour of South Korea.

The repressive military regime

South Korea's intention to host these two large-scale sporting competitions was closely related to the government policy to control domestic political environments. From 1963 to 1987, a series of military regimes ruled the South Korean parliament. While the country had witnessed remarkable economic development during this period, this was done at the expense of freedom and democracy (Lee and Lee 2015). The state-controlled economic development plan required citizens to devote themselves to economic growth, while repressing any desire to establish a more democratic political system. When the second military regime gained power via a coup in 1980, General Chun lacked political support from the people (Choe and Kim 2012). The idea of hosting the Asian Games and the Olympics was therefore part of his populist policy to attract people's political support for his regime. In fact, General Chun deliberately exploited sport as a means to control the domestic political environment (Joo 2012). Indeed, when a democratic movement was on the rise in the early 1980s, the military government introduced professional sport leagues as a form of mass entertainment so as to direct people's attention away from internal political affairs. Similarly, when Seoul was awarded the right to host the Olympics and the Asian Games in 1981 and 1982 respectively, the government presented these two pieces of news as a major national achievement and to some extent this helped consolidate General Chun's position in South Korean politics (Ha and Mangan 2002).

When the commencement of the Asian Games and the Olympics came closer, however, political protests against the military regime became more intense. As the international media began to pay more attention to the host city for these two large events, political activist groups attempted to gain publicity so that they could demonstrate their hopes for the democratisation of the nation to the world (Larson and Park 1993). In 1987, one year before the Olympic Games, the democratic movement gathered momentum and a nationwide political protest against the repressive military regime erupted (Zimelis 2011). This political situation posed a serious threat to the government's organisation of the sports mega-event. Reflecting the mood of the pro-democratic movement, the then-leader of the opposition claimed that the ruling party must accept democracy or not host the Olympics (Hill 1996). Subsequently, the regime reluctantly accepted popular demands to hold a direct presidential election in December 1987 (Han 1988). As a result, the first democratically elected president welcomed guests from around the world at the opening ceremony of the Olympic Games. In that sense, it can be argued that the two sporting occasions held in South Korea functioned as catalysts for the political transformation.

Mega-events of the 2000s

South Korea also hosted two major international sport competitions in the 2000s: the 2002 FIFA World Cup Finals, co-hosted with Japan, and the 2002 Busan Asian Games. Contrary to the political climate surrounding the Korean peninsula in the 1980s, which was largely dominated by Cold War rivalry, mistrust, and confrontation, the mood of reconciliation and collaboration was widespread in Northeast Asia in the early 2000s. The two large-scale international sporting competitions clearly reflected this political development.

The FIFA World Cup and the relationship between South Korea and Japan

In terms of South Korea's relationship with Japan, it should be noted that Korea was ruled by Japanese imperialists for thirty-six years during the first half of the twentieth century (1910–1945). In this period, the Korean people suffered from a relatively short but extremely brutal experience of Japanese imperialism (Cumings 2005). Japan indiscriminately exploited Korea's natural resources and severely repressed Korean cultural identity. The colonial authority also mobilised young Koreans by force and sent them to the war front. In particular, mobilised Korean women were forced into sexual slavery for Japanese soldiers (Soh 2008). This colonial experience left deep emotional scars on the Korean people's mentality. As a result anti-Japan sentiment has been prevalent in South Korea since its liberation in 1945. While the two countries normalised their diplomatic relations in 1965, the South Korean government still imposed restrictions on the import of Japanese cultural products such as films and music in order to prevent the diffusion of the former coloniser's culture to South Korea.

The FIFA World Cup Finals, which the two states co-hosted, contributed to ameliorating the uneasy relationship between South Korea and Japan. It is important to note that the two East Asian states originally competed with each other to win the World Cup bid. The ethos of competition and rivalry dominated during the selection process and winning the bidding war became a matter of pride for the two East Asian footballing nations (Sugden and Tomlinson 2002). As the competition between the two became increasingly serious, FIFA, unable to select one clear winner, decided to co-host the football championship in Japan and South Korea. This was a certainly an uncomfortable decision for the two competing nations, but they had to accept FIFA's choice, albeit reluctantly (Longman 1996). Furthermore, despite the fierce rivalry during the bidding campaign, Japan and South Korea soon established a strategic partnership in order to deliver the football events successfully (Lee 2002).

One of the signs that indicated improving Korea–Japan relations was a gradual relaxation of restrictions on the import of Japanese cultural commodities. In 1998, the South Korean government permitted the import of Japanese publications, and censorship of the performance of Japanese music in the theatre and the regulation concerning the showing of Japanese films in the cinema were also relaxed in the following year (Cho 2003). In 2000, a selection of Japanese television content such as documentaries and sport programmes were allowed to be broadcast by the South Korean media (Cho 2003). In 2004, the censorship of Japanese films was abolished and the selling of physical copies of Japanese music was permitted in South Korea (National Archives of Korea 2006). It seems that such deregulation in relation to Japanese mass culture during the late 1990s and the early 2000s was not unrelated to the situation wherein the two countries needed to collaborate to host the FIFA World Cup because limited cultural relations between the two sides might create an unnecessary communication barrier over the Korean Strait before and during the mega-sporting event.

Another indication that exemplifies the emerging wave of reconciliation between the two states was the meeting between the South Korean President Kim Dae-jung and the Japanese Prime Minister Junichiro Koizumi on the day after the final match of the competition. At this summit, the two heads of state signed a joint message to be sent to the Korean and Japanese people. Entitled 'Joint message for the future from the leaders of Korea and Japan: beyond the successful organisation of the 2002 FIFA World Cup Finals', this political statement highlighted the friendly relationship constructed through co-hosting the sports mega-event and the importance of maintaining and advancing this relationship further (Embassy of Japan in Korea 2002). It also stressed that the two states should expand exchange and collaboration programmes in non-sporting areas including politics, economics, and culture. Given more than half a century of mistrust and animosity towards Japan, it is difficult to claim that simply co-hosting the sporting event transformed the thorny relationship into a trustworthy one. Yet, it is equally worth noting that the Korea–Japan summit produced such a highly optimistic vision. In that sense, it can be argued that the FIFA World Cup at least offered a public forum whereby the two historical rivals were able to discuss the future relationship between them in a more constructive way.

The Busan Asian Games and North and South Korean relations

In terms of inter-Korean relations, it is important to note that the South Korean government introduced a policy of engagement with North Korea in this period. When the president Kim Dae-jung was in power in 1998, he considered improving relations between North and South Korea as one of the major political goals of his government. Instead of adopting a mutually destructive zero-sum game approach, this engagement policy, namely the Sunshine Policy, was inclined to embrace the stubborn communist regime and to help northern siblings in need (Hogarth 2012). As North Korea had suffered from a severe famine and starvation since the mid-1990s, the new South Korean administration offered economic resources and medical and food aid to the north. This generous tactic worked. The inter-Korean communication channel between the two governments reopened and the leaders of the two Korean states agreed to hold a North and South Korean Summit for the first time in the history since the division in 1948. In June 2000, the two leaders met in the North Korean capital and signed the Joint Declaration which contained an article that North and South Korea were to develop cooperation in a socio-cultural programme including sport (BBC 2000). The North and South Korean Summit facilitated collaboration and exchange projects aimed at promoting mutual understanding and affirmed shared cultural identity.

The Busan Asian Games clearly demonstrated the mood of reconciliation between North and South Korea. Importantly, it was the first time since the partition of the Korean peninsula that a North Korean delegation officially took part in an international sporting competition held in South Korea (*The Economist* 2002). Before this time, the north boycotted or disregarded any sporting events taking place in South Korea because the two Koreas did no recognise the legitimacy and political authority of the government on the other side of the border. Because sending an athletic delegation to an international meeting implies the establishment of unofficial diplomatic relations between participating and hosting nations (Strenk 1979), the two Koreas had avoided taking part in any international competitions that the other Korea hosted. The Busan Asian Games broke this stalemate. Three hundred and eighteen athletes, 22 state officials, and 335 cheerleaders from North Korea visited the South Korean city of Busan. It was the first occasion that such a large number of North Korean people had stood on the South Korean soil simultaneously since the Korean War. The South Korean officials and people warmly welcomed the visitors from the north, and the two sides displayed friendly relations throughout the event.

Another significant political issue concerning North Korean participation in the Busan Asian Games included the raising of the North Korean flag and the playing of the North Korean anthem during the Asian Games ceremony. Because the two Korean states were still technically at war, the use of North Korean symbols in South Korean public space could be interpreted as an unlawful act according to the National Security Law (Jae 2002). However, with South Korea hosting the event, it was inevitable that the North Korean flag should hang at the sporting venues. While the Asian Games were seen as a special occasion for which the National Security Law could be temporally waived, the public display of North Korean symbols still engendered controversy (Jung 2002). Despite this concern, however, when North Korean athletes won medals, communist Korea's flag was raised and their anthem was played. This marked the first time that North Korean's nationalistic rituals had been performed in South Korea. More importantly, these moments were broadcasted live to South Korean households. In consideration of more than fifty years of military tension and ideological conflict, the performance of nationalistic ceremonies for North Korea by South Korean officials was seen as a meaningful step towards peaceful co-existence and eventually the reunification of the nation.

Mega-events of the 2010s

The Asian Games took place in the South Korean city of Incheon in 2014 and the Winter Olympic Games will be held in the South Korean district of Pyeongchang in 2018. These two events concern mainly enhancing the cultural power of the country. Since Nye (2004) introduced the importance of soft power in world politics, a number of Western, developed nation-states have inclined to utilise their cultural resources, including sport, in order to increase the attractiveness of their countries (Grix and Houlihan 2014). South Korea, as a semi-core state, follows suit. It was the South Korean government's strategic decision to host these two events in an attempt to boost its cultural power (Shin 2011). At the same time, however, a sceptical view on hosting mega-events was on the rise in non-governmental sectors. Against claimed economic and social benefits, many civic organisations stated that hosting these mega-events would leave huge debts and significant environmental damage (Nam 2014). This gave rise to a situation where tension between the government and civic organisations increased. Thus, the political implications of hoisting the two sports mega-events in South Korean cities in the 2010s must be understood with reference to the government's soft power strategy and civic organisations' sceptical view of the mega-events.

South Korean culture, soft power, and sports mega-events

From the early 2000s, South Korean mass culture gradually gained popularity in East and South East Asia (Kuwahara 2014). The diffusion of Korean popular culture to the Asian entertainment market was part of the South Korean government's cultural policy that aims to enhance the reputation and image of the country in Asia and beyond (Kwon and Kim 2014). Because having an attractive cultural legacy accounted for one of the key components of acquiring soft power (Nye 2004), the South Korean government has subsidised the country's media and entertainment industry since the late 1990s. Promoting the cultural industry appropriately fits the aim of the government to enhance the nation's prestige in the post-industrial and information-based international system (Walsh 2014). Given the increasing popularity of Korean popular music, films, and television shows, it appears that South Korea's soft power strategy works.

The 2014 Incheon Asian Games took place at the moment when South Korean mass culture was widely spread over the eastern half of the Asian Continent. While the event essentially consisted of sporting competitions, the Organising Committee tended to hire South Korean celebrities in order to attract public attention from all over Asia and to introduce Korean culture through its entertainment industry (Ha 2014). For instance, a South Korean film star, Young-ae Lee, lit the Asian Games Cauldron as the final torch-bearer and a South Korean rapper, Psy, also performed during the opening ceremony. In addition, the official organisers of the event arranged cultural programmes, which consisted largely of concerts by famous Korean popular musicians. The frequent appearance of these Korean Wave stars during the Games engendered controversy and criticism because their fame might overshadow the athletic competitions (Jung 2014). Despite this concern, however, the Organising Committee and the government alike used the Asian sporting festival as a vehicle for reinforcing South Korea's emerging cultural power in Asia.

According to Nye (2004), a moral responsibility and goodwill embedded in the nation-state's foreign policy are also important elements that can enhance the soft power of the country. In this respect, the international sport development programme associated with the Pyeongchang Winter Olympic Games appears to reflect South Korea's soft power strategy. While the role and effect of sport in international development projects are contentious (Darnell 2013), a significant number of governmental and non-governmental organisations utilise sport as a tool for enhancing living conditions in developing countries in need (Levermore and Beacom 2009). The South Korean government is involved in this international development through sport initiatives. Since 2004 when the country first joined the Winter Olympic bidding campaign, the South Korean government, as part of its official development assistance activities, has invited young people from developing countries to Korea and offered free winter sport training programmes every year. The ultimate goal of this so-called Dream Programme is to foster Olympic-level athletes amongst programme participants in a way to assist them to take part in the Pyeongchang Winter Olympic Games in 2018. So far, forty-six former participants of the Dream Programme have taken part in various international winter sport competitions including the Olympic Games in 2010 and 2014. This Dream Programme exemplifies the way in which the South Korean government makes a contribution to international development through sport. By actively engaging in this project, the country can also build environments through which it can potentially enhance its soft power.

Mega-event scepticism and social protest

Since the mid-2000s, a number of South Korean regional cities have tried to host a diverse range of international sporting competitions, expecting that these events would facilitate the redevelopment of local areas and subsequently boost local economies. However, in most cases, sporting events held in these cities left very little local benefit. Instead, local governments suffered a huge financial deficit due to the large expense that hosting a sporting event incurs (Kim 2014). Having observed a series of economic failures of this sort, a sceptical view on hosting sports mega-events began to emerge amongst political activist groups.

With respect to the Incheon Asian Games and the Pyeongchang Winter Olympic Games, a number of civic organisations argue that the decision to host these two large sporting events is the outcome of provincial governments' populist policy (Choi 2014). They also warn that the host cities are in danger of being the most indebted cities in the country because of the sheer costs needed for hosting sports mega-events (Nam 2014). These groups also claim that the power elites in local areas are mainly concerned with individual political ambitions that hosting mega-events may help to fulfil (Choi 2014). Hence, according to these civic organisations, the positive economic, social and cultural legacies that sports mega-events are believed to generate are in fact myths.

The construction of the new Asian Games stadium in Incheon is perhaps the case that most vividly demonstrates financial mismanagement by a local government. In preparation for the Asian Games, the city council of Incheon drew up a plan to build a new main stadium. Yet, the advisory panels suggested renovating existing sport facilities because of the huge costs required to construct a new Asian Games facility (Kim and Lee 2014). Political activist groups also opposed the city council's proposal, as the new stadium is likely to be a white elephant without a clear plan for its use in a post-Asian Games setting (Park 2011). Despite this concern, the local government simply disregarded these oppositional views and decided to keep the original plan expecting that central government would subsidise the Asian Games project. However, after the event, the city council of Incheon was in dispute with the central government regarding the repayment of debts. Without a clear solution, the local government fell into the difficult situation of needing to pay off huge debts on its own and it was revealed that the construction of the main stadium was the main cause of the financial deficit (Kim and Lee 2014).

At the time of writing, South Korea is preparing for the Pyeongchang Winter Olympic Games. In order to avoid the economic fiasco of the Incheon Asian Games, political activist groups have initiated a campaign that requires major rearrangements of the Winter Olympic preparation project (Yoon 2015). These groups demand: (1) the relocation of the Olympic main stadium to a more densely populated urban area for reasons of sustainability, (2) the diffusion of sporting venues to various cities where facilities already exist, so that costs can be reduced, and (3) the maximum use of existing ski slopes so as to minimise environmental damage. These are surely workable rearrangements and in fact the IOC's new initiative, namely the Olympic Agenda 2020, encourages this more financially sustainable and environmentally friendly way to host the winter sport competition (The IOC 2014). However, these requirements directly contradict the interests of local businesses and developers and the Organising Committee, which largely consists of individuals from these interest groups, who refuse to accept the civic organisations' demands. The struggle between civic activists and the Organising Committee is still ongoing and only time will tell how the Winter Olympic Games unfold.

Conclusion

Sports mega-events do not take place in a political vacuum. The case of South Korea clearly shows that the organisation and delivery of international sport meetings mirrors domestic and diplomatic political environments. The events also function as catalysts for political change. In addition, various political activists and the power elites in the host cities attempt to utilise international sporting events as a vehicle for expressing their political interests. In order to conceptualise a theoretical framework for measuring the political value of hosting sports mega-events, it is important to take account of the political and historical context in which the sporting events are situated. Based on the experience of South Korea, I promulgate two ideal typical models of hosting a sports mega-event: an emerging state model and a soft power model.[1]

First, taking into consideration the political ramifications of the sports mega-events held in South Korea in the 1980s, I suggest an emerging state model of hosting a sports mega-event. Key characteristics of this model include the event as a coming out party, less democratic political regimes in power and their exploitation of the event as a vehicle for reinforcing the established political structure, and a social protest concerning internal political affairs. The Seoul Asian Games in 1986 and the Seoul Olympics in 1988 clearly correspond to the criteria of the emerging state model and, while additional empirical evidence needs to be gathered to underpin this model more rigorously, the cases of mega-sporting events awarded to other emerging nations such as Brazil and China discussed in this handbook appear to show similar patterns.

Second, the FIFA World Cup Finals and the Busan Asian Games contained elements of both the emerging state model and the soft power model. Fundamentally, the South Korean government still attempts to use sporting competitions as tools for enhancing cultural power. These were also the events that largely mirrored the government policy of engagement mainly with North Korea and to some extent with Japan. At the same time, the host country demonstrated the mood of reconciliation and collaboration with Japan and North Korea through these two large sporting events. More importantly, these were the sporting festivals that showcased a peaceful and friendly relationship built through sports, albeit temporarily, between fierce political and historic rivals. Displaying some characteristics of the two models of mega-sporting events simultaneously may be an indication that South Korea was in transition from a semi-periphery state to a semi-core country in the world system in the early 2000s.

Thirdly, the sports mega-events that South Korea delivered and will host in the 2010s seem to be geared towards the soft power model. Specific features of this type of sport mega-event involve the demonstration of global social justice through the event, the inclusion of cultural programmes that underpin universal values, the provision of inclusive sport development programmes, and the empowered role of non-governmental organisations in observing the activities of the Organising Committee and other event stakeholders. In addition, an event is largely organised in accordance with democratic principles. The Asian Games and the Winter Olympic Games offer the South Korean government a chance to reaffirm its cultural power and to be engaged in international development projects through sport. In addition, freedom of expression of mega-event scepticism to some extent indicates the democratic principle at work in society. Although it is too early to say that the Pyeongchang Olympic Games exemplify this soft power model, they certainly have that potential.

Note

1 In consideration of the entire history of the sports mega-events, a neo-liberal model can be added. This type of sporting event is mainly concerned with the commodification of the event in order to maximise commercial profits. The case of the Los Angeles Olympics in 1984 is an example of the neo-liberal model.

References

BBC (2000) *North-South Joint Declaration.* 15 June. Accessed 10 March 2015. http://news.bbc.co.uk/1/hi/world/asia-pacific/791691.stm.

Bridges, B. (2008) The Seoul Olympics: Economic miracle meets the world. *The International Journal of the History of Sport,* 25(14): 1939–1952.

Cha, V. D. (2009) *Beyond the Final Score: The Politics of Sport in Asia.* New York: Columbia University Press.

Cho, H. S. (2003) *Ilbon daejoongmunhwa gaebang younghyangbunsuk mit daeungbangan* [The deregulation on Japanese popular culture and its countermeasures]. Seoul: Korea Culture & Tourism Policy Institute.

Cho, J. H. and Bairner, A. (2012) The sociocultural legacy of the 1988 Seoul Olympic Games. *Leisure Studies,* 31(3): 271–289.

Choe, H. and Kim, J. (2012) South Korea's democratization movements, 1980–1987: Political structure, political opportunity, and framing. *Inter-Asia Cultural Studies,* 13(1): 55–68.

Choi, J. Y. (2014) Incheon Asian Game ae daehan pyunggarul huhara [It is time to evaluate the Incheon Asian Games]. *Cultural Action News Letter,* 21 October.

Chung, T. D. (1991) Korea's Nordpolitik: Achievements and prospects. *Asian Perspective,* 15(2): 149–178.

Collins, S. (2011) East Asia Olympic Desires: Identity on global stage in the 1964 Tokyo, 1988 Seoul and 2008 Beijing Games. *The International Journal of the History of Sport,* 28(16): 2240–2260.

Cumings, B. (2005) *Korea's Place in the Sun: A Modern History.* Updated ed. New York: W. W. Norton & Company.

Darnell, S. (2013) *Sport for Development and Peace: Critical Sociology.* London: Bloomsbury.

Embassy of Japan in Korea, 2002. *Haniljungsangei miraerul hyanghan gongdong message* [A joint message for the future from the leaders of Korea and Japan]. Accessed 30 April 2015. http://www.kr.emb-japan.go.jp/rel/r_worldcup/r_worldcup_005.htm#.

Grix, J. and Houlihan, B. (2014) Sports mega-events as part of a nation's soft power strategy: The cases of Germany (2006) and the UK (2012). *The British Journal of Politics and International Relations,* 16: 572–596.

Ha, J. W. (2014) K-pop festival to open with Incheon Asiad. *The Korea Herald,* 17 July 2014. Accessed 30 April 2015. www.koreaherald.com/view.php?ud=20140717001042.

Ha, N. G. and Mangan, J. A. (2002) Ideology, politics, power: Korean sport: transformation, 1945–1992. *International Journal of the History of Sport,* 19(2–3): 213–242.

Han, S. J. (1988) South Korea in 1987: The politics of democratization. *Asia Survey,* 28(1): 52–61.

Hill, C. R. (1996) *Olympic Politics: Athens to Atlanta 1896–1996.* 2nd ed. Manchester: Manchester University Press.

Hogarth, H. K. (2012) South Korea's Sunshine policy, reciprocity, and nationhood. *Perspectives on Global Development and Technology,* 11(1): 99–111.

Horne, J. and Whannel, G. (2012) *Understanding the Olympics.* Abingdon: Routledge.

Jae, S. H. (2002) Busan Asian Game gwa hanbando ki: Kookkikeyyang en 'Sangho jui' jukyong haeya [The Busan Asian Games and the Korean peninsula flag]. *Jayoo Kongron* [*Liberal Public Debate*], 37(10): 56–61.

Joo, R. M. (2012) *Trasnational Sport: Gender, Media, and Global Korea.* Durham, NC: Duke University Press.

Jung, U. J. (2002) Inkongki ungwon uro bukei daenam sunjeonhwa edo [The use of North Korean flag and North Korean propaganda]. *Wolgan Bukhan* [*Monthly North Korea*]. October 2012, pp. 54–60.

Jung, Y. S. (2014) Sayooei bingon durunan Incheon Asian Game Gaemaksik [The opening ceremony of the Incheon Asian Games reveals a poverty of reason]. *The Kyunghyang Shinmun,* 7 October 2014, p. 58.

Kim, H. D. (2014) Sustainability in hosting mega-sports events. *The Korea Times,* 24 October 2014. Accessed 10 March 2015. www.koreatimes.co.kr/www/news/opinon/2016/01/162_166916.html.

Kim, J. I. and Lee, M. W. (2014) Asian Game bitdummy Incheon, daecheganung kyungijang itnundae 4700uk bitnae kyunggijnag jeo [Inchen barrowed 47 billion won to build a new main stadium despite having an alternative facility]. *The Chosun Ilbo,* 26 October 2014. Accessed 15 March 2015. http://biz.chosun.com/site/data/html_dir/2014/10/26/2014102600918.html.

Kim, S. S. (2006) *The Two Koreas and the Great Powers.* Cambridge: Cambridge University Press.

Koh, E. (2005) South Korea and the Asian Games: The first step to the world. *Sport in Society,* 8(3): 468–478.

Kuwahara, Y. (2014). Introduction. In Y. Kuwahara (ed.) *The Korean Wave: Korean Popular Culture in Global Context.* Basingstoke: Palgrave, pp. 1–9.

Kwon, S. H. and Kim, J. (2014) The cultural industry policies of the Korean government and the Korean Wave. *International Journal of Cultural Policy,* 20(4): 422–439.

Larson, J. F. and Park, H. S. (1993) *Global Television and the Politics of the Seoul Olympics*. Boulder: Westview Press.

Lee, J. W. (2010) The Olympics in the post-Soviet era: The case of the two Koreas. In A. Bairner and G. Molnar (eds.) *The Politics of the Olympics: A Survey*. London: Routledge, pp. 117–128.

Lee, Y. I. and Lee, K. T. (2015) Economic nationalism and globalization in South Korea. *Asian Perspective*, 39(1): 125–151.

Lee, Y. T. (2002) World Cup 2002: Korea and Japan partnering for the 21st century. *Harvard Asia Pacific Review*, 6(1): 66–69.

Levermore, R. and Beacom, A. (2009) Sport and development: Mapping the field. In R. Levermore and A. Beacom (eds) *Sport and International Development*. Basingstoke: Palgrave, pp. 1–25.

Longman, J. (1996) Soccer: South Korea And Japan will share World Cup. *New York Times*, 1 June 1996. Accessed 10 March 2015. www.nytimes.com/1996/06/01/sports/soccer-south-korea-and-japan-will-share-world-cup.html.

Nam, H. W. (2014) Time bomb ticking on local government debt. *The Korea Times*, 31 March 2014. Accessed 10 March 2015. www.koreatimes.co.kr/www/news/nation/2014/04/116_154443.html.

National Archives of Korea (2006) *Ilbon daejoogmunhwa gaebang [The deregulation on Japanese popular culutre]*. Daejun: National Archives of Korea. Accessed 30 April 2015. www.archives.go.kr/next/search/list-SubjectDescription.do?id=003611.

Nye, J. J. (2004) *Soft Power: The Means to Success in World Politics*. New York: Public Affairs.

Park, H. S. (2011) Incheon Asian Game Bannaphara [Must return the Asian Games]. *Weekly Donga*, 9 May 2011, pp. 50–51.

Pound, R. W. (1994) *Five Rings over Korea: The Secret Negotiations behind the 1988 Olympic Games in Seoul*. New York: Little, Brown.

Sanford, D. C. (1993) ROK' Nordpolitik: Revisited. *The Journal of East Asian Affairs*, 7(1):1–31.

Senn, A. E. (1999) *Power, Politcs, and the Olympic Games: A History of Power Brokers, Events, and Controversies that Shaped the Games*. Champaign, IL: Human Kinetics.

Shin, C. H. (2011) *Pyeongchang Dongkye Olympic gwa Kookka Brand [The Pyeongchang Winter Olympic Games and national branding]*. Seoul: Korea Culture and Tourism Institute.

Soh, S. C. (2008) *The Comfort Women: Sexual Violence and Postcolonial Memory in Korea and Japan*. Chicago, IL: University of Chicago Press.

Strenk, A. (1979) What price victory? The world of international sports and politics. *Annals of the American Academy of Political and Social Science*, 445: 128–140.

Sugden, J. and Tomlinson, A. (2002) International power struggles in the governance of world football: The 2002 and 2006 World Cup bidding wars. In J. Horne and W. Manzenreiter (eds) *Japan, Korea and the 2002 World Cup*. London: Routledge, pp. 56–70.

The Economist (2002) The Korea united, for a day. 3 October. Accessed 20 March 2015. www.economist.com/node/1371329.

The IOC (2014) *Olympic Agenda 2020: 20+20 Recommendations*. Lausanne: The International Olympic Committee.

Walsh, J. (2014) Hallyu as a government construct: The Korean Wave in the context of economic and social development. In Y. Kuwahara (ed.) *The Korean Wave: Korean Popular Culture in Global Context*. Basingstoke: Palgrave, pp. 13–31.

Yoon, H. J. (2015) Bunsangaeche noneijocha guboohanun Jungboo and jojikwiae chakim mooleulgut [The government and the OGOC who refuse to discuss the diffusion of the Olympic venues will be responsible for the failure]. *The Hankyoreh*, 31 March 2015, p. 2.

Zimelis, A. (2011) Let the Games begin: Politics of the Olympic Games in Mexico and South Korea. *India Quarterly: A Journal of International Affairs*, 67(3): 263–278.

39

BRAZIL, POLITICS, THE OLYMPICS AND THE FIFA WORLD CUP

John Horne and Gabriel Silvestre

Introduction

Brazil has been, in less than a century and half, a monarchy, a republic, and a federation. It has been ruled by parliament, civilian presidents, military juntas, general-presidents, and by a civilian dictator.

(Rocha and McDonagh 2014: 61)

Interest in the development of the political system of the largest nation in South America has been a long-standing feature of scholarly research (see for example Rocha and McDonagh 2014; Levine and Crocitti 1999; McCann 2008). Academic interest in sport in South America has been given a significant boost by the scheduled hosting of the two largest sports mega-events – the FIFA men's football World Cup Finals and the Summer Olympic and Paralympic Games – in Brazil and Rio de Janeiro in 2014 and 2016 respectively. This is not to say that research has not been conducted until recently, but to acknowledge that the English-language literature has started to increase, and looks certain to grow even more rapidly in the coming years (for earlier research see Arbena 1999). One of the reasons is that the staging of these 'megas' focuses the attention of the global media and academics on the host nation and cities involved.

Popular involvement in sport is one of the major accomplishments of the 100 years or so since modern sport was established. But sport is not naturally followed anymore than people naturally go shopping. Sport consumers and audiences are *made* not born. This is also an accomplishment of political agencies, such as central (federal), regional and municipal government. In *Soccer Madness*, Lever (1995/1983: 6) contends that sport generally and, in Brazil, football specifically, has the 'paradoxical ability to reinforce societal cleavages while transcending them'. She argues that sport/football can 'create social order while preserving cultural identity', thus promoting rather than impeding goals of national development (Lever 1995: 22).

Anthropologists, historians, human geographers, political scientists and sociologists, amongst other scholars, have begun to investigate a number of recurring topics that enable us to begin to understand these and other developments in South America. Football, by far and away the most popular sport throughout South America, features in articles about fans, elite migrant labour, professional organizations and globalization (Gordon and Helal 2001; Raspaud and Bastos 2013; Ribeiro and Dimeo 2009). Alvito (2007) notes for example that football in Brazil has faced the twin challenges of commercialization and mediatization for at least the past 30 years. Mega-events attract accounts about the history of South American involvement, involvement in the Football World Cup and the Olympics and also the impacts of hosting on marginalized communities (Curi 2008; Gaffney 2010; Silvestre and Oliveira 2012; Sánchez and Broudehoux 2013). In addition to football, sports and other forms of physical culture discussed include surfing in Brazil and capoeira – the Brazilian martial art that combines elements of dance, acrobatics and music (Knijnik *et al.* 2010; Almeida *et al.* 2013). Specific accounts of the development of policies for sport in Brazil, and discussion of the development of leisure in Brazil and gender divisions and sport also appear in the literature (Almeida *et al.* 2013; Dias and Melo 2011; Petca *et al.* 2013).

Several articles contain overviews that summarize the history and development of sport and leisure in South America more generally, as well as those that discuss the complex composition of South American societies in the wake of centuries of immigration and colonial exploitation (Arbena 1986, 2001; Guedes 2011; Mangan 2001). Hence the diaspora of Europeans – the British, the Dutch, the French, the Germans and the Italians – as well as Portuguese and Spanish are rivalled by that of Japanese people, creating in Brazil the largest Japanese-speaking population outside of the Far East (Cuellar 2013). In future, as research grows, at least in the English-language literature, it will undoubtedly fill some of the gaps in our understanding and thus overcome the exoticization of South American culture often presented in popular travel programmes and documentaries. South America contains both economic giants, such as Brazil and relatively smaller developing economies.

In the past 30 years most of the developed and developing world has joined in the competitive marketing of places as social and economic opportunities seeking capital investment. Many 'Cariocas' (Rio de Janeiro locals) glued themselves to their TV screens at 11 am local time on 2 October 2009, awaiting the results of a decision about whether or not Rio de Janeiro would host the 2016 Olympic and Paralympic Games. On Copacabana beach, proposed site of the 2016 beach volleyball competition, a huge party was scheduled whether or not Rio was selected. The decision to award the Olympics to Rio was very much the icing on a decade of steady development. Brazil's had been one of the few economies that had remained stable and growing, leading to it being hailed as one of the BRICS, the so-called major emerging economies of Brazil, Russia, India, China (and additionally, South Africa).

The BRICS account for over 2.8 billion (40 per cent) of the world's population, but only command 25 per cent of global GDP, and hence they are also referred to as 'emerging economies'. Given the hosting of the Olympic Games by Beijing (2008), the Commonwealth Games by Delhi (2010), the FIFA World Cup by South Africa (2010), the Winter Olympic Games by Sochi (2014) and the FIFA World Cup by Russia (2018), as well as the Brazilian involvement in staging the Pan-American Games (2007), the FIFA World Cup (2014) and the Olympics (2016), some have suggested that a 'BRICS-style' of hosting sports mega-events may be emerging (Curi *et al.* 2011). Curi *et al.* point out that between 1950 and 2007, no major international sports event was hosted in Rio de Janeiro, the city lost its status as capital to Brasilia in 1960 and when it did stage the 2007 Pan-American Games, they were the most expensive of that series of competitions ever held. The 2007 Pan-AMs were marked by very tight security including the erection of walls to separate Games attendees from the local, poorer, population. Hence bidding to host these events has to be seen in a context where consumption-based development is seen as a solution to urban problems as much as national ones (Gaffney 2010).

Whilst there were no groups organized in Rio specifically against the Olympic bid, there were several groups on the ground concerned with the legacy these Olympics would bring to Rio, and especially to the marginalized communities living in *favelas* (sometimes referred to as 'slums'). While eviction in low-income, informal areas has become a not-uncommon consequence of mega-event planning worldwide, housing rights violations have reached significant proportions during recent Olympics. It is in this way that sport, and sports mega-events such as the Olympics especially, may appear superficially as credible tools of development. Yet they do so in ways that do not challenge inequalities or neo-liberal development. In fact the hosting of sports mega-events may be a most convenient shell for the promotion of neo-liberal agendas, since they do not deviate from top-down notions of economic and social development.

This chapter comprises two parts: a very brief history of socio-cultural and political aspects of sport (especially football) in Brazil that provides the background and context for the second that discusses contemporary aspects of mega-event bidding and hosting in Brazil. The first part focuses on the role of football in forging national identity and the growth in popularity of the sport. The politics surrounding Brazil's involvement in the FIFA World Cup since 1950 is discussed. The domestic politics of Brazilian football and key figures João Havelange and his former son-in-law Ricardo Teixeira are also considered. The second part will consider bidding and national politics underpinning the FIFA World Cup 2014 and the Rio de Janeiro 2016 Olympics, public protest and security, and demonstrations before and during the 2014 World Cup. The chapter concludes by considering the impact of mega-event hosting on political agendas and the outlook for football and other professional sports post-mega-events in Brazil.

Sport and politics in Brazil

There is no dictatorship in Brazil. Brazil is a liberal country, a land of happiness. We are a free people. Our leaders know what is best for (us) and govern (us) in a spirit of toleration and patriotism.

> *(Edson Arantes Nascimento da Silva (Pelé) speaking*
> *in 1972, quoted in Levine 1980: 244)*

I was kind of vague about these things, I didn't talk about politics.

> *(Pelé interviewed in 1993 about the 1970s,*
> *quoted in Levine and Crocitti 1999: 256)*

A number of more journalistic accounts of football in Brazil are available that discuss the connection with nationalism and politics (see, for example, Humphrey 1986; Goldblatt 2014; Zirin 2014). Here we briefly refer to two of the key academic sources that these journalistic accounts rely on (Lever 1995/1983; and Levine 1980) to provide a brief historical contextualization of the relations between politics and sport in Brazil.

Levine (1980: 233) recognizes the possibility of viewing sport, and especially football, as a form of opiate and distraction, and thus an agency of social control. He also acknowledges the alternative view that sport provides a source of group identity and social integration, and thus can act as a unifier of local, regional and national populations. He argues, however, that in the case of Brazil, 'futebol's chief significance has been its use by the elite to bolster official ideology and to channel social energy in ways compatible with prevailing social values'. Thus he appears to adopt a perspective more in keeping with that of Antonio Gramsci, or 'hegemony theory'.

Lever (1995/1983: 56), adopting the integration perspective, argues that 'sport promoted national integration in Brazil long before other social organizations criss-crossed the nation'. By 1914, Brazil had a national federation of sports clubs, the *Confederação Brasileira de Desportos* (CBD), or 'Brazilian Sports Confederation', and the football club as an institution dates from the late nineteenth century. Levine (1980: 234) suggests that the development of football in Brazil falls into four broad periods: 1894–1904, the development of private urban clubs for foreigners (especially the British, German and Portuguese); 1905–1933, the amateur phase which nonetheless saw a marked growth in interest; 1933–1950, professionalization and participation on the world stage, including the hosting of the fourth FIFA World Cup Finals in 1950; and since 1950, world-class recognition and the growth of commercialism. This remains a useful way of understanding the emergence of the sport in Brazil (for greater detail see Bellos 2002; Gaffney 2008; Goldblatt 2014).

The first football clubs to be established in Rio reflected the influence of foreigners – Vasco da Gama established in 1898 the Lusitania club for Portuguese merchants and bankers, Fluminense developed out of the British 'Rio Cricket and Athletic Association' in 1902, Botafogo were a spin-off from a rowing club (1904) and Flamengo, formerly another rowing club, was formed in 1915 when athletes defected from Fluminense. Thus are great sporting rivalries created within the boundaries of one city. Indicative of the growth of national pride associated with football, Levine (1980: 233) notes that:

> Following four matches in July 1929 by the touring Chelsea Football Club against Brazilian teams, Mr Steele, of the British Embassy in Rio de Janeiro, officially recommended that such future visits be discouraged, since the local partisans had behaved outrageously, intimidated the referees, and, twice victorious, 'claim as a nation to have beaten England'.

Popular interest in the sport was aided, as in other nations, by the growth of media reporting of the results by the newspaper press from the 1900s and radio from the 1930s.

Levine (1999: 44) notes how government expanded into everyday life, including sport, in Brazil in the 1930s. The government seized upon the Brazilian victory in the 1932 South American Cup and a year later football became a national institution when it was professionalized under the auspices of the CBD. In 1941 the club network in Brazil was linked to the federal government by President Vargas's centralization programme. A National Sport Council (CND) within the Ministry of Education and Culture was established to 'orient, finance, and encourage the practice of sport in all of Brazil' (Lever 1995/1983: 56). Lever (1995/1983: 59) argues that from the beginning of the diffusion and adoption of modern sport, 'sport and government more than coexist; their relationship is better described as symbiotic'. Whilst individual athletes, such as tennis player Maria Bueno, who won four times at Forest Hills and three times at Wimbledon between 1959 and 1966, and racing driver Emerson Fittipaldi, who was at his best in Formula One racing in the 1970s, may have been used to symbolize Brazilian greatness, Lever (1995/1983: 55) argues that it 'is through team sports, with their highly organised structure that precedes and outlives any particular set of athletes, that more than momentary unification of a nation is established'. She argues that in Brazil 'politicians have spurred the growth of both spectator and participant sport; sport, in return, has helped politicians court popularity and has helped the Brazilian government achieve its nationalistic goals' (Lever 1995/1983: 59). In many ways, therefore, her argument can be seen as complementary to that of Levine.

Lever (1995/1983: 59) argues that the modern history of Brazil is 'one of social and economic change through authoritarian centralization'. Sport has played its part in this in various ways.

The military coup d'état in 1964 saw the establishment of army presidents. In 1968, as repression intensified, the President, General Emílio Garrastazu Médici, began taking an interest in Flamengo and the national team. When Brazil won the FIFA World Cup for an unprecedented third time in Mexico in 1970, the team was flown directly from Mexico City to the capital Brasilia, and the players were personally received by Médici in the Planalto Palace (Levine 1980: 246). Two days of national celebration followed and shortly after the military took over the CBD (eventually renamed the *Confederação Brasileira de Futebol* (CBF) after a demand by FIFA in 1979).

Although there was considerable interest in football it is clear that less attention was paid to developing other 'Olympic sports' (Levine 1980: 249). When it was suggested to President-designate General João Baptista de Oliveira Figueiredo, that amateur sport should be given greater emphasis to improve Brazilian performance at the Olympic Games, he retorted that the Olympics were: 'political propaganda for nations who needed that sort of thing' (quoted in Levine 1980: 250). Brazil's achievements at the Summer Olympics continue to be middle ranking, including never having secured a gold medal in either the men's or women's football competition. The top medal-producing sports have been volleyball, sailing and judo.

Lever (1995/1983: 61–62; see also Goldblatt 2014: 122–157) provides several examples of the way in which football and politics mixed in Brazil during the dictatorship. When she was conducting interviews with workers in the early 1970s, a low increase in the monthly minimum wage was augmented with the giving away of 15,000 free tickets for the match between Flamengo and Fluminense (the team of the masses versus the team of the elite). At the time, the state also regulated maximum ticket prices for entrance to the 'popular' sections of public stadia, such as the 'geral' in the Maracanã in Rio. Football club directorships were also stepping-stones to political careers, and politicians have used the sport to further their interests (Kuper 1994). Admiral Helenio Nunes, President of the CBD and ARENA (the official government political party) in the state of Rio de Janeiro, used matches prior to the 1978 World Cup in Argentina as political rallies, featuring ARENA's banners and military bands. Political figures claimed to be fans even when they were not. In June 1973, when the government announced President Médici's successor, a not well-known (military) man, the newspaper *Jornal do Brasil* featured his photograph on the front page with the caption:

Gaucho [meaning from the state of Rio Grande do Sul] from Bento Gonçalves [his hometown] 64 years old, fan of International in Porto Alegre and Botafogo in Rio, brother of two generals, married, with one daughter, Ernesto Geisel will be the 23rd president of the republic.

(Lever 1995/1983: 64)

Sport, politics and the hosting of mega-events in contemporary Brazil

Since the re-democratization process in the late 1980s, sports other than football have slowly attained greater prominence in the national political agenda resulting in the creation of a dedicated ministry under the government of President Luis Inacio ('Lula') da Silva of the Workers' Party. Attention and resources have been mostly oriented towards professional sports and were lately dominated by the hosting of mega-events (Almeida *et al.* 2013). The bidding campaigns for the FIFA 2014 World Cup and the 2016 Olympic Games were fully endorsed by the national government and by the passionate support of President Lula, who on the occasion of the awards declared that football was 'more than a sport for Brazilians, it is a national passion and that with the Olympics 'Brazil gained its international citizenship . . . the world has finally recognised it is Brazil's time' (BBC Sport 2007; Rohter 2012: 223). Such claims demonstrate the political capital to be explored in relation to two audiences: the Brazilian electorate and the international opinion.

In the next two sections we pay attention to the political aspects of the preparation for the two events, here broadly defined to include the agendas of the federal and local governments, the interests of sports organizers and civil protests that have marked the build-up and staging of the football World Cup. We retrace the bidding and preparation history of the events whilst reflecting on their expected contributions and impacts, a debate that rose to international prominence with the scenes of nationwide protests.

The FIFA 2014 World Cup

Following the controversies surrounding the voting for the 2006 World Cup – when the South African bid was beaten by one vote after the sudden change of mind of one delegate – FIFA introduced a continental rotating system to designate host countries, starting with Africa and followed by South America. Since last hosting the event in 1950, Brazilian interest in organizing a World Cup was unconvincingly presented in 1988 when its candidature received only two votes to host the 1994 World Cup (US Soccer 2013). The new rotating system was thus an opportune occasion to which the then-chairman of CBF, Ricardo Teixeira, worked in getting the support of the recently elected President Lula da Silva.

Presidential support for the bid was initiated in 2004, when both Teixeira and Lula attended a friendly match between Brazil and Haiti in Port-au-Prince as part of a United Nations peacekeeping mission led by Brazilian troops. Despite expressing their interest, both Argentina and Colombia would withdraw their candidatures leaving Brazil as the sole contender. In October 2007, Brazil was confirmed as the host of the 2014 World Cup in an unusual situation since the host cities were still to be decided. From a shortlist of 18 cities 12 were finally chosen in May 2009 after FIFA conceded the request to include more host cities than the usual eight or ten. It included traditional venues in cities like Rio de Janeiro, São Paulo and Belo Horizonte, as well as less obvious football destinations such as the cities of Manaus, Cuiabá and Brasília.

A higher personal benefit seemed to hold for Teixeira, who accumulated the position of chairman of the local organizing committee, whose intentions in running for the presidency of FIFA were speculated only for him to fall into disgrace. Chairman of CBF since 1989 and a former son-in-law of João Havelange, FIFA president from 1974 to 1998, Teixeira became a powerful figure in football politics by exploiting his position and networks at CBF and as an executive member of FIFA. Despite enduring congressional probing commissions into corruption in Brazilian football, personal wrongdoings and allegations of embezzlement by the international press, he found himself at odds with Lula's successor, President Dilma Rousseff indisposed with his association to her government. Polemic declarations in the press stating that in 2014 he could do the 'most slippery, unthinkable, Machiavellian things' such as 'denying press credentials, barring access, changing game schedules' yet still nothing would happen to him (Pinheiro 2011), sparked media and public outrage on the eve of the World Cup qualifying draw, with public demonstrations calling for 'out with Teixeira'. Alleging personal health reasons he finally stepped down in 2012.

The preparations for the World Cup were poised to be one of the main symbols of Rousseff's government following the announcement of an overall programme package in

Lula's last year in office. A suite of agreements with state and municipal authorities were signed, detailing works in stadiums, public transport, airports, tourism infrastructure and roads and highways. In order to facilitate and speed up the tendering of contracts, special regulations were enacted to flexibilize both the tendering process and the cap of municipal and state levels of indebtedness. State and local governments were responsible for tendering and contracting out the projects under their responsibility, leading to varied outcomes as some projects were substantially reviewed, suspended by irregularities and even abandoned given the improbability of their conclusion on time, since many related to urban mobility such as underground transportation lines and light railways.

The progress of works was at times obfuscated by the turbulence in the relationship between FIFA and the Brazilian government leading to the approval of a general set of laws in relation to the organization of the event. These included the application of guarantees previously signed by the Brazilian government in relation to tax exemptions, the approval of visas and restrictions on ambush marketing, and also to other items that triggered heated debates such as concessionary tickets, the licensing for the sale of alcohol at the venues and the activities of street vendors in the surroundings of the venues. Minor concessions were made, such as half-priced tickets for students and the elderly and the acquiescing for the permanence of the traditional *baianas* selling Afro-Brazilian food in Salvador. Still, the relationship with FIFA became more strained as delays became all too apparent.

The immediate run-up to the event was plagued by delays, cost overruns, fatalities and nationwide protests. The national government stayed firm to the discourse of expected benefits accruing from the event, with constant reference to the legacies that would benefit the majority of the population. There was mounting criticism from the press with the escalating budget figures, particularly with the costs of stadiums and their post-event use. In one of the extreme cases, the predicted final figure for Brasilia's National Stadium was almost double the original estimate, while the future of the stadium post-World Cup remained uncertain given the absence of a competitive team in the upper tiers of the Brazilian football competitions. A similar situation beckoned for the stadiums in Natal, Cuiabá and Manaus. Up to the completion of the stadiums, ten deaths of construction workers were registered as progress was rushed to meet deadlines. Half of the venues were unveiled for the Confederations Cup in 2013, the FIFA rehearsal tournament for the World Cup, despite ongoing works visible in the venues. Up to that point the expected budget for World Cup-related expenditure had already increased to five times the original estimates. One year to go and facing mounting challenges in several planning areas, the organization of the event found itself caught in the middle of a massive public protest that swept across the country.

In June 2013, scenes of public demonstrations in the streets of Brazilian cities and heavy-handed police response were widely covered by the international press. What had started as a local protest in São Paulo against the rise in bus fares which brought some of its main thoroughfares to a halt, quickly triggered demonstrations elsewhere in the country after it was met by disproportionate repression by the police. Thousands poured into the streets of more than 350 cities to express not only their indignation to scenes of police brutality widely circulated in social networks of the internet, but also to release their discontentment with corrupted politics and the neglected state of public services.

The composition of the masses, as political scientist Andre Singer (2014) observed, was made up of two large strata, that of the middle classes and what he identified as the 'new proletariat', a young working class with formal jobs but nonetheless poorly paid and with poor working conditions (pp. 24–25). Their banners also reflected different foci: while the former expressed their anger with the continuous corruption scandals that marred national politics and the Workers'

Party, the latter manifested their revolt against issues closer to their daily lives; the poor condition of the public health, education and transport systems.

The arrival of the Workers' Party in the federal government in 2002 coincided with a period of strong economic growth, the improvement of social indicators and rising levels of consumption by the lower sections of the social scale that helped them to endure the global financial crisis relatively unscathed (Anderson 2011). Its continuance in power was sealed via a familiar political strategy in Brazil of securing support via shady deals. Exposed during the denouncement of a vote-buying scheme in 2005 that led to the sentencing of some of the party's top ranks, this long evolving story was also represented on some of the banners during the June 2013 protests. Hence, although able to afford more consumer goods, the urban poor have endured an ambiguous existence of formal jobs in precarious conditions, with poor public services. The two agendas thus converged around a related and immediate event: the FIFA Confederations Cup in 2013.

Protesting against the vilified 'FIFA standards' often evoked in official discourses justifying the spending on football venues, Brazilians demanded the same level of quality in the delivery of public services. The ever-rising budget for the event, the finding of irregularities and the suspension of projects served to confirm the general sentiment that only the powerful and rich would benefit. Long-standing campaigning groups such as the *Comitês Populares da Copa* (Popular Committees of the World Cup) highlighted the displacement of thousands of people from low-income communities by works related with the event, with estimates ranging between 170,000 to 250,000 (Montenegro 2013), and the appropriation of public improvements by private companies as the operation of the venues were privatized (Gaffney 2014). Protest videos posted online went viral. The otherwise football-crazy image that characterized the portrayal of Brazilian fans was nowhere to be seen in the Confederations Cup tournament, as chants of '*Não vai ter Copa!*' ('There won't be a World Cup') and '*Da Copa eu abro mão, quero meu dinheiro pra saúde e educação*' ('I give up the World Cup, I want my money to go into health and education') echoed in many of the host cities.

While some municipalities backtracked on their decision to raise transport fares, the federal government responded with a public announcement from President Rousseff acknowledging the demands and condemning acts of vandalism. National programmes and new governmental intentions in healthcare, education and transport were announced. If the measure managed to placate widespread demonstrations, other protests smaller in numbers continued to be carried over in the following months. This was accompanied by a wave of strikes in the professions – especially the police, teachers, road sweepers and public transport operators – for improved pay and work conditions. FIFA continued to refute criticism of its role by stating that it was Brazil's decision to bid for the event and to propose the projects associated with the stadiums.

The total cost of expenditure announced by the Brazilian government on the eve of the World Cup in 2014 was $11.3 billion (Boadle 2014; the predicted total at the time of writing in February 2015 is now closer to $15 billion). It was a far cry from initial government statements such as that of the minister of sports back in 2007 that it would be the 'World Cup of the private sector', meaning that essential works such as those destined for the venues would be covered by private companies. The final financial breakdown saw almost 83 per cent of the costs attributed to governmental spending or financed by state banks (Folha de São Paulo 2014). It was perhaps no wonder that, with the exception of one or two rather tame decorations celebrating the arrival of yet another World Cup, the vivid signs of popular excitement on the walls and streets of Brazilian cities that might have been expected with the hosting of a World Cup on home soil did not initially materialize in 2014.

The Rio 2016 Olympic Games

The 2016 Rio de Janeiro Olympic project bears some resemblances to the 2014 World Cup, in which big politics and long-time serving sports leaders played a pivotal role in securing the rights to host the event for the first time in a South American country. However, differently from the World Cup, in which football politics determined the urban agenda of hosting cities, it was the urban politics of Rio de Janeiro city that determined the Olympic project.

Rio de Janeiro had previously unsuccessfully attempted to host the 1930 and 1960 Olympic Games and the separate equestrian competition of the 1956 Olympics. A new bid would be prepared for the 2004 Olympic Games, this time as the outcome of an inter-urban policy exchange. The local elections of 1992 brought the conservative candidate Cesar Maia to government, promising to bring urban order and modernize public administration. An important element of Maia's agenda was to elaborate a strategic plan then in vogue in North American and European cities to set a vision for the city in collaboration with other representative groups. The initiative was pursued with the consulting services of policy-makers from Barcelona freshly after the organization of the 1992 Olympic Games. It was out of this relationship that the concept of an Olympic bid was born, as a way to promote urban development and city marketing.

Hastily prepared, the bid attempted to incorporate the general precepts of the 1992 Barcelona Olympic Games by earmarking declining urban areas for regeneration and a multi-cluster organization. The event was also expected to turn around the image of a city synonymous with rampant crime and police-led carnage. The bid generated great support from the public, while new promises were announced, including a bold social development agenda aimed to improve living conditions by eradicating poverty and upgrading slums. However, the bid failed to impress the IOC inspection and was not shortlisted in the final voting round. The dismal result frustrated some of the key promoters of the bid, leaving re-elected Mayor Maia and the president of the Brazilian Olympic Committee, Carlos Nuzman, to pick up the pieces and to drastically rearrange the Olympic project.

Working his way through the Olympic system and becoming a member of the IOC, Nuzman translated the message that Brazil had to first prove its credentials by convincing Maia to support a bid to host the 2007 Pan-American Games, the regional Olympic-styled competition for the Americas. Giving an otherwise modest competition an 'Olympic treatment', the event had original estimates multiplied by four as a set of venues were specially built for the event including an Olympic stadium, a velodrome, an indoor arena and an aquatics centre. This time the spatial planning privileged the expanding and wealthy district of Barra da Tijuca, with the athletes' village adding to the local gated-community stock. Criticism, particularly in relation to the inflated costs, was somehow held off as the experience was justified as an Olympic rehearsal with a new bid quickly announced for the 2016 Games.

Up to this point the national government had played a supporting and guarantor role. President Lula had confirmed in 2003 the commitment of his government with the preparations for the 2007 Pan-American Games and his backing to a short-lived bid for the 2012 Olympics. The contribution of the federal government to the total budget for the 2007 event increased substantially in the run-up period as municipal finances were compromised. The 2016 bid would then become more aligned with Brazil foreign policy discourse, reflecting the country's increasing prominent role, and having in President Lula an active poster boy. Acquired organizing expertise, geopolitics, booming national and local economies and branding opportunities in bringing the event for the first time to South America were the raw elements that the team of seasoned consultants, with previous experience in the Sydney 2000 and London 2012 candidatures, tailored to the IOC audience. Rio was then selected as the 2016 Olympic Games host in October 2009.

The masterplan of the 2016 Games reinforced the concentration of venues and facilities at Barra da Tijuca, but whereas the Pan American Games brought little contribution to the city's internal system, new transport networks and the regeneration of the port area embodied the expected material legacies. The new government of Mayor Eduardo Paes in 2009 reproduced at the local level the political coalition present at the state and national governments which then facilitated a shared agenda to release municipal, state and federal land for the regeneration of the port area. Despite not featuring any sports facilities, the project has been strongly associated as a legacy of the event, with the Olympics providing a deadline for the conclusion of several works that will transform it into a new mixed-use district of corporate towers, museums and residential areas. The other visible programme associated with the Games is the construction of 250 kilometres of segregated bus rapid transit (BRT) lanes and an extension of the underground, which together will improve the link of Barra with the other parts of the city.

Without proper disclosure of the details of the projects, a range of low-income communities learned their displacement for Olympic-related works as municipal staff turned up to mark their houses for demolition (Silvestre and Oliveira, 2012). A study of the Comité Popular da Copa e das Olimpíadas do Rio de Janeiro (2013) estimated that almost 11,000 families had been affected by these works, and were offered temporary rental assistance, financial compensation or relocation to social housing estates in the western fringes of the city. Another element that has substantially affected the lives of the inhabitants of Rio *favelas* is the security programme of Police Pacifying Units (PPU) launched in 2008. Consisting of a joint effort between the Brazilian Army and the state's elite police squad, it occupies gang-controlled communities driving away drug traffickers while constructing police bases inside the *favelas*. Despite not being directly linked with the mega-events projects, the geography of police occupations demonstrates the proximity to competition sites and tourist areas. Initial positive receptiveness by local residents has been marred by police abuse, the delayed arrival of public services, gentrification and the continuation of criminal activity.

The indignation of part of the population, together with rising living costs, helped to fuel the local June 2013 demonstrations, with some estimated 300,000 people taking to the streets of central Rio on 20 June (G1 2013). Some concessions were announced by the state governor in backtracking on the decision to demolish the athletics and aquatics centre, together with the museum of indigenous people at the Maracanã complex to make way for car parking spaces for the main stadium. The Rio mayor, Eduardo Paes, announced that evictions were to be temporarily suspended until detailed studies were produced, although these did not emerge in the following months.

The same criticisms levied at the World Cup for its lavish spending and also for worrying project delays were also directed at Rio's preparation for the Olympics as a string of negative comments on the readiness of the venues were the focus of press coverage. Two years prior to the opening ceremony Rio was reported to have just 10 per cent of facilities ready (Jenkins 2014) while the Olympic Park was still a desolate site with no erected structures and the sport cluster of Deodoro still awaited tenders for development.

Conclusion

The year 2014 marked several anniversaries for Brazil. It was 50 years since a military coup d'état brought about a 21-year-long period of dictatorship and 29 years since its replacement and re-democratization. During this time, and before, sport has remained firmly connected to politics in Brazil. When Lula became president in 2002 he inherited several problems from his predecessor, Fernando Henrique Cardoso. Public debt had doubled, the current account deficit was twice the average for South America, interest rates were over 20 per cent and the Brazilian currency was depreciating fast (Anderson 2011). Whilst Lula introduced policies that materially impacted on the poorer sections of society, such as the 'Bolsa Familia', which involves a monthly cash transfer to poor mothers against proof that they were sending their children to school and getting regular health checks, he also became aware of the potential value of aligning with those interested in hosting sports mega-events.

Through extension of Lever's argument, mentioned in the introduction, Arbena (1995: 225) argues that:

> the case could also be made that international competition can likewise diminish nationalism in favour of a greater sense of transnational community, if only through a sense of shared experiences and the consequences of operating within similar institutions and regulations.

The global impacts on the local via urban politics (Sanchez *et al.* 2014); but globalization also brings with it an amplification of existing contradictions in society and in football especially (Alvito 2007). These include the Brazilian football player diaspora, club insolvency, youth talent capture by foreign clubs, consumerization of the fans, and media monopolies' influence over the organization of football competitions and seasons. Whilst attempts have been made to resist these developments by organizing football fans, these have not had great success (Gaffney 2013). Hence the *seleção* for the 2014 World Cup featured 20 out of 23 players who played outside of Brazil, including, at the time of selection in early May, four from Chelsea in the English Premier League (EPL).

What was initially thought of as a timely opportunity for domestic and foreign politics, as well as for personal benefits for those at the heart of the project, the 2014 FIFA World Cup turned into an anathema. Anger directed towards FIFA and their expected record profit from the event affected even more the problematic reputation of the institution while it struggled with corruption scandals from other episodes (discussed elsewhere in this collection). International press coverage highlighted many problems with the preparation of the event and the contrasts between the lavish stadiums and precarious social conditions of many Brazilians. However, the forecasts of a doomed event did not materialize, at least not from where it was expected. The press, FIFA, athletes and fans alike positively reviewed the general running of the event. Contrary to the scenes of the previous year, protests did not generate the same amount of support and were fewer and smaller, if still suppressed heavy-handedly. It was rather on the pitch that Brazilian hopes for some positive vision were crushed, including the biggest defeat in the history of the *seleção*, 7–1 by the eventual World Cup winners, Germany. As Alex Bellos (2014: 388–389) had noted before the competition:

> The parallels with 1950 are strong. Brazil has more swagger than it did but it remains an insecure country, desperate to show the world that it is a serious, competent and modern nation. Its own self image could again depend on a single goal.

Or maybe seven! In 2016, however, the Summer Olympic and Paralympic Games will take place in Rio, and so a second opportunity awaits Brazilian hosts to demonstrate to the world their capacity to stage a large, multi-sport mega-event. As with all such mega-events, the political implications will comprise a mixture of the local, regional, national, and international, as well as the sporting.

References

Almeida, M., Joseph, J., Palma, A. and Soares, A. J. (2013) Marketing strategies within an African-Brazilian martial art. *Sport in Society*, 16(10): 1346–1359.

Alvito, M. (2007) Our piece of the pie: Brazilian football and globalization. *Soccer and Society*, 8(4): 524–544.

Anderson, P. (2011) Lula's Brazil. *London Review of Books*, 33(7): 3–12.

Arbena, J. L. (1986) Sport and the study of Latin American history: An overview. *Journal of Sport History*, 13(2): 87–96.

Arbena, J. L. (ed.) (1999) *Latin American Sport: An Annotated Bibliography, 1988–1998*. Westport, CT: Greenwood Press.

Arbena, J. L. (1995) Nationalism and sport in Latin America, 1850–1990: The paradox of promoting and performing 'European' sports. *International Journal of the History of Sport*, 12(2): 220–238.

Arbena, J. L. (2001) The later evolution of modern sport in Latin America: The North American influence. *International Journal of the History of Sport*, 18(3): 43–58.

BBC Sport (2007) Brazil will stage 2014 World Cup. 30 October. Accessed 12 June 2014. http://news.bbc.co.uk/sport1/hi/football/internationals/7068848.stm.

Bellos, A. (2002) *Futebol: The Brazilian Way of Life*. London: Bloomsbury.

Bellos, A. (2014) *Futebol: The Brazilian Way of Life* (2nd ed.). London: Bloomsbury.

Boadle, A. (2014) World Cup leaves Brazil costly stadiums, poor public transport, *Reuters*. 5 June. Accessed 12 June 2014. www.reuters.com/article/2014/06/05/us-brazil-worldcup-infrastructure-idUSKBN0E G23H20140605.

Comitê Popular da Copa e das Olimpíadas do Rio de Janeiro (2013) *Megaeventos e violações dos direitos humanos no Rio de Janeiro*. Accessed 12 June 2014 http://rio.portalpopulardacopa.org.br.

Cuellar, J. E. (2013) Latin America, football and the Japanese diaspora. *Soccer & Society*, 14(5): 722–733.

Curi, M. (2008) Samba, girls and party: Who were the Brazilian soccer fans at a World Cup? An ethnography of the 2006 World Cup in Germany. *Soccer & Society*, 9(1): 111–134.

Curi, M., Knijnik, J. and Mascarenhas, G. (2011) The Pan American Games in Rio de Janeiro 2007: Consequences of a sport mega-event on a BRIC country. *International Review for the Sociology of Sport*, 46(2): 140–156.

de Vasconcellos Ribeiro, C. H. and Dimeo, P. (2009) The experience of migration for Brazilian football players. *Sport in Society*, 12(6): 725–736.

Dias, C. and de Andrade Melo, V. (2011) Leisure and urbanisation in Brazil from the 1950s to the 1970s. *Leisure Studies*, 30(3): 333–343.

Folha de São Paulo (2014) O Mundial e as despesas do governo. Accessed 12 June 2014. www1.folha.uol.com.br/infograficos/2014/05/82605-o-mundial-e-as-despesas-do-governo.shtml.

G1(2013) Protestos pelo país têm 1,25 milhão de pessoas, um morto e confrontos. June. Accessed 12 June 2014. http://g1.globo.com/brasil/noticia/2013/06/protestos-pelo-pais-tem-125-milhao-de-pessoas-um-morto-e-confrontos.html.

Gaffney, C. (2008) *Temples of the Earthbound Gods: Stadiums in the Cultural Landscapes of Rio de Janeiro and Buenos Aires*. Austin, TX: University of Texas Press.

Gaffney, C. (2010) Mega-events and socio-spatial dynamics in Rio de Janeiro, 1919–2016. *Journal of Latin American Geography*, 9(1): 7–29.

Gaffney, C. (2013) Virando o jogo: The challenges and possibilities for social mobilization in Brazilian football. *Journal of Sport and Social Issues*, published online. Accessed 8 September 2014. http://jss.sagepub.com/content/early/2013/12/16/0193723513515887.abstract.

Gaffney, C. (2014) A World Cup for whom? The impact of the 2014 World Cup on Brazilian stadiums and cultures. In P. Fontes and B. Buarque De Hollanda (eds) *The Country of Football: Politics, Popular Culture and the Beautiful Game in Brazil*. London: Hurst & Co., pp. 187–206.

Goldblatt, D. (2014) *Futebol Nation: A Footballing History of Brazil*. London: Penguin.

Gordon, C. and Helal, R. (2001) The crisis of Brazilian football: Perspectives for the twenty-first century. *International Journal of the History of Sport*, 18(3): 139–158.

Guedes, C. (2011). Changing the cultural landscape: English engineers, American missionaries, and the YMCA bring sports to Brazil – the 1870s to the 1930s. *International Journal of the History of Sport*, 28(17): 2594–2608.

Humphrey, J. (1986). No holding Brazil: Football, nationalism and politics. In A. Tomlinson and G. Whannel (eds) *Off the Ball: The Football World Cup.* London: Pluto, pp. 127–139.

Jenkins, S. (2014) The World Cup and Olympics threaten to overwhelm Rio – yet there is time to create a sensation out of disaster. *The Guardian.* 23 April. Accessed 12 June 2014. www.theguardian.com/cities/2014/apr/23/world-cup-olympics-rio-de-janeiro-brazil-sensation-disaster.

Knijnik, J. D., Horton, P. and Oliveira Cruz, L. (2010) Rhizomatic bodies, gendered waves: Transitional femininities in Brazilian surf. *Sport in Society,* 13(7/8): 1170–1185.

Kuper, S. (1994) *Football Against the Enemy.* London: Orion.

Lever, J. (1995/1983) *Soccer Madness: Brazil's Passion for the World's Most Popular Sport.* Prospect Heights, NY: Waveland Press.

Levine, R. M. (1980) Sport and society: The case of Brazilian futebol. *Luso-Brazilian Review,* 17(2): 233–252.

Levine, R. M. (1999) *Father of the Poor? Vargas and His Era.* Cambridge: Cambridge University Press.

Levine, R. M. and Crocitti, J. J. (eds) (1999). *The Brazil Reader: History, Culture, Politics.* Durham, NC: Duke University Press.

McCann, B. (2008) *The Throes of Democracy: Brazil since 1989.* London: Zed Books.

Mangan, J. A. (2001) The early evolution of modern sport in Latin America: A mainly English middle-class inspiration? *International Journal of the History of Sport,* 18(3): 9–42.

Mason, T. (1995) *Passion of the people? Football in South America.* London: Verso.

Montenegro, C. (2013) Copa pode provocar despejo de 250 mil pessoas, afirmam ONGs. *BBC Brasil.* 23 June. Accessed 12 June 2014. www.bbc.co.uk/portuguese/noticias/2013/06/130614_futebol_despejos_cm_bg.shtml.

Petca, A. R., Bivolaru, E. and Graf, T. A. (2013) Gender stereotypes in the Olympic Games media? A cross-cultural panel study of online visuals from Brazil, Germany and the United States. *Sport in Society,* 16(5): 611–630.

Pinheiro, D. (2011) The president, *Revista piauí.* Accessed 12 June 2014 http://revistapiaui.estadao.com.br/edicao-58/the-faces-of-futebol/the-president.

Raspaud, M. and da Cunha Bastos, F. (2013) Torcedores de futebol: Violence and public policies in Brazil before the 2014 FIFA World Cup. *Sport in Society,* 16(2): 192–204.

Rocha, J. and McDonagh, F. (2014) *Brazil inside Out: People, Politics and Culture.* Rugby: Latin America Bureau/Practical Action Publishing.

Rohter, L. (2012) *Brazil on the Rise: The Story of a Country Transformed.* Basingstoke: Palgrave Macmillan.

Sánchez, F., and Broudehoux, A. M. (2013) Mega-events and urban regeneration in Rio de Janeiro: Planning in a state of emergency. *International Journal of Urban Sustainable Development,* 5(2): 132–153.

Sánchez, F., Bienenstein, G., Leal de Oliveira, F. and Novais, P. (eds) (2014) *A Copa do Mundo e as Cidades: Políticas, Projetos e Resistências.* Niteroi: Editora da UFF/ Universidade Federal Fluminense.

Schausteck de Almeida, B., Coakley, J., Marchi Júnior, W. and Augusto Starepravo, F. (2012) Federal government funding and sport: the case of Brazil, 2004–2009. *International Journal of Sport Policy and Politics,* 4(3): 411–426.

Silvestre, G. and de Oliveira, N. G. (2012) The revanchist logic of mega-events: Community displacement in Rio de Janeiro's West End. *Visual Studies,* 27(2): 204–210.

Singer, A. (2014) Rebellion in Brazil: Social and political complexion of the June events. *New Left Review,* 85: 19–37.

US Soccer (2013) The 1994 bid – how the US got the World Cup: part 3. 4 July 2013. Accessed 12 June 2014. www.ussoccer.com/stories/2014/03/17/14/01/the-1994-bid-how-the-us-got-the-world-cup-part-3.

Zirin, D. (2014) *Brazil's Dance with the Devil: The World Cup, the Olympics, and the Fight for Democracy.* Chicago, IL: Haymarket Books.

40

HOW DOES A LOSER WIN?

Taiwan and global sport

Tzu-hsuan Chen

Introduction

This chapter examines Taiwan, or the Republic of China, a political entity not recognised b the UN since 1971, and the appropriation of sport in the pursuit of global visibility. Not onl isolated from the political world (only 22 entities have full diplomatic relations with Taiwan but also a fringe member of the sport world, participating since 1981 under the compromise and bizarre name of 'Chinese Taipei', Taiwan's main obstacle to the world lies just across th Taiwan Strait. The People's Republic of China (henceforth, China) and Taiwan have a ver complex relationship. To put it in an extremely concise fashion, they are, on the one hand linguistically, racially and culturally intimate, and economically interdependent, yet politicall opposite and militarily hostile to each other. Taiwan, a political loser, appropriated sport as means by which to contrast itself with China, along with Japan and the US, its significant oth ers, for the construction of a national identity.

To examine this issue, the chapter takes a seemingly unorthodox detour by reviewing th unique structure of sport broadcasting in Taiwan, which embodies the tensions, cooperation competition and coercion affecting Taiwan in the world of sport since the country's Martia Law Era (1949–1987). Even though martial law ended in July 1987, the cultural rigidit of the society and the deep-rooted nationalism propagated during the Martial Law Era sti dominates Taiwan's perspective on sport. In those days, the television business in Taiwa was not a competitive commercial affair, as in the US. Nor was it a public, TV-led mod like that of the UK (BBC), Japan (NHK) or Canada (CBC). Therefore, sport broadcast ing was unlike the commonly referred to sport/media complex which Jhally (1984, 198! identifies in the Western context. This chapter establishes a de-Westernised perspective c state capitalism's impact on sport broadcasting and sport *per se* and argues that the history c Taiwan's sport and its broadcasting is a product of ideological state apparatus, in Althusser sense. Moreover, this state/sports/media complex reflects Taiwan sport vis-à-vis others o the stage of global sport.

Understandably, and deservedly so, the imposition of martial law is regarded by many schola as the watershed event in recent Taiwanese history. During the martial law era, the Kuomintan (or Chinese Nationalist Party, henceforth, the KMT) Troika, led by Chiang Kai-shek and, late his son Chiang Ching-kuo, integrated the political party, the administration and the military an established a tight network that controlled freedom of speech and assembly. Political news was taken over by the propaganda machine in order to maintain the Troika's legitimacy. However, sports news and broadcasts, with their 'soft' ideology and resonance with nationalistic doctrines, enjoyed much more breathing space.

In Western societies, sport has developed a long and stable relationship with communities and places. Local media and sport clubs enjoy 'a match made in heaven'. However, this pattern is very different from the one developed in Taiwan, where the modernisation of sport, or sportisation in Elias and Dunning's (1986) sense, was associated with Japanese colonisation from 1895 to 1945. The concepts of sport and physical education were influenced by and rooted in the educational system in that era. Since then, the narratives of sport have been associated with top-down nationalism. The predicament of political realities and national anxiety has shaped the relationship between sport and nationalism and has created an eagerness for Taiwanese to prove their existence via baseball, basketball and sporadic successes at the Olympic Games (Chiang and Chen 2013).

Nationalism and sport broadcasts

As a form of human identity, nationalism is not only a relative term but might also be a fictional one, which 'is not the awakening of nations to self-consciousness' but rather the invention of nations 'where they do not exist' (Gellner 1994: 62). Conflict is the catalyst reinforcing or arousing the sentiments of the 'imagined community', in Anderson's sense (1991). Through conflict, comparative affiliation serves as an element of collective memory and the sense of common destiny, two pillars of nationalism as Weber (1994) argues. Representing their nations, catalysed by national flags and national anthems, sportsmen and women became 'primary expressions of their imagined communities' (Hobsbawm 1992: 142). As Geertz (1973: 444) argued in his famous Balinese studies, cockfights (and, I would argue, other spectator sports as well) represent a 'mock war of symbolic selves, and a formal simulation of status tension, and its aesthetic power derives from its capacity to force together these diverse realities'.

Appadurai (1996) argues that collective experiences of the mass media can create modalities of worship and charisma. Athletes in major sporting events are mostly viewed in a synchronised and live fashion that amplifies the intensity of experience. With this in mind, Appadurai's (1996) definition of culturalism is particularly useful in the discussion of sport and Taiwanese identities:

> Culturalism, put simply, is identity politics mobilized at the level of the nation-state. . . . Culturalism is the conscious mobilization of cultural differences in the service of a larger national or transnational politics. It is frequently associated with extraterritorial histories and memories, and almost always with struggle for stronger recognition from existing nation-states or from various transnational bodies.
>
> *(p. 15)*

Taiwan had been colonised by the Spanish, the Dutch, and the Japanese from the seventeenth century. It subsequently received military and economic aid from the US after the Second World War. Above all, however, it is its relationship with China that has been particularly complicated. Seeking its own distinctive identity has been a long-standing mission for Taiwan's government and people. The construction of identity can be seen from both internal and external perspectives, with the latter being especially vital according to Appadurai's (1996) perspective. In this regard, the US and Japan have predominantly represented the modern worldview for Taiwan. Recognition, or the desire for recognition, from stronger or equal nations, especially the aforementioned two, is vital to the Taiwanese. Due to interference from its political rival China, however, the breathing room for the island on the international political stage is limited at best. Since the diplomatic crisis that jeopardised and eventually terminated the ROC's place in the UN in 1971, the US and Japan have been its two most significant allies not least because of their complex and tangled shared history. For Taiwan, the world of sport is largely a world constituted by the US and Japan. This helps to explain why baseball, the national game for these two allies, has played such a prominent role in Taiwanese sport nationalism.

The power of sport nationalism can reach members of a nation via the spectating experience. A baseball team consists of only nine players, but its influence may extend to a nation of 23 million people or more. Geertz (1973) believed that his cockfighting spectating experience revealed symbolic mock warfare and the mass media ensures that such experiences become more than merely local. The charm of sport depends heavily on its collective projection of emotion and live, synchronised broadcasts enhance feeling of common destiny and history and further contribute to the construction of collective memory and identity.

Collective memory and the construction of national identity are intertwined. The former involves the production of a series of creative and purposeful processes. The past it re-creates is filled with fabricated, rearranged, over-interpretive and even excluded elements. Authenticity and accuracy are sacrificed in order to achieve consistency and cohesiveness from these 'histories' (Zelizer 1998). The formation of collective memory is undoubtedly a dynamic process. It too is interwoven with society and the mass media (Wertsch 2002). Although not everyone shares the same exact elements of these collective memories, there is a shared orientation towards the past nonetheless. Therefore, the reinforcement of national identity is achieved by way of re-visiting these memories – no matter whether they are one's own or others' or authentic or fabricated.

Anderson (1991) argues that print capitalism is a key adhesive for binding together imagined communities. The advance of communication technologies has further accelerated this trend by penetrating our intimate locales, from televisions in our living rooms to mobile phones in our hands. Newcomb (1974) believes that television is most successful in transmitting human facial expressions and emotional reactions. As a result, the audience and the figures on television share intimacy and emotional bonds. Continuity is also a crucial aesthetic element. These two features arguably work best in sport broadcasting. Other than the skills and abilities demonstrated by the athletes, the emotions they project are etched into the memories of the television audience as well. The emotional tears of Taiwanese legend Hsi-hsin Chen, the taekwondo athlete who won Taiwan's first ever Olympic gold medal at the 2004 Athens Olympics, was more memorable than any of her kicks during the matches. The continuity of sport and its broadcasting, be it of the quadrennial Olympics or of daily professional baseball games, make the audience familiar not only with the athletes but also with their emotional projections.

Sport broadcasts mediate these narratives in order to draw in the audience. They do not simply channel the pictures and the sounds; they also recreate them. Television turns sport into an appealing, yet open-ended story. It is a genre of spectacle, personal performance, human interest, competition and unknown adventure (Gruneau 1989). Hero worship and national identity are particularly common motifs of these sport narratives.

Mediated sport viewing is by no means limited to the television set in the living room. The 'ambient television' (McCarthy 2001) is another crucial element in enhancing collective viewing and memory building. For those who cannot make it to the stadium but want to feel togetherness with fellow fans, sport bars and plazas with giant screens become their second-best choice, giving the audience an 'environmentally enhanced live sport experience'. Through this kind of collective viewing, a synchronised imagined community has been formed. In Taiwan's early years, when television was not yet an everyday luxury, broadcasters installed sets in community centres and city halls for citizens to follow the Little League World Series taking place in Williamsport, Pennsylvania.

During the Martial Law Era, the Taiwanese administration operated through its various state apparatuses, which included quasi-state-owned media, to broadcast sporting events in order to buttress its authority and governance. The structure remains mostly intact to the present day. Even when broadcasting foreign professional sport, 'the Glory of Taiwan', such as baseball pitcher Chien-ming Wang (Chen 2012) and female golfer Yani Tseng were viewed during their heydays as nationalistic symbols and attracted much attention. In this respect, what Foucault (1997) calls 'governmentality' best exemplifies Taiwan.

In a society with perfect governmentality, each and every person analyses and self-reflects upon his or her own processes and actions vis-à-vis the community, thus self-governing himself or herself. In other words, in such a society, the ruled share the same philosophy and rationality held by the ruler. If we set the concept of governmentality in a global context, Taiwan has willingly and happily been incorporated into what Hardt and Negri (2000) called 'Empire'. In this Empire, Euro-American sports are adored. In addition, Taiwan's own sports culture is inevitably becoming a vehicle for the nation to be, or imagined to be, a part of the world. It was in this context that the three major terrestrial television channels that were affiliated to the KMT, the government and the military, respectively, broadcasted the nation's popular sports and propagated them as much as possible in order to support KMT governance in the period of martial law. Furthermore, although martial law was lifted in 1987, commercial television channels continue to carry the nationalistic torch in every possible way during their sport broadcasts.

The origins of the nation/sport/media complex

In the Martial Law Era, Taiwanese people were stripped of their freedom of movement. Since they were not allowed to travel abroad for leisure purposes until 1979, television was basically the window to the world for most Taiwan citizens. Therefore, controlling this very window was crucial for Chiang and the KMT.

The shaping of the nation/sport/media complex

The authoritarian KMT and its Troika of apparatuses, which comprised the state, the political party and the military, controlled mass media through policy regulation and ownership. Each television channel was affiliated to a specific division of the Troika. The Taiwan Provincial Government owned Taiwan Television (TTV). The KMT owned China Television (CTV). The military owned the Chinese Television System (CTS). The names CTV and CTS may be confusing. However, at that time, Taiwan was a synonym for (the Republic of) China and the names were interchangeable. Many state-owned corporations, such as China Steel and China Airlines, also bore the name China following the retreat of the KMT administration to Taiwan after its 1949 defeat by Mao Zedong and his Communist Party in the Civil War.

When TTV was being prepared for its launch in 1962, it was 49 per cent part-funded by six banks affiliated to the government. Japanese corporations, including Fuji Television, Toshiba, Hitachi and NEC contributed 10 per cent each. The remaining 11 per cent of the company was owned by local businessmen approved by the government. Because the public funds did not exceed 50 per cent, TTV was still nominally a private corporation. It was this very loophole created by the KMT Troika that allowed TTV to operate as a for-profit corporation, while sti being in reality under government control.

Political news was undoubtedly scrutinised during the Martial Law Era. However, spor was accorded high priority status, especially basketball and baseball (Y.-m. Ho, 2002). A bas ketball friendly between Taiwan and New Zealand was broadcast one day after the launc of the channel (11 October 1962). Games featuring the Akron Goodyear Wingfoots an Taiwanese men's national basketball team were also broadcasted on 21 and 22 October. Th broadcast of baseball games was intriguing, especially considering the roots of the sport i Taiwan and the complicated relationship between Chiang Kaishek's 'Big-China' ideolog and Japan.

It has been argued that baseball in the early 1950s was strictly forbidden by the KMT as way to decolonise Japanese culture (Bairner and Hwang 2011; Yu 2007). However, based o the evidence, the KMT did not appropriate baseball as a decolonising tool in the embryoni stage of local sport broadcasting. The first baseball broadcast in Taiwan was of a match betwee traditional Japanese university rivals, Keio and Waseda, staged in Taiwan on 2 January 196. No Taiwanese baseball player was involved. If the KMT Troika was really so concerned abou the colonial implication of baseball, how could it allow the broadcasting of such a game dur ing the New Year holidays? The KMT administration did indeed pursue the decolonisation c Taiwan with various policies and laws. For example, it banned Japanese-language newspaper and magazines. Japanese-dialogue films and television shows were also forbidden. However, t say that baseball was banned or discouraged to the same extent is inaccurate, not to mentio the fact that Japanese funds were essential to TTV at that time.

As Table 40.1 shows, television set ownership was initially low, as would be expected c any new form of media. Thus, the degree to which it rapidly increased in the early years wa scarcely surprising given that the base number from previous year was relatively low. Howeve the significant growth rate in 1968 is worth further examination.

In the early years, TTV could not compete with newspapers. Television news gatherin was hindered by the bulky equipment, which gave radio the competitive edge. The only genr through which TTV could demonstrate its value as an audio-visual media provider was th broadcast of live events (Y.-m. Ho 2002). According to one columnist:

> There were many people watching women's basketball and kids' baseball in front of TV. They rarely watched any sport before. However, they not just watched this time but watched addictively. . . . Public or private institutions turned on the TV and allowed their employees to watch sport, like in sport-advanced countries. For those who did not know what baseball was, they could grasp what the sport was about. Understanding brings appreciation and the reports in newspapers definitely helped. However, it is television which deserves the most credit. This wave of sport craze should be appropriated and channeled into better use.
>
> *(F. Ho 1968)*

Table 40.1 Number of television sets in Taiwan

Year	1962	1963	1964	1965	1966	1967	1968	1969	1970	1971	1972
Number	3,334	16,279	36,026	62,434	108,415	163,918	343,735	438,816	510,228	672,721	835,27
Growth rate (%)	–	388	121	73.3	73.6	51.2	109	27.7	16.3	31.8	24.

The women's basketball and kids' baseball referred to in the column are the Second Asian Women's Basketball Tournament in July and the Little League baseball friendly between Hung-yeh and Japanese Wakayama Team in the August of 1968, respectively. These two historical events were broadcast live on TTV and the increased rate of television set ownership that year was proof of the impact of sport broadcasting.

However, despite the proliferation of television sets and the success of sport broadcasting in 1968, when Taiwan sent out its representative for the first time to the Little League World Series in 1969, TTV showed no interest in being a part of this history. According to Shen (2002), a famous television anchorman, then General Manager Chou said, 'It is just a kid's game, why bother sending a crew across the ocean just for a summer camp-esque event?' TTV had successfully broadcast the moon landing earlier that summer when Neil Armstrong made his famous walk, so a failure to broadcast the Little League World Series might seem surprising, but not if we take a closer look. While Taiwan's perspective on sport has always been nationalistic, there was a tendency to cherry-pick the 'Other' for fear of risking humiliation in international competitions. However, there was also a meticulous filtering of the information that the public could receive, successfully orientating Taiwan nationals to a glorious collective past, even in a game for 12-year-olds.

Interference of the Troika

When the *Ching-lung* (Golden Dragons) made the trip to Williamsport for the Little League World Series in 1969, no one in Taiwan could be sure how they would fare. Even though Hung-yeh had beaten the 'World Champion' Wakayama team a year before in a friendly game on home soil, travelling across the Pacific Ocean and competing with teams from the US was a different matter altogether. TTV failed to deliver the broadcast because they underestimated the local passion for Little League baseball. Surely, that decision incurred a huge financial cost for the channel. However, it was also because TTV was the sole TV channel at the time that it was lukewarm. When CTV became the second TV channel in Taiwan later in 1969 and baseball fever swept the nation, the broadcasting of baseball became a serious business.

A year after Chou downplayed Little League baseball as just a kid's game and was reluctant to broadcast the games in Williamsport, TTV and CTV took part in an all-out bidding war for the 1970 tournament. After a series of negotiations initiated by the powers behind the channels, TTV won the exclusive rights (CTV was awarded the 1971 rights). That the KMT Troika used Little League baseball for propaganda purposes has been well documented (Morris 2011; Yu 2007). The development of Taiwanese Little League baseball ran parallel to volatile and dire international political realities. Since the late 1960s, Taiwan's status in the UN had been fragile and its seat was eventually lost on 25 October 1971. Chiang Kai-shek and his administration seized the chance to appropriate baseball, the annual Little League World Series in particular, as a political device to bolster the administration and exalt its legitimacy in relation to China. In a speech to the World Champion *Chu-jen* (Giants) team, this appropriation is apparent in the official language of government:

> Our country is in a very difficult situation. Your victory accomplished the President's instructions. It raised people's morale. . . . I believe that all the compatriots must have felt the passion and encouragement from your victory. We should accomplish what we have to do. We should work harder to recover Mainland China.
>
> ('*Kuo Tai She Cha Hui, Ying Chu Jen Hsiao Chiang*',
> The Central Daily *1971: 3*)

The young players were regarded as warriors who would fight for Taiwan and restore the faith of its people. Baseball in Taiwan has been constructed around the exaggerated but enticing title of 'world champion'. As a consequence, the state apparatuses misappropriated a summer camp-esque tournament by using it as an ideological tool to compensate for its difficulties in the 'real' world. Diplomatic operatives distributed national flags and mobilised Taiwanese crowds to travel to Williamsport. The sea of flags and the cheers could be seen and heard on television in Taiwan as a demonstration of overseas unity, reinforcing Taiwan's fragile nationalism and ambitions towards re-territorialisation, with Williamsport as an enclave. Baseball has since become an icon of Taiwanese nationalism.

The KMT Troika would do anything to maximise the glory to be gained from Little League baseball. In 1972, the Far Eastern qualifying tournament was held in Guam, which had no equipment for broadcasting in colour TV. So TTV contacted the U.S. Army through the Ministry of National Defense and eventually got a military aircraft to transport the outdoor broadcast vehicle along with dozens of technicians and local performing artists to Guam. This shows how much investment the KMT and its media affiliates would now put into broadcasting 'a kid's game'.

Taiwan's three terrestrial channels were private corporations only in name. Each operated as an apparatus of the state machinery while simultaneously making profits. This was especially true in sports broadcasting. On the one hand, baseball teams competing in the US were manoeuvred as nationalistic symbols to help stabilise the KMT administration, even after Taiwan was expelled from the UN. On the other hand, sports events guaranteed high ratings that were attractive to advertisers. As long as these sport programmes generated revenue and did not conflict with the Troika's ideology, they were protected. Baseball fever spread across the nation, focused not only on national teams but also on broadcasts of American and Japanese baseball. In 1970, the CTV started to broadcast the World Series in which the Baltimore Orioles defeated the Cincinnati Reds 4–1. That was the inception of Taiwan's broadcasting of Major League baseball games. In the same year, the Japan Series was also broadcast in Taiwan, with Sadaharu Oh's Yomiuri Giants beating Lotte Orion 4–1. In the 1980s, Taiwanese players, Yuan-Chi Kuo, Tai-yuan Kuo and Sheng-hsiung Chuan shone in the Japanese professional league and just as the Japan Series was exempted from the No-Japanese policy, their performances were shown to Taiwanese fans to boost national morale.

All of these channels had to strike a delicate balance between generating profit and acting as part of a propaganda machine. Before the 1970 Far Eastern qualifying tournament, one director said, 'We've got a lot of advertising waiting to be broadcast. The game better go slowly. Also, be aware not to catch any pro-independence flag or signs' (Shen 1995: 91). During the championship game in 1971 featuring *Chu-jen* (Giants), ABC's cameras caught a plane trailing a banner with pro-independence messages sponsored by exiled dissidents. However, neither the message nor the image reached Taiwan, as the KMT's monitoring apparatus used the six-second delay to its advantage and kept both from view.

In addition to baseball, in 1972 TTV launched 'World Wrestling Ring', which also attracted high audience ratings and advertising revenue. However, due to wrestling's violent character, the KMT Troika subsequently ordered the cancellation of the show. In 1973, TTV also obtained the exclusive broadcasting rights to the heavyweight fight between George Foreman and Jose Roman in Tokyo. However, the contest lasted only 55 seconds, as Foreman knocked out Roman and TTV was forced to replay the round numerous times in order to be able to air all of the advertising it had secured for the match. CTS also broadcast the Mohammad Ali versus Larry Holmes bout in Tokyo in 1980. The channel started broadcasting World Cup Soccer in 1982, and continued to do so over the following 20 years. Since 1987, TTV has been broadcasting NBA games on a weekly basis. Although these broadcasts were actually of matches from the previous season, due to a lack of information, most viewers were unaware of this. When NBA broadcasts became more popular, TTV started showing tape-delayed games of the same season as well as live games.

To sum up, the three terrestrial channels established a comfortable modus operandi under the auspices of KMT state capitalism. While each had a profit motive, they also served as the mouthpiece of the Troika. During certain sporting events, nationalism and capitalism worked hand in hand for the three channels to deliver a match truly made in heaven. To pursue the marriage metaphor, they were the third person in the sport/media complex. Nevertheless, there were occasional conflicts.

The broadcasting of the Taipei Invitational International Baseball Tournament in 1985 led to an infamous incident in which the Troika interfered, even though the end of Martial Law Era was approaching. When the classic final featuring Taiwan and Japan went into extra innings, CTV was forced to cut the broadcast at 7.30 pm so that scheduled evening news could be aired, even though the ratings stood at an unbelievable high of 62.8 per cent. The furious audience was forced to turn to radio for the final few innings. When they learned that their beloved team had come from behind to beat Japan in the fourteenth inning, with Ming-tse Lu's three-run walk-off home run, matters went out of control. The beleaguered broadcaster had to play the home run over and over during the evening news to assuage its viewers' discontent. After all, it was almost the end of the Martial Law Era and baseball was, and remains, the national pastime.

In the 1970s, Little League baseball (U–12), Senior League baseball (age 14–16) and Big League baseball (age 16–18), the so-called 'three-level baseball', were the most important sporting events in Taiwan. In 1974, the year in which Taiwan won the Triple Crown (becoming champions in all three LLB-sanctioned tournaments), the three channels simulcast all three tournaments and shared all advertising revenue. This type of cooperation showed the emphasis placed on these competitions by the KMT Troika. However, this was not necessarily the most efficient way to collaborate. When the Senior League and Big League schedules overlapped in 1974, the three broadcasters did not distribute the games across their channels. Instead, they simulcast the same Senior League game live and showed the tape-delayed Big League game afterwards.

Under the oligopoly protected by the Troika, the three channels strategically cooperated and yet at times also crowded one another out. After CTS won the exclusive broadcasting rights to the Los Angeles Olympics in 1984 and enjoyed huge success commercially, TTV and CTV sought revenge by forming an alliance for the 1988 Seoul Olympics and blocking CTS out. According to Shen,

> CTV tried everything possible to force TTV into an alliance. What I understand is that CTV passed the message through General Chief of Staff of the Army Po-tsun Hou and put pressure through the KMT core. As then TTV General Manager Yung-kuei Shi was also a member of the board of KMT, the message was passed through. TTV had to ally with CTV to broadcast the Seoul Olympics.[1]

So it was that sometimes the three channels joined forces for simulcasts, sometimes fought one another for exclusive rights, and sometimes formed a two-party alliance to crowd the third one out. This did not necessarily lead to the best political or commercial benefits for the broadcasters. Yet the compromise, negotiation and rivalry reflected the KMT Troika perfectly. This was a reasonable outcome for the industry under state capitalism. However, these struggles occurred only because sport as a genre still mattered to the Troika, be it in the form of three-level baseball or of the Olympics.

The decline of the Troika and the shadows of the nation

When sport cable channels emerged in the 1990s, the influence of the three terrestrial channels in sport broadcasting began to fade. At the same time, with martial law a thing of the past, the KMT Troika was also being dismantled. The penetration rate of cable TV in Taiwan ranks among the highest in the world (see Figure 40.1), making the three terrestrial channels now just three of over 100 cable and satellite channels. Moreover, they now face further competition from a fourth terrestrial channel. Ownership of mass media companies by political parties, the government and the military was outlawed after the Martial Law Era. Left without the support of the state apparatuses under state capitalism, the redundant and rigid bureaucracies of the three channels from the Martial Law Era became less competent in Taiwan's new mass media era. Their impact and market share declined in every possible way – sport broadcasting included – even though the government still grants them priority in relation to broadcasting the Olympics. As an example, sport news is virtually non-existent on non-game days, as there is no specialist staff for sport broadcasting. A particularly low point for the broadcasters occurred in 2008, when the National Communications Council held public hearing to address complaints about the low quality of Beijing Olympics broadcasts. In addition, the three broadcasters' social responsibility to provide free-to-air channels has become a burden for them. Sport might have been the goose that laid the golden egg for the three terrestrial channels under state capitalism. However, with shifts in the politico-economic environment, the influence and business advantage that sport broadcasting afforded them has now disappeared.

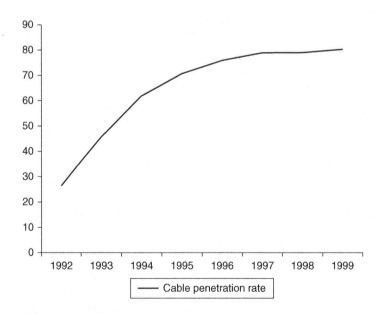

Figure 40.1 Cable TV penetration rate, Taiwan

Conclusion

A review of the history of sport broadcasting in Taiwan from 1962 to 1989 highlights the role sport played in Taiwan in that period. Due to the unique state capitalist system led by the KMT Troika, sport became a national tool that the state apparatuses could appropriate and manipulate. Although basketball raised the curtain for sport broadcasting in Taiwan, it was baseball that eventually carried the weight of national identity and narratives.

Under state capitalism, TV struck a delicate balance between propaganda and money-making. While this led to conflicts, in terms of sport, it worked perfectly for the ruling Troika. Sport in Taiwan has been central to nationalistic narratives ever since, with a significant turning-point coming in the 1970s when the country was expelled from the UN and significant allies severed ties. This relationship between sport and nationalism has continued into the twenty-first century, especially when Taiwanese athletes compete in professional sport overseas.

Sport in Taiwan did not professionalise until 1990. The concept of professionalism was not accepted during the Martial Law Era, when the purity of amateurism and the appropriation of sport as a symbol for 'recovering' Mainland China were the main missions. The success of Little League baseball was a godsend for the struggling KMT administration as well as for Taiwan as a nation. Success in Williamsport was like a parade of the emperor's new clothes; no one even dared to question the connection between a baseball tournament for 12-year-olds and national glory. Indeed, this connection provoked much debate for a decade and more. The three incumbent terrestrial channels were definitely responsible for this success story or farce, depending on one's perspective. They helped to provide stability to the administration supporting them and made tremendous profits from sport broadcasting along the way.

When professionalism arrived in 1990, nationalism stopped being the sole function of sport. However, this transformation could not happen overnight. While the window to the world for the Taiwanese has widened with the emergence of increasing numbers of cable channels and other media forms, sport in Taiwan is still largely a nationalistic affair, with sport in general and local athletes in particular selectively summoned and promoted as winners for a country that remains a political loser in the international community.

Note

1 Interviewed on 2 April 2012.

References

Anderson, B. (1991) *Imagined Communities: Reflections on the Origin and Spread of Nationalism* (Rev. and extended ed.). New York: Verso.

Appadurai, A. (1996) *Modernity at Large: Cultural Dimensions of Globalization*. Minneapolis, MN: University of Minnesota Press.

Bairner, A. and Hwang, D.-J. (2011) Representing Taiwan: International sport, ethnicity and national identity in the Republic of China. *International Review for the Sociology of Sport*, 46(3): 231–248.

Chen, T.-H. (2012) From the 'Taiwan Yankees' to the New York Yankees: The glocal narratives of baseball. *Sociology of Sport Journal, 29*: 546–558.

Chiang, Y., and Chen, T.-H. (2013) Adopting the diasporic son: Jeremy Lin and Taiwan sport nationalism. *International Review for the Sociology of Sport*, published online 18 June 2013. doi: 10-1177/1012690213491263.

Elias, N. and Dunning, E. (1986) *Quest for Excitement: Sport and Leisure in the Civilizing Process*. New York: Blackwell.

Foucault, M. (1997) Governmentality. In *The Essential Works of Foucault*. New York: New Press, pp. 87–104.

Geertz, C. (1973) *The Interpretation of Cultures: Selected Essays*. New York: Basic Books.

Gellner, E. (1994) Nationalism and modernization. In J. Hutchinson and A. D. Smith (eds) *Nationalism*. New York: Oxford University Press, pp. 55–63.

Gruneau, R. (1989) Making spectacle: A case study in television sports production. In L. A. Wenner (ed.) *Media, Sport, and Society*. Newbury Park: Sage, pp. 134–154.

Hardt, M. and Negri, A. (2000) *Empire*. Cambridge: Harvard University Press.

Ho, F. (1968) Talking Sport on Sport Day. *The United Daily*. 9 September 1968, p. 9.

Ho, Y.-M. (2002) *Taiwan Tien-Shi-Feng-Yun-Lu (The History of Taiwan Television)*. Taipei: The Commercial Press.

Hobsbawm, E. J. (1992) *Nations and Nationalism since 1780 : Programme, Myth, Reality* (2nd ed.). Cambridge: Cambridge University Press.

Jhally, S. (1984) The spectacle of accumulation: Material and cultural factors in the evolution of the sports media complex. *Insurgent Sociologist*, 12: 41–57.

Jhally, S. (1989) Cultural studies and the sports/media somplex. In L. A. Wenner (ed.) *Media, Sports, and Society*. Newbury Park: Sage, pp. 70–93.

McCarthy, A. (2001) *Ambient Television: Visual Culture and Public Space*. Durham, NC: Duke University Press.

Morris, A. (2011) *Colonial Project, National: A History of Baseball in Taiwan*. Berkeley, CA: University of California Press.

Newcomb, H. (1974) *TV: The Most Popular Art*. Garden City, NY: Anchor Press.

Weber, M. (1994) The Nation. In J. Hutchinson and A. D. Smith (eds) *Nationalism*. New York: Oxford University Press, pp. 21–25.

Wertsch, J. V. (2002) *Voices of Collective Remembering*. New York: Cambridge University Press.

Yu, J. (2007) *Playing in Isolation: A History of Baseball in Taiwan*. Lincoln, NE: University of Nebraska Press.

Zelizer, B. (1998) *Remembering to Forget: Holocaust Memory through the Camera's Eye*. Chicago, IL: University of Chicago Press.

41

THE POLITICS OF THE COMMONWEALTH GAMES

Stuart Whigham

Introduction

In comparison to the two major sporting 'mega-events', the Olympic Games and the FIFA World Cup, the Commonwealth Games is a relatively neglected event in terms of past academic consideration (Black 2014; Palmer 2013). This is unsurprising given that, first, these two 'mega-events' have been given a great deal of attention in the sociological study of sport (Black 2014); and, second, 'mega-events' have increasingly drawn attention from academics from non-specialist fields outside of sport, including sociology, politics, history, economics and tourism, amongst others. Furthermore, the common definitional offerings regarding which international sporting events qualify as 'mega-events' have resulted in a degree of exclusion for the Commonwealth Games, with leading authors such as Horne (2007) arguing that the only events which successfully meet the criteria to be deemed true mega-events are the Summer Olympic Games and the FIFA World Cup.

The work of Black (2008; 2014) distinguishes between 'first-order' sporting mega-events such as the Summer Olympics and FIFA World Cup, 'second-order' international sporting events such as the Commonwealth Games, the IRB Rugby World Cup and the ICC Cricket World Cup, and 'third-order' regional or continental events such as the Pan American Games, the Asian Games and the African Cup of Nations. Given that only the 'first-order' mega-events possess a truly global appeal in terms of media coverage and significance within the global sports system (Black 2008, 2014; Horne 2007; Roche 2000, 2006), it is understandable that 'second-order' and 'third-order' events have received less academic attention (Polley 2014). In the case of the Commonwealth Games, for example, Miller *et al.* (2001) highlight the lack of attention given to the event outside of Commonwealth countries, stating that the 1998 Commonwealth Games only attracted 500 million viewers in comparison to the 32 billion viewers of the 1994 FIFA World Cup and the 35 billion viewers of the 1996 Atlanta Olympics.

Despite this relative neglect, a select number of previous academic studies have focused on the history, economics and politics of the Commonwealth Games, thereby providing an opportunity to contextualise the status of the Games in the contemporary global sports field. This chapter offers an exploration of the historical and contemporary politics of the Commonwealth Games, and the relationship between the Games and the politics of the Commonwealth as an evolving geopolitical entity. Discussion begins with a consideration of the political context within which the event originated as the 'British Empire Games' in the inter-war period. There follows an examination of the role played by the Games during the decline of the British Empire, especially in the second half of the twentieth century. Attention will also be paid to the political uses of the Commonwealth Games by considering particular case studies, such as the averted boycott of the 1978 Edmonton Games, the completed boycott of the 1986 Edinburgh Games, the hosting of the 2010 Delhi Games in the emerging 'BRIC' nation of India, and the politics of the 2014 Glasgow Games in the run-up to the Scottish independence referendum in September 2014.

The early political history of the Games: from 'Empire' to 'Commonwealth'

An appropriate starting point for this consideration of the politics of the Commonwealth Games movement is an account of the machinations which led to the establishment of the first 'British Empire Games' in Hamilton, Canada, in 1930. In contrast to a number of other academic within the field, Houlihan (1994) explores the political history of the Commonwealth Games in significant depth in his discussion of the relationship between sport and international politics. He argues that the successful establishment of the Olympic Games movement in the early twentieth century resulted in a delay between the original proposal for an Empire Games as mooted in 1891 and the inaugural event which took place in Hamilton, Canada, in 1930. Given the success of the Olympic movement in this period as a means of fostering international relationship through the medium of sport, the proposed Empire Games became of secondary importance within the fledgling international sporting system.

Holt's (1989) analysis of the initial motivations for establishing the Empire Games concurs with the position of Houlihan, emphasising the inhibitory effect of the global Olympic Games movement on the establishment of an event which would be restricted to constituents of the British Empire. However, Holt also argues that the further momentum for establishing the Empire Games was derived from the gradual decline of British control over its imperial territories, arguing that part of the rationale behind the introduction of the Games was linked to the implementation of the Statute of Westminster in the late 1920s which would establish 'full constitutional autonomy of the Dominions' and a 'loosening of the formal bonds of Empire' (Holt 1989: 224). Whilst Holt (1989) stresses that the Games were not 'simply devised to hold together through the bonds of sport an institution which was under constitutional and economic strain' (p. 225), he also acknowledges that the ability to maintain cultural links within the Commonwealth and the opportunities to use the Games for economic 'boosterism' remained significant motives for the successful inauguration of the Games in 1930.

Another of the central historical developments in the Commonwealth Games movement highlighted by Houlihan (1994) is the changing title of the event. This is demonstrated in the shift from the 'British Empire Games' at its inauguration in 1930; the 1950 revision to the 'British Empire and Commonwealth Games' following the 1949 'London Declaration', which led to the creation of the modern British Commonwealth; the short-lived amendment to the 'British Commonwealth Games' from 1970 to 1974; and the final change to its current title of the 'Commonwealth Games' in 1978 (Houlihan 1994; Polley 2014). The political symbolism of the semantic evolution of the Games' title was clearly not an arbitrary development indeed, it can be argued that these changes are indicative of the shifting diplomatic relationship between the countries of the Commonwealth and the rebalancing of power relations within this evolving geopolitical entity. Given the rapid process of decolonisation within the British

Empire in the post-1945 period and the resultant establishment of numerous independent and sovereign states within the Commonwealth, the removal of the phrases 'Empire' then 'British' from the title of the Games symbolises and reflects the declining power of the United Kingdom as a global power throughout the twentieth century (Houlihan 1994; Muda 1998; Phillips 2000; Roche 2000; Whannel 2008).

Although this process of decolonisation has undoubtedly had a positive effect in terms of the partial rebalancing of political and symbolic power within the Commonwealth, Dheenshaw (1994) argues that the decline of British influence in global politics has resulted in some questioning of the continuing political significance of the Commonwealth as a geopolitical entity:

> Together, the countries of the Commonwealth serve no strategic military or geo-graphic purpose, and little economic purpose. They try to serve a political purpose, although one wonders what the former colonies of a spent nineteenth century world power can do in the rapidly changing realpolitik of the late twentieth century.
>
> *(Dheenshaw 1994: 2)*

Despite the validity of Dheenshaw's observations, the Commonwealth remains an important medium for the diplomatic actions of a number of its constituent members, providing the opportunity for relatively small states to achieve increased political representation for their inter-ests within this large intergovernmental organisation. The sustained allure of Commonwealth membership is further demonstrated in the willingness of states which were not historically associated with the British Empire to join the organisation, such as in the case of Mozambique and Rwanda. In addition, Houlihan (1994) argues that:

> the Games provide a useful political resource both as an additional medium for policy communication, but more importantly as a safety valve for political positions that the CHOG [Commonwealth Heads of Government] meetings might not be able to accommodate.
>
> *(p. 146)*

These meetings have had significant ramifications within the political history of the Commonwealth Games movement. Attention now turns therefore to the examination of the impact of a number of political issues in the Games' history and their implications for diplo-matic relationships with the Commonwealth, considering, first, the embroilment of the 1978 Edmonton and 1986 Edinburgh Games within protests against the apartheid regime of South Africa and, second, the political uses of the Games in the post-apartheid era in the examples of the 1998 Kuala Lumpur, 2010 Delhi and 2014 Glasgow iterations of the event.

The Commonwealth Games, apartheid and political boycotts

The shifting power balance and political dynamics within the Commonwealth were reflected in the diplomatic ramifications relating to the apartheid regime and policies of pre-1990s South Africa, an issue which dogged the Commonwealth Games movement more than any other. Given the significance of this issue, and the related proposed and actual boycotts of the Games, for diplomatic relationships within the Commonwealth, it is appropriate to consider instances where specific events were entangled in political controversy throughout much of the history of the Games.

The first instance of political controversy linked to the issue of apartheid occurred with the 1934 Games. The hosting of the second Empire Games event was originally awarded to Johannesburg, South Africa. However, concerns regarding the potential negative treatment of black and Asian athletes by the South African authorities were expressed by a number of countries, with Canada playing a particularly pivotal role in forcing the Empire Games Federation to rethink its decision to award the Games to Johannesburg (Dheenshaw 1994; Majumdar and Mehta 2010; Phillips 2000, 2002). This led to a decision to switch the hosting of the 1934 Empire Games to London instead, thus heading off the first sign of political controversy relating to the discriminatory policies of the South African government. Despite the success of this intervention, Dheenshaw (1994: 21) identifies this incident as 'epic foreshadowing', arguing that 'South Africa would continue to bedevil the Games – whether it was taking part in them or not – for many decades to come'.

In the period following the 1934 Games through to the mid-1970s, subsequent iterations of the Games managed to avoid significant political controversy between members of the British Empire and Commonwealth. For Kidd (1998), the exclusion of South Africa from the Empire/Commonwealth Games Federation in 1961 acted as an important diplomatic intervention and ensured support for the Games movement during this period. However, the risk of potential boycotts of the Games re-emerged in the run-up to the 1978 Edmonton Games, with the issue of apartheid again the central causal factor (Coghlan 1990; Dheenshaw 1994; Houlihan 1994; Jeffreys 2012; Kidd 1988; Whannel 2008).

Given the potential threat of a repeat of the 1976 Montreal Olympic Games boycott at the forthcoming 1978 Edmonton Commonwealth Games, a meeting of leaders from the Commonwealth nations was convened at the Gleneagles Hotel in Scotland in July 1977, with the aim of addressing this issue prior to the full CHOG meeting taking place in London later that year. A formal agreement was reached at the Gleneagles meeting, resulting in the production of the 'Commonwealth Statement on Apartheid in Sport' and the proposed withdrawal of all sporting contact with South Africa by other Commonwealth countries (Coghlan 1990; Jeffreys 2012; Macfarlane 1986; Whannel 2008). This 'Gleneagles Agreement' proved sufficient to ensure that all African nations (with the obvious exception of South Africa) agreed to cancel the proposed boycott of the 1978 Edmonton Games. These diplomatic machinations therefore testify to the intertwining of the racial and post-colonial politics of the Commonwealth with the continuing fortunes of the Games, further demonstrating the growing political influence within the Commonwealth of countries outside of the traditional 'white dominion' nations (namely Australia, Canada, England, New Zealand, Scotland, and Wales). The establishment of the Gleneagles Agreement therefore highlighted the relative success of the Commonwealth Games in terms of political diplomacy in comparison to the Olympic Games in this period, given the political boycotts which dogged the Olympic Games held in Montreal in 1976, Moscow in 1980 and Los Angeles in 1984 (Coghlan 1990; Houlihan 1994; Jeffreys 2012; Macfarlane 1986).

However, the success of the Gleneagles Agreement was short-lived. In his memoirs of his time as the Minister for Sport in the United Kingdom from 1981 to 1985, Macfarlane (1986) notes that the Agreement was frequently breached in the years shortly after its establishment. For example, a number of cricket and rugby tours involving the British Lions, and English and New Zealander representative teams with South Africa as both hosts and guests, took place in the period after the 1978 Edmonton Games (Bateman and Douglas 1986; Macfarlane 1986; Majumdar and Mehta 2010). Macfarlane argues that the continuing existence of these 'rebel' tours was indicative of the prevailing political stance of non-interference in sport of the Conservative government of British Prime Minister Margaret Thatcher during this period, citing a response from Thatcher to a House of Commons question on the topic in 1981 to illustrate this stance:

> We do not, however, have the power to prevent our sportsmen and women from visiting South Africa or anywhere else. If we did we would no longer be a free country. The Gleneagles Agreement recognized that we can act only by persuasion.
>
> *(Thatcher 1981, cited in Macfarlane 1986: 121)*

Unsurprisingly, this stance undermined any possibility of long-term diplomatic success for the Gleneagles Agreement in the eyes of many Commonwealth countries with more robust oppositional attitudes towards apartheid. Whilst the 1982 Brisbane Games was able to successfully stave off the repeated threat of a sporting boycott by a number of Commonwealth nations, the 1986 Edinburgh Games was unable to similarly prevent the issue of sporting contacts with the South African regime from damaging participation in the event (Coghlan 1990; Holt 1989; Macfarlane 1986; Monnington 1993; Phillips 2000, 2002).

Having previously hosted the Games in 1970, it had been hoped that Edinburgh's 1986 Games would emulate the relative success of the earlier event. The 1970 Edinburgh Games had been argued to have lived up to its billing as the 'Friendly Games' in terms of its organisation and atmosphere, having also left a positive impact on the city due to its resultant infrastructure and sporting facility improvements (Bateman and Douglas 1986; Dheenshaw 1994; Skillen and McDowell 2014; Thomson 2000). However, this did not prove to be the case in 1986, with the widespread boycott of the Games arguably representing the nadir of the Commonwealth Games movement. Monnington (1993) argues that the catalyst for the boycott of the 1986 Games was the perceived political support for the South African regime from the Conservative government in the UK, resulting in the refusal of 32 Commonwealth nations from Africa, Asia and the Caribbean to participate.

Bateman and Douglas's (1986) account represents the most thorough analysis of the political and financial controversy surrounding the 1986 Edinburgh Games. Concurring with Monnington (1993), Bateman and Douglas highlight Thatcher's refusal to support sanctions against the South African regime as the immediate cause of the Games boycott, arguing that 'governments in Africa saw Mrs Thatcher as Great Britain and vice versa . . . whereas the truth was that a majority disagreed with a Premier whose party was in a minority in Scotland' (1986: 68). Given the political furore regarding her role in causing the Games boycott, Thatcher's decision to attend the Games in person resulted in further political controversy, with the presence of several protest groups and the bold challenging of Thatcher by the English rower Joanna Toch during a face-to-face meeting attracting negative media coverage for Thatcher and her Conservative government (Bateman and Douglas 1986; Monnington 1993).

The boycott of the 1986 Games resulted in financial difficulties for the organising committee, further compounding the organisational challenges which the host city had already faced. The reduced level of international participation, media coverage, sponsorship income and the resultant underselling of the television rights for the Games to the British Broadcasting Corporation led to a perilous financial predicament for the organising committee (Bateman and Douglas 1986; Dheenshaw 1994; Macfarlane 1986). Given the lack of political willingness to support the event from the public purse, the organisers were forced to depend upon a bailout from Robert Maxwell, the high-profile and controversial proprietor of the Mirror Group Newspapers media corporation, and a controversial right-wing Japanese benefactor. Bateman and Douglas argue that 'Edinburgh's troubles began when they failed to win the backing of big businesses in the UK and Commonwealth but even more importantly when they agreed to take on the task of organisation without Government financial backing' (1986: 10). The folly of this decision in light of the increasing financial burden of hosting the Commonwealth Games in the 1980s became increasingly apparent, as host governments and organising committees for major sports events grappled, with various degrees of success, with the rapid shift towards the commercialisation of international sports events following the success of the 1984 Los Angeles Olympics. The 1986 Edinburgh Games therefore served to illustrate the potential risks of an over-reliance on private investment by a right-wing Thatcher government wedded to a political ideology which sought to reduce state intervention and levels of public funding wherever possible.

The politics of the Commonwealth Games in the post-apartheid era

The catalogue of problems blighting the 1986 Edinburgh Games rendered it the lowest point in the history of the Commonwealth Games movement; in contrast, the 1990 Auckland Games and 1994 Victoria Games successfully reaffirmed support for and participation in the event from all Commonwealth members (Dheenshaw 1994; Majumdar and Mehta 2010; Phillips 2000). Indeed, the events of the 1986 Games appeared to have demonstrated the requirements for political intervention in the sporting domain, with the British government quickly condemning a proposed 'rebel' cricket tour of an English team to South Africa in order to prevent a sporting boycott of the 1990 Auckland Games (Majumdar and Mehta 2010). Furthermore, and more importantly for the long-term stability of the Commonwealth Games movement, the success of the anti-apartheid movement in South Africa resulted in the release of Nelson Mandela and an end to the apartheid policies of the South African government. This led to the reintegration of South Africa into the wider international community and the restoration of international diplomatic relations for South Africa, which in turn facilitated a similar reintegration into the domain of international sporting competition (Cornelissen and Swart 2006; Majumdar and Mehta 2010). These developments thus negated the risks of sporting boycott linked to the issue of apartheid in all subsequent iterations of the Games, rendering the 1986 Edinburgh Games the sole victim of this political controversy.

In the immediate post-apartheid era, attention has turned to addressing the dominance of 'white dominion' nations, both in terms of the hosting of the Games and their influence within the internal politics of the Commonwealth Games movement. Until the 1998 Games were awarded to Kuala Lumpur, Malaysia, the only past instance of the Games taking place outside of these countries was Kingston, Jamaica in 1966 (Dawson 2014; Dheenshaw 1994). Furthermore, the relatively negative portrayal of the organisation of the 1966 Kingston Games in the 'white dominion' countries has been argued to be indicative of post-imperialist stereotypes regarding the capabilities of developing nations to host such events (Dawson 2014; Miller *et al.* 2001). For Majumdar and Mehta (2010), the decision to award the Games to Kingston was initially 'looked upon as a serious step forward to democratize the Games in an era of decolonization' (p. 98); subsequently, however, the significant financial costs faced by Jamaica in hosting the 1966 Games has been argued to have dissuaded developing nations from bidding to play host (Majumdar and Mehta 2010; Muda 1998).

Nonetheless, the 1990s saw increased interest in hosting the Games from outside of the traditional host countries, with governments seeking to replicate the success of the 1984 Los Angeles Olympics in its ability to make a commercial success of a major sporting event. Such a shift is evidenced in the successful bid by the Malaysian government to host the 1998 Kuala Lumpur Games. Whannel's (2008) analysis discusses the motivations of the Malaysian government in their decision to bid for hosting the 1998 Games:

the Malaysian government utilised the Commonwealth Games as a global media spectacle, both to gain international publicity and as an opportunity to celebrate its multicultural national identity and thus 'market' Malaysia as a model modern Muslim society.

(pp. 215–216)

The use of the 1998 Games as a tool for 'marketing' a positive image of the modern Malaysian nation is repeated in a number of other academic analyses of this iteration of the event (Black 2008, 2014; Muda 1998; Phillips 2000; van der Westhuizen 2004). Phillips (2000) argues that the hosting of the 1998 Games acted as part of a long-term strategy for the Malaysian government, representing a stepping-stone to demonstrate the country's capability of hosting future larger 'mega-events' such as the Olympic Games. Black (2014) reaches similar conclusions to Phillips, arguing that this strategy aligns with that of other 'springboarder' host nations for 'second-order' sports events who aim to host larger international sporting events in the future, whilst Muda (1998) emphasises the importance of this strategy within Malaysian foreign policy in the particular sense of increasing the nation's influence within Asia.

Upon the return of hosting responsibilities to the 'white dominion' nations in the subsequent cases of the 2002 Manchester and 2006 Melbourne Games, the growing political support for using major sporting events as a tool for promoting a 'legacy' of social and urban regeneration, tourism development and infrastructural projects became evident (Majumdar and Mehta 2010; Palmer 2013; Stewart 2014). However, Stewart (2014) contends that the 2006 Melbourne Games demonstrated little evidence of long-term benefits to the city following the event apart from the fact the Games 'consolidated its positions as a world leader in delivering major sports events' (p. 70). Indeed, the 2006 Games also resulted in the establishment of various grassroots political protest groups such as the 'Stolenwealth Games' and 'Graffiti Games' organisations which used the event as an opportunity to raise awareness of specific political issues such as the mistreatment of the indigenous Australian population, and the mass removal of street art from Melbourne, respectively (Stolenwealth Games 2006). The development of protest groups such as these illustrates the requirement to conceptualise the politics of sports event hosting as a multi-layered phenomenon, with the possibility for political considerations evident at the global, national and local levels to be highlighted by actors operating inside and outside of the traditional domains of political power.

Another recent trend in the hosting of major sporting events is the increased number of successful bids from 'BRIC' (Brazil, Russia, India, China) and other emerging non-Western economies (Cornelissen 2014; Curi *et al.* 2011; Grix 2014; Palmer 2013). Such developments have often been framed within a wider consideration of the links between sports event hosting and Nye's (2004) conceptualisation of 'soft power', given contemporary arguments regarding the growing importance of 'soft power' in global politics and diplomacy (Brannagan and Giulianotti 2014; Grix and Houlihan 2014; Manzenreiter 2010). The hosting of 2010 Commonwealth Games in Delhi is a case in point for such a thesis, whilst simultaneously demonstrating the high political stakes for emerging economic nations when acting as hosts of major sporting events.

Delhi had previously failed in its bid to host the 1994 Commonwealth Games, losing out to eventual hosts Victoria despite the appeals of the Indian government (Dheenshaw 1994). However, the success of Delhi's bid for the 2010 Games offered an opportunity for India to establish itself as a capable host for major international sporting events, mimicking the strategy of the Malaysian government in the case of the 1998 Kuala Lumpur Games. Given this emphasis of the Indian government on using the 2010 Games as a 'springboard' for future bids to host 'first-order' sports mega-events such as the Olympics or the FIFA World Cup, the challenges faced by both the Delhi Games organisers and the central government were magnified (Black 2008, 2014). According to Baviskar (2014), a central plank of this strategy revolved around promoting an image of Delhi as a 'world-class' city on the global stage, whilst using the Games as a catalyst for forcing through rapid social and infrastructural developments given that the

> Games legitimized social and spatial changes that would have been more difficult to achieve through political and administrative processes . . . by focusing on the importance of the Games for national prestige and, in particular, the Indian state's ambition to be recognized as a global superpower.
>
> *(p. 131)*

Despite these positive intentions, the 2010 Delhi Games act as a cautionary tale regarding the use of a major sporting event as part of a 'springboarding' strategy. In particular, the Delhi Games were plagued with concerns regarding financial mismanagement and severe budgetary miscalculations, with the costs of the Games sky-rocketing by over 1000 per cent from an original estimate of US$1.3 billion to $15 billion, resulting in the most expensive Commonwealth Games in history (Majumdar 2011; Majumdar and Mehta 2010). This was compounded by high-profile infrastructural problems, such as the collapse of a spectator walkway during the construction phases and delays in the preparation of the official athletes' village, leading to the intervention of the Commonwealth Games Federation which formally raised its concerns with the Indian government (Majumdar and Mehta 2010). Curi *et al.* (2011) argue that such incidents served to reinforce dominant Western beliefs regarding the inadequacy of developing nation-states for hosting major sporting events, with negative stereotypes regarding political disorganisation prevalent within media discourse in Western countries.

Whilst acknowledging these 'Orientalist assumptions' of the Western media, Black argues that the problems which blighted the Delhi Games 'decisively set back the prospect of an Indian Olympics' (Black 2014: 18), despite the many successes of the Games during the competition period itself. Such conclusions have been reiterated in a number of other academic reflections on the 2010 Delhi Games, with these studies emphasising the damage caused to 'brand India' by examples of financial mismanagement, infrastructural failures and accidents, social injustices and inequalities, and allegations of corruption associated with the event (Baviskar 2014; Majumdar 2011; Majumdar and Mehta 2010). Finally, the Delhi Games have illustrated the potential political ramifications for a governing party following a perceived failure in hosting a sporting mega-event, with Baviskar (2014) concluding that:

> The Games spectacularly failed to bind the citizens of Delhi to their city's government. Instead, they confirmed the sense of a citizenry being ripped off by its political leaders, a realization that led to a resounding electoral defeat for the Congress in Delhi in 2013.
>
> *(p. 138)*

The Glasgow 2014 Commonwealth Games: an apolitical event?

The final example of the inter-relationship between the Commonwealth Games and politics to be considered in this analysis is the most recent iteration of the event, the 2014 Glasgow Games. In contrast to the examples cited above which were primarily embroiled in international politics (e.g. Edinburgh 1986, Kuala Lumpur 1998 and Delhi 2010) or the politics of protest (e.g. Melbourne 2006), the 2014 Glasgow Games can instead be closely linked to domestic politics in Scotland given its proximity to the Scottish independence referendum, which took place in September 2014. However, despite the obvious potential for campaigners from both sides of the political debate, whether pro-independence or pro-union, to exploit the event in order to promote their political arguments regarding Scotland's constitutional future, the Glasgow Games remained a relatively politics-free zone, at least on the surface. Scratching beneath the surface of this apolitical facade, however, reveals a number of political issues which have remained intertwined with this event.

The first such example of the relationship between the Glasgow Games and Scottish politics lies in the original motives for bidding to host the 2014 Games. Following the re-establishment of a Scottish Parliament in 1999 with a limited range of devolved powers, Scottish politicians have had the opportunity to pursue distinct strategies to promote certain Scottish economic, social and political goals. One such strategy has seen Scotland actively pursue a range of sporting events as part of a economic development strategy underpinned by tourism promotion, infrastructural improvements and urban regeneration (EventScotland 2008; VisitScotland 2011). The 'Year of Homecoming 2014' is of particular interest when considering the importance of sport for this strategy, given that Scotland hosted two major sporting events during this year, with the Glasgow Commonwealth Games and the Ryder Cup at Gleneagles. As noted above, the growing financial costs of hosting major sports events has led to the necessity of governmental support in terms of contributions to hosting costs, thus leading to increasing political scrutiny of the economic returns on the initial investment of these public funds. Black (2014) argues that 'second-order' events such as the Commonwealth Games are of great importance to 'locales for whom second-order games are the only realistic means of pursuing event-centred development strategies' (p. 16), claiming that any attempts to 'springboard' to larger sporting events is unfeasible for smaller host nations such as Scotland. Instead, Haynes and Boyle (2008) argue that the strategic goals for Glasgow 2014 were limited, suggesting that the 'aim of the organisers will be to offer a distinctively Scottish version of the relationship between sport and society (more than may have been on show at the London-based 2012 Olympics)' (pp. 267–268). Given that events such as the Commonwealth Games must therefore act as the pinnacle in terms of the potential use of an events-based strategy for the Scottish government, the political importance of a successful event was arguably magnified.

Nonetheless, despite the proximity of the Glasgow Games to the Scottish independence referendum, the significant public investment in the Games preparations, and the high-profile nature of the event for the Scottish economy, the general political consensus was that the Games should remain a politics-free zone. However, the process by which this consensus regarding the apolitical nature of the Games was manufactured ironically demonstrates a significant degree of political positioning in rendering this major event unusable by certain campaigners. For example, the first such intervention regarding the Games came from Lord McConnell, the former First Minister of Scottish Parliament from 2001 to 2007, who appealed for a political 'truce' in the Scottish independence referendum campaign during Glasgow 2014 due to:

> genuine concerns that the Games, and the image of Scotland, could be damaged by attempts by either side – for and against – to use the Games to promote their cause, or to use the venues for campaigning. There is a real possibility that worries over politicisation will distract organisers, athletes and performers in their preparation.
>
> *(McConnell 2014)*

This pre-emptive strike from the Labour politician acted to head off concerns from strategists within the pro-union 'Better Together' campaign that the pro-independence 'Yes Scotland' campaign would seek to exploit the Games as a means of furthering the cause for independence. However, given that McConnell himself had been highly influential in both Scotland's unsuccessful bid for the 2008 UEFA European Championships and the successful bid for 2014 Commonwealth Games during his time as First Minister of Scotland, thus generating significant personal political capital in the process, his appeal for a truce arguably demonstrates a degree of double standards, given its attempts to prevent politicians from reaping similar benefits from the 2014 Games for their own political ends.

Nonetheless, McConnell's intervention resulted in sufficient media coverage to require a response from both sides of the constitutional debate regarding the politicisation of the event. Those aligned with the pro-independence campaign, such as Shona Robison (SNP MSP and Cabinet Secretary for the Commonwealth Games, Sport, Equalities and Pensioners' Rights) and Blair Jenkins (Chief Executive, Yes Scotland) moved to dismiss concerns regarding the political exploitation of the Games, arguing that the cross-party political consensus which underpinned the planning and delivery of the event ruled out the possibility of political gain for any sole party (BBC 2014; *The Herald* 2014). However Robison and Jenkins were more dismissive of McConnell's suggestion for a complete cessation of referendum campaigning, arguing that such a move would be unmanageable given the broad and grassroots nature of a number of campaign groups. Whilst prominent pro-union campaigners such as Blair McDougall (Campaign Director, Better Together) conceded the latter point regarding the difficulty of maintaining a truce (*The Herald* 2014), the pro-union side attempted to reinforce McConnell's key message regarding the importance of ensuring an apolitical Games, thus negating the possibility of pro-independence campaigners using the success of the Games as a tool to support their campaign.

The pre-emptive appeal of Lord McConnell thus proved to be an effective intervention for those who wished the 2014 Glasgow Games to be an apolitical event, with the figurehead of the pro-independence campaign Alex Salmond, First Minister of the Scottish Parliament publicly announcing a 'self-denying ordinance' to avoid discussing the independence referendum in relation to the Games (Johnson 2014; Wade 2014). Nonetheless, the extent to which McConnell's intervention was altruistic in nature, concerned with preventing damage to the Games, rather than a political manoeuvre designed to primarily benefit the pro-union campaign, is open to debate. Furthermore, the extent to which all actors on the pro-union side of the debate avoided politicking in relation to the Games was undermined by Ruth Davidson, the Leader of the Scottish Conservatives, when she raised a question regarding problems with the ticketing procedures for the Games in First Minister's Questions (Scottish Parliament Official Report 15 May 2014). It appears therefore that the apolitical nature of the Games only applied in those circumstances where their organisation proved a success, and political scrutiny of any problems relating to the Games was still deemed appropriate. Although the significant investment of public funds in the region of half a million pounds in the Games renders such scrutiny necessary and appropriate, the contradictions evident in such an approach are evident to those who may be critical of McConnell's suggested 'truce' when it is not applied in all circumstances.

Furthermore, given that the extended nature of the Scottish independence referendum campaign and the exhaustive list of issues which became politicised by both sides of the debate (ranging from central issues of economics, currency, defence, and social justice to relatively marginal issues such as broadcasting rights of BBC programming, the future of the 'Union Jack' flag and Scottish representation at the Olympic Games), it is striking that the 2014

Glasgow Games remained one of the few issues mutually declared as apolitical. Regardless of this position, the extent to which any political exploitation of the 2014 Games would have made any impact on the final result of the referendum remains highly speculative, with the result of a 55.3 per cent 'No' vote and a 44.7 per cent 'Yes' vote surely proving too significant a margin for an event such as the successful hosting of the Commonwealth Games to have had any sort of impact on the final outcome of this important decision for Scotland's constitutional future.

Conclusion

This brief synopsis of the political history of the Commonwealth Games movement has aimed to identify some of the central issues which have demonstrated the intersection between the Games and the interventions of political actors at various levels. At the international level, the declining influence of the United Kingdom within the British Empire and subsequent Commonwealth are evident in the shifting power dynamics within this geopolitical entity, with the issue of apartheid-related boycotts dogging the history of the Games movement for many years whilst simultaneously underlining the declining abilities of the United Kingdom to set the political agenda within the Commonwealth. Furthermore, the post-imperial era of global politics is evident in recent trends in the political motivations of host countries for the Commonwealth Games, as numerous states endeavour to use sport as a part of a 'soft power' strategy to promote their own interests in an increasingly competitive global economy. However, the case of Delhi 2010 serves as a cautionary tale for potential 'springboarder' hosts of both the Commonwealth Games and other international sporting events. Finally, the cases of Melbourne 2006 and Glasgow 2014 demonstrate that political implications of the Games are not restricted to international politics, with the ongoing potential for these events to become embroiled in domestic and local politics evident. It can therefore be argued that, despite its afore-mentioned status as 'second-order' international sporting event (Black 2008, 2014) which lacks the comparative global reach and media attention of the Olympic Games and FIFA World Cup, the Commonwealth Games remain equally worthy of academic analysis given the complex and multi-layered political dynamics evident in the history of the Games movement to date.

References

Bateman, D. and Douglas, D. (1986) *Unfriendly Games: Boycotted and Broke: The Inside Story of the 1986 Commonwealth Games*. Edinburgh: Mainstream Publishing Projects and Glasgow Herald.

Baviskar, A. (2014) Dreaming big: spectacular events and the 'world-class' city: the Commonwealth Games in Delhi. In J. Grix (ed.) *Leveraging Legacies from Sports Mega-Events: Concepts and Cases*. Basingstoke: Palgrave Macmillan, pp. 130–141.

BBC (2014) Scottish independence: call from 'truce' during Glasgow 2014. *BBC News Online*. 8 January. Accessed 7 October 2014. www.bbc.co.uk/news/uk-scotland-scotland-politics-25645859.

Black, D. (2008) Dreaming big: the pursuit of 'second order' games as a strategic response to globalization. *Sport in Society*, 11(4): 467–480.

Black, D. (2014) Megas for strivers: the politics of second-order events. In J. Grix (ed.) *Leveraging Legacies from Sports Mega-Events: Concepts and Cases*. Basingstoke: Palgrave Macmillan, pp. 13–23.

Brannagan, P.M. and Giulianotti, R. (2014) Qatar, global sport and the 2022 FIFA World Cup. In J. Grix (ed.) *Leveraging Legacies from Sports Mega-Events: Concepts and Cases*. Basingstoke: Palgrave Macmillan, pp. 154–165.

Coghlan, J. (with Webb, I.) (1990) *Sport and British Politics since 1960*. London: Falmer.

Cornelissen, S. (2014) South Africa's 'coming out party': reflections on the significance and implications of the 2010 FIFA World Cup. In J. Grix (ed.) *Leveraging Legacies from Sports Mega-Events: Concepts and Cases*. Basingstoke: Palgrave Macmillan, pp. 142–153.

Cornelissen, S. and Swart, K. (2006) The 2010 Football World Cup as a political construct: the challenge of making good on an African promise. *The Sociological Review*, 54: 108–124.

Curi, M., Knijnik, J. and Mascarenhas, G. (2011) The Pan-American Games in Rio de Janeiro 2007: consequences of sport mega-event on a BRIC country. *International Review for the Sociology of Sport*, 46(2): 140–156.

Dawson, M. (2014) Breaking away from the 'big boys'? Jamaican and 'White Commonwealth' expectations at the 1966 British Empire and Commonwealth Games, *Sport in History*, 34(3): 431–453.

Dheenshaw, C. (1994) *The Commonwealth Games: The First 60 Years 1930–1990*. Harpenden: Queen Anne Press.

EventScotland (2008) *Scotland – The Perfect Stage: A Strategy for the Events Industry in Scotland 2009–2020*. Edinburgh: EventScotland.

Grix, J. (2014) Preface: why do states invest in sports mega-events? In J. Grix (ed.) *Leveraging Legacies from Sports Mega-Events: Concepts and Cases*. Basingstoke: Palgrave Macmillan, pp. x–xii.

Grix, J. and Houlihan, B. (2014) Sports mega-events as part of a nation's soft power strategy: the cases of Germany (2006) and the UK (2012). *The British Journal of Politics & International Relations*, 16(4): 572–596.

Haynes, R. and Boyle, R. (2008) Media sport. In N. Blain and D. Hutchinson (eds) *The Media in Scotland*. Edinburgh: Edinburgh University Press, pp. 253–270.

Holt, R. (1989) *Sport and the British: A Modern History*. Oxford: Oxford University Press.

Horne, J. (2007) The four 'knowns' of sports mega-events. *Leisure Studies*, 26(1): 81–96.

Houlihan, B. (1994) *Sport and International Politics*. London: Harvester Wheatsheaf.

Jeffreys, K. (2012) *Sport and Politics in Modern Britain: The Road to 2012*. London: Palgrave Macmillan.

Johnson, S. (2014) Alex Salmond pledges unpolitical Commonwealth Games – then attacks George Osborne. *The Telegraph Online*. 22 July 2014. Accessed 7 October 2014. www.telegraph.co.uk/news/uknews/scottish-independence/10983781/Alex-Salmond-pledges-unpolitical-Commonwealth-Games-then-attacks-George-Osborne.html.

Kidd, B. (1988) The campaign against sport in South Africa. *International Journal*, 43(4): 643–664.

Macfarlane, N. (with Herd, M.) (1986) *Sport and Politics*. London: Willow Books.

McConnell, J. (2014) Glasgow 2014 can be the best ever Commonwealth Games. *Lords of the Blog*. Accessed 7 October 2014. http://lordsoftheblog.net/2014/01/08/glasgow-2014-can-be-the-best-ever-commonwealth-games.

Majumdar, B. (2011) Commonwealth Games 2010: the index of a 'new' India. *Social Research*, 78(1): 231–254.

Majumdar, B. and Mehta, N. (2010) *Sellotape Legacy: Delhi and the Commonwealth Games*. Noida: HarperCollins.

Manzenreiter, W. (2010) The Beijing games in the Western imagination of China: the weak power of soft power. *Journal of Sport & Social Issues*, 34(1): 29–48.

Miller, T., Lawrence, G., McKay, J. and Rowe, D. (2001) *Globalization and Sport*. London: Sage.

Monnington, T. (1993) Politicans and sport: uses and abuses. In L. Allison (ed.) *The Changing Politics of Sport*. Manchester: Manchester University Press, pp. 125–150.

Muda, M. (1998) The significance of Commonwealth Games in Malaysia's foreign policy. *The Round Table*, 346: 211–226.

Nye, J. (2004) *Soft Power: The Means to Success in World Politics*. New York: Public Affairs.

Palmer, C. (2013) *Global Sports Policy*. London: Sage.

Phillips, B. (2000) *Honour of Empire, Glory of Sport: The History of Athletics at the Commonwealth Games*. Manchester: The Parrs Wood Press.

Phillips, B. (2002) *The Commonwealth Games: The History of All the Sports*. Manchester: The Parrs Wood Press.

Polley, M. (2014) Introduction: the Empire and Commonwealth Games and the challenge of history. *Sport in History*, 34(3): 383–389.

Roche, M. (2000) *Mega-Events and Modernity: Olympics and Expos in the Growth of Global Culture*. London: Routledge.

Roche, M. (2006) Mega-events and modernity revisited: globalization and the case of the Olympics. *The Sociological Review*, 54: 25–40.

Scottish Parliament Official Report (2014) 15 May, col 31065-31067.

Skillen, F. and McDowell, M. (2014) The Edinburgh 1970 British Commonwealth Games: representations of identities, nationalism and politics. *Sport in History*, 34(3): 454–475.

Stewart, B. (2014) A tale of two Australian cities. In J. Grix (ed.) *Leveraging Legacies from Sports Mega-Events: Concepts and Cases*. Basingstoke: Palgrave Macmillan, pp. 62–72.

Stolenwealth Games (2006) Home page. Accessed 7 October 2014. http://stolenwealthgames.com/?p=home.

The Herald (2014) Shona Robison rejects calls for indyref debate truce during Glasgow 2014 Commonwealth Games. 8 January. Accessed 7 October 2014. www.heraldscotland.com/news/home-news/shona-robison-rejects-calls-for-indyref-debate-truce-during-glasgow-2014-commonwealth.1389179849.

Thomson, I. (2000) Athletics. In G. Jarvie and J. Burnett (eds) *Sport, Scotland and the Scots*. East Linton: Tuckwell, pp. 19–38.

van der Westhuizen, J. (2004) Marketing Malaysia as a model modern Muslim state: the significance of the 16 Commonwealth Games. *Third World Quarterly*, 25(7): 1277–1291.

VisitScotland (2011) *The Winning Years: VisitScotland Corporate Plan 2012/2015*, Edinburgh: VisitScotland.

Wade, M. (2014) Politicians on both sides fail to keep the referendum out of Games speeches. *The Times Scotland Online*. 23 July 2014. Accessed 7 October 2014. www.thetimes.co.uk/tto/news/uk/scotland/article4155220.ece.

Whannel, G. (2008) *Culture, Politics and Sport: 'Blowing the Whistle' Revisited*. London: Routledge.

42

THE POLITICS OF INTERNATIONAL CRICKET

Dominic Malcolm and Devra Waldman

The origins of cricket are fundamentally political. In 1747, matches between Kent and England were postponed due to players' commitments in the General Election. British parliamentarians were the first to write the laws (note laws, not rules) of cricket (Malcolm 2013) and the historical governing body of cricket in Britain, the Marylebone Cricket Club (MCC), was known as the "Parliament House of Cricket" due both to its authority in the game and the number of members who were politicians (Bradley 1990).

From the 1890s, the outlook of the MCC became increasingly imperial and many notable members were colonial administrators. Cricket became the "Imperial Game", proof of a successful "civilizing mission" and the cultural yardstick against which many colonial societies measured their relations with Britain (Stoddart 2006). The first international governing body for cricket was the Imperial Cricket Conference (ICC), from which America was excluded because it was not (or no longer) an imperial nation (Gemmell 2011). While the English were reluctant participants in early global governance of football and rugby union, the MCC hosted the meetings which led to the ICC's 1909 formation. (Post)colonialism, therefore, is the overarching theme to the politics of international cricket.

The inherent inequality of colonialism remains evident in the contemporary organisational structure of cricket, with the 105 current members organised into three tiers (Full, Associate and Affiliate).[1] While in 1997, ICC President Jagmohan Dalmiya increased the voting power of the associate members (previously associate members had one vote whereas permanent members had two), and thus reduced the relative power of traditional cricket powers (Mehta *et al.* 2009), the game remains dominated by former imperial colonies. The dominance of these countries is such that access to the cricketing elite has been granted just three times since 1954 and once attained, has never been revoked, either during extended periods when teams have failed to win or even to play (Malcolm 2013).[2] Indeed, for much of its history the ICC has effectively been an adjunct of the MCC. Both had offices at Lord's (the ICC relocated to Dubai in 2005 but retain a presence at Lord's through ICC Europe) and until 1989 the ICC's key administrative positions were automatically filled by counterparts at the MCC. For four years after this system was revised, England and Australia retained privileged voting rights as founding members. FIFA, by way of contrast, provides all member states with equal voting rights. England hosted the first three Cricket World Cups, yet the first dozen FIFA World Cups were held in twelve different countries.

Thus while cricket manifests many aspects characteristic of the politics of international sport, as illustrated in the first political-sociological treatise on cricket, C. L. R. James's (1963) seminal *Beyond a Boundary*, these are uniquely contoured by specific sets of relations which have historical roots in British imperialism. While there is not scope in this chapter for a fuller conceptual discussion of (post)colonialism, we recognise the dangers of falsely homogenising colonial communities, dichotomising settler and subaltern in oppositional relations, or ignoring the cultural specificity of colonial relations (Malcolm 2013; Waldman 2014). Fundamentally, the politics of international cricket need to be viewed through a theoretical perspective informed by a (post)colonial sensitivity towards the fluidity of social life, and cognisant of the context specificity of human action.

Consequently this chapter explores how cricket has become embroiled in diplomatic relations, been a tool in negotiating identity politics, experienced major power shifts towards emerging economies and became a vehicle in development projects. Throughout, we see the complexities of sport politics as emergent and established groups interact via the mobilisation of material and ideological power resources. We are conscious that this overview excludes a discussion of cricket's gender politics. This omission partly relates to space issues, to the authors' expertise, and the discussion of gender provided elsewhere in this volume. Ultimately however this is dictated by the emphasis on (post)colonialism as the central organising theme of this chapter (for a discussion of gender politics and cricket see Velija *et al.* 2010, 2014)

Boycotts

Sanctions represent the most significant non-military political intervention a nation can take. The most overt sporting sanction is the boycott of competitive relations and the sporting isolation of a country. The two main boycotts in cricket – of South Africa (SA) and Rhodesia/Zimbabwe – were shaped by the broader processes of (post)colonialism.[3]

In many respects the South African state was formed out of a desire to secure a political platform for British economic interests. The receptiveness of the MCC to the initial call by South African cricket administrator Abe Bailey to form an international governing body is indicative of the close relations between the respective countries' cricketing elites. Consequently the British (as well as Australia and New Zealand) were relatively supportive of SA when, in the 1950s, the UN began to formally oppose apartheid, and SA were excluded from the 1964 Olympic Games. When SA withdrew from the Commonwealth in 1961 it was not their membership but the title of the ICC that altered, the *Imperial* becoming the *International* Cricket Conference in 1965.

It was partly because South African cricket authorities saw the English as amongst their strongest allies that it was the "D'Oliveira Affair" of 1968 that marked a watershed in political relations. While the Indian cricket board called for the West Indies to cancel their 1959 tour to SA, and there were protests when SA toured England in 1960 and 1965 and Australia–New Zealand in 1963/64, it was the selection of the South African born "Cape Coloured" to tour SA as an England player that precipitated cricketing isolation. D'Oliveira moved to England because of limited cricketing opportunities in SA. Though he represented England during the summer of 1968, he wasn't initially selected for the winter tour. Many viewed this as a concession to the racist policies of SA, but when D'Oliveira subsequently replaced the injured Tom Cartwright, others viewed this as a concession to anti-apartheid protesters. Ultimately, SA cricketing authorities rejected the team the MCC selected and cancelled the tour (Gemmell 2010).

English cricketing authorities, buoyed by an extraordinary meeting of the MCC in 1968 which showed that a clear majority of members were keen to retain cricketing relations with

South Africa, sought to enable the proposed 1970 SA tour of England to take place. The UK Home Secretary requested (but did not demand) cancellation due to the potential impact of the tour on domestic race and inter-Commonwealth relations. Ultimately opposition led by the *Stop the Seventy Tour,* and lobbying by India, Pakistan, Ceylon (later Sri Lanka) and various Caribbean high commissions, combined to overcome support for the tour within Britain. Following the tour's cancellation, British cricket withdrew from competition with SA until the game was administered and played on a multi-racial basis. SA did not take part in any international cricket between 1970 and 1991 (Williams 2001).

These moves reflected international political developments. During the 1970s the UN heightened pressure on SA and requested all sporting bodies to suspend links in protest against human rights abuses. Subsequently, in 1977, the Commonwealth Heads of State signed the Gleneagles Agreement, which stated that governments would discourage contact or competition by their nationals with those from SA or other racially structured societies (Gemmell 2004). The ICC (at this time closely integrated with the MCC) conformed to the letter if not necessarily the spirit of this agreement. In 1979 a delegation visited SA and recommended that a multinational ICC team tour SA, and in 1981 the ICC passed a resolution encouraging links which fostered multi-racial cricket. The ICC did, however, denounce pseudo-national "rebel tours" by English players in 1982 and 1990, and by West Indian players in 1982–1983 and 1983–1984.

Players and coaches could, however, still visit SA as individuals rather than national representatives, and those who did often justified it in terms of their freedom to trade. While the British cricketers and administrators, particularly under the Thatcher government, were receptive to that argument, such individuals subsequently became the focus of Indian, Pakistani and West Indian protests. There was a reluctance to issue visas to certain players, and some England tours were cancelled. Such was the prominence of cricket in the sporting boycott that West Indian captain Clive Lloyd addressed the UN outlining his support for sporting sanctions. It is widely believed that sporting isolation was "a major factor" in breaking down apartheid both in the sport, and in South African society more generally (Williams 2001: 85), but colonial legacies, and political tensions within international cricket had considerable bearing on the success (and at times what looked like the potential failure) of the SA boycott.

The other major cricketing boycott – of Rhodesia/Zimbabwe – similarly has "race" connotations, but very different (post)colonial politics. During negotiations about the move to postcolonial self-government, Rhodesian whites rejected moves towards majority (i.e. black) rule. Disagreement led to Rhodesia's Unilateral Declaration of Independence (UDI) in 1965, which the UK government, backed by the UN Security Council, declared illegal. Various trade and diplomatic sanctions – including sporting boycotts – were imposed on the premise that contacts were an "aid and comfort to the illegal regime" (Little 2010: 95).

Cricket, as the primary sport of white Rhodesians, became the focus of the boycott. British government lobbying effectively dissuaded Worcestershire, Yorkshire and an MCC/England team from touring. The MCC President, former Prime Minister Sir Alec Douglas-Home, played a role in negotiations, indicative of ongoing interdependence between English cricket administration and broader structures of British political power. As with SA, the British took the most liberal view of individuals' continued links, while the Indian, Pakistani and West Indian cricket authorities sanctioned individual players.

International political pressure led to fundamental changes in Rhodesia. In 1979 political power finally shifted to the black majority (the last in the former Empire to do so), and the country was renamed Zimbabwe. Zimbabwe was admitted to the ICC in 1982 and became a full member in 1992. But political (and cricketing) crisis returned in 2002, following a rigged general election. Subsequently opposition leaders were imprisoned and martial law was declared, drawing attention to issues of poverty, low life expectancy, land reforms and economic instability. Cricket was implicated because SA and Zimbabwe were due to co-host the 2003 ICC Cricket World Cup. Some questioned whether participation in that event would be seen as an endorsement of the Zimbabwean political regime, especially given that Zimbabwean Prime Minister, Robert Mugabe, had famously said that "cricket civilizes people and creates good gentlemen. I want everyone in Zimbabwe to play cricket. I want ours to be a nation of gentlemen" (cited in Holden 2010). Others argued that participation was simply immoral in light of the abuse of political and human rights.

Consequently, the UK government *advised* the ECB against playing a match scheduled for the Zimbabwean capital, Harare. The dilemma was that the ICC only recognised lack of personal safety or *direct* government instruction as legitimate bases for withdrawal. If the ECB complied with UK government advice, it would anger the international cricket community, be fined, and be unlikely to progress in the tournament. Cricket Australia's decision to fulfil their Zimbabwe-based fixture undermined the ECB's case about poor security, but with strong public support at home, England withdrew. The ICC withheld £2.33 million of England's revenue from the tournament, and Chief Executive Malcolm Speed stated that England's stance was unpopular because, "Some of the things said in relation to Zimbabwe had an imperial, colonial overhang about them" (Gemmell 2010: 77).

England was due to tour Zimbabwe again in 2004, when in many respects social conditions had worsened. It became more apparent that Zimbabwe's cricket selectors were directed by politicians, there were claims of corruption, and players and officials critical of the regime had been banished (e.g. Andy Flower and Henry Olonga wore arm bands during Zimbabwe's 2003 World Cup match against Namibia to symbolise the death of democracy). The government again issued guidance rather than instruction and rejected ECB claims for financial compensation. After a failed appeal to the ICC to change regulations regarding boycotts, the ECB decided to go ahead with the tour though one player, Steve Harmison, withdrew citing moral/political objections. In 2009 the UK government finally instructed the ECB to cancel Zimbabwe's proposed 2010 tour of England, shortly after Cricket SA initiated a boycott. While other countries (including SA) retained and reinstated cricketing links with Zimbabwe, England has not played bilateral matches against Zimbabwe since.

Identity politics

Less overt than a boycott, but equally fundamental, is the role cricket plays in (post)colonial identity politics. A key element in cricket's structuring of (post)colonial relations is the ability to recognise other countries through granting "first class" status. For instance, four "private" English teams and two "official" MCC teams toured New Zealand before the country was deemed worthy and test matches began (Ryan 2004). Cricket was and is, to a greater or lesser extent, implicated in national identity politics and independence movements of all major cricket playing nations, but due to limitations of space, this section will focus on just the first country to achieve this status (Australia) and the most overtly conflictual case (the West Indies).

Initially at least, Australian cricket was particularly pro-imperial. Early Australian cricket was nostalgically anglophile, with clubs adopting English conventions and replicating the English rural environment. This both created a sense of normalcy within otherwise alien environments, and symbolised cultural unity. However, Australia's victories over England (winning their first "test match" in 1877) supported mounting claims for greater equality in political relations. By playing the game in a distinct way (hard, competitive, but somewhat dour), cricketers also contributed to an emerging Australian national identity (Bradley 1995).

Ironically then, the first major political crisis in international cricket stemmed from Australian objections to the English tactics during the "Bodyline" series of 1932–1933. Following multiple injuries, the Australian Board of Control sent a telegram to the MCC. Bodyline, they complained, "(made) protection of the body by the batsman the main consideration. This is causing intensely bitter feeling between the players as well as injury. In our opinion it is unsportsmanlike" (reported in *Wisden Cricketers Almanack 1934*: 328). The MCC defended their team and resisted Australian challenges to the unilateral right of the English to define civilised behaviour. Though many relevant records were destroyed shortly afterwards, "the amount of backroom diplomacy that transpired . . . [was] quite extraordinary" (Frith 2002: 242).

The more complex role of cricket in the identity politics of the Caribbean stems from the mixture of racial and (post)colonial factors. In particular, the ability of whites to dominate cricket's administrative structures long after they had acceded power in the islands' political structures reveals the importance of cricket in structures of ideological dominance. C. L. R. James (1963), for instance, self-consciously reflected on the contradiction between devotion to the game (its values and behavioural mores), and his lifetime resistance to colonial subordination. The remarkably late choice of Barbadian Frank Worrell to become the first black West Indian captain (in 1960), came at a time when the case for a region-unifying West Indian government was being made most vociferously.

Identity politics came into sharper focus when the West Indies became the dominant team in world cricket, *c.* 1980–1994. Success was attributed to a style of bowling which became inextricably bound to the assertion of a West Indian "national" identity (Patterson 1995) and resisted by the established powers (notably Britain and Australia) as excessively violent and contrary to the "spirit of the game". Various rule changes were implemented under the guise of player safety, but West Indians suspected that the real motive was to curb their success. This view was encapsulated by the West Indies' most politically active player, Viv Richards, who publicly questioned if there was "a white supremacist plot to undermine Westindies long-standing status as kings of cricket" (Williams 2001: 125). West Indian cricket thus "mirror[ed] an entire people coming into their own, rejecting colonial divisions imposed upon them and bringing a new confidence and will for cultural construction" (Searle 1990: 36).

Finally, it is important to reflect on how cricket impacted identities within the (post)colonial power. Most recently perhaps has been the symbolic annihilation of "internal empire" nation Wales through the use of the initials ECB to represent the England and Wales Cricket Board, but perhaps most notorious is the way diaspora communities have interacted with cricket in the contestation of identity politics. Notably cricket has been the choice sport when the British have voiced exclusionary and/or racial discourses. For instance, in 1990 Norman Tebbit, a leading member of Margaret Thatcher's Conservative government, proposed a "cricket test" which effectively used support for national cricket teams other than England as the basis on which minority ethnic groups in Britain could be castigated for "failing" to assimilate into British society. Five years later Michael Henderson wrote the article "Is it in the Blood?", which applied comparable questions to players born or raised in former British colonies and selected to play for England. The way each event foregrounded cricket in debates of race and ethnic identity politics in British society is unparalleled in other sports as a consequence of cricket's fundamentally colonial structure. The barracking of British-Asian cricketers (e.g. Sajid Mahmood and Moeen Ali) by (largely British-based) fans supporting Pakistan and India is the most recent manifestation of these (post)colonial diaspora identity politics (Malcolm 2013). While some interpret a multi-ethnic English team as a sign of an inclusive cosmopolitan state of hybrid identities, others see these players as deserting their ancestry and (literally) siding with the enemy.

"Indianisation" of cricket, the Indian Premier League (IPL) and (post)colonial politics

Within the last twenty years, the power centre of cricket has fundamentally shifted. Cricket is unique in that it is a global game that is played internationally, yet is no longer directly controlled by countries located in the "West" (Rumford 2007). In 1989, reflecting on the power of cricket within India, social critic Ashis Nandy said, "Cricket is an Indian game accidentally discovered by the English" (1989: 1). While mostly speaking about the importance of the sport in shaping Indian social and national identities, it is undeniable that the financial nerve centre of world cricket has shifted out of "traditional" cricket nations such as England and Australia and into India specifically. This shift in power has been described as the "Indianisation" of the sport, and reveals the (post)colonial tensions that continue to shape the politics of international cricket. This section focuses on the rise of Indian dominance in the game, the influence of the IPL, and explores how shifts in economic dominance have led to more covert, political-ideological battles designed to reassert (post)colonial understandings and assumptions about the sport and those that play it.

The rapid growth of satellite and televisual technology harnessed the appeal of cricket in India, and transnational corporations found cricket a good outlet to target this new consumer market (Gupta 2004). Recognising that India had the largest audience in the world – both domestically and amongst its diaspora – in 1994 the Board of Control for Cricket in India (BCCI) negotiated a partnership with ESPN to set up an Indian version of the network to broadcast their cricket matches (Gupta 2009). Because of the size and commitment of the cricket-watching audience in India, sales of broadcasting rights have been extremely lucrative. As a direct result of the globalisation of the game, the BCCI currently represents at least 80 per cent of the annual income for the ICC (Mehta *et al.* 2009). Cricketing boards outside India also reap benefits from selling the broadcast rights for home games against India, and some poorer cricket boards depend on this as a major source of revenue (Holden 2008). As an example of the significant shifts in the power and practices of the sport internationally, all companies advertised during the Champions Trophy held in England in 2004 were from the subcontinent (Majumdar 2007). More recently, the BCCI used its financial muscle to win the rights to host the 2011 World Cup "out of order" by "buying" votes from the struggling WICBC in exchange for financial support (Mehta *et al.* 2009).

The proliferation, popularity and influence of the IPL illustrate how the power centre of the sport has been reshaped by (post)colonial relationships between cricket nations. BCCI Vice-President at the time, and visionary behind the IPL, Lalit Modi, explicitly stated "we are trying to change the world order" (Mehta *et al.* 2009: 699). In its inaugural year (2008), the IPL raised $1.8 billion before the first ball was bowled – more than the ICC expected to receive from the 2011 and 2015 Cricket World Cups combined – and had an estimated viewership of 220 million in India alone. These numbers are impressive, indicating that the League did not require a global market to be successful (Gupta 2009).

Uniquely in cricket, the IPL utilises an auction structure where the franchise owners bid for prospective players. During the first year there were twenty-seven Indian players drafted to the league, and fifty-one foreign players and team owners spent an average of $518,518 per Indian native player, compared to $352,941 per foreign player (Mehta *et al.* 2009). That young Indian cricketers with limited international experience were more highly rewarded than international cricket "legends" reflects the decisions of franchise owners to invest in Indian nationalism as a way of establishing club loyalties (Mehta *et al.* 2009). These auctions are also highly symbolic of a reversal in (post)colonial politics, as cricketers from the former colonial powers are now traded, and others simply rejected, by a new economic elite.

The IPL-instigated movement of international players raises new dilemmas for cricket organisations. Specifically, IPL salaries are so lucrative that players are increasingly negotiating playing schedules with their home cricket boards in order to accommodate their participation (Mehta *et al.* 2009). Additionally, because many cricket boards rely heavily on the infusion of capital through outside audiences (Australia, New Zealand, SA, etc.), they must reorganise domestic playing schedules to accommodate the IPL in order to ensure that their players are available (Gupta 2011). Of course, these (post)colonial shifts in power have not gone uncontested. The ECB has been particularly uncooperative and not allowed contracted players to participate fully in the IPL because of clashes with England cricket fixtures (Gupta 2011).

The rise of India as the dominant force in international cricket has also brought about increased suspicions around cheating, corruption, racism and violence – all of which reflect anxieties of the colonial past, postcolonial assertions and profound changes afflicted by economic forms of globalisation. For example, in 2000 Delhi police recorded telephone conversations between South African cricket captain Hansie Cronje and an Indian bookmaker in which Cronje agreed to underperform in games against India. In public discourses that followed, media outlets and individuals from SA, Australia and England were in denial that such a heroic, patriotic and Christian athlete could be guilty (Sen 2001). These groups initially asserted that the Indian investigators were incompetent and/or malicious but, when Cronje confessed, explored how Cronje was corrupted by the inherent immorality of the Indian subcontinent (Sen 2001). Cronje himself participated in this blame game, claiming that he was hooked by the Indian bookmakers and felt under increasing pressure to produce results (Vahed 2013). Regardless, the responses from the wider (primarily anglo) cricket community, were infused with an imperial Orientalist (Said 2003) perspective that portrayed essential and unbridgeable differences between East and West.

The 2008 racism case between Australia's Andrew Symonds and India's Harbhajan Singh further demonstrates the (post)colonial tensions associated with the rise of Indian dominance. During the Third Test between India and Australia, Symonds accused Singh of uttering a racial slur. Despite a significant lack of available evidence ICC match referee, retired South African cricketer Mike Proctor, found Singh guilty and implemented a temporary playing ban (Mehta *et al.* 2009). The guilty verdict caused uproar in India. Australian and Indian officials worked behind the scenes to diffuse the crisis, but the BCCI made it clear that if the charges remained, India would withdraw from the Australia tour (Mehta *et al.* 2009). This would have resulted in ESPN issuing a $60 million lawsuit against Cricket Australia over lost television rights, and thus the Australian players were forced to change their stand in order to clear Singh. Mehta *et al.* (2009) suggest that the crisis split the cricket world along the lines of Asians versus the Rest, with those from Australia and England lamenting over cricket authorities "caving" to threats from the newest cricket superpower, and thus their own lost political dominance.

A final example of (post)colonial anxieties is the decision to move the IPL to South Africa in 2009 following the terrorist attacks in Mumbai. The ways in which the IPL, led by Lalit Modi, ran the league and interacted with local cricket boards, administrators and facilities, drew significant criticism. Even though "Affiliates" were paid R125,000 per match hosted in their spaces, they were requested to give up their stadium, parking, ticketing and prime corporate suites to the IPL (Vahed 2013). Gideon Haigh, English-born Australian journalist, criticised these actions (although they are common for other sporting mega-events) as indicative of the privileging of

Indian fans over host nation audiences (matches were scheduled for the convenience of domestic Indian television audiences). He went on to argue that the "Indianness" of the tournament was apparent because the IPL did not 'bring an attraction to another country, but . . . create[d] a satellite India on that country's soil'. He further argued that "there is an old fashioned word for such a form of exploitation: imperialism" (2011: 136). The controversial sentiments put forward by Haigh – along with the other examples provided above – reflect how the increasing economic power of the subcontinent provides a clear opportunity for national self-assertion, which is met with a framework of (post)colonial ideological resistance. Combined, this fundamentally alters the politics of international cricket.

Cricket and international development

Over the last twenty years, the politics of sport has also increasingly been shaped by a growing Sport for Development and Peace (SDP) sector. Consequently the ICC, MCC and national cricket associations have become involved in using cricket to achieve "development" in various ways. For example, in 2009 the ICC partnered with UNAIDS, UNICEF and the Global Media AIDS initiative to create the Think Wise Campaign to use cricket to promote HIV/AIDS prevention initiatives (ICC 2013), and in 2013 ICC Europe partnered Cricket for Change to deliver Street 20 cricket programmes to increase participation and enhance social integration. The MCC is also involved in such initiatives, using the sport to support reconciliation in Afghanistan and Rwanda and to provide educational opportunities in Sri Lanka; they have also cooperated in the building of MCC-branded "cricket communities" across India. Throughout these programmes, the processes of policital contestation outlined above can be seen to have continued.

Sport, some argue, is an international language and inherently lends itself to cooperation and teamwork, therefore making it useful for delivering broader development messages (Beutler 2008). This perspective is reflected in Khoo *et al.*'s (2014), analysis of cricket for development programmes in Samoa, which found that cricket was useful in promoting social inclusion, breaking down gender barriers to sport participation and spreading messages of HIV/AIDS awareness (see also Bateman and Binns' 2014 study of grassroots cricket and development in Mumbai). On the other hand, critiques of the international development through sport movement argue that these programmes are neo-colonial and (re)inscribe geopolitical privilege, imperial relationships and global relations of inequality as these programmes are often conducted by "Western" countries and imparted on those in the Global South who are assumed to need "developing" (Darnell 2012). Consequently, this section focuses on ongoing implications and constraints of (post)colonial relationships and politics in cricket development policies. The first example illustrates attitudes of ICC and MCC executives to their organisations' international development work, and the second investigates the partnership between the MCC and the real estate investment company Anglo Indian.

The rationales made to support international development work, and the perspectives of key administrators on development-related issues, reveal how (post)colonial hierarchies are preserved in international development practices and policies. Specifically, Waldman (2014) illustrates that those with the power to make development-related decisions (for programmes conducted across Europe, India, Sri Lanka, Afghanistan and Rwanda) are almost exclusively White, British and male, and either working at the ICC headquarters in Dubai, the MCC offices at Lord's Cricket Ground or the ICC Europe office. Furthermore, they often make decisions about these programmes with little consultation with recipients. Importantly, the exclusivity of decision-making processes is an example of how development-related decision-making processes are a manifestation of (re)colonisation on a national and inter national scale, as power is problematically reserved by former colonial elites who defin and determine development strategies and solutions on behalf of those to be "developed" (Waldman 2014). Colonial residue remains as decision-making power is retained by top executives in the ICC and MCC and marginalised groups (often those receiving develop ment programmes) continue to struggle for representation and voice in decision-making dialogue (Darnell and Hayhurst 2011).

Colonial relations are preserved and reproduced through the maintenance of hierarchies o power and knowledge (Nicholls 2009), as ICC and MCC executives promote their organisa tions as the 'legitimate' institutions to conduct development work on the basis of their expertise knowledge and professionalism. These understandings, combined with the lack of consultatio in decision-making, position their organisations as the "benevolent" providers of development while also positioning the participants as passive, grateful recipients of development (Darnel 2007). In this way, broader (post)colonial hierarchies are reinforced as Northern/Western (an in the past, exclusively British) organisations retain power to conduct development, where oth ers are only in the position to "receive" (Waldman 2014).

Consequently the international development practices and policies of the ICC and MCC could be interpreted as a form of "imperial nationalism" that exists in the sport. In that th British executives in these two organisations emphasised spreading specific "assumed" charac teristics of cricket such as discipline, fair play, teamwork, and personal responsibility through their international development work, these development programmes continue the historica process of using cricket – to know, play and understand the game – as a signifier of inclusio into the British Empire, a medium for recognition and acceptance, and to embody the essenc of "Englishness" (Malcolm 2013; Waldman 2014). The result is that the exclusive and hegem onic development-related decisions and programmes produced by the ICC and MCC fur ther privilege (post)colonial hierarchical relations, as the unequal power structures that existe through the sport continue to be preserved and accepted (Waldman 2014).

A second example – the case of the building of MCC-branded cricket communities in India – has a different "development" context, but is equally implicated by (post)colonial politics. I 2011, the MCC entered a partnership with an international real estate investment compan called Anglo Indian. The goal of this partnership is to build twelve gated, MCC-branded cricket-focused communities across India that feature a "Lord's style" cricket ground, an MCC private members club (with associated recreational facilities), an MCC cricket academy, an a Lord's Tavern restaurant and merchandise outlets. These developments entail a reassertio of the power of the MCC and Lord's – and by extension Englishness – through the build ing of MCC-modelled communities that speak to complex (post)colonial mutations of spac (Waldman *et al.* forthcoming).

Most notably, these future communities will be imagined, sold, built, and operated b these two British-based organisations. Anglo Indian and the MCC are explicitly looking t "duplicate" the prestigious (and previously colonially significant) MCC cricket academies an amenities – all of which speak to (post)colonial sentiments of power and prestige. The "legiti macy" of the MCC (as the custodian of the cricket laws) and Lord's (as a venerated coloni institution) reinforce these (post)colonial sensibilities and position England/Britain as the tru "home" and standard of the sport. By privileging the history and tradition of Lord's and th assumed "excellence" and superiority of the MCC cricket academy and coaching techniques – which simultaneously positions the culture and tradition of Indian cricket as inferior – thes developments can be read as a problematic (re)assertion of power by these British organisatio in the face of the growing dominance of Indian cricket (Waldman *et al.* forthcoming).

Thus the development of these communities is reflective of very specific ideologies of both community and cricket. Because these two organisations have the power to prescribe the imagi-nations and identities of the spaces within these communities, they also have the power to control the possible meanings of these spaces (Silk 2004; Waldman 2013). Notably the facilities which duplicate MCC institutions – the tavern, the cricket ground, etc. – are positioned at the core of the communities, while "local retail", temples, and cultural quarters are placed at the periphery (Anglo Indian 2013). By placing these distinct markers of Englishness in the centre of the community, Englishness is positioned as the desirable standard to be achieved. In this way, the Indian consumer is seen as needing "development"; excluded but also invited in through assimilation into these spaces (Waldman *et al.* forthcoming). The ways in which Anglo Indian and the MCC are working together to create and promote these communities are reflective of (post)colonial racial politics, where development of space represents the (re)affirmation of the superiority of highly exclusive English/imperial sentiments.

Conclusion

It can therefore be seen that the politics of international cricket have been fundamentally shaped by the game's location in relation to (post)colonialism. It was for this reason that cricket featured so prominently in debates about apartheid and the construction of a post-1945 international political community. It has mediated the identity politics within the colonial as well as so many (post)colonial nations, its place at the centre of India's rise as a global power, and its relevance for the recently emerged and continually growing SDP movement.

Evident within this is that, over time, the nature of political contestation has shifted from the overtly, materially and formally unequal, to the covertly, ideologically and formally more equal. From a position of imperial dominance, the British were able to directly and effec-tively resist initial challenges to their authority in and over the game, but in the post-World War II era, which favoured democracy and national self-determination, the ability to play whomever they wished, and in a style they dictated, eroded. As compelling economic forces have undermined the traditional presumptions of authority, the (re)assertion of dominance is confined, albeit relatively successfully, to practices which (re)present notions of colonial supe-riority. While it has not been the focus of this chapter, similar processes are evident in relation to women's cricket and the continuation of ideological contestation, which inhibits moves towards gender equality in the game.

The overall conclusion to be drawn from this analysis is that various power resources are mobilised within the politics of international sport. Economic dominance is important but not determinant. The effectiveness of ideological challenges is contoured by the broader context of social relations. While cricket provides a particularly apposite example of the way that the fun-damentally processual character of sport politics functions – structured by historical specificities and structuring the parameters of future conflict – a more adequate understanding of the broader phenomenon relies on the employment of such conceptual lessons.

Notes

1 See www.icc-cricket.com/about/96/icc-members/overview.
2 In January 2014, the ICC established a formal route for aspirant full members, to be ultimately decided by playing a match against the lowest-ranked test nation.
3 There has been an international boycott of playing cricket in Pakistan since 2009, when a number of Sri Lankan players were injured during a terrorist attack. However, we have not discussed this here as the boycott is not of Pakistan per se, and the team remain active playing international matches away from home.

References

Anglo Indian (2013) *Frequently Asked Questions*. Accessed 10 January 2013. www.angloindian.net/faqs-3/.

Bateman, A. (2009) *Cricket, Literature and Culture: Symbolising the Nation, Destabilising Empire*. Farnham: Ashgate.

Bateman, J. and Binns, T. (2014) More than just a game? Grass roots cricket and development in Mumbai, India. *Progress in Development Studies*, 14(2): 147–161.

Beutler, I. (2008) Sport serving development and peace: Achieving the goals of the United Nations through sport. *Sport in Society*, 11(4): 359–369.

Bradley, J. (1990) The MCC, society and empire: A portrait of cricket's ruling body, 1860–1914. *International Journal for the History of Sport*, 7: 1–22.

Bradley, J. (1995) Inventing Australians and constructing Englishness: Cricket and the creation of a national consciousness, 1860–1914. *Sporting Traditions*, 11(2): 35–60.

Darnell, S. C. (2007) Playing with race: Right to play and the production of whiteness in "development through sport". *Sport in society*, 10(4): 560–579.

Darnell, S. C. (2012) *Sport for Development and Peace: A Critical Sociology*. London: Bloomsbury Academic.

Darnell, S. C. and Hayhurst, L. M. (2011) Sport for decolonization: Exploring a new praxis of sport for development. *Progress in development studies*, 11(3): 183–196.

Frith, D. (2002) *Bodyline Autopsy*. London: Aurum.

Gemmell, J. (2004) *The Politics of South African Cricket*. London: Routledge.

Gemmell, J. (2010) So far beyond the pale: International morality and cricket boycotts. In C. Rumford and S. Wagg (eds) *Cricket and Globalization*. Newcastle: Cambridge Scholars Publishing, pp. 60–83.

Gemmell, J. (2011) "The Springboks were not a test side": The foundation of the imperial cricket conference. *Sport in Society*, 14(5): 701–718.

Gupta, A. (2004) The globalization of cricket: The rise of the non-West. *The International Journal of the History of Sport*, 21(2): 257–276.

Gupta, A. (2009) India and the IPL: Cricket's globalized empire. *The Round Table*, 98(401): 201–211.

Gupta, A. (2011) The IPL and the Indian domination of global cricket. *Sport in Society*, 14(10): 1316–1325.

Haigh, G. (2011) *Sphere of Influence: Writings on Cricket and Its Discontents*. Melbourne: Simon and Schuster.

Holden, G. (2008) World cricket as a postcolonial international society: IR meets the history of sport. *Global Society*, 22(3): 337–368.

Holden, R. (2010) International cricket: The hegemony of commerce, the decline of government interest and the end of morality? In D. Malcolm, J. Gemmell and N. Mehta (eds) *The Changing Face of Cricket: From Imperial to Global Game*. London: Routledge, pp. 213–226.

ICC (2013) *Social Responsibility*. Accessed 12 February 2013. www.icc-cricket.com/about/93/social-responsibility/partners.

James, C. L. R. (1963) *Beyond a Boundary*. New York: Pantheon.

Khoo, C., Schulenkorf, N. and Adair, D. (2014) The benefits and limitations of using cricket as a sport for development tool in Samoa. *Cosmopolitan Civil Societies: An Interdisciplinary Journal*, 6(1): 76–102.

Little, C. (2010) Rebellion, race and Rhodesia: International cricketing relations with Rhodesia during UDI. In D. Malcolm, J. Gemmell and N. Mehta (eds) *The Changing Face of Cricket: From Imperial to Global Game*. London: Routledge, pp. 93–104.

Majumdar, B. (2007) Nationalist romance to postcolonial sport: Cricket in 2006 India. *Sport in Society*, 10(1): 88–100.

Malcolm, D. (2013) *Globalizing Cricket: Englishness, Empire and Identity*. London: Bloomsbury.

Mehta, N., Gemmell, J. and Malcolm, D. (2009) "Bombay sport exchange": Cricket, globalization and the future. *Sport in Society*, 12(4/5): 694–707.

Nandy, A. (1989) *The Tao of Cricket*. London: Viking.

Nicholls, S. (2009) On the backs of peer educators: Using theory to interrogate the role of young people in the field of sport-in-development. In R. Levermore and A. Beacom (eds) *Sport and International Development*. Hampshire: Palgrave Macmillan, pp. 156–175.

Patterson, O. (1995) The ritual of cricket. In H. Beckles and B. Stoddart (eds) *Liberation Cricket: West Indies Cricket Culture*. Manchester: Manchester University Press, pp. 141–147.

Rumford, C. (2007) More than a game: Globalization and the postwesternization of world cricket. *Global Networks*, 7(2): 202–214.

Ryan, G. (2004) *The Making of New Zealand Cricket 1832–1914*. London: Frank Cass.

Said, E. (2003) *Orientalism* (3rd ed.). London: Penguin Books.

Searle, C. (1990) Race before wicket: Cricket, empire and the white rose. *Race and Class*, 31(3): 31–48.

Sen, S. (2001) Enduring colonialism in cricket: From Ranjitsinhji to the Cronje affair. *Contemporary South Asia*, 10(2): 237–249.

Silk, M. L. (2004) A tale of two cities: The social production of sterile sporting space. *Journal of Sport & Social Issues*, 28(4): 349–378.

Stoddart, B. (2006) Sport, cultural imperialism and colonial response in the British Empire. *Sport in Society*, 9(5): 809–835.

Vahed, G. (2013) Cricket and corruption: The post-apartheid relationship between India and South Africa within and beyond the boundary. *Diaspora Studies*, 6(2): 80–91.

Velija, P., Ratna, A. and Flintoff, A. (2010) Women at the wicket: The development of women's cricket in England and overseas. In C. Rumford and S. Wagg (eds) *Cricket and Globalization*. Newcastle: Cambridge Scholars Publishing, pp. 103–121.

Velija, P., Ratna, A. and Flintoff, A. (2014) Exclusionary power in sports organisations: The merger between the Women's Cricket Association and the England and Wales Cricket Board. *International Review of the Sociology of Sport*, 49(2): 211–226.

Waldman, D. (2013) A postcolonial analysis of sport for development, cross-sector partnerships, and urban redevelopment: The case of the partnership between Anglo Indian and M.C.C./Lord's Cricket Ground. Paper presented at the *World Congress of Sociology of Sport*. Vancouver, British Columbia.

Waldman, D. (2014). Behind the scenes of sport for development: Perspectives of Executives of a multi-national sport organization. Paper presented at the *North American Society for the Sociology of Sport: The Sporting Arena – Academics, Activists, and Activism(s)*. Portland, Oregon.

Williams, J. (2001) *Cricket and Race*. Oxford: Berg.

INDEX

535